W9-ATK-676

GLOBAL POLITICS

A NEW INTRODUCTION

Global Politics: A New Introduction is an innovative textbook that provides a new way of teaching and learning about world politics. Its aims are:

To provide an introductory textbook that will appeal to students and teachers of politics in the contemporary world by addressing student concerns directly and providing the basis for courses that

- address the questions students are interested in
- provide the intellectual basis for students to proceed to higher level courses
- foster and support student interest in current affairs and the difficult questions this raises.

To offer an alternative to existing introductory textbooks in different fields which tend to focus on theory and abstraction by

- presenting detailed discussion and analysis of current or historical cases in order to elaborate a sophisticated theoretical argument clearly
- ensuring that the chapters present their material in an easily comprehensible manner and develop their arguments slowly and carefully.

To offer an alternative to textbooks that focus on issues in world politics as if they were separate from theoretical questions by

- elaborating theoretical ideas and concepts in conjunction with the issues they identify and address
- demonstrating the inseparability of theory and practice.

To locate thinking about political life in the contemporary world within general thinking in social theory by

- highlighting the theoretical questions raised by issues in world politics
- making use of arguments made across disciplines in, for example, political theory, postcolonial studies, sociology, geography, peace studies, development, history, legal studies, economics and international relations.

Jenny Edkins is Professor of International Politics at Aberystwyth University.

Maja Zehfuss is Professor of International Politics at the University of Manchester.

What reviewers said about *Global Politics: A New Introduction*

'This text takes students on an important intellectual journey . . . it offers a fresh perspective with a different purpose, especially in its focus on political questions. The chapters are of a high standard written by scholars with established reputations for critical-creative thought.' – *David Campbell, Durham University, UK*

'A very good text that deals with current concerns in an engaging way. The conceptual depth of the chapters is sometimes really wonderful. Because of the range of authors and the organization of each chapter, it presents many theoretical and ideological points of view.' – *Mary Ann Tetreault, Una Chapman Cox Distinguished Professor of International Affairs, Trinity University, San Antonio, Texas, USA*

'Global Politics: A New Introduction is without doubt an outstanding textbook that will revolutionise the way in which IR is taught. It meets the demands of enquiring minds who all too often come to study IR only to be frustrated and distracted by the parochialism of intra-disciplinary squabbles. The question-based approach is a stunning innovation that opens up the field of IR: overall a teaching and learning aid worthy of its title.' – *Nick Vaughan-Williams, University of Exeter, UK*

GLOBAL POLITICS

A NEW INTRODUCTION

Edited by
Jenny Edkins and Maja Zehfuss

Routledge
Taylor & Francis Group

LONDON AND NEW YORK

First published 2009 by Routledge
2 Park Square, Milton Park, Abingdon, Oxon OX14 4RN

Simultaneously published in the USA and Canada
by Routledge
270 Madison Avenue, New York, NY 10016, USA

Routledge is an imprint of the Taylor & Francis Group, an informa business

Selection and editorial matter © 2009 Jenny Edkins and Maja Zehfuss
Individual chapters © 2009 the individual contributors

Typeset in Galliard by
Florence Production Ltd, Stoodleigh, Devon
Printed and bound in Great Britain by
MPG Books Ltd, Bodmin

All rights reserved. No part of this book may be reprinted or reproduced or utilised in any form or by any electronic, mechanical, or other means, now known or hereafter invented, including photocopying and recording, or in any information storage or retrieval system, without permission in writing from the publishers.

The publisher makes no representation, express or implied, with regard to the accuracy of the information contained in this book and cannot accept any legal responsibility or liability for any efforts or omissions that may be made.

British Library Cataloguing in Publication Data
A catalogue record for this book is available from the British Library

Library of Congress Cataloging in Publication Data
A catalog record for this book has been requested

ISBN10: 0–415–43130–1 (hbk)
ISBN10: 0–415–43131–X (pbk)
ISBN13: 978–0–415–43130–9 (hbk)
ISBN13: 978–0–415–43131–6 (pbk)

Contents

Figures

Boxes

Contributors

Roland Bleiker is Professor of International Relations at the University of Queensland. From 1986 to 1988 he worked in the Korean Demilitarised Zone as Chief of Office of the Swiss Delegation to the Neutral Nations Supervisory Commission. He is the author of *Popular Dissent, Human Agency and Global Politics* (Cambridge University Press, 2000) and *Divided Korea: Toward a Culture of Reconciliation* (University of Minnesota Press, 2005, 2008). He is also the co-editor of *Security and the War on Terror* (Routledge, 2007). He is currently finishing a book on *Aesthetics and World Politics* for Palgrave. His most recent research examines the emotional dimensions of security threats through a range of aesthetic sources, including literature, visual art and photography.

Joanna Bourke is Professor of History at Birkbeck College, University of London. She has published eight books, on Irish history, gender and 'the body', the history of psychological thought, modern warfare, the emotions and sexual violence. Her most recent books are *Fear: A Cultural History* (Virago, 2005) and *Rape: A History from the 1860s to the Present* (Virago, 2007). Her books have been translated into Chinese, Italian, Portuguese, Spanish, Catalan and Turkish. *An Intimate History of Killing: Face-to-Face Killing in Twentieth Century Warfare* (Granta, 1999) won the Fraenkel Prize in Contemporary History for 1998 and the Wolfson History Prize for 2000.

Paul Cammack is Head of the Politics and Philosophy Department at Manchester Metropolitan University. His research explores Global Governance, with particular reference to the relationship between states and international institutions. He is author of *Capitalism and Democracy in the Third World* (Continuum, 1997) and *Third World Politics: A Comparative Introduction* (with David Pool and William Tordoff, Palgrave, 1993). His current work is available through the website of the research project on the Politics of Global Competitiveness (http://www.politicsofglobalcompetitiveness.net), of which he is a member.

Simon Dalby is Professor of Geography and Political Economy at Carleton University in Ottawa. He is author of *Creating the Second Cold War* (Pinter and Guilford, 1990) and *Environmental Security* (University of Minnesota Press, 2002). He is co-editor of *Rethinking Geopolitics* (Routledge, 1998) and *The Geopolitics Reader* (Routledge, 1998, second edition 2006). His current research interests include the debate about empire and the geopolitics of the Bush doctrine in addition to matters of environmental security and sustainability. He is political geography section editor of the Blackwell Publishers Geography Compass online review journal.

Michael Dillon is Professor of Politics in the Department of Politics and International Relations at the University of Lancaster. He has published widely in international relations and in cultural and political theory. He is currently researching the problematisation of security and war from the perspective of continental philosophy with particular interest in what happens to the problematisation of security when security discourses and technologies take life rather than sovereign territoriality as their referent object (www.keele.ac.uk/biopoliticsof security). He is the author of *Politics of Security* (Routledge, 1996), co-author of *The Liberal Way of War* (Routledge, 2009) and co-editor of *Foucault on Politics, Security and War* (Palgrave Macmillan, 2008). He is working on a new book project, *Biopolitics of Security in the 21st Century* (Routledge). He also co-edits the *Journal of Cultural Research*.

Roxanne Lynn Doty is Associate Professor in the Department of Political Science at Arizona State University. She is the author of *Imperial Encounters: The Politics of Representation in North–South Relations* (University of Minnesota Press, 1996) and *Anti-Immigrantism in Western Democracies: Statecraft, Desire, and the Politics of Exclusion* (Routledge, 2003). Her forthcoming book, *The Law into Their Own Hands: Immigration and the Politics of Exceptionalism*, is being published by University of Arizona Press in spring 2009. Her current research interests include critical international relations theory, various border issues, identity and the politics of academic writing.

Jenny Edkins is Professor of International Politics at Aberystwyth University and has also taught at the University of Manchester and at the Open University. She has published widely, including most recently *Sovereign Lives: Power in Global Politics* (edited with Véronique Pin-Fat and Michael J. Shapiro, Routledge, 2004), *Trauma and the Memory of Politics* (Cambridge University Press, 2003) and *Whose Hunger? Concepts of Famine, Practices of Aid* (University of Minnesota Press, 2000, 2008). She is co-editing a textbook (with Nick Vaughan-Williams) entitled *Critical Theorists and International Relations*, forthcoming with Routledge.

Stuart Elden is Professor of Political Geography at Durham University and the editor of the journal *Society and Space* (*Environment and Planning D*). He is the author of three books of social/spatial theory, including most recently *Speaking Against Number: Heidegger, Language and the Politics of Calculation* (Edinburgh University Press, 2006). He is currently working on a history of the concept of territory, funded by a Leverhulme Major Research Fellowship, and has a book, entitled *Terror and the State of Territory*, forthcoming with University of Minnesota Press.

Naeem Inayatullah is Associate Professor of Politics at Ithaca College. He is co-author (with David Blaney) of *International Relations and the Problem of Difference* (Routledge, 2004) and co-editor (with Robin Riley) of *Interrogating Imperialism* (Palgrave, 2006). He is working on a book titled *Savage Economics*. He was the President of the Global Development section of the International Studies Association 2007–8.

Debbie Lisle is a Senior Lecturer in International Politics and Cultural Studies in the School of Politics, International Studies and Philosophy at Queen's University Belfast. She is the author of *The Global Politics of Contemporary Travel Writing* (Cambridge University Press, 2006) and has also written on contemporary art, graffiti, museums, war films, tourism and travel. In general, her research explores how global politics is represented in the cultural realm, and how audiences come to understand certain accepted 'truths' about their world. Her current research reimagines the relationship between tourism and war by demonstrating how both practices are intimately connected.

Peter Mandaville is Associate Professor of Government and Politics and the co-director of the Center for Global Studies at George Mason University in Washington DC. He is the author of *Global Political Islam* (Routledge, 2007) and *Transnational Muslim Politics: Reimagining the Umma* (Routledge, 2001), as well as co-editor of the volumes *The Zen of International Relations* (Palgrave, 2001), *Meaning and International Relations* (Routledge, 2003), and *Globalizing Religions* (Sage, 2008). Much of his recent work has focused on the comparative study of religious authority and social movements in the Muslim world. He is currently working on a project on 'Global Migration and Transnational Politics' funded by the MacArthur Foundation of Chicago (with Terrence Lyons).

Kate Manzo is Senior Lecturer in International Development in the School of Geography, Politics and Sociology at the University of Newcastle. She is author of *Domination, Resistance and Social Change in South Africa: The Local Effects of Global Power* (Praeger, 1992) and *Creating Boundaries: The Politics of Race and Nation* (Lynne Rienner, 1996). Her current research interests include Africa in the politics of development, images of Africa in Western media, and the iconography of climate change.

Anne Orford is an Australian Professorial Fellow, Chair of Law and Director of the Institute for International Law and the Humanities at the University of Melbourne. She researches in the areas of international law and legal theory, with a particular interest in the law relating to the use of force, international economic law and the international legal legacies of (particularly British) imperialism. Her publications include *Reading Humanitarian Intervention: Human Rights and the Use of Force in International Law* (Cambridge University Press, 2003) and the edited collection *International Law and Its Others* (Cambridge University Press, 2006). She was awarded a research-only Australian Professorial Fellowship by the Australian Research Council for work on a project entitled *Cosmopolitanism and the Future of International Law from 2007–2011*.

Mustapha Kamal Pasha is Professor of International Relations at the University of Aberdeen. He specialises in International Relations theory, globalization, and contemporary islam (with particular reference to confluence of globalization and Islam under conditions of late/post-modernity). He is the co-editor of *Human Security in a Post-9.11 World* (Palgrave, 2007) and *International Relations and the New Inequality* (Blackwell, 2002). He has also authored *Colonial Political Economy* (1998) and *Out from Underdevelopment Revisited: Changing Structures and the Remaking of the Third World* (with James Mittelman, Macmillan, 2002). Currently, he is completing a book on *Islam and International Relations: Modernity, Nihilism, and Politics*.

V. Spike Peterson is Professor in the Department of Political Science at the University of Arizona. She is the author of *A Critical Rewriting of Global Political Economy: Integrating Reproductive, Productive, and Virtual Economies* (Routledge, 2003), *Global Gender Issues* (with Anne S. Runyan, Westview Press, 1999, second edition) and co-editor of *Gendered States: Feminist (Re)Visions of International Relations Theory* (Lynne Rienner, 1992). Her current research focuses on informalisation in the global political economy. In 2004 the International Studies Association held an Eminent Scholar Panel Honoring V. Spike Peterson at its annual meeting. She is a Leverhulme Visiting Professor to the London School of Economics in 2007 and 2008.

Véronique Pin-Fat is Senior Lecturer in International Politics at the University of Manchester. She was awarded the Bernard Crick Prize for Outstanding Teaching in Politics by the Political Studies Association in 2006. She has a particular interest in the relationship between language, ethics and global politics. She is co-editor with Jenny Edkins and Michael J. Shapiro of *Sovereign Lives: Power in Global Politics* (Routledge, 2004) and with Jenny Edkins and Nalini Persram of *Sovereignty and Subjectivity* (Lynne Rienner, 1999). Her present research is an inquiry of universality.

Michael J. Shapiro is Professor of Political Science at the University of Hawaii. He is the author of numerous books, including *Violent Cartographies: Mapping Cultures of War* (University of Minnesota Press, 1997), *Methods and Nations: Cultural Governance and the Indigenous Subject* (Routledge, 2004) and *Deforming American Political Thought: Ethnicity, Facticity, and Genre* (University Press of Kentucky, 2006). His research covers political theory and philosophy, critical social theory, global politics, politics of media, politics of culture and indigenous politics. He has been involved in co-editing two books series, *Borderlines* (University of Minnesota Press) and *Taking on the Political* (University of Edinburgh Press). His most recent book is *Cinematic Geopolitics* (Routledge, 2008).

Annick T.R. Wibben is Assistant Professor of Politics at the University of San Francisco, where she also directs the Peace and Justice Studies Program. She continues to be affiliated with the Watson Institute for International Studies at Brown University where she was working with the Information Technology, War and Peace Project (infopeace.org) from 2001 to 2005. She is currently working on her book on *Feminist Security Studies* (Routledge, forthcoming in 2009). She has also co-produced a documentary, *After 9/11*, with James Der Derian and Udris Productions (2004). Her *Narrating Experience: Raymond Aron and Feminist Scholars Revis(it)ed* (1998) was published by the University of Tampere.

Maja Zehfuss is Professor of International Politics at the University of Manchester. She is the author of *Constructivism in International Relations: The Politics of Reality* (Cambridge University Press, 2002) and *Wounds of Memory: Politics of War in Germany* (Cambridge University Press, 2007). Her current research examines the politics of ethics in the context of war. She is a member of the National Academy of Teaching. She is also a member of the Governing Council of the International Studies Association for 2008–9.

Teaching with *Global Politics: A New Introduction*

This textbook offers a new way of teaching global politics. Many of us have become dissatisfied with existing introductions, which seem to fall into two camps – either starting with various 'theoretical approaches', or introducing global politics as a series of 'issues', or indeed offering some combination of the two. Beginning with contending approaches, while radical and inspiring when first introduced in the late 1980s, has become well worn and somewhat formulaic. Beginning with issues as an alternative can be equally frustrating. Although this new book includes both approaches and issues, it does not prioritise either. Instead, it begins with questions.

People come to the study of world politics with a series of questions about how to conceptualise the world and their place within it, motivated often by a desire for change. To give an example, many of these questions concern how we live in a world where so many people are brought together in such proximity. Who are 'we' anyway? Are we individuals, first and foremost, or social beings? What forms of identity do we adopt and why? What happens when things go wrong and we end up with wars and conflicts or severe economic inequalities?

The approach that this book presents takes questions like these as its starting point. Rather than asking students to set their questions aside whilst they study 'theory' or 'issues', the book tackles the questions head on. It uses them to draw out the concrete historical and geographical locations within which the questions are situated, examine the challenge and complexity of response, and emphasise the need to think carefully about the broader assumptions or theoretical approaches that underlie the questions we ask as well as the responses we give. Each chapter thus follows the same structure, with sections examining the question, an example, what responses there might be and broader issues raised. Taking students' questions seriously in this way fosters engagement, empowers and inspires students, and provides a sound basis for further study.

CHAPTER STRUCTURE

- The question
- Illustrative example
- Responses
- Broader issues

The book employs a number of pedagogical tools to do its job. Although the book tackles profound questions, it addresses these in a clear and accessible way. The language used is straightforward; any terms that might be difficult are carefully explained, sometimes in brackets, sometimes in marginal comments. Because the different questions that the book examines are intertwined, there are links from chapter to chapter. Throughout the book, more information about particular thinkers, detailed explanations of issues referred to and background about historical events are given in boxes that appear alongside the main discussion. The numerous illustrations aid understanding as well as emphasising the actual people and places involved in global politics. Cartoons provide pointed reflections and humorous asides.

Marginal comments are a feature of the book. They explain concepts, make links from one chapter to another and raise questions to think about.

PEDAGOGICAL TOOLS

- Accessible language
- Marginal comments
- Links between chapters
- Boxes
- Images, maps and cartoons

In its illustrative examples, the book covers many parts of the world and is wide in its historical scope. A range of different issues and events are covered, and thinkers who have addressed global questions in a variety of ways discussed. Two mappings of the book give a sense of its scope: a global mapping of issues and topics, and an historical mapping of thinkers and events. A further mapping in terms of the various concepts, ideologies and theories introduced indicates where each is covered in the book and points up how interconnected the questions are.

MAPPINGS OF THE BOOK

- Global mapping of places and topics
- Historical mapping: philosophers and world events
- Mapping of concepts: an intricate network of the overlapping concepts, theories and ideologies covered

As editors, we have learnt a lot about global politics in putting this book together. What is more, we have really enjoyed reading the chapters and seeing what this new way of approaching the subject makes possible. We hope that *Global Politics: A New Introduction* will enable students to think through the intriguing questions that they have and we hope that you will enjoy teaching with this book.

GLOBAL MAPPING OF PLACES AND ISSUES COVERED

Nuclear proliferation: Ch 19

Tiananmen Square 1989: Ch 6

Conflict in Korea: Ch 19

Microfinance in Bangladesh: Ch 14

Media/war in Vietnam: Ch 7

Intervention in Timor L'Este: Ch 18

Poverty in South Asia: Ch 14

Rise of European state: Ch 9

East European Revolutions of 1989: Ch 6

Bombing of Dresden 1945: Ch 1

Break-up of Yugoslavia: Ch 4, 18

Islam and Islamism in the Middle East and South Asia: Ch 5, 14

Global economy: Ch 12

Cold War 1947–1989: Ch 19

Media/war in Iraq 1991 and 2003–: Ch 2, 7, 20

Muslim Brotherhood in Egypt: Ch 5

San people in Botswana: Ch 9

Religion in Europe in sixteenth century: Ch 6, 5, 15

Nation in US and Europe: Ch 10

Israel/Palestine conflict: Ch 5

Killing in World Wars in Europe: Ch 1, 16

Hutu and Tutsi in Rwanda: Ch 4, 16

Global climate change: Ch 3

US Feminist identity politics: Ch 4

September 11 2001 and the 'war on terror': Ch 2

IMF, World Bank: Ch 11, 13, 14

Colonialism in Cote d'Ivoire: Ch 11

Extraordinary rendition: Ch 2

Torture debate in US: Ch 2

Earth Summit, Rio de Janerio 1992: Ch 3

US Warfare in 21st century: Ch 17

Migrant rights demonstrations 2006: Ch 8

US-Mexico border: Ch 8

Torture in Guantanamo: Ch 2

Spanish Conquest of the Americas: Ch 15

Global inequality: Ch 13

N

0   600   1800   3000   4200 Kms

HISTORICAL MAPPING: Philosophers and world events

1483–1546	**Martin Luther**	Reformation	Chapter 6
1485–1546	**Francisco de Vitoria**	International law	Chapter 15
Reformation in Europe 1517 Spanish conquests in South America			
1588–1679	**Thomas Hobbes**	Leviathan	Chapters 6, 10
Peace of Westphalia 1648			
1711–1776	**David Hume**	Political thought	Chapters 5, 10
1723–1790	**Adam Smith**	Political economy	Chapters 5, 12
1724–1804	**Immanuel Kant**	Cosmopolitan law	Chapters 5, 18
French Revolution 1789–92 American Revolution 1763–83			
1780–1831	**Carl von Clausewitz**	Strategy	Chapters 16, 17
Industrial Revolution in Europe Slave trade Colonial empires in Africa and Asia			
1809–1882	**Charles Darwin**	Evolution	Chapter 4
1818–1883	**Karl Marx**	Capitalism and Communism	Chapters 12, 13
1844–1900	**Friedrich Nietzsche**	Philosophy	Chapters 10, 19
First World War 1914–18 Russian Revolution 1917			
1856–1939	**Sigmund Freud**	Psychoanalysis	Chapter 4
1858–1917	**Emile Durkheim**	Sociology	Chapter 6
1864–1920	**Max Weber**	Sociology/Protestant ethic	Chapters 6, 9
Second World War 1939–45			
1888–1985	**Carl Schmitt**	Politcal theorist and jurist	Chapter 18
1889–1951	**Ludwig Wittgenstein**	Philosophy	Chapter 2
1891–1937	**Antonio Gramsci**	Marxist theory	Chapters 1, 7, 12
UN Charter 1945 Indian subcontinent: partition and independence 1947			
1901–1981	**Jacques Lacan**	Psychoanalysis	Chapter 4
1921–2002	**John Rawls**	Political theory: justice	Chapter 2
1925–1995	**Gilles Deleuze and Felix Guattari**	Philosophy	Chapter 10
Korean War 1950–53 18 African states regain independence 1960			
1926–1984	**Michel Foucault**	Power/knowledge	Chapters 1, 4, 6, 9, 17
1927–	**Samuel Huntington**	Clash of civilisations	Chapters 5, 8
1929–	**Jürgen Habermas**	Cosmopolitanism	Chapters 10, 18
Vietnam War 1959–75			
1930–2002	**Pierre Bourdieu**	Sociology	Chapter 10
1930–2004	**Jacques Derrida**	Philosophy	Chapter 20
1931–2003	**Neil Postman**	Media and cultural theory	Chapter 7
1932	**Stuart Hall**	Cultural theory	Chapter 7
1935–2003	**Edward Said**	Orientalism	Chapter 5
End of the Cold War 1989 Failure of Chinese democracy movement			
1935–	**Michael Walzer**	Communitarianism	Chapter 2
1936–	**Carol Gilligan**	Feminist ethics	Chapter 4
Gulf War 1991 Break-up of Yugoslavia 1991–			
1942–	**Giorgio Agamben**	Philosophy	Chapter 14
1948–	**Patricia Hill Collins**	Intersectionality	Chapter 4
1956–	**Judith Butler**	Performativity	Chapter4
September 11 2001 and the war on terror Iraq War 2003–			

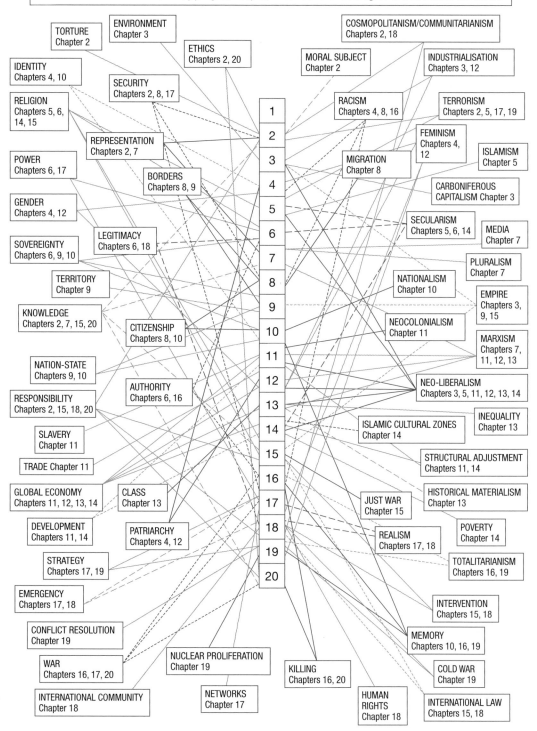

MAPPING OF CONCEPTS:
An intricate network of overlapping concepts, theories and ideologies is covered in the book

TORTURE
Chapter 2

ENVIRONMENT
Chapter 3

ETHICS
Chapters 2, 20

COSMOPOLITANISM/COMMUNITARIANISM
Chapters 2, 18

MORAL SUBJECT
Chapter 2

INDUSTRIALISATION
Chapters 3, 12

IDENTITY
Chapters 4, 10

SECURITY
Chapters 2, 8, 17

RACISM
Chapters 4, 8, 16

TERRORISM
Chapters 2, 5, 17, 19

RELIGION
Chapters 5, 6, 14, 15

FEMINISM
Chapters 4, 12

ISLAMISM
Chapter 5

REPRESENTATION
Chapters 2, 7

MIGRATION
Chapter 8

CARBONIFEROUS
CAPITALISM Chapter 3

POWER
Chapters 6, 17

BORDERS
Chapters 8, 9

SECULARISM
Chapters 5, 6, 14

MEDIA
Chapter 7

GENDER
Chapters 4, 12

LEGITIMACY
Chapters 6, 18

PLURALISM
Chapter 7

SOVEREIGNTY
Chapters 6, 9, 10

NATIONALISM
Chapter 10

EMPIRE
Chapters 3, 9, 15

TERRITORY
Chapter 9

KNOWLEDGE
Chapters 2, 7, 15, 20

CITIZENSHIP
Chapters 8, 10

NEOCOLONIALISM
Chapter 11

MARXISM
Chapters 7, 11, 12, 13

NATION-STATE
Chapters 9, 10

AUTHORITY
Chapters 6, 16

NEO-LIBERALISM
Chapters 3, 5, 11, 12, 13, 14

RESPONSIBILITY
Chapters 2, 15, 18, 20

ISLAMIC CULTURAL ZONES
Chapter 14

INEQUALITY
Chapter 13

SLAVERY
Chapter 11

STRUCTURAL ADJUSTMENT
Chapters 11, 14

TRADE Chapter 11

GLOBAL ECONOMY
Chapters 11, 12, 13, 14

CLASS
Chapter 13

HISTORICAL MATERIALISM
Chapter 13

JUST WAR
Chapter 15

DEVELOPMENT
Chapters 11, 14

PATRIARCHY
Chapters 4, 12

REALISM
Chapters 17, 18

POVERTY
Chapter 14

STRATEGY
Chapters 17, 19

TOTALITARIANISM
Chapters 16, 19

EMERGENCY
Chapters 17, 18

INTERVENTION
Chapters 15, 18

CONFLICT RESOLUTION
Chapter 19

MEMORY
Chapters 10, 16, 19

WAR
Chapters 16, 17, 20

NUCLEAR PROLIFERATION
Chapter 19

KILLING
Chapters 16, 20

COLD WAR
Chapter 19

INTERNATIONAL COMMUNITY
Chapter 18

NETWORKS
Chapter 17

HUMAN
RIGHTS
Chapter 18

INTERNATIONAL LAW
Chapters 15, 18

1
2
3
4
5
6
7
8
9
10
11
12
13
14
15
16
17
18
19
20

Acknowledgements

This project has only been possible because of the support and enthusiasm of numerous people all along the way, from first concept to finished book. First of all the many anonymous reviewers who looked at the proposal and responded with enthusiasm and support – sometimes qualified support, but support none the less – and the smaller group who read the initial manuscript in its entirety or in part and gave us detailed feedback. As well as this formal seal of approval, the excitement of numerous colleagues whom we bored with accounts of what we were up to has sustained us along the way. Perhaps the biggest thanks are of course owed to our band of contributors, who agreed readily to our requests for contributions, and put up with good grace with a pair of very intrusive editors and the demand for numerous revisions, expansions and explanations. That they remained nothing short of enthusiastic throughout all this was more than we could have hoped for. We have been overwhelmed by the quality of the chapters – their content and their style – which has in all cases not only met but exceeded our expectations from what we knew at the start were a very high-calibre bunch of authors. We hope you will all enjoy the finished product. We would also like to thank our students: the initial idea for the book would not have taken shape without them – their engagement and disengagement during the courses we have taught provided the inspiration for a new approach. Their detailed input in terms of identifying questions that they brought to the study of global politics provided the basis for the design of the book. Finally, the project would never have seen the light of day without the energetic support of the team at Routledge. Craig Fowlie believed in the project from the start, and this made us think that maybe we had a concept worth pursuing. Moira Taylor was unstinting in her support and hard work through all the difficulties along the way. Finally, although in the end his name is not in our list of authors, thanks are due to Rob Walker for his insistence at the beginning that we pursue our idea. He told us we should write it ourselves – I hope he will agree with us that had we done so the end product would have been nothing like as strong as what we have now. It has been worth all the hard work along the way. Each time we have re-read the manuscript our enthusiasm has been redoubled. Global politics is fascinating. We are delighted that our contributors have been able to bring this out and we have been particularly impressed by their commitment to engaging with readers. Thank you all.

CHAPTER 1

Introduction

Jenny Edkins and Maja Zehfuss

- *The question*
  WHAT DOES THIS INTRODUCTION TO GLOBAL POLITICS DO?

- *Illustrative example*
  HOW DO WE USE ILLUSTRATIVE EXAMPLES?

- *Responses*
  WHAT SORTS OF RESPONSES MIGHT THERE BE?

- *Broader issues*
  WHAT ASSUMPTIONS DO WE START FROM?

- **CONCLUSION**

THE QUESTION
WHAT DOES THIS INTRODUCTION TO GLOBAL POLITICS DO?

This is a textbook, but it is more than that. It is a guide for students to the questions about world politics that puzzle all of us. There are no easy answers to be had, and none of the chapters pretend that there are. There are only difficult and challenging questions – that lead to more difficult and more challenging questions. We think this is because the difficulties of global politics reflect the difficulties of 'life, the universe and everything'. This makes this book in some sense a sort of hitchhiker's guide. We don't give you answers, not even Douglas Adams' (1979) answer – you will need to read his *Hitchhiker's Guide to the Galaxy* (if you haven't already) if you want to know his answer – but we do try to give you a guide to how other people have formulated questions and how they have attempted to respond to them. Many textbooks behave as if the 'great minds' had come up with the answers: they haven't. The questions remain open and intractable, there for each new generation to formulate and tackle for themselves. This section of the introduction explores what questions we address, and discusses how the approach this book takes relates to that taken by other textbooks of world politics or international relations. So, instead of starting from the sorts of explanations of global politics that 'great minds' have given (as those textbooks do that start from 'theories') or starting from some problem in global politics (as those textbooks do that start from 'issues'), in this book we start with questions. As we have been teaching global politics, our students have asked us very intriguing questions. Often we have found that our students' curiosity is motivated by the same sorts of questions that stimulate our own interest in global politics. In this book we have tried to put together a set of these questions. Each

FIGURE 1.1
Martin Freeman as Arthur Dent and Mos Def as Ford Prefect in Touchstone Pictures' *The Hitchhiker's Guide to the Galaxy*. Ronald Grant Archive

chapter starts by introducing its main question. So this book tackles nineteen main questions. But often when we start thinking about one particular question we realise that it raises a number of other questions. Each chapter therefore focuses on one main question – the one you see in the chapter heading – but it will also discuss related questions and make reference to other chapters and their questions. We sometimes use a feature called 'marginal comments' to alert you to how the discussion in one chapter links to the question or explanation in another. Let us briefly explain what we mean by questions being related in this way.

The way we plan to use comments in the margins of the textbook is explained here.

You might, for example, wonder why people can't freely decide where they want to live (Chapter 8). Some of you may indeed have encountered this problem when you applied to a university: you may have wished to go to a university that is not in the state of which you are a citizen and this might have set off a series of problems. You may have had to apply for a visa and pay higher tuition fees, and you may at the same time have been ineligible for (some of the) available scholarships and found it difficult to acquire the right paperwork to be able to get a part-time job. Your citizenship has a material impact on how you can live your life.

So, in some way, you know the answer to the question: people can't move freely because states can decide who may and may not legally live within their borders. But how is it that states have this right? And why is the world divided into states in the first place (Chapter 9)? As you think about this you may notice that we often talk of this division in terms of 'nation-states'. But how and why have nations and states come to be related in this way? Does our allegiance to a particular nation overlap with our relation to a state (Chapter 10)? You have now started thinking about how we think about our identity. So now you need to figure out who we think we are (Chapter 4) and how we even begin to think about the world. For example, in determining how we behave towards others (say, whether we should give them financial assistance) does it matter whether these others belong to the same or another community (Chapter 2)? If how we think about the world has an impact, then what about particular ways of conceptualising the world and our place within it, such as religious beliefs. How do they affect politics (Chapter 5)? And how do we come to believe what we believe in the first place? In order to understand that, perhaps we need to know how we find out what's going on in the world (Chapter 7). And, come to think of it, did we start in the best place to think about global politics? We started with you: as good a place as any, you may think. But is there not more to the globe than the people that live on it? As we increasingly worry about climate change, we might wonder whether we don't need to figure out what it might mean not to think in human terms (Chapter 3).

So, you see, many of our questions are connected with each other. We invariably start with a particular question or concern, and often we may not even realise that it is related to global politics. But as we pursue ways of thinking about and

FIGURE 1.2
'Like all of us, he asked many different questions throughout his life'. Artist: Richard Jolley. CartoonStock Ref: rj00698.
www.CartoonStock.com

responding to the question we find that new questions are raised, often questions that concern global issues.

ILLUSTRATIVE EXAMPLE
HOW DO WE USE ILLUSTRATIVE EXAMPLES?

What you will find in this book are a lot of fascinating, and at times moving, accounts of what is going on or has gone on in particular places at specific historical points in global history. Sometimes these stories will be large-scale histories and at other times they will recount the experiences of maybe one person and their life. You will get to know a lot about many different places: this section of the introduction will map some of them for you.

When we just explained why questions are often related to each other, we did not have space to say very much about why we are asking the question or who might be affected by it. We briefly showed you how you yourself might have been affected by citizenship regulations, but we did not go into any detail. In each of the chapters, however, the authors tell you at some length about a particular context in which the question they examine has arisen. We call this an illustrative example. It's an example because for each question there will be many other cases that one could look at in relation to the question and, of course, another case may highlight different issues. But the example chosen will illustrate what issues arise when we explore the question in a particular context. It will show you why

The book contains many illustrative examples. We tell you here what we mean by that, and why we think they are important.

the question is important, who is affected by it and what is at stake in responding to it in one way or another. You will, of course, have realised that in order to cross a border legally you need the right documentation. And you probably know that many people in different regions of the world attempt to enter countries illegally and often they risk their lives in the process. But by looking at the particular example of the US–Mexico border, the author of Chapter 8, Roxanne Lynn Doty, is able to show how the US border enforcement policies of the 1990s led to a sharp increase in the number deaths along the border and how these policies were linked to larger developments in economics and security.

For many people the question of which country they are authorised to live in is one of life and death. We think it is important to acknowledge this when we ask why people cannot simply choose where they wish to live. This is also the case with the other questions explored in the book. When we ask what we can do to stop people harming others, we need to understand why people are harming each other in the first place (Chapter 18). The precise circumstances matter. What you will come across in the chapters of this book is a series of detailed accounts, sometimes heart-rending, of things that have happened or are happening in particular places at particular times. This means that as you read the book you will learn quite a bit about different places across the globe, the places where 'global politics' happen. We'll try to map some of these places in this section of the introduction.

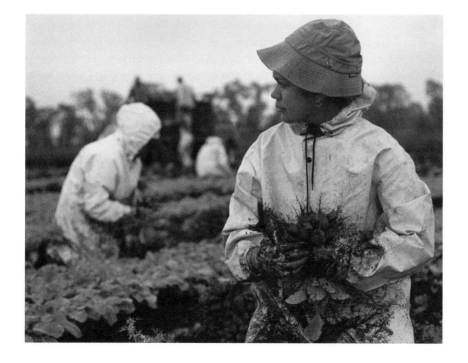

FIGURE 1.3
Migrant workers harvest radishes on the K.W. Zellers and Son family farm in Hartville, Ohio. This photo is published in *Growing Season: The Life of a Migrant Community*, published by Kent State University Press. Photo: Gary Harwood

What counts as a 'global' issue is not obvious, and people will have different views on this. And the terms people use are different too: some people talk of 'global politics', as this book does, and others of 'world politics'. The traditional term is 'international politics' or 'international relations', but we don't use either of these traditional terms here since they seem to limit global politics to relations between states or nations.

Some chapters explore phenomena that are obviously global in scope, such as climate change (Chapter 3), but they might still affect people in different places differently. This is important in order to understand the politics: those people who are in danger of losing their livelihoods and homes because of the impact of hurricanes, for example, are likely to think that climate change is a very pressing issue, whereas people living in areas not so affected might not want to assign resources to avoiding environmental change. Similarly, while there is global inequality across the globe and within each country, what this means, and what it means to be poor, depends on where you live. Chapter 13 examines developed countries in Europe, North America and Japan, but also developing and emerging countries such as Brazil, Russia, India and China.

You will also learn about many other places and how they relate to each other, creating what we call global politics and responding to it. Asia, for example, is prominent in this book. We have already noted that Chapter 13 gives you information about inequality in Japan, India and China. Chapter 14 examines responses to poverty in South Asia, Bangladesh in particular. Chapter 19 takes you to a different part of Asia, North and South Korea, and looks at the difficult relations between these two countries and how they relate to wider issues in global politics, especially the Cold War. Chapter 18 looks at East Timor's development and recent attempts to constrain violence there. As in many other cases, the question of independence for East Timor cannot be understood in separation from other countries or regions and their involvement, such as, in this case, Portugal, Indonesia and Australia. Similarly, Chapter 5 focuses on Islamic states in the Middle East, but it also discusses countries located in Asia and, of course, Africa. Chapter 11 focuses on an African country, Ivory Coast, and its role in the cocoa trade. This, again, only makes sense if we also look at the history of colonisation by France and the way in which the global economy impacts upon Ivory Coast.

It will come as no surprise to you that the United States often comes into the story of these examples. In a number of the chapters there is a clear focus on the United States (Chapters 4, 8, 10, 15 and 17), but many of the others also make reference to this country. Europe is also significant. Chapter 9 focuses on Europe and in particular the state as we now understand it, and Chapter 6 looks at the end of the Cold War in Europe, but many other chapters tell you something about Europe or particular European states.

So our 'illustrative examples' allow us to take you on something of a tour around the globe and let you learn something about places that you might not know that much about yet. But there is another reason why we examine such particular examples. In the last section, we showed you that often, when we try to respond to one question, we come across a lot of other questions. So, when we ask why people cannot simply choose where to live, we may say that this is because states can decide who may live within their borders. But this really is only a partial answer:

BOX 1.1 THE THIRD WORLD

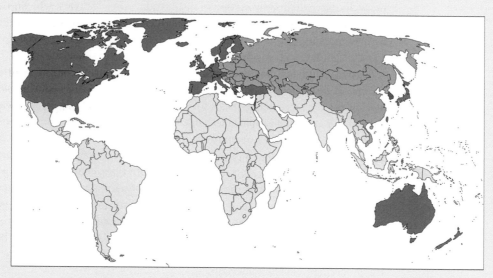

FIGURE 1.4
The three 'worlds'. Public domain

The term 'third world' was first coined in 1952. At that time, during the Cold War, the world seemed to be made up of three groups of countries: the 'modern', liberal, industrialised countries of the 'West' (US, UK and other European states, Japan, Australia, Canada and so on), the communist states of the USSR, or Soviet Union, and the 'underdeveloped' or non-industrialised states: states in Africa, Asia, South America. These groups were seen as making up the first, second and 'third' worlds, respectively. The term 'third world' was problematic, not only because this picture of the world was oversimplified from the start and became increasingly so as countries in Asia, for example, began to industrialise rapidly, and later when the communist regimes of the Soviet Union collapsed, but also because of the implicit hierarchy of 'first', 'second' and 'third'. Alternative terminologies have been suggested: 'developing world', 'emerging countries' or the division North–South, for example, but none of these is satisfactory either and the term 'third world' remains in common use.

we don't yet know why it is that states may do that. In other words, there are often many other things that we need to know in order to think through particular questions. Sometimes we actually don't really appreciate quite what it is we need to know unless we think a bit more about why we are actually asking the question, what it means for particular people, for example. In other words, the devil is often in the detail. Let us explain this in relation to a particular example.

Why are there wars?

To illustrate how looking at the detail of what happens at particular points in time in specific places helps, this section of the introduction will do just that with respect to the question 'Why are there wars?' This is certainly a question that has intrigued and vexed many thinkers. You have probably asked yourself this very question at one point or another. Most likely you were prompted by a particular war. So you may have wondered, for example, about why a group of other countries led by the United States intervened militarily in Iraq in 2003. You may have seen pictures of the destruction caused on television or read about the deaths of service personnel and Iraqi civilians in the press. You may even know people who are involved in this war in some way, and you may be concerned for their lives. So you would be asking the question 'Why are there wars?' very much with a sense of dissatisfaction in mind. What you really are asking might very well be: 'Why are there wars when they cause such destruction and misery, when they kill people?' This is, incidentally, why you have quite possibly not asked yourself in the same sort of way why there is peace, for example. Intuitively, we would prefer peace over war. If there are wars nevertheless, we would like to have an explanation for that. We don't seem to require an explanation for peace – or peace, say, in Sweden – in the same way.

At least part of the reason why we want an explanation for war is that wars involve deliberate and significant destruction. Using military force means intentionally destroying things. Ideally, the destruction is aimed at and limited to military targets, that is, basically, enemy combatants and those things that enable them to act as combatants, such as, most obviously, their weaponry. Often other things and people get destroyed, too, however. If this was not the aim of the action that brought about the destruction, then this is called 'collateral damage' and is not illegal under international law, unless it is excessive. Nevertheless people are killed.

Chapter 20 engages further with the dilemmas that arise in considering war as a response to perceived wrong in the world.

You probably don't much like the idea of killing people and, if so, you are likely to think that war is not such a good idea. But it's not that simple. First, sometimes people claim that, while wars do kill people, particular wars kill fewer people than the alternative. So, if Saddam Hussein's Iraq really had had weapons of mass destruction and had used them, many more deaths might have ensued. The argument therefore is that we must go to war in order to avoid deaths. But of course you can immediately see that this is a really problematic claim: you have to make all kinds of assumptions about what might happen in order to argue this. And, as the case of Iraq shows, one can very easily be wrong about such things. Second, if you are really against war because war kills people, you should probably also be against cars. 3,180 people were killed on the United Kingdom's roads, for example, in the twelve months ending in March 2006 (Wilkins 2006). That means almost nine people died as a result of road traffic accidents every day. This is a considerable number of deaths, and people certainly campaign to reduce the number of these deaths, but there is not the widespread condemnation of cars (as a cause of death) that there is of wars.

Bombing of German cities in the Second World War

In order to think through why this might be the case it is helpful to think about a particular example. We could look at the war in Iraq, but we actually want to examine something different, an aspect of the larger set of events that is called the Second World War. You probably already know something about this war. You will be aware that the Allies won. When we say 'the Allies', we generally mean the United States, the Soviet Union, the United Kingdom and France, although it really is all a bit more complicated. Germany and Japan surrendered to the Allies in May and August 1945, respectively. This 'world' war was fought in a large number of places across the planet, but we want to look at only one aspect of it: the bombing of German cities.

For more on the Second World War, see **Chapter 16**.

From 1940 onwards the British Royal Air Force bombed 131 towns and cities across Germany, some of them repeatedly (Sebald 2004: 3). From 1943 the United States Army Air Force was also involved in what was then called the combined strategic bombing offensive. It is often said that there was a significant difference between how the US and the UK went about the bombing. The US is said to have been involved in 'counterforce' targeting (that is, they aimed to attack militarily relevant sites only), whereas the UK engaged in 'countervalue' targeting (that is, they deliberately targeted cities and the people who lived within them). One strategy was meant to disable the Germans from continuing the war by taking away from them the means for conducting the war, the other to demoralise the population such that they would overthrow the government or in some other way give up the fight. Another way to put this is to say that the US was involved in 'precision' bombing of particular, militarily valuable targets whereas the UK was involved in what is variously called 'area bombing', 'carpet bombing' or 'obliteration bombing'. Of course, things were not that straightforward: there was considerable debate in both countries throughout the war about bombing strategies, and as a result approaches to bombing changed over time. And it was the Americans who actually built a replica of Berlin in the desert in Utah in order to figure out how to destroy the city by setting off a fire-storm through the bombing (Davis 2002).

The precise extent of the destruction caused by these operations is difficult to measure precisely, but it was certainly considerable. A.C. Grayling notes that '485,000 dwellings were completely destroyed and 415,000 severely damaged' (Grayling 2007: 103) and this constituted 20 per cent of Germany's housing stock at the time. W.G. Sebald uses slightly different figures. He speaks of 3.5 million homes destroyed and 7.5 million civilians rendered homeless. There were 31.1 cubic metres of rubble per inhabitant in Cologne and 42.8 in Dresden (Sebald 2004: 3).

We know that hundreds of thousands of people died in these raids, though there is no precise figure that is agreed. According to the US Strategic Bombing Survey of September 1945, 305,000 German civilians were killed by bombs and another 780,000 injured (Grayling 2007: 104). A figure of about 600,000 civilian deaths is also often cited. One of the problems in determining the death toll is that human remains could often not be recovered, in particular where bombing had led to a fire-storm. There is a bit more clarity about the airmen who were killed: 55,000 members of the British Bomber Command died – that is, an astonishing 44 per cent of them, according to Jörg Friedrich (2002) – and 7,700 aircraft were lost (Grayling 2007: 104).

The bombing of Dresden is particularly infamous. This is in part because it happened so late in the war, on 13 February 1945, but also because the destruction caused was particularly devastating. Dresden, like Hamburg in 1943, was one of the cities where the bombing set off a fire-storm. A variety of bombs were used on cities. Some were designed to create a shock-wave that would reduce buildings to rubble or, at a greater distance, break windows and strip roofs. A much bigger effect could, however, be achieved by using incendiary bombs. These would start a fire, sometimes using phosphor, which could not be put out with water. Other bombs, involving a timed delay mechanism, would stop firecrews from putting out the blazes. Eventually, the fire would create a wind that would fan the flames even more. The heat would become unbearable. The fire in Dresden was such that later waves of bombers had to fly at a higher altitude.

FIGURE 1.5
Dresden, 1945: Cremation on Altmarkt. Photo: Library of Congress. Digital Ref: 3b40632

No markers could be made out any more and in at least one instance an order was given to simply bomb 'the middle of the fires' (Taylor 2005: 320). The fires were visible for about 100 miles (Taylor 2005: 325)

In fire-storms many died not from blasts, but from asphyxiation. They died because they stayed in the air-raid shelters. In some shelters in Dresden, several thousand people were killed by lack of oxygen, smoke poisoning and carbon monoxide poisoning (Taylor 2005: 329). Others were buried alive underneath buildings that had collapsed (Taylor 2005: 330). Those who left the shelters had to contend with new waves of attack, time-delayed bombs that would continue to go off and, of course, the fire. The fire in Dresden was strong enough to suck people towards its core. They also had to attempt to escape the 'tornadoes of burning sparks and debris'. In the city centre, many were simply burnt to death (Taylor 2005: 331–2).

Frederick Taylor quotes at length from a letter by one survivor, Hans Schröter, to a woman whose parents' deaths he had seen:

> We had got through both raids and thought we would now survive. This unfortunately was not to be the case. The door of the basement of No. 38 [Marienstrasse] was buried under rubble, so the only option was the emergency exit to No. 40 and 42. When we got through to No. 40, flames were already pouring down the steps, so that to save our lives we had to act with the utmost haste. . . . To push through the exit required enormous courage, and many could not summon it – including, perhaps, your beloved parents. They may have thought we'll be all right in the basement, but they had not reckoned with the oxygen shortage. As I emerged, I saw my wife and son standing by the security post on the *parterre* of No. 42. . . . When we got back [after two minutes], however, my loved ones had disappeared. I checked every shelter and basement on the street. Nowhere were they to be seen, everything wreathed in flame, no entry possible. Unable to find my family, I summoned my last instincts for survival, got as far as the Bismarck Memorial.
>
> (Taylor 2005: 336)

The following day Schröter returned to his home.

> The sight that greeted my eyes was appalling . . . Everywhere charred corpses. I quickly headed home, hoping to find my loved ones alive, but unfortunately this was not so. They lay on the street in front of No. 38, as peacefully as if they were asleep. What I went through at that point you can easily imagine. Now I had to find out if my parents-in-law or other friends could be rescued from our basement alive. . . . As we opened up the emergency exit from No. 38, the heat that came out was so intense that we could not go down

there. . . . The basement of No. 42 was full of bodies. I counted about fifty. Eulitz was among them. I could not see your parents, as everyone was piled on top of each other.

(Taylor 2005: 337)

RESPONSES
WHAT SORTS OF RESPONSES MIGHT THERE BE?

Reading these harrowing accounts, you may well be at a loss to know quite how to respond. No response seems adequate in view of the horrors described here. We find ourselves engaged and moved by such accounts in a way quite different from the way we might engage with an 'academic' argument. We wonder whether our emotional response is acceptable, or whether we are required to put this aside and take a dispassionate view – though whether or to what extent we may find that possible is questionable. Just for the sake of argument, let's differentiate between two sorts of responses as we think about this. On the one hand, you may think that it is extremely important to engage with what happened to individual people in this war, and with the horrific effects that the bombing had on people's lives, and deaths. These effects are likely to produce strong emotions in those who read about them. You may be appalled, for example, that people were burnt alive. You are prompted to imagine yourself or your family members in a similar situation, and think about how you would feel and react. You may then feel a strong desire to do something about it – a responsibility, if you like, to prevent others from having to suffer in this appalling way.

On the other hand, you may think that these individual stories and hardships have to be put into some sort of context, and that thinking about them in that way is equally, or even more, central. You may consider that, whilst clearly you would not wish such suffering on anyone, there are other important issues to be considered here, and that we could lose sight of these if we were to allow ourselves to be overwhelmed by an emotional response. Some people want to respond in what they consider to be more 'rational', objective or abstract terms. Some might want to say that we should weigh up the pros and cons of the bombing campaigns which led to such horrendous suffering, rather than simply react to the suffering itself. The bombing of German cities was part of the Allies' larger fight against the Third Reich. It is often said to have been a response to the bombing of cities by the Nazis, in particular the bombing of Rotterdam in May 1940. The Second World War is often represented as a necessary or even 'good' war. Note that what is meant here is the war fought by the Allies, even if that is often not mentioned. People often assume that 'we' all look at this war from the perspective of the Allies, the victors. It was a good war because the Third Reich was such an appalling political system. Many people, it is argued, were saved from the murderous

You might like to look at Chapter 7, where the author discusses her emotional response to a film about war.

This is related to the idea of 'just war' discussed in Chapter 15.

policies of the Third Reich by the victory of the Allies, and the death of several hundred thousand German civilians is not such a large price to pay in this context.

Does it matter that this way of waging war killed many civilians? Does it matter how people died? Is there something particular about how people die in war? Usually we don't look at deaths in detail. But if we want to understand why there are wars, do we not need to grasp what wars are in this sort of way? Arguably, war is, precisely, about killing people (Bourke 1999). Some people might say that getting too involved with the deaths and their gruesomeness detracts from thinking about the 'real' issues. What they usually mean by this is that we need to focus on the need to fight the Third Reich. But now we are already talking about how people think about war, how they respond to the question of why there are wars. Responses to questions are what we look at in the next section here. In the last we just wanted to show you how examining a particular example can affect how you might think about a question, what you might think is important.

Each chapter begins by discussing detailed, grounded historical practices, such as the example that we have just set out, one situation within which the chapter question might have arisen. So we now know how the question has affected particular people, for example. You might be impatient to know by now how to respond to the question. So far we have shown how difficult it can be to know how to respond. In the section called 'Responses', each of the chapters therefore looks at how people have responded in general to the question at issue. When we say 'respond to a question', there seem to be two senses in which we might do this. We might think through the question, in the way in which scholars do, for example, looking for an answer. We mentioned earlier that some textbooks seem to suggest that the 'great minds' have come up with the answer to your questions and this is the sort of thing that we will be exploring in this part of the chapters. You already know that we don't really believe that there are such answers that we can turn to. But it's still important to engage with such attempts at answers. Doing so, not least, helps us understand better why we might not be satisfied by such answers.

There is another way in which we might think about responses: we might look to act in response to the question by doing something about it. So, if we were to further explore the question of why there are wars, we could examine groups that have opposed war and try to understand how they have aimed to overcome the problem. Of course, these two senses of response are not separate. How you aim to get rid of war is likely to be informed by the way in which you think about the question of why there are wars. But some of our chapters stress one sense of 'responding' to the question, whilst others focus on the other. Whichever way they interpret responses, these chapters always give you a range of different responses to think about and compare.

Chapter 16 discusses killing in war.

There are a number of ways of responding to questions. In this section we examine what we mean by 'responses' and what different types of responses there might be.

Let's first look at ways of thinking through the question as a form of response. One thing you will notice is that some of the ways of responding to different questions are actually similar to each other. Some ways of thinking – or what will be called pictures of the world in Chapter 2 – have a lot to say about a whole range of issues in global politics. A number of the chapters examine Marxism as a response to the chapter question (Chapter 7, 11, 12, 13 and, briefly, 9). Marxism takes economics to be fundamental to understanding politics, and so it's no surprise that the chapters that focus on obviously economic issues use this way of thinking about the world. But, of course, the point is that economics also matters when we might not notice it right away, for example when we try to understand the media (Chapter 7). A number of the responses explored in the different chapters highlight the significance of the history of colonisation and its effects in the present (Chapters 3, 11 and 15), which is related to this way of thinking. Liberalism or neoliberalism also holds that economics is really important, but, as you will see, this way of thinking has a rather different idea of how the economy 'works' and therefore a very different idea of how we should respond to particular questions (Chapter 12, 13 and 14). You will also notice that 'pluralism' (Chapter 7) is very similar to liberalism.

Other ways of thinking start in a different place. One important question in politics is often who you are or, put differently, which group you belong to. Chapter 4 examines different ways of thinking about this important issue of identity: it makes a difference whether we think identity is static or dynamic. Chapter 2 looks at different ways of conceptualising what we should do in the world and, again, this is related to who we think we are. The chapter compares and contrasts the cosmopolitanism of Charles Beitz and the communitarianism of Michael Walzer. The latter sees the community we belong to as significant in responding to the question, whereas the former sees individuals as the subjects of global politics. Chapter 10 looks at a different set of thinkers and ways of thinking that tell us about why we might feel allegiance to a community, such as Thomas Hobbes, John Locke and Jean-Jacques Rousseau.

Some chapters think of responses more in terms of actions in response to the question at issue. Chapter 8, for example, examines ways in which citizenship has been organised by states and the problems this creates. Chapter 15, which examines why some people think they know what is good for others, looks at two contemporary expressions of this attitude: the Euston Manifesto and the idea of benevolent imperialism. When there is conflict in the world, we often want to know how to move beyond it. Chapter 19 examines two different responses to this problem, confrontation or engagement.

But these two senses of 'response' are not as separate as they may appear. The examination of indigenous perspectives in Chapter 3, for example, not only represents a completely different way of thinking our place in the world, a different

BOX 1.2 SUSAN MEISELAS, PHOTOGRAPHER

The cover photograph by Magnum's Susan Meiselas shows a rebel in Nicaragua in 1978 wearing a traditional mask to conceal his or her identity. Meiselas returned to Nicaragua ten years after she took her photos of the revolution to 'step back through the looking glass to find the people she once photographed, to forge connections and return their pictures to them' (Brothers 2007). She produced a documentary in 1991, *Pictures of a Revolution,* to mark this return. On the cover of the DVD is an image of youths wearing similar masks practising to throw contact bombs.

According to Meiselas, 'We take pictures away and we don't bring them back. That became a central quest for me – relinking, revisiting, the repatriation of work: it's become a kind of motif in my thinking'. A number of her images involve identity and its masking, whether she is photographing revolutionaries or demonstrators in disguise, or forensic odontologists who attempt to trace the missing through the reconstruction of facial features from skulls. Meiselas' website is at http://www.susanmeiselas.com/.

(*Pictures from a Revolution*. Directors: Susan Meiselas, Richard P. Rogers, Alfred Guzzetti. DVD, 2007. 88 mins)

FIGURE 1.6
Nicaragua. June 1978. Youths practise throwing contact bombs in forest surrounding Monimbo. Photo: Susan Meiselas. Magnum. Image Reference NYC15590 (MES1981016 K023)

cosmology, if you will, but this directly implies a different way of relating to the natural world, that is, a different way of acting. Similarly, the idea that politics and religion are best kept separate, called secularism, has practical implications: politics is in many states organised in accordance with this belief (Chapters 5 and 6). Different conceptions of the law favour different ways of responding to political problems (Chapter 18). Ideas about geopolitics or strategy (Chapter 3, 9, 16 and 17) also have an effect on how we think it is appropriate or profitable to act in the world. This interconnection is shown very clearly in Chapter 17. Changes in technology may in turn affect how we think and act (Chapters 9 and 17).

BROADER ISSUES
WHAT ASSUMPTIONS DO WE START FROM?

Looking at the general responses that people have come up with to the questions that our chapters address often leads to broader questions, questions that might need to be thought about before we can even begin to think about the particular question at issue in the chapter. Sometimes, the responses we examine will already have assumed certain answers to these broader questions. In other words, they will have taken certain things for granted, without even examining or thinking about them. This is often not deliberate. Sometimes it is very difficult to identify what has been taken for granted, precisely because it *is* 'taken for granted' and so widely assumed to be the case that it is not subject to question. We don't even see that we have made certain assumptions before we start. It seems to be 'common sense': there seems to be no alternative way to think about it.

However, if we want to delve more into how we might respond to the questions that concern us, we need to try to identify some of the assumptions that ground our usual ways of thinking. Knowing (or, rather, trying to think about) what assumptions we start from is standard practice in much academic and scholarly reflection. If we don't do this, we may end up with answers to our questions that are limited in ways we can't recognise, and that don't enable us to think beyond (or even be aware of) the constraints that 'common sense' imposes, or come up with useful ways of addressing our concerns. Robert Cox (1981) has characterised two ways of thinking about global politics. One he calls 'problem-solving theory'; the other he calls 'critical theory'. Problem-solving thinking works *within* the assumptions of what counts as common sense at a particular point in time. It looks at the problem, or in our case the question, on its own terms, and seeks an answer within the same framework or set of assumptions that raised the question in the first place. Critical thinking seeks to *question* the problem itself, and the common sense it takes for granted. Our thinking is conditioned by social, cultural and ideological influences, and critical theory seeks to uncover this conditioning. A critical approach would seek to ask why a particular issue had been put forward as a problem to be solved in the first place: what were the common-sense assumptions hidden behind thinking of that as a problem? Such an approach would also ask who would *benefit* from the problem being solved if we were to solve it on the terms in which it is posed. In general, Cox argues, problem-solving theory works to reinforce what is called the status quo – it keeps in place accepted ways of thinking and the structures of political and economic power that go along with those ways of thinking. As he famously said, 'Theory is always *for* someone and *for* some purpose' (Cox 1981: 128); his argument was that in order to think critically we had to make sure we examined the power relations in which our thinking was inevitably embedded. Critical thinking, in other words, 'stands apart from the prevailing order and asks how that order came about' (Cox 1981: 129) because, if we do want to change anything, we first have to understand the world as it is. Many of the chapters of this book attempt to think in this critical type of way when examining the responses that have been given to the questions they address.

Chapter 20 further discusses the idea of change and the sorts of assumptions that are behind it.

Identifying the assumptions within which our thinking might be working is much more difficult and challenging than it might seem. However, it is also very rewarding: once we pinpoint our hidden assumptions, we open up the possibility of different ways of thinking about the world. These different ways of thinking are not, of course, ways that avoid making assumptions, but they are based on *different* assumptions. And, since theory and practice are not as separate as they seem, as we will discuss in a minute, this also opens up the possibility of *doing* things differently. It doesn't mean that we can change the world overnight, of course not, but it does open up ways of thinking about how we might work for the change we want, a question that we look at in more detail in the concluding chapter of the book. Perhaps just as importantly, it enables us to see how what we do has been constrained by the common sense within which we have been thinking.

BOX 1.3 ANTONIO GRAMSCI

Italian Marxist thinker Antonio Gramsci (1891–1937) was imprisoned by Mussolini's fascist regime in Italy between 1926 and 1937, and he wrote his most famous works during that period. As a result of these circumstances, they are written in the form of fragmentary notes, avoiding the use of words such as 'Marx' and 'class' (a key concept in Marxist thought, as Chapter 13 explains). Gramsci's eleven years in prison led to a complete breakdown of his already far from robust health. His thirty-three prison notebooks were smuggled out of his clinic room to safety by his sister-in-law Tatiana Schucht when he died in April 1937.

FIGURE 1.7
Antonio Gramsci

It is very important to ask how the common sense that limits our thinking is produced. Antonio Gramsci argues that 'in all periods there co-exist many systems and currents' of thought, which are first born and then spread or diffused in society; in this process of diffusion 'they fracture along certain lines and in certain directions' (Gramsci 1971: 327). We need to examine how these processes work. But these ways in which accepted ways of thinking are produced and circulated are not something that can be thought of as separate from academic enquiry itself. As students of global politics we are not outside common sense: it influences us too. We all have what Gramsci called a 'spontaneous philosophy', contained in language, common sense, and the collections of beliefs, religious or otherwise, that we hold (Gramsci 1971: 323). There is not just one common sense: common sense is a product of history and circumstance. We are each, Gramsci says, the 'product of the historical process to date which has deposited in [us] an infinity of traces, without leaving an inventory' (Gramsci 1971: 324).

Our task, then, if we want to think critically, is to make such an inventory, or, in other words, to attempt to figure out what those influences might be that have made us think and act the way we do. The job is to track down our assumptions, and to acknowledge what is unquestioned or taken for granted in our ways of thinking. Common sense needs to be replaced by criticism, or what we might call critical theory, in the sense that Cox used this term, as we discussed just now.

There is one further point that needs to be made about our ways of thinking – or what Gramsci calls our 'philosophies' and what we might here want to call, in our terminology, our 'theories'. Let's look at what Gramsci (writing at a time when it was common sense to assume that the pronoun 'he' could unproblematically be taken to refer to 'he or she', and 'man' to encompass 'woman') says in one of his *Prison Notebooks*:

> Philosophy in general does not in fact exist. Various philosophies or conceptions of the world exist, and one always makes a choice between them. How is this choice made? Is it merely an intellectual event or is it something more complex? ... Which ... would be the real conception of the world: that logically affirmed as an intellectual choice? Or that which emerges from the real activity of each man, which is implicit in his mode of action? And since all action is political, can one not say that the real philosophy of each man is contained in its entirety in his political action?
>
> (Gramsci 1971: 326)

How we think about the world and the impact this has is discussed in more detail in **Chapter 2**.

The important point that he is making here is that the way people choose to think about and explain the world is, after all, part of 'the world' and influences what happens. It cannot be separated from other things people do.

These two things, 'theory' and 'practice', if you like, are often kept separate by people who think about global politics. However, one of our starting points in this book is that the distinctions that are often made between the detailed, historical study of events and things people do in the world and the more general explanations that are put forward to help us account for the things we observe – the distinction between practice and theory, as it is often called – are in many senses artificial, as Gramsci argues.

Gramsci is by no means the only writer to have tackled the question of what role common sense or our conceptions of the world play in our thinking and our politics. Michel Foucault, whose work you will come across in Chapters 4, 6, 9 and 17, has also examined the intimate relation between theory and practice, or, in his terminology, knowledge and power (Foucault 1980). He argues that at any particular period in history there is a particular 'regime of truth' in place that validates what should count as true. Certain people are authorised to determine what is true, and there are specific ways of assessing truth. In the modern era, in the Western world, it is predominantly the scientific method that has been assumed to be capable of guaranteeing truth. What we call knowledge for Foucault is not something that is independent but rather something that is always tied up with power structures. He offers us what he calls a toolbox which we can use to prise open these systems of truth and, if we like, destabilise them: demonstrate their contingent, historical character, or, in other words, the way in which they are not universally true or valid. His genealogical method uses a combination of detailed historical excavations and localised, specific knowledges. Ludwig Wittgenstein, too, has looked closely at the role language plays in limiting our thought. His work is explained in Chapter 2, so we won't say much about it here. Wittgenstein talks in terms of language games and pictures. He argues that when we think we are explaining the world we are only tracing again and again a picture of the world that frames our ideas of it. We are always operating within what he calls a 'language game' or a certain 'grammar'.

We have seen here a number of different ways of thinking about how we might look at the relation between thinking about the world and doing things in the world, and we have found several different views on how to approach this. Gramsci, Foucault and Wittgenstein differ in the terminology they use and in the specific arguments they put forward, but they would all agree that direct access to 'the world' is not possible: we always think about the world and the questions of global politics starting from within a particular 'common sense' (Gramsci), 'regime of truth' (Foucault) or 'language game' (Wittgenstein).

Of course there is another group of views entirely, which we haven't discussed here. There are people who argue that there is no problem at all – or, less strongly, no real problem – in separating theory and practice. For these people, it is possible to have an independent, neutral position (or one that is more or less independent or neutral) from which an objective view of the world can be formulated. Truth can be found, and our job as academics, for these people, is precisely to be seekers after truth. This is called a 'correspondence theory of truth', and it is discussed in Chapter 2.

CONCLUSION

The question of whether there is any possibility of objective knowledge of the world is one of the broader questions that many of the other chapters in this book raise, too. In our view the diversity of accounts and explanations of events in global politics demonstrates that there is no neutral view to be had. Different accounts of cosmology and what the world is, different common senses and different philosophies, lead to different approaches. And different political starting points are linked with different explanations. We would ask that you bear in mind as you read through this book that what the authors of the various chapters give are their own arguments and their own interpretations. They are not in a position to give an unbiased, neutral view: no one is, as far as we are concerned. They make every effort to present to you arguments that they disagree with, and they indicate where those arguments can be found. We would encourage you to follow this up in the further reading that is given so that you can form your own views. You may well come to different conclusions. As we said at the start of this introductory chapter, there are no answers: the questions remain open and intractable, there for each new generation to formulate and tackle for themselves.

FURTHER READING

Cox, Robert W. (1981) 'Social Forces, States and World Orders', *Millennium: Journal of International Studies* 10, 2: 126–55.
> This article sets out the difference between 'critical theory' and 'problem-solving theory' in thinking about global politics, and why this is important.

Donald, James and Stuart Hall (1986) *Politics and Ideology*, Milton Keynes: Open University; Beechey, Veronica and James Donald (1985) *Subjectivity and Social Relations*, Milton Keynes: Open University Press.
> If you want to follow up on the relationship between politics and the way we think, these two readers extend the discussion in interesting ways.

Hall, Stuart (1996) 'Gramsci's Relevance for the Study of Race and Ethnicity', in David Morley and Kuan-Hsing Chen (eds) *Stuart Hall: Critical Dialogues in Cultural Studies*, London: Routledge.
> In this chapter, Stuart Hall gives a very clear explanation of the main features of Gramsci's work and its contemporary importance.

Hollis, Martin and Steve Smith (1991) *Explaining and Understanding International Relations*, Oxford: Clarendon Press.

Hollis and Smith make a distinction between 'explaining' and 'understanding', which is similar to the distinction between critical and problem-solving theories discussed here.

REFERENCES

Adams, Douglas (1979) *The Hitchhiker's Guide to the Galaxy*, London: Pan Books.

Bourke, Joanna (1999) *An Intimate History of Killing: Face-to-Face Combat in Twentieth-Century Warfare*, London: Granta.

Brothers, Caroline (2007) 'Susan Meiselas: Photographs from the Edge', *International Herald Tribune*, 1 August, http://www.iht.com/articles/2007/08/01/arts/magnum.php?page=1.

Cox, Robert W. (1981) 'Social Forces, States and World Orders', *Millennium: Journal of International Studies* 10, 2: 126–55.

Davis, Mike (2002) *Dead Cities*, New York: The New Press.

Foucault, Michel (1980) *Power/Knowledge: Selected Interviews and Other Writings 1972–1977*, trans. Colin Gordon, Brighton: Harvester Press.

Friedrich, Jörg (2002) *Der Brand: Deutschland im Bombenkrieg 1940–1945*, Munich: Propyläen Verlag.

Gramsci, Antonio (1971) *Selections from the Prison Notebooks*, London: Lawrence and Wishart.

Grayling, A.C. (2007) *Among the Dead Cities: Is the Targeting of Civilians in War Ever Justified?*, London: Bloomsbury.

Sebald, W.G. (2004) *On the Natural History of Destruction*, trans. Anthea Bell, London: Penguin.

Taylor, Frederick (2005) *Dresden: Tuesday 13 February 1945*, London: Bloomsbury.

Wilkins, Lucy (2006) 'Are Britain's Roads Getting Safer?', BBC News Online, 17 August, http://news.bbc.co.uk/1/hi/uk/5256506.stm.

CHAPTER **2**

How do we begin to think about the world?

Véronique Pin-Fat

- *The question*
  THINKING AND LANGUAGE

- *Illustrative example*
  THINKING ABOUT TORTURE: THE TICKING BOMB SCENARIO

- *Responses*
  THINKING ABOUT ETHICS: TWO RESPONSES

- *Broader issues*
  THINKING ABOUT THINKING

- **CONCLUSION**

THE QUESTION
THINKING AND LANGUAGE

How we think about the world matters in very important ways. It impacts on what we do from day to day, for a start. For example, if, as a student, you have a poor opinion of a particular lecturer at your university or college – if you have decided that he or she is boring or difficult to follow – you will be less likely to attend the lecture, unless of course you think there are strong conventions in place to compel you to go. If you think of the world as a dangerous place, this may impact on how you travel to the lecture: you may avoid public transport, for example, and decide to walk, because of the possibility of a terrorist attack. Such an attack may be statistically very unlikely, but the way you picture the world will affect how you interpret such 'evidence' and how you behave. Other students may see travelling on the bus or the train as a way of making a political statement, a way of 'defying' those who want to prevent life going on as usual.

This chapter explores the notion that how we think about the world affects how we live in it. It is of course not just a matter of how we live in it on our own, but how we live in it with others. You encounter lots of people in your life from the moment you wake up to the moment you go to bed. Some of them may be close to you and you may even love them. Some you don't know so well, but may see regularly, such as students and lecturers. Some you've never met but have heard or read about, such as people all over the globe who appear in the news. And, of course, there may be some people you just do not like, find 'weird' or plain annoying. Either way, we don't live in the world on our own and somehow need to find ways of accommodating each other.

Living in the world with other people is the realm of politics and ethics. Broadly speaking, ethics is about how we should live with other people in the world and politics is about what kinds of living and ways of thinking about who we are are made possible. So, for example, should someone whom you regard as 'weird' be treated any differently from someone you love? Furthermore, what counts as 'weird'? What does that tell us about 'normal'? Are people whose lives are different from ours, perhaps because they live in a different country from us or practice a different religion, 'weird'? Ethics and politics look at both how we should regard and accommodate each other and what kinds of things make it possible to, for example, treat each other with respect and what kinds of things don't. That I might view you as 'weird' or even 'inhuman' (politics) may very much dictate how I then treat you (ethics). When we examine more closely how we think about the world, it turns out that ethics and politics are inseparable.

Is thinking about the world something that just happens in our heads? Perhaps, but our thinking about the world must in some way be public, or accessible to others. We formulate and communicate ideas and thoughts by means of language. Language is public. It consists of shared rules and vocabularies, for example. Language seems a strong candidate for giving us access to how we think about the world and, as such, the relationship of language to the world is a central theme of this chapter.

The thoughts we have about the world reveal a number of things: the types of things that we believe are in the world, the kinds of people that we think we live amongst, what we think is important, what we think is possible, and even how we believe we should think about the world. These thoughts are all attempts to make sense of the world and our place in it. So, the questions that we are going to look at here are:

These broad questions are examined in the context of thinking about danger in section 3 of **Chapter 17**.

1   How do we begin to think about the world and make sense of it?
2   Does the world exist independently of any thoughts we might have about it?
3   Is the way we think about the world simply a representation of what it is?

This may seem a bit abstract, but let's look more closely now at the effects that our thinking has in the world.

Some people regard thinking and language as separate from the world. They see the world as carrying on independently of what we think. According to this way of thinking, we produce various representations of the world, but the world continues regardless. However, as I mentioned above, what we are going to explore in this chapter is how what we think about the world actually impacts on the world: it changes the world. We also examine how, if we ignore the impact our ways of thinking have on the world, we can find ourselves complicit in what happens in ways we might not wish to be.

ILLUSTRATIVE EXAMPLE
THINKING ABOUT TORTURE: THE TICKING BOMB SCENARIO

We will begin by looking at an example of thinking. Although we will be engaging with *thinking* about torture here, it is important to be clear that this does not necessarily mean we are engaging with the practices of torture and their justification or otherwise. In fact, as we shall see, sometimes our thinking about torture avoids engaging with it in important ways. To illustrate these points, we will examine one way of thinking about torture that is called 'the ticking bomb scenario'.

Torture obviously affects people's bodies and lives; it causes great physical suffering and pain and has profoundly negative emotional and psychological effects. Elaine Scarry, in her book *The Body in Pain* (1985), goes as far as to say that torture in a sense destroys – or, in her words, 'unmakes' – the world: it destroys ideas of the world and our place in it that have been painstakingly put together. Some governments have condoned torture and created official policies around its use. The particular way of thinking about torture that I want to examine – the ticking bomb scenario – has been an important part of recent debates. Examining the use of the ticking bomb scenario to think about torture, and the practical implications of that way of thinking, provides an example of how ways of thinking about the world have very real effects.

Since September 11, 2001, the debate about whether torture can be justified has once again come to the fore, especially in the United States. On that date, thousands were killed when hijacked passenger aeroplanes hit a number of

FIGURE 2.1
Map of Iraq showing Abu Ghraib

high-profile targets, including the World Trade Center in New York and the Pentagon near Washington, DC. The Bush Administration considered these events to be acts of war against the US perpetrated by terrorists: Osama bin Laden and Al-Qaeda. President George W. Bush declared a 'war on terror' nine days later. The 'war on terror' involves secret commando operations and two 'hot wars', one in Afghanistan and one in Iraq. At the time of writing, these operations are still ongoing. The 'war on terror' provides the context within which the torture debate takes place.

Although there had been secret US military investigations into allegations of torture and reports of its use from organisations such as the International Committee of the Red Cross, it was not until May 2004 that accounts and images of US military personnel torturing detainees in Abu Ghraib prison, Iraq, burst into public view. This had the effect of pushing the torture debate controversially but firmly into the public domain.

An absolute prohibition against torture is embodied in a convention to which many states have agreed, the United Nations Convention Against Torture and Other Cruel, Inhuman or Degrading Treatment or Punishment. In the Convention Against Torture (1984), torture is prohibited because it violates 'the inherent dignity of the human person' (Preamble). Torture is defined as

> any act by which severe pain or suffering, whether physical or mental, is intentionally inflicted on a person for such purposes as obtaining from him or a third person information or a confession, punishing him for an act he

The 'war on terror' has also been used by the United States to identify other states as 'rogue states'.
See Chapter 19

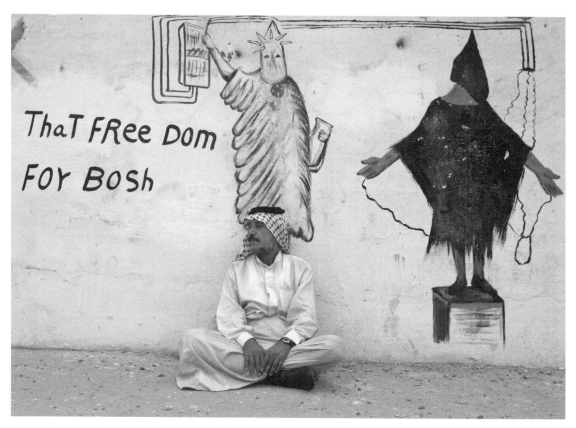

FIGURE 2.2
Iraqi Graffiti mural depicting prisoner abuse on a wall in Sadr City, Baghdad. Photo: Ali Jasim/Reuters

or a third person has committed or is suspected of having committed, or intimidating or coercing him or a third person, or for any reason based on discrimination of any kind, when such pain or suffering is inflicted by or at the instigation of or with the consent or acquiescence of a public official or other person acting in an official capacity. It does not include pain or suffering arising only from, inherent in or incidental to lawful sanctions.

(United Nations 1984: Article 1)

The Convention continues: 'No exceptional circumstances whatsoever, whether a state of war or a threat of war, internal political instability or any other public emergency, may be invoked as a justification of torture' (Article 2, section 2). The Convention Against Torture, therefore, prohibits any circumstances from being used as a justification for torture. However, the argument has been made that there are circumstances when torture can be justified. This argument often begins with the positing of a particular scenario. Here is how the scenario goes:

Imagine this: there is a time-bomb planted in the centre of a large city somewhere in the United States or a European capital, in Washington, Paris, London or Berlin, for example. It is armed, ticking and counting its way down towards detonation. You have the person who planted it in custody. He won't talk. Hundreds, if not thousands, will die if the information on the whereabouts of the bomb is not revealed. Should you torture the person whom you are holding in custody in order to find out where the bomb is and stop it from exploding?

This hypothetical situation is called the ticking bomb scenario. The scenario is often used as a starting point in thinking about whether torture can ever be justifiable. It is used to test the limits of the absolute prohibition against torture: the idea that we shouldn't use torture under any circumstances. The ticking bomb scenario challenges this prohibition by asking whether it can be displaced or disregarded in exceptional circumstances, even though the Convention Against Torture prohibits this explicitly, as we have seen. Often, the answer that the scenario leads to is that it can. Let us examine how this comes about.

A scenario can mean an imagined or hypothetical sequence of events; the word also refers to the outline of the plot of a play or film.

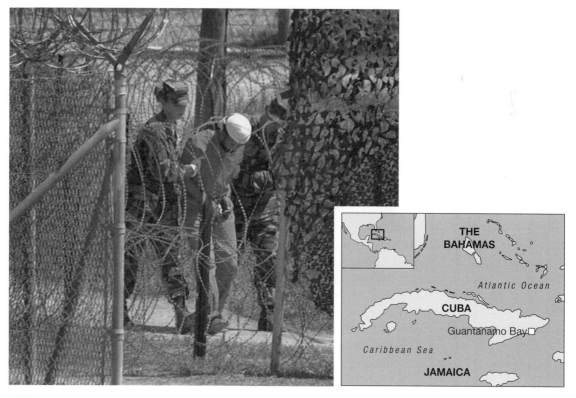

FIGURE 2.3
Guantánamo Bay: a detainee is escorted for interrogation in 2002.
Photo: Andres Leighton/AP

FIGURE 2.4
Map of Cuba showing Guantánamo Bay

BOX 2.1 EXTRAORDINARY RENDITION

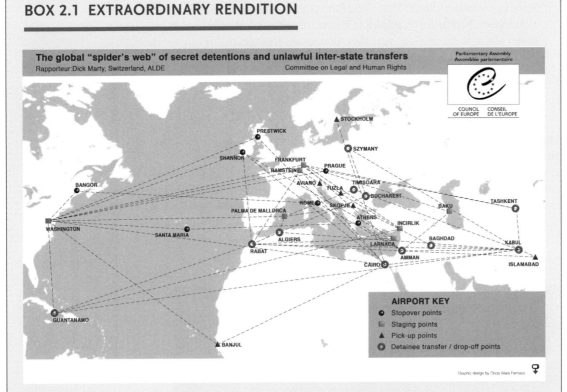

FIGURE 2.5
Map of detentions and renditions. Council of Europe. Graphic design by Once Were Farmers

During the 'war on terror', the United States has detained people in prisons outside its own territory: the US Naval base in Guantánamo Bay, Cuba; the US airbase in Bagram, Afghanistan; and Abu Ghraib prison in Iraq. In 2006 nearly 400 detainees of approximately 30 different nationalities were being held in Guantánamo without charge. In 2007 the UN Committee against Torture called for its closure based on allegations that treatment of detainees amounted to torture, in addition to questions regarding whether they legally could be held indefinitely without charge. Similar allegations concerning detention without charge and torture have also been made in relation to Bagram airbase and Abu Ghraib.

There appears to be growing evidence that the US has also been operating a policy of 'extraordinary rendition' with 'the complicity, collusion or acquiescence of a number of European and other governments'. This policy is one where 'hundreds of people have been unlawfully transferred by the USA and its allies to countries such as Syria, Jordan and Egypt . . . [where] they risk enforced disappearance, torture and other ill-treatment' (Amnesty International 2007: 9).

How does a hypothetical scenario like the ticking bomb function to justify torture in practice? It does so by providing *only* the kind of information we need to conclude that we might be justified in torturing the person we have in custody.

Using this hypothetical scenario gives us certainty about a number of things:

- We are certain that the person we have in custody is the person who planted the bomb and not someone who is lying about having planted it or an innocent person.
- We are certain that we know that the bomb has been planted in a large city and that it will kill lots of people rather than just one or two.
- We are certain that the bomb will go off, that is to say, we are confident that it won't just fizzle, splutter and fail to detonate.
- We are certain that if we torture the person in custody he or she will tell us the true location of the bomb and not lie.
- We are certain that it is possible to torture the person for the short period of time that the bomb is ticking and not a moment longer (weeks, months, years) in order to extract the information on the location of the bomb.
- We are also very confident that when we do torture that person our torture methods won't kill him or her before he or she tells us where the bomb is planted. We assume, then, that we (or our agents) are trained, effective torturers with a practical knowledge of torture techniques. We are certain that our torture methods work; torture will make the person in custody tell us where the bomb is and therefore allow us to find it, disarm it and save many valuable lives.
- We also know that saving lives is an appropriate justification.

The scenario is neat and tidy. It has been constructed very carefully to eliminate many difficult issues. This isn't deliberate deception particularly. Rather, it is a function of the hypothetical scenario. It deliberately eliminates specific aspects of a situation in order to focus solely on the core issue: whether the prohibition against torture is absolute. By abstracting the core issue in this way, the idea is that we can 'test' the limits of the prohibition.

The scenario works by providing compelling reasons for torture being justified under certain circumstances. However, it is a scenario set up in such a way that we *already* know that torturing the detainee is justifiable. Since the scenario tells us that saving lives is good and torture saves lives, it must be the case that torture can be justified. The scenario is a purely theoretical construct, and deliberately so. In order to construct a hypothetical scenario such as this, one must believe that theory (thinking about the world) and practice (doing things in the world) can be separated. A separation is made and assumed to be possible.

When we read the ticking bomb scenario more closely, we notice that it does two other things, as well as separating theory and practice.

When we buy into a scenario we no longer have to worry about things that the scenario already tells us are one way rather than another – we put them to one side.

You will often find that people simply assume that saving lives is a good thing. But we don't always act to save everyone's lives. In fact, we routinely endanger some people's lives, and not always in order to save others. Soldiers and enemy civilians are only the most obvious cases here; arguably, the global economy also relies on putting some lives at immediate risk.

Rationality came to be seen as incredibly important in the period called the Enlightenment, but it was also a quality attributed to men in particular.
See Chapters 4 and 5

First, the scenario suggests that we need to employ our rationality and come to conclusions based on either certainty or, at a minimum, reasonable belief. There are certain things we need to know before we can make a decision and we need to balance them up rationally. Often what we are balancing are competing values. In the case of the ticking bomb it is the value of the strict prohibition of torture *versus* the value of saving a significant number of lives. As we have seen, the scenario suggests that abstraction is helpful. The ticking bomb scenario is deliberately and consciously designed to reduce the problem of torture to only two competing values and to compel us to choose which value is more significant. It is, necessarily, a simplification. But, in the view of those using this scenario, simplification can help us determine more accurately what we should do.

Second, although the scenario suggests that all human life has value – not only the lives that are at risk from the bomb's explosion, but also that of the person we have in custody – it is clear that 'we' are not the person who planted the bomb, nor are 'we' associated with them. The scenario is not constructed from the point of view of the person who is in custody. There is no mention of what justifications he or she may have, or what reasons there may be, for planting the bomb. Of course, this does not mean that there are any justifications, but the scenario does not explore whether there are any reasons for planting the bomb or not. For example, the ticking bomb scenario is not one where a person plants a bomb that threatens hundreds of lives in order to prevent others from taking hundreds of other, different, lives. The scenario is completely silent about the purported bomber's motivations other than the desire to kill people with the explosion of

© Mike Baldwin / Cornered

"I found out what makes him tick, but he still won't tock."

FIGURE 2.6
'I found out what makes him tick . . .' Artist: Mike Baldwin. CartoonStock Ref: mba0459. www.CartoonStock.com

the device. This means that 'we' are the potential (albeit righteously reluctant yet well trained) torturers in the scenario. Furthermore, 'we', as potential torturers, feel more akin to those whose lives are at risk from the bomb than to the person we have in custody. Whoever he or she is, it seems that he or she is not 'us'. Whoever 'we' are, we are not in Kabul, Addis Ababa or Shanghai, for example, as the scenario, interestingly, always imagines that the bomb is planted in an advanced industrialised country.

As an abstraction, then, the ticking bomb scenario shows much more than might be supposed at first glance about the way of thinking about the world that it involves. When we look at what the scenario leaves out, what it does not allow us to consider, we find that it ignores the question of how far our feelings and responsibilities may stretch: should or do they include others who are not part of what we think of as 'us'? Perhaps our obligations are limited to those who belong with us in a particular community or perhaps they extend to the whole of humanity.

In practice, things are more complicated than the abstract scenario. The situation may not be one of choosing between the value of one life (the person in custody) and that of many others (the potential victims of the bomb). We cannot always be sure that we have the right person in custody. We are often uncertain. This implies that we may have to torture others as well, since they might equally know where the bomb is planted. We are more likely to be dealing with several (or even hundreds of) possible 'knowers' who would need to be tortured to reveal the location of the bomb *versus* hundreds of lives to save. Indeed, it is precisely the kind of logic employed in the ticking bomb scenario that leads to large numbers of people being detained in the 'war on terror': they may be 'knowers'. In practice, the logic of the ticking bomb scenario provides a justification for detaining people in great numbers. If so, the neatness of the scenario begins to break down, and with it its strict separation of theory and practice. The scenario no longer refers to an exception that applies to only one life (the bomber's) but begins to implicate many others.

The prohibition of torture, as set out in the Convention Against Torture (United Nations 1984), does not treat torture as an act that is perpetrated on only one individual either. The Convention Against Torture's references to 'a public official or other person acting in an official capacity' (Article 1) as perpetrators of torture make it clear that the Convention is concerned with prohibiting the institutional-isation and widespread political use of torture by states. The Convention Against Torture and the abundant evidence of torture being used globally show that, in practice, torture implicates many, many lives. In global politics, then, what is at stake in the practices of torture is not a question of the justifiability of an isolated incidence of the action of one person (the torturer) on only one other (the person in custody). It is, more accurately, the actions of many ('us') on many ('them').

Our short study of the ticking bomb scenario has served as a way of introducing questions about a way of thinking about the world: one that employs an abstract rationality and separates thinking about the world, or theorising, from the world itself, or practice, and one that ducks the question of whether our obligations are limited to people who share the same community with us or whether they extend to the whole of humanity. We have seen that this way of looking at the world can provide a justification for actions that in practice can lead to the torturing of many people, not just one.

RESPONSES
THINKING ABOUT ETHICS: TWO RESPONSES

The ticking bomb scenario implies that the decisions that we have to make about whether or not to use torture should be thought of as *moral* decisions. They are decisions about what we *ought* to do or what we *should* do. Very often, moral decisions are seen to be the result of applying some kind of rule governing our treatment of others and understanding exactly how the rule should apply. For example, the ticking bomb scenario rationally examined the limits of applying the rule 'torture is an absolute moral prohibition' and found that the rule was not absolute after all. We noted at the start of the chapter that, roughly speaking, *ethics* is about how we should live with other people in the world. Thinking about ethics means broadly thinking about moral rules and how they govern the ways in which we treat each other. Often such rules are phrased in terms of moral duties, moral obligations and/or moral responsibilities. When we come to explore how people have thought about the question of ethics in global politics, straightaway we encounter discussions about the rules that should govern our duties and obligations and how far they should apply: whether our duties and obligations should extend only to those within the political community or state in which we find ourselves, or whether they should extend to the whole of humanity. We have already encountered this debate in our exploration of the ticking bomb scenario

The work of different thinkers is often grouped into different schools of thought, perspectives or approaches. While it is sometimes useful, 'boxing' people like this risks oversimplifying complicated questions.

Two thinkers, Charles Beitz and Michael Walzer, have sustained answers to these questions. Their respective answers arise in two approaches called cosmopolitanism and communitarianism. I will look at the work of each thinker in turn. In order to begin to understand and unravel the implications of each set of answers, I will focus on the pictures or representations they use. I will say more about what we mean by pictures or representations in the next section, but for the time being it is sufficient to note that thinking about the pictures they use is helpful in highlighting the way in which each answer is an attempt to provide an accurate and true representation of the realities of global politics.

1 A focus on *pictures of reason* will serve to reveal traditional, differing, views on what an academic study of global politics is supposed to focus on as most relevant to ethics and how we should think about it.

2 *Pictures of the subject* tell us what or who, supposedly, 'we' are and, more particularly, what it is about 'us' as moral subjects that provides us with moral value or character. This is vitally important because such pictures tell us not only who or what has the highest moral value in global politics, but also the moral subject towards which we are primarily ethically responsible in practice.

3 *Pictures of ethico-political space* tell us where the possibility of ethical action in global politics is believed to take place. They seek to depict what the 'world' of global political reality is 'really' like and its hostility, or otherwise, to the accommodation of ethics in practice.

Communitarianism: Michael Walzer

In the work of Michael Walzer we find a communitarian set of answers to questions of ethics in global politics. Communitarians focus on the state as a moral subject in global politics. As Walzer's picture of ethico-political space will reveal, the moral value of the state lies in its political community.

To understand the moral significance of the community we first need to examine Walzer's *picture of the subject*. According to Walzer, being human is about being complex: creating meaning and culture which 'we' both reflect and are reflected in (Walzer 1994: 85). Human beings have equal moral value because they are all culture- and meaning-producing creatures. Each subject participates in his or her own community. Globally, there is a vast plurality of differing social and cultural meanings because, whilst 'we' all produce meanings and culture, 'we' do not all produce the same ones. Is it possible to talk of a common humanity since there will be differing opinions about what 'humanity' might mean? Yes, says Walzer, although 'our common humanity will never make us members of a single universal tribe. What members of the human race have in common is particularism (that is, attachment to particular groups over humanity as a whole): we participate, all of us, in thick cultures that are our own' (Walzer 1994: 83).

For Walzer, being human is about creating meanings and therefore different cultures; unsurprisingly, his *picture of reason* is a picture of shared understandings, which are radically particularistic. In contrast to the cosmopolitan thinker Beitz, whose view we examine on pp. 34–6, for Walzer reason is not separate from its social, historical and cultural contexts. What is rational depends on what those of us who share the same understandings mean by the word. Applying this to ethics, Walzer's position is one that emphasises that standards of rightness and wrongness, justice and injustice, etc. depend on particular socio-cultural practices.

For other views of what the state, or what is sometimes called the nation-state, is as a form of political community, and how it is held together, see **Chapters 9 and 10**.

Of course, what counts as human and what doesn't is historically and culturally changeable. See **Chapters 4 and 15**

Having prepared the ground, we can now better appreciate Walzer's *picture of ethico-political space*. In the final analysis, he produces an international ethics that centres on states as the moral subjects (Walzer 1977). States, he argues, have moral value because they contain a political community. The community is the expression of a common life that its members have produced, sustained and participated in as meaning-producing human beings. A state, for Walzer, consists of a political community and its government (Walzer 1985 [1980]: 220, 235). The political community has rights to territorial integrity and sovereignty and these rights belong to the state through the consent of its members. Through consent, members form a metaphorical 'contract' with the state that it should protect the common life which they have shaped over a long period of time.

For Walzer, upholding the state rights of territorial integrity and sovereignty should form the basis of an international morality. However, only legitimate states' rights should be respected. He says that states are only legitimate if there is a fit between the government and community such that the former represents the peoples' political life in accordance with their own traditions and specific way of life. The problem, of course, is how can we judge fit when 'our' opinions about being governed according to 'our' traditions will be so different from those of others? For example, 'we' might think that only democratic forms of governance provide a fit and hence provide legitimacy to governments. Well aware of this, Walzer says that most of the time states should presume that other states are legitimate and should not intervene in their affairs. Nevertheless, there may be very rare occasions when the principle of non-intervention can be overridden. For Walzer, these would be when the absence of fit is radically apparent, as in the case of either a struggle for national liberation, a civil war or the massacre, enslavement or expulsion of a mass of people.

Cosmopolitanism: Charles Beitz

The second answer to who we are is a cosmopolitan one, found in the work of Charles Beitz. In contrast to Walzer, Beitz considers individuals who are rational, free and equal to be the moral subject of global politics.

Beitz applies John Rawls' theory of justice to international politics (Beitz 1999 [1979]; Rawls 1971). He seeks to find out which principles of justice would be chosen to create a perfectly just world order (an 'ideal theory'). But how would such a principle, where 'social and economic inequalities are to be arranged . . . to the greatest benefit of the least advantaged', be chosen? To think about this, Beitz uses a hypothetical scenario called the global original position. He sees using this scenario as a purely theoretical exercise of moral reasoning – like the ticking bomb scenario – and one that is impartial. It requires that we suspend any bias and put to one side being a particular self with particular interests: according to

The state's claim to territorial integrity and political sovereignty is discussed in **Chapter 9**

Changing attitudes to intervention are the subject of **Chapter 18**

Chapter 10 examines ways of conceptualising the political community by looking at a number of novels. One of the characters is a committed cosmopolitan.

BOX 2.2 JOHN RAWLS

John Rawls (1921–2002) is widely regarded as the late twentieth-century's greatest liberal political philosopher. His major intellectual preoccupation was to defend the notion that civil and political rights are inviolable and that such rights are the first duty of a liberal state. His most important book, *A Theory of Justice*, was first published in 1971. In it he explores the contours of a just society with the argument that 'Each person possesses an inviolability founded on justice that even the welfare of society as a whole cannot override. Therefore, in a just society the rights secured by justice are not subject to political bargaining or to the calculus of social interests'.

FIGURE 2.7
John Rawls. Photo: Jane Reed,
University of Harvard

his *picture of reason* this is possible. In the scenario, state representatives would not know their nationality or whether their state had large natural resources, but they would know that resources are unevenly distributed globally and that each state needs adequate resources for there to be a successful and just global society. Consequently, Beitz argues, the parties would rationally choose a global principle that redistributed natural resources justly, because no state representative would want to find that they had few or no natural resources.

For Beitz's cosmopolitan ethics to work, he needs to argue that principles of justice can apply to the non-ideal environment of global politics. Why? It all has to do with Rawls. Rawls thinks his principles can only be applied to domestic societies as 'cooperative ventures for mutual advantage' (Rawls 1971: 4). Beitz disagrees and argues that international politics is sufficiently similar to domestic politics to count as a cooperative scheme, even though international institutions and practices may not be genuinely cooperative. Beitz's point is that there is enough transnational activity – trade, international investment, aid and communications – to mean that burdens and/or benefits are produced which need to be justly distributed. Beitz offers us a *picture of ethico-political space*, then, that emphasises the similarity between domestic and international politics. Because of their similarity the principles of justice discovered by ideal theory and the hypothetical scenario apply.

The problem of the distribution of benefits across the globe is certainly a major issue in global politics today.
See Chapter 13

But who are 'we' according to Beitz? For whom are global burdens and benefits to be redistributed in the name of justice? Beitz's answer is the individual: persons who have rights and interests. Beitz rejects the view that non-person-based interests are appropriate or relevant from the moral point of view. According to his *picture of the subject* it is persons, rather than states, nations or communities who should benefit. This is the badge of a cosmopolitan position. Furthermore, Beitz believes that persons have a natural duty to create and sustain just institutions. In other words, the principles of justice (which ideal theory locates using the hypothetical scenario of the global original position) can become part of the non-ideal world because it is a natural duty of moral subjects to secure justice *and* because the international context is sufficiently like the domestic to make acting on such a duty appropriate and realistic.

We summarise Walzer and Beitz's different pictures in the table in Figure 2.8.

BROADER ISSUES
THINKING ABOUT THINKING

Surveying the way two thinkers in global politics approach ethics gave us two sets of *pictures* of reason, the subject and ethico-political space. *Importantly, both approaches share the impulse to picture.* Regardless of the content of the pictures, each approach believes that theirs is an accurate and true representation of the *reality* of reason, the subject and ethico-political space.

Attempts to describe global political reality are forms of representation, or what I have called pictures. The assumption is that the truth or falsity of a picture or representation depends on how accurately it corresponds with reality. This

	Walzer (Communitarian)	Beitz (Cosmopolitan)
Reason	Reason cannot overcome interests, biases and socio-cultural meanings	Reason transcends our interests and biases
The subject	The state or the political community is the moral subject	The individual (as a member of humanity) is the moral subject
Ethico-political space	Ethics takes place within states; those outside are not our primary moral concern	Ethical responsibility extends to every person regardless of where they live

FIGURE 2.8
Table summary of Walzer and Beitz

depends on postulating what we call a *word–object relation*. The meaning of a word depends on it naming or accurately representing the correspondent object that exists independently in reality. So, for example, 'political community' refers to a common way of life; and so on. In this way of thinking, all the things referred to exist outside language and act as the foundation of the word. They exist in a reality that is independent of any thoughts or words we might have about it. Our words simply refer to the foundation or essence of such things as political community and principles of justice. This is what picturing assumes. It is called a correspondence theory of truth. When a picture accurately portrays reality, or when our words name the correct 'thing' or object, then the picture is true. The picture is false if it is inaccurate.

But what happens if you begin to wonder about the whole endeavour of picturing and the pictures themselves? What happens if we shift our attention towards pictures as the problem rather than the answer to ethics? If we did make such a shift we would be involved in something different: another approach. This different approach questions whether pictures can fully capture reality at all. In other words, it questions how and where we draw the lines around what we think reality is and what impact these lines have on people's lives and the ways in which they are able and unable to live them with each other.

Pictures, framing and language games

Before we return to looking at torture and ticking time bombs as an example of how pictures impact on people's lives and our treatment of each other, we first need to ask why pictures might be problematic. The philosopher Ludwig Wittgenstein argued that when we provide answers they tend to be of the kind 'This is how things are'. However, as Wittgenstein says:

> one thinks that one is tracing the outline of the thing's nature over and over again, and one is merely tracing round the frame through which we look at it. A *picture* held us captive. And we could not get outside it, for it lay in our language and language seemed to repeat it to us inexorably.
>
> (Wittgenstein 1958: §§114–15)

Wittgenstein implies that pictures are part of the practice of language that he calls language games. Rather than picturing reality as though reality were outside our language, pictures constitute or create reality. This does not mean that there is no external reality. But it does mean that we are wholly dependent upon language to make sense of and understand the world we live in. And if this is so, then language tells us *what* to think about the world or what we call reality. The importance of this cannot be overstated. It means that how we think about the

Holding a mirror up to reality and checking whether the image accurately reflects reality is another way of thinking of this. **See Chapter 17**

You will have come across references to 'discourses', 'ideologies', 'images', 'ways of thinking' or 'ways of understanding': these often mean the same thing, or something very similar, to what are called 'pictures' here.

Chapter 20 takes up the issue of language and our relation to what we call reality in a slightly different way.

BOX 2.3 LUDWIG WITTGENSTEIN

Ludwig Wittgenstein (1889–1951) is one of the most influential philosophers of the twentieth century. His major intellectual preoccupation was with the relationship between language and the world and how our misunderstandings of it lead to philosophical problems. In his lifetime he published only one work, the *Tractatus Logico-Philosophicus* (1922), perhaps most famous for its phrase 'Whereof one cannot speak one must remain silent'. His later philosophy was posthumously published as *Philosophical Investigations* (1958). His influence remains important outside philosophy, including in thinking about global politics.

FIGURE 2.9
Ludwig Wittgenstein

world is regulated by our language games or practices. In turn, if our thoughts are regulated by language, it means that our thoughts are practices: ways of being in the world. This is why pictures, as snapshots of what we think about things and people in the world, affect the world we live in. For example, calling a person who plants a ticking bomb a 'terrorist' or a 'freedom fighter' matters beyond the choice of mere vocabulary. Using the term 'freedom fighter' seems to suggest that the person may have a justifiable reason for their actions, whereas 'terrorist' does not. Another way of putting this important point would be to say that our language games constitute the limits of possibility: they tell us what it is possible to do and how it is possible to exist and act in the world.

In summary, thinking about language games emphasises how language makes a difference to how we live and act in the world with others. Pictures tell us what we think 'reality' is and therefore regulate how we act and live in it. Elaborating this further, we can say that pictures are practices of telling us what shall count as 'true', 'false', 'the subject': any 'thing' (object) or any 'body' (subject). Therefore, the pictures that relate to ethics are a set of practices that tell us what ethics is. Making pictures the problem rather than the answer makes the job of asking how we think about the world and ethics in global politics very different. Thinking about the world becomes a questioning of how thinking or picturing regulates the ways in which we act and the impact this has on people's lives.

Let's now return to thinking about torture and the ticking bomb scenario in order to illustrate the shift towards an approach that sees pictures of reason, the subject and ethico-political space as the problem, not the answer.

Pictures of reason, the subject and ethico-political space

The ticking bomb scenario is the practice of a specific kind of picture of reason: a particular idea of what we think 'thinking about' the world requires. In this case, we will see that Charles Beitz and the United States Administration practice the same picture of reason as that underlying the ticking bomb scenario. There is a good chance that you are familiar with this picture. It is often associated with liberalism.

Liberalism is a pervasive ideology. Many of the chapters mention it, in particular those that explore the global political economy.

The ticking bomb scenario operates with a picture of reason as abstraction. It operates in three steps. *Step one* presents us with a dilemma: whether the value of the life of the bomber can be overridden in order to save other lives. However, this dilemma is not generated by the scenario. It is what the scenario is *about* and why it has been constructed. Having constructed it for this purpose, *step two* requires imagining or thinking hypothetically of anything that might be an exception to an absolute prohibition against torture. Obviously, the candidate for an exception is a ticking bomb. The scenario is asking us whether we think that a ticking bomb really is an exception. Once we've decided that, then *step three* in this picture of reason is to find 'real-world' cases or practices where the justifications for torture appear. The shape of this picture of reason is one where there is a clear separation between theory and practice. How we are to act in the world is first determined by theory as the exercise of reason in the abstract. The next issue is then to apply theory to the world. These steps are also how Beitz generates his principles of justice. He identifies the issue, provides a hypothetical scenario (the global original position) and from that deduces global principles of justice that should be applied to the world.

How can we engage with this picture of reason differently? One way is to trace the effects of this picture rather than engage with its 'truth' or 'falsity'. There are many effects, but we can highlight an important one here. Separating theory and practice means just that: separating them. This then raises the obvious problem of how the two can be reunited, if at all, as the practice of theory. But, more importantly, we might want to think about whether theory and practice can be separated in the first place. One way we could do this would be by asking what kind of people are included in this picture of reason. The scenario is not interested in, nor does it include, actual cases of torture: who was tortured, how, why and by whom. The only people who are in the picture are people using abstracted reasoning. They don't have feelings of guilt, humiliation, fear, enjoyment or confusion, nor do they feel pain or scream, for example. The scenario also does not include any politics: why the 'bomber' might have planted the bomb, why he planted it where he did, who has captured him, who has labelled him as a 'terrorist' and why, etc. The scenario is deliberately designed to strip away all this information and ask us to make decisions in the absence of the much messier, complicated fabric of global politics.

This section has argued that pictures are practices even if, as in this case, they are conceived as purely theoretical. Examining the ticking bomb scenario's picture of reason as the problem involves exploring the possibility that, through its separation of theory and practice, it may be a practice that sanitises torture through its lack of reference to any specific people or political context. Arguably, this has the effect of making torture seem more rational, more palatable and less objectionable. If so, the creation of a scenario that allows for the possibility that torture *is* justified may well be implicated in the actual practice of torture. This would mean that the strict separation of theory and practice that the scenario depends on for making torture justifiable might not be possible in the first place.

So those talking about torture in this way are in some sense responsible for the actual torture that takes place: their talk has made that torture possible.

In August 2004, the Final Report of the Independent Panel to Review [US] Department of Defense Detention Operations was published as a response to accounts of the torture of prisoners in Abu Ghraib prison, Iraq, by US military personnel in late 2003. The Report was commissioned by the then US Secretary of Defense, Donald Rumsfeld, to provide independent advice on the abuse of detainees. The Report states that, 'For the US, most cases for permitting harsh treatment of detainees on moral grounds begin with variants of the "ticking time bomb" scenario' (Schlesinger *et al*. 2004, Appendix H: 2). Why does this matter? The point is that the report clearly accepts that the ticking bomb scenario *can* justify torture and that this is a position shared by the United States. Therefore, the picture of reason that underlies the ticking bomb scenario is part of a set of shared practices employed by the US Administration. Given this, for the US and the report the issue now becomes how 'harsh treatment' can be used, by whom

FIGURE 2.10
Samrong Military
Hospital, Cambodia.
Photo: Olivier Pin-Fat,
Agence Vu

and under which circumstances, but no longer *whether* it should be used. Bearing this in mind, we must ask whether the ticking bomb scenario is complicit in the use of torture because the use or practice of its picture of reason makes torture possible.

Pictures of reason are also related to pictures of the subject. In the bomb scenario, it is clear that subjects are meant to come to their decisions rationally and this is what matters most. Our alternative approach would ask what kind of subject this is: what does it include and exclude? It is fascinating that the ticking bomb scenario does not mention pain, as pain is, perhaps, what we most associate torture with. The subjects in the scenario (the torturer and the tortured) are pictured as disembodied. That is to say that they are viewed as people with reason but with no body that can feel pain. Nor are they pictured as having emotions. Not only does the bomber in the scenario not scream, he does not cry, he has no relationships of love and he holds no beliefs in his heart rather than his head. It is very difficult to explore how far our bodies and emotions matter in global politics and ethics, but the point is that we can ask whether this picture of the subject that excludes them seems to miss something important about being human. Insofar as this picture of the subject is a practice, it has the effect of excluding emotions and embodiment from consideration. This is, furthermore, a political act since it is telling us what matters most about being human. So, for example, if the tortured bomber begins begging for the torture to stop, should we listen to him? Or should we only listen if he is presenting us with rational reasons to stop? Is compassion, for example, irrelevant to global politics and ethics?

Apart from this picture of the subject as disembodied, without emotions and without emotional ties to others, the subject is neither social nor political. Again this is a picture most associated with liberalism and is also shared by Beitz. In the ticking bomb scenario the bomber and the potential torturer do not belong to any specified society or culture, have no specified citizenship, no specified notions of belonging or identity and no political reasons for acting. In section 3, we traced how this is a picture of the subject that Beitz employs and we saw Walzer's objections to it. However, instead of asking which thinker has the 'true' picture, what we need to do using our alternative approach is to trace the effects of the practice of each picture. As we have seen in the ticking bomb scenario, the picture of the subject is employed in a way that contributes to the separation of theory and practice by abstracting people from the context within which they are living and acting. Consequently, the ticking bomb scenario does not ask whether there might be any justification for the bomber planting the bomb.

This leads us nicely into thinking about the relationship between pictures of reason and the subject and the picture of ethico-political space. *Where* does ethics or politics take place? Ironically, the pictures of reason and the subject in the ticking bomb scenario do not explicitly suggest a particular place because of

When we talk about other forms of violence – war, for example – we also tend to talk as if there were no actual bodies involved.
See Chapter 16

their commitment to the absence of a specific society and a disembodied subject. Place lies in the background as a hidden assumption. However, it is clear from the practice of these pictures that the scenario is supposed to apply to the United States or a state much like it. The clues are in the setting-up of the scenario. The bomb is planted in Washington, Paris or London, for example. There are two things to notice about this: (1) the potential victims of the bomb will be people living in the US or an advanced industrialised state; (2) therefore the potential torturers will be the US or an advanced industrialised state. This is the ethico-political space within which the ticking bomb scenario is set. We could see this as a problem and we could ask what happens to the scenario if it is set elsewhere. What if, for example, a ticking bomb is planted somewhere in Afghanistan and the bomber is a US soldier being held by the Taliban? Does this make a difference to how we would come to a decision about the justifiability of torture? And, if you feel that it does, why does it? Regardless of your answers, in the ticking bomb scenario we have a picture of ethico-political space as one occupied by states; more specifically, liberal democratic states.

We might want to ask whether it is only liberal democratic states that can justifiably use torture. Moreover, we can go further by asking whether the spaces within which ethics and politics take place in global politics must be territorial spaces like states, nations or political communities. *Perhaps ethics is all around us and is unavoidable.* We live in a world of pictures, where what we think about the world matters. If, as this chapter has suggested, pictures are the problem, then ethico-political space, and the need and occasion to think about the problem of picturing, is everywhere: it is in the state, at home, in the lecture theatre, in this textbook, in abstract thoughts and hypothetical scenarios. If we fail to be aware of how we think about the world and its effects, we may find ourselves blindly complicit in a variety of practices, such as torture. It should make us pause to think about how we think about the world.

CONCLUSION

This chapter has traced how and why what we think about the world matters. It began by posing questions about how the way we think about the world impacts upon who we think we are and the setting within which ethical issues arise in global politics. It then moved on to well-established answers about what pictures of reason, the subject and ethico-political space consist of through a detailed examination of the thought of Charles Beitz and Michael Walzer. Finally, it examined a different approach: a way of thinking that sees pictures as the problem, not the answer, a way of thinking that can be seen as an ethico-political endeavour in itself. In the final analysis, it is a plea for us, whoever 'we' may be, to be mindful of how we live in the world and our ethico-political relations with others.

FURTHER READING

Edkins, Jenny and Véronique Pin-Fat (2005) 'Through the Wire: Relations of Power and Relations of Violence', *Millennium: Journal of International Studies* 34, 1: 1–26. Examines violent practices of drawing lines.

Fierke, K.M. (2002) 'Links across the Abyss: Language and Logic in International Relations', *International Studies Quarterly* 46, 3: 331–54. An introduction to the relevance of Wittgenstein for global politics.

Greenberg, Karen J. (ed.) (2006) *The Torture Debate in America*, New York: Cambridge University Press. A detailed survey of aspects of the torture debate in the US.

Heyes, Cressida J. (ed.) (2003) *The Grammar of Politics: Wittgenstein and Political Philosophy*, Ithaca, NY, and London: Cornell University Press. Useful for detailed consideration of the relevance of Wittgenstein to politics and ethics.

Pin-Fat, Véronique (2005) 'The Metaphysics of the National Interest and the "Mysticism" of the Nation State: Reading Hans J. Morgenthau', *Review of International Studies* 31, 2: 217–36. Examines the international ethics of Morgenthau using pictures of reason, the subject and ethico-political space.

Walzer, Michael (2004) *Arguing about War*, New Haven, CT, and London: Yale University Press. A more recent meditation on war and intervention.

WEBSITES

Amnesty International, http://www.amnesty.org. A human rights non-governmental organisation that monitors human rights around the world.

United Nations, Committee Against Torture, part of the Office of the High Commissioner for Human Rights, http://www2.ohchr.org/english/bodies/cat/. This Committee is responsible for monitoring the prevention of torture.

REFERENCES

Amnesty International (2007) *Report 2007: The State of the World's Human Rights*, London: Amnesty International.
Beitz, Charles (1999 [1979]) *Political Theory and International Relations*, Princeton, NJ: Princeton University Press.

Rawls, John (1971) *A Theory of Justice*, Cambridge, MA: Harvard University Press.

Scarry, Elaine (1985) *The Body in Pain: The Making and Unmaking of the World*, New York and Oxford: Oxford University Press.

Schlesinger, James R., Harold Brown, Tillie K. Fowler and Charles A. Homer (2004) *Final Report of the Independent Panel to Review Department of Defense Detention Operations*, August.

United Nations (1984) *Convention Against Torture and Other Cruel, Inhuman or Degrading Treatment or Punishment*, December.

Walzer, Michael (1994) *Thick and Thin: Moral Argument at Home and Abroad*, Notre Dame, IN: University of Notre Dame Press.

Walzer, Michael (1985 [1980]) 'The Moral Standing of States: A Response to Four Critics', in Charles R. Beitz, Michael Cohen, Thomas Scanlon and A. John Simmons (eds) *International Ethics*, Princeton, NJ: Princeton University Press.

Walzer, Michael (1977) *Just and Unjust Wars: A Moral Argument with Historical Illustrations*, London: Allen Lane.

Wittgenstein, Ludwig (1958) *Philosophical Investigations*, trans. G.E.M. Anscombe, ed. G.E.M. Anscombe and Rush Rhees, 3rd edn, Oxford: Basil Blackwell.

Wittgenstein, Ludwig (1922) *Tractatus Logico-Philosophicus*, trans. C.K. Ogden, London: Routledge and Kegan Paul.

CHAPTER 3

What happens if we don't think in human terms?

Simon Dalby

- ■ *The question*
  FROM ENVIRONMENT TO BIOSPHERE

- ■ *Illustrative example*
  CLIMATE CHANGE

- ■ *Responses*
  HOW DO WE FRAME THE ISSUE IN TERMS OF GLOBAL POLITICS?

- ■ *Broader issues*
  CHALLENGING CARBONIFEROUS CAPITALISM

- ■ **CONCLUSION**

THE QUESTION
FROM ENVIRONMENT TO BIOSPHERE

There is much more to existence than solely human concerns. We are part of a complicated biosphere: a thin layer of air, soil, ocean and life surrounding a small planet (Smil 2003). The food we eat, the water, and other things, we drink, the clothes we wear, the buildings we live in, the cars we drive and, yes, the sewage we flush away each day, are all essential to human life, and, as such, matters that concern how we organise our lives and how we interact with each other. In other words they are very much a matter of politics even if they are frequently not thought about in quite this way.

FIGURE 3.1
'Human Watch:
Conference'. Artist:
Patrick Hickey.
CartoonStock
Ref: phin28.
www.CartoonStock.com

"Everything is going according to plan. The ocean levels are rising faster than expected so world domination could be sooner than later. Our only fear is that these dumb beasts will destroy themselves before their work is done."

Many of the non-human aspects of existence are discussed these days in terms of the environment. There are numerous discussions about pollution, water quality, diseases in animals that we eat, the extinction of some species and the protection of others, loss of forests in many places in the world and, above all now, concerns about climate change. But the term 'environment' itself only became a matter of public concern in the mid-twentieth century. The term 'nature' referred to more or less the same things in Western cultures before then, and still does today. Nature has long been contrasted to culture, and understood in contrast to civilisation too (Williams 1973). Nature is rural, culture is urban. Towns are about industry and commerce, places of progress and innovation. Rural areas are for farming, for recreation and enjoying, well, nature. Thus there is a separation of modern humanity, people who live in cities, from more backward rural areas. And yet so many people who live and work in cities now wish to escape the stress and business of city life by living in or at least visiting the 'countryside', as it is known in Britain.

'Environment' is technically a word that means that which surrounds something else. Originally the word 'environs' usually meant the area around a town. Updated in the twentieth century, it came to mean what surrounds humanity, the outside factors of air, land and water that provide the context for human living. Environmental discussion from the 1960s onwards focused in part on the human

The changing use of terms such as 'environment' and 'nature' reflects changing pictures of the world, or what are also called 'discourses', as discussed in **Chapter 2** disruptions of parts of this environment. Oil spills and smoke, pesticide poisonings and chemical contamination combined with discussions of urban congestion and suburban sprawl to suggest that humanity was doing damage to the environment, and wasting resources in the process too (Ward and Dubos 1972). This concern about wasting, or running out of, key minerals, fuel supplies and even food added to the worries about pollution. Conservation of resources linked up with the pollution discussions in this discourse of environment, which arrived on the political scene as a series of protest movements in developed countries in the late 1960s and 1970s (Sandbach 1980). Governments responded in various ways and most states now have environment departments; environmental movements continue to push matters onto national and international agendas (Wapner 1996).

But while environmental thinking is understood to be essential to discussing the future intelligently, it is now complemented by a growing realisation of the need to think much more carefully about the whole biosphere. But when we try to do

BOX 3.1 GROWTH AND THE ENVIRONMENT

In the early 1970s some thinkers revived concerns usually linked to the name of Thomas Malthus that resources would run out, stopping economic growth. In the much discussed report on *The Limits to Growth*, early computer projections about when resources would run out were coupled with pessimistic concerns about pollution, and the eventual collapse of industrial society was forecast (Meadows *et al.* 1974). The arguments about the limits to growth in the 1970s suggested that the planet was running out of essential resources so development would have to come to a halt one way or another. It also suggested that pollution would be a major cause of societal collapse. All of this suggested that economic growth couldn't go on indefinitely on a small planet. Vehement criticisms came from many who argued that the poor would be denied the benefits promised by economic development.

Thus, to make environmental concerns palatable, discussions focused on a strategy to overcome the deleterious aspects of economic growth in terms of sustainable development. Designed to promote economic activity that would not deny future generations the necessities for their livelihood, sustainable development was the key theme in the widely cited final report of the World Commission on Environment and Development (1987) headed by Gro Harlem Brundtland, *Our Common Future*. The suggestion in its pages, that development had to continue to add to human wealth so as to deal with problems of poverty and all the social and health ills that came with it without destroying the global environment, became the core of the discussion about development and environment in the United Nations and provided the background for the huge Earth Summit in Rio de Janeiro in 1992.

that, when we try to think about the planet as a whole, and start with the natural systems within which humanity exists, big important questions about how we got here and what kind of a planetary home we are making for future generations quickly get raised. In all the discussions about biodiversity, mad cows, genetically modified crops, ethical consumption and, above all, climate change, how society is organised does get discussed, but frequently in terms of the appropriate role for experts and government regulations. But the categories we use in this discussion, and the term 'environment' itself, frequently don't help either in describing our present predicament or in trying to work out how to proceed in particular circumstances. Mostly this is because in these present circumstances the distinctions between town and country, city and rural areas are making less and less sense. Environment as a separate nature outside cities, a matter of rural affairs or a distant concern, has gradually given way to understandings, however vague and imprecise, that we all live in a single biosphere.

Is future human well-being the most important thing?

ILLUSTRATIVE EXAMPLE
CLIMATE CHANGE

The recognition that human actions are inadvertently causing changes to remote parts of the planet has been emphasised recently by the discussion of climate change. Climate change is a complicated process, but one that is now partly driven by human actions. The complexity arises because the atmospheric system and its links to both land and ocean involve numerous flows of energy and matter which vary with the seasons and from place to place. Human actions change the land fairly directly, and so may cause direct effects: a black asphalt car park radiates heat on a sunny day very differently from the hayfield that it replaced. But by far the greatest change that humanity is introducing into the climate system is the addition of carbon dioxide, methane and other so-called greenhouse gasses that trap heat in the atmosphere.

Over long geological time-scales of the past, forests and other life-forms have absorbed carbon dioxide from the air. Some of them, when they died, have been covered with silt and buried. Over millions of years various chemical processes underground have turned the organic matter into coal, petroleum and natural gas. In the last few centuries humanity has been rapidly reversing this long-term trend. Now by literally turning rocks into air, for that is what we are doing every time we burn coal to make electricity, drive a car or use fossil fuels in countless other ways, we are changing the make-up of the atmosphere and in the process changing the systems that drive the biosphere's climate and creating a new set of circumstances for humanity (Flannery 2006). Environment is no longer something 'out there', separate from humanity, but something we are increasingly remaking by our actions.

You will often notice that people assume that culture is 'made' but nature is 'given'. Our impact on the environment suggests that it is much more complicated than that.

VAUNA LOA OBSERVATORY, HAWAII
MONTHLY AVERAGE CARBON DIOXIDE CONCENTRATION

FIGURE 3.2
CO_2 concentrations from the Mauna Loa Observatory, Hawaii. Global Monitoring Division, Earth System Research Laboratory, National Oceanic and Atmospheric Administration. Permission granted

Capitalism and industrialisation

Climate change is especially important in any discussion of global politics both because it has global ramifications and because its causes stem from how we collectively organise our contemporary urban society. While coal and to a very small degree petroleum have been used by people for thousands of years, it is only since the beginning of what is called the industrial revolution late in the eighteenth century that using them has begun to have a noticeable effect on the earth's atmosphere. Once the steam engine was put in motion, first in railway engines, then as the power system for steamships, the global economy rapidly became connected: 'Suddenly the price of wheat in Liverpool and the rainfall in Madras were variables in the same vast equation of human survival' (Davis 2001: 12). The substitution of fossil fuels for labour both dramatically changed the structure of British and, subsequently, other societies and simultaneously set in motion the accumulation of carbon dioxide in the atmosphere.

Changes during industrialisation and the rise of capitalism are discussed in **Chapter 12.**

This whole process of what Lewis Mumford (1934) once called carboniferous capitalism, because the coal that powered industrial society came from the carboniferous period in geological history, was accelerated dramatically when petroleum was refined and oils and gases started being used for lighting, heating and then, crucially, in the internal combustion engines used to power cars and lorries (Dalby 2002). When one adds in the energy used in road, parking and bridge construction, a very substantial part of the energy used in contemporary society is directly related to automobiles and their infrastructure. Cars have become status symbols, recreational toys, temporary offices and much more than transportation in our lives. They are frequently advertised as instruments of the domination of nature and of the freedom to go anywhere without consequences (Paterson 2007). They have become the symbols of modernity.

But much more than just cars are involved in the use of carbon fuels. Power-generating stations using coal are a substantial source of carbon emissions; at least part of the electricity used to power the computer used to write this chapter came from coal-powered generation; very little came from solar or wind power. Many of the items of everyday life are made from plastics and petroleum, including the keyboard on which this chapter was typed. The container ship and the trucks that brought it round the world from the factory to my office were also powered by fossil fuels. These things are simply part of our everyday world, and the consequences of these modes of life have, until recently, rarely been considered as a matter of world politics.

FIGURE 3.3
Traffic congestion

Accelerating change and unpredictable effects

Climate has been relatively stable for the last 10,000 years or so since the end of the last ice age. There have been some dramatic short-term disruptions like when the Krakatoa volcano in Indonesia blew its top in 1883 and put huge quantities of material into the atmosphere, shading the sunlight for a couple of years (Winchester 2003). But mostly over this period of the planet's existence, climate has stayed within a fairly narrow range close to what we became familiar with before the 1980s. While some societies, perhaps most notably Mayan civilisation in the Americas, have collapsed, possibly because of environmental change, this stable set of circumstances allowed for the emergence of agricultural societies and the beginnings of human civilisations (Diamond 2005). Now numerous indications of climate change are becoming obvious, not only to scientists and those who use satellites and weather stations to monitor change, but also to bird-watchers, who pay attention to bird migrations, gardeners and farmers, who have to plant and harvest according to the seasons, not to mention the people who plan such things as winter snow removal budgets in many cities of the Northern Hemisphere.

The processes changing the atmosphere, the phenomena of global warming, are fairly simple to outline. Increased burning of fossil fuels puts more carbon dioxide (CO_2) into the atmosphere. Plants and oceans can't absorb all this increased volume of gas so it starts to accumulate. Prior to the Industrial Revolution carbon dioxide was fairly stable at about 270 parts per million in the atmosphere. Now it's getting close to 400 parts per million and forecasts for the rest of this century suggest that it might get as high as 500 parts per million or close to double its pre-industrial levels. Because we know from the geological record that global climate varies very closely in line with CO_2 concentrations and there is no record in the last half a million years of CO_2 anywhere close to existing levels, there is great concern in the scientific community about what the future holds for the biosphere and for humanity (Flannery 2006).

While the details of how all these factors play out in the biosphere are complicated, some general trends are clear and some are very worrisome. Not least, what worries scientists is that many of the likely responses to increased atmospheric temperatures will be neither gradual nor predictable. Feedback loops are already beginning to accelerate trends that speed up heating. Neither will changes be evenly spread geographically. Already it is clear that heating is having dramatic effects in the polar regions of the planet. Ice and snow reflect a lot of sunlight because they are white. Where ice and snow melt, and either ground or ocean is exposed, more sunlight is absorbed as heat because of the darker colour. This warms the area, encouraging further melting. While sea ice melting doesn't affect the level of oceans, both warming of the ocean water and melting of ice on land does raise sea levels.

BOX 3.2 GREENHOUSE GASES

Carbon dioxide is a relatively large molecule among atmospheric gases and large molecules trap infrared radiation, keeping the heat that would otherwise escape back into space in the atmosphere. Methane turns out to be an even more potent gas, and it stays in the atmosphere longer than carbon dioxide; human activities have also so far caused nearly a doubling of methane in the atmosphere. The CFCs (chlorofluorocarbons) that are the cause of so much worry about ozone layer depletion are also very potent greenhouse gases. (The international agreement in the late 1980s to phase out the production of CFCs will also in the long run help reduce the amount of this greenhouse gas in the atmosphere (Soroos 1997)). Water vapour, too, is sometimes a powerful greenhouse gas. Cloudy nights in temperate climate zones are usually less likely to have frost than clear ones. But in the daytime when those clouds reflect sunlight back into space they act to cool the surface. This makes water a very difficult gas to work into predictions of climate change. Other ironies of atmospheric change include the fact that while aeroplanes flying high in the atmosphere are pouring carbon dioxide into the air they are also emitting other polluting gases, or aerosols, that act to reflect sunlight and cool the earth's surface, which counteracts the warming of the carbon dioxide. This strange fact was confirmed by measurements over the United States in the few days after September 11, 2001 when air traffic was grounded. Likewise, air pollution in Asia from fires and inefficient engine combustion both is a local health hazard and is probably reducing the warming from the sun by its shading effects. Clean combustion may be a benefit for reducing smog, but may add to climate change.

FIGURE 3.4
NASA image shows increase in the hole in the ozone layer. Photo: NASA

In the Northern polar region adding fresh water to the oceans may have other unforeseen effects. One obvious one is the possibility of disrupting the global circulation of the oceans. The Gulf Stream, which flows north in the Atlantic from the Gulf of Mexico up to Iceland and the coast of Norway, sinks in these northern latitudes because the water it contains is denser than the surrounding water it meets. But if the water in these northern waters becomes less salty because of the

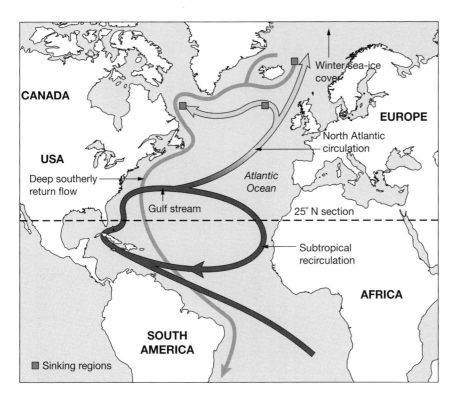

FIGURE 3.5
The North Atlantic conveyor. Redrawn from graphic on website at
www.thewe.cc/...abrupt_climate_change_event.htm

melting glacier ice in Greenland and elsewhere in the far north, then the Gulf
Stream waters may not be denser when they get there, and hence may not sink
the way they have done for many thousands of years. In this situation, where the
Atlantic conveyor switches off, the warm air that comes with the Gulf Stream may
not warm Europe the way it normally does and, at least temporarily, Europe might
get much colder as the rest of the planet heats up.

While this may not be a very likely outcome in the next few decades, it emphasises
the key point that climate is very complicated and change is likely to happen very
unevenly. Thus climate change may have many unpredictable effects. Droughts
in Australia might further reduce its grain production. Likewise, if the Northern
Hemisphere becomes cooler and drier perhaps the production of wheat in Canada
and the US will also be reduced. If such things happen when a major disruption
of the monsoon in South Asia occurs, then there may not be much surplus grain
in the world system to offer emergency aid in the face of famine. This will be
especially so if farmland is converted to grow biomass to make fuel to replace the
use of petroleum and so reduce carbon dioxide emissions.

It is important to think
about how many of these
changes are likely to
affect particular people
more severely than
others.
See Chapters 13 and 14

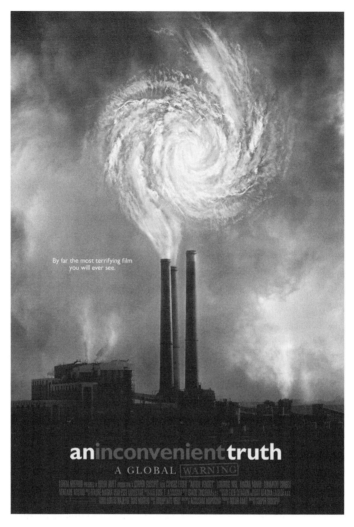

FIGURE 3.6
Image of smokestacks producing hurricanes from *An Inconvenient Truth*. Lawrence Bender Productions. Poster courtesy the Kobal Collection

One other possible effect of climate change is the increased severity of large storms. The 2005 hurricane season in the Caribbean, and the fact that hurricane Katrina devastated Louisiana and, due to a failure of the dyke system round New Orleans, flooded that city, focused attention on the vulnerability of populations to storms. Hurricanes, or typhoons as they are called in the Pacific, are fed by warm ocean water, and as the oceans warm it is likely but far from certain that more severe storms will occur (Shepherd and Knutson 2007). It might transpire that more frequent but less severe storms happen, but the real danger comes with the possibility of bigger and more severe storms. Not least, this is because so many people now live in harm's way. Many poor people have no choice but to live on marginal land in coastal areas, river valleys and hillsides vulnerable to flooding or landslides. If extreme weather events become more frequent people in these areas and in large low-lying delta areas may be especially vulnerable. New Orleans may not be the last coastal city to suffer the consequences of storms and rising sea levels.

That said, it is also worth pausing to consider the simple fact that emergency measures, if taken in time, do frequently save lives and reduce the damage to property. The example of the Cuban system, where a complicated and flexible system of neighbourhood and community responsibility and an effective shelter programme, work to protect people from the impacts of hurricanes that regularly hit the island, shows that much can be done to reduce vulnerabilities if appropriate preparations are undertaken (Sims and Vogelmann 2002). And yet in numerous countries there has been a reluctance to tackle these issues. Activists attending the Earth Summit in Rio de Janeiro in 1992 sketched out some basic principles for acting as though we collectively live in a vulnerable biosphere,

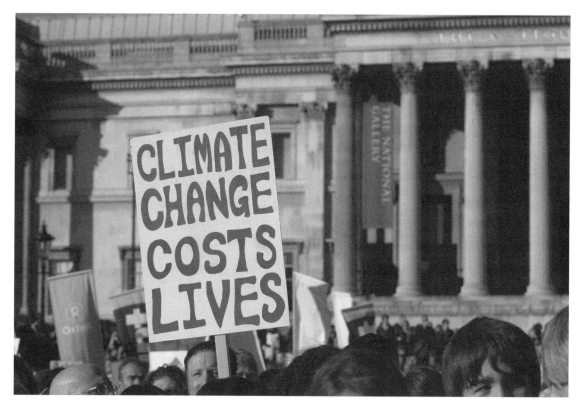

FIGURE 3.7
Demonstration on climate change, London, November 2006. Photo: Dave Walsh, Greenpeace

BOX 3.3 THE UN AND THE ENVIRONMENT

The Conference on the Human Environment held in Stockholm in 1972 marked the first attempt by the United Nations to discuss global environmental matters in a comprehensive manner (Ward and Dubos 1972). While the United Nations Environment Program (UNEP) was established in the 1970s to deal with environmental matters, it was not a major United Nations priority in the years that followed. Nonetheless, in the 1980s UNEP was involved in discussions about the global atmosphere, stratospheric ozone depletion and the establishment of the Intergovernmental Panel on Climate Change (IPCC), the scientific body that evaluates and summarises climate change science for governments.

The early IPCC technical reports (see http://www.ipcc.ch/index.html) fed into the deliberations at the huge Earth Summit, the United Nations Conference on Environment and Development (UNCED), which was held in Rio de Janeiro in 1992 (Chatterjee and Finger 1994). Among the agreements that came from this conference attended by most of the heads of state on the planet was the Framework Agreement on Climate Change (Soroos 1997). This in turn produced the much more talked about Kyoto Protocol late in the 1990s, an agreement that entered into force on 16 February 2005 when Russia finally became part of the agreement. This protocol, and the numerous elaborations and modifications worked out at subsequent conferences of the parties, has become the key focal point of international efforts to limit greenhouse gas emissions.

But most of this remains a matter of regulating emissions, and frequently of intense arguments about how to allocate responsibilities, quotas and measurements. Neither the Kyoto Protocol nor the Framework Convention is a forum for planning global sustainable development or ensuring the rapid spread of technological innovations such as photovoltaic cells, solar water heaters or green building designs. It remains mostly focused on environment, rather than on building a sustainable economy, although discussions of such programmes as clean development mechanisms at least suggest the possibility of the United Nations playing a more active role in building a green economy. The real test for the United Nations system and its ability to shape the future will be what comes after the Kyoto agreement when additional states are incorporated into more extensive climate change arrangements.

Attempts to act on environmental concerns are often not helped by the way the world is divided into territorial units called states.
See Chapter 9

principles that subsequently became the 'Earth Charter', the closest thing there is to an international manifesto for sustainable living. While the government delegations did enact some international agreements in Rio, notably the Framework Convention on Climate Change, progress on dealing with greenhouse gas emissions has been very slow in most states.

RESPONSES
HOW DO WE FRAME THE ISSUE IN TERMS OF GLOBAL POLITICS?

But how are we to understand all this politically? What modes of thinking might we invoke to think through these new circumstances? Perhaps more important, in what sense are these apparently new circumstances actually new? If they are not new, what lessons from the past might we draw on in analysing the problem and in thinking about the issue of climate change as a matter of global politics? In this section three different ways of thinking about this issue, drawing from environmental history, indigenous perspectives and geopolitics, address the question of whether human-centric or, perhaps more precisely, modern urban human perspectives are all that are required. Looking back into history we can see how the current ecological circumstances came about and come to understand in what senses our climate change predicament is really new. Looking outside Western thinking to the sometimes very different views from indigenous peoples who were conquered by modern societies provides an interesting contrast with modern understandings of environment. Finally, by looking at where the fuels come from and the consequences of the waste products from their combustion we can see where the problem lies and how power on the largest scale matters.

Environmental history

Environmental history has emerged in the last few decades as a discipline that links geography, ecology, natural history and the traditional concerns of the discipline of history with the unfolding of human events. The crux of the matter is captured in the title of one of the key texts in the field, Alfred Crosby's (1986) *Ecological Imperialism*, where human matters of imperialism are linked directly to the ecological consequences of European conquest. Although it is frequently not thought of in these terms, the history of imperialism is all about changing landscapes and ecologies. Much of this is not done deliberately, but the introduction of horses and cattle in the Americas, not to mention rabbits in Australia, has dramatically altered the environments of these continents. In addition, growing wheat and other crops, as well as clearing large forests to make agricultural fields, involves a complete change in the plants and animals in areas where colonisation occurs.

Processes of imperialism and colonial conquest are discussed in **Chapters 11 and 15.**

Not all the ecological changes of European colonisation were a matter of introducing European plants and animals into distant areas where they could flourish, the 'neo-Europes' in Crosby's terms. Some of the plants found in the Americas found their way back to Europe. In particular, the humble potato became a crucial part of the diet of Europe after some varieties were taken back across the Atlantic. Indeed one can argue that it was precisely the dependence of peasants in Ireland in the 1840s on a few potato breeds that rendered them so vulnerable when a warm summer spread a blight to which the potatoes were susceptible. The massive starvation that followed killed perhaps a million inhabitants and forced many more to flee the island in search of a living elsewhere. To this day the human population of the island has not grown back to the level it was a century and a half ago.

Looking to the huge changes wrought on the landscapes of North America, in particular in the nineteenth century, as what quickly started to look like an American empire spread rapidly across the continent, suggests clearly that what we now take for granted as 'the environment' is much more of an artificial construction than a natural entity. Widespread slaughter of the buffalo herds, the eradication of many bird species and the clearing of forests for cultivation of crops changed the ecology of the continent fundamentally. The wilderness was enclosed, farmed and above all rendered tame and safe for European settlement. On the western frontier, beyond the area easily farmed, the 'Wild West' became ranching country, the buffalo replaced by roaming cattle overseen by the ever-present 'cowboy'. This part of ecological imperialism has become part of popular American, and now global, culture, where the western has generated a genre of movies and books.

Accounts by people whose ancestors were displaced by the changes in the United States are interesting. See **Chapter 10**, where the writings of Sherman Alexie are discussed.

But this expansion of human control over environments, and the conversion of wilderness into tamed landscape, is a larger part of the human experience as agriculture has gradually eliminated or pushed hunter-gatherer peoples into marginal areas. It has been followed by the emergence of an urban civilisation, one that has expanded dramatically in the last century to appropriate minerals, fuel and land from the distant corners of the planet to supply essential materials to the cities. The human species, this colonising medium-sized mammal, has expanded its range to the whole planet, and the consequences are so dramatic that we are now shaping the evolution of the biosphere in new ways. The total scale of this transformation has led to discussions of the novelty of this situation; to borrow the phrasing from another major book (McNeill 2000) in the field of environmental history, there now is *Something New under the Sun*.

Indigenous perspectives

In the process not only have animals and plants, trees, fish and birds been displaced and frequently simply annihilated, but indigenous cultures have also perished. Much of the expansion of European power, and its appropriation of land and resources through direct colonisation in the Americas and Australia, was at the expense of the indigenous cultures that were there before Europeans encountered them. Indigenous perspectives on history now make this clear (LaDuke 1999). Many cowboy movies are about fighting 'Indians' in the Wild

West, a theme that reflects the fact that the native societies were caught up in the conquest and frequently fought back in the face of invasion. The cavalry didn't always get there in time.

One of the key assumptions in the conquest of the Americas was that the land Europeans were entering was 'empty', at least in the sense that it wasn't being farmed and used 'productively'. If native peoples were using the land they weren't doing so in ways that the European conquerors thought were significant, so the removal of the natives wasn't seen as a problem. The legal doctrine of *terra nullius* literally specified the land as empty. Civilisation was about dominance and control over land and resources; the benefits of civilisation came only with the adoption of these modes of controlling the environment. The fact that indigenous peoples frequently had complicated and sophisticated understandings of their local eco-systems, and that they often harvested animals in ways that ensured their reproduction in the long term, was rarely understood by settlers, who assumed that the land was not being used because it was not being farmed in European ways.

See **Chapter 9** for a discussion of territoriality.

Native cosmologies in North America, and frequently in the case of indigenous peoples elsewhere, do not start with the assumptions of a humanity apart from nature. Living within ecosystems, native peoples frequently don't make that fundamental separation between people and everything else (LaDuke 1999). What 'modern' societies might designate as native religion, but what might be much better understood as an integral part of local cultures, frequently requires some notion of respect for the animals one captures and kills to eat. This is not a picture of an environment external to humanity for it to dominate and control, an external entity to mine and exploit for resources and commodities; it is seen as a place to

For a discussion of the place of religion in global politics, see **Chapter 5**

"There is nobody else. I'm afraid we've wiped out all of the other species."

FIGURE 3.8
'There is nobody else'.
Artist: Stan Eales.
CartoonStock.
Ref: sea0186.
www.CartoonStock.com

inhabit, a home that provides the necessities of life and will continue to do so if cared for appropriately. Thus long-term consequences, and the possibilities of ecological renewal, are integral to the political considerations of native cultures.

The radical separation on which modernity rests is just that when viewed from many non-Western cultural perspectives. Thus the disregard for other species, the willingness to introduce new crops and the destruction of 'pests' that might threaten the agricultural systems of the settlers are viewed askance by native activists. The connections between life and land are ignored by modern modes of thinking that reduce fecund ecologies to resources, and land to a commodity that should be exploited for short-term commercial gain. None of this is to take a romantic view of traditional societies. The assumption that native societies and environments were a paradise prior to the disruptions of colonisation is neither historically accurate nor politically helpful, but the dramatic contrast in cosmologies is useful in thinking about the assumptions of an external nature that can be managed in present circumstances. Native cosmologies challenge the separation of nature and society that modernity is based upon.

> Is the easy distinction between humans and other species a particular feature of modern thinking?

Geopolitics

Looked at on the largest scale, that of geopolitics and power on the global scale, the pattern of resource exploitation and disruption of local ways of living continues as ever larger appropriations of resources are made to feed and fuel consumption in the metropoles. Nowhere is this more evident than in the case of petroleum, the substance that is at the heart of the problem of climate change, and a matter once again at the heart of discussions of geopolitics (Klare 2008). Because it is used so widely in contemporary society, petroleum has become an essential commodity. Some of the oil wells in current use are in remote places where indigenous peoples live. These peoples have been involved in numerous struggles against the environmental despoliation caused by wells and pipelines and also in attempts to gain some of the financial benefits of oil extraction. Once again the pattern of colonisation and the displacement of indigenous peoples continues (Gedicks 2001).

Many of the oil production facilities on the planet are far from where the petroleum is refined and used. Most obviously in the region round the Persian Gulf huge reserves of oil lie under the sands where until recently nomadic peoples lived on the Arabian peninsula, or where traditional centres of civilisation flourished in Persian lands further north. In this region a struggle to control the oil trade has repeatedly plunged local states and Western powers into conflict. Violence comes with oil. It is valuable enough to fight over. Given its importance for the global economy, those who would control that economy are tied into struggles to control both the supplies directly and the profits that can be made

FIGURE 3.9
Oil refinery. Stock photo

from selling the products. In particular, American efforts to control the petroleum supplies in the Gulf are tied directly into rivalries with Iran and formerly with Iraq (Bacevich 2005). But this is not a simple matter of the American government doing the bidding of the oil companies to protect its supplies. It's a much more complicated situation than that, not least because oil company profits go up when supplies are tight and prices rise.

Here the most obvious contradictions in the global politics of our times become very evident. The violence involved in trying to control the petroleum trade is in fact a violence to perpetuate the production of a substance that is a direct threat to the stability of the planet's climate. Thus America is at war in the Middle East in part to protect an unsustainable global society; it is fighting to maintain a way of life that is imperilling all our futures. In part it is doing so out of sheer inertia: things have long been done this way so they continue to be done this way. In part it is also a belief in technology and the power of the internal combustion engine and a globalised economy to provide wealth that ensures that the overall lot of humanity continues to improve. It's a mode of existence that simply doesn't think that environment matters that much. It perpetuates the assumption that environment is an externality to the important matters of human society, and the provision of commodities and status in particular. Power in human societies these days is still mostly understood in these terms.

There are many views as to what gives rise to violence as a method of action to solve problems. **See Chapter 16**

BROADER ISSUES
CHALLENGING CARBONIFEROUS CAPITALISM

We have to think about environment, social change and geopolitics simultaneously and try to see how political economy links all of them together, tying the fate of marginalised people into the economic and security priorities of political elites in the metropoles. But we also need to think about arguments that challenge the continued operation of carboniferous capitalism and about how social change might happen if environment and the consequences of imperial geopolitics for indigenous peoples were taken into account. We can no longer operate on the assumption that there is a separation between us and the planet; there is no external nature that we can manipulate without having to deal with the consequences. The changing composition of the air makes this fact unavoidable. There is no distant place we can safely put our waste, pollution or sewage. Neither can we ignore the consequences of our modes of consumption for the lives of marginalised people growing the crops we use or struggling with the disruptions caused by mines, oil wells and pipelines in many places (Sachs and Santarius 2007).

Despite the growing recognition of this as the appropriate starting point, and all the discussions about the Kyoto Protocol and subsequent climate change negotiations over the last decade (see Box 3.2, p. 52), the growth in the use of fossil fuels has continued apace. Asian economies are booming and the large economies of India and China in particular seem determined to catch up with Western models of urban carboniferous capitalism (Worldwatch Institute 2006). Car ownership is rising rapidly; national pride is linked to the existence of national car production facilities in many states in Asia in particular. This economic growth is based on petroleum fuels, following on from American, Japanese and European practice rather than innovating with new fuels. Oil is still king. This is not surprising for developing economies where playing catch-up is the dominant mode of economic activity, but as oil becomes increasingly scarce and supplies are potentially disrupted by instabilities and wars in the Middle East, the wisdom of such a development strategy seems highly doubtful. If climate change is taken seriously this is doubly the case.

Potential disruptions as a result of storms, cooling in Europe, droughts in agricultural regions and such things as sea level rises are what drives much of the concern about climate change. While affluent consumers in the global economy, and in particular in the urban metropoles of that economy, may be relatively insulated from droughts and agricultural disruptions, rural residents, and those living in marginal landscapes susceptible to flood waters in particular, are not. Many diseases will also spread to areas where they have not been known for generations, if at all. If these disruptions coincide with major warfare in the Middle East or some other source of trade disruption, the potential for human suffering will be

To what extent does capitalist economics rely on growth? Is sustainable growth a contradiction in terms?

Development strategies have a range of serious consequences for the people subject to them.
See also Chapter 11

immense. All these constitute the case to be concerned about environmental change on the big scale.

While environmental change isn't new in the human experience, as environmental historians have made clear, the potential for rapid shifts in climate makes numerous people vulnerable now in ways that are perhaps similar to the situation in the late nineteenth century, when famine swept through areas in the European empires in part because of the economic disruptions caused by the globalisation of the grain trade and the effects this had on regional agriculture (Davis 2001). If all this happens while hurricanes and droughts become more severe, there is a potential for major human disasters. Beyond that, the most worrisome dimension of environmental change is the potential for a dramatic flip in the climate system that radically changes the whole arrangement of climate zones (Alley 2004). This is why many scientists have recently focused on the Atlantic conveyor and the Gulf Stream. While no one expects a series of changes on the scale of the plot of the 2004 Hollywood disaster movie *The Day after Tomorrow*, the possibility of a very nasty climate surprise is of great concern, especially because there is little evidence that, at least at the moment, international political institutions could deal effectively with such an event.

In particular, this is suggested by the pattern of thinking that appears in much of the negotiating about climate change, not least by the frequent assumption that Northern consumers can sink their carbon emissions in plantations in poor countries (see Box 3.4). Rather than dealing directly with reducing consumption, part of the strategy has been to export the pollution and plant trees where labour and land are relatively cheap in other states (Lohmann 2006). All of this reminds historians of the story of colonial plantations designed to supply commodities for markets in the metropoles. Poor peoples are once again displaced to grow tree crops that are at best a temporary way of soaking up some of the carbon emissions, but a way that lets Northern consumers off the hook for the moment and allows them to claim to be carbon neutral. This postpones dealing with the industrial and transportation systems that continue to turn rocks into air so we can all enjoy having cool toys, big and small. The costs are displaced onto poor people in the South and onto our grandchildren, who will bear the brunt of the disruptions today's fuel use sets in motion in the future. Environmental justice for whom?

Some people might see carbon offsetting as an example of neo-colonialism. **See Chapter 11**

The political and economic arguments against tackling environmental change have usually asserted that change is simply too expensive. Only recently have economists and politicians begun to take seriously the opposite and altogether more compelling argument, that it will be a lot cheaper to act now to reduce the dangers, rather than paying potentially huge costs later. As the Stern Report on climate change, the British government document that investigates in detail the costs of climate change, put it: 'we have never seen a market failure like this'

BOX 3.4 CARBON OFFSETS AND TRADING

If too many greenhouse gases are being produced by economic activities, is it possible to get them out of the air? If so, why not deal with the problem of greenhouse gases by offsetting production against activities that reduce gas production and remove gases from the atmosphere. If tropical trees grow quickly and in the process absorb carbon from the atmosphere, then why not invest in plantations that can soak up emissions, and offset the use of fossil fuels against tree growth? This argument is the basis of a growing social movement and investment market in carbon offsets, as well as a part of the larger international markets for carbon dioxide credit trading designed to reduce the growth of greenhouse gases. Insofar as it provides a constituency in business groups to promote action on climate change and facilitates social movements which wish to offset consumer lifestyles and make them carbon neutral, carbon offsets may by useful.

But critics are quick to point out various flaws in offset thinking (Lohmann 2006; Monbiot 2006). Most obviously, if industries are offsetting their emissions they may not have the same incentives to reduce greenhouse gases, which is what really needs to be done. If consumers offset their emissions, and hence stop feeling guilty about the ecological consequences of what they are doing, rather than changing how they live to actually reduce their emissions, then offsets aren't helpful. If quick-growing but ecologically inappropriate trees, like eucalyptus, which needs lots of water, are grown they may badly affect water supplies and other aspects of the environment. Badly designed programmes of plantation farming may aggravate the problems faced by marginal farmers or indigenous peoples on whose lands the plantations are created. Plantation agriculture was key to colonial development; calling the forests carbon offset trees and having local governments administer the forests doesn't change this old pattern.

Al Gore was US Vice President from 1993 to 2001. More recently he has been noted for his campaign to promote environmental awareness and in particular his documentary film *An Inconvenient Truth*, which won him both an Oscar and a share of the Nobel Peace Prize in 2007.

(United Kingdom Treasury Department 2006). This brings the discussion back to politics, and who should do what to deal with the 'failure' of the existing mode of organising human affairs to consider the consequences of our modes of life for the future, or for marginalised native peoples struggling to adapt to the influx of modernity on their lands and cultures. In Al Gore's (2006) words, we now simply have to deal with 'the inconvenient truth' of climate change; but how to do so remains very difficult.

There is now no mechanism in human affairs to decide on what should be produced or how and where to ensure that catastrophe is avoided. Global agreements on everything from ozone depletion, through bans on the trade of endangered species, to climate change are attempts to rectify this gap. But mostly they look to limit damage rather than change modes of living so as not to do damage in

BOX 3.5 THE STERN REPORT

The *Stern Review Report on the Economics of Climate Change* was released by the United Kingdom Treasury Department in October 2006. In the 700-page report Sir Nicholas Stern makes the case that spending money now to head off the worst effects of climate change is much more sensible than waiting to deal with the consequences later. Whatever the finer points of the economic discussion, his case is simple and direct. If nothing is done the economic disruptions caused by climate change will be dramatic and painful to future generations. Relatively modest intelligent investments now can head off future economic disruptions and are hence good public policy designed to benefit economies in the future. Even if these investments slow economic growth slightly now, Stern argued, they are well worth it in terms of avoiding future losses. The Stern Report is noteworthy because it clearly focuses on the costs of doing nothing, whereas most of the economic arguments about climate change suggest that it is economically rational to do little or nothing because the costs of trying to change economic systems will be very considerable. By reversing this logic Stern has had a fairly immediate political effect on the larger debate about how to think about the future of the global environment. What the Stern Report also suggests clearly is that policy needs to deal with both adapting to climate change, some of which is already inevitable, and mitigating some of its worst effects by taking actions now to slow down the rate of increase of greenhouse gas concentrations in the air. Mitigation is needed not just to buy time for humans and their economies to adapt, but, crucially, to give natural ecosystems the time they need to adapt to the coming changes. In the words of the United Nations Development Program (2007: vi), 'While we pursue adaptation we must start to reduce emissions and take other steps at mitigation so that the irreversible changes already underway are not further amplified over the next few decades. If mitigation does not start in earnest right now, the cost of adaptation twenty or thirty years from now will become prohibitive for the poorest countries'.

the first place. The focus on regulations and legislation driven by environmental groups, and in some states the presence of a green political party, to force business to stop emissions of pollution is now frequent (Lipschutz 2004; Clapp and Dauvergne 2005). Many of these regulations are highly technical matters worked out by experts in the industries being regulated. Reducing politics to such technical negotiations suggests that what matters is fine detail about chemical formulas, trading quotas and industrial standards. The big questions about what kind of a society is best, how we might live together and what needs to be done to ensure the safety and wellbeing of our children and those in distant places too, are frequently squeezed out of the discussion.

Facing major changes in the circumstances of human existence, which is what the climate change discussion is all about, demands that different questions be posed

Liberals believe that there is an informal mechanism that determines what is produced and so on – what Adam Smith called the 'invisible hand'.
See Chapter 12

Are we talking about how we should ensure the survival of humanity or is it the case that the planet as a whole is indifferent to human survival? Are we still placing humans at the centre of the world, as in the picture of the world prior to the Copernican revolution? Copernicus argued that the earth was not the centre of the universe, with the sun moving round it, as had previously been thought. Do we still think 'man' is the centre of the universe?

and the big issues of how to live collectively in a changing biosphere be discussed much more carefully. We clearly need institutions that arrange matters so that we produce the things we actually need to live well without completely disrupting natural cycles in the biosphere (Sachs and Santarius 2007). Our existing political institutions have so far mostly failed to grapple with the new circumstances of human existence (Dodds and Pippard 2005). Native cosmologies, and their insistence that we are all part of the cycles of life, might have many lessons to teach us about how we reconsider those institutions and think about how to live well within a small vulnerable biosphere. Ecological science, too, shows us that we are part of the environment, not the masters of it. It's not out there in the wild spaces distant from civilised cities; it's part of the systems of life that we have dramatically changed by our industries and our profligate use of energy and materials.

CONCLUSION

Climate change challenges many of the modern assumptions about politics. The whole modern mode of thinking, of managing an external environment to maximise the production of things rather than human wellbeing, has shaped public administration and regulation in national and international discussions. Science has now made it abundantly clear that we are living in a biosphere that our actions are reshaping, and that we now need to rethink these modern assumptions. Environment is no longer just a matter of pollution and resource constraints, parks and conservation. It is now a much more important matter, which enters directly into any discussion of how we should live. Climate change now makes dealing with environmental matters urgent and unavoidable. New institutions and new ways of making decisions about what we make, and hence what kind of world we produce for future generations, need a lot more attention from politicians and scholars.

But we can learn from history as well as from science. The indigenous focus on living within one's surroundings, inhabiting rather than controlling, is one valuable lesson. Another lesson is that distinctions between rural nature and urban civilisation are no longer useful when it comes to thinking about politics or public administration. A focus on the flows of material and energy in the biosphere becomes necessary; looking at the connections between things and people makes political responsibility for one's actions unavoidable. In short, starting from natural systems and thinking about the interconnections between our actions and distant places where the energy and commodities we use come from, rather than thinking from the viewpoint of modern consumers disconnected from the rest of the world, makes life more complicated but in turn gives us a very useful perspective on global politics.

FURTHER READING

The best popular explanation of the science of global warming is probably Tim Flannery's (2006) *The Weather Makers*. Vaclav Smil's (2003) guide to *The Earth's Biosphere* is precisely what its title suggests and is useful for the rest of the science that matters in discussing environmental politics. An overview of the current state of the world's natural environments and how all this relates to development is in the United Nations Environment Program report *Geo4 Global Environmental Outlook: Environment for Development*, released in October 2007.

Wolfgang Sachs and colleagues (2007) book on a *Fair Future* is excellent on the principles of thinking ecologically while seeing the interconnections between the South and North. Ronnie Lipschutz (2004), in *Global Environmental Politics*, is also good on the interconnections between commodities and how environmental politics actually works. George Monbiot's (2006) critical book *Heat* is very useful for thinking seriously about the politics of change and what needs to be done. The larger scholarly discussion of environment and global political economy is in Jennifer Clapp and Peter Dauvergne's (2005) *Paths to a Green World*.

WEBSITES

The rapidly changing science of global change is summarised by the International Geosphere Biosphere Program (IGBP) at http://www.igbp.kva.se/. The 2007 Nobel Prize-winning Intergovernmental Panel on Climate Change (IPCC) can be found at: http://www.ipcc.ch/. Al Gore's Inconvenient Truth site is at http://www.climatecrisis.net/. The United Nations Environment Program's *Global Environmental Outlook* is online at http://www.unep.org/geo/.

The United Kingdom Treasury Department *Stern Review Report on the Economics of Climate Change* (2006) made a substantial impact when it was published because it clearly showed that it was cheaper to act now to prevent the worst effects of climate change than pay to deal with the effects in the future; the report is online at http://www.hm-treasury.gov.uk/independent_reviews/stern_review_economics_climate_change/stern_review_report.cfm.

Background information on the writing of the text of the Earth Charter and details about current campaigns based on it can be found at http://www.earthcharter.org. The Worldwatch Institute, at http://www.worldwatch.org/, publishes numerous well-researched articles and reports on many environmental matters, including climate change. Greenpeace International's climate campaign can be found at http://www.greenpeace.org/international/campaigns/climate-change.

REFERENCES

Alley, Richard B. (2004) 'Abrupt Climate Change', *Scientific American* 291, 5: 62–9.

Bacevich, Andrew (2005) *The New American Militarism: How Americans Are Seduced by War*, New York: Oxford University Press.

Chatterjee, Partha and Matthias Finger (1994) *The Earth Brokers: Power, Politics, and World Development*, London: Routledge.

Clapp, Jennifer and Peter Dauvergne (2005) *Paths to a Green World: The Political Economy of the Global Environment*, Cambridge, MA: MIT Press.

Crosby, Alfred (1986) *Ecological Imperialism: The Biological Expansion of Europe 900–1900*, Cambridge: Cambridge University Press.

Dalby, Simon (2002) *Environmental Security*, Minneapolis, MN: University of Minnesota Press.

Davis, Mike (2001) *Late Victorian Holocausts: El Niño Famines and the Making of the Third World*, London: Verso.

Diamond, Jared (2005) *Collapse: How Societies Choose to Fail or Succeed*, New York: Viking.

Dodds, Felix and Tim Pippard (eds) (2005) *Human and Environmental Security: An Agenda for Change*, London: Earthscan.

Flannery, Tim (2006) *The Weather Makers: How We are Changing the Climate and What It Means for Life on Earth*, Toronto: HarperCollins.

Gedicks, Al (2001) *Resource Rebels: Native Challenges to Mining and Oil Corporations*, Boston, MA: South End.

Gore, Al (2006) *An Inconvenient Truth*, New York: Rodale Books.

Klare, Michael (2008) *Rising Powers/Shrinking Planet: The New Geopolitics of Energy*, New York: Metropolitan.

LaDuke, Winona (1999) *All Our Relations: Native Struggles for Land and Life*, Cambridge, MA: South End.

LeBillon, Philippe (2005) *Fuelling War: Natural Resources and Armed Conflict*, Adelphi Paper 373, Oxford: Routledge.

Lipschutz, Ronnie D. (2004) *Global Environmental Politics: Power, Perspectives, and Practice*, Washington, DC: CQ Press.

Lohmann, Larry (ed.) (2006) *Carbon Trading: A Critical Conversation on Climate Change, Privatisation and Power*, Development Dialogue, No. 48, http://www.dhf.uu.se/publications.html.

McNeill, J.R. (2000) *Something New under the Sun: An Environmental History of the Twentieth-Century World*, New York: Norton.

Meadows, D.H., D.L. Meadows, J. Randers and W.W. Behrens III (1974) *The Limits to Growth*, London: Pan.

Monbiot, George (2006) *Heat: How to Stop the Planet from Burning*, London: Penguin.

Mumford, Lewis (1934) *Technics and Civilization*, New York: Harcourt.

Paterson, Matthew (2007) *Automobile Politics: Ecology and Cultural Political Economy*, Cambridge: Cambridge University Press.

Sachs, Wolfgang and Tilman Santarius (eds) (2007) *Fair Future: Resource Conflicts, Security and Global Justice*, London: Zed.

Sandbach, Francis (1980) *Environment, Ideology, Policy*, Oxford: Blackwell.

Shepherd, J. Marshall and Thomas Knutson (2007) 'The Current Debate on the Linkage Between Global Warming and Hurricanes', *Geography Compass* 1, 1: 1–24.

Sims, Holly and Kevin Vogelmann (2002) 'Popular Mobilization and Disaster Management in Cuba', *Public Administration and Development* 22, 5: 389–400.

Smil, Vaclav (2003) *The Earth's Biosphere: Evolution, Dynamics and Change*, Cambridge, MA: MIT Press.

Soroos, Marvin (1997) *The Endangered Atmosphere*, Columbia, SC: University of South Carolina Press.

United Kingdom Treasury Department (2006) *Stern Review Report on the Economics of Climate Change*, London: HM Treasury.

United Nations Development Programme (2007) *United Nations Development Report 2007–2008 Fighting Climate Change: Human Solidarity in a Divided World*, New York: United Nations Development Program.

United Nations Environment Programme (2007) *GEO4 Global Environmental Outlook: Environment for Development*, Nairobi: United Nations Environment Programme.

Wapner, Paul (1996) *Environmental Activism and World Civic Politics*, Albany, NY: State University of New York Press.

Ward, Barbara and Rene Dubos (1972) *Only One Earth: The Care and Maintenance of a Small Planet*, Harmondsworth: Penguin.

Williams, Raymond (1973) *The Country and the City*, London: Chatto and Windus.

Winchester, Simon (2003) *Krakatoa: The Day the World Exploded, 27 August 1883*, New York: HarperCollins.

World Commission on Environment and Development (1987) *Our Common Future*, Oxford: Oxford University Press.

Worldwatch Institute (2006) *State of the World 2006*, New York: Norton.

CHAPTER 4

Who do we think we are?

Annick T.R. Wibben

- ■ *The question*
  NARRATIVES AND POLITICS

- ■ *Illustrative example*
  THE US FEMINIST MOVEMENT

- ■ *Responses*
  HOW CAN WE CONCEPTUALIZE IDENTITY?

- ■ *Broader issues*
  DO WE NEED TO IDENTIFY WITH A GROUP?

- ■ **CONCLUSION**

THE QUESTION
NARRATIVES AND POLITICS

Our idea of who we think we are is often based on something called identity: national, ethnic, racial, gender, class, sexual and religious identity are among the categories that are used in discussions. To think about the question of identity, we need to do two things: (1) begin to see how we are always already subjected to identity politics and (2) examine what some of the implications of being identified (or identifying) with a particular group can be in global politics.

Once we have come to understand why identity is such an important concept, we can take a closer look at how identity politics plays itself out in the particular case of the women's movement in the United States and what the experiences of this movement can teach us about identity politics in other settings. Identity politics is inspired by the interests of, and intended to benefit, a particular group with a shared identity. It has been a key form of political activism, though one that is much criticized, as we shall discover shortly.

As soon as a baby is born, people begin to identify this new person in various ways. Besides assuming the baby's ethnicity or nationality, this very often means identifying the baby's gender. Today, with the advent of new technologies, many people will seek to find out whether they are having a girl or a boy even before birth. The consequences of this early identification range from 'getting ready' by selecting a name and painting a nursery in the 'right' colour, to selective abortions in countries like India (where a preference for males is common) or China (where the preference for males is coupled with a one-birth policy). Thus, from an early age, before birth even, identity politics matters.

Narrative theorists have pointed out that we are all *homo fabulans* – storytellers. Narratives are 'the primary way by which human experience is made meaningful' (Polkinghorne 1988: 1). Through narratives we make sense of the world, produce meaning, articulate intentions and legitimize actions. While our lives begin with us being subject to the stories of our parents and others around us, we soon begin to tell our own stories about who we are and where we belong. As we grow, and as the stories of who we are change over time, we might be disappointed when we realize that how our family or community sees us does not match how we identify ourselves.

As we enter new life situations the process of identification continues: We might be confronted with racism for the first time and begin to rethink our identity in terms of race (Winddance Twine's classic on 'Brown-Skinned White Girls' (1996) discusses the case of girls who in college become identified as black). We might realize that having children can mean not ever reaching a leadership position in the workplace. We might find that our religious heritage or nationality limits our movement, as is the case for Palestinians living under occupation in Gaza and the West Bank or for Mexican immigrants to the US. Our image of ourselves and what others see in us (and how they expect us to act) is always unfinished. And there are always multiple stories of who we are intersecting at any one time. Most of these are beyond our control and many times they offer conflicting accounts.

As we identify ourselves through these stories, we draw on various markers of identity that have been passed down to us through the stories we were told. In this ongoing process we are constantly comparing our experiences with those of the rest of the group that we identify with. We discover a shared tradition, a feeling of belonging when our experiences match the standards of identification. We devise new stories, and challenge or reject those that others tell (about us or themselves), when they do not match our experience.

We tell stories about who we are, and these stories are closely related to the pictures we form of the world.
See Chapter 2

The way our stories relate to belonging to a nation (or national identity) is discussed in **Chapter 10.**

Chapter 8 discusses Mexican immigration to the US in some detail.

Of course, identities are often not mutually exclusive. Many people consider themselves to belong to two groups that others may consider to be separate. This is visible in the proliferation of hyphenated identities, such as Mexican-American.

What it might mean to think in non-human-centred terms is discussed in **Chapter 3**.

Chapter 5 examines the example of Islam as a source of identification.

The markers of identity that are emphasized in these stories – whether they be national, ethnic, racial, gender, class, sexual or religious in kind – always signal the belonging to a particular group. In other words, they identify us as a member of a particular group and not of another in the same category (accordingly, when applied strictly, as in the case of fundamentalist movements, one cannot be Hindu and Muslim at the same time, and most countries in the world will still only allow their citizens to hold one passport). That is, at the same time as they place us *inside* this particular group, they also place us *outside* another group.

What is more, by identifying certain traits of belonging to this particular group, they also tell us who the Other is. We cannot understand what it means to be inside without at the same time identifying who or what is outside. Without this 'constitutive outside', something seen as fundamentally different, identity would no longer be meaningful. Even the broad identifier 'human' relies on a juxtaposition with the 'non-human' (e.g. animals, plants or rocks). The latter tell us what it means to be 'human' (e.g. not an animal, not a plant, not a rock). As such, at base, members of a group may have little more in common than not being 'them.'

In addition to marking this boundary, those on the inside are privileged over those on the outside in a number of ways: they can decide what it means to belong and consequently who does not. They often enforce purity inside with the threat of being outside, thus marking what is outside as inferior to those traits identified with the group (e.g. heterosexuality might be considered the norm and people with other sexual orientations will be not only excluded but considered deviant, sinful or appalling in some other way). This holds true whether the group is in a hegemonic or a subjugated position (whether it is the group in charge or not). In a hegemonic position, however, the in-group has easy access to resources (economic, military and cultural) as well as control thereof. Important institutions (e.g. the education system) will be shaped to conform to its members' needs and to transmit their values. Thus, 'although the boundaries are ideological, they involve material (biological, legal, social) practices and therefore have material origins and effects' (Yuval-Davis 1994: 410). At the extremes, being identified (or identifying) with one or another group could mean the difference between life and death.

We have seen that identity is an important concept because it is fundamental to the way we think of ourselves today: it gives us a sense of belonging and it is the marker of our tradition, history and heritage. Identity politics is comforting as it promises security and meaning: 'Stability lies in part in clearly defined sex roles, family life and religious orientation' (Moghadam 1994: 19).

We have noted that identity politics is also a boundary politics that prescribes what is accepted and expected for members of the in-group, the good people. As such,

BOX 4.1 THE BREAK-UP OF YUGOSLAVIA

During the break-up of the former Yugoslavia, ethnic and national identities were harnessed in an intense struggle over power and resources. For several decades, while the state known as Yugoslavia existed, the identities that were soon to become a source of intense and bloody conflict were fluid and not politically significant. Yugoslavs lived together in broad-based communities. During the early 1990s, at the end of the Cold War, different groups within Yugoslavia began to signal their belonging to a particular group (e.g. Serb). In doing so, they placed themselves outside another group (e.g. Bosnian) and began also to distinguish other traits that were reasons for being considered other (e.g. being Muslim in the case of many Bosnians). For many Yugoslavs this was the first time that their religion and heritage came to matter, since they had led an entirely secular life before then.

Serbia and Montenegro have asserted the formation of a joint independent state, but this entity has not been formally recognized as a state by the United States.

Macedonia has proclaimed independent statehood, but has not been formally recognized as a state by the United States.

FIGURE 4.1
Former Yugoslavia, based on 1991 census

As the politics of identity intensified, every Yugoslav had to identify with one of the emerging groups: Albanians, Bosnians, Croats, Macedonians, Montenegrins, Serbs and Slovenes. The leaders of these different groups began to claim the right to national self-determination (asking for the international community to recognize their group as independent). Some of them, especially Serbs but also Croats, began to 'purify' the regions that they identified as belonging to their group. This meant that those who were seen as other were subjected to increasing oppression and even armed violence (see Campbell 1998).

Whether woman or man, being identified as other (e.g. Bosnian) could lead to being held in concentration camps, where rape, hard labour and random execution were common. What is more, age mattered too: in Srebrenica a large number of refugees had gathered under the protection of the United Nations. In July 1995 the Serb military, in their efforts to 'cleanse' the area seen as belonging to Serbia, attacked the safe zone. While they allowed women and children to leave, men of fighting age were massacred. Three markers of identity – gender, age and nationality – came to matter greatly for these men (see Carpenter 2003).

identification takes place by identifying against others, not just excluding but oppressing them and the traits associated with them. The result is that being identified (or identifying) with a particular group is always potentially dangerous.

How can we draw strength from identifying with a group and at the same time curtail the violence it so often entails? The next section looks at a specific example of identity politics – the case of the feminist movement in the United States in the second half of the twentieth century. By looking at the history of the movement and the challenges it has faced, we will be able to better understand the complexities of identity and how we may address identities in conflict without recourse to violence.

ILLUSTRATIVE EXAMPLE
THE US FEMINIST MOVEMENT

Feminist identity politics relies on the idea that some groups are oppressed because they are identified in a particular way: being identified as women, with the associated traits of femininity, leads women to have a shared experience of oppression. Some feminists have argued that this experience that *all* women share, and which is fundamentally different from that of *all* men, should be the basis for feminist politics. Feminists who began thinking along these lines in the 1960s are called second-wave feminists (first-wave feminism refers to feminist activism

FIGURE 4.2
Women's Liberation March, Sydney, 1980. Photo: The Search Foundation – Tribune, State Library of NSW

of the late nineteenth and early twentieth century, in particular that of the suffragettes, who were fighting for a woman's right to vote and to hold public office). Most second-wave feminists, inspired by liberal political thought, sought to overcome oppression by working to achieve equality between women and men. Therefore they are also referred to as liberal or equality feminists.

Emergence of feminist activism

Feminist activism and scholarly activity emerged in many locations and were inspired by a broad range of disciplines (e.g. history, literature, philosophy, politics, psychoanalysis, sociology) and oppressive circumstances. The work of these women (and some men) produced some important insights that challenged

"I heard they spent all day arguing
whether to let women into the
boardroom."

FIGURE 4.3
'I heard they spent all day arguing'. Artist: John Morris. CartoonStock Ref: jmo1622.
www.CartoonStock.com

the foundations of the social and political order as well as what is today considered worthwhile knowledge.

Asking the basic question 'Where are the women?', feminists found that often no one had looked for them before.

Much of the knowledge that had been collected in massive volumes on library shelves, that was being taught in schools and universities and that was being used to make important policy decisions was based on the experiences of men. Even knowledge about women-centred processes like pregnancy, birthing, childrearing and other activities that involved women's bodies or activities largely assigned to women was dominated by men.

Feminists decided that the bias of science and policy could only be corrected by gathering knowledge about women. They argued that these new insights, based

BOX 4.2 CAROL GILLIGAN

FIGURE 4.4
Carol Gilligan.
Photo: Joyce Ravid

Carol Gilligan, a feminist psychologist, wrote a well-known book called *In a Different Voice* (1982). In it she examines theories of childhood development to find that 'The disparity between women's experience and the representation of human development, noted throughout the psychological literature, has generally been seen to signify a problem in women's development' (Gilligan 1982: 1–2).

Her studies, however, led her to suggest that it is not that girls are failing to develop properly, but rather that the models used to assess development are based solely on the experiences of men. Reviewing studies of play, for example, she instead suggests that girls develop differently because they have a different value system. They tend to give preference to the continuation of relationships over the setting and following of rules.

These types of observations led Gilligan to develop an ethics of care as an alternative moral framework, also for politics. While her work has been criticized by many feminists for essentializing women's voices and experiences – saying that she makes a virtue out of qualities that are the result of subordination – her work continues to resonate with many women. Joan Tronto, in *Moral Boundaries* (1993), and Virginia Held, in *The Ethics of Care* (2006), have thought more about some of the implications of Gilligan's approach for global politics.

on women's experiences, would transform ways of thinking and cultural categories. A very important and innovative approach to examine and challenge patriarchy (structures of male domination) was feminist consciousness-raising. The premise of this approach was that 'through discussion women would begin to see what they had once been convinced were personal problems are actually political problems' (Kauffmann 1990: 28). Indeed, when women began to share their experiences in partnerships, friendships, the workforce or the marketplace, they discovered systematic patterns of male domination in all of these areas.

This pervasiveness of patriarchy led feminists to question the entire setup of the private/public dichotomy and the assumptions underlying some of the primary categories of political thought. Jean Bethke Elshtain, in *Public Man, Private Woman* (1981), did a re-reading of canonical texts and rethinking of classic political concepts from a feminist perspective. Another effort focused on recovering women's writing (see, e.g. Spender 1983) to see what historical trends could be uncovered and to develop a broader appreciation of women's experiences.

Traditionally, women and their concerns were seen to belong to the private sphere, whereas politics took place in the public sphere, to which only men were admitted.

FIGURE 4.5
Betty Friedan

In addition, some women began to write about their experiences of oppression due to their identification as women. Betty Friedan's *The Feminine Mystique* (2001 [1963]) was one of the most influential books of this type. Published in the early 1960s, many credit it with jumpstarting second-wave feminism. Friedan began writing the book after she attended her college reunion where she gave a questionnaire to two hundred of her fellow female classmates asking them about their life expectations and experiences. The survey confirmed that many women were unhappy and did not know why – Friedan began calling this 'the problem which has no name'. She eloquently linked the symptoms to an idealized image of femininity – the 'feminine mystique' – which encourages women to confine themselves to the narrow roles of housewife and mother, forsaking education and career aspirations in the process. Her book is still an eye-opening read for many women, but its concerns and suggestions reveal her white middle-class experience.

María C. Lugones and Elizabeth V. Spelman, while not addressing Friedan's work directly, worry about the consequences of extrapolating from specific women's experiences to arrive at an account of *the* woman's voice. They worry that changes perceived as making life better for some women might not be at all liberating for women 'whose lives would be better if they could spend more time at home, whose identity is inseparable from their religious beliefs and cultural practices . . ., who

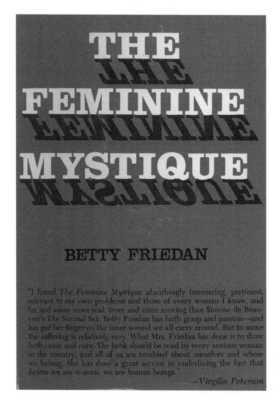

"I found *The Feminine Mystique* absorbingly interesting, pertinent, relevant to my own problems and those of every woman I know, and far and away more real, truer and more moving than Simone de Beauvoir's *The Second Sex*. Betty Friedan has both grasp and passion—and has put her finger on the inner wound we all carry around. But to name the suffering is relatively easy. What Mrs. Friedan has done is to show both cause and cure. The book should be read by every anxious woman in the country, and all of us are troubled about ourselves and where we belong. She has done a great service in underlining the fact that *before* we are women, we are human beings."
—*Virgilia Peterson*

FIGURE 4.6
The Feminine Mystique.
Cover: W.W. Norton

have ties to men – whether erotic or not – such that to have them severed in the name of some vision of what is "better" is, at that time and for those women, absurd' (1983: 579). While the situation might still *seem* oppressive, and even *be* oppressive, they argue that feminist theory should aim to be 'respectful, illuminating, and empowering' (1983: 580) to women in particular settings rather than true or false in an abstract sense. Feminisms should always remain contextual.

This exchange reveals a major problem with second-wave feminism: many of the women who were part of the movement at the time assumed that their experiences were the same as those of *all* women. They assumed that the oppression they experienced was the same as that experienced by *all* women. They imagined their avenues for empowerment, such as equality with men, would free *all* women from oppression. Or, maybe, they did not think about their bias because their identity as white middle-class women had not been challenged.

The problem that speaking for a group implies that the group shares experiences is not, of course, unique to the women's movement, but rather an issue that all movements have to deal with.

bell hooks (she never writes her name with capitals) suggests that the very idea that the feminist movement aims for equality between women and men should raise a number of questions. 'Since men are not equals in white supremacist, capitalist, patriarchal class structures, which men do you want to be equal to?' (hooks 1984: 18). She argues that this very question reveals the bias in liberal, second-wave feminism. Lower-class and poor women, especially if they are not white, immediately recognize that this definition of feminism is flawed since the men in their communities are not in a powerful position. Being like them would not entail an end to oppression. Therefore, liberal (equality) feminism is revealed to be part of the problem, rather than the solution. The framing of the problem as one of equality with men illustrates an unwillingness on the part of white middle-class feminists to examine their own privilege and their complicity in the structures of oppression.

FIGURE 4.7
bell hooks. Photo:
http://www.lib.utk.edu/
news/diversity/archives/
images.bell.jpg

Intensification of identity politics

The famous feminist slogan – the personal is political – which is central to feminist consciousness-raising in second-wave feminism, takes on new meaning as black, Chicana (that is, Mexican American), lesbian and Third World feminists begin to demand that their experiences and their voices be taken seriously:

> We want to express to all women – especially to white middle-class women – the experiences which divide us as feminists; we want to examine incidents of intolerance, prejudice and denial of difference within the feminist movement. We intend to explore the causes and sources of, and solutions to these divisions. We want to create a definition that expands what 'feminist' means to us.
>
> (Moraga and Anzaldúa 1983 [1979]: xxiii)

BOX 4.3 PRIVILEGE

Let us take a moment to examine privilege. Privilege is a structure of unearned assets that we take for granted and that are considered 'normal.' Peggy McIntosh, in 'White Privilege and Male Privilege' (1993 [1988]), argued that the privilege of some is always premised on the denial of advantages to others, but we are not encouraged to see this – after all, few of us want to consider ourselves oppressors.

If we think about it, however, most of us will be able to identify some form of privilege we enjoy: white privilege, class privilege, male privilege, heterosexual privilege and more. Being privileged means that society reflects your worldview and that what you do goes uncensored. Think about it: as you go about your daily life, do people ever censor your behaviour? When you access various media, do you hear about or see people with your lifestyle, your ethnicity or your sexual orientation? Are your religious holidays and customs celebrated by the majority of people in your country? Do you ever limit your movement for fear of being attacked violently because of your gender, race or sexual orientation? Has someone questioned your affection for your partner or described your interaction with your children as unnatural? How many times have you been oblivious to the needs, language and customs of others without being affected by this ignorance?

Unacknowledged privilege is dangerous both personally and politically because it means that we *are* oppressors without even realizing it. 'Whites are taught to think of their lives as morally neutral, normative and average, and also ideal, so that when we work to benefit others, this is seen as work that will allow "them" to be more like "us"' (McIntosh 1993 [1988]: 32). If we want to change structures of domination, we have to first challenge our complicity in their perpetuation.

As this excerpt from *This Bridge Called My Back* shows, feminists can no longer assume that there is an experience that *all* women share and which can therefore be the basis of the women's movement.

A phase of intensified politics around identity, what Kauffmann has called the anti-politics of identity (1990), begins. Rather than basing political action on supposedly shared identities, identity itself becomes the subject of politics and the focus of examination. Consequently, various previously accepted elements of our life-stories become sites of political contestation. We might develop new ways of thinking and being, transform cultural categories to match new ideas or even develop separate cultural programmes for each specific subcategory of identity. Hyphenated identities like 'Black-lesbian-radical-feminist' or 'White-working-class-eco-feminist' are adopted to specify the belonging to a particular group.

An increasing number of feminists consequently begin to focus their attention on identity itself, even though many of the initial criticisms by black, Chicana, lesbian and Third World feminists of second-wave feminism specifically pointed to the material consequences of identity politics. This shift is evoked not just by the political critiques outlined above, but also by a philosophical shift that will be outlined in more detail in the next section. Suffice it to say at this point that gender and sex came to be seen as socially constructed. This means they are no longer thought to have a base in nature, anatomy or anthropological essence, but are seen to be constructed in a process of social, cultural and political struggles. This conceptual development allows us to examine the processes involved in identity formation more closely and to recognize the power struggles involved in identifying different markers and creating group hierarchies. It also alerts us to the fact that identity shifts both contextually (e.g. the same person might be identified as Ashanti in Ghana, Ghanaian in Africa, African in Europe) and over time (e.g. as we discover our sexuality, we might realize that we differ from the heterosexual norm).

Notwithstanding these advantages, the move toward examining identity without reference to the social, economic and political order within which it is embedded proved problematic for feminism for a number of reasons. First, the specificity that is sought by an ever-increasing number of hyphenations creates the illusion that people indeed possess a single, fixed identity (rather than one that is continually in flux). What is more, it also suggests that this identity can be captured if only we can dissect all its details (rather than accepting that it is impossible to portray all the facets of a person). An increasing fragmentation and a new wave of exclusions ensues as the sub-groupings become smaller and smaller. The focus on personal experience swiftly becomes an inward focus away from the commonalities that consciousness-raising sought to discover.

Instead, (trendy) subcultures and a politics of lifestyle evolve which closely resemble the logic of the marketplace. The outcome is a culture of political correctness and a focus on personal conduct, rather than revolutionary change. Identity politics in this vein is anti-politics (Kauffmann 1990), since the focus is on what people wear, eat and say (individually) rather than what they are doing politically (as a social movement). Says Carmen Vasquez,

> We can't even agree on what a 'Feminist' is, never mind what she would believe in and how she defines the principles that constitute honour among us. In key with the American capitalist obsession for individualism and anything goes as long as it gets you what you want, feminism in America has come to mean anything you like, honey. There are as many definitions of Feminism as there are feminists, some of my sisters say with a chuckle. I don't think it's funny.
>
> (quoted in hooks 1984: 17)

The focus on individualism and the market in the context of modernization in South Asia also leads to the diversion of collective struggle for change.
See Chapter 14

Vasquez does not think it is funny because these practices lose sight of common-alities that, arguably, form the basis for collective struggles such as that of the women's movement. Preoccupied with its own micro-politics, this type of feminist identity politics neglects to analyse shared oppression and thus to build a basis for solidarity. As it assumes that a person's racial, religious, sexual or class identity and that person's political views are one and the same, it repeats the flaws of second-wave feminism: where second-wave feminism unproblematically spoke for *all* women – these feminists no longer speak for anyone (but them-selves). Either way, the structures of (male) oppression remain unchallenged. When feminists no longer communicate across the diverse groupings that make up the women's movement, they stop engaging in a shared political process.

When seeking a unified feminist project, no homogeneous group of women can be assumed. To form a movement that accommodates all women, feminists need to engage in a politics of identity that examines privilege. When occupying a position of privilege, it is necessary to acknowledge one's complicity in upholding the structures of oppression (sexism, racism, homophobia, etc.). Only then can feminist and other activists strategically inhabit whatever privileged status they may enjoy to change the status quo.

This requires a reform of consciousness-raising as a feminist strategy. Whereas in the past 'consciousness-raising techniques assume[d] as a basis for political action a reality that has to be discovered and then changed', Nira Yuval-Davis suggests thinking of it as 'a reality that is being created and re-created when practiced and discussed' (1994: 414). Consciousness-raising can no longer be a simple uncovering of experience but has to become a way to challenge representation and to confront privilege and power. Two separate questions need to be asked here: (1) 'How are our identities represented in and through the culture and assigned particular categories?' and (2) 'Who or what politically represents us, speaks and acts on our behalf?' (Brundt quoted in Yuval-Davis 1994: 415).

RESPONSES
HOW CAN WE CONCEPTUALIZE IDENTITY?

The previous section examined the case of feminist struggles with identity politics in the United States. It is fair to say that those struggles mirror as well as intersect with a wider debate about identity and questions of belonging. For example, while both sex and gender used to be seen as natural, we now think of them as broadly socially constructed. The same holds true for the way we understand identity more generally. This is a very recent phenomenon, however, since it was only during the twentieth century that scholars began to think in these terms. This section looks at these different ways of thinking about identity and the markers used to signify it – e.g. nation, ethnicity, race, gender, class, sex or religion – and what some of their limitations are.

Biology and natural history

Before discussing different ways of thinking (theories) that offer competing explanations today, it is important to examine their historical precursors. Understanding how ideas have developed over time helps to imagine them changing again. Take the example of female and male identity: until quite recently, they used to be thought of as determined by biology and now are seen as socially constructed. However, the whole field of biology only developed about two hundred years ago, so how did people think of this difference before then? What about other markers of identity, such as race or nation?

Chapter 10 explores how nations are made and **Chapter 8** explores the significance of race in relation to migration.

Biology developed out of a larger field of study called natural history. During the eighteenth century and beyond, natural history encompassed all descriptive

FIGURE 4.8
The depiction of supposed essences, as imagined in natural history. From S. Wells, *New Physiognomy or Signs of Character . . .*, New York: American Book Co., 1871

aspects of the study of nature, including humans. When describing what was later called race, for example, scholars of natural history included everything 'from the morphology of the skin, to the discussion of sexual desire, to music and poetry' (Appiah and Gutman 1996: 49). A person was perceived to possess an essence of some sort that gave rise to all of these traits. Only during the nineteenth century did fields like anatomy, physiology, anthropology, sociology and biology develop. With the emergence of these fields new concepts and frameworks were pioneered which broadened the horizons of scholars and lay people alike.

The work of Charles Darwin (1809–82) introduced new ways of thinking about inheritance and natural selection as well as new categories like species and race. Darwin used the term 'race' to refer to animals and plants as well as to people. The increasing acceptance of Darwin's theories gave scientific support to the idea that different kinds of human groupings – races – could be clearly distinguished. The traits associated with different races would become the subject of studies, called race science or raciology (Gilroy 2000). From the association of facial features (e.g. nose, lips, shape of the eyes) to assumptions about intelligence and sexual inclination, we find raciology produced material that has been used time and time again to justify discriminatory policies at home and abroad. What is more, entire ideologies like Orientalism (that is, the inevitably prejudiced representation of Eastern cultures and peoples by outsiders) and anti-semitism are based on raciology.

Orientalism is explained in **Chapter 5**.

Static and dynamic approaches to identity

Whereas identity used to be thought of as having its roots in nature or some sort of spiritual or anthropological essence, most scholars today subscribe to some variant of the idea that identity is socially constructed. As noted above, this implies that identities are seen to be constructed in a process of social, cultural and political struggle, rather than given by nature. That being said, there are some important differences in the manifold approaches to identity that are bundled under this label.

A stark contrast exists between those approaches that have a static conception of identity and those that take a dynamic approach to subjectivity. The static perspective presumes the existence of an individual and asks questions about that person's identity, whether this be their race, sexuality, gender, class or some other marker of significance. The competing approach, what might be termed the dynamic perspective, does not assume subjectivity prior to its identification with these markers. To concretize these distinctions, we will discuss each perspective in turn.

R.W. Connell, in his book *Masculinities* (1995), provides some examples of ways of thinking about gender that follow the static perspective. A very common

BOX 4.4 HUTU AND TUTSI IN RWANDA

Through colonialism, European ideas of biology and natural history spread throughout the world and with them assumptions about the superiority of European races. The Hamitic myth and its role in the 1994 genocide in Rwanda is a case in point. The Hamitic myth, whose origins can be traced to the Bible, originally provided justification for the enslavement of people of African descent. It was re-evaluated after the discovery of the achievements of ancient Egypt and from then on used to describe those peoples who appeared most 'European-like' in appearance and achievement.

During the colonization of Africa, the Tutsi of Rwanda were identified as Hamitic and therefore preferable to the Hutu, who were not considered worthy of cultural redemption. While these ideas were first introduced by German colonizers, the subsequent Belgian colonial administration perfected the idea of two distinct races by issuing identity cards which indicated racial belonging (in 1935). Prior to colonization the distinction between Tutsi and Hutu seems to have been largely one of caste (with the Tutsi being cattle keepers and the Hutu farmers, though movement between the two groups was common and the distinction largely associated with the type of work undertaken). What is more, they spoke the same language, shared similar customs and frequently intermarried.

The colonial authorities expanded existing hierarchies by using the Tutsi as a proxy government for Rwanda. The Belgians also supported the expansion of Tutsi power by providing the Tutsi with better education (with the help of Catholic missionaries). When the Tutsi demanded greater decision-making power and even independence, in 1959 the Belgians reversed the hierarchy and thereafter supported Hutu demands. Meanwhile, based on the same Hamitic myth used to justify colonial violence, anti-Tutsi propaganda like the *Hutu Manifesto* began to proclaim that if the Tutsi were indeed foreign invaders with European ancestry, the country should rightfully be governed by Hutu.

After the achievement of independence in 1961 and government by the Hutu majority, rumours of plots by Tutsis to resubjugate the Hutus marred Rwandan politics and were used to justify supposedly preventive killings of thousands of Tutsi. The erstwhile culmination of this 'Hutu power' movement was the 1994 Rwandan genocide, during which approximately 800,000 Tutsi and moderate Hutu were killed in a period of 100 days. (See Gourevitch 1998; Mamdani 2001.)

approach associated with this perspective is positivism (an approach based on the view that the scholar can take up a position outside the world that is being studied). Here the focus is on what we can observe in relation to a particular marker of identity – the way women or men actually are, for example. John Gray's well-known self-help book *Men Are from Mars – Women Are from Venus* (2002) uses this type of approach to list characteristics that statistically seem to be more common to either gender's relationship behaviour. The picture that is painted as a result can only provide broad brushstrokes and, while claiming to be universal, will actually be quite specific and directly match only a few people's experience.

A main criticism of this approach is that it is very conservative (in the sense of traditionalist) – it can only ever observe the current status quo and it does not lend itself well to imagining alternative options. What is more, often the variation among one group (e.g. in the relationship behaviour of different women) is greater than the differences that exist between different groups (that is, between the behaviours of women and men). As such, this approach easily becomes self-referential – it describes what it observes and then observes what it has previously described. In the case of *Men Are from Mars – Women Are from Venus* the author observes how women or men are more likely to behave and then writes a book about it. When people read the (self-help) book, they begin to behave according to these ideas and their actions then seem to support the initial observation. However, they could just as well be a consequence of having read the book.

Another way of thinking that matches the static perspective is a normative approach. While it is often contrasted with positivism because it may explicitly challenge the status quo, a normative approach is similar: from a position assumed to be outside the world that is being analysed, it describes how things ought to be (rather than how they are, as the positivist approach does) and then observes whether individuals comply with the norm. Yet strong normative ideals often mean that few actually ever reach them.

For example, while a norm for masculinity is that everyone be as tough as a cowboy in John Wayne films, we might find that many men never dream of riding a horse and 'roughing it'. What is more, some men might match the depiction of cowboys in *Brokeback Mountain* (a film that chronicles the complex twenty-year love story of two cowboys) and not the heterosexual norm often associated with masculinity. This raises some questions: how normative (widespread) is the norm? Can the description of some normative behaviour or appearance help us understand multiple masculine identities? Or is there just one norm and do men who do not meet the standards of heterosexuality or toughness become less manly?

To reiterate, what makes both of these approaches static approaches is that they rely on the observation of characteristics of already-known entities (e.g. female and male individuals). That is, they list the characteristics that supposedly identify a person after having already decided that a certain sample of them belongs to one group (e.g. Asian Americans) and not to another (e.g. Native Americans). What is more, neither approach leaves much room for variations within the group, such as feminine men or masculine women. There is little or no room for greyscales here (e.g. what happens to people of mixed descent, that is, both Asian-American and Native American?). As such, the world easily becomes black and white.

BOX 4.5 JACQUES LACAN

FIGURE 4.9
Jacques Lacan. Photo:
www.ildiogene.it/Ency/
Pages/Immagini/Lacan

Psychoanalysis, a field that arose at the end of the nineteenth century as a result of the work of Sigmund Freud (1856–1939), is concerned with the role of the unconscious. Regarding the question of identity, the work of Jacques Lacan (1901–81) in particular is of interest. Lacan, himself trained in psychoanalysis, reviewed many of Freud's original ideas proposing that the unconscious should be understood as structured like language. Doing so, he linked psychoanalysis and semiotics (the study of signs).

Lacan introduced the idea of the 'mirror stage', which describes the formation of the conscious self via the process of identification. Simplified, for Lacan the act of identifying with one's own image in the mirror provides the illusion of wholeness. Yet, he also argues, the act creates a fundamental misunderstanding: the image is always partial. There is always a lack that we seek to compensate for to become whole again. Or, conversely, there is an excess which cannot be captured no matter how hard we try to examine all details of who we are. An important element of the Lacanian mirror stage is also the caregiver (Lacan refers to the mother), who represents the Other to whom the child turns for recognition and who provides the first experience of being a subject – an I. (For a discussion of the relevance of Lacanian and other psychoanalytically inspired approaches for global politics, see Edkins 1999.)

The dynamic approaches discussed here agree that a main mistake of static accounts of identity is that they assume a cohesive, fixed subject that can be identified (a subject which we can know). They suggest instead that subjectivity is always already a product of discourses – national, ethnic, racial, gender, class, sexual or religious – that circulate at any given time and place (some are local, some regional and some global, which also means they can be quite different and then conflict with each other). From this perspective the possibilities for who we can be are not up to the individual, but set out in advance and also limited by society. Identification (the creation of subjectivity), then, takes place in the process of articulating the relationship between subjects and discourses – between ourselves and the principles, expectations and constraints of society. This means that who we are is always a matter of becoming rather than one of being: we should thus ask how we have become identified and who we can become, rather than who we are or have been.

What sort of a subject is at the heart of our thinking is also discussed in **Chapter 20**.

Since these are the types of questions thinkers espousing dynamic approaches are interested in, they examine the processes through which the body is identified (or inscribed) to become a recognizable subject in a particular location (e.g. of a

Jacques Derrida was particularly interested in thinking through the impact of such dichotomies. Some of his ideas are discussed in **Chapter 20.**

nation, a class or a religious group). In addition, drawing on psychoanalytical insights, they consider difference to be a key to the development of identity – without an Other that cannot be subsumed, there would be no distinctness to ourselves. This is also exemplified in many languages, e.g. in the dichotomies that are so prevalent in Western thought: weak/strong, female/male, black/white. It is possible to analyse this difference through a semiotic approach that contrasts the meanings assigned to different markers (or signifiers) in a particular symbolic structure (see Connell 1995: 70 for a discussion in relation to gender).

The dynamic conception of identity, particularly its constitutive relation to difference and its argument that subjects do not pre-exist discourse, has been criticized for lacking a conception of agency. Seyla Benhabib notes, 'if these agents retain capacities for resistance, resignification or for "subverting gender codes" in Butler's language, from where do they derive?' (1994). If who we are is determined by discourses that predate our existence, how can change occur

Chapter 20 also explores the issue that we always confront language as already existing.

BOX 4.6 JUDITH BUTLER AND PERFORMATIVITY

FIGURE 4.10
Judith Butler. Photo: Berkeley University

An influential application of psychoanalytical and other insights is Judith Butler's conception of identity as performance. She first introduced it in her book *Gender Trouble* and has refined it since. Her main argument is that 'gender is always a doing, though not a doing by a subject who might be said to pre-exist the deed' and therefore that 'identity is performatively constituted by the very "expressions" that are said to be its results' (Butler 1990: 33). In other words, by acting out what signifies being a certain kind of person, e.g. a white woman, one's subjectivity as a white woman is constituted and one is identified as such.

Butler uses the example of drag queens to make her point, arguing that drag performance enacts the way in which any (gender) identity is assumed. In his performance the drag queen also denaturalizes femininity by exaggerating its elements and by disturbing its coherence since the performed gender does not match the expected behaviour for a man.

It is important to note that Butler does not consider gender performance a choice. Rather, drawing on the work of Michel Foucault (1926–84), she argues that the performance is disciplined by regulative discourses of gender. This means that we are made to conform and our performance is constrained by the repetition of certain expected standards of behaviour (norms), which consequently appear to constitute a core of identity.

that moves beyond these structures? We will look at some possible answers to this question in the next section when we turn again to looking at identity politics in a broader context.

Notwithstanding the discussion of these two approaches as though they are entirely separate frameworks, it should be noted that not all discussions of identity can be neatly separated in this way. The distinction is useful, however, to tease out some broader conceptual issues that help us understand the variety of approaches: a main difference between the two approaches discussed here concerns their assumptions about what type of knowledge is possible (epistemology). Whereas the static approach believes that it is possible to clearly identify various markers that make up a person's identity, the dynamic approach is less certain about this possibility and sees different markers as together constituting, through processes of identification, a subject.

In addition, the two approaches conceptualize agency differently: the static approach often considers the possibility of multiple identities, also suggesting the option of a choice between them (or at least of emphasizing different markers). Scholars associated with the dynamic approach, on the contrary, tend to spend considerable time focusing on identity politics as a disciplinary tool that limits who we can become. How these differences matter when we answer the question that guides this chapter is the topic we will turn to now.

BROADER ISSUES
DO WE NEED TO IDENTIFY WITH A GROUP?

So far we have discussed why we need to pay attention to identity at all, how identity politics have played out historically in the US feminist movement, and how identity has been conceptualized. What we have yet to address is the question posed at the outset of the chapter: if our identity is often linked to group identification, do we need to identify with a group? Thinking this through raises other questions.

To begin, whenever someone uses the term 'we' it is a good idea to ask who 'we' includes. In this case, who is the 'we' that is asked to identify with a group? The answer to the question whether 'we' have to identify with a group might depend on our position of privilege, for example. Few white people ever have discussions about how their whiteness affects their ability to go about their daily lives, get an education or to be treated equally before the law. Black people who live in countries where they are not the majority, however, need to teach their children from an early age how to navigate everyday racism for their own survival. Thus, while they might not want to identify as black so as not to be subject to the effects

BOX 4.7 BLACK POWER

The Black Power movement exemplifies this conundrum of identity politics: in an effort to reverse the script of racism, being Negro is reconstructed as being black. This requires a refusal to assimilate to white norms of behaviour and the building of 'complex traditions of politics, ethics, identity and culture' (Gilroy 2000: 12). The goal is to be respected *as a black person*, not despite being a black person. Over time this movement has 'gone far beyond merely affording protection and reversed the polarities of insult, brutality and contempt, which are unexpectedly turned into important sources of solidarity, joy, and collective strength' (Gilroy 2000: 12).

Yet like all identity politics this one too requires 'that there be some script that go with being [black,] there will be expectations to be met; demands will be made' (Appiah and Gutman 1996: 99). The question that arises is whether one tyranny is being replaced by another that still leaves too little room to diverge from the norm (it is just a different norm now). What is more, we might wonder, as black-lesbian-feminist Audre Lorde famously did, whether the master's tools will ever dismantle the master's house. While rejecting all things associated with whiteness might be a source of strength and even a necessary step in challenging racial hierarchies, only when the idea of race itself is abandoned can real change occur. However, as long as groups on either side of the divide hold on to the notion (usually those that benefit from its existence in some manner) this is unlikely.

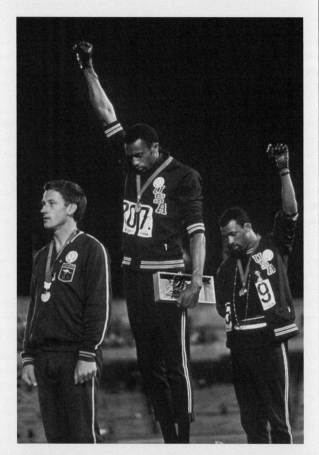

FIGURE 4.11
The Black Power salute in the 1968 Summer Olympics: Tommie Smith (centre) and John Carlos (right) salute, while Silver medallist Peter Norman (left) wears an Olympic Project for Human Rights badge to show his support for the two Americans.
Photo: AP/PA Photos

of racism, considering that they are always already identified as such, they might decide to claim a black identity. Doing so can provide them with a support network and avenues to challenge discriminatory policies as a group – but it can also lock them into another cycle of identity politics (Box 4.7).

We might further ask – and the formulation of this question depends on our theoretical orientation – whether it is even up to us to identify with a group or whether others identify us. The static approaches discussed in the previous section would contend that it is up to us to choose our identity (within limits) and that we are also identified by those around us according to the markers of each identity category. The dynamic approaches would likely argue that the question itself reveals a misunderstanding of the processes of identification. Instead of us being able to identify with a group, who we can be is limited by the parameters of belonging to a particular group and is constantly in flux. Processes of identification are ambivalent from the start and there is no point at which a unified subject is possible: 'There is always "too much" or "too little" – an overdetermination or a lack, but never a proper fit, a totality' (Hall 1996: 3).

This conceptualization also suggests a response to the criticism that no agency is possible in a framework that stresses the constitutive role of discourse. Since identity never properly fits and is constantly challenged due to encounters with other people and varying discourses that increasingly circulate globally, there are continuous ruptures where identities can be negotiated. Where identity is already under revision, there is also room for agency. Besides, challenges arise in the name of anticipated or actual suffering – 'visions of what is better are always informed by our perception of what is bad about our present situation' (Lugones and Spelman 1983: 579).

Finally, the question suggests that we have to identify with *one* group. Yet none of us is *only* Asian or *only* Christian or *only* woman. Can we have multiple identities? What happens when they conflict? Does being a member of many oppressed groups (e.g. being Chicana and lesbian) imply that the oppression adds up? Or multiplies? What if one is part of both an oppressing (e.g. male) and an oppressed (e.g. working-class) group? Again, the way the questions are asked reveals some of the underlying assumptions behind them. For example, when people talk of having multiple identities, they often try to signal that identities need to be viewed in context and that some of them might be strategically more useful for the particular social, cultural and political struggle for hegemony (that is, the dominance of one group over other groups). All the while, such language also seems to suggest a maximum of autonomy – as though one has a closet full of identities that may be worn as one chooses. Most scholars will agree that such a conception, one that entirely disregards any structural limitations, is unhelpful and inaccurate.

BOX 4.8 PATRICIA HILL COLLINS: INTERSECTIONALITY

Patricia Hill Collins, pioneer of *Black Feminist Thought*, writes in the preface to the second edition of her book (2000 [1990]) about the importance of combining the work of revisioning individual black women's consciousness with challenges to larger structures of oppression and injustice. Failure to do so will only replace one form of domination with another. To do away with all forms of domination, she specifically locates her thinking in relation to other projects that share a concern for social justice and urges activists to recognize similarities among these varied projects. To this end, she develops the idea of intersectionality to conceptualize the complexities of multiple and conflicting identities.

Intersectionality 'refers to particular forms of intersecting oppressions, for example, intersections of race and gender, or of sexuality and nation'. Collins further notes that thinking about identity in terms of intersectionality 'reminds us that oppression cannot be reduced to one fundamental type, and that they work together in producing injustice' (2000 [1990]: 18). She gives the example of African-American women who are subject to three interdependent dimensions of oppression:

- economic, which describes the exploitation of black women's labour, initially under slavery and in service occupations since;
- political, which refers to the routine denial of rights and privileges accorded to white male citizens, such as voting, holding public office, getting a good education and being treated fairly in the justice system; and
- ideological, which covers both controlling images and certain qualities attached to black women (Collins 2000 [1990]: 4–5).

The dimensions of oppression are interdependent and can be located in a matrix of domination. Collins argues that 'regardless of the particular intersections involved, structural, disciplinary, hegemonic and interpersonal domains of power reappear across quite different forms of oppression' (2000 [1990]: 18). What they have in common, just like the intersections highlighted with regard to African-American women's oppression, is that they constitute a highly effective system of social control to keep people in their assigned, subordinate place.

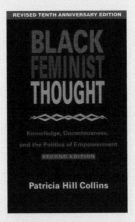

FIGURE 4.12
Black Feminist Thought.
Cover: Routledge

FIGURE 4.13
Patricia Hill Collins.
Photo: University of
Maryland, College Park

Adopting Collins' framework of intersectionality to think of varied dimensions of identity, and the oppressive effects of identity politics, limits the ever-present tendency to think of identity in overly individualistic terms. When asking questions about domination and oppression, we always also have to look at the structures that facilitate and perpetuate them. We might then find that discourses of identity both enable and limit who we might become, how we have been represented and how we might represent ourselves (Hall 1996). Our task is to recognize them as temporary resting points, to see in them the workings of power (and struggles for hegemony) and to challenge their effects.

CONCLUSION

In this chapter we have begun to develop some tools to understand different conceptions of identity and the complex consequences of identity politics. Yet much of what this chapter focuses on relates to the negative, indeed deadly, effects of identity politics, and one might wonder why not do away with the concept once and for all? The simple answer is that it gives us a sense of belonging and a sense of direction. This might explain why greater attention is paid to identity as people become increasingly mobile and as ideas circulate ever widely in this globalized world such that we may now talk of an 'explosion of usage' (Hall 1996: 1).

What is more, it is particularly those approaches that question the idea of an essential, primary and cohesive identity that have proliferated in recent years. What they suggest is that the way we have thought about identity, with a core self that may be adjusted slightly but remains largely stable through time and space, is no longer adequate. Yet, while these approaches are 'no longer serviceable – "good to think with" – in their originary and unreconstructed form' (Hall 1996: 1), they are still needed due to the centrality of questions of agency and politics. As Stuart Hall summarizes, it is 'an idea which cannot be thought in the old way, but without which certain key questions cannot be thought at all' (1996: 2).

Thus, even if we cannot agree on how identity should be conceptualized, which markers should triumph or even whether the preoccupation with identity is only a symptom of late modernity – we can maybe ask better questions about the occurrence of identity politics and its material effects. And we can begin to recognize how our own privilege oppresses others, but also how it gives us the power to promote change.

FURTHER READING

Campbell, David (1998) *National Deconstruction: Violence, Identity and Justice in Bosnia*, Minneapolis, MN: University of Minnesota Press.
A detailed analysis of the identity politics at play during the break-up of the former Yugoslavia. In 1999 the book received a prize for being the best English-language publication on the topic.

Collins, Patricia Hill (2000 [1990]) *Black Feminist Thought: Knowledge, Consciousness, and the Politics of Empowerment*, Boston, MA: Unwin Hyman.
For students who want to learn more about the intersections of gender and race (but also other forms of oppression) this is a 'must read'. It also provides some of the best ideas out there for moving beyond identity politics and toward justice.

Gourevitch, Phillip (1998) *We Wish to Inform You that Tomorrow We Will Be Killed with Our Families: Stories from Rwanda*, London: Picador.
Probably the best account of the Rwandan genocide, based on a series of interviews with Rwandans between 1995 and 1998. Not for the faint-hearted.

Hudson, Valerie M. and Andrea den Boer (2004) *Bare Branches: The Security Implications of Asia's Surplus Male Population*, Cambridge, MA: MIT Press.
Examines how global security might be affected by the preference for males in many Asian societies and thus offers a great case study of the importance of identity politics today.

Kaldor, Mary (2006) *New and Old Wars: Organized Violence in a Global Era*, 2nd edn, Cambridge: Polity Press.
A major work for those who want to understand the role of identity politics in today's wars. Kaldor locates the difference between old and new wars in the latter's distinctive war economies, their genocidal tendencies and the use of identity politics as a means to political power.

Ryan, Barbara (ed.) (2001) *Identity Politics in the Women's Movement*, New York: NYU Press.
This collection has most classic and recent statements on feminist identity politics (in the US) and offers a great overview for students interested in the subject.

WEBSITES

American Anthropological Association, *RACE: Are We So Different?*, http://www.understandingrace.org/home.html.
An extensive website (and exhibition) that examines race through multiple lenses.

BBC World Service, *Yugoslavia History File*, http://news.bbc.co.uk/hi/english/static/map/yugoslavia/.
A timeline with a series of maps and historical information on Yugoslavia (1900–2003).

The World Wide Web Virtual Library, *History: Yugoslavia (1918–1995)*, http://vlib.iue.it/history/europe/yugoslavia.html.
An extensive website useful for further research on historical information (it also has some maps).

Deutsch, Barry, *The Male Privilege Checklist: An Unabashed Imitation of an Article by Peggy McIntosh*, http://www.amptoons.com/blog/the-male-privilege-checklist/.
A checklist and links to further privilege discussions.

Heyes, Crissida (2002) *Stanford Encyclopedia of Philosophy: Identity Politics*, http://plato.stanford.edu/entries/identity-politics/.

Part of the extensive online Stanford Encyclopedia of Philosophy, this entry on identity politics explores many of the issues raised in this chapter from a philosophical perspective (in reference to many different markers of identity) and provides additional links.

Human Rights Watch (1999) *Leave None to Tell the Story: Genocide in Rwanda*, http://www.hrw.org/reports/1999/rwanda/.

A detailed report on the genocide in Rwanda, with an update on the tenth anniversary in 2004.

Korenman, Joan, *Women of Color Websites*, http://research.umbc.edu/~korenman/wmst/links_wc.html.

A regularly updated list of women of colour resource websites.

PBS, *African American Lives: Beyond Genealogy*, http://www.pbs.org/wnet/aalives/science.html.

This section of a larger site on the four-part PBS series *African American Lives* examines how advances in genetics may help trace the roots of African Americans – with some surprising results.

SSRC, *Is Race 'Real'?*, http://raceandgenomics.ssrc.org/.

This forum, organized by the Social Science Research Council, discusses recent controversies surrounding race after recent advances in genetics.

REFERENCES

Appiah, K. Anthony and Amy Gutman (1996) *Color Conscious: The Political Morality of Race*, Princeton, NJ: Princeton University Press.

Benhabib, Seyla (1994) 'From Identity Politics to Social Feminism: A Plea for the Nineties', *Philosophy of Education Yearbook 1994*, http://www.ed.uiuc.edu/eps/PES-Yearbook,94_docs/BENHABIB.htm.

Butler, Judith (1990) *Gender Trouble: Feminism and the Subversion of Identity*, London: Routledge.

Campbell, David (1998) *National Deconstruction: Violence, Identity and Justice in Bosnia*, Minneapolis, MN: University of Minnesota Press.

Carpenter, Charli (2003) 'Women and Children First: Gender Norms and Humanitarian Evacuation in the Balkans, 1991–1995', *International Organization* 57, 4: 661–94.

Collins, Patricia Hill (2000 [1990]) *Black Feminist Thought: Knowledge, Consciousness, and the Politics of Empowerment*, Boston, MA: Unwin Hyman.

Connell, R.W. (1995) *Masculinities*, Berkeley, CA: University of California Press.

Edkins, Jenny (1999) *Poststructuralism and International Relations: Bringing the Political Back In*, Boulder, CO: Lynne Rienner.

Elshtain, Jean Bethke (1981) *Public Man, Private Woman*, Princeton, NJ: Princeton University Press.

Friedan, Betty (2001 [1963]) *The Feminine Mystique*, New York: W.W. Norton & Company.

Gilligan, Carol (1982) *In a Different Voice: Psychological Theory and Women's Development*, Cambridge, MA: Harvard University Press.

Gilroy, Paul (2000) *Against Race: Imagining Political Culture beyond the Color Line*, Cambridge, MA: Harvard University Press.

Gourevitch, Phillip (1998) *We Wish to Inform You that Tomorrow We Will Be Killed with Our Families: Stories from Rwanda*, London: Picador.

Gray, John (2002) *Men Are from Mars – Women Are from Venus*, London: HarperCollins.

Hall, Stuart (1996) 'Introduction: Who Needs "Identity"?', in Stuart Hall and Paul du Gay (eds) *Questions of Cultural Identity*, London: Sage Publications.

Held, Virginia (2006) *The Ethics of Care: Personal, Political, Global*, Oxford: Oxford University Press.

hooks, bell (1984) *Feminist Theory: From Margin to Center*, Cambridge, MA: South End Press.

Hudson, Valerie M. and Andrea den Boer (2004) *Bare Branches: The Security Implications of Asia's Surplus Male Population*, Cambridge, MA: MIT Press.

Kauffmann, L.A. (1990) 'The Anti-Politics of Identity', *Socialist Review* 90, 1: 67–80; reprinted in Barbara Ryan (ed.) (2001) *Identity Politics in the Women's Movement*, New York: NYU Press.

Lugones, María C. and Elizabeth V. Spelman (1983) 'Have We Got a Theory for You! Feminist Theory, Cultural Imperialism and the Demand for "The Woman's Voice"', *Women's Studies International Forum* 6, 6: 573–81.

McIntosh, Peggy (1993 [1988]) 'White Privilege and Male Privilege: A Personal Account of Coming to See Correspondences through Work in Women's Studies', in Anne Minas (ed.) *Gender Basics: Feminist Perspectives on Women and Men*, Belmont, CA: Wadsworth.

Mamdani, Mahmood (2001) *When Victims Become Killers: Colonialism, Nativism, and the Genocide in Rwanda*, Princeton, NJ: Princeton University Press.

Moghadam, Valentine M. (1994) 'Introduction: Women and Identity Politics in Theoretical and Comparative Perspective', in Valentine M. Moghadam (ed.) *Identity Politics and Women: Cultural Reassertions and Feminisms in International Perspective*, Boulder, CO: Westview Press.

Moraga, Cherríe and Anzaldúa, Gloria (1983 [1979]) *This Bridge Called My Back: Writings by Radical Women of Color*, New York: Kitchen Table, Women of Color Press.

Polkinghorne, Donald E. (1988) *Narrative Knowing and the Human Sciences*, Albany, NY: SUNY Press.

Spender, Dale (1983) *Feminist Thinkers: Three Centuries of Women Thinkers*, New York: Random House.

Tronto, Joan C. (1993) *Moral Boundaries: A Political Argument for an Ethics of Care*, London: Routledge.

Winddance Twine, France (1996) 'Brown-Skinned White Girls: Class, Culture and the Construction of White Identity in Suburban Communities', *Gender, Place, and Culture: A Journal of Feminist Geography* 3, 2: 205–24.

Yuval-Davis, Nira (1994) 'Identity Politics and Women's Ethnicity', in Valentine M. Moghadam (ed.) *Identity Politics and Women: Cultural Reassertions and Feminisms in International Perspective*, Boulder, CO: Westview Press.

CHAPTER 5

How do religious beliefs affect politics?

Peter Mandaville

- ■ *The question*
  THE ROLE OF RELIGION TODAY

- ■ *Illustrative example*
  ISLAMIC STATES AND MOVEMENTS

- ■ *Responses*
  DO RELIGION AND POLITICS MIX?

- ■ *Broader issues*
  CULTURE, FUNDAMENTALISM AND RELIGIOUS IDENTITIES

- ■ **CONCLUSION**

THE QUESTION
THE ROLE OF RELIGION TODAY

What do we mean when we talk about religion? Scholars have struggled and argued for many years about how to define religion. Some emphasize the idea that religion is concerned primarily with conceptions of God, divinity and the meaning and order of human existence. Others have tended to emphasize the way religion serves to draw distinctions between *sacred* (that is, transcendent or other-worldly) forms of space and belief and more mundane, or *profane*, domains of 'worldly' human endeavour. Some definitions, such as that of anthropologist Clifford Geertz (1973), focus on the symbolic power of religion and its ability to influence how people understand their place in the world and also to impart meaning to the actions they undertake. Other scholars have pointed out that the idea of religion as a distinct category or sphere of human activity reflects a specifically Western worldview and historical tradition. Talal Asad (1993) points out that in other cultural traditions it is not so easy to make a firm separation between religion and other spheres of life such as politics, culture, society and economics. This point will be important later when we discuss the meaning and nature of secularism, the belief that the state and morals should be independent of religion. For now, however, let us assume that when we are talking about religion we are referring to individuals and groups who base their identities and ethics at least in part on a tradition and set of beliefs about the creation of the world and the order within it that locates the source of this creation and order outside purely human or natural agency.

Often whether we hold religious beliefs or not is central to our picture of the world, to use the terminology from **Chapter 2.**

So where do we see religion at work in global politics today? Many people if asked this question right now might think first and foremost of the Islamic world. Particularly since the events of September 11, 2001 – when hijackers associated with the terrorist group Al-Qaeda flew aeroplanes into several targets in New York City and Washington, DC – and subsequent attacks such as the London bombings of 7 July 2005, Islam has been a major subject of discussion. Much of this debate has been around questions of terrorism and support for violence. The United States, for example, declared militant Islamic extremism to be the major target of its new 'war on terror'. Considerable attention has also been paid to Islamic movements in other countries that have used violence in the pursuit of their political goals, such as HAMAS in the Palestinian territories and Hizbullah in Lebanon. Other examples where Islam or 'Islamic' groups have been seen to

Chapters 2 and 19 have more on the 'war on terror'.

BOX 5.1 DEFINITIONS OF RELIGION

For anthropologist Clifford Geertz, religion is '(1) a system of symbols which acts to (2) establish powerful, pervasive, and long-lasting moods and motivations in men by (3) formulating conceptions of a general order of existence and (4) clothing these conceptions with such an aura of factuality that (5) the moods and motivations seem uniquely realistic' (Geertz 1973).

For theologian George Lindbeck, religion is 'a kind of cultural and/or linguistic framework or medium that . . . makes possible the description of realities, the formulation of beliefs, and the experiencing of inner attitudes, feelings, and sentiments' (Lindbeck 1984).

Marxist writers such as Louis Althusser tend to emphasize the idea that religion functions as a form of 'false consciousness' which socializes us into accepting as normal certain historically and materially contingent relations of social power (Althusser 2001).

play a role in world politics include the period when Afghanistan was under the rule of a highly conservative movement known as the Taliban. Well before the United States accused and eventually overthrew their regime for supporting terrorism, the Taliban had attracted widespread criticism from the world community for violating human rights and for their harsh treatment of women. Finally, countries such as Iran, which regard themselves as Islamic states, are seen by some as a challenge when they assert that they are subject to divine authority. Within Europe, a number of recent incidents such as the Danish cartoon affair have fuelled debates about whether 'religious' Muslims and 'secular' Europeans can co-exist peacefully.

Despite the current tendency to focus on the Islamic world, there are many other examples where religion seems to play a role in global politics. A number of recent conflicts have had strong religious dimensions. Think, for example, of Northern Ireland, where the divisions between the two conflicting sides broke down along

Whether people who subscribe to fundamentally different values can live together, and how, has vexed many thinkers across the centuries. What do you think?

FIGURE 5.1
'Do you believe in God?' Artist: Bryan Bartholomew. CartoonStock Ref: bbrn51.
www.CartoonStock.com

BOX 5.2 THE DANISH CARTOON AFFAIR

In September 2005, the Danish newspaper *Jyllands Posten* published a series of cartoon depictions of Muhammad, the Prophet of Islam. Most famous among them was an image depicting the turban on Muhammad's head as a bomb. Several months after the publication of the cartoons, protests broke out in a number of Muslim countries almost simultaneously (an interesting globalization story in itself, involving the internet, satellite TV and transnational activist networks). Angered by what they perceived as an attack on the Prophet and an insult to Islam at a time when global tensions were high in the aftermath of September 11, 2001 and the US invasion of Iraq, rioters attacked Danish embassies and several countries initiated an embargo on Danish goods. In Europe the Danish cartoon affair prompted a debate about how to strike a balance between freedom of speech and respect for cultural difference. It also further fuelled an ongoing debate about whether the values of Europe's rapidly growing Muslim community were compatible with Western norms.

The situation in Northern Ireland was long considered an intractable conflict but is now more stable. **See Chapter 19**

Understanding these conflicts requires an exploration of the politics of identity. **See Chapter 4**

For more on capitalism, see **Chapters 12 and 13.**

the Protestant and Catholic denominations of Christianity. For more than twenty years, Sri Lanka has seen a civil war pitting Hindus and Buddhists against each other. In the former Yugoslavia, much of the bloodshed in the 1990s was explained in terms of ethnic rivalries between Catholic and Orthodox Christians as much as between Christians and Muslims. While many of the participants in these conflicts did not define their actions and motivations by direct reference to religion, the religious factor was important because it allowed the leadership of certain parties to raise the stakes by appealing to a greater cause. Religion is also present in world politics in ways far less dramatic and violent. For example, millions of Catholics around the world recognize the spiritual authority of the Pope as the final arbiter, globally, of matters relating to Church doctrine. We can also see today the role of various religious groups in seeking to build new bases of mass popular support, such as the recent upsurge in conversions to Pentecostal Christianity in Africa. The strength of the Christian Evangelical movement in the United States has been a major factor in the political success of that country's Republican party in recent years. The United States represents a very interesting case in which church and state are formally separated, but where religion features very heavily in political discourse. This has led some, such as the political theorist William Connolly (2005), to see in the United States a new form of theocracy (that is, government by religion) premised on affinities between belief in God and absolute faith in market capitalism. Religious institutions can sometimes also form alliances of the sort traditionally seen in global politics. For example, at the United Nations International Conference on Population and Development in 1994, the Vatican (the authority of the Catholic Pope) sought to make common cause with a number of conservative Muslim states in opposing birth control and abortion.

Globalization has also promoted the emergence of 'New Religious Movements' that combine aspects of various faith traditions while addressing concerns relating to environmentalism, social justice and the search for meaning and spirituality in a complex world (Clarke 2006). Some of these groups, such as the Falung Gong movement in China, seek to challenge the political status quo.

ILLUSTRATIVE EXAMPLE
ISLAMIC STATES AND MOVEMENTS

Much of the discussion about religion in global politics today focuses on the Muslim world. This is not only because of the events of September 11, 2001 or the Danish cartoon episode mentioned in Box 5.2 on p. 100. Even for some time before these events, it was not uncommon to find claims being made that Islam was problematic because in its belief system religion and politics could not be separated – meaning that the Muslim world was resistant to secularism and modernization (see pp. 111–13). Those advancing such ideas – many of whom are scholars associated with the Orientalist worldview discussed on p. 116 – seemed to assume that Islam was something quite static and unchanging: a rigid set of beliefs impervious to change or progress. When we look at the evolving relationship between religion and politics throughout Islamic history, however, quite a different perspective emerges. We find not only that Islam has been remarkably dynamic and diverse as a belief system, but also that the motivations and patterns of political behaviour displayed by Muslims are wholly amenable to explanation through conventional themes and theories of political analysis.

History of the Islamic world

From humble beginnings in the western part of present-day Saudi Arabia, the religion of Islam expanded rapidly in the second half of the seventh century and soon encompassed most of the Middle East, Persia and North Africa. In subsequent eras, Islam spread further east to South Asia and eventually to the furthest southeastern reaches of the Asian continent into present-day Malaysia and Indonesia. Various Islamic dynasties rose and fell during the Middle Ages, and at their height these empires represented the apex of human civilization, science and learning.

The most important Muslim power in the early modern period was the Ottoman Empire (*c.* 1300–1922). The Ottomans were the first Muslim rulers to interact with European powers after the formation of the modern state system in the seventeenth century, and were well integrated into the structures and processes of global politics. In the late nineteenth century an anti-colonial movement

The emergence of the state in Europe is traced in **Chapter 9**.

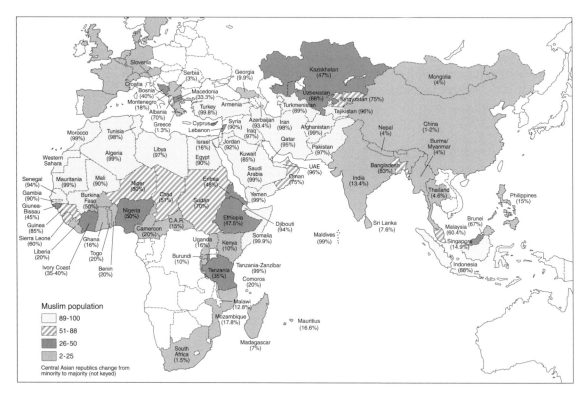

FIGURE 5.2
Map of Muslim populations. Source: Peter Mandaville, *Global Political Islam* (Routledge, 2007)

known as Pan-Islam emerged. The Pan-Islamists argued that Muslims were facing a similar condition of imperial bondage at the hands of European colonial powers. Their solution was to encourage the political unity of Muslims, invoking the centuries-old religious idea of the *umma* – an Arabic term that refers to the world community of Muslim believers. The leaders of this movement did not advocate returning to a conservative, literalist interpretation of Islam, but rather emphasized the compatibility of Islam with modernity and science. For them, the imperative was to *reform* Islam.

The Ottoman Empire found itself on the losing side of World War I and was dissolved in its aftermath, with Britain and France gaining control of many of the territories that had previously been under its control (such as Syria, Lebanon, Palestine, Iraq, Egypt). This war also effectively marked the beginning of the end for the various European empires, with some of them fragmenting into various new nation-states. On the Anatolian peninsula, heartland of the former Ottoman lands, a new country, the Turkish Republic, was founded in 1922 by Mustapha Kemal. 'Kemalism' – the ideology deriving from the major project of sweeping political, economic and cultural reform he initiated – emphasized the ideals of

On the significance of territory, see **Chapter 9**

Europeanization and *secularism* as the proper way to 'be modern'. To this day, Turkey enforces a strict separation between religion and state; this is embodied in laws and policies that restrict the public role of religion more strongly than in many countries we usually think of as secular (not concerned with religion), such as France, the UK or the USA.

After World War II, many of the former Ottoman territories under British and French control became independent states. Many of these were led by governments that embraced various models of national secular politics – chief among them Egypt under Gamal Abdel Nasser (r. 1952–71), who became the iconic leader of a regional Arab Nationalist movement. This secular-nationalist model had quickly trumped the emerging project of Pan-Islamism early in the twentieth century, and as the modernizing drive of these new governments proceeded in countries such as Egypt, some sectors of Egyptian society began to feel that the country risked becoming corrupted by foreign ideologies.

Islamism: Islamic political movements

The early postcolonial period in the Middle East saw the consolidation of a political ideology, commonly referred to as Islamism, that rejected the national-secular model in the name of a vision of social order deriving from the direct application of Islam to the governance of modern states. In its totalizing, systematic approach, Islamism was no different from other contemporary ideological counterparts such as socialism or capitalist democracy. Islamism, hence, needs to be understood as expressing a distinctly modernist approach to politics. Its supporters, known as Islamists – who were generally highly educated members of the Muslim world's new middle classes (doctors, engineers, etc.) – saw in Islamism a way to embrace new institutions and technologies without having to abandon their values and beliefs – in other words, it was a way to be modern without having to become Western.

The most important social movement embodying this new vision of political Islam was founded in Egypt by a schoolteacher named Hassan al-Banna. In 1928 he established a group known as the Muslim Brotherhood. The Brotherhood sought to ensure a continued role for religion in society and saw itself as an antidote to the Westernizing and secularizing tendencies of the political elite. Many Islamist leaders also argued that the doctrine of modern nationalism was incompatible with the teachings of Islam and the ideal of the *umma*. While not a political party, the Brotherhood became implicated in the evolving political landscape of Egypt in the 1930s and 1940s. Branches were established throughout the Arab world, and similar groups founded in Pakistan (the Jama'at-i Islami) and Turkey (the Refah Party). With its enormous popularity and rapid inroads into the country's new educated and middle classes, Nasser began to see the

Muslim Brotherhood as a political threat. Banned and driven underground from the 1950s, the movement became radicalized. This phase of its existence is commonly associated with its chief thinker at the time, Sayyid Qutb. Qutb – whose ideas became very influential on successive generations of radical Islamists (including groups such as Al-Qaeda) – had become convinced, like a number of Third World activists, that it had become impossible to work within the existing political system to achieve social justice. Revolutionary politics and armed struggle (*jihad* – from the Arabic word for 'strive'), in Qutb's teaching, were required to achieve social change in the Muslim world.

Qutb's views appealed only to a fringe minority in the Muslim world and, in the successive generation, to only a small fraction of Islamists. His views on *jihad*, for example, were generally regarded as a highly unorthodox departure from traditional understandings that emphasized the defensive nature of *jihad*. In other Muslim-majority countries during this period, Islamist parties had evolved into opposition movements. Banned from formal politics in Egypt, the Muslim Brotherhood instead began to build a strong base of social support at the neighbourhood and municipal levels, establishing social service and charity networks, and gaining control of all leading professional associations and syndicates.

Globalization and its effects are discussed in **Chapter 12.**

While these may seem to be highly localized developments, an important part of what allowed the Islamists to build up this kind of support within Egypt's civil societal spaces was what we refer to today as *globalization*. As Anwar Al Sadat (President of Egypt 1970–81) opened up Egypt's economy to world markets and the country undertook neoliberal economic reforms at the behest of institutions such as the International Monetary Fund (IMF), the scale of state welfare and employment provision was scaled back significantly. This created 'gaps' in the provision of basic services that the Islamists were able to fill, gaining widespread support and popular legitimacy in the process.

Islamic states

In 1979, Iran experienced an 'Islamic Revolution' led by religious scholars (chief among them the Grand Ayatollah Khomeini) but carried out by a combination of religious and secular social forces, including socialists and urban merchants. In its aftermath, the radical wing of the clergy purged all non-religious political elites to establish a new Islamic Republic of Iran and impose a conservative and literalist interpretation of Islamic law (*shari'ah*) on a largely unsuspecting population. Iran thus joined the ranks of the world's 'Islamic states', alongside two other countries, Saudi Arabia and Pakistan. Saudi Arabia was founded between the two World Wars as a theocratic monarchy (that is, one governed by religious leaders) based on a political alliance between a princely family (the Sa'ud) and a religious establishment seeking to purvey an indigenous form of Islam – highly austere and

FIGURE 5.3
Ayatollah Khomeini
returns from exile on
1 February 1979.
Photo: PA Photos

puritanical – known as Wahhabism. With the discovery of vast oil wealth under its deserts, Saudi Arabia was catapulted to a position of geopolitical prominence, establishing a close alliance with the United States that has endured for many years. The second Islamic state already in existence was Pakistan, established in 1947 at the time of the postcolonial partition of India. Initially established as a homeland for the Muslims of the Indian subcontinent, the exact nature and meaning of Pakistan's status as an Islamic state have constituted a chief source of political debate in the country for decades. For some, Pakistan was an Islamic state in the same sense in which Israel is a Jewish state – that is, as a national homeland for the members of a given religion rather than a state whose political and legal systems are derived directly from religion. Others in Pakistan argued that the government of Pakistan should be actively working to extend the remit of *shari'ah* to all sectors of society.

Development and
modernization in states
in South Asia according
to principles of Western
modernity conflict with
ideas of Islamic
modernity.
See Chapter 14

Radical Islamist groups

The 1980s saw a significant increase in the global visibility of political Islam – the ideology of Islamism and its adherents, known as Islamists – as it became increasingly entwined with Cold War geopolitics. Several events and movements formed during this decade help us understand the contemporary interface between Islam and global politics. After the Soviet Union's invasion of Afghanistan in 1979, a number of volunteer fighters from the Arab world travelled to Afghanistan to assist in repelling what they interpreted as an atheist incursion into Muslim territories. These 'Arab-Afghans' were important insofar as their experience during

The Cold War and its
geopolitics are explained
in **Chapter 19**.

these years (1980–8) helped to crystallize the ideological and geopolitical vision that would later define Al-Qaeda. Among this group of supporters from the Middle East was Osama Bin Laden, a member of the wealthiest commercial family in Saudi Arabia who had renounced his family's business in the name of what he saw as a larger struggle against new forms of global, imperial atheism (disbelief in the existence of God). The eventual withdrawal of Soviet forces from Afghanistan was interpreted by Bin Laden as a victory and as evidence of Islam's ability to triumph over the world's superpowers (at that time the USSR and the USA). Out of this experience was born Bin Laden's vision Al-Qaeda: an effort to globalize the Afghan experience.

FIGURE 5.4
Women demonstrate: at Ramallah's Al Manara plaza, two schoolgirls take part in a solidarity demonstration of Palestinian women – the wives, mothers and sisters of many killed in the first days of the uprising. Photo: Ingeborg Moa

Two other important Islamist groups active today were also established during this period. Although Hizbullah in Lebanon and HAMAS (an acronym for *Harakat al-Muqawwama al-Islamiyya* – the Islamic Resistance Movement; the word also means 'zeal' in Arabic) in the Palestinian territories have been linked to Al-Qaeda in contemporary discussions because of their militant tactics, such direct connections are inaccurate and mask the fact that Al-Qaeda and groups such as Hizbullah and HAMAS are motivated by and pursuing distinct political agendas. Chief among these differences is the fact that HAMAS and Hizbullah are primarily movements of religious nationalism. Hizbullah was established in the wake of the Israeli invasion of Lebanon in 1982 with an Islamist agenda limited to Lebanon. Likewise HAMAS, which emerged in the context of the first Palestinian *intifada* (uprising, or 'shaking off') in the late 1980s, has always defined its political agenda in terms of Palestinian national liberation from Israeli occupation and, subsequently, the establishment of an Islamic state in its territories.

While their political aims may be geared towards nationalist aspirations, both of these groups have received significant support from neighbouring states and various transnational fundraising networks. Hizbullah, for example, has strong ties to Iran and Syria, while HAMAS – as a branch of the Muslim Brotherhood – has been able to tap into that group's funding infrastructure in addition to receiving direct support from various states in the Middle East. In recent years, the nature and role of both organizations has become increasingly ambiguous. Hizbullah and HAMAS both have at least three dimensions to their activities:

1   They provide basic social services such as education and healthcare to the disenfranchised (that is, those deprived of the rights of citizenship) populations of Lebanon and the Palestinian territories, ensuring strong measures of grassroots support.
2   They have political bodies that compete in parliamentary elections alongside other parties. Hizbullah has enjoyed strong representation in the Lebanese legislature since the end of the civil war and HAMAS gained control of the Palestinian Authority in 2006.
3   They maintain armed wings that permit them to employ violence when they find it expedient to do so.

Why politics turns to violence is discussed in **Chapter 16**.

While not globally organized like Al-Qaeda, both HAMAS and Hizbullah factor heavily in the global politics surrounding the Israel/Palestine conflict and Lebanon. Hizbullah, for example, taps into the media infrastructure of contemporary globalization via its own satellite television station Al-Manar ('The Beacon').

On the media in general, see **Chapter 7**.

Thus, Al-Qaeda – for many, the group that most readily springs to mind today when speaking of Islam and global politics – needs to be situated within a diverse

BOX 5.3 SUNNI AND SHI'ITE ISLAM

The instability and violence experienced by Iraq in the years following the US invasion of 2003, much of which occurred along sectarians lines, prompted discussion about the difference between two major branches of Islam. The distinction between Sunnis and Shi'ites goes back to the time of the death of the Prophet Muhammad and a debate over who should succeed him as the leader of the Muslim community. One group argued that leadership should stay within the Prophet's family and rallied around the candidacy of Ali (hence *Shi'i* or 'Partisans' of Ali), Muhammad's cousin and son-in-law. Others favoured choosing a leader from among the Prophet's longest-serving and most trusted companions, and their view prevailed. A distinctive Shi'ite political identity, however, did not emerge until several decades later when Ali's family were killed by the army of a rival noble clan seeking to consolidate its ruling position. In the ensuing centuries, Shi'ites developed their own parallel institutions and schools of religious law. Indeed, in its conventional usage the term 'Sunni' refers to the orthodox schools of religious jurisprudence. As Shi'ites faced persecution over the ensuing centuries, their identity came to be defined in part in terms of dispossession and disenfranchisement. That said, Shi'ite leaders eventually established a number of important empires, notably the Fatimids in Egypt (910–1171) and the Safavids in Persia (1501–1736). There are different denominations within Shi'ism, the largest group being the 'Twelvers' – so named because they recognize a line of twelve leaders in the *imamate*, a religio-political institution unique to Shi'ite Islam. Shi'ites today constitute approximately 10–15 per cent of the world's Muslim population, or 130–195 million. Over half are found in two countries, Iran (90 per cent of the population) and Iraq (around 60 per cent of the population).

and multifaceted ecology of world political Islam. Al-Qaeda was established in Afghanistan by Arab-Afghan fighters following the decision by the Soviet Union to withdraw its troops after a failed occupation effort. Emboldened by this seeming victory, Al-Qaeda sought to export the Afghan model to other countries in which Muslims were understood to be fighting foreign invasions or resisting imposed secularism. The move to establish the group also represented a major shift away from the worldview of earlier radical Islamists such as Qutb and the groups he inspired. For them, the goal was to successfully attack and supplant the 'near enemy', that is the leaders of secular-national regimes in the Middle East and other Muslim majority countries who were perceived as the proxies of Western powers. Bin Laden and Al-Qaeda's new emphasis on the 'far enemy', inspired by the Afghan experience, emphasized instead the idea of directly attacking what they understood to be the source of global imperialism and atheism – namely, the United States. Al-Qaeda's goals are the liberation of Muslim territories from occupying infidel forces and the making of a world that is 'safe for Islam' – a world in which a social political order based on *shari'ah* can be realized. Some within this camp understand this to mean the re-establishment of centralized political authority in the Muslim world via a new Caliphate, an institution that had existed since the seventh century but was abolished by Kemal at the end of the Ottoman Empire.

Al-Qaeda today is better thought of as a discourse of resistance whose material reality is found in a transnational coordinating network highly skilled in forging temporary operational ties with local/regional movements or individuals in order to engage in violent activism. Far from representing a kneejerk reaction to globalization, Al-Qaeda appropriates the logistical and communicative infrastructures of globalization to pursue the fulfilment of a narrative, a 'story', internalized by its leadership, about the necessity and inevitability of Islam's triumph over the infidel (unbelieving) forces of world power – particularly the United States and its allies in Europe and elsewhere. Al-Qaeda as a radical Islamist group is quite unorthodox even within the wider *jihadist* movement, many of whose members did not agree with Bin Laden's decision to carry out the September 2001 attacks. While Al-Qaeda's model of global Islamic politics has attracted only a few thousand of the world's 1.25 *billion* Muslims as actual members, some in the Muslim world are drawn to Bin Laden as a symbol of anti-Americanism (even while they usually disagree with the methods he employs). In the wake of the attacks of September 11, 2001 (and subsequent bombings in Europe and elsewhere attributed to Al-Qaeda and its affiliates), we have seen Muslim identity around the world being increasingly regarded as a political question – particularly among Muslim populations in Europe and North America. This has meant that debates around Islam and Muslims have come to take on wider significance beyond the question of terrorism and violence, reinvigorating discussions of whether 'Islam' and 'the West' are compatible in cultural or civilizational terms. We have seen aspects of this in events such as the 2006 Danish cartoon affair and the controversy surrounding the Pope's speech later that same year, in which the head of the Catholic Church seemed to imply that Islam was violent by nature and Muslims incapable of exercising reason.

Al-Qaeda is sometimes seen as an entirely new terrorist threat because it is a network, but contemporary Western warfare also revolves around the idea of network.
See Chapter 17

Moderate Islamic politics

While much of the public debate and discussion of Islam is focused on Al-Qaeda and the minority of extremist groups in the Muslim world, there are a number of other important trends to recognize. Some scholars have claimed that the global *jihad* movement has essentially failed and become re-domesticated (Gerges 2005), while others argue that the Islamist movement as a whole has become so thoroughly integrated into the norms and structures of global modernity as to represent the onset of 'post-Islamism' (Roy 2004). Other analysts see in this something more akin to the normalization of Islamist politics, meaning that we are beginning to see signs that the old, rather constraining model of the Muslim Brotherhood no longer holds sway. Certain observers suggest that the inclusion of Islamist parties in the political systems of countries such as Jordan, Yemen and Kuwait has had a moderating effect on the Islamist movement (Schwedler 2006). This trend toward Muslim Democracy, as it has been termed (Nasr 2005), can be seen in the victory of 'semi'-Islamist parties such as the Justice and Development Party in Turkey (commonly known by its Turkish acronym AKP). This is a new form of conservative politics, comparable to the Christian Democratic parties of Europe, in which religion functions primarily as a reference point for public morality rather than a direct source of legislation. In other words, these are Islamically based political parties which accept the legitimacy of the formally secular state and which are willing to work pragmatically alongside other parties (secular liberals, socialists, etc.) to pursue shared goals. It is too early to know whether or not such a trend is taking hold, but it is certainly noteworthy that 'new Islamists' (Baker 2006) of this sort have sprung up in countries as diverse as Morocco, Turkey, Egypt, Jordan, Pakistan and Indonesia in recent years.

It is impossible to provide a single, overall characterization of the role of Islam in global politics. As a community of faith encompassing over a billion people and spanning multiple continents, Islam is itself highly diverse, and so are the ways in which it impacts and interacts with global politics. Multiple streams of Muslim politics are clearly recognizable today, and one cannot easily determine which of them predominates. Indeed, in many cases the ebb and flow of various trends is a function of the prevailing global political climate. What has become clear, however, is that an overview of the recent history of political Islam helps

FIGURE 5.5
Muslim Brotherhood deputies in the Egyptian Parliament, 2006. Getty Images

to lay bare a set of presumptions about both the relationship between religion and politics (i.e. the question of whether they should be kept separate in a properly 'modern' world) and also the extent to which religion helps us to understand the supposed motivation of political players.

RESPONSES
DO RELIGION AND POLITICS MIX?

The idea of the interface or mixing of religion and politics being problematic and potentially dangerous is a byproduct of the rise of secularism, often regarded as one of the hallmarks of modern society. But where did the assumptions and expectations associated with secularism come from, and how have they come to play such an important role in mediating our understanding of how (and whether) religion matters in politics? There is an almost total absence of references to religion in books about global politics prior to the 1990s. It is as if scholars were blind to religion as a force in global affairs, or did not find it to be helpful in explaining international politics.

Secularism

In formal political terms, secularism refers to the idea of a separation between the institutions of church and state. Its origins are to be found in the rise of European modernity and the establishment of the sovereign state. Aspects of the discourse on secularism are, however, to be found throughout the historical record and within the core texts of world religions such as Christianity and Islam. In the Christian tradition, for example, the famous passage of the Bible about 'rendering unto God what is God's and unto Caesar that which belongs to Caesar' is generally regarded as acknowledging a categorical distinction between worldly political power and the transcendental other-worldly mandate of religious authority. In the Islamic tradition, while there is no formal theological division between religion and politics, Islamic history is replete with the rise and fall of empires whose day-to-day affairs seemed to reflect a similar distinction in the minds of rulers.

The modern history of secularism is associated with two important developments in European intellectual and political history: the philosophical Enlightenment and the birth of modern political sovereignty.

The Enlightenment was associated with a shift in how people thought about the origins and status of knowledge. Where truth was previously understood to derive from religion and faith, the Enlightenment – and modernity more generally –

This 'rational, thinking subject' is modelled on what is considered to be male, and therefore women and supposedly feminine qualities have often been considered less significant or even entirely excluded. **See Chapters 4 and 12**

entailed a shift to the idea that truth and knowledge could be determined through the effort of human reason. Furthermore, the human condition was no longer seen as subject to divine providence. Rather, human beings were now understood to possess the capacity to change the world around them. One aspect of secularism, then, is a shift away from relying on religious belief to provide knowledge and understanding of the world, and the rise of a belief in the ability of the autonomous, rational, thinking subject to comprehend the world and to change it for the better.

The use of statistics to analyse and explain the social world is one such phenomenon. See **Chapter 13** for some of the problems with this.

This new orientation gave rise to the attitudes and methods that underpin the modern natural sciences, many of which were later reproduced in an effort to create social science. Eventually, some scholars began to associate the advent of modernity with an evolutionary model of human development. According to this model, societies that have undergone modernization are further along in terms of developmental progress than those societies characterized by the persistence of traditional beliefs and practices, such as religion (Lerner 1958). Modernization is generally understood as a process whereby societies 'evolve' according to the trajectory of the Western political economy from about the sixteenth century – meaning that they adopt capitalism, industrialization and, increasingly today, also political liberalism and democracy.

The emergence of states in Europe is traced in **Chapter 9**, which also explains the Peace of Westphalia. **Chapter 6** discusses secular forms of authority.

The political-institutional understanding of secularism is associated with the emergence of modern sovereign states in Europe, a development commonly dated to the Peace of Westphalia in 1648. After the Wars of Religion in the preceding

---

BOX 5.4 KEY ENLIGHTENMENT THINKERS

- Voltaire (1694–1778): a leading French critic of organized religion who emphasized the power of human reason and agency in shaping society.
- David Hume (1711–76): a Scottish philosopher who argued that knowledge and understanding of the world derive from the human senses – an approach known as empiricism – rather than from divine sources.
- Immanuel Kant (1724–1804): one of the leading German philosophers of the Enlightenment, whose work remains highly influential today. Kant exhorted people to 'dare to know'. He used the Latin phrase for this: *sapere aude*.
- John Locke (1632–1704): an English thinker whose ideas on liberty, the individual and property were central to the development of political modernism.
- Adam Smith (1723–90): a Scottish economist and moral philosopher generally regarded as the leading theorist – in his book *The Wealth of Nations* – of modern capitalism.

century, it was agreed among rulers that religion should be kept separate from matters of state. This was to ensure that the legitimacy of the sovereign would remain free from attempts by church authorities to interfere in politics, and produced a situation in which many found themselves subject to official state religions. The rise of liberalism in political thought – in large measure a reaction against this idea – soon produced the form of government known as republicanism. In a modern republic, the location of sovereignty and the responsibility to govern are understood to shift from being the preserve of monarchs to being the right of the peoples so governed – hence *res* ('concern') *publicus* ('of the people'). In the republican model, public affairs are to be regulated by the rule of law, popularly legislated, rather than by the whim of monarchs or the faith-based 'irrationality' of religion. As part of this shift away from official religions of state, religion came to be seen as a private matter – that is, a sphere of activity belonging to realm of the individual and whatever voluntary associations might arise between consenting individuals outside the influence and determination of the state.

> These are different 'pictures' of political space in the sense explained in **Chapter 2.**

> Being confined to the private realm means being excluded from the public sphere where decisions are made about who gets which resources. This is why feminists have challenged the boundary between private and public.
> **See Chapter 4**

In recent years, a number of interventions by scholars coupled with political events in the world have led to a reconsideration of some of the conventional thinking about secularism and the place of religion in the world today. Some sociologists of religion for whom a general trend towards greater secularization in the modern world was once taken for granted have since backed off from that position (Berger 1999). Others have argued that in fact we are seeing a greater public role for religion around the world (Casanova 1994), with some connecting this to an increased search for meaning and purpose in a highly complex, globalizing world (Laidi 1998). Scholars of non-Western societies have also been critical of the secularization thesis, but in a different way. For them, it is not so much that the supposed trend towards secularism has been reversed, but that it was never an appropriate account of the world in the first place. Writers such as Talal Asad (1993) have argued that the very idea of religion and politics as wholly distinct and separate spheres is itself a Eurocentric proposition, reflecting the particular experience of modernity as it evolved in Europe and North America. For him, it is therefore inappropriate to try and apply this schema as a universal explanation of the relationship of religion and politics. Several Indian political theorists have argued along similar lines that the notion of secularism is inappropriate for understanding the relationship between religious communities and national society in that country (Nandy 1995; Chatterjee 1998).

Religion in the social sciences

One well-known social science account of international affairs is Samuel Huntington's 'Clash of civilizations' thesis, in which 'civilizational' blocs pursue security and interests defined in terms of cultural values. Huntington also provides

BOX 5.5 HUNTINGTON'S *CLASH OF CIVILIZATIONS*

Samuel Huntington's thesis first appeared in the influential policy journal *Foreign Affairs* in 1993, and several years later in book form as *The Clash of Civilizations and the Remaking of World Order* (1998). Huntington's book was about the role of culture and religion in world politics. He argues that in the post-Cold War world, cultural blocs – which he labels 'civilizations' – will become the major protagonists of global affairs. 'The fault lines of civilizations', he says, 'will be the battle lines of the future'. In Huntington's view, each civilization expresses a unique worldview and set of values. As contact between these cultural or symbolic systems intensifies in the face of global pressure to integrate economies, political communities and cultures, the incompatibility of different civilizations leads to increased tension and eventually actual conflict between them. What are the civilizations he is talking about? For Huntington, many of the divisions between civilizations are religious in nature. His Western civilization is largely composed of the Protestant and Catholic Christian majority nations (except Latin America, a sort of Western sub-civilization according to Huntington). Others in his list include the Muslim world, the Orthodox Christian world, the Hindu world and the Buddhist world. To these can be added three others, the Sinic world (covering China and areas of Southeast Asia), Japanese civilization and also Sub-Saharan Africa, whose status Huntington leaves unclear.

us with a rigid understanding of culture with little space to account for the considerable diversity and nuance that exist within and between his civilizations.

Claims about civilizations and religions as the new primary blocs in world politics have been subject to considerable critique (Huntington 1996; Hall and Jackson 2007) in recent years. Likewise the popularity of Huntington's thesis has ebbed and flowed, with the attacks of September 11, 2001 seeming for some to give credence to the idea of a civilizational struggle between Islam and the West. Numerous criticisms have been levelled against Huntington's thesis. His concept of civilization is so large and heavily abstracted that it is difficult to map it on to any kind of social reality – in other words, it is difficult to think of civilization in terms of lived experience. The blocs that Huntington identifies as civilizations are, in some cases, so enormously diverse that it becomes nearly impossible to treat them analytically as a single cultural unit. Furthermore, Huntington's thesis operates with a very static and stultifying conception of culture. In order to make the argument about civilizational difference as a source of conflict, he is forced to reduce highly complex and fluid belief systems to rather stagnant and essentialized ideal-types that, again, bear little resemblance to social reality. It is difficult to see the dynamic and intersubjective qualities that define culture in Huntington's reified (that is, in a way that makes the abstract concept appear real) civilizations. In terms of our discussion so far, it is important to examine

Huntington paints a picture of the world that seems to provide an easy explanation for recent terrorism and the responses to it. But, as **Chapter 2** shows, such pictures do not simply enable us to see what is already there: they make the world we see. They also make invisible what does not fit into the picture.

Huntington's argument critically because of the way in which it ends up having to reduce complex, multifaceted human subjects to their religious identities in order to maintain its own logic.

BROADER ISSUES
CULTURE, FUNDAMENTALISM AND RELIGIOUS IDENTITIES

Before Huntington's analysis of clashing civilizations other scholars of world politics were beginning to stress the importance of cultural and religious forces in world politics, but in considerably more subtle terms (Der Derian and Shapiro 1989). These writers asked us to consider the relevance of wider social theory for understanding some of the central problems in contemporary global politics. They argued, for example, that it is difficult to understand many of today's problems without recognizing the inherently postcolonial nature of global affairs (Darby 1998; Doty 1996).

The importance of colonial history in understanding the postcolonial present is discussed in **Chapters 11, 14 and 15**.

Others have argued that culture is the very terrain upon which conceptions and practices of world order and power have played out throughout modern history. For these scholars, culture is crucially important because of its intimate relationship with processes of identity formation and the making of 'others' (see Chapter 4). The ideas of Edward Said are particularly relevant in this regard.

FIGURE 5.6
An example of 'Orientalist' art in Edward Said's sense: *The Snake Charmer*, Jean-Léon Gérôme, 1870. © Sterling and Francine Clark Art Institute, Williamstown, Massachusetts, USA

Examining 'representation' is a different way of saying that you are interested in the 'picture' that a particular view generates.
See Chapter 2

These colonial hierarchies of power continue to have significant effects.
See Chapters 11 and 14

Edward Said's landmark text *Orientalism* (1978) made the argument that culture and power are closely related in the historical establishment of particular forms of world order. More specifically, Said delves into various domains of cultural production (literature, art, scholarship) in the European world during the colonial period in order to understand the relationship between *representation* and geopolitical power. His focus on representation was prompted by the fact that in reviewing depictions of various peoples the West seemed to regard as 'outside' or Other – particularly in the Islamic (or 'Oriental') world – Said found that the stories told about the non-Western world seemed to regularly and systematically associate these cultures with traits that were the opposite of Western values and that carried strongly negative connotations. For example, Muslim peoples were often represented as exotic, overly sensualized, lazy or violent as opposed to rational, orderly and hard-working – all characteristics, supposedly, of Western modernity. Said argues that this is something more than just subjective bias, however. He suggests that this system of cultural representation, which he terms Orientalism, was a core component of the exercise of colonial power. In other words, Said argued that one of the ways in which the West constituted its own identity and legitimized its dominance was to construct the non-Western world – the object of its imperial geopolitics – as its absolute Other. This helped to justify and naturalize the hierarchies of power between various (culturally defined) world regions, and eventually to institutionalize the European sovereign state model as a global system.

For Said, culture is not simply one factor in understanding global politics, but a core terrain upon which it is played out: global politics, on this reading, *is* culture. Some scholars have argued that Said overstates his case and ignores reciprocal processes of Western objectification and representation by non-Western peoples (Buruma and Margalit 2004), while others suggest that Said's theory continues to hold some merit in terms of understanding not only the underlying logic of Huntington's neo-Orientalist vision but also the central thrust of US foreign policy in the aftermath of the Cold War (Ó Tuathail 1996).

Writers such as Tariq Ali have engaged this issue through the theme of fundamentalism. It is important for us to consider the term since it is generally associated with religion, and particularly with Islam. A term that originally came into usage to describe certain forms of American Christianity in the nineteenth century, 'fundamentalism' emerged as a common designation of danger in reference to various Islamist movements from the 1980s. Some critics have dismissed its utility simply because it does not provide any analytical value (Pieterse 1994). They argue by emphasizing one's adherence to the 'fundamentals' of a given religion does not tell us much about the nature and behaviours associated with a given religious identity. For example, one might easily follow the fundamental beliefs of Islam and never even consider becoming involved with political movements or violent groups. Ali's (2003) intervention in this debate is interesting because he seeks to decouple the term 'fundamentalism' from an exclusively religious connotation and to associate it instead with any form of thought or ideology that is uncompromising in its worldview and which represents itself as the sole source of truth or the only solution to global problems. Viewed in this way it becomes possible to recognize today the existence in global politics of various kinds of fundamentalism, some of which are not religious in nature. For example, sometimes the assumptions and practices associated with the neoliberal economic policies that underpin organizations such as the International Monetary Fund and the World Trade Organization take on the aura of 'religion' when, in the absence of no strong proof of their remedy, global policymakers place considerable faith in these approaches as a route to salvation from global poverty.

Ali's depiction of fundamentalism takes a different direction, however. He tries to show that in the wake of the attacks of September 11, 2001 there emerged a curious form of parallel fundamentalism that can been seen through a comparison of the discourses and worldviews contained in the rhetoric of US President George W. Bush and the statements of Al-Qaeda leader Osama Bin Laden. Each of these global political actors represented himself as the guardian and purveyor of absolute morality. Bin Laden promised to work to establish a world system based on Islamic law, while the subsequent policy choices of the Bush Administration seemed to suggest that it was driven by a worldview (commonly described as neo-conservative) that sought to remake the world in its image. In this sense, the 2003 war with Iraq can be interpreted as an effort by the United States to transplant its own model of good governance (liberal democratic, capitalist)

There is evidence that neoliberal economic policies have changed the way we view poverty but are unable to end poverty as they claim to. **See Chapter 14**

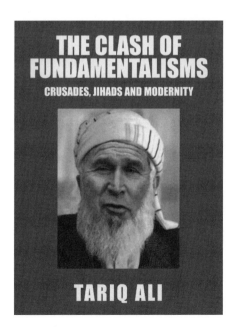

FIGURE 5.7
President Bush dressed as Bin Laden on the cover of Tariq Ali's *The Clash of Fundamentalisms*. Verso

to the heart of the Middle East. This way Bush and Bin Laden both revealed themselves to be pursuing projects of absolute and universalizing morality – much in the vein of religion even where religion was not explicitly invoked. Neo-conservatism is an example of ideology – that is, a template of meaning-making with a singular horizon that allows people to understand the world in ways that lead to certain unavoidable conclusions about what must be done in response to the circumstances of the world. Ideology not only mediates how we perceive the world around us, but also prescribes all-encompassing solutions for dealing with the world it hands us (Eagleton 1991). It hence becomes possible to draw strong parallels between religion and ideology, rather than treating religion as something unique.

This point is all the more important to bear in mind due to the tendency on the part of some analysts of global politics to privilege religious affiliations as if they are forms of identity that trump all others. We see this in commonplace practices such as the use of the term 'Muslim world' or when writers refer to large categories such as 'Muslims in Europe.' While such terminology is often merely trying to be descriptive, it becomes problematic when it begins to ascribe behaviours to religion – that is, when we begin to make assumptions that because a country happens to be part of something called the Muslim world, or because someone happens to be a Muslim, then they will necessarily think or act in a certain way. This is, in essence, a point about the danger of projecting religiousness on to people who hold multiple identities and whose considerations and decisions regarding their political behaviour cannot be reduced to religion. For example, it can be argued that in many cases the views and motivations of people in the so-called Muslim world can just as easily, if not more accurately, be understood in relation to the problems and concerns of Third World or developing world identities – that is, in relation to issues of global inequality in socioeconomic terms, and politically in terms of the asymmetry of power between countries in the global North and the global South. Further complicating the analysis is the fact that even where religious language is deployed to mobilize political identity, the root causes of the antagonism underpinning these claims are sometimes better found in other domains (e.g. the political disenfranchisement of a minority group). Projecting religious identities on to large groups can even mask the true sources of political discontent in some cases. For example, during the Paris riots of 2006, it was not uncommon to find the participants in these riots being described as 'Muslim protesters' even though none of their claims was couched in terms of Islam. It would have been more accurate in that case to approach the issue in terms of the mobilized discontent of unemployed immigrants.

Also of great importance is the need to recognize the inevitability of great diversity within the various traditions of world religion. Christianity, Judaism and Islam all contain within them multiple currents, denominations and sects, and all of them vary considerably depending on where in geographical and cultural terms they

It is interesting to compare the discussion of the role of 'pictures' in Chapter 2 with the discussion of 'ideology' here.

For a discussion of other sorts of identity and the complications involved in thinking about identity, see Chapter 4.

See Chapter 10 for a picture of the 2006 Paris riots and a discussion of how they related to the question of the nation.

are practised. In the Muslim world there is certainly a highly visible yet numerically very small radical fringe prepared to use violence to subvert the current world order. There are many more Muslims, global public opinion surveys suggest (Pew Global Attitudes Project 2005), committed to an interpretation of Islam that is in harmony with values of tolerance, pluralism and democracy. A majority of the world's Muslims are not affiliated with any kind of political movement; nor do they understand their religion as a system of beliefs that requires them to behave politically in any particular way. This fact strengthens the point made above about the need to look beyond religion to understand the political identities and worldviews of peoples that we often too easily categorize in terms of their religion.

Do you consider that your political worldview is informed by religion?

Finally, we need to resist the idea that religious identities or political claims framed in terms of religion are somehow beyond the comprehension of what we otherwise regard as political reason. Conflicting parties in Sri Lanka's armed dispute whose primary desires can be understood in relation to social stability and personal security, for example, may appeal to aspects of Hinduism and Buddhism that emphasize peace. In countries such as Turkey and Indonesia, parties whose political platform is defined in terms of eliminating government corruption will often speak of Islam as the source of their public morality without having any interest in setting up Islamic states. Furthermore, we can even see evidence today of religious and secular parties forming coalitions in support of shared goals. For example, within the broad Global Justice and 'alter-mondialisation' movements today, one can find socialists, environmentalists and religious parties of various denominations trying to achieve social justice (a key value in Islam and certain interpretations of Christianity) and preserve the planet. While their languages may differ – e.g. 'Mother Earth' vs the human relationship with the planet as a sacred covenant – all of these people are committed to a common vision of participation and cooperation in world affairs. Viewing religion in this way allows us to identify it as just one among many similar ideational sources at play in global politics. Rather than viewing and treating religion as a space of exception in global politics – as a unique force beyond reason and comprehension – we are better off treating it as one of many terrains and languages through which the global political is engaged. Islam, for example, needs always to be understood in relation to *Muslims* – that is, to the people who profess its belief and interpret its meaning in terms of their life experience and circumstances. Only by contextualizing religion in this way, in terms of lived experience, can we understand how and where it intersects with the global political.

Environmentalism is interesting here because it does not place the human at the centre. **See Chapter 3**

CONCLUSION

The question of religion in global politics is nothing if not highly complex. In addressing the framing question with which we opened the discussion, 'Does religion matter in global politics?', it would seem that we need to answer this in the affirmative, but with certain very important qualifications. More specifically, three points bear drawing out by way of summary and conclusion: (1) the importance of understanding when and how to grant importance to religion in seeking to understand global politics – in other words, recognizing that religion is present in a given global political situation does not mean that that situation should be read exclusively or even primarily in terms of religion; (2) the importance of recognizing the presence of enormous diversity within world religions and the dangers entailed in treating them as monoliths; and (3) the fact that religious identities and world political claims framed in terms of religion are not necessarily categorically distinct from or unconnected with other kinds of political and ideological claims. Indeed, as several examples today can show, these sorts of claims are often motivated by a desire on the part of both the 'religious' and the 'non-religious' to achieve similar goals even where the language they use may differ.

FURTHER READING

Haynes, Jeff (1998) *Religion in Global Politics*, Harlow: Longman.
   A survey of key religious trends in all major world regions with an emphasis on the dynamic and increasingly interdependent relationship between them.

Jenkins, Phil (2006) *The New Faces of Christianity: Believing the Bible in the Global South*, New York: Oxford University Press.
   An analysis of the phenomenal growth of Pentecostal Christianity in Africa and other parts of the developing world in recent years.

Juergensmeyer, Mark (1994) *The New Cold War? Religious Nationalism Confronts the Secular State*, Berkeley, CA: University of California Press; (2003) *Terror in the Mind of God: The Global Rise of Religious Violence*, Berkeley, CA: University of California Press and (2006) *The Oxford Handbook of Global Religions*, New York: Oxford University Press.
   A leading sociologist reflects on the relationship between religion, conflict and nation-states in the global era across a broad range of faith traditions.

Kurtz, Lester (2006) *Gods in the Global Village*, 2nd edn, Thousand Oaks, CA: Sage.
   Examines the impact of globalization on how people understand the role of religion and the structure of its organization.

Mandaville, Peter (2007) *Global Political Islam*, London: Routledge.
   A broad overview of the history and evolution of Muslim politics with a particular focus on the interface between globalization and political Islam.

WEBSITES

BeliefNet, http://www.beliefnet.com.
   The leading website on global religions.

Islam Online, http://www.islamonline.net.

> A portal for Muslim issues and information. The site is closely associated with Yusuf al-Qaradawi, a leading Islamic scholar-jurist with a global audience. It represents the perspective of mainstream conservative Islamic orthodoxy.

Muslim Wakeup!, http://www.muslimwakeup.com.

> A self-described 'progressive' Muslim site, featuring articles dealing with various social issues such as the relationship between Islam and feminism. An interesting contrast to Islam Online.

The ISIM Review, http://www.isim.nl.

> A forum courtesy of the Institute for the Study of Islam in the Modern World in the Netherlands, this publication frequently features short articles on the Muslim world with a strong global politics focus.

IslamiCity, http://www.islamicity.com.

> One of the major Islamic portal websites, with a variety of articles on contemporary Muslim issues, search engines for Islamic textual sources and information on Muslim media and local services (mainly in the USA).

REFERENCES

Ali, Tariq (2003) *The Clash of Fundamentalisms: Crusades, Jihads, and Modernity*, London: Verso.

Althusser, Louis (2001) *Lenin and Philosophy and Other Essays*, new edn, New York: Monthly Review Press.

Asad, Talal (1993) *Genealogies of Religion: Discipline and Reasons of Power in Christianity and Islam*, Baltimore, MD: Johns Hopkins University Press.

Baker, Raymond (2006) *Islam without Fear: Egypt and the New Islamists*, Cambridge, MA: Harvard University Press.

Berger, Peter (ed.) (1999) *The Desecularization of the World: The Resurgence of Religion in World Politics*, Washington, DC: Ethics and Public Policy Center.

Buruma, Ian and Avishai Margalit (2004) *Occidentalism: The West in the Eyes of Its Enemies*, London: Penguin.

Casanova, Jose (1994) *Public Religions in the Modern World*, Chicago, IL: University of Chicago Press.

Chatterjee, Partha (1998) 'Secularism and Toleration', in Rajeev Bhargav (ed.) *Secularism and Its Critics*, New Delhi: Oxford University Press.

Clarke, Peter (2006) *New Religious Movement in Global Perspective: A Study of Religious Change in the Modern World*, London: Routledge.

Connolly, William E. (2005), 'The Evangelical-Capitalist Resonance Machine', *Political Theory* 33, 6: 869–86.

Darby, Philip (1998) *The Fiction of Imperialism: Reading between International Relations and Postcolonialism*, London: Cassell.

Der Derian, James and Michael Shapiro (eds) (1989) *International/Intertextual Relations: Postmodern Readings of World Politics*, Lexington, MA: Lexington Press.

Doty, Roxanne Lynn (1996) *Imperial Encounters: The Politics of Representation in North–South Relations*, Minneapolis, MN: University of Minnesota Press.

Eagleton, Terry (1991) *Ideology: An Introduction*, London: Verso.

Geertz, Clifford (1973) *The Interpretation of Culture*, New York: Basic Books.

Gerges, Fawaz (2005) *The Far Enemy: Why Jihad Went Global*, Cambridge: Cambridge University Press.

Hall, Martin and Patrick Thaddeus Jackson (eds) (2007) *Civilizational Identity: The Production and Reproduction of 'Civilizations' in International Relations*, New York: Palgrave.

Huntington, Samuel (1998) *The Clash of Civilizations and the Remaking of World Order*, New York: Simon and Schuster.

Huntington, Samuel (ed.) (1996) *The Clash of Civilizations? The Debate*, New York: Council on Foreign Relations.

Laidi, Zaki (1998) *A World without Meaning: The Crisis of Meaning in International Politics*, London: Routledge.

Lerner, Daniel (1958) *The Passing of Traditional Society: Modernizing the Middle East*, Glencoe, IL: The Free Press.

Lindbeck, George (1984) *The Nature of Doctrine*, Louisville, KY: Westminster John Knox Press.

Nandy, Ashis (1995) 'An Anti-Secularist Manifesto', *India International Quarterly* 22, 1: 35–64.

Nasr, Vali (2005), 'The Rise of Muslim Democracy', *Journal of Democracy* 16, 2: 13–27.

Ó Tuathail, Geraóid (1996) *Critical Geopolitics: The Politics of Writing Global Space*, Minneapolis, MN: University of Minnesota Press.

Pew Global Attitudes Project (2005) 'Islamic Extremism: Common Concern for Muslim and Western Publics', Washington, DC: Pew Research Center.

Pieterse, Jan Nederveen (1994) 'Fundamentalism Discourses: Enemy Images', *Women against Fundamentalism Journal*, 5: 2–6.

Roy, Olivier (2004) *Globalized Islam: The Search for a New Ummah*, New York: Columbia University Press.

Said, Edward (1978) *Orientalism*, New York: Pantheon Books.

Schwedler, Jillian (2006) *Faith in Moderation: Islamist Parties in Jordan and Yemen*, Cambridge: Cambridge University Press.

CHAPTER 6

Why do we obey?

Jenny Edkins

- ■ *The question*
  OBEDIENCE, RESISTANCE AND FORCE

- ■ *Illustrative example*
  THE REVOLUTIONS OF 1989

- ■ *Responses*
  AUTHORITY AND LEGITIMACY

- ■ *Broader issues*
  THINKING ABOUT POWER

- ■ **CONCLUSION**

THE QUESTION
OBEDIENCE, RESISTANCE AND FORCE

On the whole we seem to be fairly obedient creatures. We go from day to day doing mostly – not always, of course – what is expected of us. We usually respect conventions about property and ownership, we are polite and well mannered to our friends as a general rule, and we tend to do as we are told – by our boss, the traffic warden, the doctor, the tax inspector and so on. Why do we obey people like this? Is it because we have to? Well, clearly we risk losing our job or falling foul of the law if we don't. But do we make this calculation every time, or do we just do what is expected because that is easiest? Or are we obeying some internal voice – our conscience – or, if we are religious, the precepts of our faith?

What happens if we disagree with the way things are organised – if, for example, it has been decided that the government is going to build new nuclear power plants and that part of the money we pay in taxes will go towards this? If we disagree with this decision, what do we do? Most of us accept that the government is entitled to make such decisions, even if we think it is doing something very unwise, even criminal, and we do nothing: we pay our taxes and let the government get on with it. Some of us maybe don't: we organise a demonstration, we challenge the decision, we withhold our taxes. We are disobedient, usually in a non-violent sort of way, called 'civil disobedience' – we disobey, but we are civil about it. And usually, of course, our action makes no difference: the decision we disagree with doesn't change.

Of course, if we live in a democracy we get the chance every so often to express our disagreement with the decisions of a particular government by voting it out of office. This really does not give us much of a voice in what goes on, but if we want to be more involved we have various routes open to us. We could stand for election ourselves, become a political activist and help formulate party policy, lobby the government, perhaps through joining or working for a campaigning organisation. To take any of these routes, we would have to follow a series of conventions and jump a number of hurdles, all of which rely on us doing what's expected in a particular context. At this point it is beginning to seem as though the whole of social and political existence involves 'doing what's expected'. Even if we decide that the whole system of government that we live under is so appalling that we should work to change it, we still have to organise politically – even revolutions can demand some obedience along the way, although ultimately major *dis*obedience, even violent disobedience, may be what is planned.

In many respects, it is good to be able to do what is expected – to know what that is without giving it too much thought, and to just do it. Fairly automatic obedience can be much easier than trying to work out what on earth we are supposed to do in a totally unfamiliar or chaotic situation. It is good to have a framework of conventions and rules in place, even though some of them may not be ideal, and for there to be someone else, in a leadership position, who is responsible for dealing with any crises that may come along. We know where we are and who we are in such a case. When we come across a situation where there is nothing to guide us – when a major accident happens, when our life changes suddenly – we can find ourselves having to completely rethink what to do, from scratch.

What happens when we are asked to do something that we really think we shouldn't be doing – if we are asked to injure someone, for example? This isn't something that happens under normal circumstances to most of us, but if, as we have seen, we are generally obedient creatures, we might want to think about what would happen if, for example, someone whose authority we respected, or someone who was in a position to enforce their authority, told us that it was

Chapter 20 discusses some of the problems with the idea of changing the world.

"I am going to close my eyes and cover my
ears. I expect the student who took my chair, my
desk, and my chalkboard to bring them back."

FIGURE 6.1
'I am going to close my eyes'. Artist: Aaron Bacall. CartoonStock. Ref: aba0400.
www.CartoonStock.com

necessary for us to injure someone. A famous experiment by Stanley Milgram
seems to show that people in general are willing to cause fairly severe injuries to
others if told to do so by someone in a position of authority – in Milgram's case,
someone wearing a white coat. There are, of course, many examples where people
are ordered to do something that normally they might consider they shouldn't
do: soldiers who kill in combat, for example. There are cases that perhaps
seem less extreme, too, for example when civilians in Nazi Germany carried on
with mundane administrative tasks even though they knew or suspected that
what they were doing was part of the bureaucracy of killing (Bauman 1991;
Lanzmann 1995).

Milgram's experiment is
discussed in **Chapter 16**.

How do those in authority enforce their demand that we obey? How do they
make us obey if we don't want to? Usually, they persuade us that we should, first
of all: if we are tempted to drink and drive, then they show us advertisements
designed to bring home the damage we might do as a result, or impose a fine if
they catch us. But if persuasion doesn't work, we move to the next stage: they
will forcibly stop us from driving, ultimately by confining us behind prison bars.
'They', the agents of the government, are entitled to use force, in the form of
the armed forces or the police, to guarantee obedience. Of course, this is not a
carte blanche: when the Ohio National Guard shot dead four student demonstrators and injured others during an anti-Vietnam War protest at Kent State
University in 1970, this was widely regarded as an unreasonable, and hence
illegitimate, use of force by the state government.

Although shooting fellow citizens who are demonstrating peacefully is not something we would expect our armed forces to do, the fact that it could happen, and does occasionally, must be at the back of our minds when considering any action that challenges the government. If we are seriously intending to overthrow a government, then we need to think of the possibility that the government will use force to resist this challenge to its authority. Indeed, often a challenge to the government that seeks to replace it with another political order will take the form of an armed rebellion, in anticipation of the armed response.

ILLUSTRATIVE EXAMPLE
THE REVOLUTIONS OF 1989

To understand more about the questions of authority and obedience that we've raised, let's look at some instances where a political order was challenged, people were disobedient and authority, at least temporarily, collapsed. We will not be looking here at violent revolutions, where guerrillas or insurgents (as armed resistance movements against the authorities tend to be called) confronted the armed forces of the state. Instead we focus on examples where the government was taken on or defied by its own unarmed citizens. What happens when a number of people stand up and refuse to obey? We will be exploring in some detail what people who were involved in one way or another in events of this type thought and did.

We will talk particularly about examples of acts of disobedience, performed in some cases by an individual person and in others by large gatherings of people. In each case we need to think about why and to what extent these acts of disobedience succeeded, and whether, ultimately, they failed. Theda Skocpol's work on social revolutions is interesting here (Skocpol 1979). She argues that although revolutions are often directed against the authority and power of the state, what happens in the end is not the reduction of state power but actually the reverse: its reinforcement. A different set of rulers, with perhaps different ideological commitments, take over the running of the state apparatus after a revolution, but the state itself, as an institution, is strengthened rather than weakened.

What exactly we mean by the state is discussed further in **Chapter 9**.

A number of events that could be described – indeed *were* described – as revolutions took place in 1989, in different parts of the world and with apparently vastly different outcomes. The 1989 democracy movement in China came to an abrupt end on 3 June 1989, when the armed forces of the state violently dispersed demonstrators who had gathered in Tiananmen Square in the heart of Beijing. Their demands had been expressed through peaceful demonstrations throughout the city, where it seemed that students and workers – indeed the entire population of Beijing – had turned out in support. Some of the Communist Party leaders also supported the movement, but not those at the head of the then party leadership. Hunger strikes by students took place on the square itself, and they constructed a huge 'goddess of democracy' from white plaster. There were attempts at negotiation and calls for the students to return to their universities. After a lengthy period of demonstrations and many weeks of hunger strike, it became clear that the hard-line voices within the communist leadership had won out and that the order had been given for troops to enter the city and suppress the demonstrations. Despite this, for some time things continued as before: the troops of the 'People's Army' were persuaded by demonstrators who spoke to them face-to-face to turn back and not to fire on their fellow citizens. However, in the end, on the night of 3 June 1989, the tanks moved into Tiananmen Square.

These events in China were watched around the world. Scenes of buses carrying flag-waving and cheering supporters, small tents crowded into Tiananmen Square in which the hunger strikers lay, the square itself – vast, but looking more like a city within a city than the huge and daunting empty space of ceremonial and power that it was supposed to be – all these images were broadcast worldwide. Images of the violence in the square on the night of 3 June were also shown worldwide: students fleeing before the advancing soldiers, the injured being rushed away by friends, the tanks crushing everything in their path.

A very famous image from that time is the photograph of one man standing in front of a column of tanks advancing down Chang'an Avenue a few days later, on 5 June. This picture shows a lone person, carrying nothing but what looks like a shopping bag and a jacket and wearing a white shirt, who places himself in the road precisely in the path of an advancing column of tanks. People around

FIGURE 6.2
Tiananmen Square, Beijing, China, 1989. Photo: Stuart Franklin, Magnum

the world watching the video images of this saw the tank driver's several attempts to drive around the man – first to the right and then to the left – thwarted by the man determinedly repositioning himself in front the tank, time and time again, eventually so close to it that the tank could not get around at all. The tank stopped – and the demonstrator climbed up onto the tank to speak to the driver or get inside the tank, before climbing down. The tank then started up its engine again, and the whole incident repeated itself, before the tank once more came to a stop. Finally, the man disappeared, two other men hustling or helping him away, depending on how you see it – we don't know the outcome, and we don't know who the man was, or whether he is still alive (Thomas 2006).

This image of how one man, apparently fearless, could stop the advancing might of the state, embodied in the armoured car, was and remains an iconic image. Later that year came the revolutions of 1989 in what was at that time called Eastern Europe. These upheavals formed part of the end of the Cold War and the eventual collapse of the Soviet Union. The people involved in the protests demanding change in Eastern Europe had seen what had happened in China. Although in East Germany, for example, the state had limited the information available to that which conformed to the official Chinese line, people had been able to pick up broadcasts from West Germany (Prins 1990: 211). They knew what was at stake: the tanks could arrive. On 17 June 1953 Soviet tanks had been sent in as part of the violent suppression of strikes and demonstrations in Berlin which left at least fifty people dead. And in 1968 Soviet tanks had rolled into Czechoslovakia in response to the reform movement known as the Prague Spring. It could well happen again. Communist leaders, too, those who could call in the tanks, had seen what this had led to in China: a period of destabilisation.

In East Germany that autumn, the situation was confused. There had been a series of major street demonstrations calling for change in Leipzig, where the numbers of people demonstrating rose from 50,000 on 9 October 1989 to 100,000 on the 16th, 150,000 on the 23rd and 300,000 on the 30th, and in East Berlin, where 500,000 people marched on 4 November (Prins 1990: 81, 227–8). Soviet leader Mikhail Gorbachev had made statements to the effect that he would not intervene in the changes going on in the various states that at that time formed part of the Soviet bloc. The communist leadership in East Germany had changed – Erich Honecker had given way, to be replaced by Egon Krenz. In countries all around East Germany, in Hungary, Czechoslovakia, Romania and Poland, as well as in places such as Ukraine and Estonia which at that time were part of the Soviet Union itself, similar unrest was being expressed. By the beginning of November it had become clear to the party leadership that changes would have to be made to travel restrictions on East German citizens – by then large numbers of East Germans had been leaving the country for the West via the newly opened borders to the West, first in Hungary and later in Czechoslovakia – 50,000 had left between 3 and 8 November via the latter route (Prins 1990: 81, 228).

For more about what the Cold War involved see **Chapter 19**.

BOX 6.1 THE BERLIN WALL

At the end of the Second World War in 1945, Germany was divided, for administrative purposes, between the four allied powers: Britain, France, the US and the Soviet Union (the USSR, or Union of Soviet Socialist Republics). The sector allocated to the USSR became East Germany, or the Deutsche Demokratische Republik (DDR), and the remaining three sectors became West Germany, the Federal Republic of Germany (FRG). The former capital city of Germany, Berlin, situated in the Soviet zone, was also divided, and in 1961 a wall was constructed around West Berlin, to prevent citizens from the communist zone crossing to the West. The wall embodied in concrete the Iron Curtain that divided West and East during the Cold War.

FIGURE 6.3
Berlin and the division of Germany at the end of the Second World War

Then, on 9 November at a press conference at about 7 p.m., the government Press Officer Günter Schabowski made a statement about new travel regulations that were to be established, permitting East Germans to travel to the West with appropriate visa documentation. Questioned repeatedly by the press as to when these new regulations were to come into effect, Schabowski eventually replied 'immediately': he had not been fully briefed – this was not the intention. To those listening to his announcement, the implications were unclear.

One of those who heard the announcement over the radio was Harald Jäger, on duty that evening at Bornholmer Strasse, one of the checkpoints between East and West Berlin, in his role as deputy director of the Passport Control Unit (PKA). This is his account of what happened as he was having dinner:

> I heard Schabowski's words that we had come to an arrangement whereby citizens of the GDR were permitted to travel to West Berlin or the FRG without any preconditions. In response to a question from a journalist when this would be valid the gist of Schabowski's response was: immediately. Upon this wording my dinner got stuck in my throat. I said: What is all this? What sort of intellectual diarrhoea is this? I left my dinner and immediately went into the pre-(passport) control area for leaving the country at Bornholmer Strasse in order to ring Colonel Ziegenhorn. Colonel Ziegenhorn was our superior at the time and director of the operational headquarters of the Main Division VI [Passport Control and Search] of the Ministry for State Security. The gist of Colonel Ziegenhorn's response was: 'Have you also heard the television broadcast of Schabowski'. I said: 'Yes. What should we do?' Colonel Ziegenhorn said: 'Wait for now. There is no possibility of leaving the country under these conditions. Continue to monitor the situation at Bornholmer Strasse and call me regularly about the developing situation.'
>
> (Chronik der Mauer, undated a)

Within about half an hour, there were a large number of people – Jäger estimates around a hundred – at the checkpoint. They had heard Schabowski's statement, like Jäger, and were demanding to go through to the West. Over the next minutes and hours the crowd swelled from a few hundred to many thousands, as more people arrived to find out what was going on and to demand to be let through. Many ordinary East Berliners had heard the radio announcement but decided at first that it was meaningless and carried on with what they were doing. Later, however, the mood changed, and people made their way to the checkpoints. This was an extremely risky thing to do: 'no East German without a visa on his passport

FIGURE 6.4
Bornholmer Strasse, Berlin. The displeasure is growing. Those who are waiting are demanding the new freedoms that the ZK [Central Committee] decided on in the afternoon. Spiegel TV

– vetted by the secret police, the Stasi, and rarely granted – ventured near any of the city's checkpoints . . . It was a criminal offence – "unwarranted intrusion into a border area"' (Hilton 2001: 325), and there was a shoot-to-kill policy for anyone trying to climb the wall. Many people had died in the attempt since it had been built.

At Bornholmer Strasse checkpoint, Jäger called his superior again, several times, and eventually the colonel agreed that they should let a small number of people through, to ease the pressure. Those who were most pushy were to be let past, and their passports stamped on the photograph, such that they were effectively disbarred from returning. As well as the most 'provocative', others were to be let through as well, so that the crowd would not have the impression that to get through all that was needed was for them to be particularly aggressive. This was 'the bureaucracy of madness', but passport huts were opened and at around 9.20 p.m. the first people began to filter through, some with their passports stamped over the photo, some not (Hilton 2001: 331).

This action did not solve the problem for Jäger, but exacerbated it:

> The pressure increased even more. The citizens of the GDR now saw that we were letting some persons leave the country. The reason for this was not clear to them. They assumed that it would now start, that they would be permitted to leave. We had to continue to prevent them because we had the order to only let some persons leave the country and not all of them. The pressure continued to increase and the number of people at the checkpoint Bornholmer Strasse also continued to increase.
>
> (Chronik der Mauer, undated b)

FIGURE 6.5
Bornholmer Strasse, Berlin. The first step into the West: the woman from East Berlin has made it. She has passed the border control. Spiegel TV

FIGURE 6.6
At the barrier the situation is worsening. The border guards have no order to open the border. Meanwhile 20,000 to 30,000 people are jammed into Bornholmer Strasse. Spiegel TV

It became clear to Jäger that something had to give. His guards were looking to him for solutions, but he was getting no help from his superiors. The crowd was waving and chanting; there was a risk, he thought, that people could panic and have been crushed, or that one of the guards might panic and fire a shot, despite the instructions they had not to use their pistols (Hilton 2001: 341–2). Jäger made up his mind:

> When I saw what could develop, that our members of staff had been driven into a corner and that the demand by the citizens of the GDR became stronger and stronger, I decided to open everything and to immediately stop passport controls.
>
> (Chronik der Mauer, undated c)

He was taking a great risk. 'Normally, you'd expect something to happen to you. I had refused to carry out – well, implement – the orders' (Hilton 2001: 343).

But although he didn't know it, Jäger was not alone. A similar situation was repeated at other checkpoints around the city: the pressure of ordinary East Berliners who had decided to test out the meaning of the announcement that evening for themselves, confused border guards without instructions as to what to do, and a general air of excitement and anticipation.

Once news that the wall had been opened spread, people from all over Germany – and indeed from further afield – travelled to Berlin to see for themselves. Andreas Ramos, a Dane, writes of his visit:

> I stood with several East German guards, their rifles slung over their shoulders. I asked them if they had bullets in those things. They grinned and said no. From some houses, someone had set up loudspeakers and played Beethoven's ninth symphony: Alle Menschen werden Brüder. All people become brothers. On top of every building were thousands of people. Berlin

FIGURE 6.7
At 11.30 p.m. the checkpoint at Bornholmer Strasse is *de facto* open. The police report a stream of people from East to West 'like ants'. Spiegel TV

was out of control. There was no more government, neither in East nor in West. The police and the army were helpless. The soldiers themselves were overwhelmed by the event. They were part of the crowd. Their uniforms meant nothing. The Wall was down.

(Ramos 1994–2008)

RESPONSES
AUTHORITY AND LEGITIMACY

There are a number of writers who have looked at how we should think about revolutions. We have already mentioned Theda Skocpol; others include, for example, Ted Gurr (1970), Charles Tilly (1993) and John Dunn (1989). You might be interested in following up this strand of the literature, but what we want to do here is not look at how people have thought about revolutions but rather examine a number of approaches to the question of social and political authority and community. The question that interests us in this chapter is 'Why do we obey?' and we want to turn now to focus not on revolutions but on the times in between, when we all do as we are told, or seem to.

Two thinkers who have explored the question of why we generally seem to obey sources of social and political authority, though in different ways, are Max Weber and Emile Durkheim. These two writers were part of the wave of intellectual effort that produced the disciplines of social and political theory and, more specifically, sociology in the late nineteenth and early twentieth century. One of the inspirations behind this work was the notion that religious sources of authority – the belief in something or someone outside human society, something that transcends human experience, rather than something inside or immanent to it – were no longer what was most significant. As anthropologist Talal Asad puts it, in this period 'religion was considered to be an early human condition from which modern law, science and politics emerged and became detached' (Asad 1993: 27). Before the eighteenth century, religious sources of authority were deemed to provide the answers. A transcendent being or god was regarded as the source not only of creation but of the ethical rules and standards that we were to aspire to. Most often, punishment for disobedience to the commands of a deity was not to come in this life, but in the next. Rewards for obedience would come in heaven, not on earth. These religious views began to lose their hold with the rise of discourses of secularisation in Europe. The source of authority came to be seen as being in the individual person, or in the social and political order which individuals subscribed to. This led to the urgent need for accounts of those non-transcendent forms of authority: if what or whom we obeyed was not a transcendent godhead, what or who was it, and how were we to think through what was going on here? The social and political sciences both attempted to provide an

For a discussion of the rise of secularism and the European Enlightenment, and the contrast between the religious and the secular, see **Chapter 5** answer and, in doing so, reinforced the move from religion to secularism that seemed to be taking place. The source of authority was relocated from a transcendent source to a source in the individual or in the society or the political order (Mavelli 2008). We return to this point when we discuss Hobbes and the English Civil War in the final part of this section.

Alongside, and part of, the driving force of the discourse of secularism was the notion that the social sciences ought to be able to explain the social world in much the same way as the physical sciences had succeeded (as it seemed then) in explaining the natural world. In other words, it should be possible to discover the laws of social behaviour, just as scientists had discovered the laws of nature – like gravity, thermodynamics and so on. If we weren't to explain the natural world as God's creation but as the result of scientific laws, perhaps we should be able explain the social world in the same way. However, although some later sociologists who draw on this work do see Weber and Durkheim as having striven for 'scientific' laws of society, or, in other words, for generalisations that would enable us to predict and control social affairs, it is perhaps best to think of them rather differently.

Note here the link between sources of authority (what we obey, or what authorises what we do) and ideas of truth (how we know, or what authorises knowledge).

For Max Weber, the social world was a complicated affair. Although he was interested in the questions raised by Marx, concerning the interrelation of 'all institutional orders making up a social structure' (Gerth and Mills 2007: 49), he wanted to contest the Marxist view that in the end history could be accounted for by economic factors, as in historical materialism, which he saw as a monocausal account (Gerth and Mills 2007: 47). For Weber an account that tried to simplify everything down to a single overriding cause would be misleading: in social life what happened had a multiplicity of causes. He was interested how social structures of power worked through bureaucracy and discipline, for example, and how social differentiation in terms of economic class and social status were interrelated. He studied social structures and religion in India and in China, where very different forms of differentiation – by caste or by education – arose. He was fascinated by the way that capitalist industrialisation had happened in Europe but not in China or India. Perhaps his most famous book is *The Protestant Ethic and the Spirit of Capitalism* (Weber 1930), where he traces how the development of Calvinist religious practices of duty in a calling contributed to the conditions of possibility for the growth of capitalism in Europe. Of course, once capitalism had taken root and material goods had 'gained an increasing and finally inexorable power' over people's lives, it continued even when the practices associated with it had long ceased to have any religious meaning. As Weber so poignantly puts it, 'the idea of duty in one's calling prowls about our lives like the ghost of dead religious beliefs' (Weber 1930: 182). In putting forward this argument, it was *not* his aim 'to substitute for a one-sided materialistic an equally one-sided spiritualistic causal interpretation of culture and of history' (Weber 1930: 183) but rather to point to another possible starting point for further

For more on historical materialism, see **Chapter 13**.

investigation, investigation which would always have to focus on the specifics of particular historical conjunctures.

One of the reasons that Weber has been misread as attempting a simple causal analysis might be his use – as an analytical tool – of what he called constructed or ideal 'types' (Gerth and Mills 2007: 294). These 'types' are an aid to thinking, and are consciously ahistorical: any real-life historical situation will, Weber insists, be much more complex. In his discussion of forms of authority he uses this method. He identifies three 'types' of authority:

> All ruling powers, profane and religious, political and apolitical, may be considered as variations of, or approximations to, certain pure types. These types are constructed by searching for the basis of *legitimacy*, which the ruling power claims. Our modern 'associations' are of the type of 'legal' authority. . . . The past has known other bases for authority, bases which, incidentally, extend as survivals into the present . . . 'charismatic authority' [and] 'traditional authority'.
>
> (Gerth and Mills 2007: 294–6)

In the modern form of legal-rational authority, 'the legitimacy of the power-holder to give commands rests upon rules that are rationally established by enactment, by agreement, or by imposition' (Gerth and Mills 2007: 294). This rests in turn on a constitution. Orders are based on these impersonal rules, not on the authority of the person giving the orders as a person. A hierarchical organisation of officials who wield power and the separation of public and private spheres go along with this form of authority. The other two 'types' of authority are different. The first of these, charismatic authority, is a form of rule to which those who obey submit because of 'their belief in the extraordinary quality of a specific person' (Gerth and Mills 2007: 295). Charismatic authority is legitimised through heroic feats, victories, miracles and the like, and disappears if these magical powers appear to vanish. The second, traditional authority, is based upon a belief in 'what actually, allegedly, or presumably has always existed' (Gerth and Mills 2007: 296). The most familiar types of traditional authority are the rule of father or husband over the household, the lord or master over the serf, the prince over officials, nobles and vassals, and the sovereign prince over subjects. In particular historical situations, these last two forms of authority exist alongside each other, and both remain significant, even under legal-rational systems of authority.

For more on Max Weber, in particular his ideas about the state, see **Chapter 9**.

What is important here is that we have an analysis that sees power or authority as possessed by a specific and identifiable few in any society who can command the obedience of others. They are obeyed because their authority or power to command is deemed legitimate – because of either its legal-rational, charismatic or traditional basis.

For Emile Durkheim, the social realm is not just a collection of individuals, but something more, something unique and quite distinct: 'Society is a reality *sui generis*; it has its own characteristics' (Durkheim 1995: 15). This leads to certain implications:

> Precisely because society has its own specific nature that is different from our nature as individuals, it pursues ends that are also specifically its own; but because it can achieve those ends only by working through us, it categorically demands our cooperation. Society requires us to make ourselves its servants . . . It subjects us to all sorts of restraints, privations and sacrifices without which social life would be impossible. And so, at every instant, we must submit to rules of action and thought that we have neither made nor wanted and that sometimes are contrary to our inclinations and our most basic instincts.
> (Durkheim 1995: 209)

We obey these rules, not just because of any superior physical force that compels us to do so, says Durkheim, but because of the moral authority that society has: 'we defer to society's orders not simply because it is equipped to overcome our resistance but, first and foremost, because it is the object of genuine respect' (Durkheim 1995: 209). Indeed 'a society is to its members what a god is to its faithful' (Durkheim 1995: 208). In ordinary circumstances, the weight of the general view or shared convictions has enormous force; when people come together in a large gathering this is amplified and things happen and emotions are aroused that each person as an individual would be incapable of, and that all look back on afterwards with surprise (Durkheim 1995: 212). In revolutionary periods it is because of such heightened interaction and what it generates that 'people live differently and more intensely than in normal times' (Durkheim 1995: 213). We depend on society in the way that we might depend on a religious figure, and we do what society expects us to because of that dependence.

So far, then, we have looked at the way two leading figures in the new discipline of sociology – located specifically in the turn to secularism in Europe – thought about questions of power, authority and obedience. There is one further response to these questions that I want to examine, before we turn to what some of the broader questions these responses lead to might be. I want to examine the thought of Thomas Hobbes (1588–1679). His work was not part of the nineteenth-century movement towards a social science at all; he was a seventeenth-century political philosopher, concerned to rethink forms of authority in the absence of a divinity. Living in England at the time of the English Civil War, one of Hobbes' priorities was to find some arguments for stability and peace, rather than the chaos and instability into which the country had sunk. The Civil War had lasted from 1642 to 1651 and the questions at stake concerned whether the monarch should rule alone by divine right or only with the consent and under the authority of parliament – or, indeed, whether parliament could rule without a sovereign.

BOX 6.2 THE REFORMATION IN EUROPE

The Reformation is located in what historians call the 'early-modern' period in Europe, which runs from the late fifteenth to the early eighteenth century (MacCulloch 2004). It took place in Western Christendom – an area 'almost equivalent to what would become "Europe"' (Collinson 2003: 1). According to *The Cambridge Modern History*, written in 1903,

> the Reformation of the sixteenth century had its birth and growth in a union of spiritual and secular forces such as the world has seldom seen at any other period of its history. On the secular side, the times were full of new movements, intellectual and moral, political, social, and economic; and spiritual forces were everywhere at work, which aimed at making religion the birthright and possession of the common man – whether king, noble, burgher, artisan, or peasant – as well as of the ecclesiastic, a possession which should directly promote a worthy life within the family and the State. These religious impulses had all a peculiar democratic element and were able to impregnate with passion and, for a time, to fuse together the secular forces of the period. Hence their importance historically.
>
> (Ward *et al.* 1903)

One of the best-known figures is Martin Luther, born on 10 November 1483 at Eisleben. His Ninety-Five Theses, nailed to the door of the Castle Church at Wittenberg at noon on All Saint's Day, 1 November 1517, were a forthright critique of the practice of the Sale of Indulgences – for the forgiveness of sins – by the Catholic Church. His case was not just that this had become a corrupt practice, but that the Church could not in this way stand between the believer and their God. Forgiveness came from God alone, and could not be bought or sold.

On the one hand, the authority of the Pope as head of the Catholic Church had been challenged. In England the Reformation set in train a series of struggles that led eventually to the developing view that religion should be regarded as a private affair, a matter for individual conscience, not an affair of state: different religious practices could be tolerated within one political community. The modern sovereign individual, conceived of as a separate, self-contained and self-accountable entity, was emerging. On the other hand, the authority of the monarch or sovereign was still seen as coming from God, and how this could be otherwise was yet to be thought through. Hobbes' contribution to the debates of his time did not please the royalists: he argued for a strong central authority, sovereign or commonwealth, to avoid the chaos of a war 'of every man against every man' (Hobbes 1651), but sovereign power or sovereignty – the supreme authority of the sovereign – came not from the divine right of kings but from the people, who, as sovereign individuals combining together, entered into a social contract to ensure their peace and security. In other words, sovereignty for Hobbes came not from above but from below, not from outside this world but from within it.

According to Hobbes, when individuals combine and enter into a social contract, their individual power or authority is added together to form a power greater than any of them (Hindess 1996: 24). He calls this the Leviathan: a giant man, made up of the bodies of small individual men and carrying a sceptre and a sword, as the famous illustration on his title page shows. This quantitative view of power – as something that can be added up – forms the basis of many understandings of power in social and political life. Power is seen as something that 'determines the capacity of actors to realize their will or to secure their interests' (Hindess 1996: 26). Alongside the capacity to act is the right to act: the question of the perceived *legitimacy* of the one who possesses power to exercise it. This, of course, as we have seen, was the question that exercised Weber.

FIGURE 6.8
Title page from Thomas Hobbes' *Leviathan* (1651).
http://cache.eb.com/eb/image?id=99235&rendTypeId=4

BROADER ISSUES
THINKING ABOUT POWER

To think of power in this simple, quantitative way, as some mysterious entity or substance that we can't see but that can be possessed and exercised, and which means that someone gets to do what they want to do, doesn't really help us very much. We can talk about how much power a particular person (or state) *has*, but when someone we think of as powerful – as *having* lots of power – doesn't get to do what they want, then we simply admit that maybe they had less power than we thought. In other words, this conception of power leads to some very circular arguments. People with power can do things, so we can tell who is powerful by looking at what people do. Those who look as though they do pretty much what they want we describe as powerful.

There seems to be no way of telling in advance, however, who will turn out to have been the most 'powerful' in any particular situation. Nor, indeed, is there any obvious way of knowing for certain who *has* got what they wanted: people are too complicated in terms of motivations and desires for that. And people tend not to behave all the time as the sovereign individuals they are deemed to be in modern liberal economic and political theory in any case: they may be more concerned to do what they think others want them to do than to satisfy their own wishes and desires.

This argument that people might be more complex than is allowed in this notion of the sovereign individual is also explored in **Chapter 10**.

A different way of thinking about questions of power, authority and obedience is found in the work of French political thinker Michel Foucault. He poses a basic challenge to the ways of thinking about power that we have encountered so far, ways of thinking that see a clear dividing line between those that have power or authority and those that obey, and thus see power as fundamentally repressive. In the thinking we have examined, power in someone else's hands is something that prevents us from doing what we want to do. Foucault finds this way of thinking curious:

> In defining the effects of power as repression, one adopts a purely juridical conception of power, one identifies power with a law that says no, power is taken above all as carrying the force of a prohibition. Now I believe that this is a wholly negative, narrow, skeletal conception of power, one which has been curiously widespread. If power were never anything but repressive, if it never did anything but to say no, do you really think one would be brought to obey it? What makes power hold good, what makes it accepted, is simply the fact that it doesn't only weigh on us as a force which says no, but that it traverses and produces things, it induces pleasure, forms of knowledge, produces discourse. It needs to be considered as a productive network which runs through the whole social body, much more than a negative instance whose function is repression.
>
> (Foucault 1980: 119)

In fact, Foucault argues, it is best not to talk of 'power' at all, but of 'power relations'. In all social interaction, relations of power are involved. When two people talk over coffee, when a group meets for a lecture in a university setting, when we take a walk along the beach or when we chat over the internet, in all these social relations, relations of power are involved. In some cases it might seem that power relations are all one way – for example that your lecturer gets to do what he or she wants, despite disruptive students such as those shown in the cartoon at the start of this chapter. And some people these days, influenced by Foucault's work in some way but not fully taking on board what he meant, talk continually of 'power relations' as if that meant the relations that people who 'have' power can exert over those that don't. In the student–supervisor relationship, when they say there are 'power relations' involved, in a dark tone of voice, these people tend to mean that one side is more power-ful than the other. That is not what Foucault meant.

Foucault wanted to draw our attention to the way in which in any social relations there is a tension or a negotiation going on which traverses what is happening. Power, for Foucault, means nothing unless there is resistance. And in all social relations or interactions there are interactions of power and resistance. I will suggest a walk on the beach, perhaps, and when we get there, you might suggest which way we should go. Although you might have preferred a climb up the hillside to the beach in the first place, or I might have wanted to walk inland whereas you fancied taking a walk round the headland, we agreed on what to do and we did it. If we went our separate ways instead, we would no longer have enjoyed each other's company – which, presumably, we both wanted to do. There is clearly difference and deference – distinctions of age or gender, familiarity with the terrain, willingness to be led or to lead – which will come into play. And the interaction as we take our walk on the beach will reinforce or perhaps dislodge those differences. In other words, when we get back to the car, things will have changed: we won't be quite the people we were when we set out. Our relationship may be different; we may be different. This, I think, is something of what Foucault means when he says that power is a productive network that runs through all interaction, which 'traverses and produces things', 'induces pleasure, forms of knowledge, produces discourse' – and by 'discourse' he doesn't just mean the conversation we enjoyed on our walk.

What has all this talk of walks on the beach to do with the serious business of politics, authority and obedience? The point I think is that we can take this talk too seriously – by which I mean we can believe too much in the fiction of an authority that we have to obey. It is useful to have such a fiction; as we have said before, it simplifies daily life. It also gives us something to believe in – some power above ourselves, something that will survive us, or that in the meantime, enables us to make sense of our lives. If we follow Foucault's suggestion and cut off the king's head, then there are other ways of thinking about politics.

Of course, in the English Civil War the King's head was literally cut off. What Foucault means here is somewhat different. He means that we should stop thinking in terms of some larger legitimate central authority or source of rules, which we just then have to work out how to obey. We need instead to rethink politics without the sovereign. To return to our walk – maybe our walk on the beach was not particularly significant in the grand scheme of things, but what of one man's walk along Chang'an Avenue in Beijing, or the walk thousands took to the checkpoint at Bornholmer Strasse? These were in many senses just walks too, with similar debates about whether to go, when to go, where to go and so on: in all these instances, what we are looking at is forms of social interrelations. Maybe the notion of power relations that Foucault is asking us to consider is more help here than notions of centralised, validated authority. Maybe that authority is constituted through numerous interactions and power relations. Maybe it doesn't have some sort of independent, separate existence before those interactions. Certainly, as we have seen, it is vulnerable to challenge by individuals or groups who are not what we could call 'powerful'.

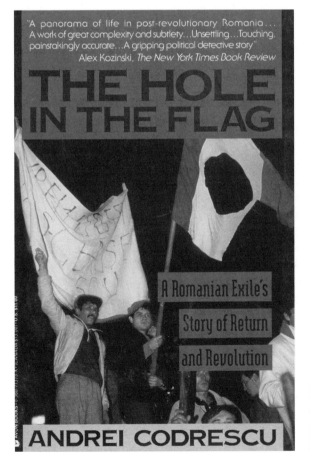

FIGURE 6.9
The hole in the Romanian Flag, 1989. Source: Andrei Codrescu, *The Hole in the Flag: A Romanian Exile's Story of Return and Revolution* (Avon Books, a division of the Hearst Corporation,1991). Cover photo: Gamma Liaison, published by arrangement with the author

Slavoj Žižek writes in 1993: 'The most sublime image that emerged in the political upheavals of the last years . . . was undoubtedly the unique picture from the violent overthrow of Ceausescu in Romania [in December 1989]: the rebels waving the national flag with the red star, the Communist symbol, cut out, so that instead of the symbol standing for the organising principle of the national life, there was nothing but a hole in its center' (1993: 1). The communist authorities had been overthrown, but nothing had yet been put in place instead. Where there is no organising principle, nothing to tell us to obey, this makes a certain lack or gap in the social order visible. Žižek argues that the social order is always incomplete in this way, but that this incompleteness is generally hidden from sight by the symbol that we put at the centre of things (God, communism, the sovereign, the nation, the people). We think we are obeying an authority of some sort, one that has the force to make us comply, but what we are following is a symbol – and we need a symbol like this to conceal the emptiness, the meaninglessness, at the heart of social life.

Foucault complains that we still think of politics in terms of centralised power and the legitimation of particular forms of authority. We need, he says, to cut off the king's head – and here he means the head of the Leviathan as well. Foucauldian conceptions of power point to the need to 'think about politics in the absence of its defining constitutive fiction' (Hindess 1996: 158). This fiction is not just sovereignty, but the notion of political community – or 'society' in the Durkheimian sense.

When the revolutionaries of Eastern Europe cut the communist symbol from the centre of the flag, they did not just cut out sovereign power – the communist rule that had been overthrown – they highlighted the notion of what Žižek calls 'tarrying with the negative': the possibility of not replacing that sovereign with anything at all, not even with what we call, vaguely, 'political community', but rather 'tarrying with', or remaining in, a state of the absence of rule. Is there not perhaps always a certain 'absence' or 'incompleteness' to any social order or form of authority? Is it not always in some sense little more than a fiction?

Taking this sort of approach would lead us to think of *relations* as what we should be studying – relations of *power* in the Foucauldian sense among them, of course – and how those relations produce the entities at their nodal points as well as the hub (community, society, etc.) that the relations appear to centre around. Note that we do not need to say *social* relations, or limit ourselves to relations between *people*. In his approach to Actor-Network-Theory, Bruno Latour is interested in exploring the role of things in the interrelationships that he studies. Things – materialities – he says, should be seen as part of the collectives we study – 'collective' being the word he chooses to replace the word 'society' (Latour 2005: 25). Think of the role of the Berlin Wall in the example we discussed in this chapter: do materialities like these not form a vital part of the relations we want to think about?

The fence between Mexico and the US discussed in **Chapter 8** might be a similar example.

In their study of Paris, Latour and the photographer Emilie Hermant explore the networks of interactions that produce the city of Paris – the work of individuals and agencies that designate the streets with the names that then appear on the maps that visitors use to make their way around the city and on the walls of the buildings that line those streets, for example, or the way that the fabric of the city is continually built and rebuilt, and its changes and famous inhabitants charted in wall plaques and signs, by a network of engineers, surveyors and stonemasons (Latour and Hermant 1998). The body of the city, like a human body, 'resembles', according to Latour, 'a jet of water that maintains its shape through the swift movement of countless tiny drops, each adding its minute contribution to the slightly trembling form' (Latour and Hermant 1998: Plan 52). Both the body and the built fabric of the city can be re-built, stone by stone or cell by cell, and can remain the same and yet different. Stop the movement and there is nothing: 'a gurgling at the bottom of a greenish basin; a corpse; a crumbling ruin' (Latour and Hermant 1998: Plan 52). Latour argues that political bodies like the French state or the municipal council of Paris are similar, and neither more nor less durable.

At the end of their study, they return to the question of power. They argue that the networks that frame life occupy only a tiny space: 'The word "power" changes meaning. It no longer denotes states of unquestionable things . . . There is indeed power; that is, force, virtualities, empowerment, a dispersed plasma just waiting to take shape . . . Yes, the power is invisible, but like the virtual, like the plasma, like the perpetual transformations' of buildings and bodies (Latour and Hermant 1998: Plan 53). The power of the sovereign or the king or the state is no more fixed than is a human body or a building: like these, it is always in the process of transformation, always being re-built. Relations of power and their intricate movements are what matter, in other words, not the power-ful and the power-less.

CONCLUSION

We have taken a journey in this chapter, a walk even, beginning with the question of why we obey, how we might think about what makes forms of power and authority in 'society' work, and what it might mean to disobey. We examined moments when it seemed that the authority of well-established and repressive systems of government might be being challenged – in one case the challenge seemed to fail, whereas in the other it seemed, for a moment at least, to succeed. We have not of course examined what happened next in East Germany or the rest of what was the Eastern European communist bloc. Some commentators might argue that the hope for new possibilities – talk of a 'third way' between communism and capitalism, for example, was widespread in 1989 – did not materialise. After all, the former communist states became in short order obedient parts of the capitalist world. And, finally, we explored some other ways of thinking about the workings of relations – through notions of power relations and networks – in what we used to call social life.

FURTHER READING

Foucault, Michel (2000) 'The Subject and Power', in *Essential Works of Foucault 1954–1984*, ed. Paul Rabinow, New York: The New Press.
  This short piece by Foucault, which first appeared in 1982, gives a good account of how he sees his work on power, including why we should study the 'subject' and how one should analyse power relations.

Hindess, Barry (1996) *Discourses of Power: From Hobbes to Foucault*, Oxford: Blackwell.
  Useful discussion of power that distinguishes power as capacity and power as right, and contains chapters on notions of power in critical theory and John Locke, as well as Hobbes and Foucault.

Latour, Bruno (2005) *Reassembling the Social: An Introduction to Actor-Network-Theory*, Oxford: Oxford University Press.
  Elaborates on Actor-Network-Theory and how it differs from other approaches to sociology; the website 'Paris: Invisible city' (listed below) does the same job in a different format.

Weber, Max (1930) *The Protestant Ethic and the Spirit of Capitalism*, trans. T. Parsons, London: Unwin.
  A fascinating and classic account of the relation between the particular rationalism underlying industrial capitalism in the West and the ethics of certain Protestant sects.

WEBSITES

The Berlin Wall/Berliner Mauer 1961–1989, Senate Chancellery, Governing Mayor of Berlin, http://www.berlin.de/mauer/oeffnung/index.en.html.
  Gives full details, with maps, of remaining sections of the wall, memorial sites and former border crossing points, as well as a section on the opening and fall of the wall.

Chronik der Mauer (in German), Bundeszentrale für politische Bildung, Deutschlandradio and Zentrum für zeithistorische Forschung Potsdam e.V., http://www.chronik-der-mauer.de/index.php.
  Gives a day-by-day account of events with links to video clips and broadcasts.

Lutteroth, Jule (2004) 'Wir kommen jetzt öfter', 9 November, Spiegel Online, http://www.spiegel.de/panorama/zeitgeschichte/0,1518,326184,00.html.
  An article about the events of the night of 9 November 1988 that has links to photographs taken at the time.

Foucault on Bachelard (in French), http://www.youtube.com/watch?v=kAwWwQZ_3FQ.
  A gem of a clip (two minutes) of Foucault talking about the problem of obediently following prescribed reading lists or sticking to canonical texts.

Latour, Bruno and Emilie Hermant (1998) *Paris: Invisible City*, available online at http://www.bruno-latour.fr/virtual/EN/index.html.

In this online essay, Latour introduces Actor-Network-Theory (ANT) through a study of 'Paris' accompanied by Hermant's photographs.

Thomas, Antony (2006) *Tiananmen Square: The Tank Man*, Cutting Edge Documentary, 90 mins. PBS Frontline, 11 April 2006, http://www.pbs.org/wgbh/pages/frontline/tankman/ or at http://video.google.com/videoplay?docid=472778793 0108202470

Documentary about the man who stood in front of the tank, and the surrounding events during the Tiananmen Square protests in 1989 and since.

REFERENCES

Asad, Talal (1993) *Genealogies of Religion: Discipline and Reasons of Power in Christianity and Islam*, Baltimore, MD: Johns Hopkins University Press.

Bauman, Zygmunt (1991) *Modernity and the Holocaust*, Ithaca, NY: Cornell University Press.

Chronik der Mauer (undated a), http://www.chronik-der-mauer.de/index.php/de/Media/VideoPopup/day/9/field/audio_video/id/14521/month/November/oldAction/Detail/oldModule/Chronical/year/1989.

Chronik der Mauer (undated b), http://www.chronik-der-mauer.de/index.php/de/Media/VideoPopup/day/9/field/audio_video/id/14524/month/November/oldAction/Detail/oldModule/Chronical/year/1989.

Chronik der Mauer (undated c), http://www.chronik-der-mauer.de/index.php/de/Media/VideoPopup/day/9/field/audio_video/id/14538/month/November/oldAction/Detail/oldModule/Chronical/year/1989.

Collinson, Patrick (2003) *The Reformation*, London: Weidenfeld and Nicolson.

Dunn, John (1989) *Modern Revolutions: An Introduction to the Analysis of a Political Phenomenon*, 2nd edn, Cambridge: Cambridge University Press.

Durkheim, Emile (1995) *The Elementary Forms of the Religious Life*, trans. K.E. Fields, New York: The Free Press.

Foucault, Michel (1980) 'Truth and Power', in *Power/Knowledge: Selected Interviews and Other Writings 1972–1977 by Michel Foucault*, ed. Colin Gordon, Brighton: Harvester; also published as Michel Foucault (2000) 'Truth and Power', *Essential Works of Foucault 1954–1984*, ed. P. Rabinow, New York: The New Press.

Gerth, H.H. and C. Wright Mills (2007) *From Max Weber: Essays in Sociology*, London: Routledge.

Gurr, Ted R. (1970) *Why Men Rebel*, Princeton, NJ: Princeton University Press.

Hilton, Christopher (2001) *The Wall: The People's Story*, Stroud: Sutton Publishing.

Hindess, Barry (1996) *Discourses of Power: From Hobbes to Foucault*, Oxford: Blackwell.

Hobbes, Thomas (1651) *Leviathan*, available in several editions and online at, for example, http://oregonstate.edu/instruct/phl302/texts/hobbes/leviathan-contents.html.

Lanzmann, Claude (1995) *Shoah: The Complete Text of the Acclaimed Holocaust Film*, New York: Da Capo Press.

Latour, Bruno (2005) *Reassembling the Social: An Introduction to Actor-Network-Theory*, Oxford: Oxford University Press.

Latour, Bruno and Emilie Hermant (1998) *Paris: Invisible City*, http://www.bruno-latour.fr/virtual/EN/index.html.

MacCulloch, Diarmaid (2004) *Reformation: Europe's House Divided 1490–1700*, London: Penguin.

Mavelli, Luca (2008) 'Beyond Secularism: Immanence and Transcendence in the Political Thought of William E. Connolly', in Alan Finlayson and Samuel Chambers (eds) *Becoming Plural: The Political Thought of William E. Connolly*, London: Routledge.

Mommsen, Wolfgang J. (1990) *Max Weber and German Politics 1890–1920*, trans. M.S. Steinberg, Chicago, IL: University of Chicago Press.

Prins, Gwyn (ed.) (1990) *Spring in Winter: The 1989 Revolutions*, Manchester: Manchester University Press.

Ramos, Andreas (1994–2008) *A Personal Account of The Fall of the Berlin Wall: The 11th and 12th of November, 1989*, http://www.andreas.com/berlin.html.

Skocpol, Theda (1979) *States and Social Revolutions: A Comparative Study of France, Russia and China*, Cambridge: Cambridge University Press.

Thomas, Antony (2006) *Tiananmen Square: The Tank Man*, Cutting Edge Documentary, 90 mins, PBS Frontline, 11 April 2006, http://www.pbs.org/wgbh/pages/frontline/tankman/.

Tilly, Charles (1993) *European Revolutions 1492–1992*, Oxford: Blackwell.

Ward, A. W., G. W. Prothero and Stanley Leathes (1903) *The Cambridge Modern History, Vol. 2*, Cambridge: Cambridge University Press, http://www.questia.com/reader/.

Weber, Max (1930) *The Protestant Ethic and the Spirit of Capitalism*, trans. T. Parsons, London: Unwin.

Žižek, Slavoj (1993) *Tarrying with the Negative: Kant, Hegel and the Critique of Ideology*, Durham, NC: Duke University Press.

CHAPTER 7

How do we find out what's going on in the world?

Debbie Lisle

- ■ *The question*
  THE MEDIATION OF INFORMATION

- ■ *Illustrative example*
  MEDIA BIAS: REPRESENTATIONS OF WAR

- ■ *Responses*
  FREEDOM VS CONTROL: THE MEDIA AND POWER

- ■ *Broader issues*
  HOW TO READ THE MEDIA

- ■ **CONCLUSION**

THE QUESTION
THE MEDIATION OF INFORMATION

All of our questions about global politics – about war, famine, migration, protest, violence – assume that we *already know* something about world events. Too often, discussions and debates about global politics assume that we are all-knowing and God-like creatures – swirling around the heavens and looking down on all sorts of fascinating activities. Much as we would like such omniscient powers, the reality is that we are all stuck here on earth, each of us rooted to a particular time and place, and each of us armed only with specific and partial knowledge about the world. Moreover, nobody has first-hand access to activities going on outside their specific and immediate context. That information must be gathered, constructed and sent to us through various forms of technology (for

Of course, we may think we have exclusive knowledge that we should convey to others. **See Chapter 15**

example television, the internet, the radio, mobile phones), and we must have the appropriate equipment and skills to receive and understand this information. This chapter explores this process of communication by looking at how information about global politics is gathered, constructed, represented, disseminated and interpreted. In short, it looks at what happens to information as it moves through the media.

Some form of media – some technology of representation – is necessary in any form of communication. As Neil Postman argues, we couldn't know anything in the world without different forms of media to convey information:

> The information, the content, or, if you will, the 'stuff' that makes up 'the news of the day' did not exist – could not exist – in a world that lacked the media to give it expression. I do not mean things like fires, wars, murders and love affairs did not, ever and always, happen in places all over the world. I mean that lacking a technology to advertise them, people could not attend to them, could not include them, in their daily business.
>
> (Postman 1987: 7–8)

What happens when we apply Postman's argument to the study of global politics? We see that the objects, issues and events we usually study (for example, wars, revolutions, invasions, treaties) do not even exist without the media – without the technologies of communication – to express them. So while it is certainly important to study objects, issues and events in global politics – the 'stuff' that makes up 'the news of the day' – it is also important to study the process by which we receive information about such objects, issues and events. Indeed, most of us do not form our opinions about global politics by going directly to Baghdad, or Kabul, or the Pentagon (the US Department of Defense). But we do form our opinions based on what we receive about these places from the media. But even those people who do travel directly to war zones – diplomats, soldiers, journalists, experts – form their opinions and create solutions based on information they receive from the media. Another way to say this is that all objects, issues and events in global politics are mediated. That is, we know about them, and formulate our opinions on them, by consuming media representations. Surely, then, it is important to explore how our opinions about global politics – about whether it was right to intervene in Iraq, about whether human rights should be universal, about the extent of American dominance – are shaped and influenced by the media.

Of course global politics is about many things as well as these, as the various chapters in this book show.

It is important to study the media because the information we get from it is never neutral or innocent: it is always – and I mean *always* – biased. Whenever we talk about bias, we mean that a media product 'leans towards a particular view of a given issue' (Burton 1997: 226). This notion runs counter to our usual understanding that the media – especially the news media – is there to deliver the

BOX 7.1 NEIL POSTMAN

Postman was one of the pioneers of media and communication studies, and wrote a very important book entitled *Amusing Ourselves To Death* (1987). He was interested in how television, as a specific technology of communication, shapes the information we receive. Postman argues that American television privileges image over content, and therefore feeds the audience 'dumbed-down' entertainment rather than rational political argument. As an example, Postman offers the following:

> it is implausible to imagine that anyone like our twenty-seventh President, the multi-chinned, three-hundred pound William Howard Taft, could be put forward as a presidential candidate in today's world. The shape of a man's body is largely irrelevant to the shape of his ideas when he is addressing a public in writing or on the radio, or, for that matter, in smoke signals. But it is quite relevant on television. The grossness of a three-hundred-pound image, even a talking one, would overwhelm any logical or spiritual subtleties conveyed by speech . . . You cannot do political philosophy on television. Its form works against the content.
>
> (Postman 1987: 7)

In short, a fat person – no matter how persuasive their views – would never be elected President because he or she would not look good on television. Postman's argument is that we have allowed television to set the agenda for political debate, and because television favours image-friendly sound-bites, we ignore many sane and viable political ideas that may not be easily conveyed through such an image-conscious medium. For Postman, the *form* that this information passes through (that is, television) is shaping the *content* of political debate (that is, it only allows those arguments that can be made quickly by beautiful people relying on images and sound-bites). He contrasts the current situation of television with nineteenth-century public meetings when large audiences regularly gathered to listen to political debates that lasted up to seven hours (Postman 1987: 45–50). Can you imagine that? *Seven* hours! Postman argues that television has shrunk our attention span so much that we can barely focus on political issues for seven minutes, let alone seven hours.

truth. My point is that bias in some form is built into all forms of communication and operates across all styles of media – from the most factual news programme to the most innocent children's cartoon. Indeed, *all* media representations come from somewhere, and try to advocate a particular agenda. The media never have access to some clear, unmediated truth that they can deliver to us unchanged and untainted. Every story the media tell, every image they construct, every sound bite they repeat is shaped in a way that advocates a pre-existing agenda – a dominant picture of the world that privileges some people and excludes others. Does this mean that the media is biased because journalists are lazy and doing their jobs badly? That if only they *searched harder* they would be able to break

We all have strong views on particular issues, which are inevitably partial or biased. This is because whenever we begin to think about the world we operate with already established pictures of the world that influence and shape our thinking, often without our realizing it.
See Chapter 2

through all this bias and find the truth in all its shining glory? No. This means that it is *impossible* for any journalist – even the best and most respected – to represent the world in an unbiased, neutral or objective manner. Bias is not something the media can escape from – there is no way to represent the world in a way that doesn't also advocate a particular – and necessarily biased – picture of the world.

The question of bias is important in the study of global politics because it reveals a very difficult and ambivalent relationship between the media and the government. In the UK, for example, the media are understood as the 'Fourth Estate' – they are the fourth most important political body after the clergy, the House of Lords and the House of Commons. But the media are different from all these other official institutions because they act as a kind of watchdog on the government, and are therefore seen to advocate the public interest. But the media's ability to act as a check and balance on the government is seriously tested during times of war. Often, the government puts pressure on the media to support its decision to go to war and help to mobilize public support in their readers, viewers and listeners. In other words, the government wants to discourage the watchdog tendencies of the media during times of war. Governments can do this by protecting and classifying information in the name of national security – in effect, they practise a form of official censorship. When the media fail to question such efforts by the government, a rather cosy three-way consensus is established between government policy, media stories and public opinion. In this mode, the media do not act as a 'watchdog', but rather as a mouthpiece for the government. It is as if the government is willing to tolerate the pesky watchdog antics of the media during the normal course of events, but when we go to war the media must get in line, stop asking difficult questions and act as a mouthpiece for the government's decision.

ILLUSTRATIVE EXAMPLE
MEDIA BIAS: REPRESENTATIONS OF WAR

To further examine the conflicted role of the media during war, let us study three modern conflicts and ask how the government tries to use the media as a mouthpiece to generate consensus, and how the media would rather act more like a watchdog.

The Vietnam War (1960–75)

This war was an important lesson for any government that seeks to control the media during times of war. The historical context of the war is important: it was

BOX 7.2 DON McCULLIN, WAR PHOTOGRAPHER

FIGURE 7.1
Portrait of a shell-
shocked marine,
Hue, Vietnam, 1968.
Photo: Don McCullin

Don McCullin started his photography career on the streets of North London, but became famous for covering conflicts in Cyprus, Beirut and Vietnam. This image of a shell-shocked US Marine was taken in Vietnam during the Battle for Hue City in 1968. Like many photographers, McCullin started out by wanting to get close to the action: 'I don't believe you can see what's beyond the edge unless you put your head over it; I've many times been right up to the precipice, not even a foot or an inch away. That's the only place to be if you're going to see and show what suffering really means' (Bannon and George Eastman House 2003: 677). But after years of covering war zones, McCullin became depressed about the morally ambiguous position of the war photographer: if you are a witness to such suffering, shouldn't you try and help instead of standing back and taking pictures? McCullin himself has done both – he has helped wounded soldiers, but he has also taken pictures when he could have intervened. This tricky position made McCullin seriously question the morality of his chosen profession and he spent much of the 1990s taking pictures of the tranquil Somerset landscape. Recently, however, he has turned his lens on wider social issues such as AIDS in Africa.

taking place at the same time as the mass media were developing with unprecedented speed in the Western world. Radio was still popular, but television quickly became the medium of choice; indeed, Vietnam is often referred to as the first television war. As well, this was the era when photojournalism flourished, and many photographers such as Tim Page, Larry Burrows and Don McCullin became famous when their picture essays were published in broadsheet newspapers and Sunday supplements.

What makes the Vietnam War significant is that journalists, photographers and cameramen had unprecedented access to the battlefield and covered all aspects of the war. While they started off in mouthpiece mode, writing stories that generally aligned with military policy, they became much more critical as the war dragged on. After 1968 the media shifted into watchdog mode and grew increasingly critical of American military action in the region (Hallin 1986: 3–12). As this shift in the media's position was taking place, audiences were confronted with increasingly graphic images of conflict every morning in their newspapers and every night on the evening news. These media stories were much different from the

Even though the 'patriotic newsreels' did not show this, World War II was extremely violent.
See Chapter 16

patriotic newsreels people remembered seeing at the cinema during World War II, and soon audiences began to turn against the war. One of the most famous images that galvanized anti-war sentiment across the world was taken by Nick Ut in 1972. It shows a young girl named Phan Thi Kim Phuc running down the street fleeing a Napalm attack. Her clothes have been burned off, and her face conveys both shock and terror.

It was images like this that prompted media theorist Marshall McLuhan to state that 'Television brought the brutality of the war into the comfort of the living room. Vietnam was lost in the living rooms of America – not on the battlefields of Vietnam' (1975). The shift in the media's position – from mouthpiece to watchdog – and the public's negative reaction to the images disseminated by the media taught the American government two valuable lessons: (1) never allow the media unrestricted access to the battlefield; and (2) always practise news management by controlling the stories that are given to the media and, by extension, to the public.

The Gulf War (1990–1)

By the time the Gulf War started in 1990, the American government had fully taken on board the lessons it had learned during the Vietnam War. It created a new body – the Department of Defense News Media Pool (DoDNMP) – that was put in place to effectively control and manage the media's access to the

FIGURE 7.2
Napalm attack.
Photo: Nick Ut, AP

battlefield. Structurally, this involved organizing reporters into official pools with military escorts, giving official news briefings about military operations, restricting the travel and movement of journalists and subjecting all copy written by journalists to a 'formal security review' (Tumber and Palmer 2004: 3). Unsurprisingly, this situation was very unpopular with the media, who argued that they could not do their jobs properly – as watchdogs – if they were not given direct access to the battlefield. As war correspondent P.J. O'Rourke explained at the time:

> You may wonder what the job of being a Gulf War journalist is like. Well, we spend all day broadcasting on the radio and TV telling people back home what's happening over here. And we learn what's happening over here by spending all day monitoring the radio and TV broadcasts from back home. You may also wonder how any actual information ever gets into this loop. If you find out, please call.
>
> (O'Rourke 1992: 196)

What is important to remember about the Gulf War is that despite these practices of news management, the overriding relationship between the media and the government was consensual. Either because the media were successfully managed – and even censored – by the military or because they agreed in principle with the military intervention, the media generally supported this war.

But it is also important to remember that the media–military relationship changed significantly in the Gulf War. If Vietnam was the first television war, then this was

---

BOX 7.3 THE CNN EFFECT

Piers Robinson defines the 'CNN effect' as 'the ability of real-time communications technology, via the news media, to provoke major responses from domestic audiences and political elites to both global and national events' (2002: 2). Certainly there are significant historical examples of media images provoking public and government action – Vietnam, for one – but also the images of the Ethiopian famine in 1984 that mobilized millions to donate money and put pressure on their governments to send aid (Philo 1993). After the Gulf War, however, the media seemed to have more power to determine foreign policy decisions. For example, Robinson argues that the infamous media images of a dead American marine being dragged through the streets of Mogadishu prompted President Clinton to immediately withdraw American troops from Somalia (2002: 46–63). The CNN effect continues to be debated by media analysts, military press officers and governments. There is disagreement over how the CNN effect can be measured, and many argue that the media only speed up foreign policy actions that were already in preparation.

the first information war, where, for the first time, news was broadcast 24/7 all around the globe. This meant that news was conveyed in real time on channels like CNN, and people could watch live footage of scud missiles being launched, bombs exploding and troops firing weapons. Journalists, reporters, military press officers, editors and news producers were forced to adapt to a drastically reduced news cycle in which they responded to 'live-feed' images without the usual context or background – and they did this around the clock. Such intense media saturation during the Gulf War increased the power of the media to determine how governments respond to international crises. Indeed, throughout the 1990s people identified the 'CNN effect', in which the military no longer works in a *pre-emptive* mode (that is, controlling and censoring reporters during war), but now works in a *reactive* mode where it is forced to respond – sometimes militarily – to issues raised by the media.

The Iraq War (2003)

At the time the decision to invade Iraq was taken, the world was still recovering from one of the biggest media events in history: the attack on the Twin Towers on September 11, 2001. The intense media scrutiny that surrounded this event carried over into the reporting of the subsequent invasions of Afghanistan and Iraq. Once again, the US military sought to re-establish its control over the media – this time by implementing a system of embedding more than 600 US and international reporters, who lived, worked and travelled with selected military units.

September 11, 2001 was followed by the 'war on terror', and the Iraq War is part of that.
See Chapters 2 and 19

Indeed, by offering 'a first-hand, up-close view of combat missions', the military used the strategy of embedding to get the media back 'on side' after the contentious relationship that had developed between the two during the 1990s (Pfau *et al.* 2004: 75). But the strategy of embedded journalism actually allowed the military to exercise a new and more subtle form of information management. For example, all embedded journalists had to sign a lengthy contract which restricted what they were allowed to report (for example nothing on future operations, no photographs of prisoners of war) and prevented them from carrying private mobile phones or satellite telephones, or travelling in their own vehicles (Tumber and Palmer 2004: 16). Such strategies of information control seriously compromised the media's ability to act as a watchdog. Each reporter effectively became a member of the military troop – they bonded with soldiers and often used 'we' in their stories – and were entirely dependent on the military for transport, food and security. As a result, even the most experienced journalist became, in effect, a propaganda tool for the government (McLane 2004: 82–3).

One of the things that distinguished the Iraq War from previous conflicts was the increasing use of internet news sources and blogs. For those fed up with the spin emanating from Western news agencies and looking for war coverage not compromised by embedded reporting or vetted by the Pentagon, it was possible to access news from independent media sites such as the Independent Media Centre (www.indymedia.org), or from Arab media sources such as Al Jazeera (http://English.aljazeera.net/News). Moreover, many people were taking control of this medium in an active way by posting ideas, images and commentary on web pages and blogs. Indeed, the Iraq War ushered in the era of the 'warblog', where established journalists (for example Arianna Huffington on www. Huffingtonpost.com/theblog), soldiers stationed in Iraq (for example 'My War: Killing Time in Iraq', at http://cbftw.blogspot.com) and concerned citizens offered personal interpretations and generated web-based discussion about the war. One of the most popular warblogs during the conflict – 'Where is Raed?' (http://dear_raed.blogspot.com/) – was run by Salam Pax, an ordinary Iraqi citizen who uploaded reports about daily life in a war zone. It was on these websites and warblogs that the information war charted a new course. This was where infamous images from the war – digital photographs of American soldiers torturing and humiliating Iraqis at the Abu Ghraib prison, video clips of Al-Qaeda beheading one of its kidnap victims and mobile phone shots of Saddam Hussein being hanged – were circulated and discussed. This is not to suggest that the internet is always truthful or accurate, but it is to recognize that during the Iraq War the internet became a crucial forum where ordinary people could access both official and alternative news sources, participate in online discussions about the war, and disseminate controversial links and images. As James Der Derian (2001) has argued, we can no longer understand the operation of modern war without examining its *virtual* character – how military organizations, diplomats and statesmen are making use of computer technology and virtual networks in order to better mobilize for combat.

For more on what happened at Abu Ghraib and how this became possible, see **Chapter 2**.

These examples of the changing media/military relationship during war are instructive, for they provide a powerful example of how information is transformed during the process of communication. Whether it is the government trying to control journalists' access to the battlefield, or reporters trying to reveal the military's less palatable actions to audiences back home, it is clear that nobody remains neutral in their efforts to use and abuse information during war. Winning 'hearts and minds' is a serious business, especially when people's lives are at stake. But the experience of war reporting is significant in a wider sense as well: it reveals a fundamental contradiction that underscores the role of the media in society. Are they able to act effectively as a watchdog on government? Or are they only ever beholden to power, and therefore consigned to the role of mouthpiece?

BOX 7.4 JAMES DER DERIAN'S MIMENET

James Der Derian argues that we can no longer think of society as a simple 'military-industrial complex' in which the government, business elites and the military run things in a cosy triad. Contemporary society must now be understood as a 'military-industrial-media-entertainment-network' – or MIMENET – in which technologies such as computer simulations have erased the line between the virtual world and the real world. He explains, for example, how Hollywood has joined forces with the military to produce computer-generated 'simulation-based training environments' in order to make combat *more real* for soldiers in training. Why practise killing 'fake' enemies when you can kill very realistic computer-generated ones? Such simulations are also shaping the thoroughly digitized battlefield as soldiers now rely on computer technologies to transform foreign territory into fully functional 3-D images that help them effectively track, expose and target their enemies. Der Derian is concerned with how all this computer technology effectively sanitizes the consequences of war: what happens when enemies are reduced to pixels on a screen – when war is effectively reduced to a video game? He argues that we are living in an age of *virtuous war* where violence is actualized and executed 'from a distance – *with no or minimal casualties*' (Der Derian 2001: xv). This distance radically changes the soldier's moral proximity to the enemy, who has now become thoroughly dehumanized and digitized. As Der Derian argues, 'virtuous war has an unsurpassed power to commute death, to keep it out of sight, out of mind. Herein lies its most morally dubious danger. In simulated preparations and virtual executions of war, there is a high risk that one learns how to kill but not to take responsibility for it' (Der Derian 2001: xvi).

RESPONSES
FREEDOM VS CONTROL: THE MEDIA AND POWER

It seems there is no way to resolve the contradictory position of the media in society: it will always be both watchdog and mouthpiece. At the heart of this debate is a fundamental disagreement over the extent to which the media can influence government actions – especially with respect to foreign policy. Those from the Pluralist tradition argue that the media are only ever there to serve the public interest and keep democratic values alive. In this sense, the media are always in watchdog mode, keeping an eye on the government and making sure it doesn't get out of control and neglect what the electorate want. Those from a more Marxist tradition argue that the media operate primarily as a mouthpiece for government interests. Because the media are beholden to those in power, they use its influence to persuade the masses that the government's decisions are the *right* decisions for everyone.

Pluralist perspective

The Pluralist position is really an acceptance of, and a belief in, the values and realities of liberal-democratic societies. In essence, Pluralists see the media as simply an extension of the public sphere in ancient Greece, where people went to receive information and debate the issues of the day. For pluralists, the media performs two crucial democratic tasks: (1) it informs the public and (2) it acts as a watchdog on those in power. What is interesting, of course, is that all governments, no matter what their ideological orientation, always accuse the media of exploiting their position as the fourth estate and filing deliberately biased reports against them. So, for example, while the Clinton Administration claimed to be fighting a right-wing bias in the media throughout the 1990s, Figure 7.3 illustrates the Bush Administration's current belief that the media has a left-wing bias against its policies in Iraq. For Pluralists, such balanced accusations demonstrate that the media are getting it right: they should *always* keep the government on their toes.

Along with the protection of free speech, the reduction of government interference in the media and an increase in people's access to information, Pluralists advocate the principle of consumer choice. For example, if a newspaper or news channel is too right-wing for you, then you can choose a more left-wing broadsheet or television station. Pluralists always emphasize the range of media products available to the consumer – from small circulation newspapers like *The Socialist Worker* to broadsheets like *The New York Times*. Pluralists accept that each different media outlet presents a partial and slanted view of the world, but it is the consumer who ultimately decides which partial view prevails and becomes

The Greek city-state or *polis* was one of the earliest forms of political unit in Europe. **See Chapter 9**

Bill Clinton was President of the United States from 1993 to 2001. Donald Rumsfeld's role in the US Administration is discussed in **Chapter 17**.

FIGURE 7.3
'Leftist media'. Cox & Forkum © 2004. In a town hall meeting with soldiers at Camp Buehring in Kuwait on 8 December 2004 Donald Rumsfeld said, 'You go to war with the army you have. They're not the army you might want or wish to have'. http://www.washingtonpost.com/wp-dyn/articles/A132-2004Dec14.html

accepted by the mainstream. In this approach, a basic symmetry exists between media outlets and their audiences. If a marginalized viewpoint is unpopular, it is squeezed out and becomes commercially unviable. As O'Sullivan *et al.* argue, such a variety of media outlets 'act as a barometer of changing tastes and preferences. Diverse audience interests are reflected in a diversity of media choice. If there is a demand, media corporations will respond' (O'Sullivan *et al.* 2003: 146). In this sense, Pluralism is founded on the notion of consensus: there is a consensus on the predominant social values in society, which is reflected in mainstream and popular media.

Marxist perspective

Those who approach the media from a Marxist perspective start from the assumption that we live in a hierarchical society where power is concentrated in the hands of only a few people at the top. This does not just mean those in government, but also those who control wealth (business leaders) and those who control information (media leaders). These elites make up the membership of the ruling class. The basic assumption of Marxist approaches is that the media will work to secure the interests of this ruling class. In effect, the media operate as a mouthpiece for elite power by *encouraging* the idea that the hierarchical structure of society is beneficial for everyone (including those at the bottom) and *discouraging* the idea that the ruling class benefits disproportionately from such a social structure. For Marxists, the ruling class uses the media as a tool of persuasion: they try and convince everyone that the hierarchical structure of society is serving *everyone's* interests, not just their own.

This does not mean that the media relinquish their role as the fourth estate. Indeed, a Marxist approach argues that the media are perfectly capable of attacking the occupants of political office; that is, whatever party and group of politicians happens to be in power at any particular time. However, this watchdog role is very limited. While the media *are* able to critique politicians, they are *not* able to critique the foundations and structures of political power itself. This is how the media works in tandem with elite power: it offers superficial critiques of particular parties and policies (for example, 'George Bush's foreign policy agenda is flawed'), but it never goes so far as to question the foundations of the system itself (for example, 'If we live in an egalitarian society, how come so many families still live in poverty?'). And this is why the hierarchical and unequal structure of the system – a structure which, remember, serves to protect the dominant position of the ruling class – continues to persist. Marxists argue that the media give the *impression* of being a check on governmental power and stimulating debate, but what it actually does is control and confine the terms of that debate so that the foundations of the system are never questioned. In effect, the media work to engineer consent from the public – they manage and control public

Media that promote different views arguably don't offer a simple choice as we are not necessarily aware of the 'picture' of the world which informs what we can see and think.
See Chapter 2

You'll come across Marx and his ideas in a number of chapters in this book: **Chapters 11, 12 and 13**, for example.

For a discussion of power and authority, see **Chapter 6**.

Chapter 13 looks at inequality within the United States.

debate so that the fundamental structure of society is not disrupted (Wheeler 1997: 19–26).

Given their view that the media are members of the ruling class, it is not surprising that Marxists are very concerned with questions of media ownership and influence. If the media are effectively a mouthpiece for elite power, any information that does not serve their ruling class values will be suppressed. This suppression can be active, direct and violent; for example, in totalitarian regimes press freedom is replaced by a system of propaganda. But, more often, the manipulation of information to serve ruling-class needs is more subtle and difficult to detect. We saw an example of this in the Gulf War when the close relationship between the media and the government resulted in a widely held consensus in which dissenting voices were silenced. Many Marxist scholars argue that the same kind of consensus is currently being established between the Bush Administration and powerful media conglomerates such as Rupert Murdoch's News Corporation. Indeed, Robert Greenwald's documentary *Outfoxed: Rupert Murdoch's War on Journalism* provides a compelling argument about how private media conglomerates like Murdoch's manipulate news content – especially about the 'war on terror' (www.outfoxed.org). When this kind of cosy relationship between elite groups is established, citizens are discouraged and actively prevented from asking difficult or subversive questions. Graphic artist Micah Wright's 'Propaganda Re-Mix Project' (http://homepage.mac.com/leperous/PhotoAlbum1.html) effectively illustrates how the American media is complicit with Bush's pro-war policies.

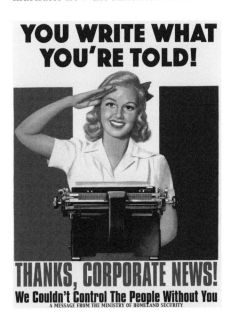

FIGURE 7.4
'You write what you're told'. Micah Wright poster from the Propaganda Re-Mix Project.
Poster © 2008 by Micah Wright, courtesy of AntiWarPosters.com

The power of the audience

One of the limitations of the Pluralism vs Marxism debate is that it doesn't pay enough attention to the power of the audience. Pluralists assume that audiences interpret media products according to the same dominant values of consensus, whereas Marxists believe that audiences are so pacified by cultural products that they are not able to identify how the media reproduce elite power. Cultural theorist Stuart Hall (1993) offers a compelling alternative to this debate in his encoding/decoding model.

BOX 7.5 STUART HALL

FIGURE 7.5
Stuart Hall.
Photo: Stuart Hall

Stuart Hall is one of the most prominent Cultural Studies theorists of our time. His work analyses how cultural and media products are part of a struggle between elites who want to secure their hegemonic (or dominant) position in society and those who want to stop them. The media, of course, are central to this struggle; indeed, this 'representational arena' is where the struggle for hegemony takes place. For example, the media bolster the elite's position when they construct 'moral panics', reproduce stereotypes and scapegoat non-mainstream identities, but they also challenge that elite position when they give voice to marginalized groups and individuals (Hall *et al.* 1978; Hall and Jefferson 1993). For Hall, much depends on the audience, who *may* read cultural and media products in a passive and uncritical manner or *may* actively construct alternative and oppositional meanings. While Hall's work, which draws on that of Italian Marxist Antonio Gramsci, is indebted to Marxism – indeed, he claims to always be 'within shouting distance of Marx' – he remains uncomfortable with how some Marxists privilege the category of class and neglect our complex identity negotiations of race, gender and sexuality. Much of his later work examines how these negotiations play themselves out in the 'circuit of culture' where representations are produced, disseminated and consumed (Hall 1997: 15–63; Du Gay *et al.* 1997). For example, newspaper representations of black British athletes reveal a much wider struggle over multiculturalism and national identity in Britain (Hall 1997: 223–34). When these athletes are winning races, newspapers emphasize their British qualities – but when they are losing races (or, worse, when they are failing drug tests), newspapers accentuate their identities as black men and women. Central to all of Hall's work is the idea that hegemonic elites intervene in the 'circuit of culture' to produce and stabilize dominant or consensus meanings. The job of any critical reader is to identify, analyse and resist those moments of domination by offering independent and critical readings.

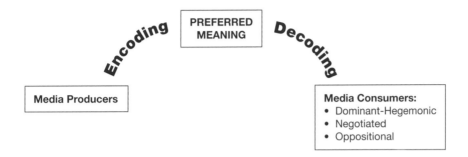

FIGURE 7.6
A simple formulation of Hall's model of encoding/decoding. Stuart Hall

Hall argues that any media message is made up of codes, or signs. During the process of communication, media producers arrange these codes so that they convey a preferred meaning, which is then sent through media channels and delivered to audiences. Hall makes two important moves here. First, he suggests that all media texts are *polysemic*; that is, each document – a television show, a photograph, a novel – contains a number of possible interpretations. What happens in the process of communication is that all these different interpretations are gathered up and squashed into a preferred meaning that serves dominant political agendas. Second, he suggests that there is no guarantee that the preferred meaning encoded into a media text by its producers will be read in the intended way by its consumers. Certainly many people will 'get the message', but many people will not – and some will deliberately refuse it. For Hall, this is because the audience can never be seen as a homogeneous group. When consuming the media, each audience member will take up a different position depending on their own context.

People who watch and read the media uncritically are in the Dominant-Hegemonic position: they decode and accept the preferred meaning because it accords with their own political values. People in this position do not question the motives or agendas behind a media product, but simply enjoy it as an innocent leisure practice. People who watch and read the media with some critical awareness are in the Negotiated position: that is, they accept the basic message of a programme or story, but they may differ or disagree on certain specific points. These critical moments can arise when the reader has more personal knowledge or experience than is being expressed. So, for example, you may read a newspaper story about why Britain is being 'swamped' by refugees and asylum seekers, and while you may agree that this is a growing political issue, you may disagree with the judgemental tone of the story. In this case, you may have written an essay on this subject for one of your classes, and you may have discovered a number of

You may in fact wonder why people cannot simply choose where they wish to live.
See Chapter 8

alternative reasons why refugees and asylum seekers are now a permanent feature in global politics. Hall argues that most audience members adopt this negotiated position with respect to the media. Finally, people who watch and read the media with a critical eye are in the Oppositional position: they understand perfectly well what the preferred meaning of the story is, but they deliberately reject it and draw on alternative values. This last position is important for Hall, for it suggests that audiences are not the passive and duped creatures that Marxist approaches would have us believe. Rather, audiences have the capacity to resist the preferred meanings in any media text, and therefore question any consensus that might develop between the media and the powers-that-be.

BROADER ISSUES
HOW TO READ THE MEDIA

To follow through on Hall's understanding of audience interpretation, let's analyse competing reactions to a popular media representation of war – Stephen Spielberg's *Saving Private Ryan* (1998). This film depicts the famous Allied D-Day landings in Northern France during World War II. It follows a group of soldiers who have been assigned a special task: to locate and retrieve a Private

FIGURE 7.7
Tom Hanks, Matt Damon and Ed Burns in *Saving Private Ryan* (1998), dir. Stephen Spielberg. Dreamworks SKG, Paramount Pictures and Amblin Entertainment. Ronald Grant Archive

Ryan, whose three brothers have been killed in action, and who is to be returned home to his mother. The preferred meaning of the film, encoded by Spielberg, is about the courage, bravery and heroism of ordinary American soldiers during World War II. Those who enacted a dominant-hegemonic reading of the film were swept away by Spielberg's narrative – not just the awesome and 'realistic' visuals of the opening D-Day landing scenes, but also by the touching moments of male camaraderie as a disparate group of soldiers banded together for a humanitarian mission. Viewers in this position were deeply moved not only by the graphic horrors of war, but also by the many sacrifices made by American soldiers in the name of freedom. As one veteran of the D-Day landings explained, 'Spielberg has given us what we used to call an optimistic tragedy. We come away sobered but feeling better about the strength of our democracy' (Metcalf 1999: 46). Those who enacted a negotiated reading were also moved by the narrative trajectory of the film, but were able to point out some inconsistencies in Spielberg's project. For example, the film makes it seem as if the Americans were the only forces involved in D-Day, and effaces the participation of British, Canadian and other European troops. Indeed, French viewers reacted badly to the 'Americentric' portrayal of war, especially the patriotic flag waving at the beginning and end of the film (Hedetoft 2000: 278–97). Those who enacted an oppositional reading of the film took issue with Spielberg's claim that the horrific and detailed opening landing sequence constituted an anti-war statement – the idea being that after seeing such horrors on screen nobody would ever support war again. As World War II veteran Howard Zinn explains, the film does nothing but glorify and romanticize the myth of combat: 'I disliked the film intensely, indeed, was angry at it. Because I did not want the suffering of men in war to be used, yes, exploited, in such a way as to revive what should be buried along with all those bodies in Arlington cemetery – the glory of military heroism' (Zinn 1998: 138). For critics like Zinn, the film was not in any way critical of the military establishment and, as a result, worked like all seductive Hollywood war films – as a recruitment tool for the military.

This example is particularly interesting because it demonstrates how two veterans of World War II – men who actually fought on the European battlefields – derived totally different meanings from the same film. This brings up the question of whether we *know* something better if we are there, experiencing an event first hand. But by the time both Metcalf and Zinn watched *Saving Private Ryan* in 1998, their 'first-hand' experience of World War II had been filtered, refracted and shaped by over fifty years of media and cinematic representations of that event. Indeed, these representations helped them transform the incoherent, traumatic and terrifying experiences of battle into a clear and concise narrative of 'what happened'. For Metcalf – and for many people who live in Allied countries, including Steven Spielberg – World War II was a heroic, noble and just battle against an evil enemy. Indeed, this is the *preferred meaning* of the film. But Zinn rejects this message and takes a more *oppositional* stance: no war – not even World

How we should remember wars is itself a significant question. See Chapter 16

War II – is ever worth the sacrifice and loss of innocent life, and all patriotic and uncritical commemorations of such events should be resisted. Here we have two radically different interpretations of World War II – there is not just disagreement over 'what happened', but also disagreement over the meaning of such an event, and how that meaning is conveyed in a film like *Saving Private Ryan*.

When we study the effect of the media, it is very tempting to think that the answer to such disagreements – indeed, the answer to any bias, misrepresentation or propaganda – is to actually go there and witness a key event in global politics for yourself, or to privilege accounts of people who were actually there and witnessed or participated in these events. But this is not a satisfying answer – not least because we can't all be budding journalists dashing around the world in order to encounter key events first hand. Rather, it is not a satisfying answer for two main reasons. First, when we tell stories about important historical events, those stories are directly shaped by the issues of *the present* rather than the past. Very simply, it is not some overarching, finally settled and uncontested notion of 'the truth' that dictates how we talk about the past – it is our *present* concerns and struggles that shape such discussions. In this sense, *Saving Private Ryan* is much more about conflict in the 1990s than it is about World War II: it encourages us to remember a 'good and just' war in order to *forget* the moral complexities of recent interventions (for example Kosovo, Somalia, Afghanistan, Iraq). Media representations such as *Saving Private Ryan* are absolutely crucial in shaping the past according to more contemporary concerns and agendas. Second, none of us – not World War II veterans, not journalists, not soldiers, not victims – can stand outside the media and claim that they don't affect our political judgements. We are, all of us, profoundly shaped by the information we receive in the media every day: there is no magic place outside their reach and influence where we can deliberate and come to the *right* conclusion in an unmediated sense. Rather, our own personal views on global political issues have been shaped by all the television news programmes, newspaper articles, movies, advertisements, photographs and stories we have seen, heard and read over the years. More importantly, major political decisions are also shaped by this condition of media saturation: foreign policy advisors, security consultants, Navy Seals and seasoned diplomats all formulate their decisions about an event, in part, from the media sources they watch, read, download and listen to. Now, such an intense form of media saturation wouldn't be a problem if the information delivered by the media was neutral – if it came to us untouched by producers, editors, comptrollers, focus groups, governments and advertisers. But as we know, all media information comes from somewhere, and is trying to advance someone's agenda. This is why Stuart Hall's insistence on critical reading strategies is so important. It is only by identifying the dominant agendas being encouraged by the media – especially in the area of global politics – that we can challenge those moments when dominant agendas masquerade as 'the truth' in order to squeeze out, exclude and silence more uncomfortable or unpalatable accounts of global events.

Is it a bad thing that all media information advances someone's agenda? Is it a bad thing if they pretend not to have an 'agenda'?

One of the difficulties of studying the media is an assumption that our responses to it are always rational, judicious and measured. This is, of course, seldom the case: we react to media representations instantaneously and emotionally. Think of the way avid sports fans watch their favourite teams compete live on television: they shout at their own players to do better (and they swear at the opposition for being terrible); they scream and whoop and jump and go crazy when victory is assured; they are outraged when 'unjust' refereeing decisions are awarded; and they sometimes weep with depression when their beloved team loses. It is almost as if they believe that if they shout loud enough at the television their favourite player will listen to their tactical suggestion (crafted carefully from the sofa), or the referee will reverse a penalty decision. This is not rational behaviour by any means. But it is one example of how *all* audience members – including you and me – become emotionally engaged in media representations. When media producers are trying to convince us of something – the *rightness* of a policy, the *hilarity* of a pratfall, the *guilt* of a prisoner, the *trauma* of a victim, the *joy* of a victory, the *pain* of a death – they don't do it by appealing to our rational natures. They do it by appealing to our emotions. And it works: we giggle, we scoff, we roll our eyes, we bury our head in our hands, we laugh out loud, we raise our eyebrows, we look away when it gets scary, we shout and cheer, and sometimes we cry.

This introduces a very important question: does the media facilitate a genuine expression of emotion? Or does it deliberately manipulate our emotions for political ends? Let's go back to the way *Saving Private Ryan* uses the past to reshape present anxieties about military intervention. I remember being entirely moved by this film the first time I saw it on its release in 1998. I was pinned to my seat for the initial D-Day landing scene, I fell half in love with the wise but tough Captain Miller (played by Tom Hanks), I hated the Germans – especially the traitorous prisoner of war – I was full of admiration for a military that wanted to protect Mrs Ryan's only remaining son, and I wept buckets at the film's rendering of heroic sacrifice. But I was very perplexed at this response: why was I so moved by this film? I wasn't alive during World War II, and I didn't personally know anyone who fought during that war. This was a different world from my own. And then I started thinking about how *Saving Private Ryan* related to the world I was living in – a decade in which violence was returning to the global stage with great force, but a decade in which the moral justifications for violence were, at best, hopelessly complex. In fact, my overblown emotional response was precisely what Spielberg ordered: his nostalgic commemoration created a 'comfortable surrogate' for the uncomfortable world I faced every day when I watched the television news or read the newspaper headlines (Kolker 2000: 257).

I was shocked, to say the least, at the way I had been so successfully manipulated by Spielberg's story. In every subsequent viewing, I discovered another layer to this deception: the rather obvious musical score, the cynically timed combat sequences punctuated by slower narrative elaboration, the faceless German

Can you think of a film you've seen recently that has appealed to you emotionally in these sorts of ways?

enemy, the stereotypical troop of 'characters' (that is, the wise-ass from the Bronx, the innocent rookie, the thoughtful doctor) and the unabashed patriotism of the American flag. Every time I watched it I got angrier at Spielberg's ability to manipulate the audience. And yet, despite all this 'rational' knowledge, I still could not help but be moved, somehow, by the larger themes of sacrifice, brotherhood and heroism. This contradiction frames all my media encounters with warfare. On the one hand, I am desperate to work out how such representations are manipulating me and trying to convince me of someone else's political agenda. But, on the other hand, I am moved when I see images depicting the consequences of war – when people's cities are destroyed, when their loved ones are killed and when their homelands implode in violence. Images such as these invoke empathy, compassion, anger and concern – not rational responses by any means, but incredibly powerful *emotional* responses.

My point is not to deny such emotional responses; indeed, these are precisely the kind of feelings that connect people across the world and inspire many common practices in global politics (for example aid packages, debt relief, humanitarian interventions). My point is simply that we must look carefully at how the media mobilizes both our reason *and* our passion in trying to put its point across. Too often, emotional appeals mask the dominant political agendas that are being served by the media. By all means, we must maintain the capacity to be moved by powerful media representations – to be inspired into debate, discussion and action. But we cannot exempt the media – as a political institution – from critical examination in this regard. We must call attention to those moments when the media deliberately manipulate our emotions in an effort to encourage a specific political position (for example, going to war).

CONCLUSION

There is, of course, an easy answer to the question 'How do we find out what's going on in the world?' Very simply, we ask questions. This is always the first step – be curious and take an active role in discovering the ins and outs of global politics. But this chapter has taken a further step by asking us to think about *where* we direct our questions, about the forum within which we discover, debate and discuss global politics. And this forum is undoubtedly the media in the broadest sense – television, radio, film, magazines, the internet, pod casts, advertising, etc. The main point of this chapter has been to demonstrate that the media do not constitute a neutral space; rather, they play an active role in shaping and influencing our opinions about global politics. The influential role of the media is nowhere more apparent than during times of war: indeed, there are many examples of the media acting as a mouthpiece for government during war, to the point of becoming a vehicle for propaganda. In this sense, we cannot leave it up to the media to provide a balanced view. We, as consumers of the media, need

The emotions set off by witnessing others' suffering raise questions: what can we do to stop people harming others? And what issues arise when we believe that we know what is good for them?
See Chapters 18 and 15

It might be worth asking where the questions we ask come from. Are they neutral, or do they come from who we think we are, and what we think is important, before we start asking questions?

to develop critical reading skills so we can identify when and how the media try to manipulate and shape our views about the world.

FURTHER READING

Lawrence Grossberg, Ellen Wartella and D. Charles Whitney (1998) *Mediamaking: Mass Media in a Popular Culture*, New York: Sage Publications, is the most comprehensive introduction to the complex relationship between the media and society in general. It develops a politically sophisticated account of the media, and provides good examples and illustrations of the main theoretical concepts.

John Fiske (1990) *Introduction to Communication Studies*, London: Routledge, and Dennis McQuail (2005) *McQuail's Mass Communication Theory*, London: Sage Publications, both give a more in-depth look at the theoretical framing of communication. They help to explain the complicated transfer of information from producers, through the media, to the consumer, and both books tackle the difficult question of how meaning is generated in this process.

Mark Wheeler (1997) *Politics and the Mass Media*, Oxford: Blackwell. Chapter 1 provides a good review of the main debates between Pluralist and Marxist approaches to the media.

Georgia Chondroleou's (2002) review article 'Studying the Media and Politics in Britain: A Tale of Two Literatures?', *British Journal of Politics and International Relations* 2, 2: 359–73, gives a fuller account of the main differences between Pluralist and Marxist approaches and their respective strengths and weaknesses.

Tim Allen and Jean Seaton (1999) *The Media of Conflict: War Reporting and Representations of Ethnic Violence*, London and New York: Zed Books and Susan Carruthers (2000) *The Media at War: Communication and Conflict in the Twentieth Century*, London: Palgrave, are good starting points that provide general accounts of the relationship between the media and war within the context of global politics. There are numerous books about the media's role in specific conflicts (for example Vietnam, Kosovo), and given the increasing importance of information during war, there will be many more books published in this area.

WEBSITES

Communication, Culture and Media Studies Infobase, http://www.cultsock.ndirect. co.uk/MUHome/cshtml.
Also known as 'Cultsock'.

Media Communication Studies site at the University of Aberystwyth, http://www. aber.ac.uk/media.
These two sites are the best of some very good websites that provide a comprehensive introduction to the theories, debates and methods of media studies.

Indymedia, http://www.indymedia.org.
> A collection of independent media resources.

Fairness and Accuracy in Reporting, http://www.fair.org/index.php.
> A media watch group.
> There are a variety of websites dedicated to independent media reporting, of which these two are among the best.

The War and Media Network, http://www.warandmedia.org.

The Global Media Project at the Watson Institute for International Studies at Brown University, http://watsoninstitute.org/globalmedia.
> Interdisciplinary research into the role of the media during war is developing rapidly, and these two websites in particular help to navigate, foster and promote this work.

The Iraq War Archive, http://www.iraqwararchive.org.
> More specifically, a useful website about media coverage of the Iraq War.

OTHER RESOURCES

Outfoxed: Rupert Murdoch's War on Journalism, Documentary by Robert Greenwald (www.outfoxed.org).

REFERENCES

Bannon, Anthony and George Eastman House (2003) *1000 Photo Icons*, Cologne: Taschen.

Burton, Graeme (1997) *More than Meets the Eye: An Introduction to Media Studies*, 2nd edn, London: Arnold.

Der Derian, James (2001) *Virtuous War: Mapping the Military-Industrial-Media-Entertainment Network*, Boulder, CO: Westview Press.

Du Gay, Paul, Stuart Hall, Linda Janes, Hugh Mackay and Keith Negus (1997) *Doing Cultural Studies: The Story of the Sony Walkman*, London: Sage Publishers and the Open University.

Hall, Stuart (1997) *Representation: Cultural Representations and Signifying Practices*, London: Sage Publishers and the Open University.

Hall, Stuart (1993) 'Encoding/Decoding', in Simon During (ed.) *The Cultural Studies Reader*, London: Routledge.

Hall, Stuart and Tony Jefferson (eds) (1993) *Resistance through Rituals: Youth Subcultures in Post-War Britain*, London: Routledge.

Hall, Stuart, Charles Critcher, Tony Jefferson, John Clarke and Brian Robert (1978) *Policing the Crisis: Mugging, the State and Law and Order*, London: Palgrave Macmillan.

Hallin, Daniel C. (1986) *The 'Uncensored War': The Media and Vietnam*, Oxford: Oxford University Press.

Hedetoft, Ulf (2000) 'Contemporary Cinema: Between Cultural Globalization and National Interpretation', in Mette Hjort and Scott MacKenzie (eds) *Cinema and Nation*, London: Routledge.

Kolker, Robert Phillip (2000) *A Cinema of Loneliness*, 3rd edn, Oxford: Oxford University Press.

McLane, Brendan R. (2004) 'Reporting from the Sandstorm: An Appraisal of Embedding', *Parameters* 34, 1: 77–88.

McLuhan, Marshall (1975) *Montreal Gazette*, 16 May.

Metcalf, Roy (1999) 'So Costly a Sacrifice: Saving Private Ryan', *Social Policy* 29, 4: 44–7.

O'Rourke, P.J. (1992) *Give War a Chance*, London: Picador.

O'Sullivan, Tim, Brian Dutton and Philip Rayner (2003) *Studying the Media: An Introduction*, 3rd edn, London: Hodder and Arnold.

Pfau, Michael, Michel Haigh, Mitchell Gettle, Michael Donnelly, Gregory Scott, Dana Warr and Elaine Wittenberg (2004) 'Embedding Journalists in Military Combat Units: Impact on Story Frames and Tone', *Journalism and Mass Communication Quarterly* 81, 1: 74–88.

Philo, Greg (1993) 'From Buerk to Band Aid: The Media and the 1984 Ethiopian Famine', in John Eldridge (ed.) *Getting the Message: News, Truth and Power*, London: Routledge.

Postman, Neil (1987) *Amusing Ourselves to Death: Public Discourse in the Age of Show Business*, London: Methuen.

Robinson, Piers (2002) *The CNN Effect: The Myth of News, Foreign Policy and Intervention*, London: Routledge.

Tumber, Howard and Jerry Palmer (2004) *Media at War: The Iraq Crisis*, London: Sage.

Wheeler, Mark (1997) *Politics and the Mass Media*, Oxford: Blackwell.

Zinn, Howard (1998) 'Saving Private Ryan', *Social Justice* 25, 3: 138–43.

CHAPTER 8

Why is people's movement restricted?

Roxanne Lynn Doty

- ■ *The question*
  BORDER CROSSINGS

- ■ *Illustrative example*
  THE US–MEXICO BORDER AND THE IMMIGRATION CRISIS

- ■ *Responses*
  IDEAS OF STATES AND CITIZENSHIP

- ■ *Broader issues*
  CULTURAL RACISM

- ■ **CONCLUSION**

THE QUESTION
BORDER CROSSINGS

On 22 February 2006 US Border Patrol agents found the body of the first undocumented border crosser to die in Cochise County, Arizona for that year (*Arizona Daily Star* 2006). The man's name was Antonio Dominguez Callejas, from Vera Cruz, Mexico. He was 47 years old and had died of exposure and dehydration approximately 35 hours before he was found. Antonio's death was just one of over 400 undocumented border crossers who would die in 2006 and one of the 3,600–4,000 who have died in the past 10–12 years (Rubio-Goldsmith *et al.* 2006; United States Accountability Office 2006). Approximately 20 per cent of these deaths have been women and children. The situation on the

US–Mexico border is not unique. According to the United Nations Economic and Social Council, over 3,000 migrants died between 1997 and 2000 attempting to reach Europe, most of these while attempting to cross the Straits of Gibraltar (United Nations Economic and Social Council 2002). These deaths painfully illustrate that while it is undoubtedly true that advances in transportation and communication have facilitated the relatively easy movement of some people across the globe, some movements entail unspeakable tragedy.

Globalization has been accompanied by increasing numbers of people moving across borders for various reasons. Many forms of border crossing are whole-heartedly welcomed by governments. For example, almost all governments encourage and actively seek to promote the movement of peoples across their borders in the form of international tourism, which is the world's largest export earner as well as one of the most important sources of employment. In many countries it is the number one industry. In January 2007, the Secretary-General of the World Tourism Organization reported that world tourism had entered a historically new phase of growth which began in 2004. In 2005, there were 800 million international arrivals. In 2006 international arrivals surpassed 840 million, representing over 20 per cent growth in the span of three years (United Nations World Tourism Organization 2007). Another form of movement across borders that is increasing and that is encouraged by governments involves education. In 2004, approximately 2 million students were enrolled in institutes of higher education outside their country of origin (Freeman 2006; Thorn 2005). Indeed the movement of people across borders for the purpose of higher education not only is encouraged by governments, but has also become part of the global marketplace, with the World Trade Organization taking it on as an area of concern (Altbach 2001).

Changes in the global political economy are discussed in **Chapter 12**.

Other forms of movement across borders such as international business travel, overseas employment and some types of immigration are also welcomed and facilitated by governments. Economically motivated migration is described by immigration scholars in terms of 'push' and 'pull' factors. The lack of job opportunities, low wages and poverty 'push' people to leave a country. They are 'pulled' to those places where employment opportunities exist and/or where they can earn higher salaries (Isbister 1996: 95–8; Hollifield 2000). As the world continues to become increasingly interconnected in numerous ways, so the movement of people across borders accelerates. A couple of examples illustrate this. In the United States, the number of persons granted permanent legal residency in 1986 was 601,708 (Migration Policy Institute 2004). By the year 2006 this figure was 1,266,264 (Migration Policy Institute 2007). The inflow of people from other countries to the United Kingdom for 1991 was 53,900. By 2006 this number had increased to 143,205 (Migration Policy Institute 2007). Clearly these various realms of movement are part and parcel of the phenomenon of globalization. However, not all movement is welcomed and it often encounters

The term 'globalization' is a contested one. Some people argue that changes are exaggerated; others see globalization as a key change in the contemporary world.

strong and at times ugly opposition. This is most obviously the case when it comes to the movement of peoples who, for various reasons, do not have the proper authorization. Many human beings who have crossed sovereign, national borders without the proper documentation have met with a similar fate to Antonio. Those who do make it often encounter intense, passionate and sometimes violent opposition in most of the Western industrialized countries. Almost all Western industrialized countries have enacted increasingly restrictive immigration policies over the past decade. This has been the case especially when it comes to unskilled immigrants.

Why is this the case? Why is it that some can move relatively freely across borders, but many others face often insurmountable hurdles? Why are people free to move within national borders, but not across them? At one level there are obvious answers to these questions. People can generally move freely *within* national borders if they are citizens or if they are in the country legally. People can move freely *across* national borders if they have legal authorization to do so. However, these simple, straightforward answers are not entirely adequate to this extra-ordinarily complex issue. Both citizenship and legality are complex concepts and practices. The ways in which citizenship has been granted as well as the ways in which it has been denied have been linked to social and political phenomena that involve power and struggles over meaning and identity. The same is true for the realm of legality and illegality. For example, it is important to remember that at various times in the history of the United States some practices were legal that

Of course, we need to ask why national borders exist in the first place. Why is the world divided in this way?
See Chapter 9

European
African (slaves)
Indian
Chinese
Japanese   •••••••• Majority of population descended from immigrants

FIGURE 8.1
Map of world migration routes since 1700. After A. Getis (1991) *Introduction to Geography*, 3rd edn, Dubuque: W.C. Brown Publishers

would be considered totally unacceptable today, e.g. the enslavement of African Americans, the internment of Japanese Americans, and the denial of voting rights to Native Americans and women. Those practices created severe constraints on what citizenship could mean and who could possess it. If the human beings who fell into these categories attempted to exercise the rights that were granted to others it was considered illegal. However, laws change as a result of peoples' fights for rights. Both citizenship and legality are dynamic rather than static. They are undergoing continual change. So, pointing to citizenship and legality as reasons why people's movements are restricted provides us with only partial answers. We still must ask *why* movement should be restricted based on these two things. The term 'illegal' conveys a black and white world in which those who cross without the proper authorization are considered criminals regardless of the circumstances that led them to cross. If we are satisfied with citizenship and legality as reasons why people's movements are restricted, our analysis stops and we go no further. We do not explore the meaning of these concepts themselves and the contexts within which they become significant. We do not examine the powerful forces underlying official policies that pertain to citizenship or the right to move across borders legally. We do not ask *why* they should be accepted as valid reasons for immigration policy.

To understand why people cross borders and why movements are often restricted it is important to explore the contradictory forces that are at work in the world. If we dig deeper we may rethink our preconceptions about citizenship and legality. A more in-depth, critical exploration is essential if we are to understand why, despite the absence of citizenship and the absence of proper authorization, people still move across borders in very large numbers and often at very great risk. A more in-depth analysis is also important if we are to begin to explore the possibilities for change in how we think of borders. In light of the immense consequences restrictions on free movement have for human beings and the society they create, it is necessary for us to engage in a more critical examination as to why and how peoples' movement is restricted and what the outcomes of such restrictions have been.

Chapter 10 examines another aspect of citizenship: the life stories of those who are exiled from their 'home' and those who are uneasy in their allegiance to the nation-state in which they live.

The UN Secretary-General Ban Ki-moon has suggested that the free migration of peoples should be welcomed as a way to tackle problems such as poverty (*Guardian (London)*, 10 July 2007).

ILLUSTRATIVE EXAMPLE
THE US–MEXICO BORDER AND THE IMMIGRATION CRISIS

La linea, as the line separating Mexico from the United States is sometimes referred to, extends 1,951 miles (3,141 km) from the Pacific Ocean in the west to Brownsville, Texas and Matamoros, Tamaulipas in the east. It is the longest contiguous border (shared physical boundary) in the world between a First World country and a Third World country. It is also the most frequently crossed

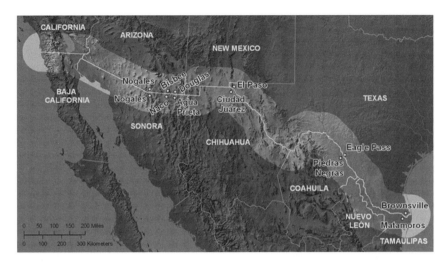

FIGURE 8.2
Aerial photo-map of US–Mexico border. Public domain, USGS

international border in the world. This border over which many peoples' movement is restricted is a place where, in the words of one writer, 'the Third World grates against the first and bleeds' (Anzaldua 1987). While there are many unique aspects of the current US immigration crises revolving around this particular border, it speaks to and exemplifies the more general phenomenon that the entire world is experiencing. The movement of peoples across national borders without authorization is truly a global phenomenon. This section presents the

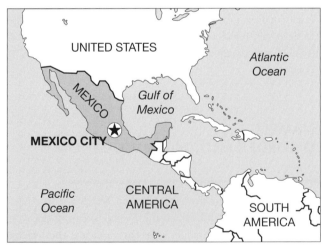

FIGURE 8.3
Map showing US and Mexico in context

background to the contemporary issue of undocumented immigration from Mexico into the United States, detailing the border enforcement policies of the 1990s that gave rise to skyrocketing numbers of deaths of migrants as they attempted to cross through dangerous terrain. It also discusses the consequences in terms of the increased use of human smugglers, the efforts of citizen border patrol groups who have taken it upon themselves to guard the US–Mexico border, the formation of migrant rights groups and an anti-immigrant movement. This section concludes with a review of policies that have been proposed and some that have been adopted.

The contemporary immigration crisis can be traced to several events far removed from the US–Mexico border. In 1993 New York's World Trade Center was bombed by suspected unauthorized immigrants. In the same year two Central Intelligence Agency employees in Virginia were assassinated by an unauthorized immigrant from Pakistan. These two events, as well as the economic recession that persisted in the United States at the time, helped to fuel anti-immigrant sentiment (Nevins 2002). They also contributed to the framing of undocumented immigration as a national security issue. Against this background, in the early morning hours of 6 June 1993 a ship carrying 286 human beings without authorization to enter the United States ran aground on Rockaway Beach in Queens, New York. The name of the ship was the *Golden Venture* and the unauthorized passengers were from China, mostly from the province of Fujan. Ninety of the passengers had boarded that ship in February off the coast of Thailand. Another 200 boarded in March off Mombasa, Kenya, having been stranded there for a year after the other smuggling ship they were on, *Najd II*, broke down. Ten passengers drowned and the others were immediately detained by the US Immigration and Naturalization Service (INS) and jailed. While this had little to do with the southern border of the United States, it brought the issue of undocumented immigration to the forefront of national attention. It also contributed to notions of the US being 'invaded' by 'illegal aliens'.

Border control strategies

Around the same time, Silvestre Reyes, then Border Patrol Chief in El Paso, Texas, launched a border operation called Operation Blockade, later renamed Operation Hold the Line because the first name was considered offensive. On 19 September 1993 he deployed 400 agents and their vehicles in a highly visible show of force along a twenty-mile section of border between El Paso, Texas and Ciudad Juarez, Mexico. This marked a departure from the previous strategy of pursuit and apprehension *after* the border had been crossed. Almost immediately apprehensions fell dramatically. Reyes and Operation Hold the Line thus received a great deal of favourable national publicity.

Why might people find the name 'Operation Blockade' offensive? Is the changed name any better? Why?

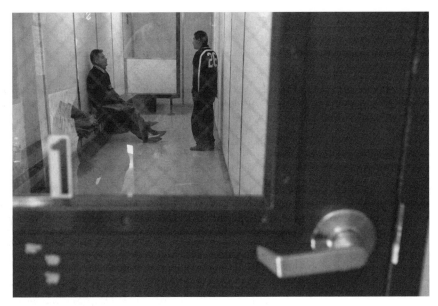

FIGURE 8.4
Martin Margas Posadas,18, from Puebla, Mexico (right) and another man wait in the US Border Patrol holding cell in Campo near California's border with Mexico. Photo: Marc Campos, *Inland Valley Daily Bulletin* Staff Photographer

Based on the 'success' of Operation Hold the Line, in 1994 the US Immigration and Naturalization Service, in consultation with the US Defense Department's Center for Low Intensity Conflict, developed a new comprehensive border strategy, 'prevention through deterrence'. This became and continues to be the official border enforcement strategy of the United States (United States General Accounting Office 2001). The logic of this strategy was to deter migrants from crossing in the more populated areas. Operation Hold the Line in El Paso, Texas was joined by Operation Gatekeeper in San Diego, California. The strategy initially targeted these two border areas because at the time they accounted for approximately two thirds of all undocumented entries into the United States. Operation Gatekeeper entailed the installation of high-intensity floodlights to illuminate the border day and night as well as eight-foot steel fencing along fourteen miles of the border beginning at the Pacific Ocean. Border Patrol agents were stationed every few hundred feet behind this wall (Dunn 1996; Andreas 2000; Nevins 2002).

As had been the case in El Paso, this strategy drastically reduced the number of undocumented crossings and the San Diego area went from being the busiest port on the entire border to a relatively quiet area. 'Prevention through deterrence' was deemed a success and these two operations were joined by Operation Safeguard in Nogales, Arizona in 1995. This operation was extended to the cities of Douglas and Naco in 1999. Attention was also heavily focused on deterrence

What do the names 'Operation Gatekeeper' and 'Operation Safeguard' suggest?

with the passage of the Illegal Immigration Reform and Immigrant Responsibility Act in 1996. Funds were authorized for the construction of additional layers of fencing in San Diego, for the purchase of new military technology and for the hiring of 1,000 Border Patrol Agents a year through the year 2001. In 1997 Operation Rio Grande was put into effect in South East Texas, sixty additional miles of fencing were added to Gatekeeper and ten additional miles to Hold the Line. The overall effect of these border enforcement policies has been to push migrants to increasingly remote and dangerous crossing routes and to engage the services of human smugglers or *coyotes*. While crossings may decrease in certain areas, the overall numbers of undocumented border crossers has continued to rise. The Binational Migration Institute (BMI) at the University of Arizona in Tucson recently reported that the 'funnel effect' created by the US border policies of 'prevention through deterrence' is the 'primary structural cause of death of thousands of North American, Central American, and South American unauthorized men, women, and children who have died while trying to enter the US' (Rubio-Goldsmith *et al.* 2006).

It is interesting, and important to note especially in terms of locating this issue in the context of globalization, that the North American Free Trade Agreement (NAFTA) was being negotiated during the same period of time that the new border enforcement strategies were being put into place. Significantly NAFTA sought to promote the free movement of goods and capital, but not people.

BOX 8.1 NAFTA

NAFTA is a trade agreement between the United States, Canada and Mexico. NAFTA eliminated all non-tariff trade barriers to agricultural trade between the US and Mexico. Many other tariffs were also eliminated immediately, with others being phased out over a 5–15 year period. Some experts argued that NAFTA would lead to more economic development in Mexico and thus reduce the incentive for undocumented migration to the US. Others said it would increase migration. Both of these seemingly opposed viewpoints were supported by the US Commission for the Study of International Migration and Cooperative Economic Development in 1990. This commission argued that free trade and economic integration was the best long-term remedy for unwanted immigration, but that in the short to medium term immigration would likely increase. This has been referred to as the 'migration hump' (Martin 2003). NAFTA was expected to displace millions of Mexican corn farmers (Martin 1993). In an important sense, NAFTA exemplifies the more general contradiction of a world characterized on the one hand by the increased desirability and ease of movement across borders for commodities, services and some people and on the other hand by severe restrictions placed on others who are nonetheless compelled to move across those very same borders.

Virtually no attention was given to the movement of people for jobs or any other reasons. Efforts to increase border enforcement intensified around the time that NAFTA took effect in 1994. Operation Gatekeeper and the other border operations can be seen as efforts to appease those who held the view that NAFTA would increase immigration. It contained no provisions for labour and thus ignored any affects it would have on workers.

Anti-immigration legislation

The contemporary immigration crisis in the United States has met with various proposals, bills and new laws, especially at the local level of cities and towns. The state of Arizona passed Proposition 200 in November 2004, which denies undocumented migrants access to jobs, healthcare and legal protection. This was a catalyst for a rash of nationwide measures. As of August 2006 more than half of the states in the United States had passed anti-immigrant measures. The city of Hazelton, Pennsylvania passed one of the nation's harshest laws, approving $1,000 fines for landlords who rent to undocumented migrants. In August 2006 landlords in Valley Park, Missouri began evicting tenants who were not in the United States with the proper documents. In September 2006 US Immigration and Customs Enforce (ICE) agents fanned across three counties in the state of Georgia in raids targeting undocumented migrants. Citizens and non-citizens alike were rounded up because of physical appearance. These are just a few of the many examples of local responses to undocumented migration. At the national level, in December 2005 the US House of Representatives passed House Bill 4437, Border Protection, Anti-Terrorism, and Illegal Immigration Control Act of 2005, commonly referred to as the Sensenbrenner Bill, after its sponsor Representative James Sensenbrenner. This bill is considered by migrant rights groups and many others to be one of the most draconian in recent history. It would have required all employers to use an electronic data base to verify employee's eligibility to be in the US, authorized a high-tech fence along sections of the US border and made it a criminal offence to come to the aid of migrants in distress. Many humanitarian, religious and medical workers would immediately become criminals. The House bill would have also required immediate detention and deportation of any undocumented person. In response to this bill, the US Senate introduced a compromise bill that proposed a guest worker programme and created paths to citizenship for *some* of the estimated 12 million undocumented migrants who currently live and work in the United States. National-level immigration legislation is currently stalled, but continues to be one of the country's most important and divisive issues.

Another proposed piece of legislation that seeks to reinforce a different kind of border is the current effort in the United States to deny birthright citizenship to babies born to undocumented parents. Almost every anti-immigrant organization,

The European Union (EU) is an example of an area of free movement of goods like NAFTA, though in the EU movement across internal borders between states is normally free for people as well. In the EU too there has been concern about the effect of the ensuing internal labour migration.

In many parts of the world there is no right to citizenship of a country as a result of birth within its borders alone; often one's parents' citizenship counts too.

as well as some policy makers, is in favour of revoking this long-standing right that is guaranteed in the 14th amendment to the US Constitution. House Bill 698, which was sponsored by 49 members of the US House of Representatives in 2006, would have eliminated this right. The bill was defeated in December 2006 but it is predicted that it will continue to resurface.

Vigilante groups

Some individuals and groups have responded to unauthorized immigration into the United States by taking it upon themselves to engage in the unofficial and unauthorized, though not necessarily illegal, patrolling of the US–Mexico border regions. This phenomenon received much national and international attention with the April 2005 Minuteman Project in southeastern Arizona. By autumn 2005 over 40 other anti-immigrant border vigilante groups had formed in the United States. These groups not only engage in the physical patrolling of the border, but also often hold rallies at day labour sites where migrant workers gather waiting for work and at state capitals and Mexican consulates. Despite these responses people continue to cross without the proper documents and border crossing continues to be a dangerous undertaking. Every year with the approach of spring and summer, as the temperatures begin to rise in the southwestern United States another season of death begins.

FIGURE 8.5
Day of the Dead, 2 November 2004, Anapra, Mexico. Mass celebrated at the border in memory of undocumented migrants who died while crossing the US–Mexico border. AP/PA Photos

RESPONSES
IDEAS OF STATES AND CITIZENSHIP

US immigration laws and border enforcement strategies implicitly and explicitly make many assumptions about nations, states, territorial borders, citizenship and identity that underlie efforts to restrict the movement of peoples. The assumptions that make US border policies possible are mirrored in academic literature that describes a world where the insides of societies are clearly distinguished from the outside. Such a view presents a world that is neatly divided into nation-states separated legally by sovereign territorial borders that are mutually recognized and respected by other states. People living within states' sovereign territorial borders share certain legal, political, social and cultural marks of identity whose ultimate expression is that of citizenship. On such a view, even though there is much movement across borders, ultimately there exists a link that is impossible to disentangle between the sovereign legal territorial state and its inhabitants, its citizens. These are 'givens' and if they seem to be under threat they must be protected. The nation consisting of citizens who share a national identity is generally assumed to be naturally connected to the state.

Such a view is also inherent in other concepts such as sovereignty, national identity and national security. These concepts which we draw upon to understand the world and which inform policy makers contain within them the notion of a unitary identity for both individuals and collectives. Such an understanding of the world is also ingrained in our ways of being and acting in the world. When it comes to unauthorized movements of people, this view presumes that it is natural for the world to be disturbed by people who move across sovereign borders without authorization because some people belong in some places and other people belong in other places. Given sufficient money, enough border patrol agents, military troops, high enough walls, sophisticated enough technology and the political will of leaders, territorial borders can be fortified and secured. The safety and sanctity of the citizen can thus be ensured. The world can be restored to its 'natural' state.

The way of thinking described above is very powerful today. One of the reasons for this may be the fact that it contains a certain commonsensical element. At first glance, it may seem to us simply an accurate description of 'how the world is'. Our lives contain many things that contribute to this sense of 'naturalness', e.g. flags, national anthems, passports and so on. However, if we pause to critically reflect upon the situations described in sections 1 and 2, we come away with a much different picture that suggests the 'givens' that we begin with are outdated. We can ask if the 'givens' contained in conventional ideas are sustainable and at what cost. A great deal of effort is required to maintain the 'truth' of idealized pictures of the world, and the conventional view of states, nations, citizens and identity is increasingly one that does not match the way the world actually is. When

There are other ways the world could be ordered. For a discussion of how the world of sovereign states with territorial borders came into being and is sustained, see **Chapter 9**.

The problems with this view of the nation-state and citizens sharing a national identity are discussed in **Chapter 10**. Many of the inhabitants of a nation-state do not identify with it in any straightforward way.

The way idealized pictures of the world help us begin to think about the world is discussed in **Chapter 2**.

such idealized views are called into question by what is happening on the ground, in peoples' everyday lives, and when conventional ideas seem to be becoming unravelled, these efforts generally intensify. We see this happening today in the United States with calls to 'close our borders' and 'protect our sovereignty' on the part of segments of the general populace. We also see it in the various laws and proposals dealing with undocumented immigration discussed above. We must ask, though, what is sacrificed in such efforts to sustain these ideas and categories that may no longer suit the world? Crossing borders without the proper documentation obviously entails many sacrifices that stem from restrictive policies that prevent migrants from obtaining the proper documentation; leaving home and family, paying huge sums of money to smugglers, and often paying with their lives. We also need to ask what society as a whole sacrifices when restrictive immigration laws are put into place and when laws aimed at those who already live here without the proper documents are enacted. Further, we need to question the very meaning of society and the values and ideals that have generally been associated with it. We need to rethink our understanding of citizenship and the identities it encompasses and those that it excludes.

Currently, about 12 million undocumented immigrants reside in the United States, although we should remember that it is very difficult to obtain a completely accurate count simply because these people are undocumented. The most widely used method of calculating the undocumented population in the United States is referred to as the 'residual method'. This method estimates the unauthorized population by subtracting the legally resident foreign population from the total number of foreign-born counted in a census (Migration Policy Institute 2004). Some have been here most of their lives, some arrived yesterday. Some live next door to 'us' and send their children to 'our' schools, and pay taxes to 'our' government. Some even fight in 'our' wars. Some live in shacks in the canyons and hills around 'our' most upscale housing developments. Some own their own businesses. Others are 'day labourers' who stand on street corners waiting for work. 'They' reflect the diversity that defines what the United States is today. Still, none of 'them' have very many rights because their identities are primarily defined by the absence of citizenship. This privileged status is currently out of reach for most of these people. They are therefore subject to arrest and deportation at any time. In the United States the number of undocumented migrants detained has jumped over the past year to 28,000 during fiscal year 2007, up from 19,700 the previous year (*Arizona Republic* 2007). Undocumented migrants are held in city and county jails as well as detention facilities all over the country, some of which are privately run. Whole families are often detained. An example is the T. Don Hutto Family Residential Detention Center in Taylor, Texas, which is owned and operated by the private Corrections Corporation of America. This centre, which was opened in May 2006, has come under fire from civil liberties and immigrant rights groups, who accuse it of being run like a prison (Rutland 2007). Immigration raids at work and other places are also on the increase. It is

How many undocumented migrants live in Europe? See http://www.picum.org/HOMEPAGE/Numbers/Numbers.htm.

not uncommon for routine traffic stops to result in deportation for those who are undocumented. In March 2007, three high-school students in the Phoenix, Arizona area were deported to Mexico after being stopped for drag racing. An honours student in the Justice Studies programme at Arizona State University who has lived in the United States since he was a toddler is currently facing deportation proceedings after being stopped in March 2007 for making an improper right turn (Nanez 2007).

Such a situation makes a statement about the limitations of citizenship as it is currently understood. Citizenship, as a legal category and a category of identity that is attached to a piece of geographical territory, is extremely problematic today. Globalization presents challenges to this concept and raises serious questions as to whether the conventional concept of the citizen in political and legal practices which function to exclude and deny rights to those who are not citizens can ultimately survive. The human beings who contribute to society but live in fear because of their undocumented status make a silent statement about the limitations of current understandings of 'the citizen'. Recently, this contestation has taken a more visible and openly articulated form, as illustrated in the massive migrant rights demonstrations that took place throughout the US in the spring of 2006.

FIGURE 8.6
Los Angeles immigration demonstration, 25 March 2006. Photo: Lucas Jackson, Reuters

Citizenship has always contained an exclusionary element. Inherent in the concept of citizenship is the notion of an insider, which necessarily implies an outsider. For example, for Aristotle, one of the most influential of the ancient Greek philosophers, women, foreigners and slaves were outsiders.

What has been touted as 'universal' citizenship in the United States has, at various moments in history, excluded women, African Americans and others. It currently excludes millions of people who are physically present on the inside of US territory but are officially deemed outsiders. This situation has led many to call for immigration reform that grants 'amnesty' to some undocumented migrants who have lived in the United States for various lengths of time. Anti-immigrant activists and policy makers have been quite vocal in opposing any pathway to future citizenship for any migrants who are in the United States without authorization. Granting legal status and the opportunity for citizenship to unauthorized migrants is not a new idea. The Immigration Reform and Control Act of 1986 (IRCA) created a process whereby more than 2.7 million authorized migrants gained lawful permanent residence in the United States (Papademetriou 2005). France undertook a similar policy in 1966 with 'regularization', which allowed migrants who had entered without authorization or overstayed their visas to receive legal working papers (Freeman 1979). More recently, in 2005, Spain launched a programme that granted 'amnesty' to undocumented migrants who had entered the country prior to August 2005, had a job contract and no criminal record (BBC News 2005).

As the above examples show, it is possible to find instances in which unauthorized immigrants have been granted the opportunity for citizenship. Still, such programmes generally encounter widespread opposition. Currently, in the United States such opposition has prevented any policy solutions. To understand such opposition it is useful to examine some of the issues raised by citizenship itself. While the notion of citizenship is extremely complex in itself, we need to probe even further. The following section discusses the issues of race and culture that have historically been linked in various ways to citizenship.

BROADER ISSUES
CULTURAL RACISM

'The border' is multifaceted and the territorial line that slices through the ocean, mountains, desert, rivers and canyons of the United States is only one aspect of a much larger phenomenon that artificially divides human beings from one another. There are many borders in the world that create a self and an other, a subject who belongs and one who does not, a subject who can be called 'citizen' and one whose very existence in a particular place is deemed illegal. The

Identity can take many forms, and national identity is only one of them. **Chapter 4** discusses the process of identification in general, and gender and racialized identities in particular; **Chapter 5** examines religion; and **Chapter 15** the distinction between 'civilized' and 'barbarian'.

FIGURE 8.7
'Australian citizenship test'. Artist: John Ditchburn 1/05 2006-240 © John Ditchburn

movement of peoples without the proper authorization is a 'site' where many manifestations of various understandings of borders come together and where issues of identity and belonging are brought to the fore. The ways in which a society responds to the human beings who enter its sovereign territory without proper authorization say much about how it conceives of itself and 'others'. It also says much about how the issue of identity intersects with notions of justice, fairness and equality. Particularly pertinent to identity within the context of the movement of peoples are the issues of race and culture.

How, then, does one begin to think of the relevance of race and culture when it comes to the issue of restricting the movement of peoples? One way to approach this very difficult issue is to consider our understanding of identity itself. If we understand identity as stable and fixed, as something that defines the essence of individuals and groups and differentiates them from other individuals and groups, we are likely to come away with an essentialist understanding of humanity. Such an understanding suggests that we can determine essential characteristics of peoples that define who they are and that differentiate them from others. However, if we question this view and think of identity as inherently unstable, multiple and often full of tension, we will be less quick and less certain about categorizing people, defining them by the colours of their skin, the places they

Identity was discussed in **Chapter 4**; a distinction was made there between static (essentialist) and dynamic (socially constructed) views of identity.

BOX 8.2 RACE AND CULTURE

Balibar and Wallerstein (1991) have observed that national identity and citizenship have a long history of being linked with racial categories of identity and racial identity has often been linked to culture. Race and culture are impossible to define in a 'scientific' way that would permit one to proclaim with certainty that current immigration policies in the United States are racist or that anti-immigrant positions are racist. Like the concept of identity, race and culture are not static phenomena. It is notoriously difficult to say with absolute certainty what elements make up a culture. Ironically this is one of the reasons this term is so powerful. Vagueness and ambiguity are often what make concepts powerful. For example, political leaders use the term 'national interest' quite frequently and never say with any degree of precision what it means exactly. Nonetheless, it often functions to arouse much passion and support amongst the populace. Similarly, when political leaders and scholars express the concern that immigration, and especially undocumented immigration, poses a threat to a nation's culture they very rarely say precisely what they mean. Furthermore, when one begins to examine the things they could possibly mean, we are often left with very little that is concrete. Some thinkers have suggested that culture can function as a smokescreen for race. Biological notions of race have been thoroughly debunked and yet race as a category of identity lingers and it retains quite a bit of power despite the elusiveness of what it 'is'. Culture is equally slippery. While some markers of culture, such as language, seem relatively straightforward, it remains a notoriously 'slippery' and contested concept.

come from, their ancestors and so on. In other words we can think of identity in a more complex way as a phenomenon that is socially constructed. We can think of identity as something that does not necessary come before political and social practices, but rather is constructed by these things.

These two understandings of identity are relevant when it comes to the issues of race and culture. Race and culture throughout history have often been thought of as stable markers of identity that define a group of people. The consequences of this when it comes to race have been particularly odious, e.g. slavery, lynching, the Holocaust, colonialism. Historically, race has also been an important element in US immigration policy. The US Immigration Act of 1924 was praised by Adolf Hitler: 'Compared to the old Europe, which has lost an infinite amount of its best blood through war and emigration, the America nation appears as a young and racially select people. The American union itself, motivated by the theories of its own racial researchers, [has] established specific racial criteria for immigration' (quoted in Romo 2005). As part of the general 1924 restrictions, the

Chapter 4 also explores the issue of race.

Oriental Exclusion Act banned all immigration from Asia (Reimers 1992). Such blatant forms of racism are easy to recognize. In contemporary times, thinking of race as a fixed, genetic marker (phenotype) has been thoroughly debunked. Studies indicate that there really is no such thing as race in any biological, genetic sense.

Today, it is a great deal more difficult today to justify political and social practices that are blatantly racist. Still, it would be a gross and dangerous mistake to claim that racism no longer exists. If this is the case, then perhaps the term 'race' is not only linked to one's skin colour or any other biological or genetic indicator. Even in earlier times, the concept of race extended beyond blood or genetics and was often linked to other factors such as nationality, tradition, geography and culture (Doty 2003). All of these factors have come into play in constructing identities for peoples. What this suggests, then, is that it is possible to have a kind of racism that draws upon something other than skin colour. This is what the concept of cultural racism, or what some have referred to as neo-racism, is meant to convey (Barker 1981; Balibar and Wallerstein 1991; Doty 2003; Taguieff 1990). Neo-racism suggests that it is natural for antagonisms (hostilities) to develop between members of a bounded community, i.e. a nation, and 'outsiders' (Barker 1981: 21).

> See **Chapter 4** for a discussion of early biological views of difference.

The notion of cultural racism has been applied to immigration issues in Britain and Europe and is also a useful way to understand at least a portion of the immigration 'crisis' in the United States today. This is clear in popular notions that immigrants, especially those from Mexico, pose a threat to the cultural integrity of the United States, to 'our way of life' and to the very definition of who 'we' are. Over the past ten years or so we have witnessed a proliferation of writings that expound upon the presumed dangers that immigrants pose to the cultural integrity of the United States. These range from extremist internet blogs to highly respected academics. Samuel Huntington's *Foreign Policy* article 'The Hispanic Challenge' (2004a) and his subsequent book *Who Are We?* (2004b) are highly controversial and much criticized but they resonate with other popular publications. The most recent of these is Pat Buchanan's *State of Emergency: The Third World Invasion and Conquest of America* (2006). These are all examples of precisely what the term 'neo-racism' is meant to capture. They create the notion of 'others' whose 'assimilability' is questionable and who therefore threaten 'our' very existence. This way of thinking about peoples and cultures and borders provides a simplified and dangerous way of interpreting the consequences of the movement of human beings, with or without the proper authorization. This is not to suggest that the 'old-fashioned' racism does not still exist. A recent study of traffic stops in the state of Arizona found that Highway Patrol officers were more than twice as likely to search vehicles driven by Hispanics and blacks than those operated by Anglos (Wagner 2007).

> For more on how such discourses of danger work and affect politics, **see Chapter 17.**

CONCLUSION

The immigration 'crisis' in the United States today raises questions that are pertinent to most other advanced industrialized democracies who have experienced and continue to experience immigration from countries deemed 'Third World' and who find themselves with a substantial number of human beings who have arrived without the proper legal documents. The European Union is often cited as an example of a case in which freedom of movement has triumphed over sovereign national borders. When the provisions of the Schengen Agreement came into force in 1995, travellers between member states were no longer required to show passports (Gelatt 2005). However, the existence of the European Union has not eliminated undocumented migration and freedom of movement is only granted to citizens of member states. It has not eliminated exclusionary practices (Balibar 2004). In an important sense the question raised by Samuel Huntington, i.e. 'Who are we?', is a pertinent one, but not necessarily in the sense in which he poses it. Constructing categories of human beings who are defined in large part by their lack of documents raises important questions about the values that have traditionally been attached to 'us'. The restriction of people's free movement raises important questions about what values such as democracy and human rights can mean in an age of globalization when borders mean very little and very much at the same time.

In our contemporary world borders are easy and difficult to cross at the same time. Exclusion is increasing and decreasing at the same time. From a critical perspective there are very few satisfactory responses to the question of why people's movement is restricted. Restrictive legislation on the part of the United States as well as many European countries has for the most part failed in terms of reducing immigration. Efforts to limit and/or prevent people from moving across sovereign territorial borders without the proper documentation have given rise to numerous other problems such as an increase in human smuggling, deaths of migrants in their dangerous journeys and an underground world of human beings who live amongst us but do not enjoy the same privileges as citizens.

FURTHER READING

Andreas, Peter (2000) *Border Games: Policing the US–Mexico Divide*, Ithaca, NY: Cornell University Press.
> Useful for background to recent US policies pertaining to its southern border.

Balibar, Etienne (2004) *We the People of Europe? Reflections on Transnational Citizenship*, Princeton, NJ and Oxford: Princeton University Press.
> This book reflects upon the ways of understanding what citizenship means and how this may be changing due in part to migration.

Brian, Barry and Robert E. Goodin (eds) (1992) *Free Movement: Ethical Issues in the Transnational Migration of People and Money*, University Park, PA: Pennsylvania State University Press.
This book presents several essays addressing the movement of goods, services and people across borders and the ethical questions raised by these movements.

Brubaker, William Rogers (ed.) (1989) *Immigration and the Politics of Citizenship in Europe and North America*, Lanham, MD: University Press of America.
Addresses the issue of citizenship in the context of immigration.

Cornelius, Wayne, Philip Martin and James F. Hollifield (eds) (1994) *Controlling Immigration: A Global Perspective*, Stanford, CA: Stanford University Press.
Good general overview of immigration from a global perspective.

Massey, Douglas S., Jorge Durand and Nolan J. Malone (2002) *Beyond Smoke and Mirrors: Mexican Migration in an Era of Economic Integration*, New York: Russell Sage.
Essays on Mexican migration into the United States.

Massey, Douglas S., Joaquin Arango, Graeme Hugo, Ali Kouaouci, Adela Pellegrino and J. Edward Taylor (2005) *Worlds in Motion: Understanding International Migration at the End of the Millennium*, Oxford: Oxford University Press.
Good general overview of contemporary immigration issues from a global perspective.

Reimers, David M. (1998) *Unwelcome Strangers: American Identity and the Turn against Immigration*, New York: Columbia University Press.
History of anti-immigrant groups and activities in the United States.

Sassen, Saskia (1996) *Losing Control? Sovereignty in an Age of Globalization*, New York: Columbia University Press.
Focuses on governance in an age of globalization, of which immigration is a major issue.

WEBSITES

Congressional Research Service (CRS) http://www.opencrs.com is the public policy research arm of the US Congress. It issues about 3,000 briefs, reports and issue papers per year, including papers on immigration issues.

Immigration Policy Center (IPC) http://www.ailf.org/ipc is part of the American Immigration Law Foundation (AILF) and was established in 1987 as a tax-exempt, not-for-profit educational, charitable organization. The Foundation is dedicated to increasing public understanding of immigration law and policy and the value of immigration to American society, and to advancing fundamental fairness and due process under the law for immigrants.

Migration Policy Institute (MPI) http://www.migrationinformation.org is an independent non-partisan, nonprofit think tank in Washington, DC that provides analysis, development and evaluation of immigration policies at the local, national and international levels. It was founded in 2001 by Demetrios G. Papademetriou and Kathleen Newland, and grew out of the International Migration Policy Program at the Carnegie Endowment for International Peace (http://carnegieendowment.org/).

The Southern Poverty Law Center (SPLC) http://www.splcenter.org was founded in 1971 as a small civil rights law firm. Today, SPLC is internationally known for its tolerance education programmes, its legal victories against white supremacists and its tracking of hate groups. Located in Montgomery, Alabama – the birthplace of the US Civil Rights Movement – the Southern Poverty Law Center was founded by Morris Dees and Joe Levin, two local lawyers who shared a commitment to racial equality. Its first president was civil. This organization publishes news items and reports on hate groups, including border vigilantes.

More information about the European Union (EU) can be found on the website Europa: The European Union at a Glance http://europa.eu/abc/index_enhtm. The reasons why the EU was founded are detailed and the history of its most recent expansions is charted. The rules for the movement of workers are given on another part of this site: http://ec.europa.eu/youreurope/nav/en/citizens/index.htm#.

REFERENCES

Altbach, Philip G. (2001) 'Higher Education and the WTO: Globalization Run Amok', *International Higher Education*, Center for International Higher Education, Boston College, www.bc.edu/bc_org/avp/soe/cihe/newsletter/News23/text001.htm.

Andreas, Peter (2000) *Border Games: Policing the US–Mexico Divide*, Ithaca, NY: Cornell University Press.

Anzaldua, Gloria (1987) *Borderlands: La Frontera*, San Francisco: Spinsters/Aunt Lute Book Company.

Arizona Daily Star (2006) 'Cochise Reports 1st Death of Illegal Entrant in '06', 22 February, http://www.azstarnet.com/SN/printDS/117018, accessed 24/02/06.

Arizona Republic (2007) 'Number of Immigrants Detained in the US Increases', 5 November.

Barker, Martin (1981) *The New Racism*, London: Routledge.

Balibar, Etienne (2004) *We the People of Europe? Reflections on Transnational Citizenship*, Princeton, NJ and Oxford: Princeton University Press.

Balibar, Etienne and Immanuel Wallerstein (1991) *Race, Nation, Class*, London: Verso.

BBC News (2005) 'Spain Launches Immigrant Amnesty', September. Online http://newsvote.bbc.co.uk/mpapps/pagetools/print/news.bbc.co.uk/1/hi/world/europe/4242411.

Buchanan, Patrick J. (2006) *State of Emergency: The Third World Invasion and Conquest of America*, New York: Thomas Dunne Books, St Martin's Press.

Doty, Roxanne Lynn (2003) *Anti-Immigrantism in Western Democracies*, London and New York: Routledge.

Dunn, Timothy J. (1996) *The Militarization of the US–Mexico Border 1978–1982*, Austin, TX: Center for Mexican American Studies, University of Texas at Austin.

Freeman, Gary P. (1979) *Immigrant Labor and Racial Conflict in Industrial Societies: The French and British Experiences*, Princeton, NJ: Princeton University Press.

Freeman, Richard B. (2006) *People Flows in Globalization*, National Bureau of Economic Research, Working Paper 12315.

Gelatt, Julia (2005) 'Schengen and the Free Movement of People across Europe', *Migration Information Source*, 1 October, Washington, DC: Migration Policy Institute.

Hollifield, James F. (2000) 'The Politics of International Migration', in Caroline B. Brettell and James F. Hollifield (eds) *Migration Theory: Talking across Disciplines*, New York: Routledge.

Huntington, Samuel P. (2004a) 'The Hispanic Challenge', *Foreign Policy* 141: 30–45.

Huntington, Samuel P. (2004b) *Who Are We? The Challenge to America's National Identity*, New York: Simon and Schuster.

Isbister, John (1996) *The Immigration Debate*, West Hartford, CT: Kumarian Press.

Martin, Philip (2003) 'Immigration: Shaping and Reshaping America', 10 October, Monograph, Michigan: University of Michigan, http://ww.npc.umich.edu/news/events/PRB-Monograph-Final.pdf.

Martin, Philip (1993) 'Trade and Migration: NAFTA and Agriculture', Washington, DC: Institute for International Economics, www.iie.com.

Migration Policy Institute (2007) 'MPI Data Hub – Migration Facts, Stats, and Maps', http://www.migrationinformation.org/DataHub/countrydata/data.cfm, accessed 05/11/07.

Migration Policy Institute (2004) 'Where the Numbers Come From', http://www.migrationinformation.org/feature/062005_explan.cfm, accessed 01/09/05.

Nanez, Dianna M. (2007) 'Don't Ask, Don't Tell Immigration Era Ending', *Arizona Republic*, 24 April.

Nevins, Joseph (2002) *Operation Gatekeeper: The Rise of the 'Illegal Alien' and the Making of the US–Mexico Boundary*, New York and London: Routledge.

Papademetriou, Demetrios G. (2005) 'Reflections on Restoring Integrity to the United States Immigration System: A Personal Vision', *Migration Policy Institute Insight*, No. 5, September.

Reimers, David. M. (1992) *Still the Golden Door: The Third World Come to America*, New York: Columbia University Press.

Romo, David Dorado (2005) *Ringside Seat to a Revolution*, El Paso, TX: Cinco Puntos Press.

Rubio-Goldsmith, Raquel, M. Melissa McCormick, Daniel Martinez and Inez Magdalena Duarte (2006) 'The "Funnel Effect" and Recovered Bodies of Unauthorized Migrants Processed by the Pima County Office of the Medical Examiner, 1990–2005', report submitted to the Pima County Board of Supervisors by the Binational Migration Institute, Mexican American Studies and Research Center at the University of Arizona, Tucson, Arizona, October 2006; Latin America Working Group, www.lawg.org/countries/mexico/death-stats.htm.

Rutland, Patricia J. (2007) 'T. Don Hutto: Homeland Security Bars U.N. Inspector', *Austin Chronicle*, 11 May.

Taguieff, Pierre-Andre (1990) 'The New Cultural Racism in France', *Telos* 38: 109–22.

Thorn, William (2005) 'Regulation of the Cross-Border Supply of Higher Education Services – an Australian Perspective', paper presented at the World Trade Organization Symposium on Cross-Border Supply of Services, Geneva, 28–29 April 2005, www.wto.org/English/tratop_e/serv_e/sym_april05_e/thorn_e.doc.

United States Accountability Office (2006) 'Border-Crossing Deaths Have Doubled Since 1995; Border Patrol's Efforts to Prevent Deaths Have Not Been Fully Evaluated', report to Bill Frist, Majority Leader, US Senate, August, GAO–06–770, Washington, DC: USGAO.

United Nations Economic and Social Council (2002) E/CN.4/2002/NGO/45, http://daccessdds.un.org/doc/UNDOC/GEN/G02/103/78/PDF/G0210378.pdf.

United States General Accounting Office (2001) 'INS Southwest Border Strategy: Resource and Impact Issues Remain after Seven Years', Report to Congressional Committees, August, GAO–01–842.

United Nations World Tourism Organization (2007) 'UNWTO Secretary-General Opens FITUR 2007', news release of the World Tourism Organization, www.world-tourism.org/newsroom/Releases/2007/January/opensfitur.htm.

Wagner, Dennis (2007) 'Racial Trends Found in DPS Traffic Stops', *Arizona Republic*, 7 November, http://www.azcentral.com/news/articles/1107dps1107.html.

CHAPTER 9

Why is the world divided territorially?

Stuart Elden

THE QUESTION
FORMS OF POLITICAL AND GEOGRAPHICAL ORGANISATION

If we look at an atlas, we find that it often begins with two maps of the world. One of these is physical, the other political. The first shows relief, depicting mountain ranges and plains, significant rivers, land masses and oceans. The second shows the same land and water, but this time the earth is brightly coloured, divided up and with clear lines separating out states from each other, and capital or other major cities marked as signs of human impact. We find the same divide when we move to maps of the continents later in the atlas.

The physical maps show a world that has barely changed in human history, although our knowledge of it certainly has. The political maps, though, bear almost no relation to the situation a few hundred years ago, let alone a few thousand. Territorial changes were common until the 1940s, many new states emerged from the process of decolonisation after World War Two and certain areas – notably Eastern Europe and Central Asia – will have dramatically changed in the lifetime of readers of this book. The final settlement of some areas remains an issue today.

Taking this kind of perspective shows us that the division of the world into separate territorial units, called states, is both artificial and arbitrary. Today it is generally accepted as the norm for political and geographical organisation. Yet this has not always been the case. Looking at older maps shows a very different perspective. Until relatively recently, large parts of the world were either unknown entirely – such as desert, mountain or polar regions – unknown to people in other parts or known to them only in the vaguest of ways. Land masses and key rivers appeared on maps of the world drawn in Europe, but the inland areas of islands or continents were largely undiscovered by Europeans and unmapped by them.

Maps of Europe in the Middle Ages show a jumble of political allegiances, with different rulers having control over a patchwork of land. Take a map of the situation in the fourteenth century, for instance (Figure 9.1). There are lands owned by the Church in Rome, lands within the Kingdom of France that owe allegiance to German princes, and the reverse. England has areas of strategic control on the continent, while the houses of Austria and Luxembourg have power far beyond their nominal location. The rulers of contemporary cities or regions such as Naples or Burgundy control vast swathes of land. Focusing in on a smaller area would show more complications. And, as noted above, at this time large parts of the rest of the world were unknown either in whole or in part to European cartographers. Much later, Africa's land was divided by European powers in the late nineteenth century into 'spheres of influence', which only later evolved into definite control on the ground (Figure 9.2).

The division of the world into territorial units called states reflects a particular relation to space. Yet, just as not all human communities have been the same as modern states, so too with their relation to the land they inhabit. Hunter-gatherer communities have a very different relation to space from those societies that cultivate land and domesticate animals. They tend not to have fixed dwellings and may move with the seasons in search of water and food. A recent legal case may help to illustrate this.

The modern state of Botswana includes large parts of the Kalahari Desert (Figure 9.3). The indigenous San or Basarwa people of this area, often known as the Bushmen, are looked at as one of the oldest peoples in the world. The Central

Although this division of the world into states is accepted as the norm, it does create problems in terms of tackling important issues, such as climate change.
See Chapter 3

This division also means that not everyone is authorised to live where they choose, creating many serious difficulties.
See Chapter 8

FIGURE 9.1
Map of Central Europe in 1360. From *Atlas to Freeman's Historical Geography*, edited by J.B. Bury, Longmans, Green, and Co., 3rd edn 1903

The history of colonialism continues to have an impact in a range of ways.
See also Chapters 11, 14 and 15

This idea that we must protect the environment is one that has historically emerged and changed.
See Chapter 3

Kalahari Game Reserve in Botswana was created by the British as colonisers in 1961 to allow them to remain in their ancestral lands. On independence in 1966 the government of Botswana proposed that they move into new settlements outside this area, in which hospitals and other social services were provided. One of the reasons given was for the protection of the wildlife in the Reserve. The discovery of diamonds in the 1980s meant that this movement took on a new urgency for the government, despite the resistance of the San people. In 2002 this eviction was facilitated by violence, refusal of hunting licences and ceasing food rations. In late 2006 a Botswana court ruled that the eviction was illegal and that the people could return.

In this example we can see the clash between a modern state and its territorial claims, including the desire to exploit its natural resources, and a different understanding of space of a nomadic people who live from and on the land, rather than

FIGURE 9.2
Map of Africa in 1892. From *A School Atlas of English History*, edited by Samuel Rawson Gardiner, London: Longmans, Green, and Co., 1892, p. 62.

cultivate it (see Townsend 2004). Even looking at the geometric boundaries of the Reserve and the western border of the state imposed over a physical and human landscape shows two very different spatial logics.

Standard definitions of territory suggest that it is an area of space under the control or jurisdiction of a group of people, which might be a state, but which might potentially be other types of political organisation. Jean Gottmann notes that

> Although its Latin root, *terra*, means 'land or 'earth', the word territory conveys the notion of an area around a place; it connotes an organisation with an element of centrality, which ought to be the authority exercising sovereignty over the people occupying or using that place and the space around it.

> (Gottmann 1973: 5)

The desire to exploit natural resources is often a source of conflict.
See Chapter 3

FIGURE 9.3
Map of Botswana and Central Kalahari Game Reserve
Redrawn after: www.merriam-webster.com/cgi-bin/nytmaps.pl?botswana

The geographer David Storey suggests that

> The term 'territory' is most usually used in reference to the area of land claimed by a country. However territories exist at a variety of spatial scales from the global down to the local. Territory refers to a portion of geographic space which is claimed or occupied by a person or group of persons or by an institution. It is, thus, an area of 'bounded space'.
>
> (Storey 2001: 1)

The claim that a territory is a bounded space leads to the idea of a state as what the sociologist Anthony Giddens called 'a bordered power container' (1985; see Taylor 1994, 1995). The notion of a bounded space is important not just as one

BOX 9.1 MAX WEBER

FIGURE 9.4
Max Weber. Deutsches
Historisches Museum,
Berlin Ref: F52/2693

Max Weber (1864–1920) was a German historian
and political economist. He is seen as one of the
founders of sociology, and is known for his
writings on the city, religion and the historical
development of the state. He was involved in the
negotiations for the Treaty of Versailles (1919)
and helped to draft Germany's Weimar
Constitution, which came into force in 1919.
His most famous works are *The Protestant Ethic
and the Spirit of Capitalism* (1958, written 1904–5),
Economy and Society (1968, written 1914) and the
essay 'Politics as a Vocation', from which the
quotation on this page is taken.

of the key ways in which territories are defined, but because it brings us to the
notion of a boundary or border.

The relation between the state and its territory is therefore crucial to understanding both terms. The German sociologist Max Weber famously declared that
'a state is that human community which (successfully) lays claim to the monopoly
of legitimate physical violence within a certain territory, this "territory" being
another of the defining characteristics of the state' (1994: 310–11).

Weber therefore stresses four key things: community; legitimacy; violence; and
territory. The state is a particularly human grouping, within a discrete area, and
within that area it makes a claim to complete control. He is suggesting that this
type of political rule is inherently tied to a particular place, and the people within
it. The state is able to command absolute authority within that discrete area,
without the involvement of other forces – be they other states or political
groupings. Its authority is absolute because it is both undivided (no other body
has that power) and unlimited (the state can do what it wants, without reference
to other bodies). Other political groups, such as private armies or rebel forces, or
independence movements are, by their nature, illegitimate, that is, without moral
or legal justification. This is the notion of sovereignty – the power to command
and rule, which is rendered legitimate through a claim to authority. The international political system, such as that set out in the United Nations Charter, largely

For more on Weber's
work on power and
authority, see
Chapter 6.

For some of these agreements regarding the environment, see **Chapter 3**.

subscribes to this view of the relation between politics and place. States are held to have exclusive internal sovereignty (jurisdiction within their own borders) and equal external sovereignty. Equal external sovereignty, or equal jurisdiction, means that no state should be a puppet of another, and that there should be no hierarchy of states. In practice there are many instances where this is clearly not the case, but these assumptions function as an important legal and political fiction that structures the world and helps to maintain the international order. Today, though, international agreements increasingly do put limitations on state sovereignty, including on actions that impact on the environment, the use of nuclear power and the treatment of refugees.

Why, then, is the world divided territorially? Why are borders drawn where they are? Has the world always been divided in this kind of way? Why do some rivers and mountain ranges form borders, yet others do not? Why do some lines of division take on such importance, while other lines drawn on maps or on the ground do not? Contrast, for example, the heavily militarised line of control between India and Pakistan in the mountains of Kashmir with the largely uncontrolled border region between Pakistan and Afghanistan. Why have the borders of Germany, for example, moved so dramatically over the twentieth century? Why are the borders in Africa drawn in such a way, with so many straight lines cutting through the landscape? Why, with the notable exception of Antarctica, where territorial claims are suspended, is almost every piece of land on the planet under the control of a single state, which claims exclusive rights to what happens in this area? This is not to say that there are no disputed territories – examples would include Kashmir, the Occupied Territories of the Palestinian West Bank and the Gaza Strip, and many others in the Middle East – but rather that the norm is that they are 'owned' by a state. Why, increasingly, are the oceans being similarly divided? Why should geographical location dictate citizenship, rights and responsibilities? The place where you are born, or where your parents are from, determines many of the conditions that will affect the rest of your life.

For more on the complex relationship between citizenship, geography and rights, see **Chapter 8**.

Chapter 18 examines in detail whether we are able to stop people from being harmed and, in particular, the case of East Timor. **Chapter 18** also discusses what it means to look to the 'international community' for answers.

Although some people are able to move where they live, taking on citizenship of or permanent residence in another state, this is not an option for many people. Questions of immigration and the status of refugees show the close relation between geography and rights. Many indigenous peoples find themselves excluded from their historical lands, either entirely or because modern borders cut across them. Many states treat those who live within their territory in terrible ways, but what possibility do these people have to leave; and what rights or responsibilities do regional or international organisations have to protect them? This question has been raised especially in the last few years with the examples of Rwanda, East Timor, Kosovo and Sudan, but the international community does not yet seem to have come up with a satisfactory answer.

ILLUSTRATIVE EXAMPLE
THE DEVELOPMENT OF THE EUROPEAN TERRITORIAL STATE

In order to get some sense of how territory emerged, and why this model of ordering political space spread across the world, I will outline the history of the European state, with an emphasis on its geographical aspects. This allows us to see that not all political organisations have the same relation to space.

Ancient Greece, the Roman Empire and the Middle Ages

The ancient Greek city-state, known as a '*polis*', was one of the earliest forms of political unit in Europe. It dominated Greek political culture between the eighth and third centuries before the Common Era (the period before the birth of Jesus Christ) and is discussed by writers such as the philosophers Plato and Aristotle and the historians Thucydides and Herodotus. Although it had an urban centre, this human community spread into the neighbouring countryside and cultivated land in this region. It thus had a centralised source of power, and a broader extent where it reached out to neighbouring land. Although there were wars between *poleis*, there was often lots of unclaimed land between them. Unlike modern states they did not take over all of the land in the broader region, and some rural shrines, for example, were shared between neighbours. We therefore have a model of political rule that is strongly centralised, with power being less strong as we move away from the centre.

The *polis* and political thought related to it have had a lasting impact on the political imagination. **See Chapters 4 and 8**

Rome began as something similar to a Greek city-state, but as it waged wars against its neighbours in the region it began to accumulate more and more land. By the time the republic fell and it became an empire, it had expanded further and further away from the Italian peninsula. Roman political geography is complicated, with different parts of the empire ruled in different ways, either through allegiance, paying tribute (goods, slaves or money) or incorporation into Roman systems. Rome did not recognise other political units as being on the same level as it – unlike the way neighbouring states do today. Land was, effectively, part of the Roman Empire, or it could become so at some point in the future. This is the idea of *terra nullius* – empty or no-man's land. This meant that they did not accord other groups the same rights of possession that they gave themselves, something that European powers later used to justify colonisation of large parts of the rest of the world. While Rome sometimes built walls or barriers, such as Hadrian's Wall in northern England or the fortifications on the Rhine River in modern-day Germany, these were more for defensive purposes than to mark the final borders of Roman expansion. Land on both sides of Hadrian's Wall was cultivated, for example, and another wall was built further north (the Antonine Wall) as Rome expanded its reach. At this time the idea of a frontier – as an area

The idea of *terra nullius* was also used by the European conquerors in relation to the American continent. **See Chapter 3** of land between different political rulers – predominated over a boundary as a single line of control. While today a boundary is, nominally, a line with zero width between two political units such as states, at this time the idea of a frontier as a zone, or something having width, was much more common. What is important about this is that a frontier zone will usually have people living in it, as well as resources within it. A border can be either a line or a zone, but today most are lines, even though there is a lot of discussion of border regions looking at areas across these lines.

With the collapse of the Western Roman Empire in the fifth century of the Common Era, Europe became a much more jumbled and complicated political unit. Various kings, tribes and other political groupings, including the Church, had power over land. This was often on a very small scale, and there were frequent invasions and transfers of authority. Large parts of Western Europe were unified under the Carolingian Empire, and the King of the Franks, Charlemagne, was crowned Holy Roman Emperor by the Pope on Christmas Day 800. Three centuries after the fall of the Western Roman Empire, therefore, an attempt was made to re-establish it as the Holy Roman Empire. Despite the French author Voltaire's joke that this was neither holy, Roman nor an empire, this was a way for the Church in Rome to exercise political power across much of Europe for several hundred years.

The Treaties of Westphalia

With the fractures in religion around the Reformation – a period of conflict over the trajectory of the Catholic Church, particularly over corruption and the power of the priesthood – there arose a particular kind of political problem. If the prince or king of a region within the Empire converted to Calvinism or Lutherism, which religion would be dominant in his lands? Would it be the religion of the local ruler or that of the Church in Rome? This caused a great deal of conflict in the sixteenth and seventeenth centuries, leading to various agreements between the units within the empire. The two most famous are the Diet of Augsburg in 1555, which laid down the principle of *cuius regio, eius religio* – to whom the rule, or region, his religion – and the Treaties of Westphalia in 1648. Augsburg's settlement, which allowed for Lutheran princes or free cities to have this as the official religion, was effectively extended to Calvinists in 1648.

While Westphalia brought to an end most of the fighting in the Thirty Years War, France and Spain continued fighting until the Treaty of the Pyrenees in 1659. This is in some senses even more important, as it led to a joint commission for setting the exact border between Spain and France, and can be said to have created the first modern boundary from what had previously been more of a frontier (see Sahlins 1989).

For more on how the relationship between religion and politics is understood and organised, see **Chapters 5 and 6.**

Chapter 6 tells you more about the Reformation, and Martin Luther in particular.

BOX 9.2 THE PEACE OF WESTPHALIA

The Peace of Westphalia (1648) comprised two treaties negotiated in the north-west of modern Germany, at the towns of Münster and Osnabrück. The treaties brought to an end the Thirty Years War (1618–48). The Osnabrück Treaty was between Sweden and the Emperor of the Holy Roman Empire, the one at Münster between France and the Emperor. There were a number of things at stake in the negotiations, including religion and political power. The Westphalian treaties are often used to mark the beginning of the modern era of politics, with the introduction of the idea of absolute state sovereignty, sometimes known as the Westphalian System. A range of characteristics we would associate with modern states are indeed given to political units within the empire by the treaties. For example, they are given the right to declare war and peace, and are entitled to make laws, raise taxes, keep a standing (permanent) army and to make new fortifications and alliances without the prior consent of the Emperor.

The treaties importantly stress the 'free exercise of territorial right' (Treaty of Münster, Article 64; Treaty of Osnabrück, Article VIIII, 1) or the 'territorial right and superiority' (Osnabrück, Article V, 30) that the princes have, thus linking political rule, or sovereignty, to land, to territory.

FIGURE 9.5
'The Swearing of the Oath of Ratification of the Treaty of Westphalia at Münster, 24th October 1648' by Gerard Ter Borch (1648). © The National Gallery, London

Note that the presumption against interference is ignored in various ways. **Chapter 13** highlights the interference of global financial institutions in the domestic policies of 'developing' states and **Chapter 15** examines why some people sometimes think it's good to interfere in other states.

Chapter 10 examines how nations have to be made and are always challenged by alternative stories of community.

The situation in North and South Korea is examined in **Chapter 19** and the end of the division between East and West Germany is explored in **Chapter 6**.

There were, of course, also non-European empires. **See Chapter 15**

From this period on, the state model began to become the standard form of political organisation in Europe. This was not entirely a result of the Peace of Westphalia, since many states – such as England, France and Sweden – existed before this time. The emergence of city-states in northern Italy during the Renaissance is also important as they began to develop more modern forms of political rule, developing from classical ideas. Equally, many of the features of the modern system of states – such as equal sovereignty and the presumption against non-interference in domestic affairs – clearly did not become norms until much later. Yet around this time states or individual rulers began to pay much more attention to the importance of clearly demarcating where their rule extended to.

It is worth noting that the state predates the nation. The nation is often taken to have developed in the late eighteenth century. The development of the nation, and ideas of national identity and nationalism, is a similarly contested and historical one. Today people often talk about the nation-state. This is problematic for at least two reasons. First, it assumes that the two are the same thing, when one is a grouping of people and the other a political unit. The borders of each *can* coincide, but most states include people of different nationalities, and at times the same nationality has been found in more than one state, such as in North and South Korea today, or East and West Germany in the late twentieth century. Second, a straightforward equation of the nation with the state generally fails to note the historical and contingent development of each term.

Imperialism and empire

The European model for dividing states was gradually spread across the world between the fifteenth and twentieth centuries (see Badie 2000). These European empires differed from many earlier empires, such as the Roman Empire, in their spatial extent. Whereas the Roman Empire had expanded contiguously – that is, to land immediately bordering its existing possessions – European empires occupied land at a distance. Other parts of the world became the location for inter-European rivalries. These included French and English competition in North America and Spanish/Portuguese claims on different parts of the world. Later these took on a particularly concentrated form in the late nineteenth century with the 'scramble for Africa'. This was a process by which European powers carved up Africa for their own purposes.

Thus the Western European model of territorial division between states was exported to much of the rest of the world. Initially this was as colonial possessions, but as these places gained independence they largely inherited the boundaries of colonial division. In South America, for instance, the division between Spanish and Portuguese possessions and internal divisions between parts of the Spanish Empire became the boundaries of the newly independent states. This became known as the doctrine of *uti possidetis*, a Latin phrase meaning that what you will have is 'what you possess'. In 1964 the Organisation of African Unity passed a motion that suggested that this should be the principle of decolonisation for that continent too. While this had the benefit of preventing a territorial free-for-all, it has meant that the largely arbitrary boundaries of Africa remain, creating many ongoing problems (see Lalonde 2002).

Within Europe the break-up of empires has led to the emergence of a number of new states. After the First World War the defeated powers of Germany, Austria-Hungary and the Ottoman Empire were either broken up or had territory removed as part of a punitive settlement. In the various treaties of the Peace of Paris, which included the Treaty of Versailles, the victorious powers sought to rebuild the map of Europe. Germany lost territory to many of its neighbours, including Belgium and Poland. The Habsburg Empire was fragmented into a number of smaller states, including Austria, Hungary and a number of states in Central Europe and the Balkans. To avoid lots of small states, some rather artificial ones were created such as Czechoslovakia, which included Czechs and Slovaks, and Yugoslavia. Yugoslavia means the federation of the Southern Slavs, and was effectively created by a line being drawn around a large number of different peoples – Slovenes, Serbs, Croats, Albanians, Montenegrins and Macedonians. From the Ottoman Empire modern Turkey was created – still a multi-ethnic state – and a number of new states in the Near and Middle East. Many of the world's most insuperable territorial problems – such as Iraq and Israel/Palestine – date from this time.

Yugoslavia broke apart in the 1990s amidst violent conflict. For more on this and a map of the region, see **Chapter 4**.

FIGURE 9.6
Map of ethnic distribution of the Habsburg Empire, 1914. Source:
http://www.historyonmaps.com/BWSamples/HabsburgEthnic.html

At the end of the Cold War many of these states fragmented into smaller entities. Some of these split along broadly nationalist lines, though there is much debate as to whether these pre-existed the division or were in some way produced by that process. Self-determination – the idea that a group of people in a discrete area should be able to govern themselves – again became very popular. Earlier uses of this ideal, such as those that shaped the Peace of Paris, had been tempered by recognition of considerations concerning the viability of new states. Equally, as can be seen from Figure 9.6, it is rare for national groups to fit neatly into discrete geographical areas, with the situation on the ground often far more complicated, with a mosaic of different identities. In addition, some people do not identify in this way. The compromise that the international community fell upon was that republics within federal states could become independent states. This meant that Czechoslovakia was able to split into the Czech Republic and Slovakia in a largely peaceful way. This is known as the Velvet Divorce, a reference to the Velvet Revolution in 1989, which overthrew Communist rule without much bloodshed. The Soviet Union similarly broke up along republic lines – its full title was the Union of Soviet Socialist Republics (USSR) – into fifteen separate states. This led to independence for the European states of Ukraine, Belarus and the Baltic States of Estonia, Latvia and Lithuania, as well as a number of new states in Central Asia such as Uzbekistan and Tajikistan. Many of these states, especially those in Central Asia had no experience of independence before and were often unable to deal with some of its implications. In addition, many of the republics' boundaries were poorly specified.

The break-up of Yugoslavia is extremely complicated, but again largely occurred along the lines of the former republics of that federal state. Bosnia did not work on this basis, since its multi-ethnic nature and the interests of its neighbours led to prolonged civil war and forcible movement or destruction of populations, known as ethnic cleansing. These problems were solved to some extent by a complicated cartography of division and incorporation at the Dayton Conference. Yet this did not end the problems in Yugoslavia, with Kosovo, an autonomous province of Serbia, seeking independence. NATO went to war in 1999, ostensibly to protect the civilian population of Kosovo from Serbia. While the aerial bombardment produced the desired outcome of a Serbian withdrawal, it also produced problems of a different nature. One was the status of Kosovo itself, which caused much discussion concerning its future either within Yugoslavia or Serbia, as an international protectorate or as an independent state. While Russia objected because of its support from Serbia, even states that supported Kosovo's declaration of independence in 2008 feared it would create a precedent for other states to break up. The republics within the Yugoslav federation, or those within the Soviet Union, were able to gain recognition for their independence and take on the boundaries of internal division. Kosovo, though, was a province within a republic, and so was not of the same constitutional standing. Among

The break-up of Yugoslavia involved a particular kind of identity politics, as discussed in **Chapter 4.**

NATO's Kosovo operation and its legality were controversial. **See Chapter 18** other examples, this is the same kind of distinction that Chechnya has within Russia or Abkhazia within Georgia. These complications will be returned to on pp. 214–15.

RESPONSES
THE EMERGENCE OF TERRITORY

There are many explanations for the emergence of territory as a particular way of ordering the relation between political rule and space.

Some writers use the idea of territoriality to understand territory. These accounts suggest that human relations to space can be understood through modes of behaviour. Some valuable studies have been made of 'human territoriality', looking at how humans, both individually and collectively, encounter, work and change the spaces around them. Some of this work begins from a biological perspective, deriving insights from comparing human behaviour to that of animals (see Malmberg 1980). While this way of approaching the topic can produce some valuable insights, the problem with it is that human social organisation has changed more rapidly than our biological drives.

Chapter 4 notes such biological perspectives in relation to the way we think about gender and race.

Some work on territoriality does not suggest such a purely biological approach, but incorporates a more social angle (Sack 1986). For Sack territoriality is a geopolitical strategy, not a basic vital instinct. Territory is a social construct – produced through interaction and struggle – and therefore thoroughly permeated by social relations. To analyse the territory as a mere container of social action is to miss a vital part of the picture. Sack's analysis, as well as that of a number of other writers, incorporates elements of a range of approaches to understanding territory.

These can be usefully schematised as political-economic, political-strategic and technique-based.

Political-economic approach

Some accounts see territory as a form of property. Marxist accounts particularly suggest that developments in economics are important. In *The German Ideology*, Karl Marx and Friedrich Engels suggest that antiquity is tied to the city-state and its 'little territory' and the Middle Ages to the country (1970: 45). Though the economic system of the Middle Ages, feudalism, thus put a great deal of focus

Chapter 13 introduces Marx and Engels' work.

on land, it was only with capitalism and the emergence of the modern state that there was a real emphasis on people and land as significant taxable assets. To have land under a system of centralised control, and to remove overlapping jurisdiction, became an imperative. This was tied to the emerging focus on the importance of private property, the growth of new towns and cities and a shift of power toward the middle classes with increased industrialisation. This led to a stress on the importance of national markets rather than local ones, and a widespread centralisation of the state, and therefore a control of its land, as territory.

Chapter 12 shows the impact of industrialisation upon people and their work situation.

One of the best examples of this argument is found in the work of the Marxist theorist Perry Anderson, particularly in his books *Passages from Antiquity to Feudalism* (1974a) and *Lineages of the Absolutist State* (1974b). Anderson offers a broad analysis of the material forces shaping the development of successive historical periods, suggesting that this is a Marxist account. However, his account is broader than the merely economic.

> The typical medium of inter-feudal rivalry, by contrast, was military and its structure was always potentially the zero-sum conflict of the battlefield, by which fixed quantities of ground were won or lost. For land is a natural monopoly: it cannot be indefinitely extended, only redivided. The categorical object of noble rule was territory, regardless of the community inhabiting it. Land as such, not language, defined the natural perimeters of its power.
>
> (P. Anderson 1974b: 31)

This is a complicated series of claims. Anderson is suggesting that feudal power structures revolved around possession of land, often fought over. If one feudal lord gained land, another would have lost it. Land is a scarce resource and cannot be produced, only redistributed. Given that political control revolved around possession of land, people were much less important. Changes in economic structures produced a different social structure.

Political-strategic approach

Hinted at in Anderson's quotation above, and more explicitly stressed in other accounts, is the fact that territory emerges as important for more strategic reasons. States wanted to ensure that their land was practically manageable, and so were concerned with issues around security. France, for example, following the Treaty of the Pyrenees, began a process of mapping and surveying its land, moving towards what it called its 'natural frontiers'. These were the Alps and the Pyrenees, the English Channel, Atlantic and Mediterranean, and the River Rhine. This gives rise to the roughly hexagonal shape of modern France. To ensure this, France exchanged some land to the north-east to even up its boundary with the Netherlands, and employed technical specialists to map and reinforce its borders

Territory is now much less central to thinking about security.
See Chapter 17

more generally. The unifications that produced Germany and Italy in the nineteenth century were instances of national projects that included the bringing together of disparate political entities in a unified territory.

These accounts stress the importance of power relations in understanding control of space, either explicitly, as in some work by and influenced by Michel Foucault, or through other terms such as 'sovereignty' or 'authority'. Weber's analysis of the historical development of the state would fit in this category. The sociologist Michael Mann has provided a very detailed account from this broad perspective (1986, 1993), stressing the changing dynamics of power and in particular military and strategic interests in the development of the state, though, like Anderson, he only tangentially discusses territory.

Foucault's work is also discussed in **Chapter 6**.

The political-economic and political-strategic models for understanding territory have much merit, and it is undoubtedly the case that there were a number of interlinked changes that impacted on political rule over space. Both types of analysis are vital to understanding how territory emerged as an organising category. However, elements of both ways of understanding territory can be

---

BOX 9.3 MICHEL FOUCAULT

Michel Foucault (1926–84) was a French historian and philosopher. His studies of madness, medicine, punishment and sexuality have had a significant impact in a range of disciplines. His work on power and its relation to knowledge has been particularly important. Foucault argues that power flows throughout society rather than from a central source, and that it is best analysed through a series of relations. Power is *exercised*, which means we should study how it is used rather than nominal possession of power. Especially in his later works he is interested in how power can be creative, rather than simply repressive, and how both forms of power are important in understanding the modern human subject. His most influential work for those interested in politics is *Discipline and Punish* (1976), but the ongoing publication of his lecture courses, such as *Society Must Be Defended* (2003, from 1975–6) and *Security, Territory, Population* (2007, from 1977–8) is beginning to have an important impact.

FIGURE 9.7
Paris, 1973. Demonstration in support of immigrant workers. In the foreground: the French philosopher Michel Foucault. Photo: Gilles Peress, Magnum

found in earlier political systems. The first, of land as a form of property, can be found in ancient Greek texts such as Plato's *Laws* and was clearly a crucial factor throughout the Middle Ages. The Domesday Book, from 1086, was a survey of the lands in England for the knowledge of William the Conqueror, who had invaded twenty years before. The second is closer to a sense of land as terrain, and in this sense can be found in any number of ancient texts such as Thucydides' *History of the Peloponnesian War* or Julius Caesar's accounts of the *Gallic War* or the *Civil War*.

Technique-based approach

One thing that was significantly different in the period when territory, at least in its modern sense, emerged was the availability of a number of techniques. The mapping and control of territory is, in large part, dependent on them.

They include advances in geometry, such as the coordinate or analytic geometry pioneered by René Descartes (a form of geometry that uses algebra, coordinates and equations); developments in cartography and land surveying; and improvements in the accurate measurement of time through more advanced clocks. Knowing the exact time both in your current location and at another known point was essential to getting an accurate measurement of longitude. This is because the sun circles the earth in twenty-four hours and there are 360° of longitude. Therefore one hour time difference from your starting point is 15°; four minutes is 1°. In order to accurately measure distances, and especially to know where ships were at sea, this was of enormous importance. Latitude is easier to measure, as it can be obtained from the angle of the sun or known stars to the horizon, though this too requires a certain calculative ability and the right instruments. Only with these kinds of facilities could modern boundaries be established as more than a line staked out on the ground. For mountainous regions, for deserts or tundra, or particularly for the abstract division of unknown places in the colonised world, such techniques were crucial.

The development of new forms of technology often has an impact on how our lives are organised and how we relate to the world. **See Chapters 7, 12 and 17**

Just as Mann stresses the development of certain military techniques, so the geographer Edward Soja suggests the importance of cartographic ones alongside purely economic factors:

> Conventional Western perspectives on spatial organisation are powerfully shaped by the concept of property, in which pieces of territory are viewed as 'commodities' capable of being bought, sold, or exchanged at the market place. Space is viewed as being subdivided into components whose boundaries are 'objectively' determined through the mathematical and astronomically based techniques of surveying and cartography.
>
> (Soja 1971: 9)

BOX 9.4 GEOMETRIC TERRITORIAL DIVISION

Examples of these kinds of geometric territorial division include:

- The western boundary between the USA and Canada, which runs along the 49th parallel of latitude. Compare this to the eastern boundary between the states, established much earlier between colonial possessions of the British.
- The surveying of the Mason-Dixon Line in the 1760s, which was to settle a boundary dispute between Maryland and Pennsylvania when they were both British colonies. The line runs at approximately 39° 43′ 20″.
- The rectangular land survey of the lands of the United States west of the Mississippi in the late eighteenth and nineteenth centuries, leading to the geometric shape of many of the western states. There is a town called Four Corners which is the only place in the USA where four states (Utah, New Mexico, Arizona and Colorado) meet at a single point.
- The straight-line boundaries of the states within Australia.
- The division of Africa between colonial powers at the 1884–5 Berlin Congress.
- Some of the borders in the Middle East and in the Arabian peninsula, many of which were set after the break up of the Ottoman Empire following World War One.

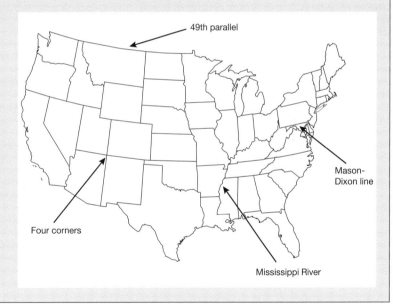

FIGURE 9.8
Map of mainland USA

As can be seen from the Soja and Anderson quotations on pp. 208 and 206 and from Mann's analysis, it is rare to find any of these ways of understanding territory – the political-economic, the political-strategic and the technique-based – in isolation. Nonetheless they are important component parts of any analysis. If the first allows an understanding of territory as land and the second of territory as terrain, perhaps only the third really sets 'territory' apart as a distinct form of social/spatial organisation.

Boundary making

One of the key techniques is in the practice of actually making boundaries and the process of taking this from the map to the land. In political geography a three-stage process of boundary making is usually outlined:

- *allocation*, which sets the general shape, making use of straight lines, coordinates of latitude/longitude, and depiction on a map;
- *delimitation*, which involves the selection of specific boundary sites on the ground;
- *demarcation*, where the boundary is marked by pillars, cleared vistas, fences, etc.

(Jones 1945)

It is clear that the first stage, and even elements of the second, can be done without any detailed knowledge of the land itself, whereas the third necessarily requires presence on the ground. Many colonial boundaries were only allocated or loosely delimited, leading to many subsequent problems. Today, maintenance and management of previously demarcated boundaries and the effective demarcation of those that were merely allocated or delimited is an ongoing concern. Poorly maintained borders often lead to conflict, such as the war between Ethiopia and Eritrea in 1998–2000.

One may of course ask whether this cavalier attitude towards colonial borders was due to technical difficulties or an indifferent attitude.

Recognising this historical aspect of territorial division is important, because it allows us to see that the modern way of ordering the world is not the only possible system. It allows us to escape what the geographer John Agnew has called the territorial trap. Agnew suggests that this is a threefold assumption: that modern state sovereignty is a given that requires clearly bounded territories; that there is a necessary opposition between foreign and domestic affairs; and that the territorial state is the geographical 'container' of modern society (Agnew 1994). Similarly, for Gottmann, it is all too easy to uncritically assume the modern, or legal sense of territory as a 'portion of geographical space under the jurisdiction of certain people' (1973: 5).

BROADER ISSUES
THE FUTURE OF THE TERRITORIAL STATE

States have not always existed, and territorial division is neither fixed nor the only way in which humans have encountered and organised space. The emergence of certain techniques, dependent in part on changes in scientific and philosophical ways of viewing the world, shows that this is a historical development.

The kinds of techniques that allowed states to map and control their own territory and to abstractly divide up other places are not isolated. Rather they are part of a much wider range of developments in the natural and human sciences around that time. This was a historical period that included the Renaissance, literally a *rebirth* of interest in the literature, science and politics of classical Greece and Rome. Many modern inventions emerged at this time, and scientists, writers and philosophers discussed a whole range of ideas. The beginning of modern political theory in the work of writers such as Niccolò Machiavelli, Jean Bodin and Thomas Hobbes; modern philosophy (René Descartes, John Locke, Baruch Spinoza and Gottfried Leibniz); and modern science (Galileo, Isaac Newton) are all closely related. There is a concentration on reason – both in terms of abstract science and thought and also in terms of political practice. The emergence of a number of mathematical and calculative techniques, such as land surveying, triangulation and geometry, is closely linked to state practices, with many of the sponsors of cartographers being states or other rulers. In addition, the development of political arithmetic, which later became known as statistics – literally the knowledge of states – began at this time (Elden 2007).

Chapters 6 and 10 note Thomas Hobbes' influence, too.

Chapter 5 explains how this concentration on reason is related to the Enlightenment.

Recent innovations in technology have led to developments in how boundaries are discussed at peace conferences and put into practice on the ground. Some of the more technologically inspired methods were used at the Dayton Peace Conference in 1995 to set the boundaries of Bosnia. These included digitised maps that could be redrawn and calculated far more quickly than by hand, allowing the cartographers to work at the same speed as the negotiations; statistical analyses that would quickly compute what percentage of territory different political groups would get depending on the placing of lines; and visualisations. These last were perhaps the most stunning innovation, allowing the negotiations to see the terrain they were dividing as if they were flying over it (Johnson 1999). For political leaders unable to read maps, such as Slobodan Milošević, these were a powerful technique. Since Dayton, techniques have further evolved, and GIS (Geographical Information Systems) software is extensively used in boundary making, as it has been for the Ethiopia–Eritrea border, maritime boundaries and as a tool of the discussions in the Israel/Palestine 'peace process'.

Statistics are extremely important to how we understand and govern the world. **See especially Chapter 13**

The emergence of a particular model of the state and its control of territory emerged at a particular historical juncture and in a specific geographical context. This was then spread to most other parts of the world through colonisation. Recognising that the territorial state is a historical development shows both that it has not always existed and that there is no essential reason why it always should. This leads to the question of whether this particular model of the state will endure, and whether territory is as important in the twenty-first century as it has been for the past few centuries.

Thinking territorially is a powerful way of operating, for among other things it enables states to claim exclusive internal jurisdiction – the right to do anything

Chapter 18 examines in more detail how sovereignty is significant in the context of conflict and possible resolutions.

they want within their boundaries. States are unlikely to give up this control without a struggle. Nonetheless, several challenges to this way of working have occurred over the last few decades.

One of these is the rise of supra-national organisations, such as the European Union. This is taking over key aspects of the role of states, such as making laws and monetary policy, and the rejected European constitution pushed for moves toward a common defence and foreign policy. With the weakening of internal borders to allow the free movement of goods and people, the European Union has challenged a number of the territorial aspects of the states which have joined as members (see James Anderson 1996; Bialasiewicz *et al.* 2005).

Globalisation has also challenged the idea of self-contained territorial states, with suggestions that flows of information, goods and energy around the world now transcend state boundaries. This has led some to suggest that globalisation can be understood as deterritorialisation or supra-territorialisation. Deterritorialisation means that territory is no longer fixed, and supra-territorialisation that spaces of interaction can no longer be contained with the borders of states (see Scholte 2005).

Some writers suggest that globalisation is productive of new ways of under-standing space, suggesting that new techniques have emerged. Manuel Castells, for example, has suggested that we have moved from a 'space of places' to a 'space of flows' (Castells 1989; 1996: 405–59). His suggestion is that location is no longer as important as it once was, but connection, through networks, has superseded it:

> Our societies are constructed around flows: flows of capital, flows of information, flows of technology, flows of organizational interactions, flows of images, sounds and symbols. Flows are not just one element of social organization: they are the expression of the processes dominating our economic, political, and symbolic life . . . Thus, I propose the idea that there is a new spatial form characteristic of social practices that dominate and shape the network society: the space of flows. The space of flows is the material organization of time-sharing social practices that work through flows. By flows I understand purposeful, repetitive, programmable sequences of exchange and interaction between physically disjointed positions held by social actors.
>
> (Castells 1996: 412)

Technologies of communication are discussed in Chapter 7.

There is undoubtedly much to be said in favour of this analysis. New forms of technology, particularly in terms of communication and the passage of informa-tion, have transformed social relations. In this interlinked and interdependent world we are now often supposed to be closer – in the sense of our concern and interaction – to people many miles away than to our nearest neighbours. Proximity is not the same as distance.

BOX 9.5 THE EUROPEAN UNION

The EU was set up in the aftermath of World War Two to bring peace, stability and prosperity to Europe. From the Schuman Declaration and the six-nation EU of the 1950s the EU has grown and after its 2007 enlargement includes 27 countries. The three main decision-making bodies in the EU are: the Parliament, the Council of Ministers of the EU, and the Commission. Its annual budget is over €120 billion [$190 billion] in fields like regional and social development, agriculture, research and energy. The EU is a single market . . . Citizenship of the EU brings with it a series of fundamental and political rights, including the right to travel, live and work anywhere in the EU. Countries of the EU work closely together on trade issues and development policy, and the EU is developing a common foreign and defence policy.

(From: Pascal Fontaine (2006) 'Europe in 12 lessons' http://europa.eu/abc/12lessons/index_en.htm)

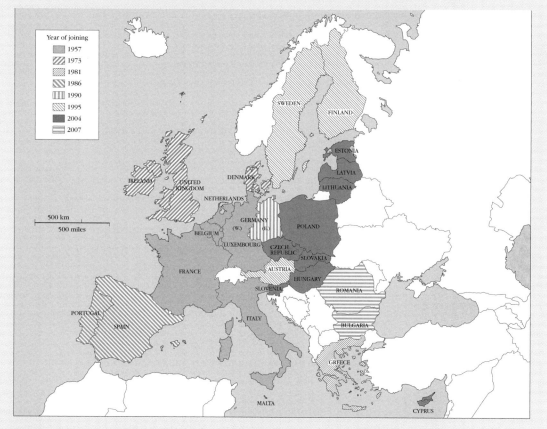

FIGURE 9.9
Member states of the European Union, 2007

See Chapter 8 for a map of migration flows.

The movement of people around the world, and in particular wide-scale economic migration, has also produced a series of challenges to the exclusive territorial power of the state. Yet while in the 1990s a series of suggestions were made about the decreasing power and importance of state borders, a number of more recent changes, notably the attacks of September 11, 2001, have produced a movement in the opposite direction. The building of the security wall in the Palestinian Occupied Territories by Israel and the reinforcing of the USA's borders are two of the most obvious examples of this trend.

Andrew Linklater has suggested that these broad processes require us to rethink notions of identity, national ties, rights and belonging. This will open up 'new forms of political community which sever the links between sovereignty, territory, citizenship and nationalism' (Linklater 1998: 213).

Other challenges, notably those of an environmental nature, produce problems and require solutions that transcend the territorial nation-state. Pollution, infectious diseases such as HIV/AIDS, SARS and avian flu, nuclear proliferation, poverty and global climate change all show the limitations of individual countries trying to resolve problems, and have led to a number of supra-national and therefore supra-territorial initiatives. For many analysts, these show the broader context in which we need to understand contemporary politics.

The environment and the challenges it poses are discussed in Chapter 3.

Yet a notion of supra-territorialisation or deterritorialisation requires a more detailed analysis of territory itself, in order that we can see what we are supposedly moving beyond. Given these changes, the stress should be on the remaking of spatial relations (reterritorialisation) in this new configuration of power, rather than simply assuming that such relations have been superseded (see Elden 2005a; Sassen 2006). In addition, while the techniques deployed today in terms of control of territory and its division are different in degree from those of several centuries ago, they still rest on essentially the same calculative understanding of space. The network society is still a connection of mathematically determined locations. In these terms globalisation is an extension of the idea of territory as calculative space to the world, the globe, as a whole. Just as territory is not simply land or terrain, the globe is more than merely the Earth. It is a geometric and political category, increasingly owned, distributed, mapped, calculated, bordered and ordered or controlled.

The involvement of the international community in the internal affairs of states has developed over the post-Cold War era. As well as the debate over the war in Iraq, there have been a number of other instances. International intervention, albeit belatedly, in Bosnia and later in Kosovo was framed as protecting civilian populations. US Assistant Secretary of State Richard Holbrooke famously described the former as 'bombing for peace'. In the latter case it effectively gave autonomy to Kosovo from Serbia, leading to its later recognition as an independent state. International intervention was not forthcoming in Rwanda in 1994, when the two main ethnic groups in the country were massacring each other. In East Timor, international intervention helped to protect that country's desire for independence from Indonesia.

All of these can be seen as limitations to the ability of a state to do as it chooses within its own boundaries (see Yamashita 2004; McQueen 2005). In the context of the 'global war on terror' this logic of intervention has been extended to states that allow terrorist groups to operate from within their territory and to those that pursue weapons of mass destruction. The first was used to justify the bombing of Afghanistan and the overthrow of the Taliban, as well as more recent attacks on Lebanon and Somalia by America's allies; the second was the primary reason advanced for the invasion of Iraq and the deposing of Saddam Hussein, and the current tensions over North Korea and Iran.

In international law, the idea of territorial integrity requires both the preservation of existing boundaries and the sovereignty of states within them (see Elden 2005b). If the second, *territorial sovereignty*, is held to be contingent – that is, dependent on particular behaviour – can the first, *territorial preservation*, remain unchallenged? Why should a state be limited by what it can do within its boundaries but those boundaries not be open to question? Can Iraq be maintained as a unified state when it is clear that it has descended into sectarian civil war? How will Kosovo develop in the future, and how will it not create a precedent for the fragmentation of other states? Russia's war with separatists in Chechnya and China's conquest of neighbouring lands like Tibet and its independence movements in Xinjiang province (also known as East Turkistan) help to explain why both countries are very wary of opening up this question.

It is therefore clear that the question of territorial division is at the very heart of contemporary debates about global politics. It is interesting to consider what specific types of space and place are implied by political practice, which of course extends to scales below those of nation-states and the world as a whole. Contemporary political changes, particularly in relation to globalisation, are producing profound changes in the constitution of the state, but the developments in terms of political geography, namely territory, are much less certain. Territorial issues, especially when thought through the notion of territoriality, can say much about the spatial organisation of regions, towns, rural development and other forms of the relation between people and place.

The international interventions in East Timor and Kosovo are further discussed in Chapter 18.

North Korea and the invasion of Iraq are both discussed in Chapter 19.

CONCLUSION

This chapter has attempted to show how the modern territorial division of the world is both contingent in its specifics and in its general ordering. The relation between territorial issues and contemporary politics works in a number of ways, from issues concerning national identity, war, globalisation and rights. The history of the concept of territory helps us to understand how some of these issues came to be decided in the way that they have been. Yet while there are numerous territorial disputes current in the world, and widespread debate about the relation between territory and sovereignty in the era of 'globalisation', there seem to be no generally agreed principles for changing the way in which the world is divided territorially.

FURTHER READING

There is extensive literature on topics relating to territory, especially the state, and on specific territorial issues, but relatively little on the idea of territory itself. Storey (2001) and Delaney (2005) provide accessible introductions to the topic, along with a range of examples, as does Malcolm Anderson (1996), although this is now a little out of date. Jönsson *et al.* (2000) provide some useful historical detail in the European context, which Badie (2000) usefully expands. Ruggie (1993) and Taylor (1994, 1995) provide a survey of work in the field, continued and supplemented by Paasi (2003). Jones (1945) is still unparalled as a technical guide; and Anderson (2003) is useful for information. Huth and Allee (2002) is rather methodological, but the appendices are very useful. Black (1997) and Pickles (2004) are very readable and provide lots of good examples of the relation between politics and cartography. Soja (1971) and Gottmann's (1973) accounts are still very valuable, and, for the most comprehensive analysis of territory from the perspective of territoriality, see Sack (1986).

WEBSITES

Borderbase, http://www.nicolette.dk/borderbase/index.php.
  Site with lots of information. Choose a country at top left to see a map and often a photo of its borders.

Borders and Territory, http://garnet.acns.fsu.edu/~phensel/territory.html.
  Site maintained by Paul R. Hensel, Florida State University, with a large range of useful information, particularly concerning territorial disputes.

Centre for International Borders Research, http://www.qub.ac.uk/cibr/.
  Research centre at Queen's University, Belfast.

CIA World Factbook, https://www.cia.gov/cia/publications/factbook/index.html.
  Information on boundaries and territorial disputes.

Google Earth, http://earth.google.com.
  Not always accurate, but lots of fun.

International Boundaries Research Unit (IBRU), http://www.dur.ac.uk/ibru/.
  Research Centre based at Durham University. Website contains lots of information on boundaries, including a news archive, links and newsletters. Many of IBRU's publications are available to download for free.

International Crisis Group, http://www.crisisgroup.org/home/index.cfm.
    An NGO which provides regular reports and updates on geopolitical issues, including
    those with a boundary or territorial element.

Nijmegen Centre for Border Research, http://www.ru.nl/ncbr/.
    Go to the 'Border Portal' for a list of relevant literature and links.

Perry-Castañeda Library Map Collection, http://www.lib.utexas.edu/maps/index.html.
    An excellent collection of contemporary and historical maps housed at the University
    of Texas at Austin.

REFERENCES

Agnew, John (1994) 'The Territorial Trap: The Geographical Assumptions of International
    Relations Theory', *Review of International Political Economy* 1, 1: 53–80; reprinted
    in John Agnew and Stuart Corbridge (1995) *Mastering Space: Hegemony, Territory
    and International Political Economy*, London: Routledge.
Anderson, Ewan (2003) *International Boundaries: Geopolitical Atlas*, Chicago, IL:
    Fitzroy Dearborn.
Anderson, James (1996) 'The Shifting Stage of Politics: New Medieval and Postmodern
    Territorialities?', *Society and Space* 14, 2: 133–53.
Anderson, Malcolm (1996) *Frontiers: Territory and State Formation in the Modern
    World*, Oxford: Polity.
Anderson, Perry (1974a) *Passages from Antiquity to Feudalism*, London: NLB.
Anderson, Perry (1974b) *Lineages of the Absolutist State*, London: NLB.
Badie, Betrand (2000) *The Imported State: The Westernization of the Political Order*, trans.
    Claudia Royal, Stanford, CA: Stanford University Press.
Bialasiewicz, Luiza, Stuart Elden and Joe Painter (2005) 'The Constitution of EU
    Territory', *Comparative European Politics* 3, 3: 333–63.
Black, Jeremy (1997) *Maps and Politics*, London: Reaktion.
Castells, Manuel (1996) *The Rise of the Network Society, The Information Age: Economy,
    Society and Culture*, Oxford: Blackwell.
Castells, Manuel (1989) *The Informational City: Information Technology, Economic
    Restructuring and the Urban-Regional Process*, Oxford: Blackwell.
Delaney, David (2005) *Territory: A Short Introduction*, Oxford: Blackwell.
Elden, Stuart (2007) 'Governmentality, Calculation, Territory', *Environment and
    Planning D: Society and Space* 25, 3: 562–80.
Elden, Stuart (2005a) 'Missing the Point: Globalisation, Deterritorialisation and the Space
    of the World', *Transactions of the Institute of British Geographers* 30, 1: 8–19.
Elden, Stuart (2005b) 'Territorial Integrity and the War on Terror', *Environment and
    Planning A* 37, 12: 2083–104.
Foucault, Michel (2007) *Security, Territory, Population*, trans. Graham Burchell, London:
    Palgrave.
Foucault, Michel (2003) *Society Must Be Defended*, trans. David Macey, London: Allen
    Lane.

Foucault, Michel (1976) *Discipline and Punish: The Birth of the Prison*, trans. Alan Sheridan, Harmondsworth: Penguin.

Giddens, Anthony (1985) *The Nation-State and Violence*, Cambridge: Polity Press.

Gottmann, Jean (1973) *The Significance of Territory*, Charlottesville, VA: University Press of Virginia.

Huth, Paul K. and Todd Allee (2002) *The Democratic Peace and Territorial Conflict in the Twentieth Century*, Cambridge: Cambridge University Press

Johnson, Richard G. (1999) 'Negotiating the Dayton Peace Accords through Digital Maps', United States Institute of Peace, www.usip.org/virtualdiplomacy/publications/reports/rjohnsonISA99.html.

Jones, Stephen B. (1945) *Boundary-Making: A Handbook for Statesmen, Treaty Editors, and Boundary Commissioners*, Washington, DC: Carnegie Endowment for International Peace, Division of International Law.

Jönsson, Christer, Sven Tägil and Gunnar Törnqvist (2000) *Organizing European Space*, London: Sage.

Lalonde, Suzanne (2002) *Determining Boundaries in a Conflicted World: The Role of Uti Possidetis*, Montreal and Kingston: McGill's-Queen's University Press.

Linklater, Andrew (1998) *The Transformation of Political Community: Ethical Foundations of the Post-Westphalian Era*, Cambridge: Polity Press.

McQueen, Carol (2005) *Humanitarian Intervention and Safety Zones: Iraq, Bosnia and Rwanda*, Basingstoke: Palgrave Macmillan.

Malmberg, Torsten (1980) *Human Territoriality: Survey of Behavioural Territories in Man with Preliminary Analysis and Discussion of Meaning*, The Hague: Mouton Publishers.

Mann, Michael (1993) *The Sources of Social Power: Volume 2, The Rise of Classes and Nation States 1760–1914*, Cambridge: Cambridge University Press.

Mann, Michael (1986) *The Sources of Social Power: Volume 1, A History of Power from the Beginning to AD 1760*, Cambridge: Cambridge University Press.

Marx, Karl and Friedrich Engels (1970) *The German Ideology*, ed. C.J. Arthur, London: Lawrence & Wishart.

Paasi, Anssi (2003) 'Territory', in John Agnew, Katharyne Mitchell and Gerald Toal (eds) *A Companion to Political Geography*, Oxford: Blackwell.

Pickles, John (2004) *A History of Spaces: Cartographic Reason, Mapping and the Geo-Coded World*, London: Routledge.

Ruggie, John (1993) 'Territoriality and Beyond: Problematizing Modernity in International Relations', *International Organization* 47, 1: 139–74.

Sack, Robert David (1986) *Human Territoriality: Its Theory and History*, Cambridge: Cambridge University Press.

Sahlins, Peter (1989) *Boundaries: The Making of France and Spain in the Pyrenees*, Berkeley, CA: University of California Press.

Sassen, Saskia (2006) *Territory, Authority, Rights: From Medieval to Global Assemblages*, Princeton, NJ: Princeton University Press.

Scholte, Jan Aart (2005) *Globalisation: A Critical Introduction*, 2nd edn, Basingstoke: Palgrave Macmillan.

Soja, Edward (1971) *The Political Organisation of Space*, Commission on College Geography Resource Paper No. 8, Washington, DC: Association of American Geographers.

Storey, David (2001) *Territory: The Claiming of Space*, London: Prentice Hall.

Taylor, Peter J. (1995) 'Beyond Containers: Internationality, Interstateness, Interterritoriality', *Progress in Human Geography* 19, 1: 1–15.

Taylor, Peter J. (1994) 'The State as Container: Territoriality in the Modern World-System', *Progress in Human Geography* 18, 2: 151–62.

Townsend, Jeff (2004) 'Botswana: The San (Bushmen) Rights Case', CRS Report for Congress, http://www.botsblog.com/pdf/crs_botswana_101904.pdf.

Weber, Max (1994) *Political Writings*, ed. Peter Lassman and Ronald Spiers, Cambridge: Cambridge University Press.

Weber, Max (1968) *Economy and Society*, ed. Guenther Roth and Claus Wittich, New York: Bedminister Press.

Weber, Max (1958) *The Protestant Ethic and the Spirit of Capitalism*, New York: Scribner's Press.

Yamashita, Hikaru (2004) *Humanitarian Space and International Politics: The Creation of Safe Areas*, Aldershot: Ashgate.

CHAPTER **10**

How does the nation-state work?

Michael J. Shapiro

THE QUESTION
STATES, NATIONS AND ALLEGIANCE

Modern political thinking tends to be absorbed in, if not wholly exhausted by, two closely interrelated historical trajectories. One is the process of state formation, the other that of nation-building. As a result, modern political discourse is usually understood on the basis of the geopolitical world of nation-states.

With respect to the state part of the hyphenated term 'nation-state', scholars have focused on the process by which states were formed by monopolizing violence within a bounded territory. As a variety of historical accounts have put it, the monopolizing of violence required disarming diverse sub-state affili- ated groupings, asserting fiscal control over the population and establishing recruitment procedures for armies and bureaucracies. All of these moves were aimed at securing territorial boundaries and centralizing and governmentally controlling all aspects of the population, in order to become a separately governed entity with centralized control. As a result, states are understood primarily as territorial entities with exclusive, coercively and legally supported sovereignty.

In contrast, the nation part of the hyphenated expression takes on its meaning with respect to time inasmuch as nations are understood as peoples who belong to a shared cultural community with a historical trajectory. As a result citizen-subjects receive what Jürgen Habermas calls a 'double coding'. They have both territorial and historical identities. But it is controversial as to how the second coding, the one involving historical time, is to be understood. To avoid the assumption that members of a nation-state derive their coherence on the basis of a myth of a 'prepolitical fact of a quasi-natural people', Habermas (1998) suggests that the communal attachment of nation-state members should be regarded as civic rather than organic, i.e. based on political and legal entitlement rather than hereditary belonging. However, contrary to Habermas' attempt to avoid naturalistic identity politics, the state's legitimation of its control over a population frequently involves the pseudo-histories which Eric Hobsbawm and Terence Ranger have famously referred to as the 'invention of tradition' (1992).

At the level of the individual citizen-subject, such inventions operate as a basis for allegiance. As I have noted elsewhere, that allegiance is best understood as allegiance to a story:

> Given the complex sets of forces that have been responsible both for assembling as a 'people' those groupings identified as 'nations' and the ambiguities and contentiousness associated with the ways that such assemblages claim territories, their primary national stories must bear considerable weight. Indeed, there are nothing other than commitments to stories for a national people to give themselves a historical trajectory that testifies to their collective coherence.
>
> (Shapiro 1999: 47)

The weight that the stories must bear takes on its significance in the face of competing allegiances which apply especially to those who reside in a single nation-state but understand their self-fashioning and hence loci of allegiance either as split or as existing elsewhere. While the nation-state deploys various forms of cultural governance to apply centripetal force (a force pulling toward the centre) to national coherence – ceremonies, national holidays, national museum displays and so on – other genres or forms reflect the centrifugal forces (moving away from the centre) that apply to those who exist in different imaginaries or different identity narratives.

The way identities have been thought about is also discussed in **Chapter 4**. The question of identity politics is examined there in relation to the feminist movement. Certain ways of thinking of gender and sexuality play a role in nation-building, as we see in this chapter.

The emergence of the state as the seemingly obvious form of political organization and its relation with territory and sovereignty are discussed in **Chapter 9.**

For example, the Hanif Kureishi and Stephen Frears film *Sammy and Rosie Get Laid* (1987) provides an exemplary moment of difference from national allegiance in the UK. At one point in the film, Sammy, a Pakistani immigrant, says to his wife Rosie, a native Englishwoman, 'We are not British, we're Londoners.' And the film as a whole challenges traditional geopolitical presumptions. London, like most cosmopolitan cities, contains an ethnoscape (a landscape of diverse ethnic subjects) with the kinds of differing (usually binational) experiences and thus multiple allegiances that disrupt the traditional statist political discourse. As Gayatri Spivak puts it in her reading of the film, London contains a variety of types who constitute a 'challenge to the idea of the nation' – for example, the 'homeworker' exists along with other 'super exploited women in export processing zones' and thus represents a perspective on connections with nationhood that conflict with that of the traditionally scripted citizen-subject (Spivak 1993: 252).

The significance of homeworkers and the feminization of labour in the contemporary global economy are discussed in **Chapter 12**.

Heeding Spivak's example, I want to identify one such homeworker (who ultimately became a writer), Jamaica Kincaid. She is a naturalized American who provides an alternative perspective to the mythology of the nation-building project of the US Founding Fathers. A descendant of the coerced labour force in the Caribbean (she is from Antigua), where slaves with no control over the conditions or pace of the work produced both cotton and sugar, the latter a product that by the mid-seventeenth century (and for one and one half centuries thereafter) was 'by far the most valuable product exported from the Americas'

FIGURE 10.1
'The Declaration of Independence by John Trumbull' [1756-1843]. John Trumbull's 1816 version painted for the US Capitol Building Rotunda. The Art Archive. Ref: AA401943

(Eltis 2002: 40), Kincaid became a writer after initially arriving in the US as a servant (an *au pair*). Now someone with divided national and cultural experiences, she is one who has, in her terms, her 'feet, . . . in two worlds' (2000: 123). Given her heritage of coerced labour and her experience as a bonded servant, Kincaid has a different basis for her perception of the American founding experience from those who unambivalently celebrate the creation of America's founding documents. For example, while looking at the famous portrait in Philadelphia's Liberty Hall of the signers of the Declaration of Independence, Kincaid ponders the occupational infrastructure of their studied ease and suggests we imagine those not in the picture, those whose labour has assisted in the enactment of the European thought-world in America's founding:

> America begins with the Declaration of Independence . . . but who really needs this document. . . . There is a painting in Philadelphia of the men who signed it. These men looked relaxed; they are enjoying the activity of thinking, the luxury of it. They have time to examine this thing called their conscience and to act on it . . . some keep their hair in an unkempt style (Jefferson, Washington), and others keep their hair well groomed (Franklin), their clothes pressed.
>
> (Kincaid 1997: 70)

She continues with a speculation about those who have worked to prepare the men for the occasion:

> the people who made their beds and made their clothes nicely pressed and their hair well groomed or in a state of studied dishevelment.
>
> (Kincaid 1997: 70)

Kincaid shares her ambivalent allegiance with other writers who have articulated their unease in their nation-state loci of residence.

ILLUSTRATIVE EXAMPLE
WORLDS OF UNEASE WITHIN THE NATION-STATE

French sociologist Pierre Bourdieu pointed to the difficulty of thinking outside the reasons of state that promote national allegiance with his remark, 'To endeavour to think the state is to take the risk of taking over (or being taken over by) a thought of the state' (1998: 35). He recommends a method of hyperbolic doubt, which he attributes to Thomas Bernhard's novel *Alte Meister Komödie* (1985). Bourdieu's notion of the 'genesis and structure of social space' in which creativity is possible is useful because it implies, at a minimum, that we should look at how a writer who resists or at least complicates nation-state allegiance is

Questions of gender, race and sexuality arise in **Chapters 4, 8 and 12** particularly. The modern nation-state relies on a particular picture of the family.

FIGURE 10.2
Pierre Bourdieu

socially situated. Bourdieu provides a path to the resistance of state-dominated political thinking by displacing the biographical causation model associated with mainstream literary analysis with attention to the spatio-temporality of the field within which a writer either recycles or challenges the dominant orders of intelligibility. However, if instead of seeing the existing social order as a hierarchical system of social 'fractions', as Bourdieu does, we view it as a fractal field, a historically produced amalgam or blend of diverse life-worlds that have been assembled by a history of state-directed 'nation-building' and its forms of political economy, we can identify counter-hegemonic personae whose writing challenges the myth of national coherence.

Specifically, much of the politics of contemporary writing reflects the counter-memories (alternative ways of recollecting the story of the nation-state) of those groups that have been territorially displaced by a history of political economy that is associated with the formation of the European-oriented model of political order. Global and local economic management by powerful states is responsible for depositing the diverse bodies that inhabit the social fields within the modern nation-state. For example, in the US case, many African-American, Native American and exiled writers do not (as Bourdieu would have us believe) select from existing idioms within the hierarchy of available styles that have congealed within state-dominated social orders. Rather, their writing expresses profound ambivalence toward the literary field within which their work is deployed, precisely because of the tendency of that field to be complicit with the state's presumption (its primary mode of 'thought') that it governs a unitary and coherent national culture.

The examples of structures of feeling and identity commitments that are in tension with national allegiance are legion, but, given the space available, I look at three cases, reviewing briefly some of the writing of Toni Morrison, an African American, Sherman Alexie, a Native American, and Michelle Cliff, a diasporic Jamaican. All of their texts constitute modes of thought generated from outside the spaces authorized by the conventional nation-building narrative, within which every individual is an undifferentiated sovereign citizen-subject and the social order is merely an ahistorical class structure.

> Memories and counter-memories arise in **Chapters 16 and 19**, where memories of violent conflict are discussed.

> The state's way of thinking here could be described, in the terms used in **Chapter 2**, as its picture of political space.

Michelle Cliff

I begin with Michelle Cliff because her observation on languages, expressed by one of her fictional characters, serves to characterize the agenda for writers who recognize the traps lurking in familiar systems of intelligibility (or ways of understanding). The narrator in her novel *Free Enterprise* reflects on the historical role of each language's participation in the imperial domination of her homeland. 'English', she says, 'was the tongue of commerce . . . Spanish was the language

FIGURE 10.3
Michelle Cliff.
http://www.english.
emory.edu/Bahri/cliff.gif

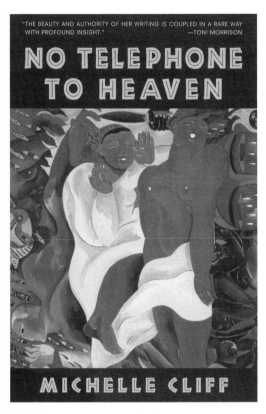

FIGURE 10.4
No Telephone to Heaven. Cover illustration Karen Barbour; a Plume Book, published by the Penguin Group, 1987

of categories', by which she means the creation of a biopolitical matrix of economically and politically ineligible, miscegenated (mixed) blood types, and Latin was the language of Christian spiritual hegemony. 'Against these tongues', she adds, 'African of every stripe collided' (Cliff 1993: 7).

Although Cliff writes in English, because of her diasporic experience, which leaves her outside ordinary national attachments, she sees the nation-state as an ontological as well as a territorial actor (one concerned as much with identity coherence as with territorial control) and, accordingly, she sees nation-state governance as symbolic as well as territorial. For example, her novel *No Telephone to Heaven* (1987) focuses on transnational lives that constitute or produce oppositional imaginaries (alternative ways of imagining the emergence and existence of the lifeworld) opposed to those of conventional national subjects. The diasporic perspective in the novel is realized both geopolitically and linguistically – geopolitically by the back and forth movement of her main character, Kitty Savage, between the US and Jamaica (as well as back and forth from England) and

The familiar 'pictures', in the terms used in **Chapter 2.**

linguistically in the collision of idioms, standard English and Jamaican patois, and in the anti-narrative structure, a set of dissociated narrative fragments.

It is important to note the form as well as the content of Cliff's writing. She uses the genre or form of the novel, which in the nineteenth and early twentieth centuries displaced other narrative forms in the Third World. Although, as Franco Moretti has pointed out, the nineteenth-century novel often functioned as a nation-building genre, especially in the case of the historical novel, subsequently Cliff and many other Third World writers have made the novel a site of resistance to the national and global imaginaries of the 'first world'. Yet Cliff shows a profound ambivalence toward writing in general because she recognizes the difficulty of extracting a thought from the outside whilst working within languages that encode (contain in coded form) structures of domination or control over others. As she has noted, her primary linguistic imaginary is silence, a form of resistant aphasia (an inability to speak or understand speech), which she sees as the ultimate location for one who would wholly resist the colonizing forces within language. Cliff's political inflection of silence is manifested in her *No Telephone to Heaven* when her character Kitty Savage is described as breaking her silence when she discovers a shop with Jamaican foods in New York. Ultimately, although Cliff's 'attempt to bound off a space of silence via the symptom of aphasia' (Aguiar 2001: 70) is never consummated – Cliff continues to write – it reflects her suspicion that, however hybrid and resistant her cacophony of voices and assemblage of narrative fragments in her novels are to the dominant idioms and historical memories of the state, she can never be wholly present to herself as a resisting body in her writing.

Sherman Alexie

FIGURE 10.5
Sherman Alexie.
Photo: Rex Rystedt/
SeattlePhoto.com

Sherman Alexie shares Michelle Cliff's ambivalence toward writing and also embodies the split consciousness of one who exists in two different life worlds. For Alexie, the contemporary Indian presence in the US, which occupies his attention, is both geographically and ethnologically (culturally) ambiguous. Accordingly, his main character, Low Man Smith, in his story 'Indian Country' (Alexie 2000) is a writer and doubtless his literary stand-in. Low Man describes himself in one of the story's conversations as one who is 'not supposed to be anywhere'. Moreover, Low Man's Indianness, along with that of other Native American characters in the story, is highly diluted. He is a 'Spokane', but he speaks and understands no tribal languages, was born and raised in Seattle, and has visited his own reservation only six times.

The 'Indian country' for which Alexie's story provides a fragmentary mapping has resonances with a prophetic remark by the Oglala, Black Elk, roughly seventy

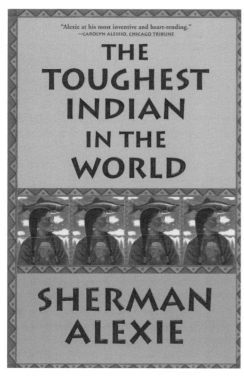

FIGURE 10.6
The Toughest Indian in the World. Cover design by Charles Rue Woods; cover art by
Wendell Minor; published by Grove Press, 2000

years earlier. Noting what was left of his Indian country after a century in which
the political economy of Euroamerica pushed a white cultural nation westward,
he remarked, 'They have made little islands for us . . . and always, these islands
are becoming smaller' (Neihardt 1932: 12). Similarly, if viewed pictorially, the
'Indian country' that emerges in Alexie's literary landscape would have to be a
few faintly visible colour flecks on a map of the US's western states. And, tellingly,
the precarious and obscure visibility of that country is reinforced throughout the
story's dialogues by continual challenges to traditional Indian practices of
intelligibility. For example, when Low Man asks an older Indian, Raymond, if he
is an elder, Raymond shifts to a non-Indian idiom: 'elder than some, not as elder
as others,' he replies. Given his awareness of the ways in which Native American
sense-making is always already colonized by a Euroamerican idiom, Alexie has his
alter ego Low Man Smith articulate a profound ambivalence toward being
immersed in the US literary field. Low Man refers to the chain bookstores that
carry his books as 'colonial clipper ships', and in the process of moving about an
urban venue in search of a non-chain bookstore he tries to divest himself of his
laptop, first trying to trade it in a 7-Eleven store and then handing it to a clerk
in a Barnes & Noble chain bookstore, pretending he found it.

The encounters of
colonizers with those
they colonized are
discussed in
Chapter 15.

Toni Morrison

FIGURE 10.7
Toni Morrison.
Photo: Kate Kunz from
cover of *Paradise*,
publisher Alfred A.
Knopf, New York, 1998

Race and its perceived
significance for
community are also
discussed in
Chapters 4 and 8.

Finally, Toni Morrison articulates the same ambivalence toward her participation in US literary culture as Cliff and Alexie. She makes her political challenge to literary culture explicit by referring to the paradox inherent in her participation as a novelist in a culture of literacy. She admits that she 'participates in the public sphere constituted by print literacy [but] . . . her fiction strains to constitute itself as anti-literature and to address a type of racial community that she herself recognizes to be unavailable to the novelist' (Dubey 1999: 188). Morrison's audience or constituency takes on its coherence as a transnational black culture of great diversity, forged as much through structures of exclusion and episodes of displacement as through practices of solidarity. And much of the cultural imaginary that forms the implied readership of her novels is preliterate. Yet, like Cliff and Alexie, Morrison continues to write. And, most significantly, her novel *Paradise* (1998), which addresses itself to a historical episode of racial exclusion, effectively enacts the critical posture that Bourdieu has identified as the antidote to 'state thinking', the necessity of creating a 'rupture' that challenges the state's '*symbolic* violence', its mobilization of and control over the mental structures that make its institutions appear '*natural*'. The conceptual strategy or 'tool for rupture' is, according to Bourdieu, 'the reconstruction of genesis', which brings 'back into view the conflicts and confrontations of the early beginnings and therefore all the discarded possibilities'.

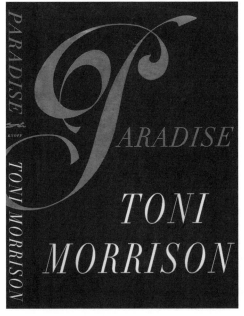

FIGURE 10.8
Paradise. Cover. Jacket design by Carol Devine Carson; Alfred A. Knopf, Publisher, New York, 1998

The 'genesis' to which Morrison's novel is addressed is the ideology and story of American exceptionalism that fuelled a major aspect of the Euroamerican nationhood project. Initially, the religious, patriarchal leaders of the early New England settlers strove to inculcate the presumption that America was to be a new Jerusalem, 'a site specifically favoured by God – perhaps the very place that he had chosen to initiate the millennial Kingdom of Christ' (Kammen 1997: 175). Subsequently, from the early nineteenth century on, a secularized or non-religious version of American exceptionalism has held sway among many American historians who have been vehicles of 'the assumption that the United States, unlike European nations, has a covenant that makes Americans a chosen people who have escaped from the terror of historical change to live in timeless harmony with nature' (Noble 1968: ix).

The idea of the covenant and the imperatives that flow from it – the need to resist change and the need to maintain the purity of the lineage that is charged with the special mission – produce the woeful consequences described at the beginning and end of Morrison's novel. The novel suggests that at best the exceptionalist narrative stifles politics and at worst it leads to violence. In addition to the closure of the political, the other consequence (violence) provides the chilling opening to the novel, whose first line is: 'They kill the white girl first'. Thereafter, an understanding of this opening event requires that the reader follow a complex and shifting narrative that eventually explains a deadly attack by a group of men from a covenanted, all-black community in Oklahoma on the women in a nearby convent that has served as a women's shelter.

The attackers are from Ruby, a small western all-black community in which the older members situate themselves in a historical narrative that celebrates the perseverance of their ancestors in the face of rejection and their subsequent redemption through adherence to the codes of a special mission. Descended from former slaves, the town's ancestors left discrimination in the late nineteenth-century American South only to be denied entry into both white and black communities in Oklahoma, which, as Morrison had learned, had 26 all-black towns at the turn of the twentieth century (Hitchens 1998: 450). The Rubyites' special mission, an African-American version of American exceptionalism, is engendered by their rejections, to which they refer in their narrative as the 'disallowing'. Having walked from Mississippi to Oklahoma, attracted by an advertisement about an all-black town, they discovered that their blackness was a threat to the lighter-skinned 'Negroes', who shunned them: 'The sign of racial purity they had taken for granted had become a stain' (Morrison 1999: 194).

Coping with the shock of a rejection (which they had expected only from whites), they founded their own all-black community of Haven in Oklahoma and subsequently moved even further into western Oklahoma to found Ruby, which they regarded as the fulfilment of their ancestors' intention to construct an Eden,

The role of religion in America today is briefly discussed in **Chapter 5.**

Chapter 15 discusses how we might think about the way in which those with 'exclusive knowledge' attempt to enlighten others, a version of the 'exceptionalism' or 'special mission' mentioned here.

a paradise on earth run by a group of racially pure blacks. The town chronicler, Patricia, summarizes the '8-rock's' (descendants from the original founders) model for maintaining purity: 'Unadulterated and unadulteried 8-rock blood held its magic as long as it resided in Ruby. That was their recipe. That was their deal. For immortality' (Morrison 1999: 217). But while 'Ruby' ('who can find a virtuous woman? For her price is far above Rubies', Proverbs xxxxi: 10) contains signs of paradise – for example, the soil seems almost miraculously fertile, so that while Haven had only barren muddy ground, Ruby has flourishing gardens – it also turns out to be a stiflingly conservative, patriarchal and even misogynist community. And rather than turning inward to confront divisive issues, when the younger Ruby generation departs from the original covenant, the patriarchs of Ruby displace their problems on a nearby community functioning with a different covenant. The assault with which the novel begins is on a shelter for women, whose inhabitants have had connections with some of the town's men. The shelter is in a former convent (in a mansion that had once served as a 'cathouse') outside the town.

Morrison's novel enacts Bourdieu's suggestion about the necessity of creating a rupture by returning to the founding myths that sustain violence, actual or symbolic. While identifying a racially fractured America, she contests both the Puritan reading of American exceptionalism and the African-American attempt to simulate that exceptionalism while accepting it as a dogma and thus attempting to preserve or freeze the meanings generated in founding acts. In accord with Bourdieu's methodological injunction, she subjects founding myths (of both Euro and African America) to hyperbolic doubt.

RESPONSES
STORIES OF COHERENT NATIONHOOD

Nation-building

In contrast to the writers I treat in the preceding section, much of the history of artistic production has been complicit with the cultural governance policies of states seeking to fashion a coherent and unitary national culture. For example, the development of French Grand Opera during the nineteenth century was structured to invite the people into the nation, various national theatre initiatives were similarly aimed at the fashioning of national culture and, without state prompting, the nineteenth-century historical novels – for example those of Sir Walter Scott – articulated a geographical dynamic that reflects a process of the cultural integration necessary for the state to claim a coherent cultural nation. His novels typically involve a process of border attenuation.

FIGURE 10.9
Paris Opera, by Charles Garnier, 1857–1874. Photo: Kevin Matthews/Artifice Images

This nation-building orientation of the arts, especially in the nineteenth century, was echoed by the dominant approaches to nationalism in the twentieth. The best-known scholars of nationalism – Benedict Anderson, Ernst Gellner, Anthony Giddens, Charles Tilly and countless others have emphasized the centripetal forces of national allegiance, primarily by focusing on mainstream media and state-run agencies and institutions. In particular, Benedict Anderson's (1991) well-known mantra that nations, as 'imagined communities', became objects of widespread symbolic allegiance through the operation of mediating genres (for example newspapers) is widely accepted by practitioners of comparative politics and international studies.

Traditional theorists of nationalism focus on two very different kinds of issues. The first and perhaps most pervasive in the literatures is the problem of allegiance, where 'nationalism' becomes a problem of the process through which citizens become identified with their nation-state. To treat that problem theorists turn to various media. In Anderson's case (1991), the primary medium is the daily newspaper. Other thinkers have looked at the roles of national cultural institutions, for example national theatres (Kruger 1992), music (Attali 1985), landscape painting (Bermingham 1986; Miller 1993; Daniels 1993), film (Burgogyne 1997; Hjort and MacKenzie 2000) and novels (Moretti 1998). In the case of each medium, idioms are adduced by the theorist to identify the way the medium encourages people to imagine the nation, e.g. to 'picture' it in the case of landscape painting, to identify its process of attenuating internal borders in the case of the historical novel, in the case of music, the collectivizing sentiments that harmony creates, in the case of film, the way founding myths are transmitted, and

Chapter 7 has a discussion of the importance of media representations in the context of war.

the way national theatres invited people into the nation by emphasizing what is distinctive about Englishness or Irishness or Frenchness, etc.

It should be noted, however, that the emphasis in the writings of Third World scholars has been very different. For example, looking at the results of the nationalist imagination in Asia and Africa, Partha Chatterjee (1993) focuses not on the centripetal aspect of identity formation but on a significant difference from the way that nationalism has been produced in the West. For Chatterjee, anti-colonialist nationalisms involved a struggle with imperialist powers and depended very much on spiritual media.

Citizens' rights

The second, and an increasingly important, issue has been a treatment of the process by which citizens have extracted rights. Within this perspective, citizenship is treated as a result of enactments, a form of 'transactional citizenship', where national affiliation is 'the outcome of historically specific processes of claim-making and bargaining between state and societal actors' (Mische 1996). However, if we recognize that nation-states contain groups that exist outside of the boundaries of society, for example indigenous peoples, 'claim-making' can be seen as a luxury of peoples who already enjoy some form of social recognition. To theorize nationalism in such cases is to develop a frame for treating the resistances of those groups who are 'ungrammatical' within the primary discourses of the nation-state (Shapiro 2004). A focus on national allegiance tends to render invisible those peoples who have not been clearly welcomed into the nation.

Chapter 8 looks at some of the implications of not being a citizen of the country you want to live in.

The mythic social contract

However misleading the assumptions of the scholarly writers who focus on the dynamics of national allegiance may be, at least their conclusions are based on analyses of concrete institutions – for example the history of the press in the case of Anderson, and the monopolization of coercion in the case of Giddens and Tilly. The dominant trend in political theory has been less attentive to actual historically developing institutions and mediating agencies. Drawing on approaches to the social contract emerging from the political theory canon, especially from the writings of Thomas Hobbes, John Locke and Jean-Jacques Rousseau, a nation-friendly model of the social order has held centre-stage in the social sciences. It has been assumed that a unitary social order has developed on the basis of an implicit contract by which each citizen agrees to forego coercive means in return for the protection offered by centralized coercion.

Thinkers who have told this mythic story base it on a model of egoism. They argue that the primary urge is toward a self-interestedness that would naturally provoke a 'war of all against all' (Hobbes 1981). What induces the social contract for Hobbes is a rational approach to one's interests, based on the recognition that only a strong centralized state can offer one protection against the predatory designs of others. Locke offers a similar view – that everyone is inclined to want to have complete autonomy over their person and possessions. Rationality prevails and they effectively agree to give up the right to punish transgressions against their person and property to a centralized state. And among thinkers of the social contract, Rousseau is another who assumed that the 'natural' state is one in which everyone provides for their own self-preservation and would rather resist any form of collective mastery but is forced to recognize that it is necessary to yield to certain collective conventions.

For a discussion of Hobbes' claims about authority and the sovereign, see **Chapter 6**.

We thus have, famously, three versions of a mythic social contract that the thinkers presume to be the basis of the collective coherence that became the condition of possibility for the control necessary to govern the modern nation-state. If we heed the dynamic situation of most social orders, created as the flows of immigrant and refugee bodies that introduce ideational and practical schisms, the idea of a social contract becomes increasingly unwarranted.

In **Chapter 8** you can find more on flows of immigrants.

Nevertheless, it is an idea that persists. While everywhere one can witness the absence of an operating social contract – evident, for example, in the periodic riots in the immigrant-filled suburbs of Paris, the *Banlieue parisienne*, in the clan antagonisms in various African countries, in the immiseration and exclusion of *los Indios* in various Latin American countries, and in the 'prison-industrial complex' disproportionately targeted at (what are constructed as) 'ethnic minorities' in the

FIGURE 10.10
Youths in Paris suburb,
Le Blanc Mesnil,
3 November 2005.
Photo: AP/PA Photos

US – the existence of a coherent and consensual society remains the legitimating alibi for the political for most political theorists.

BROADER ISSUES
AN ALTERNATIVE POLITICAL IMAGINARY

In order to provide a counter-model to the mythic consensuality that has been the basis of the presumption that states contain a unitary and coherent national society, we need an alternative image of the political. The French philosopher Jacques Rancière, writing on the politics of aesthetics (the ways in which the arts repartition experience), sees a politically acute version of aesthetics as a window onto the existence of many worlds, each of which is lived differently (2004).

In order to pursue this insight and suggest an alternative political imaginary from the mainstream social contract notion, I turn here to a piece of literature, Milan Kundera's novel *Ignorance* (2002), which is based on the ambiguous national experience of exiles who share Kundera's own experience.

The novel begins with an alienating remark delivered to Irena, a Czech ex-patriot living in Paris, by her friend, Sylvie: 'What are you still doing here?' When Irena asks in response, 'Where should I be?', Sylvie's rejoinder is 'home'. It is 1991, and Sylvie has the expectation that Irena, despite having lived in Paris for twenty years, still thinks of Czechoslovakia as home and will want to return to participate as a citizen in the new independence, after the dissolution of the former Soviet bloc (Kundera 2002: 3). The intermittently contentious dialogue continues briefly until Irena breaks off into a book- and film-influenced fantasy about emotional returns.

Irena's silent meditation about emotional returns triggers Kundera's break from his characters to a richly annotated philosophical discussion of nostalgia, with references to a range of fictional and actual émigrés who either returned or resisted returning (for example Odysseus, who returned to Ithaca, and Schoenberg, who did not return to Austria, respectively). Apart from the specifics of the particular fictional and historical characters he treats, Kundera constructs a global cartography. The novel provides a mapping not only of the post-Soviet geopolitical world but also of the way geopolitics and passion are linked. To assess the thinking that the mapping enacts, we are in need of a philosophical perspective that can address the overlay of passion on political territoriality that frames Kundera's narrative.

Many of Kundera's philosophico-literary excursions in his novels are inspired by Friedrich Nietzsche's philosophy, most famously his *The Unbearable Lightness of Being* (1984), which shares Nietzsche's sentiment that the possibility of an eternal return renders Being heavy. The thought of an eternal return gives 'to acts and

Chapter 19 explains more about Nietzsche.

events the moral import they would lack in a godless universe wherein every act or event occurred only once' (White 1990: 66). Ever since that novel, Kundera has pondered the problem of moral and emotional weight as he has connected Nietzsche's version of a mythological return with the problem of the émigré's actual or potential return. Because, for Kundera, emotional and moral registers are intimately connected, it is not surprising that toward the end of his meditation on nostalgia in *Ignorance* he refers to the way Homer sets out a 'moral hierarchy of emotions', which provides the basis for Odysseus' abandonment of Calypso, whose 'tears' are represented as less worthy than 'Penelope's pain' (Kundera 2002: 9). From Kundera's Nietzschean perspective, moral hierarchies are oppressive. Hence we are able to understand the demoralized Odysseus, who suffers from the terrible bargain he has made by giving up an intense passion for the weaker emotion of nostalgia and the self-applied pressure from his expected responsibilities as a husband and patriarch. He has become the forlorn Odysseus (the Ulysses) so well described in Tennyson's famous poem (1842), the Ulysses who laments:

> Match'd with an aged wife, I mete and dole
> Unequal laws unto a savage race,
> That hoard, and sleep, and feed, and know not me.

Most significantly for what Kundera sees this lending to his story of contemporary émigrés and returnees, Odysseus discovers that while 'for twenty years he thought about nothing but his return . . . the very essence of his life, its centre, its treasure, lay outside Ithaca', and, further, although he had enjoyed a receptive audience while in exile (for example 'the dazzled Phaeacians' who listened to his adventures 'for four long books'), in Ithaca 'he was one of their own, so it never occurred to anyone to say, "tell us"' (Kundera 2002: 34–5).

Similarly, when Irena returns to Prague, her old acquaintances show little interest in her twenty years of life outside Prague. It was one thing for her former friends to ignore the French wine she brought and instead persist in drinking beer but quite another to ignore her words: 'They can drink beer if they insist, that doesn't faze her; what matters to her is choosing the topic of conversation herself and being heard' (Kundera 2002: 37). Inasmuch as the identity of an individual, like the collective identity of a nation, requires recognition, the inattentiveness of her Prague acquaintances to Irena's Paris life deprives her of confidence in the identity narrative she has adopted.

On the other side of the self–other relationship to identity, what the women's disinterest in Irena's other life reflects is their unwillingness to extend sympathy across national boundaries. When we consider the identity issue at stake in Irena's encounter with her former acquaintances, we have to appreciate the politics of the history–memory disjuncture that Kundera is addressing through the fates of his characters.

'History', as Pierre Nora points out, is produced by the way 'our hopelessly forgetful modern societies, propelled by change, organize their past' (Nora 1989: 8). In the process of that organizing, memory tends to be eradicated: 'Memory and history, far from being synonymous appear now to be in fundamental opposition.' While memory is 'a perpetually active phenomenon' reflective of the sense-making of people coping with their life-worlds, 'history is the reconstruction, always problematic and incomplete, of what is no longer' (Nora 1989: 8).

Chapter 16 shows how memories affect politics and make wars possible.

Nora's distinction is effectively enacted in Kundera's narrative of the experience of *Ignorance*'s émigrés. While others try to impose a geopolitical allegiance on them, predicated on the way the former compatriots want to organize history, the émigrés try to maintain an intimacy with their memories, their lived temporalities. To the extent that the novel lends its characters an ethico-political outcome, it is the achievement of a refusal to give in to the identities, resident in an imposed history, which are thrown at them by their non-listening families, friends and acquaintances.

Hence, applying Nora's distinction to the historical moment of Kundera's novel, 'history' imposes allegiance, while memory, the 'perpetually active phenomenon' that ties people to an 'eternal present', is the condition of possibility for intimacy. To put it another way (in the language of the philosophers Deleuze and Guattari (1987)), 'history' involves the imposition of officially inscribed molar codes, the collective identity spaces tied to the macropolitical world of states, while memory is what contains the molecular level, the multiple layers of individual micropolitical potential for becoming, experiencing and associating.

BOX 10.1 GILLES DELEUZE AND FÉLIX GUATTARI

FIGURE 10.11
Gilles Deleuze and Félix Guattari. Photo: courtesy of Charles J. Stivale

Deleuze and Guattari collaborated on two volumes of a study of what they called 'Capitalism and Schizophrenia'. The second volume (1987) provides a radical challenge to identity politics in general and to the codes within which state allegiance is promoted. For them, the state is a 'machine of capture'. In response to such capture, they elaborate what they call 'lines of flight', ways of eluding state capture.

To be allied to the codes associated with history, which are geopolitically oriented temporalities that Irena's friends and husband impose on her, Irena must ignore her life. As Deleuze puts it, 'the sensuous signs of memory are signs of life' (2000: 65). Thus, when Irena sees Josef in Prague (she recalls him from a brief romantic liaison), her memory of a sensuous past is activated, and, crucially, she is encouraged to think. As Deleuze notes, for Proust 'truth depends on an encounter with something that forces us to think'. And here that thinking helps Irena to distance herself from the expectations of others and allow intimacy (with herself as well as with an other) to trump geopolitical allegiance. Intimacy challenges what Lauren Berlant refers to as 'the normative practices, fantasies, institutions and ideologies that organize people's worlds' (2000: 2).

Irena's experience of a return is similar to that of the man she encounters romantically in Prague. Josef is an émigré living in Denmark, whose wife, now dead, had urged him to visit his old homeland, once the Soviets had departed ('Not going would be unnatural of you, unjustifiable, even foul', she said: Kundera 2002: 139). When Josef visits his former friend N in Prague, whom he has not seen for 20 years, N and his wife ask nothing about his Danish life:

> There was a long silence and Josef expected questions: If Denmark really is your home, what's your life like there? And with whom? Tell about it! Tell us! Describe your house! Who's your wife? Are you happy? Tell us! Tell us! But neither N nor his wife asked any such question.
>
> (Kundera 2002: 159)

Before following Irena and Josef, who meet and have an affair during their brief return, we need to appreciate Kundera's approach to the politics of the identity struggle they undergo.

Kundera's attachment to Nietzschean philosophy, which he deployed in his *The Unbearable Lightness of Being* (1984), notwithstanding, I want to discuss his *Ignorance* with reference to David Hume's philosophical inquiries into the passions. While his *The Unbearable Lightness of Being* thinks in a Nietzschean way, Kundera's *Ignorance* thinks in a Humean way. The overlay of passions on the novel's literary geography complicates mappings that focus exclusively on national allegiances and summons the Humean argument that passions direct ideas.

To capture the kind of network that Kundera's novel proposes, we can extrapolate from an insight that Gilles Deleuze derives from his reading of Hume on human nature. In contrast with much of the political theory canon (often drawn, for example, from the writings of John Locke), in which the social bond within the socio-political order is ascribed to a contract between ruler and the ruled, Hume's philosophy offers 'a radical change in the practical way the problem of society is posed' (2005: 46). Given the Humean insistence that it is 'affective circumstances'

BOX 10.2 DAVID HUME

FIGURE 10.12
David Hume, by and
published by David
Martin, after portrait by
Allan Ramsay, 1766.
National Portrait Gallery

David Hume (1711–76) is recalled as a philosopher, historian and economist
and is best known for his affiliation with British empiricism. However,
Hume's version of empiricism is a radical version. Rather than basing his
empiricism on a simple and direct relationship between sensations and
intelligibility, Hume analysed the principles of human nature – the
passions and associations – that create the conditions of possibility for a
relationship between what is sensible and what is intelligible. In so
doing, Hume initiated what would later be the Kantian revolution in
philosophy and its post-Kantian revisions, which directed attention
away from things (the object world) and to the conditions (formal and
historical) of the subject.

that guide people's ideas (because the 'principles of passion' control ideational
inclinations), association within the social domain becomes a matter of modes of
partiality (Deleuze 2005: 45). Accordingly, the problem of the social is to be
understood not through the concept of the contract, which implies that the main
political problem is one of translating egotism into sociality, but in terms of
partialities, which makes the problem one of how to stretch the passions into
commitments that extend beyond them, how, as Deleuze puts it, 'to pass from
a "limited sympathy" to an "extended generosity"' (2005: 46), for, as Hume
insists, 'the qualities of the mind are *selfishness* and *limited generosity*' (Hume 1978:
494). To the extent that the extended generosity that justice represents is to
develop, 'it takes its rise from human conventions', that are necessitated by the
'*confin'd generosity of men, along with the scanty provision nature has made for his
wants*' (Hume 1978: 494–5).

The extrapolation I want to apply to Kundera's narrative locates the problem in
a global rather than merely social space. In this expanded spatial context, the issue
becomes not one of a person's moderating her/his partialities in relationships
with the consociates of a national society but with potential consociates within
alternative national spaces. Hume did contemplate the problem of extending
sympathy across national boundaries, noting that 'we sympathize more with
persons contiguous to us, than with persons remote from us. . . . With our
countrymen, than with strangers' (1978: 581). However, to appreciate Kundera's
overlay of sensibilities on the dynamic mapping that exiles have created, we have

Such broader issues
about our changing
allegiances are
also considered in
Chapter 9.

to recognize a complication that Hume's notion of 'selfishness' fails adequately to register.

The self-consciousness required to be selfish – to be in touch with one's passions – is difficult to achieve in a world in which others impose regulative ideals with respect to what those passions are supposed to be. The disruption to Irena's hard-won sense of self as a French citizen with a French 'structure of feeling' is a result not of the newly won Czech independence, which would not by itself have summoned an ambivalence, but of having to deal not only with a French friend who pressures her to reassume a former feeling and its attendant national commitment but also with pressure from a husband of Swedish origin who, ironically, has no such feeling for his 'native' country. Her husband, Gustaf, a committed cosmopolitan (one with no national allegiance), argues that although he has no nostalgia for *his* country of birth, she should have some for hers. Similarly, Josef must deal with his wife's expectation about how he should feel and behave and, subsequently, the censorious feelings of his brother and sister-in-law, who remained during the Soviet occupation. Certainly there are those who possess what Pico Ayer (2000) calls 'a global soul' or who, like Salman Rushdie, detest the 'narrowly defined cultural frontiers' implied in the very idea of a 'homeland' (1991: 19). But, however passionate cosmopolitans may be about their attachments to multicultural urban settings and their commitment to resist narrow geopolitical allegiance, the emotionally charged cartography they define looms less large, in terms of both space and affective intensity, than the one defined by exiles.

Chapter 2 has more to say about cosmopolitanism.

CONCLUSION

I began by noting that while the hyphenated term 'nation-state' has been the primary referent of modern political discourse, the focus it attracts leaves many political subjects in the shadows. It is possible to provide a counter-history – based on particular counter-memories – to the nation-state-oriented story of political modernity. Because the state sovereignty story, which is dominant within academic approaches, fails to register much of the experiences of both citizen-subjects and those without recognized political qualification, I turn primarily to literatures in which those subjects' experiences are articulated. Two dimensions of that turn are important. First, the personae whose writings are selected are drawn from those whose movements inscribe an experiential story that challenges the narratives within which the nation-state version of political subjectivity is developed. Second, the form of the writing, which among other things registers the identity ambiguities of the authors and their characters, provides a contrast with the certainties manifested in the identity discourses of the nation-state.

In order to locate the personae who challenge the nation-state story of political modernity, one must focus on the process by which bodies enter the national societies that have been mythically represented as formed by a consensual social contract. For example, émigrés whose territorial statuses have arisen from coercive forces rather than relatively free choices have different political narratives to offer. In particular, as I point out in my treatment of Milan Kundera's novel *Ignorance*, the struggle of exiles to achieve self-mastery in the face of conflicting identity pressures provides an exemplary counter-memory to the abstract narratives of entrenched or immobile citizen-subjects with unambiguous national allegiances. To place their stories within a socio-political frame, one must abandon the social contract version of national societies and turn to a version that can register the situations in which territorial allegiances are in flux, ambiguated and productive of changing sentiments toward self and other.

To recover the centrifugal political forces that undermine the mythologies of nation-state consolidation, one needs to contrast the academic and artistic texts that serve to reinscribe and/or consolidate nation-state political imaginaries with those writing events that provide challenges and alternatives, that counter the totalizing story of political modernity and that have exposed as an illusion the conceit that the nation-state is unproblematically consolidated.

FURTHER READING

Balibar, Etienne and Immanuel Wallerstein (1991) *Race, Nation, Class: Ambiguous Identities*, London: Verso.
>   This collection provides a critical approach to racism, which, influenced by the writings of the philosopher Louis Althusser and the historian Fernand Braudel, locates the phenomenon not merely in attitudes but in social relations and structures.

Bhabha, Homi (ed.) (1990) *Nation and Narration*, New York: Routledge.
>   This collection on nations and nationalism applies literary tropes in order to show how nations generate paradoxical allegiances through the narratives within which they locate themselves.

Campbell, David (1998) *National Deconstruction*, Minneapolis, MN: University of Minnesota Press.
>   This study of the violence in Bosnia refigures and extends Jacques Derrida's concept of deconstruction, turning literary tropes into political and ethical critique.

Corrigan, Philip and Derek Sayer (1985) *The Great Arch*, Oxford: Basil Blackwell.
>   This investigation of English state formation locates the emergence of national allegiance within a long historical trajectory.

Edkins, Jenny, Véronique Pin-Fat and Michael J. Shapiro (eds) (2004) *Sovereign Lives*, New York: Routledge.
>   This collection treats the geo- and biopolitical aspects of sovereignty at the level of the lives impacted by sovereign prerogatives and practices.

Giddens, Anthony (1983) *The Nation State and Violence*, Cambridge: Basil Blackwell.
This is a sociological treatment of the articulation between the development of the nation-state and the violence of its self-creation.

Lloyd, David and Paul Thomas (1998) *Culture and the State*, New York: Routledge.
This is a neglected but excellent treatment of the cultural governance perspectives and practices that have accompanied state formation.

Shapiro, Michael J. (1994) *Methods and Nations: Cultural Governance and the Indigenous Subject*, New York: Routledge.
This investigation of cultural governance and the neglect of the indigenous subject in the discourses of the social sciences on nation-building applies aesthetic theory, as it is articulated in film, music and landscape painting.

Tilly, Charles (1990) *Coercion, Capital and European States, AD 990–1990*, Cambridge, MA: Basil Blackwell.
Tilly provides a historical narrative of the role of coercion in state formation.

Walker, R.B.J. and Saul H. Mendlovitz (eds) (1990) *Contending Sovereignties*, Boulder, CO: Lynne Rienner.
This collection provides critical, interdisciplinary approaches to sovereignty.

REFERENCES

Aguiar, Marian (2001) 'Decolonizing the Tongue: Reading Speech and Aphasia in the Work of Michelle Cliff', *Literature and Psychology* 47, 1–2: 94–108.

Alexie, Sherman (2000) 'Indian Country', *The New Yorker*, 13 March.

Anderson, Benedict (1991) *Imagined Communities: Reflections on the Origins and Spread of Nationalism*, London: Verso.

Attali, Jacques (1985) *Noise: The Political Economy of Music*, trans. Brian Massumi, Minneapolis, MN: University of Minnesota Press.

Ayer, Pico (2000) *The Global Soul: Jet Lag, Shopping Malls, and the Search for Home*, New York: Vintage Books.

Berlant, Lauren (2000) 'Intimacy: A Special Issue', in Lauren Berlant (ed.) *Intimacy*, Chicago, IL: University of Chicago Press.

Bermingham, Ann (1986) *Landscape and Ideology*, Berkeley, CA: University of California Press.

Bernhard, Thomas (1985), *Alte Meister Komödie*, Frankfurt am Main: Suhrkamp.

Bourdieu, Pierre (1998) 'Rethinking the State: Genesis and Structure of the Bureaucratic Field', in Pierre Bourdieu, *Practical Reason: On the Theory of Action*, Stanford, CA: Stanford University Press.

Burgoyne, Robert (1997) *Film Nation*, Minneapolis, MN: University of Minnesota Press.

Chatterjee, Partha (1993) *The Nation and Its Fragments*, Princeton, NJ: Princeton University Press.

Cliff, Michelle (1993) *Free Enterprise*, New York: Dutton.

Cliff, Michelle (1987) *No Telephone to Heaven*, New York: Dutton.

Daniels, Stephen (1993) *Fields of Vision: Landscape Imagery and National Identity in England and the United States*, New York: Polity.

Deleuze, Gilles (2005) *Pure Immanence*, trans. Anne Boyman, New York: Zone Books.

Deleuze, Gilles (2000) *Proust & Signs*, trans. Richard Howard, Minneapolis, MN: University of Minnesota Press.

Deleuze, Gilles and Félix Guattari (1987) *A Thousand Plateaus: Capitalism and Schizophrenia*, trans. Brian Massumi, Minneapolis, MN: University of Minnesota Press.

Dubey, Madhu (1999), 'The Politics of Genre in *Beloved*', *Novel: A Forum on Fiction* 32, 2: 186–94.

Eltis, David (2002) 'Introduction', in David Eltis (ed.) *Coerced and Free Migration: Global Perspectives*, Stanford, CA: Stanford University Press.

Habermas, Jürgen (1998) 'The European Nation-State: On the Past and Future of Sovereignty and Citizenship', trans. by Ciaran Cronin, *Public Culture* 10, 2: 397–416.

Hitchens, Christopher (1998) 'Morrison's West', *Vanity Fair* 450, February.

Hjort, Mette and Scott MacKenzie (2000) *Cinema & Nation*, New York: Routledge.

Hobbes, Thomas (1981) *Leviathan*, New York: Penguin.

Hobsbawm, Eric J. and Terence O. Ranger (1992) *The Invention of Tradition*, Cambridge: Cambridge University Press.

Hume, David (1978) *A Treatise of Human Nature*, 2nd edn, Oxford: Oxford University Press.

Kammen, Michael (1997) *In the Past Lane: Historical Perspective on American Culture*, New York: Oxford University Press.

Kincaid, Jamaica (2000) *My Garden Book*, New York: Vintage.

Kincaid, Jamaica (1997) 'The Little Revenge from the Periphery', *Transition* 73: 68–73.

Kruger, Loren (1992) *The National Stage: Theater and Cultural Legitimation in England, France, and America*, Chicago, IL: University of Chicago Press.

Kundera, Milan (2002) *Ignorance*, trans. Linda Asher, London: Faber and Faber.

Kundera, Milan (1984), *The Unbearable Lightness of Being*, trans. Michael Henry Heim, London: Faber and Faber.

Miller, Angela (1993) *The Empire of the Eye: Landscape Representation and American Cultural Politics 1825–1875*, Ithaca, NY: Cornell University Press.

Mische, A. (1996) 'Projecting Democracy: The Formation of Citizenship across Youth Networks in Brazil', in Charles Tilly (ed.) *Citizenship, Identity and Social History*, New York: Cambridge University

Moretti, Franco (1998) *Atlas of the European Novel: 1800–1900*, New York: Verso.

Morrison, Toni (1998) *Paradise*, New York: Plume.

Neihardt, John G. (1932) *Black Elk Speaks*, New York: Morrow.

Noble, David (1968) *The Eternal Adam and the New World Garden*, New York: George Braziller.

Nora, Pierre (1989) 'Between Memory and History: *Les Lieux de Memoire*', *Representations* 26: 7–24.

Rancière, Jacques (2004) *The Politics of Aesthetics: The Distribution of the Sensible*, trans. Gabriel Rockhill, New York: Continuum.

Rushdie, Salman (1991) *Imaginary Homelands*, London: Granta.

Shapiro, Michael J. (2004) *Methods and Nations: Cultural Governance and the Indigenous Subject*, New York: Routledge.

Shapiro, Michael J. (1999) 'Narrating the Nation, Unwelcoming the Stranger', in Michael J. Shapiro, *Cinematic Political Thought: Narrating Race, Nation and Gender*, New York: NYU Press.

Spivak, Gayatri Chakravorty (1993) *Outside in the Teaching Machine*, New York: Routledge.

White, Alan (1990) *Within Nietzsche's Labyrinth*, New York: Routledge.

CHAPTER 11

Do colonialism and slavery belong to the past?

Kate Manzo

- ■ *The question*
  SLAVERY: ABOLITION AND CONTINUATION

- ■ *Illustrative example*
  COLONIALISM AND CAPITALIST DEVELOPMENT IN IVORY COAST

- ■ *Responses*
  THE EFFECTS OF ADJUSTMENT: DEPROLETARIANISATION AND MODERN SLAVERY

- ■ *Broader issues*
  IS TODAY'S WORLD POSTCOLONIAL OR NEOCOLONIAL?

- ■ **CONCLUSION**

THE QUESTION
SLAVERY: ABOLITION AND CONTINUATION

To what extent does the global politics of development remain influenced by colonial practices and power relations? Colonialism has been defined as 'the direct political control of a people by a foreign state' (Bernstein, Hewitt and Thomas 1992: 168), as 'the control by one group over another inhabiting a separate territory' (De Alva 1995: 262) and as 'an empire that was developed for settlement by individual communities or for commercial purposes' (Young 2001: 16). Colonialism therefore implies some degree of foreign command and political control, whether or not settlers are present. Two significant aspects of the colonialism of old were slavery in Africa and the establishment of a global trading network controlled by European powers and their various agents. The official worldwide demise of both these aspects is signalled rhetorically by two key concepts, namely abolition and national development. But the reality behind the rhetoric in contemporary West Africa suggests that today's world is *not* postcolonial in any meaningful sense.

Considering slavery first, the British Parliament's ratification of the Act for the Abolition of the Slave Trade in March 1807 marked the beginning of the end of the transatlantic trade in slaves from Africa to the British colonies. Some years were to pass before official recognition that – in the words of then Home Secretary Sir Robert Peel – 'the abominations of the slave system could not be tolerated much longer' (Peel 1833: 1). The Slavery Abolition Act of May 1833 brought an immediate end to the legal principle of property in man but it did not (as Peel himself noted in an article in *The Times*) immediately eliminate slave labour. In an effort to reconcile the competing interests of slaveholders and abolitionists, the Act made provision for the slave's eventual emancipation 'in the course of 12 years by the purchase of his freedom from the fruits of his own exertions' (Peel 1833: 2). In the meantime, all existing slaves were required to register as 'apprenticed labourers' and continue to work for their masters.

Subsequent international conventions are a sure sign of the partial success of such early abolitionist measures. The League of Nations' Slavery Convention of 1926;

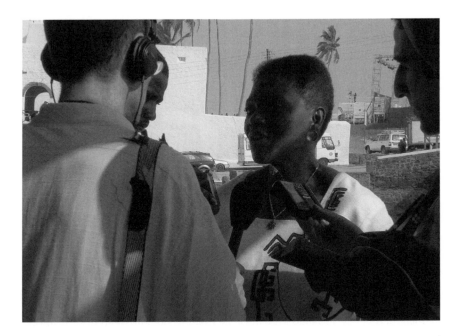

FIGURE 11.1
Baroness Amos, Leader of the UK House of Lords, at Elmina Castle in Ghana on the 200th anniversary of abolition. Photo: British Council in Ghana

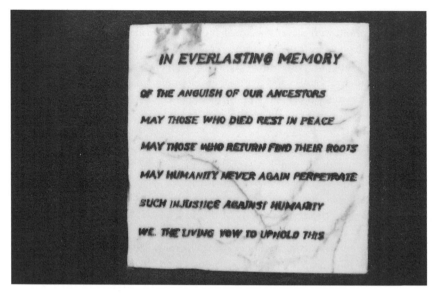

FIGURE 11.2
Plaque commemorating slavery at Elmina Castle, Ghana. From *Castles & Forts of Ghana*,
by Kwesi J. Anquandah (Ghana Museum's Monument Board, 1999)

the United Nations' 1948 Universal Declaration of Human Rights; and the Rome
Final Act of 1998 represent notable efforts to both define slavery and eradicate
it. More recently, human rights campaigners and organisations (such as Anti-
Slavery International) have taken the 200th anniversary of the abolition of the
slave trade as an opportunity to raise awareness of all forms of slavery both
historical and contemporary.

These ongoing movements for change demonstrate the need to think in terms
of abolitionism as a process rather than abolition as a finished achievement.
Furthermore, they show that the major legacy of abolitionism is not the
elimination of slavery but the illegality of the principle of 'property in man'.
Slavery is now illegal everywhere because 'freedom from slavery has been defined
in international law as a fundamental human right' (Bales and Robbins 2001: 18).

The most obvious consequences of the international outlawing of slavery are
concealment and official denial. In his classic analysis of the 'new' or modern
version of slavery that is defined by its very illegality, Bales notes that 'even when
shown photographs and affidavits, nations' officials deny its existence' (1999: 8).
Slavery is often redefined as something else, such as 'indentured labour' or (even
more benign) 'child fostering'. The inevitable outcome of all this is uncertainty
over numbers and conceptual confusion. For example, whereas Anti-Slavery
International (2007) puts the number of contemporary slaves in the world at
12 million, the 'best estimate' of Bales is 27 million – a figure considerably lower,

For a discussion of the
relation between law and
politics, see **Chapter 18**.

he suggests, 'than the estimates put forward by some activists, who give a range as high as 200 million' (1999: 8).

The current global context of secrecy, denial, uncertainty and confusion compels the question of what the concept of slavery means if not legal ownership of human beings or 'property in man'. A useful starting point is the book *Disposable People*, which defines slavery as 'the total control of one person by another for the purpose of economic exploitation' (Bales 1999: 6). In this and other writings, Bales consistently argues that while slavery has changed in form over time it has clearly not disappeared. Its defining characteristics – and the keys to understanding such contemporary forms of the phenomenon as debt bondage and enforced prostitution – are still violence, control and economic exploitation (Bales and Robbins 2001).

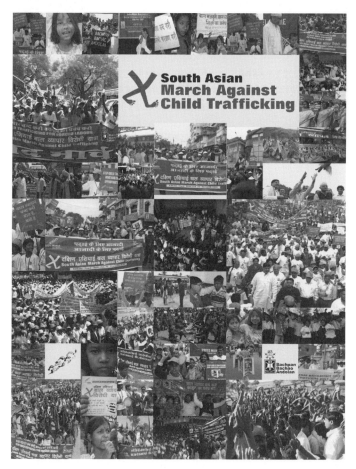

FIGURE 11.3
The South Asian March Against Child Trafficking, New Delhi, 22 March 2007.
Photo: Global March Against Child Labour

As useful as it is in distinguishing the 'old' from the 'new' slavery, Bales' work does not highlight key distinctions between *slavery* as a type of forced labour and *trafficking* (by agents, recruiters and transporters) as a means to that end (Manzo 2005). Nor does Bales address the differences between slavery and other forms of labour exploitation. Varying systems of production and labour regimes clearly co-exist now, just as they did in the colonies of old. If all forms of violence, control and economic exploitation are labelled as slavery, then the millions of illegal and badly paid migrant workers in the world necessarily belong in that category. They don't, however, if we maintain a definition of slavery as unpaid forced labour. This definition is a useful synthesis of insights drawn from two bodies of work. One is Marxist theory, notably its important distinction between slavery as a mode of labour exploitation typified by unpaid work and proletarianisation as a system of labour exploitation typified by wage labour. The other is theories of slavery, which generally emphasise forced labour (through violence and coercion) as the basis of the master–slave relationship.

Even if slavery is defined relatively narrowly as unpaid forced labour, it is still possible to find evidence of its existence. A case in point is the former French colony of Côte d'Ivoire (known also by its English name of Ivory Coast). Thanks to the efforts of investigative journalism in Britain and the United States, the West African country found itself at the turn of the twenty-first century (along with multinational corporations such as Cadbury and Mars) at the centre of the so-called chocolate slavery debate.

There may be millions of slaves globally, but it was the widespread references to 15,000 trafficked children from Mali working without payment on Ivorian cocoa farms that helped turn a regional African phenomenon into a matter of international concern. That is because the enslavement of trafficked *children* (who are defined in international law as persons under the age of eighteen years old) constitutes a triple abuse of international human rights conventions and protocols. Violated along with the fundamental human right to freedom from enslavement are the human right to freedom from trafficking and the child's right to freedom from labour.

In West Africa, as elsewhere, legal enforcement of prohibition is the other side of the coin of official ignorance and denial of contemporary slavery. Chronicles of the experiences of emancipated young people exist thanks to the efforts of the Malian government (among others) to liberate and repatriate child slaves. The oral testimonies of those typically enticed away with false promises and then held in place by violence and threats will not settle the question of exact numbers. But these stories of entrapment into unpaid forced labour are nonetheless important in offering compelling evidence that slavery (as I've defined it) actually exists in Ivory Coast.

See the discussion of forms of labour in the global political economy in **Chapter 12**.

Chapter 13 examines the expansion of the global proletariat.

Migration across borders can be forced, like child trafficking, or voluntary. For a discussion of movements of people across the US–Mexico border, see **Chapter 8**.

ILLUSTRATIVE EXAMPLE
COLONIALISM AND CAPITALIST DEVELOPMENT IN IVORY COAST

Child slavery in Ivory Coast is best understood in a wider context – in relation to the effects of global capitalist development on the West African region. The story of modern slavery in Ivory Coast (which became a colony of France in 1893) must begin in the early twentieth century – with an understanding of what Amin (1973) calls the outward-directed economic development of French West Africa. That term captures in shorthand the three key features of the colonial political economy that still epitomise the region today:

1   an economic growth pattern marked by heavy dependence on the export of a handful of primary products;
2   a forced labour system for the production of agricultural commodities;
3   last but not least, a global supply chain controlled all the way along by colonial companies, traders, intermediaries and middlemen.

FIGURE 11.4
Map of Ivory Coast

Colonial production and unequal exchange

The name Ivory Coast derives from a profitable international trade in ivory during the seventeenth century. That trade was virtually over by the beginning of the subsequent century, however, thanks to the resulting decimation of the elephant population. It therefore wasn't until after the subsequent push inland in the mid-nineteenth century that France began to establish a firm foothold in the West African colony.

Here as elsewhere, the driving force behind colonial settlement was the desire for economic exploitation, notably the promise of fertile environments for cash crop production (i.e. production of agricultural commodities for sale rather than consumption or use). By the early twentieth century, the principal cash crops in the southern forest zones of Ivory Coast were coffee and cocoa, whereas in the northern savannas the main cash crop was cotton.

Cotton was already in production for sale to local artisans before the arrival of colonial powers (Bassett 2001). However, the intervention of the French Textile Development Company (Compagnie Française de Développement des Textiles – CFDT) marked the onset of a classically colonial pattern of unequal and uneven exchange. A raw material of relatively low value produced in the colonies was exchanged for finished manufactures (in this case textile goods) produced in the metropolis. Furthermore, the entire international supply chain was controlled by an integrated network of colonial operators:

> The terms on which this cotton was exchanged reflected the manner in which production was organised: the private company [i.e. CFDT] responsible for cotton production in the colonies was a subsidiary of the sole metropolitan buyer of French West African cotton. At the same time, the sale of manufactured textile goods to the colonies was the responsibility of large trading companies affiliated to the metropolitan textile industry. These companies enjoyed exclusive rights to the French West African market, protected by trade restrictions debarring all but French textile products.
>
> (Campbell 1975: 37)

As in neighbouring Ghana under the British, the basic structure of colonial cultivation in Ivory Coast was the plantation economy. From 1912 (when cocoa became a cash crop) until the end of World War II, production by Africans was doubly enforced. Those with access to land were compelled to cultivate cocoa by colonial authorities, while, at the same, French planters were guaranteed a steady supply of workers via a system of labour conscription.

The French abolition of the forced labour system in 1945 marked the onset of a series of changes. That system was abolished thanks to the collective efforts of

BOX 11.1 FÉLIX HOUPHOUËT-BOIGNY

FIGURE 11.5
Félix Houphouët-Boigny.
Courtesy of Célestin
Mbenti Nkoudou

Among those leading the fight for the abolition of forced labour and the rights of African planters was Félix Houphouët-Boigny. A qualified physician from a wealthy family of planters, Houphouët-Boigny held political posts in French ministries prior to Ivorian independence. An ardent anti-communist, he was commonly known in the West as the 'Sage of Africa' or the 'Grand Old Man of Africa'. He was the country's president from independence in 1960 until his death in 1993.

the 20,000 indigenous planters who came together in 1944 to form the African Agricultural Union.

Post-independence economic development

Ivory Coast was one of many African states to achieve formal political independence in 1960. According to Amin (1973: 50), the abolition of forced labour was a catalyst for the plantation-based agricultural development to follow. Agriculture was not the only aspect of post-independence development, however. Infrastructure (roads, railways and ports) and import substitution industrialisation (i.e. the government policy of replacing imports with domestically produced goods) to support the development of national manufacturing (such as textile mills and food-processing plants) were also central to the new government's strategy for national development. But with formal political power in the hands of the landed plantation-based class, post-independence development not surprisingly entailed a focus on agricultural growth (Campbell 1975: 37).

Ivorian economic growth was successfully achieved in the first decade after independence via policies of agricultural expansion and diversification. Production rose for all crops – everything from domestically consumed yams, plantains and manioc to the exported commodities of coffee, cocoa, bananas and pineapples. Another significant earner was wood, exports of which 'rose from a 1950 figure of 90,000 tons to 1,250,000 tons in 1965' (Amin 1973: 52).

Despite (or indeed because of) such changes, economic development remained outward-directed. Increases in food production failed to achieve self-sufficiency. The food deficit actually worsened, leading to greater dependence on grain and rice imports (Amin 1973: 52). Added to that, the development of Ivory Coast was still based mainly on agricultural exports, with expansion and diversification relying heavily on external factors of production in the form of foreign investment, imported technology and an inflow of immigrant labour from the West African region (Amin 1973: 44; Crook 1990: 651).

Last but not least, the guiding official principle of cooperation with France in all fields only cemented the pre-existing power of French companies, managers, advisers and traders. To return to the cotton example, not only did those who had once produced and marketed raw cotton continue to do so, but 'the large export-import houses affiliated with French industry maintained sole access to the Ivorian market by virtue of a quota system, in force until February 1969, which required special licenses for any textile products from sources other than France' (Campbell 1975: 38). In sum, the entire supply chain of unequal and uneven exchange remained immediately after independence in the hands of the same controlling interests as before.

It is interesting to read this account of economic development alongside the account of changes in the global political economy in **Chapter 12.** See also discussions of global inequality and poverty in
Chapters 13 and 14.

The politics of last resort: development crises and structural adjustment

Before turning to the specific factors responsible for the appearance of modern slavery in Ivory Coast, it's necessary to consider the internal benefits of outward-directed economic development. Which domestic forces within Ivory Coast, in other words, might have profited from the pattern of development described in the previous section?

At least until 1981, when the first crisis of development became impossible to ignore, the internal benefits to growth went disproportionately to 'the original power elite' in control of the Ivorian state (Crook 1990: 651). It wasn't only that a development model founded on agricultural growth was bound to generate capital for landowners. It was also that the wealth generated from state-led industrial development, i.e. the combination of import-substitution policy and direct public investment in domestic manufacturing, enabled the new ruling elite to consolidate its political position. The key institutions, in this regard, were not only the government and civil service but also an expanding machinery of economic administration and control, notably the agricultural extension agency, the Ministry of Agriculture and the crop-marketing board (Crook 1990).

The Ivorian economy grew at an average rate of 7.2 per cent a year from independence in 1960 to 1981 (Ridler 1993: 301). For the Houphouët-Boigny regime, those decades of spectacular economic growth no doubt served the dual purpose of political and economic stability. But the limits of the Ivorian economic 'miracle' were already apparent to some well before the combined effects of a series of pressures 'finally delivered Côte d'Ivoire into the hands of the international bailiffs or, as they are quaintly called in development jargon, the "donor community"' (Crook 1990: 649).

Samir Amin argued in the early 1970s that the writing was already on the wall for an economic development model based on three limiting factors. One was the dual dependence of export-oriented agriculture on paid foreign labour (for production) and foreign markets for cash crops. A second was the dependence of import-substitution industries on domestic consumption – the growth of which was severely limited by restrictions in income. And last but not least – most damaging of all – was the method of financing development through foreign capital and investment. Thanks to high rates of investment return (a pattern of capital repatriation reminiscent of the colonial period), Ivory Coast had already passed 'from the stage of development, characterised by a net inflow of foreign capital, to that of exploitation, characterised by a reversal in the balance of flows and an increasing preponderance of re-exported profits' (Amin 1973: 56).

The subsequent crisis of development has been blamed in part on political interference in markets, notably the channelling of payments to farmers for cash crops through the *Caisse de stabilisation* or crop marketing board (see Crook 1990: 659; also Ridler 1993: 302). As implied by its French name, the basic purpose of the *Caisse* was price stabilisation. Instead of exposing traders and farmers to free market forces, the Ivorian government operated a national system of guaranteed purchase and fixed producer prices. This system was a double-edged sword, for while it safeguarded livelihoods in periods of slump, it paid sub-market prices in periods of boom. The system was thus paradoxical for farmers and traders, as it benefited them most when market prices were low. The government, on the other hand, clearly benefited from the 'good years', when 'important elements of the nation's budget for expansion and investment were funded by the *Caisse* surpluses' (Crook 1990: 659).

What finally brought matters to a head was not development policy as such but a series of external 'shocks'. The most damaging single factor was the international drop in commodity prices that followed the short-lived boom of the mid-1970s. Despite the efforts to diversify agriculture, Ivory Coast still depended for the bulk of its export earnings on cocoa and coffee. The loss of foreign exchange earnings meant that terms of trade inevitably declined, i.e. Ivory Coast was forced to pay relatively more for imports thanks to the declining value of its exports.

Matters were only made worse by the wider context in which commodity prices dropped. They fell at a time of continued foreign borrowing to sustain public

Note that economic growth does not necessarily improve everyone's wealth. **See Chapters 13 and 14**

Note that this argument shows a liberal mindset: according to liberal thought, if only markets operated freely, development would automatically occur. **See Chapter 14**

FIGURE 11.6
US Commodity Price Index adjusted for consumer price inflation. Source: Mineweb.com.
With permission

expenditures; of decline in the value of the US dollar (the currency in which commercial loans were denominated); and of rising prices for imported oil. The cumulative effect was a dramatic increase in national indebtedness. By 1981, Ivory Coast's external debt was ten times higher than it had been only three years earlier, 'and debt-service costs had increased even faster' (Ridler 1993: 303).

BOX 11.2 STRUCTURAL ADJUSTMENT

The term 'structural adjustment' is shorthand for 'the process by which the IMF and the World Bank base their lending to underdeveloped economies on certain conditions, pre-determined by these institutions' (Milward 2000: 25). Sometimes known as the 'Bretton Woods twins' or international financial institutions (IFIs), the IMF and World Bank are the product of formal negotiations that took place at Brettons Woods, New Hampshire, USA, in 1944. The aim of the Bretton Woods conference, which was orchestrated by Britain and the United States, was to initiate a post-war international economic order based on fiscal discipline, exchange rate stability, free markets and growth in international trade. The empowerment of the IFIs to oversee and manage this new order was a key consequence of Bretton Woods. All adjustment programmes reflect this background and what I have elsewhere called 'the twin pillars of the neo-liberal (essentially capitalist) development agenda, namely market-based economic arrangements and minimalist states' (Manzo 2003: 438).

That combination of factors explains why the Ivory Coast government initially turned (like so many in Africa) to the International Monetary Fund (IMF) for financial assistance.

The first structural adjustment programme (SAP) for Ivory Coast was introduced in 1981 and updated periodically throughout the decade. The changes demanded were a 'one size fits all' programme of currency devaluation, liberalisation of prices and interest rates, fiscal restraint and austerity (i.e. cuts in state expenditure), and trade liberalisation (Ridler 1993: 303).

As with so many African countries, negative economic growth and an increasingly unsustainable debt burden were for Ivory Coast the dark at the end of the adjustment tunnel. The Ivorian government has been doubly blamed for the new 'manifestly impossible austerity programme' demanded by the IMF and World Bank in February 1990 (Crook 1990: 669). The regime of Houphouët-Boigny has been faulted, first of all, for maintaining an agricultural policy of cocoa expansion – apparently with World Bank support – until April 1988 (Crook 1990: 662–3). In this way it failed to foresee the consequences of further declines in international commodity prices. Second, the regime in power failed to fully implement its SAPs – refusing, for example, to cut the salaries of public-sector employees as demanded by fiscal austerity (Ridler 1993: 304–5).

And yet, even its critics acknowledge the limited room for manoeuvre of a state such as Ivory Coast, where 'the survival of a regime often depends on the degree to which lenders restrain their demands' (Crook 1990: 650). Throughout post-independence Africa, political legitimacy has depended on economic performance and delivery. An obvious factor in this regard has been high rates of growth, which have helped to paper over the contradictions of outward-oriented development. Contradictions are more easily exposed in periods of downturn and reversal – which are inevitable for cash crop exporters in particular. Thanks to the price volatility of international commodities, declining terms of trade can be unpredictably sudden and sharp. This happened to Ivory Coast, for example, between 1985 and 1990 when the world prices of cocoa more than halved (Ridler 1993: 304).

Again, compare this account of economic development to the changes in the global political economy described in Chapter 12.

Equally significant is the state's capacity to regulate and administer the national economy. As argued by Mbembe (2001: 76), the post-independence African state's 'credit with the public' stems from a combination of financial means, administrative power and distribution of goods. In this light, the determination of the Ivorian government to keep the cocoa trade going and maintain a large civil service makes political sense. Enabling farmers to be paid (through the *Caisse*) while guaranteeing public-sector employment was perceived as key to the legitimacy of 'Houphouët and his cronies' (Crook 1990: 669).

Some Islamic movements also acquire 'credit with the public' through the provision of services.
See Chapter 5

What changes were attributable to the heightened influence of the IMF in Ivory Coast in the 1990s? The basic argument of the next section is that structural adjustment has been responsible for a redistribution of benefits. Far from undermining existing patterns of inequality, however, structural adjustment has only made matters worse.

RESPONSES
THE EFFECTS OF ADJUSTMENT: DEPROLETARIANISATION AND MODERN SLAVERY

Colonial political economy was typified by cash crop dependence, enforced production of cash crops and supply chain control. It is against each of these criteria that the effects of structural adjustment – and its redistribution of benefits – are therefore to be assessed.

Cash crop dependence has only intensified under the IMF's generalised framework of export promotion and market-led growth. Following the death of Houphouët-Boigny in 1993 and his replacement by his constitutional successor, National Assembly President Henri Konan Bedie, the Ivorian government entered into a concessional loan agreement through the IMF's Enhanced Structural Adjustment Facility (ESAF) for low-income countries. In return for a low interest loan of 0.5 per cent (to be repaid over five to ten years), the 'international bailiffs' demanded a standard policy package of currency devaluation, cuts in government spending and (most tellingly) the liberalisation of banking and trade.

This insistence on the free market is informed by neoliberal ideas. See Chapter 14

In regard to export agriculture, specifically, the donor community echoed the old 'apologists for colonialism' who argued that African farmers would derive positive benefits from the opportunity to produce coffee, cocoa and palm oil (Rodney 1982: 154). Contemporary donors insisted that a flourishing free market would benefit Ivorian farmers by freeing them from government interference and allowing them access to the true price of their commodities on the world market.

The Bedie government responded with capitulation to the long-standing demand for devaluation of the Ivorian franc. The national currency was devalued by 50 per cent in 1994 at the same time as export taxes were eliminated. These measures have been thanked for a subsequent economic comeback marked by a jump in growth rates and a drop in inflation. But fortuitous timing was equally significant. The donor-mandated reforms coincided with improved international prices for cocoa and coffee.

The combined effect of externally imposed policies and world market forces was an immediate explosion of cocoa production (up 44 per cent from 1994 to 1996) and Ivory Coast's movement to the top of the ranks of world cocoa producers. The country now accounts for 40 per cent of global supply.

So who or what might have benefited, at this stage, from structural adjustment? Certainly not Ivory Coast's forest zone – the historical site of cocoa production. The country's protected tropical forests have become increasingly vulnerable to illegal logging and cocoa expansion. As for the Ivorian government, structural adjustment initially was a double-edged sword. While it brought the traditional benefits of growth (as described earlier) it also undermined state capacity for economic administration and control at a delicate time of political transition. In this context, the Bedie government trod the familiar African path described by Mbembe (2001: 76). It became increasingly repressive and reliant on control of the forces of coercion to try to stifle dissent.

The loss of forests is now a global concern. See Chapter 3

Farmers and planters would have to be the clear beneficiaries of a programme of reforms designed to limit state power and expose them more fully to world market forces – but only as long as the price of their commodities remains high and (equally importantly) buyers pay producers the true market rate. Unfortunately for agricultural producers, the basic economic logic of supply and demand dictates that prices must inevitably fall. Cocoa (like other exportable cash crops) 'is characterised by boom and bust cycle – as global production/supply rise, price of cocoa beans fall and vice versa' (International Labor Rights Fund, undated: 4).

An apt illustration of the consequences of 'boom and bust' economics (i.e. a period of economic expansion followed inevitably by a period of recession) is what happened when world cocoa prices plummeted in 1999. Ivorian farmers were particularly hard hit because the drop coincided with the final abandonment of the *Caisse* system of guaranteed prices. Ivorian cocoa production is labour-intensive and historically reliant on workers from the West African region. With the donor-enforced completion of the process of trade liberalisation, both the migrant workforce and the 70 per cent of the Ivorian population engaged in agricultural activity were therefore negatively exposed to the full force of structural adjustment.

In response to increased rural poverty and government repression, military forces under the leadership of General Guei overthrew the Bedie administration on 24 December 1999 and replaced it with the so-called National Council for Public Salvation (Country Watch, undated: 4). After a disputed election in October 2000, General Guei was replaced as president by Laurent Gbagbo. Following an unsuccessful coup attempt by Guei's supporters in 2002, army rebels seized control of the northern regions of the country and plunged Ivory Coast into civil war. France (the former colonial power) soon dispatched thousands of troops into the country to police a dividing line between the north and the south. The French military was still there two years later – along with reinforcements from the United

Nations (UN) – as the international community (in the guise of France, the UN and the African Union) attempted to broker a power-sharing agreement (Talbot 2004).

The Marxist concept of deproletarianisation helps explain why, in a neoliberal context of shrinking state capacity, trade liberalisation and attendant political unrest, Ivorian farmers 'have been pushed to use their own children or those supplied by traffickers' in efforts to sustain rural livelihoods (International Labor Rights Fund, undated: 6). At the root of this concept is the proletarian – a person who survives by selling their labour power and working for wages. The corresponding term 'proletarianisation' has been mentioned already. Unlike slavery – which was defined earlier as unpaid forced labour – proletarianisation refers to a crucial aspect of capitalist development, namely the process whereby large numbers of people who once owned the means to produce goods and services for sale become employed solely as wage labourers.

Deproletarianisation is shorthand for a Marxist view of regression or reversal, whereby forced labour is reintroduced as a method of worker discipline and a way to cut costs under capitalism. The deproletarianisation thesis calls into question the standard explanation for the rise of modern slavery that's offered by Bales (1999: 12–13). There the emphasis is on two key contributing factors within a wider context of economic globalisation and population growth. One is socio-economic modernisation. The other is labour *supply* – the basic notion being that a ready availability of willing young workers necessarily drives labour costs down.

The problem with the 'over-supply' thesis is that it doesn't really explain why slaveholders should need to drive labour costs down beyond the point of paying a pittance to paying nothing at all. Deproletarianisation helps to answer that question, even if it is a framework for understanding all forms of agrarian forced labour and not an explanation for modern slavery per se. The underlying premise is that agricultural producers will protect their economic interests by switching labour regimes for the same reasons that Britain switched from 'informal empire' to formal colonialism. Producers of commodities will resort to forced labour when they *must* and not simply because they *can*.

The value of that suggestion is twofold. On the one hand, it would seem to make logical sense given the global illegality of slavery (and attendant risk of prosecution) discussed in the introduction to this chapter. Even if the outlawing of slavery doesn't eradicate the practice it still alters the calculus of slaveholders, turning what was once an accepted convention and best possible option into a final resort. On the other hand, deproletarianisation reflects the actual behaviour of Ivorian farmers. Modern slavery in Ivory Coast is more of a variable than a constant, ebbing and flowing with changes in commodity prices. Farmers, furthermore, have readily turned to more conventional methods of protecting their livelihoods.

How does 'deproletarianisation' compare with the 'informalisation' of labour discussed in Chapter 12 and the expansion of the global proletariat discussed in Chapter 13?

They took to the streets in 2004, for example, in protest at the changes introduced since the abolition of the *Caisse* and the abandonment of the system of minimum pricing. Uncertain of market prices and distrustful of the trio of semi-private agencies set up after 2000 to oversee the cocoa trade, growers complained of their diminished capacity to withstand economic shock. They argued that the sliding levy scale introduced to compensate for heavy losses in global markets offered far less protection than the old guaranteed minimum price (BBC News 2004: 1).

To connect deproletarianisation to structural adjustment in this way is not to excuse the behaviour of slaveholders. The point is to demonstrate the political consequences of neoliberal development. The argument thus far clearly reinforces the conventional message sent by human rights activists (such as the International Labor Rights Forum) that structural adjustment hits hardest at the poor.

It is necessary to conclude now by considering the other side of the neoliberal coin. If farmers and planters are only the winners in theory of neoliberal development, then who or what are the beneficiaries in practice?

That question returns the analysis to the issue of supply chain control. In Britain's 'informal empire', free trade agreements were a means to protect dominant commercial interests while exploiting relatively weak states. They were thus implicitly hierarchical, in both an economic and political sense. At the top (as the quotation from Rodney in Box 11.3 implies) were the 'white colonialists', who exercised political control and profited most economically from the status quo; at the bottom was the economically exploited and politically disempowered African peasantry.

BOX 11.3 COLONIALISM'S DIVISION OF LABOUR

A peasant growing a cash crop or collecting produce had his labour exploited by a long chain of individuals, starting with local businessmen. Sometimes, those local businessmen were Europeans. Very rarely were they Africans, and more usually they were a minority group brought in from outside and serving as intermediaries between the white colonialists and the exploited African peasant . . . The share of profits which went to middlemen was insignificant in comparison to those profits reaped by big European business interests and by the European governments themselves.

(Rodney 1982: 154–5)

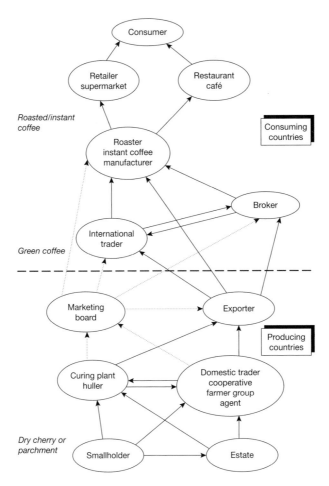

FIGURE 11.7
General structure of the global coffee-marketing chain. Stefano Ponte (2002) 'The "Latte Revolution"? Regulation, Markets and Consumption in the Global Coffee Chain', *World Development* 30, 7: 1099-122

Current global food chains are remarkably similar to the colonial division of labour, as the above exposition of coffee markets demonstrates.

With regard to Ivorian cocoa, next in line to farmers are the farmgate buyers and local exporters, who are now (thanks to trade liberalisation) in a better position to haggle with farmers over prices. These 'local businessmen' have been accused of short-changing producers by 'buying their beans cheaply and selling at big profits in the rising market' (Cowell 2002: 1). As the London-based International Cocoa Organisation (ICA) noted in a 2000 report, 'Ivory Coast's mostly illiterate farmers are ill-equipped to negotiate with [the] hard-bargaining commodity buyers' who systematically underpay (quoted in Cowell 2002: 2). For farmers, then, the consequence of the abandonment of fixed prices is only the privatisation of their exploitation and not (as promised) their payment at true market rates.

Further along the supply chain are London-based brokerage firms such as Armajaro, a company headed by the trader Anthony Ward (the man nicknamed Chocolate Finger by business associates). Serving as brokers between African exporters and Western cocoa processors, these companies stand to make fortunes in commodities futures markets from speculative buying and selling.

Beyond the brokers are the cocoa grinders and processors who buy raw beans to turn into semi-finished products such as cocoa powder and butter. The members of this group suffer from commodity price rises if they cannot pass on the rising costs to their own buyers. These, in turn, are food companies in general and chocolate and confectionary manufacturers in particular (Cowell 2002: 4).

Dominant brand-owners such as Cadbury and Mars are the 'big business interests' that arguably dominate the entire cocoa supply chain (Tiffen 2002). Their relative commercial dominance, rather than proximity to any actual slaves, placed them at the centre of the 'chocolate slavery debate' mentioned on p. 248. But the multinationals are not the end of the chain. Beyond them are two other links. One is the retail outlets that may squeeze manufacturers by refusing to countenance price increases on the finished products they sell (Cowell 2002: 4). The other is assorted consumers like us, who contribute to global demand.

> Are you eating a bar of chocolate as you read this? Which company made it? Do they tell you where they source their cocoa from?

Overseeing the whole are the new agents of 'informal empire' – the IMF and World Bank and, arguably, the World Trade Organisation. From their command centres in Washington, DC, this 'unholy trinity' of multilateral institutions governs a world economy 'that their neoliberal ideology insists is best left institutionally ungoverned' (Peet 2003: 23). This inherent contradiction exposes the triumvirate to powerful dissent and may well undermine it eventually. No empire lasts forever, not even the most powerful.

> As consumers, we are all implicated, then, in child slavery. What should we do about it? Is consumer action enough?

In the meantime, all three institutions are sustained by a combination of institutional learning and powerful support. They 'have learned that a little spin and some confessions of partial failure . . . excuse many abuses in the exercise of power' (Peet 2003: 24). Even more importantly, the 'unholy trinity' represents a conglomerate of economic and political interests. At its economic heart are the major beneficiaries of neoliberalism – multinational corporations in general and, according to Peet (2003: 202), investment banking in particular. At its political heart are the governments of the leading capitalist countries. Counted among their ranks are the former colonial powers. They (like France in the Ivory Coast) may still turn to military means to protect their vital interests – but only when informal strategies fall short of the mark or misfire.

BROADER ISSUES
IS TODAY'S WORLD POSTCOLONIAL OR NEOCOLONIAL?

Answers to questions are never simply a matter of either common sense or empirical fact. They inevitably depend on two interrelated factors. One is meaning – the issue of how key concepts in the question are understood and defined in their own terms as well as differentiated from other similar concepts. The second is perspective – how those same key concepts are interpreted from within a particular theoretical framework. Concepts and theory together determine intellectual focus and approach – the ways in which arguments are presented and evidence marshalled.

With the above points in mind, this final section, which raises the larger question of whether today's world is postcolonial or neocolonial, begins with a critical interrogation of the meaning of the key concepts 'postcolonial', 'colonial' and 'neocolonial'.

> Think about the notion of pictures of the world presented in Chapter 2. Are the concepts we use and the perspective we adopt part of our picture of the world?

Postcolonialism

The fundamental issue with the term 'postcolonial' is whether the *post* in the term signals *after*. The perspective from which this issue is considered is 'postcolonial theory' – a term that is itself open to interpretation thanks to the diversity of self-consciously postcolonial scholarship. Postcolonialism is best seen as a 'site of critical inquiry' (Slater 1998: 655) or a set of shared ideas rather than a single theory or unified body of thought (Abrahamsen 2003: 191).

Postcolonial theory, first of all, refuses to treat 'postcolonial' as a synonym for 'European decolonisation'. The world can only be considered 'postcolonial' if we assume that historic patterns of economic control and command necessarily ended with formal colonial rule. Patterns of continuity amid change mean that international power relations have moved beyond colonialism in some ways while remaining thoroughly colonial in others. There is thus still some utility (despite the criticisms levelled against it) in the Marxist concept of neocolonialism considered later in this section.

Second, postcolonial theory is fundamentally concerned with topical issues and themes and not with colonial history per se. It is interested in contemporary manifestations of historic aspects of European colonialism, such as slavery in Africa. As the discussion so far has argued, while slavery per se is an institution defined by unpaid forced labour, the defining feature of *modern* slavery is the shift in the master–slave relation from the legal ownership that obtained in the colonial era to illegal control. The trafficking of children from countries like Mali to work on cocoa plantations in the Ivory Coast exposes the covert character of modern slavery while situating its patterns of economic domination, violence and resistance in a global economic context. This focus consciously integrates the economic concerns of traditional Marxism with the politics of international human rights, thus offering an example of what Young calls 'postcolonial cultural critique' (2001: 7).

In explaining slavery's persistence, the issue once again is continuity amid change; specifically, the issue of how child enslavement can exist (if not positively flourish) in a world of international human rights law, formal decolonisation and capitalist development. The answer suggested here embeds the problematic of modern slavery firmly within the workings of the world economy as well as the frameworks and strategies designed to promote capitalist development. Attention to two key processes, namely deproletarianisation and structural adjustment, shows how the fundamentally uneven and hierarchical character of colonial power relations remains invested in contemporary theories and practices of development.

BOX 11.4 DEFINITIONS OF POSTCOLONIALISM

The postcolonial does not privilege the colonial. It is concerned with colonial history only to the extent that that history has determined the configurations and power structures of the present.

(Young 2001: 4)

Postcolonial theory involves discussion about experiences of various kinds: migration, slavery, suppression, resistance, representation, difference, race, gender and place (among others).

(Power 2003: 123)

The post-colonial . . . can be defined in relation to a period of time that is marked by the power of the colonizing process.

(Slater 1998: 653)

Colonialism, as conventionally defined in terms of formal settlement and control of other people's land and goods, is in the main over, but many of its structures and relations of power are still in place.

(Abrahamsen 2003: 195)

Postcoloniality . . . is a salutary reminder of the persistent 'neo-colonial' relations within the 'new' world order and the multi-national division of labour.

(Bhabha 1994: 6)

Colonialism

Before we return to the question of whether today's world is postcolonial in any meaningful sense, or more properly neocolonial, we need to ask what colonialism entailed. As David Slater has noted, there are crucial distinctions between the Iberian colonisation of Latin America by Spain and Portugal, on the one hand, and the pan-European colonisation of Africa and Asia on the other (Slater 1998: 653). Both colonisation and decolonisation began and ended much sooner in the American continent than they did in the other two. All of Latin America except for Cuba and Puerto Rico was formally independent by 1825, whereas the process of Asian decolonisation only began with the independence of India from Britain in 1947. At that time, the only two African countries not under colonial rule were Ethiopia and Liberia. The decolonisation of Libya in 1951 marked the onset of decolonisation in North Africa, while the trailblazer in Sub-Saharan Africa was Sudan in 1956.

So, it is safe to say (as scholars generally do) that European decolonisation has largely run its course. But, by the same token, it would be dangerous to assume that all aspects of colonialism have reached an unequivocal end, for two reasons. First, the geography of independence remains spatially uneven. Many islands as opposed to continents in the world (such as French Martinique and the Dutch Antilles) continue to fly European flags and are effectively still colonies. Meanwhile, as Young (2001: 3) points out, more recent invasions (such as that of Tibet by China and Kashmir by India) signal the arrival of a new generation of colonial rulers.

Second, there was always more to colonialism than what Potter (1992) calls its 'international political dimension', i.e. the direct control and formal political rule of a subject population by a foreign power. On the one hand, colonialism in practice was arguably marked by six other features, namely:

- bureaucratic elitism and authoritarianism;
- statism (i.e. comprehensive political control of the economy);
- use of 'traditional' authority figures;
- use of force;
- technological advantage; and
- a hegemonic ideology designed to legitimate and perpetuate the existing regime.

(Potter 1992)

According to Potter, it was only the international political dimension of colonial rule that was 'snapped at independence' (1992: 219).

On the other hand, colonialism needs to be understood in relation to motives as well as features. As the Ivory Coast case demonstrates, European colonialism was

Early colonisation in the Americas is discussed in Chapter 15.

driven by economic as well as territorial interests in land. For Britain, at least in the mid-Victorian period (roughly the 1850s to the 1870s or slightly later), 'informal empire' was the preferred means of extending supremacy. 'Refusals to annex are no proof of reluctance to control', as Gallagher and Robinson (1953: 3) have memorably said. But Victorian policy makers viewed annexation only as a method of 'last resort' to secure British interests. Formal political rule was not considered as long as commercial penetration, political influence and economic command could be achieved by other means. First among these were free trade agreements and treaties of friendship 'made with or imposed upon a weaker state' (Gallagher and Robinson 1953: 11–12).

Young suggests that different motivations (for commercial exploitation and settlement) gave rise to 'two distinct kinds of colonies' within European empires – 'the settled and the exploited, the white and the black, which would be treated very differently' (2001: 19). Colonies varied as well in terms of their systems of production and labour regimes. Bernstein, Johnson and Thomas (1992: 186) identify four broad types of colonial labour regime, namely: forced labour (of which slavery is a notorious exemplar); semi-proletarianisation; petty commodity production; and proletarianisation. Slavery was only ever a feature of plantation economies or 'colonies of domination' (Young 2001: 23). It did not typify colonialism per se.

What *did* come to typify all European colonies was their insertion into trade on the world market. Whether it was the primary motivation for it or not, the establishment of a global trading network controlled by European powers and their various agents was a significant aspect of the colonialism of old.

Neocolonialism

The conviction that nothing much has changed in the world economic order since independence, in that patterns of economic power and unequal exchange remain more or less exactly as they were, is at the heart of the neo-Marxist concept of neocolonialism. A term first coined by Kwame Nkrumah – 'the man who had been able to transform the politics of Ghana and pressurise the British into leaving without a single shot being fired' (Young 2001: 45) – neocolonialism is most obviously neo-Marxist in the sense that the framework of analysis was inspired by the writings of Russian Marxist Vladimir Lenin. The title of Nkrumah's 1965 book – *Neo-colonialism: The Last Stage of Imperialism* – is a clear echo of Lenin's earlier analysis of colonialism as a system of economic exploitation in *Imperialism: The Highest Stage of Capitalism* (Nkrumah 1965; Lenin 1939).

Nkrumah's basic argument was that a resource-rich country such as Ghana could not develop autonomously thanks to its insertion within an international division

There is a discussion of the European territorial state and its imperial expansion in **Chapter 9.**

FIGURE 11.8
Kwame Nkrumah

BOX 11.5 DEFINITIONS OF NEOCOLONIALISM

Following World War II decolonization quickly accelerated and colonialism shifted in meaning once more as the Left – now fully committed to the use of 'colonialism' to describe an economically or politically dependent condition – rechristened the predicament of the newly liberated but economically devastated nations as 'neocolonialism'.

(De Alva 1995: 267)

The imposition of the international division of labour under formal colonialism had the indirect effect of laying the foundations for the continued economic control and domination over colonial resources even in the absence of direct political overlordship and administration.

(Hoogvelt 1997: 30)

Neocolonialism denotes a continuing economic hegemony that means that the postcolonial state remains in a situation of dependence on its former masters, and that the former masters continue to act in a colonialist manner toward formerly colonized states.

(Young 2001: 45)

---

of labour centred on capitalist exploitation and external control of markets. This analysis not only inspired a more general neo-Marxist framework for the analysis of underdevelopment in West Africa (see Amin 1973). It also played well among many other leaders of newly independent states – especially those elsewhere in Africa confronted with the same 'harsh reality' of economic dependence on exports of primary commodities (Young 2001: 45).

The charge that those same new rulers were metaphorically in bed with the enemy and thus part of the problem was captured in the development of underdevelopment thesis of Andre Gunder Frank, which emphasised the complicity of the post-independence ruling class or 'comprador bourgeoisie' with the interests of international capital (see Frank 1967). Frank's analysis of capitalism and underdevelopment in Latin America exposed the internal benefits as well as costs of outward-directed development while enfolding the problem of underdevelopment within a broader analysis and critique of the expansion of capitalism into a world system.

FIGURE 11.9
Andre Gunder Frank.
Photo: Permission from
http://wsarch.ucr.edu/
archive/gunder97cd.html

As Slater (1998) points out, a degree of intellectual mud-slinging can give the impression that neocolonialism and postcolonialism are incompatible terms. The former stands accused of overemphasising the continuity of colonialism and the power of the West, while the latter has been charged with a seeming 'avoidance of political economy and in particular class politics, and more pointedly an implicit acceptance of global capitalism' (Slater 1998: 655). This whole debate raises much bigger and more troubling questions (which have been explored in more depth elsewhere) about the utility of simple binary distinctions between postcolonial theory and area studies (Abrahamsen 2003) and between culture and political economy (Manzo 2005).

> In other words, is it really helpful to try to decide whether one approach or the other is 'better'? How would we ever be able to decide this once and for all? And, in any case, aren't there many different approaches subsumed under each of these labels?

Suffice it to say here that the field of postcolonial studies is expansive enough to embrace a variety of theoretical persuasions. The concept of neocolonialism (like other Marxist concepts) is not foreign to postcolonial theory. There is no necessary contradiction in terms between neocolonialism and postcolonialism and, more generally, between neo-Marxist thought and postcolonial theory. Their common frame of reference is the contemporary effects of colonial power relations over time.

CONCLUSION

The end of formal colonial rule has not ended historic patterns of economic control and exploitation any more than the abolition of slavery has eradicated enslavement. Slavery – like colonialism itself – persists despite its official demise. While both have changed in form they are sustained in a variety of ways by economic and political interests.

Although the geographic focus of the chapter is Africa (West Africa in particular), the issues raised are global in scope and broader in character. It is necessary to think about the wider relationship between capitalism and slavery; the uneven and unequal consequences of development in theory and practice; and the prospects of meaningful change.

A general lesson to draw from this analysis is that neither colonialism nor slavery is antithetical to capitalist development. Capitalism may well benefit more in theory from the invisible hand of the free market than from mechanisms of force (be it forced labour regimes or the enforced subjugation of formal political rule). But as the history of Ivory Coast's agricultural commodities trade demonstrates, capitalism in practice has always relied for its transnational expansion on unequal relations of power. Inequalities may be inherent in the international division of labour and global supply chain. But labour exploitation and unequal exchange are not naturally occurring phenomena. They are political outcomes and the effects of global relations of power involving states and, increasingly, the agents of 'informal empire'. As such, they are always (like colonialism and slavery) subject to change.

FURTHER READING

Archer, Leonie (ed.) (1988) *Slavery and Other Forms of Unfree Labour*, London and New York: Routledge.
> An edited overview of theories of slavery.

Coote, Belinda (1996) *The Trade Trap: Poverty and the Global Commodity Markets*, Oxford: Oxfam.
> A critical analysis for Oxfam of the relationship between poverty and global commodity markets.

Laycock, Henry (1999) 'Exploitation via Labour Power in Marx', *Journal of Ethics* 3, 2: 121–31.
> An exploration of the Marxist distinction between slavery and other forms of labour exploitation.

Manzo, Kate (2005) 'Modern Slavery, Global Capitalism and Deproletarianisation in West Africa', *Review of African Political Economy* 32, 106: 521–34.
> An exploration of the relationship between capitalism and modern slavery in Africa, using Ivory Coast as a case study.

Memmi, Albert (2006) *Decolonisation and the Decolonised*, Minneapolis, MN and London: University of Minnesota Press.
> A portrait of the contemporary situation of formerly colonised areas and peoples.

Mohan, Giles, Ed Brown, Bob Milward and Alfred B. Zack-Williams (2000) *Structural Adjustment: Theory, Practice and Impacts*, London and New York: Routledge.
> A detailed exploration of all aspects of structural adjustment, including consideration of alternatives.

Mshomba, Richard E. (2000) *Africa in the Global Economy*, Boulder, CO and London: Lynne Rienner Publishers.
> An exploration of how Africa has been affected by trade-related policies and agreements, including international commodity agreements.

WEBSITES

Anti-Slavery International, http://www.antislavery.org.
> The world's oldest international rights organisation.

Free the Slaves, http://www.freetheslaves.net.
> A non-profit organisation dedicated to ending slavery worldwide.

Stop Chocolate Slavery, http://vision.ucsd.edu/~kbranson/stopchocolateslavery.
> A website dedicated to raising awareness of slavery and other labour abuses in the production of chocolate.

World Rain Forest Movement, http://www.wrm.org.uy.
> Some useful information on the environmental consequences of commodity production.

REFERENCES

Abrahamsen, Rita (2003) 'African Studies and the Postcolonial Challenge', *African Affairs* 102, 407: 189–210.

Amin, Samir (1973) *Neo-Colonialism in West Africa*, Harmondsworth: Penguin.

Anti-Slavery International (2007) 'About 1807–2007', http://www.antislavery.org/2007/about.html (accessed 12/03/07).

Bales, Kevin (1999) *Disposable People: New Slavery in the Global Economy*, Berkeley, CA, Los Angeles, CA and London: University of California Press.

Bales, Kevin and Peter T. Robbins (2001) '"No One Shall Be Held in Slavery or Servitude": A Critical Analysis of International Slavery Agreements and Concepts of Slavery', *Human Rights Review*, 2, 2: 18–45.

Bassett, Thomas J. (2001) *Peasant Cotton Revolution in West Africa: Côte d'Ivoire, 1880–1995*, Cambridge: Cambridge University Press.

BBC News (2004) 'Cocoa Delays Hitting Ivory Coast', 1 October: 1–2, http://news.bbc.co.uk/1/hi/business/3706952.stm (accessed 03/04/07).

Bernstein, Henry, Hazel Johnson and Alan Thomas (1992) 'Labour Regimes and Social Change under Colonialism', in Tim Allen and Alan Thomas (eds) *Poverty and Development in the 1990s*, Oxford and New York: Oxford University Press.

Bernstein, Henry, Tom Hewitt and Alan Thomas (1992) 'Capitalism and the Expansion of Europe', in Tim Allen and Alan Thomas (eds) *Poverty and Development in the 1990s*, Oxford and New York: Oxford University Press.

Bhabha, Homi K. (1994) *The Location of Culture*, London and New York: Routledge.

Campbell, Bonnie (1975) 'Neo-Colonialism, Economic Dependence and Political Change: A Case Study of Cotton and Textile Production in the Ivory Coast 1960 to 1970', *Review of African Political Economy*, 2, 2: 36–53.

Country Watch (undated) 'Overview – (Côte d'Ivoire) Ivory Coast', http://countrywatch.altavista.com (accessed 29/03/07).

Cowell, Alan (2002) 'War Inflates Cocoa Prices but Leaves Africans Poor', *New York Times*, 30 October, http://www.globalpolicy.org/socecon/develop/Africa/2002/1030cocoa.htm (accessed 25/03/03).

Crook, Richard C. (1990) 'Politics, the Cocoa Crisis, and Administration in Côte d'Ivoire', *Journal of Modern African Studies* 28, 4: 649–69.

De Alva, Jorge K. (1995) 'The Postcolonization of the (Latin) American Experience: A Reconsideration of "Colonialism," "Postcolonialism," and "Mestizaje"', in Gyan Prakash (ed.) *After Colonialism: Imperial Histories and Postcolonial Displacements*, Princeton, NJ: Princeton University Press.

Frank, Andre G. (1967) *Capitalism and Underdevelopment in Latin America: Historical Studies of Chile and Brazil*, New York: Monthly Review Press.

Gallagher, John and Ronald Robinson (1953) 'The Imperialism of Free Trade', *Economic History Review* 6, 1: 1–15.

Hoogvelt, Ankie (1997) *Globalisation and the Postcolonial World: The New Political Economy of Development*, London: Macmillan.

International Labor Rights Fund (undated) 'The World Bank and IMF Policies in Côte d'Ivoire: Impact on Child Labor in the Cocoa Industry', http://www.laborrights.org/projects/childlab/WBIMFcocoa.pdf.

Lenin, Vladimir I. (1939) *Imperialism: The Highest Stage of Capitalism. A Popular Outline*, New York: International Publishers.

Manzo, Kate (2005) 'Exploiting West Africa's Children: Trafficking, Slavery and Uneven Development', *Area* 37, 4: 393–401.

Manzo, Kate (2003) 'Africa in the Rise of Rights-Based Development', *Geoforum* 34, 4: 437–56.

Mbembe, Achille (2001) *On the Postcolony*, Berkeley, CA and Los Angeles, CA: University of California Press.

Milward, Bob (2000) 'What Is Structural Adjustment?', in Giles Mohan, Ed Brown, Bob Milward and Alfred B. Zack-Williams (eds) *Structural Adjustment: Theory, Practice and Impacts*, London and New York: Routledge.

Nkrumah, Kwame (1965) *Neo-Colonialism: The Last Stage of Imperialism*, London: Heinemann.

Peel, Sir Robert (1833) 'Abolition of Slavery in the British Colonies', *The Times*, 14 May, http://dspace.dial.pipex.com/town/terrace/adw03/peel/economic/abolition.htm (accessed 12/03/07).

Peet, Richard (2003) *Unholy Trinity: The IMF, World Bank and WTO*, London: Zed Books.

Ponte, Stefano (2002) 'The "Latte Revolution"? Regulation, Markets and Consumption in the Global Coffee Chain', *World Development* 30, 7: 1099–122.

Potter, David (1992) 'Colonial Rule', in Tim Allen and Alan Thomas (eds) *Poverty and Development in the 1990s*, Oxford and New York: Oxford University Press.

Power, Marcus (2003) *Rethinking Development Geographies*, London and New York: Routledge.

Ridler, Neil B. (1993) 'Fixed Exchange Rates and Structural Adjustment Programmes: Côte d'Ivoire', *Journal of Modern African Studies* 31, 2: 301–8.

Rodney, Walter (1982) *How Europe Underdeveloped Africa*, Washington, DC: Howard University Press.

Slater, David (1998) 'Post-Colonial Questions for Global Times', *Review of International Political Economy* 5, 4: 647–78.

Talbot, Chris (2004) 'Ivory Coast: Two Years of French and United Nations Occupation', *World Socialist Website*, 14 August: 1–4, http://www.wsws.org/articles/2004/aug2004/ivry-al4.shtml.

Tiffen, Pauline (2002) 'A Chocolate-Coated Case for Alternative International Business Models', *Development in Practice* 12, 3/4: 383–97.

Young, Robert (2001) *Postcolonialism: An Historical Introduction*, Oxford: Blackwell.

CHAPTER 12

How is the world organized economically?

V. Spike Peterson

THE QUESTION
ECONOMICS FROM FEUDAL MARKETS TO INDUSTRIALIZATION

We begin with the apparently easy question: 'What is economics?' A simple answer is that economics is the study of the production and distribution of goods and wealth. Like most dictionary definitions, this gets us started – but what do the additional words in the definition mean? They look reasonably familiar: production is about 'making' things, distribution is about 'dividing things up', and goods are various sorts of things, usually the kinds we can see or use (plates, watches, trucks). Wealth is a bit trickier: it may refer to 'money' generally, or more specifically to 'financial investments' – like stocks and bonds. Or it may refer to 'riches' in the broadest possible sense.

People have been making and exchanging goods for at least several thousand years, but they did not think about this in terms of the whole world. Indeed, *they did not think about this as 'economics'*. The earliest markets were areas where people came together to simply exchange one good – primarily food or functional items – for another. Because transportation was difficult, only goods considered very valuable were worth carrying long distances. For most of human history, then, markets were quite small, goods were primarily local and exchanges in the market were simply part of reproducing everyday life. In other words, exchange activities were embedded in social relations more generally; like growing food or preparing meals, there was no reason to think about 'economics' separately.

For a map that shows what Europe looked like in the Middle Ages, see Chapter 9.

As long as belief in and practices of subsistence agriculture prevailed, the scale and effects of markets were limited. During the Middle Ages in Europe such feudal conditions involved a complex web of kingdoms and other sites of power. Monarchs granted noblemen rights to land in return for loyalty and military services. Noblemen could in turn grant land to those who served them. The vast majority of people, called peasants, lived on and worked the land owned by others. Reciprocity was the norm: estate-owners granted access to land-based resources in return for military services and agricultural labour and products. Goods produced through agriculture and market activities in towns were important for funding military exploits, but cultural norms and aristocratic expropriation of wealth made the pursuit of profit for private gain quite difficult. An additional site of power was the Christian Church, with the Pope at its head; this provided over-arching moral authority and constituted perhaps the most significant unifying cultural force.

From roughly the 15th century, Europeans built upon inventions and developments elsewhere to move from this decentralized system of agricultural production to state-centric and technologically enhanced forms of capitalist industrialization. The shift involved profound changes in people's identities, ways of thinking and ways of structuring human behaviour. Centralizing European states promoted capitalist arrangements that favoured the accumulation of wealth by a minority, whose decision-making power shaped the choices of and resources available to the majority. Eventually, capitalist markets extended worldwide. To answer our chapter's question we must therefore familiarize ourselves with this transition. The following highly simplified account emphasizes changes that are especially important for understanding *today's* global political economy:

- the role of states in creating capitalist markets;
- how technologies matter;
- how work is organized; and
- whose work is valued.

Increasing consolidation of power in nation-states altered loyalties as well as 'economics'. Church-based authority declined due to religious debates, the development of rationalist thinking and a new sense of 'man's' control over social and physical forces. From roughly the 16th century, centralized states adopted mercantilist policies to enhance their wealth through foreign exploration, trade, appropriation, slavery, plantation economies and military conquest. Internally, mercantilism promoted positive trade balances (more exports than imports) and protection of domestic production; externally, it increased aggressive exploitation of 'new' lands and prompted conflicts as European powers fought over control of markets.

After the 18th century, capitalist industrialization consolidated and extended European power. As long as animals, humans, wind and flowing water were the only sources of energy, forms of power and production remain limited. The industrializing transition to making machines and harnessing steam power had vast consequences. The power of merchants who traded goods faded in favour of industrial capitalists who invested in machines and factory production that enabled greater productivity. Lives and landscapes were forever changed. Labour was increasingly commodified: peasants were driven off of or drawn from the land by new policies enforced by states; without access to land, they were compelled to become wage workers (referred to as members of the proletariat in Chapter 13) – selling their labour power to factory owners – for survival. Industrial capitalism transformed the scale of production, who produced what goods, by what means and with what value. The site of 'work' shifted away from households to workshops and factories where it was paid in wages, considered (economically)

For a discussion of states and nations and how we come to think of them as inextricably linked into 'nation-states', see **Chapters 9 and 10.**

Rationalist thinking has been extremely important since the Enlightenment, which is discussed in **Chapter 5.** The decline in the significance of church-based authority is also explored in **Chapter 6.**

The effects these changes have had on the environment are discussed in **Chapter 3.**

FIGURE 12.1
Textile mill in Lancashire, England.
Photo: Getty Images

BOX 12.1 ADAM SMITH AND POLITICAL ECONOMY

FIGURE 12.2
Portrait of Adam Smith.
Photo: Vanderblue
Collection

In the late 18th century, Adam Smith produced the first systematic analysis of 'political economy'. He wrote about the state's essential role in managing flows of goods, facilitating exchange between nations and ensuring that the state's wealth be used for the benefit of its population. He did not separate economics from politics, nor did he write about the whole 'world'. He criticized mercantilism and its promotion of state interference, arguing instead for a liberal 'free market' model of *laissez-faire* ('let it be') policies. He believed that these would permit the invisible hand of the market to operate and enable nations to prosper through pursuing their comparative advantage. Smith also cultivated a distinction between public and private and initiated a devaluation of household labour as not 'productive'.

'productive' and associated with 'bread-winning' men. These profound changes, and the emergence of liberalism, were a turning point in organizing economic activities, assigning value and institutionalizing power (Rupert and Solomon 2006).

Liberalism marked a decisive shift in thinking about reason, rights, individuals and power-wielding institutions. Its 18th-century form rejected arbitrary power in favour of rights to private property, religious choice and individual freedom. These rights were the cornerstone of Europe's 'democratic' 'revolutions'. At the same time, liberalism produced an unstable tension: between freedom expressed in economic terms (through private property and unconstrained market arrangements) and equality expressed in socio-political terms (through democratic processes and requisite constraints to ensure equality of access, opportunity and participation).

ILLUSTRATIVE EXAMPLE
THE GLOBAL POLITICAL ECONOMY AND INCREASING INFORMALIZATION

Capitalist industrialization generated an unprecedented abundance of goods, but at considerable cost. It was especially devastating for all who lost access to land-based subsistence and were forced to earn wages – in typically harsh conditions

– as the only way to survive. Moreover, the expansion of European wealth and power depended on the disruption of societies far from its shores: colonial practices cost Africa approximately 14 million people to slavery, destroyed India's flourishing cotton industry in favour of British exports, forcefully exploited the Chinese market, and directly and indirectly killed innumerable indigenous peoples of Oceania and the Americas. Early liberalism extended political equality to propertied males only. European claims to scientific progress and rational superiority were used to position 'whites' at the top of emerging racialized hierarchies and lent legitimacy to colonizing practices. And, in spite of romanticism, women and the family sphere of social reproduction lost resources and status to the masculinized public sphere of politics and 'real' (waged) production.

Slavery persists today.
See Chapter 11

Although they faced various forms of resistance, Europeans continued to consolidate their cultural, economic, political and military power (Held *et al.* 1999). They moved massive resources of raw materials and foodstuffs from non-industrialized areas to Europe, and ensured – through loans and precluding other options – that developing countries purchased Europe's manufactured goods. In advanced industrialized countries (AICs), a middle class emerged due to enhanced production, union organizing and the liberal-capitalist welfare state. For the first time in history, through collective bargaining workers were able to increase their power relative to that of capital. In the 20th century, advanced transportation networks and emerging information and communication technologies extended the reach of capitalist markets. This short history reveals how market activities expanded to eventually encompass the 'world'. It also reveals how, at every step, capitalist markets depended on the political power of states.

Economics is inextricable from power operating in social systems more generally. This occurs through the interaction of various agents (individuals, corporations, states and international organizations) exercising various forms of power (purchasing and investing, job creation and termination, taxation and welfare, trade policies). To emphasize how economics is inseparable from power and politics, we refer to the global political economy. We now have a 'picture' of how the global political economy was created historically. But how is it organized *today*?

The importance of 'pictures' is discussed in
Chapter 2.

One of the most puzzling and problematic developments is a phenomenal increase in the volume, value, extent and socio-political significance of informal-sector activities. Informalization refers to the growth in these activities, which involve legal and illegal practices 'outside' formal, market-based production. When economists and the media talk about 'economics' they usually mean formal – contractual, regulated, legal – exchanges, where wages and salaries are negotiated, commodified goods and services are exchanged, and some degree of profit-seeking is assumed. Because they occur outside the formal sector, informal activities are rarely 'counted' in economic studies or analyses. But research reveals that these activities constitute more than half of *all* economic output and equal

For more on how economic activity is measured, see **Chapter 13.**

Reliable data is a problem in general for analysing the global economy.
See Chapter 13

75 per cent of the gross domestic product of some countries. While size alone suggests that informalization matters, the invisible, irregular and often illegal aspects of informalization pose additional challenges – illustrated starkly by criminal networks that funnel money into conflict zones. Yet informalization is poorly understood because until recently it was largely ignored.

How to document and measure informalization is controversial, and how to secure reliable data is problematic (*Journal of International Affairs* 2000; Bajada and Schneider 2005). Yet globalization scholars agree that economic restructuring has dramatically increased the volume, value and extent of informal economic activities (Schneider and Enste 2002; Kudva and Benería 2005). These range from socially necessary labour and voluntary work, where cash is rarely exchanged and 'regulatory authorities' are absent (e.g. childcare, housework, neighbourhood projects) to secondary, 'shadow' and 'irregular' activities, where some form of enterprise and payment is expected but legal regulation is either difficult to enforce or intentionally evaded (e.g. street vending, petty trade, sex work, drug dealing, arms trading).

This phenomenal growth is interesting in part because it was unexpected. On the one hand, economists have traditionally neglected informal activities in favour of focusing on the 'formal' sector. On the other hand, economists expected informal activities to wane as industrialization inexorably 'formalized' (through waged labour and regulations) most economic processes (Tabak and Crichlow 2000).

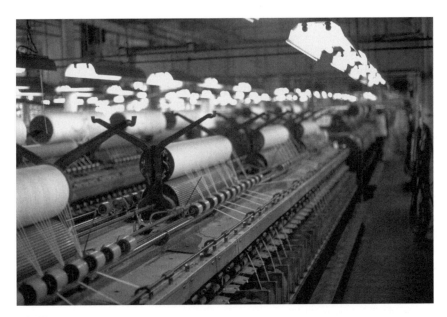

FIGURE 12.3
Computerized textile mill. Photo: Mark Antman, Phototake, New York City

In the context of neoliberal globalization, however, informal activities have continued and even increased. If we include work in caring and reproductive labour, subsistence agriculture and the shadow economy, the time spent in informal activities far exceeds that of formal market exchanges.

One source of this growth is flexibilization. In advanced economies, mass production of consumer goods in the 20th century involved large and integrated factory worksites where workers gradually unionized. The power of organized labour translated into relatively secure, well-paying jobs with good benefits. In recent decades, these arrangements have been transformed by global restructuring. Flexibilization is the buzzword that characterizes the changes: production processes shift to spatially dispersed networks (the global assembly line; subcontracting; smaller enterprises); increasingly casualized (non-permanent, part-time) and informalized (unregulated, non-contractual) jobs; small batch, 'just in time' (short-term rather than long-term) production planning; and avoidance of organized labour (Cerny 1995).

Flexibilization feminizes the workforce: an increasing proportion of jobs require few skills and the most desirable workers are those who are perceived to be unorganized (undemanding), docile but reliable, available for part-time and temporary work, and willing to accept low wages (Benería 2003). Prevailing stereotypes depict women as more attractive candidates for these jobs. Prevailing realities are that women – in spite of decades of activism and legal advances – continue to earn 30–50 per cent less than men worldwide. And in spite of heading almost one-third of the world's households, women are still thought of as secondary earners, not primary (that is, male) breadwinners. This assumption is used to 'justify' lower wages for women, as if their earnings were marginal to family well-being and the 'real' economy of men's work (Chang 2000; Parreñas 2001). Feminization then refers to how flexibilization is simultaneously a material,

Chapter 4 discusses feminist activism and the problems it has encountered.

BOX 12.2 GENDER AND FEMINIZATION

Gender is related to, but more complicated than, the conventional distinction between females and males. It refers to socially learned identities and ways of thinking and acting that are characterized as masculine or feminine. For example, 'reason' and assertiveness, appearing unemotional and 'in control', and being the 'breadwinner' are masculinized (associated with masculine characteristics). In contrast, 'emotion' and 'dependence', appearing uncertain and submissive, and being the 'homemaker' are feminized. The key pattern to recognize is that, in general, and with powerful consequences, qualities associated with masculinity are valourized over, and at the expense of, those associated with femininity.

embodied transformation of labour markets (more women workers) and a conceptual characterization of devalourized labour conditions (poorer pay and less secure work arrangements).

In general, flexibilization increases the power of management and decreases the choices available to most workers. The rhetoric of neoliberalism invokes flexibility as essential for competitive success and as an inherently positive policy. As this rhetoric becomes common sense it obscures how these policies are in fact politically and economically motivated; they benefit some at the expense of others. In the absence of regulatory frameworks that protect workers' rights and generate living wages (adequate for sustaining households), flexibilization translates into greater insecurity of employment, income and benefits for the majority of the world's workers.

The terms 'liberal globalism' in **Chapter 13** and 'neoliberal globalization' in **Chapter 14** are roughly equivalent to the term 'neoliberalism' in this one.

As the subcontracting, homework and casualization of labour associated with flexibilization become 'normal', so do the less formal and regulated work conditions of informalization. Insofar as flexibilization erodes labour's organizing power, protection of workers' rights and wage expectations, it exacerbates the decline in family income that 'pushes' more people to generate income in whatever way they can; they often do so by engaging in informal economic activities. Finally, because flexibilization translates into avoidance of taxes, it exacerbates the declining resources devoted to public welfare provisioning and spurs participation in informal activities to compensate in part for this loss.

We know, then, that informalization matters economically. The sheer size of it has tremendous implications for everyday lives, livelihoods and sites of power (Sassen 1998). Informalization matters because it undercuts some legitimate businesses and enables others. Its avoidance of taxes alone decreases public revenues, with far-reaching economic effects, especially on the most vulnerable groups. Perhaps most significant structurally, by avoiding 'indirect wages' and regulation of labour relations and worksite conditions, informalization enhances the power of capital at the expense of labour. That is, it places downward pressure on wages more generally, which both decreases employed labour's earnings and power and has a disciplining effect on all workers.

Moreover, and inextricably, informalization matters politically. Informalization poses quandaries of documentation and measurement; policies may be misconceived and inappropriate if they are based on faulty estimates of national output, income distribution or unemployment. Societies lose when informal activities evade tax collection, decrease public revenues and enable corruption. Recent scandals regarding insider trading and fraudulent accounting practices reveal how extensive the damage can be. Similarly, the reduction in tax revenues due to informalization has political effects in terms of who wins and loses as a consequence of selective public expenditures. Societies also lose when unregulated

FIGURE 12.4
'Injusticia global'. Artist: Sergio Langer, *El Clarin*, Argentina

work practices pose safety, health and environmental risks, when criminal activities thwart collective interests in law and order, and when illicit gains are used to fund conflicts. Critics of informalization hence argue that avoidance of regulations is directly and indirectly bad for wages, workers, the environment and long-term prospects for societal well-being.

As with flexibilization, some individuals prosper by engaging in entrepreneurial activities – legal and illegal – made possible by a less regulated environment. This is especially evident in micro-enterprises favoured by neoliberals, in developing countries where informal activities are crucial for income generation and in criminal activities that are increasing worldwide (Friman and Andreas 1999; Naylor 2002). Women, migrants and the poor do the majority of informal work (Benería 2003; Hoskyns and Rai 2007). And, like flexibilization, this work is polarized between a small, privileged group (that includes some elite women) able to take advantage of and prosper from deregulation and flexibilization and the *majority* of the world's workers, who participate less out of choice than necessity due to economic *and* ideological devalourization (Peterson 2003). Mainstream accounts emphasize elites and entrepreneurs, but the majority of flexible and informal workers have few choices about the work that they do. And they do a great deal of it.

In short, informal activities are growing. They span a wide range of activities, and crucial to their significance is how they *blur* conventional boundaries separating public and private, legal and illegal, production and reproduction, national and international. The majority of informal activities are also feminized – involving devalued identities, statuses, working conditions and forms of compensation. Informalization thus poses fundamental questions about global political economy in relation to family livelihoods, conditions of employment, what counts as economic activity and how activities are valued.

RESPONSES
EXPLAINING THE GLOBAL POLITICAL ECONOMY

The imposition of policies of structural adjustment in developing countries such as Ivory Coast is part of neoliberalism and has had a huge impact.
See Chapter 11

We know that neoliberal globalization is powerfully affecting how life is lived and work is done throughout the world. We also know that the explosive growth in informal activities was unanticipated and that its effects are economically and politically important. Those who study global politics debate how and why these changes are occurring, and who the winners and losers are. What are the most familiar approaches, what do they include, what do they omit?

The disciplinary separation of economics from politics (and from sociology, anthropology, communications and psychology) works against understanding the overlapping and interdependent dimensions of these disciplines. When Adam Smith initiated the study of political economy in the 18th century, he focused on market activities. He did so because the forces of industrial capitalism were dramatically altering conditions of social life and posed the most challenging problems. But he understood markets as inextricable from other social, institutional and political dynamics. How, then, did the study of political economy become fragmented into economics and politics?

After the 18th century, forms of social organization based on state-driven market exchanges were intensified. Western-centric ideologies of progress, national self-determination, secularism, science and liberal capitalism were spread around the world, with extensive, though not homogeneous, effects. Advanced industrial countries dominated the world order and cultivated economic development models that sustained Western supremacy. In these countries, mass production, collective bargaining and the liberal-capitalist welfare state fostered the growth of a middle class. These cumulative developments had diverse effects. On the one hand, successful industrialization was associated with enhanced productivity, a proliferation of goods, greater consumer pleasures and new identities. On the other hand, unemployment, harsh work conditions and relentless competition meant new miseries, labour migrations and increasing disparities between 'haves' and 'have-nots' within and among nations.

As universities became central to the production of knowledge, studies of social life fragmented into disciplinary specializations. The study of political economy was 'divided' into economics and politics, and the lure of 'scientific methods' encouraged those who identified as 'economists' to narrow and formalize their analyses. By the 20th century, 'neoclassical economics' became the predominant school of economic theory, and it is subscribed to by most economists who advocate today's neoliberal restructuring. This school presupposes that resources are scarce, human wants are unlimited, and that rational ordering of preferences determines how individuals and firms optimize their self-interests. Formal mathematical models and manipulation of statistical data are preferred methods.

In effect, this orientation focuses on 'objective' phenomena and excludes from analyses that which is not quantifiable or not valued enough to be 'counted'. Until recently, the study of global politics tended to marginalize consideration of race, gender and even class. Related to this is a tendency to neglect the fact that emotional investments and social identities – 'who we are' – have tremendous importance. They shape our desires, expectations, self-esteem, attitudes, values and how we act – especially toward 'others'. These 'subjective' factors are difficult to measure but they matter to politics. Neglect of identities and subjective factors is in turn related to an avoidance of 'cultural' phenomena, for example, popular music, television programmes, videos, films, YouTube and other forms of leisure. Information and communication technologies expand the global 'reach' of these media and powerfully shape what information people have access to and what ideological assumptions they then internalize. In sum, disciplinary boundaries and an emphasis on objective phenomena shape what we know about global politics, and especially the global political economy.

> Chapter 4 discusses who we think we are, and how gender and race are significant.

> The question of how we know what is going on in the world and the way this influences how we think is the subject of Chapter 7.

Liberal and neoliberal approaches

Conventional – and hence the most familiar – accounts of global political economy are associated with the liberal tradition and its promotion by neoclassical economists of 'free market' policies. Basic assumptions of this position include: markets are efficient and morally desirable; the unfettered movement of trade and capital will result in optimal investment flows; countries benefit by emphasizing their comparative advantage; growth is imperative and will 'trickle down', to the benefit of all; open borders ensure the most efficient and equitable distributions of goods worldwide. The role of governments is to facilitate the operation of markets but otherwise not intervene in decision-making.

> Chapter 13 discusses how the free market in fact leads to global inequality.

The policies of neoliberalism clearly emerge from this liberal tradition. The restructuring they entail is 'new' because it is elevated to the global level. At the same time, it penetrates to the individual level: as public services and welfare supports decline, individuals alone are expected to ensure their well-being

FIGURE 12.5
'Don't stop believing'. Artist: Barry Deutsch

through 'smart' consumerism and investing wisely for their retirement. 'Market fundamentalism' aptly conveys the meaning of neoliberalism: to promote the power of market-based decision-makers over that of public or government-based decision-makers. The overriding objective of private and corporate capital (market forces) is to make profits for owners and shareholders. For capital, unlike governments, the well-being of ordinary workers and citizens is not the primary concern. In the absence of government regulation, market forces are not accountable to workers or citizens and tend to undercut collective (democratic) efforts to direct production processes and determine how society's goods are distributed. In this sense, neoliberal policies of deregulation and privatization subject workers and citizens to regulation primarily by market forces, where the motivation is pursuit of profits rather than provision of public goods. The tension between promoting private gains and improving public welfare complicates both how we theorize global political economy and how we evaluate neoliberal capitalism.

The pursuit of profit impacts on the environment, arguably a public good.
See Chapter 3

If we liken restructuring to a global 'game' of neoliberal capitalism, its enthusiasts fundamentally believe in the game at play. That is, they subscribe to the model of human nature attributed to the players (atomistic, competitive and rational individuals or states), to the expectations that flow from this model when no additional constraints are imposed ('each-to-his-own', winner-takes-all strategies) and to the projected long-term, system-wide benefits from playing what they understand anyway as the 'only game in town' ('there is no alternative'). In an important sense, these accounts render structural hierarchies invisible, by being either depoliticized (as 'the way things are' due to nature or ineluctable globalization) or marginalized (as perhaps regrettable but nonetheless subordinated to, or a distraction from, more pressing analytical concerns). This theoretical perspective dominates in economic analyses and mainstream media. Because most people hear little other than this account, they tend to believe it is the only one.

Liberal and neoliberal economists have focused on 'formal' market activities, where commodified goods and services are exchanged and some degree of profit-seeking is presupposed. Those who study the global economy have focused on the role of large corporate firms and advanced industrial economies. Both were considered historically the most successful choices and developmentally the most probable. For example, modernization theory assumed that 'the rest would follow the West' in terms of how they developed economically. It was assumed that informal activities would be displaced by industrialization, which involved the expansion of 'waged' labour and increasing forms of regulation. Little theoretical attention was paid to activities that did not conform to these assumptions and expectations. As a result, economic theory ignored informal activities in favour of more familiar market processes that predominated in advanced industrial economies. From a critical vantage point, this silence reflected a relative lack of interest in issues of greater importance to poor and developing countries, and of greater consequence for vulnerable (devalourized, feminized) populations.

Theoretical reassessment was spurred by growth in informal activities worldwide and, especially, as a prominent feature of economies in 'transition' from centralized state-planning regimes toward neoliberal ones. For the most part, informalization that does not involve criminal activity tends to be interpreted positively by liberal economists. It is seen as a breeding ground for microenterprise or a creative and flexible response to 'inefficient' or 'excessive' regulation. Some argue that informally earned income has a stimulating effect on the formal economy. But there are different reasons for participating in the informal sector. The tendency to focus on the positive effects of entrepreneurial activities, undertaken primarily by middle- and upper-income groups, leads to a neglect of informalization among lower-income groups. The latter participate more for sheer survival and have too few resources to be engaged in activities that 'stimulate the economy'.

The idea that microenterprise has positive effects is behind the promotion of microfinance discussed in **Chapter 14**.

At the same time, there are growing networks of organized crime (Naylor 2002). These engage in illegal activities – drug smuggling, sex trafficking, arms trading

– that are often very lucrative. The implications are especially disturbing when we consider how both legal and, especially, illegal operations are important sources of funding for conflicts and wars. These forms of informalization have become very important in terms of international military and security concerns (Ballentine and Sherman 2003). This of course has increased the attention that liberal analysts give to informal activities. In spite of theoretical reassessments, however, social reproduction and household labour continue to be marginalized in mainstream accounts (Himmelweit 2002). Also neglected are the effects of historical and growing inequalities worldwide and how these both reflect and are exacerbated by informalization (Tabak and Crichlow 2000).

Liberal and neoliberal analyses tend to dominate in economic theory, media accounts and public consciousness. But there are dissenting voices too, as some economists criticize the viability of neoliberal restructuring as currently practised. They are troubled by the adverse effects of rapid restructuring, especially its tendency toward destabilization of social conditions and the larger problems this can create. Given recurring financial crises and recent corporate accounting scandals, critics are also concerned about deregulation of financial arrangements and the difficulties of ensuring transparency and accountability.

To stay with the global game metaphor, these players subscribe to the assumptions and objectives of neoliberalism, but are concerned about the negative effects of applying them so rapidly and indiscriminately. Responses focus on 'adjusting' the implementation of policies, especially to ameliorate their most deleterious effects. In this sense, the rules of the game are not fundamentally challenged but the major players are encouraged to take a longer and broader view, to ease up on the immediately devastating practices so that the game itself proceeds with less conflict and loss, and fewer crises.

Marxist approaches

See the discussion of historical materialism in **Chapter 13.**

The most widely recognized alternative to liberal and neoliberal approaches emerges from the Marxist tradition. This includes a variety of perspectives and important distinctions, but what they share are critiques of capitalism (Rupert and Solomon 2006). The basic argument is that capitalism promotes the concentration of resources and power in a minority, at the expense of the majority. Marxist global political economy attempts to develop more holistic or structural explanations of how markets, firms and governments interact. This approach takes institutions seriously and analyses them in relation to power differentials. For example, institutions may serve as mechanisms for establishing and maintaining class-based inequalities, and the state may be dominated by elites but also have a remedial role in alleviating class hierarchies. Another increasingly influential variant of Marxism features the insights of Antonio Gramsci. This approach pays

BOX 12.3 KARL MARX

FIGURE 12.6
Karl Marx

Karl Marx (1818–83) is best known for his analysis of the workings of capitalism as a mode of production, and its exploitation and commodification of workers and their labour. He argued that changes in the social *practices* of production, from slavery through feudalism to capitalism, changed the ways in which we *picture* the world. He was an active campaigner and his writings formed the inspiration for communist and socialist political programmes that placed the well-being of the collectivity above the rights of private property. He was clear that while 'the philosophers have only interpreted the world, in various ways; the point is to change it' (*Theses on Feuerbach*, XI; see McLellan 1977).

particular attention to issues of culture and illuminates how hegemonic rule occurs through ideological 'consent'. For example, the ideology of neoliberalism is promoted through multiple media, which cultivates an acceptance of capitalism as both desirable and inevitable ('there is no alternative').

Marxist-oriented approaches offer critical vantage points and extensive research on changes in the organization of production, global divisions of labour, accumulation and regulation dynamics, and class and geopolitical hierarchies. Their emphasis on historical developments is important for illuminating how systems are made and hence can be changed. Like liberal economists, they tend to focus on the formal sector but have also made significant contributions to theorizing informalization.

On one hand, Marxism is associated with the view that formalization or proletarianization would replace all other forms of labour as capitalism developed. On the other hand, Marxists more indebted to historical materialism have long understood that full proletarianization is a structural contradiction for capitalism. Briefly, they argue that capital accumulation depends not only on profits gained through formal mechanisms of production and exchange but also, and continuously, on accumulation of profits through non-capitalist, nonwaged, casual and/or informal economic activities that are not proletarianized.

A dimension of this thesis is that capital's pursuit of the highest profit entails *maintaining* a surplus ('reserve army') of labour that is not currently – or 'formally' – employed but potentially employable. This surplus both enhances profits through maintaining downward pressure on wages and disciplines

Proletarianization means an increasing number of workers are engaged in and dependent on waged labour.
See Chapter 11

employed workers through the threat of being replaced from these reserves. In other words, the availability of surplus labour compels workers to compete with each other; this competition enhances the bargaining advantage of employers by decreasing what they need to offer in terms of wages and benefits. The informal sector constitutes some of this labour surplus and tends to lower wages. First, avoidance of regulated work conditions avoids a variety of costs to firms and decreases average labour costs. Second, direct competition from informalized workers tends to decrease the number of higher-paid (formal) workers, and sometimes decreases how much they are paid. Given these dynamics, the wage contract underpinning formal work arrangements is only part and not the whole of economic activities; full proletarianization would undercut the expansionary capitalist pursuit of only the *highest* realizable profit rates.

Compare the discussion of deproletarianization in **Chapter 11**.

Moreover, Marxist analysts recognize that informalization is not a passing phenomenon. Rather, it is a structural feature of capitalist relations and plays a role in the periodic restructuring associated with capitalism's boom-and-bust cycles. During economic downturns, informal activities increase as people struggle to generate whatever income they can in whatever way possible. Similarly, the apparent 'newness' of informal growth in advanced economies is due to conceptual selectivity (a focus on industrialized production, formal activities, etc.) and relegating informal activities to theories of 'development' (focused on poor, 'third world' rather than industrialized economies).

In sum, Marxist approaches help us understand informalization as both a structural feature of capitalism (linking the informal to the formal economy through downward pressure on wages) and a long-term cyclical process (linking the expansion of informal activities to accumulation cycles). It broadens our focus to include informal activities as integral to formal waged production relations and all labour force formation. These are important advances in thinking about informalization. They remain limited, however, in two related ways. First, these analysts rarely extend their critique of structural hierarchies beyond economic indicators. Rather, they focus on 'class' (within nations) and developed versus developing countries (between nations). Second, they continually neglect social reproduction, domestic labour and intra-household dynamics.

BROADER ISSUES
THE HIDDEN COSTS OF NEOLIBERALISM

We have seen how liberal and neoliberal economists theorize global political economy, offer limited accounts of informalization and tend to ignore structural hierarchies. Analysts drawing on the Marxist tradition expand our knowledge of informal–formal linkages and improve our understanding of historical patterns and *global* dynamics. They also provide illuminating critiques of economic hierarchies.

What continues to be left out of this picture and hence weaken our understanding of how the world economy is organized? What larger questions remain unexamined? In particular, who are the actual winners and losers in this game? And what are the long-term consequences? The puzzle of informalization offers a useful vantage point for considering these questions, exploring how value is assigned and revealing the hidden costs of neoliberalism.

What does it mean to think of the global economy as a 'game' in the first place?

We know that work outside the formal economy is not diminishing, as expected, but increasing dramatically with globalization. Increasing unemployment, flexibilization and erosion or prohibition of union power have meant declining real incomes and decreased job security for most workers worldwide. Deregulation and privatization undercut welfare provisioning, state employment and collective supports for family well-being. As economic conditions deteriorate, individuals and families are thus 'pushed' to engage in informal activities as a strategy for securing income however they can. The majority of informal workers are women, migrants and the urban poor. The income they generate often enables families to survive but rarely enables them to prosper. For the most part, these vulnerable (feminized) populations remain excluded from the purported benefits of neoliberalism. In this sense, informalization takes advantage of, and exacerbates, inequalities based on gender, race and economic hierarchies. In effect, the majority of the global population loses in the game of neoliberalism.

Chapter 13 examines the 'losers' of the global economic 'game' in some detail.

FIGURE 12.7
Vegetable vendors, China. Photo: Jenny Edkins

A significant component of informalization involves activities undertaken to ensure social reproduction – the labour that is characterized as 'women's work'. These activities are rarely analysed in mainstream accounts because they are not valued or easily quantified and hence not 'counted' (Waring 1999). This neglect is due in part to conceptual habits: locating men in the public sphere of power and 'real' – that is, paid – work, and women in the household sphere of emotional maintenance, leisure and caring – that is, unpaid – labour. It is also due to institutionalized practices: for example academic disciplines that study social life as separate (psychological, social, economic, political) spheres of inquiry. Critics argue, in contrast, that what is regarded as 'women's work' and 'informal' activities is crucial for analysing the global political economy.

In short, more adequate understanding of global politics requires including the role of informalization, examining who the winners and losers are, and considering the consequences of excluding so many from neoliberalism's purported benefits. Analysts who are most attentive to these issues and combine a variety of theoretical approaches are feminists – especially those who are critical of colonialism and racism. They provide the most inclusive accounts of social reproduction, gendered work and informalization. Their research is especially rich in providing empirical data and case studies; they enable us to theorize how work is assigned value; and they variously engage in theorizing *multiple* hierarchies.

There is a discussion of feminist activism, and of racism, in **Chapter 4**. The distinction between public and private spheres is also discussed in that chapter.

The gendered division of labour

Feminism has no single meaning and there are many ways of thinking about how patriarchy operates. Differences shaped by history, culture, location, disciplinary interests and theoretical orientations generate a wide range of approaches. In general, feminist economists analyse the relationship between women's reproductive labour, the formal economy and surplus accumulation. Research includes 'adding' women's labour in social reproduction (care of children and elders, housework, etc.) to existing theoretical models, examining gender differences in labour markets and work conditions, and developing policy recommendations. Feminist international development economists concentrate on non-industrialized countries. They study not only how social reproduction and informal activities affect women's empowerment, but also how gendered values and strategies affect national 'development' more generally.

Feminist economists who identify with Marxism theorize capitalism's relationship to 'women's work'. They argue that bearing, raising and appropriately socializing future workers *produces* labour power (workers) for the formal economy. The economic benefits of this unpaid labour accrue to employers who are thereby spared the full costs of producing the labour force. That is, employers do not have to 'pay' for the work of social reproduction that is assigned primarily to women but is necessary for infants to become adults who are available for work. Economic theory should address how workers themselves are produced before their labour is made available for either informal or formal deployment.

Feminists also borrow from and contribute to Marxist analyses that focus on 'households' as basic units of analysis (Smith and Wallerstein 1992). Although households vary, two key points emerge from this research. One is that the informal labour associated with the household (e.g. subsistence, homework, petty commodity production) is a structural feature of capitalist dynamics. Like social reproduction, this informal labour underpins capitalist profit-making, yet is neglected in mainstream economic theory. A second point is that wages alone – except for a small elite – provide inadequate income and resources for sustaining households. To survive, most of the world's families combine available wage income with informal activities, public welfare support and/or self-provisioning (do-it-yourself) labour.

What links these various observations is a gendered division of labour that was historically produced, extends worldwide, and assigns women and men different responsibilities. This division relegates women to the primary role in sustaining family and household well-being and depoliticizes the socially necessary work that women do and the disproportionate burden of responsibility placed on them when economic conditions degenerate. The processes involve gendered identities (breadwinner, homemaker) and ideologies (masculine work is for cash, feminized work is for love). Here the empirical studies of structural adjustment policies, flexibilization and informalization merge in exposing how women are expected to 'take up the slack' when male wage-earning and public services decline. For many women, this increasingly means working a 'triple shift' – of reproductive labour, informal work and formal employment.

Chapter 5 has more to say about ideology.

It is not simply women who suffer the costs of neoliberal globalization. As noted above, informalized workers and those with the fewest choices about how to survive include the majority of people – women *and* men – worldwide. These vulnerable populations are losers in the game of neoliberal capitalism, and their exclusion from its purported benefits has implications for all of us.

The costs of exclusions

The game metaphor enables us to see the 'whole' world through various lenses. From the vantage point of liberal and neoliberal economists, growth is the answer and unfettered capitalism is the preferred and 'inevitable' way to achieve it. From a similar starting point, but with increasing attention to global inequalities and the dangers these pose, more cautious voices are urging reforms. They advocate 'corrective' policies in the hope of softening the 'costs' of restructuring and dampening its most devastating effects. Less familiar are a number of explicitly critical perspectives. These include a range of Marxist approaches, some versions of institutionalism, many environmentalists and a variety of feminist critiques.

Because they start from different positions, their criticisms are wide-ranging. Different players among them argue that neoliberal globalization increases class inequalities, enhances the wealth and power of elites, fails to lift the poorest out of poverty, erodes the gains and prospects of organized labour, worsens un- and underemployment, displaces subsistence agriculture and local craft production, increases the unpaid work of women, fuels licit and illicit informalization, lowers standards in advanced economies, increases surveillance and discipline of workers, weakens worker demands through the threat of job losses and capital flight, reduces the state's capacity – or commitment – to prioritize domestic welfare, promotes environmental damage and toxic dumping on poor countries, fuels speculative and volatile financial markets, and poses systemic risks due to the integration of financial markets.

'Corrective' and transformative recommendations are equally wide-ranging and depend on particular issues and the perspective of the critic. In general, however, these 'players' argue that the problems of the global economy are too deep for cosmetic fixes. Adjustments to soften the negative effects, or a slower pace to ameliorate damage, may afford important and even life-saving temporary relief but are simply not enough. The costs of neoliberalism for most people and the planet are simply too great. Hence these players argue variously for different premises, different rules and even a fundamentally different game.

Common sense is discussed in **Chapter 1**.

This summary of positions reveals a singularly important factor in shaping one's assessment of neoliberalism. That factor is whether and to what extent the rules of the game and its premises are taken for granted as common sense. This common sense includes, first, believing that 'there is no alternative' to capitalism. Adherents argue that this claim is supported by the historical, cumulative success of capitalist development and the displacement or collapse of all alternatives. The second and related belief is that neoliberalism is (ultimately) good for everyone: providing efficiency, creativity, growth and even security.

What are the consequences of accepting this 'common sense' and the particular game of capitalism that it perpetuates? In the short term, marginalized populations face daunting challenges: how to secure immediate resources for family survival and well-being, and how to maintain self-esteem and optimism under stressful conditions and unpromising futures. In the long term, growing inequalities drain people's sense of inclusion in a global community; increase feelings of frustration, despair and resentment; reduce the likelihood of people working together for common goals; and undermine democratic principles, which require inclusiveness (Uvin 2003). In combination, these conditions increase the impoverishment of the majority and the probability of conflicts.

Illuminating the social exclusions of neoliberalism shifts attention to the *costs* of perpetuating it as 'common sense'. Failure to 'count' these costs is due in part to theoretical biases and disciplinary boundaries, and resistance to critical thinking. It is also due to the 'top-down' vantage point of elite decision-makers, Western states and corporate executives. In spite of advocating 'global' processes and democratic ideals, those who promote neoliberalism pay little heed to voices and viewpoints outside rich, powerful states, indeed outside elite sites of power and authority within those states. Through their selective lenses the 'reality' in developing countries, the 'discarded fourth world', urban ghettos and over-burdened families is rendered invisible and hence simply not 'counted'.

What is being suggested here is that neoliberalism is a 'problem-solving theory' in the terms discussed in **Chapter 1** and that what is needed instead is a critical theory.

CONCLUSION

Inequalities do not originate with neoliberalism, nor do its proponents claim to intentionally exacerbate them. Even the brief history summarized above reveals long and entwined histories of colonialism, racism, patriarchy and economic inequality within and among nations. These hierarchies of 'difference' were already internalized and institutionalized and could be 'used' in support of neoliberal objectives, for example by devaluing the informal work done by women, the poor and migrants. What distinguishes contemporary capitalism is its unprecedented global reach and its ability to shape how 'all' of us think. Corporations control most of the world's media, and their primary objective is the pursuit of profit for private shareholders. Hence the dominant media promote neoliberalism. But the narrow vantage point thereby broadcast to 'the world' effectively undermines critical thinking and democratic processes. People who are told only one story cannot help but believe 'there is no alternative'. Critical perspectives, lived realities and alternative visions are simply 'not counted'.

FURTHER READING

Bakker, Isabella and Stephen Gill (eds) (2003) *Power, Production and Social Reproduction: Human In/security in the Global Political Economy*, Basingstoke: Palgrave Macmillan.
    Comprehensive discussion of the importance of social reproduction to economics and security.

Dickinson, Torry D. and Robert K. Schaeffer (2001) *Fast Forward: Work, Gender, and Protest in a Changing World*, Lanham, MD: Rowman and Littlefield.
    Student-friendly account of global political economy that identifies key patterns and how people are organizing for better conditions.

Kofman, Eleonore and Gillian Youngs (eds) (2008) *Globalization: Theory and Practice*, 3rd edn, London and New York: Continuum.
Interesting and instructive collection providing diverse disciplinary treatments of globalization.

Palan, Ronen (ed.) (2000) *Global Political Economy: Contemporary Theories*, London and New York: Routledge.
Overview of major contemporary approaches and debates.

Rai, Shirin M. (2002) *Gender and the Political Economy of Development*, Cambridge: Polity.
Overview of development theory and practice with attention to gender.

Scholte, Jan Aart (2005) *Globalization: A Critical Introduction*, 2nd edn, Basingstoke: Palgrave Macmillan.
Especially accessible and comprehensive overview of globalization, including definitions, history, data, controversies and policy implications.

WEBSITES

The UC Atlas of Global Inequality, http://ucatlas.ucsc.edu/index.php.
Explores the interaction between global integration (globalization) and inequality, and provides maps, graphics and data.

Institute for Policy Studies, http://www.ips-dc.org/.
A multi-issue think tank offering a cross-cutting analysis with a historical perspective; committed to strengthening and linking social movements.

Institute of Development Studies, http://www.ids.ac.uk/ids/.
A leading global organization for research, teaching and communications on international development.

United Nations Development Programme, http://www.undp.org/.
The UN's global development network, an organization advocating for change and facilitating exchange of knowledge, experience and resources.

United Nations Development Fund for Women, http://www.unifem.org/.
The women's fund at the United Nations, providing financial and technical assistance to innovative programmes and strategies to foster women's empowerment and gender equality.

International Labour Organization, http://www.ilo.org/.
UN specialized agency, promoting social justice and labour rights; research reports on informal and formal work.

REFERENCES

Bajada, Christopher and Friedrich Schneider (eds) (2005) *Size, Causes and Consequences of the Underground Economy: An International Perspective*, London: Ashgate.

Ballentine, Karen and Jake Sherman (eds) (2003) *The Political Economy of Armed Conflict: Beyond Greed and Grievance*, Boulder, CO: Lynne Rienner.

Benería, Lourdes (2003) *Gender, Development and Globalization: Economics as if All People Mattered*, New York: Routledge.

Cerny, Philip G. (1995) 'Globalization and the Changing Logic of Collective Action', *International Organization* 49, 4: 595–625.

Chang, Grace (2000) *Disposable Domestics: Immigrant Workers in the Global Economy*, Cambridge, MA: South End Press.

Friman, H. Richard and Peter Andreas (eds) (1999) *The Illicit Global Economy and State Power*, Lanham, MD: Rowman and Littlefield.

Held, David, Anthony G. McGrew, David Goldblatt and Jonathan Perraton (1999) *Global Transformations: Politics, Economics, and Culture*, Stanford, CA: Stanford University Press.

Himmelweit, Susan (2002) 'Making Visible the Hidden Economy: The Case for Gender-Impact Analysis of Economic Policy', *Feminist Economics* 8, 1: 49–70.

Hoskyns, Catherine and Shirin M. Rai (2007) 'Recasting the Global Political Economy: Counting Women's Unpaid Work', *New Political Economy* 12, 3: 297–317.

Journal of International Affairs (2000) Special Issue: The Shadow Economy 53, 2.

Kudva, Neema and Lourdes Benería (eds) (2005) *Rethinking Informalization: Poverty, Precarious Jobs and Social Protection*, Cornell University Open Access Repository, http://hdl.handle.net/1813/3716 (accessed 11/11/07).

McLellan, David (1977) *Karl Marx: Selected Writings*, Oxford: Oxford University Press.

Naylor, R.T. (2002) *Wages of Crime: Black Markets, Illegal Finance, and the Underground Economy*, Ithaca, NY: Cornell University Press.

Parreñas, Rhacel Salazar (2001) *Servants of Globalization: Women, Migration and Domestic Work*, Stanford, CA: Stanford University Press.

Peterson, V. Spike (2003) *A Critical Rewriting of Global Political Economy: Integrating Reproductive, Productive, and Virtual Economies*, London and New York: Routledge.

Rupert, Mark and M. Scott Solomon (2006) *Globalization and International Political Economy: The Politics of Alternative Futures*, Lanham, MD: Rowman and Littlefield.

Sassen, Saskia (1998) *Globalization and Its Discontents*, New York: New Press.

Schneider, Friedrich and Dominick H. Enste (2002) *The Shadow Economy: An International Survey*, Cambridge: Cambridge University Press.

Smith, Joan and Immanuel Wallerstein (eds) (1992) *Creating and Transforming Households: The Constraints of the World-Economy*, Cambridge: Cambridge University Press.

Tabak, Faruk and Michaeline A. Crichlow (eds) (2000) *Informalization*, Baltimore, MD: Johns Hopkins University Press.

Uvin, Peter (2003) 'Global Dreams and Local Anger: From Structural to Acute Violence in a Globalizing World', in Mary Ann Tetreault, Robert A. Denemark, Kenneth P. Thomas and Kurt Burch (eds) *Rethinking Global Political Economy: Emerging Issues, Unfolding Odysseys*, London and New York: Routledge.

Waring, Marilyn (1999) *Counting for Nothing: What Men Value and What Women are Worth*, 2nd edn, Toronto: University of Toronto Press.

CHAPTER 13

Why are some people better off than others?

Paul Cammack

THE QUESTION
SOURCES OF INEQUALITY

Just by virtue of the fact that you are reading this book, you are likely to be among the better off people in the world. For a start, you are not among the estimated 20 per cent of the world's adult population classified as functionally illiterate (two thirds of them women, by the way, although this is changing fast). Even if you only stayed in school past 15, you are in the top half of educational achievement worldwide; if, as I expect, you have gone on to tertiary education (college or university), you are in the top quarter (UNESCO 2006: 293, 309). This doesn't guarantee that you are relatively well off, but it makes it very probable. Around two-thirds of students in developed countries go into tertiary education, but only one in six in developing countries, so your chance of having a college or university education is much higher if you grew up in a developed country. But wherever you grow up, your chances of making it to college or university are always better the better off you are. And if you did, you'll be pleased to know that the longer you stay in education, the more you are likely to earn: in the US, for example, full-time year-round workers over 25 who hadn't finished high school were averaging $28,000 a year in 1999, while those with bachelor's degrees or better averaged $65,000 – more than twice as much (Weinberg 2004: 3).

A thought experiment

Now, imagine that you could be someone else, and you could choose your gender and ethnicity, and when and where to live. Assuming you wanted the best chance of being well off, what would you choose?

If you chose now, rather than some time in the past, you would be right, for the richer developed countries at least. In the United States, again, average per capita GDP (the gross domestic product or total output of the country, measured in dollars, divided by the total population) was just over 50 per cent higher in 2000 than in 1979. Second, you would be wise to choose to be male – to stay with our US example for the time being, men in 1999 were earning 50 per cent on average more than women; and if you did choose to be born in the US, you certainly shouldn't choose to be Hispanic. If you did, you would find yourself on the *lowest* average earnings, at $31,000 a year – less than if you were black ($33,000), or 'American Indian' (the official classification – you might prefer 'First Nation') ($34,000). You would probably choose to be white ($46,000), but you would actually come out better if you chose to be Asian – the average salary of Asians in the US was $47,000 in 1999, perhaps because 44 per cent had at least a bachelor's degree or better, compared to 26 per cent of the white population, 14 per cent of the black population, and 10 per cent of the Hispanic population. And 8 of the 11 million who declared themselves 'Asian' in the 2000 Census are immigrants, a reminder that many people migrate in search of a better living – a poor one still, in the case of many migrants to the US from Mexico and Central America, a much better one for most of the principally Chinese, Filipino, Indian, Vietnamese and Korean groups who make up the Asian population (Malone *et al.* 2003: 6).

But if you did choose the US, you would be taking a risk. It is the richest of the large industrialized nations (the tiny Grand Duchy of Luxembourg, with a population under 500,000, is the richest country in the world by far), but it also has the highest and fastest rising income inequality in the rich world (Smeeding 2005: 968). If you were lucky, you might end up among the top 10 per cent,

Chapter 4 also examines how gender and race matter to people's lives.

Despite this inequality within the United States and other rich nations, many people try to enter these countries in search of a better living and indeed take considerable risks to do so. Chapter 8 examines the example of migration from Mexico to the United States.

with an income of close to $100,000 a year; if you were very lucky indeed you might be among the one in 10,000 who take home over $14 million a year. Even this would be twenty times less than top CEO (Chief Executive Officer) Richard D. Fairbank of Capital One Financial, who took home $280 million in stock option gains in 2005. But as you can see from Figure 13.1, your chances of ending up with a high income would not actually be very good. Although *average* incomes are among the highest in the world, wealth is actually heavily concentrated among the top 10 per cent of the population, and extremely concentrated towards the very top – the bottom 90 per cent average less than $29,000 per year. And incomes grew much more quickly for the rich than for the poor between 1979 and 2000. The poorest 10 per cent saw their incomes grow by only 8 per cent in total over those years, while the richest *doubled* their income (Smeeding 2005).

In the United States, then, inequality is dramatic, and getting worse. It has created the 'separate country' of Richistan, inhabited by just 1 per cent of the population (Frank 2007). In October 2007 the US Internal Revenue Service calculated that income distribution had reached a new post-war peak of inequality

US Average Incomes, 2005		
Income group	*Number*	*Average income*
All population	145,881,000	$46,806
Bottom 90%	131,292,900	$28,980
Top 91–95%	7,294,050	$110,424
Top 96–99%	5,835,240	$176,925
Top 99–99.5%	729,405	$370,887
Top 99.5–99.9%	583,524	$695,764
Top 99.9–99.99%	131,293	$2,316,353
Top 0.01%	14,588	$14,027,614
Top 100 CEOs	100	$34,479,120
Top 10 CEOs	10	$68,955,000
Top CEO	1	$249,420,000

FIGURE 13.1
US Average Incomes, 2005. Source: Emmanuel Saez, Updated Tables and Figures for 2005, at http://elsa.berkeley.edu/~saez/, accessed 29/07/07. Permission granted

FIGURE 13.2
'Congratulations Mr Henderson'. Artist: Clive Goddard. CartoonStock Ref: cgon253.
www.CartoonStock.com

in 2005, with the top 1 per cent of the population receiving 21.2 per cent of
income (Ip 2007). The following section looks at the comparative picture,
bringing in other rich industrial countries and the 'emerging markets' of Brazil,
Russia, India and China (sometimes referred to as the 'BRIC' countries because
of their initials). As we shall see, although the US is an extreme case among rich
countries, the over-whelming majority of the world's population lives in societies
that are becoming significantly more unequal. Sections 3 and 4 will explore some
of the different explanations for and attitudes towards this growing global
inequality, and the larger questions it provokes.

ILLUSTRATIVE EXAMPLE
INEQUALITY IN THE AGE OF NEOLIBERAL REFORM

There is nothing new about inequality between societies and individuals. It is and
always has been a defining feature of global politics. Historically, such things as
unequal ownership of land, rent from property and exploitation of political and
military power have been important means of accumulation of personal and
national wealth. In the nineteenth and twentieth centuries unequal access to
education and policies that favoured urban rather than rural development also
contributed to inequality between individuals and regions. But important as these
issues still are, they do not explain contemporary patterns of inequality.

Changes in the global economy in the late twentieth century

Three changes that took place in the late twentieth century are shaping current patterns of global inequality. The first is the reversal of the significant post-Second World War shift towards greater equality in the advanced industrial economies, initiated by neoliberal reform in the UK and the US from the 1970s onwards. The second is the creation of a genuinely *global* capitalist economy over the same period, particularly as a consequence of the rise of the Asian economies (successively, Japan, Taiwan, Korea, China and India), and the re-establishment of market economies in the former Soviet Union and in Eastern Europe after 1989. The third is the concurrent promotion by leading governments and international institutions of greater openness and competitiveness in the emerging global capitalist economy. Current sources and patterns of inequality are not the result of chance, or of some mysterious force called 'globalization', but the product of a deliberate shift in policy, increasingly coordinated on a global scale. By the early years of the twenty-first century this had created a completely new set of global circumstances. As a result, the character and dynamics of inequality today are very different than in the past. The dynamic global expansion of capitalism has raised income levels in some of the poorest and most populous countries (such as China and India), so that if you compare average incomes across countries it looks as if global inequality has been reduced. But it has also made those countries much more unequal internally – so that the benefits of rising wealth are going disproportionately to a few. It is already possible to discern the outlines of the new pattern of inequality that will dominate in the future – the global ascendancy of capital over labour, the universal shift of income from workers to owners of capital, and the concentration of global income and wealth among a new class of global capitalists. Global capitalism may in the long run reduce inequalities between *countries*, but on present evidence it sharply increases inequalities between *individuals*.

Chapter 12 examines some of the implications of this globalizing economy, in particular the phenomenon of informalization.

The graphs in Figure 13.3 offer a snapshot impression of what has been happening. They show the share of national income earned by the top 0.1 per cent of the population – the top one in 1,000 in other words – up to the year 2000 in five countries. The first graph shows the pattern for the US, the UK and Canada from 1913 to 2000 (as discussed for the US in the previous section), and the second for France and Japan from 1885 to 2000. You will see that there is a broadly similar pattern in the three countries in the first graph. There is a sharp decline from the early twentieth century to around 1945 – the end of the Second World War. Then, after a slight recovery, there is a steady decline through to the late 1970s. But from the late 1970s onwards the share of income going to this tiny proportion of the population has risen dramatically, back to where it was more than sixty years ago (or eighty years ago in the case of the US), and it is continuing to rise sharply. The second graph shows that in France and Japan, too, the share of income going to the top 0.1 per cent of the population was relatively low and

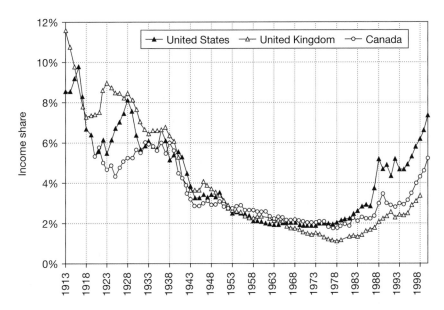

A. Top 0.1 per cent income share in English speaking countries

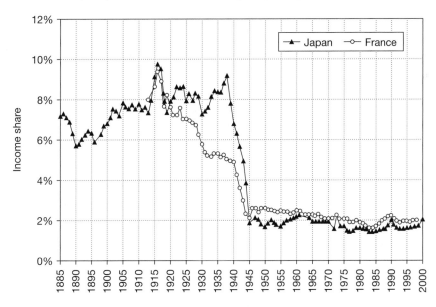

B. Top 0.1 per cent income share in France and Japan

FIGURE 13.3
Top 0.1 per cent income shares across countries. Source: Thomas Piketty and Emmanuel Saez (2006) 'The Evolution of Top Incomes: A Historical and International Perspective', *American Economic Review, Papers and Proceedings*, 96, 2: Figure 3, p. 203. Permission granted

Note that these graphs do not tell us who the top earners are, whether, for example, this group is predominantly white, predominantly male, predominantly from a privileged educational and/or socio-economic background.

stable between 1945 and 1975. But it also reveals two significant differences. First, it shows that while the share in France fell between the two world wars, as in the first three cases, in Japan it didn't fall at all until the Second World War. Second, in neither case did the share *rise* again from the early 1980s (Piketty and Saez 2006: 203). In the mid-1960s, the top 1,000th of income earners were taking home about 2 per cent of national income in all five cases – two hundred times more than what an equal share would have been, but still very roughly a quarter of the share they had enjoyed fifty years earlier. Forty years later, the very rich in the US had practically gained back all they had lost, with the UK and Canada following the same path, but no such change had taken place in either France or Japan.

We are looking here only at the changing share of income of a tiny fraction of the population of just five countries. But the graphs tell us quite a lot about changing patterns of income distribution (how income is shared, or distributed, across different groups of the population) over the last century. First, they suggest that a substantial *redistribution* of income (a significant *change* in the way income was shared across the population) took place around the time of the Second World War, and was sustained thereafter. Second, though, it shows that to the extent that this was a global phenomenon (remember, we are looking only at five of the G7 countries – along with Germany and Italy, the seven leading developed economies in the world) it was unusual and relatively short-lived. Third, it suggests at least three different patterns: a Japanese (possibly East Asian) pattern, with 1939–45 a key turning point and a stable distribution of income thereafter, and *two* 'Western' patterns – the first an 'Anglo-North American' pattern in which redistribution after the Second World War is rapidly reversed from the early 1980s, the second a French (possibly continental European) pattern in which it is not.

The G7 countries are Canada, France, Germany, Italy, Japan, the UK and the US.

Measuring and comparing inequality

Measuring and comparing inequality in and between countries over time is complicated. As Box 13.1 on pp. 302–3 explains, it cannot be done without good basic data (national statistics) and ways of comparing them; and the various ways of doing it have advantages and disadvantages. Figure 13.4 shows the measures of inequality discussed in Box 13.1 for ten countries around 2000 – three Scandinavian democracies known for their relative equality, and the seven leading developed nations known as the G7. The first column gives average levels of income (in terms of purchasing power), showing the US and Norway comfortably ahead of the rest. The remaining columns show different measures of inequality. On every one, the three Scandinavian democracies are the most equal. They have the lowest Gini coefficient (led by Denmark), and the poor receive well over half (57 per cent) of the median income (P10/P50), while the rich receive from around one-and-a-half to one-and-two-thirds the median income (P90/P50). In contrast, in the most extreme case among the developed states, that of the United States, the poor receive only 37 per cent of the median income, while the rich receive more than twice as much. As a result, the gap between the rich and poor (P90/P10) is twice as much in the United States as it is in Denmark and Norway, with the other developed G8 countries in between. So although the *average income* in the United States is the highest among these countries, if we look at the real incomes of the poor (P10 real income rank) the poor are better off in Canada, Denmark, Germany and Sweden – as they are in Austria, Belgium, Luxembourg, the Netherlands, Switzerland and Taiwan (Brandolini and Smeeding 2007, Figure 3: 33). The *poor* in the United States, in other words, do not even make it into the top ten in global terms. As the authors point out, this is a consequence of a period of 'unrelenting increases in income inequality' from the 1970s on.

Income inequality in ten developed countries, 2000 (Japan 1992)								
	1	*2*	*3*	*4*	*5*			
Country	*GDP per capita (PPP) 2000*	*Rank*	*Gini circa 2000*	*Rank*	*Comparing the poor and the rich*			
					P10/P50 (Poor)	*P90/P50 (Rich)*	*P90/P10 (Ratio)*	*P10 real income rank*
Denmark	27,828	3	0.225	1	0.57	1.55	2.8	2
Norway	33,092	2	0.251	2	0.57	1.59	2.8	1
Sweden	25,232	5	0.252	3	0.57	1.68	3.0	6
Germany	25,061	6	0.275	4	0.54	1.80	3.4	3
France	25,045	7	0.278	5	0.55	1.88	3.4	6
Canada	26,821	4	0.302	6	0.48	1.88	3.9	3
Japan	23,971	9	0.315	7	0.46	1.92	4.2	n.a.
Italy	34,365	1	0.333	8	0.35	1.99	4.5	9
US	22,487	10	0.370	10	0.47	2.12	5.7	5
UK	24,666	8	0.343	9	0.47	2.15	4.6	8

FIGURE 13.4
Income inequality in ten developed countries, 2000 (Japan 1992) Sources: Columns 1–2: Penn World Tables 6.2; Columns 3–5: Brandolini and Smeeding (2007, Figures 1 and 3)

BOX 13.1 MEASURING AND COMPARING INEQUALITY

MEASURING AND COMPARING INCOME

All measures of inequality within and across countries must be treated with caution. They are the results of very complex procedures, which have been refined in recent years, but remain fairly crude in many respects. For a start, for any one individual country it is hard to calculate real personal disposable income – the ideal common measure of the value of the income attributable to a single individual. In many countries a proportion of income for many comes from non-cash sources (such as food grown on family plots); the size of households and the number of people who depend on a particular income varies widely across the world; and while there are a wide range of sources of income that might be taken into account – wages and salaries, income from rent or investments, government transfers (such as welfare payments) – relatively few countries have good records of these, particularly for comparisons over extended periods of time. Second, it is impossible to compare incomes directly between countries. Comparisons based on exchange rates (usually made by converting local currencies into US dollars at the current rate of exchange) are very misleading – as anyone who has travelled knows, a dollar buys a lot more in China or India than in the US (and a lot less in Switzerland or Japan). This problem is overcome by calculating purchasing power parity or PPP – turning national currencies not into the equivalent in US dollars at the current rate of exchange, but into the equivalent in US dollars that you would need to buy a 'typical' basket of goods. This is a much better measure, but it is still complicated and rather rough and ready, especially as 'typical' purchases vary widely, and particularly between the rich and the poor.

MEASURING AND COMPARING INCOME INEQUALITY

There are three common ways of measuring inequality within and between countries, each with strengths and weaknesses.

The Gini coefficient

The commonest measure used is the Gini coefficient, which is a cumulative measure of overall inequality on a scale of 0 (perfect equality) to 1 (perfect inequality, or all wealth held by one person). On this measure, the lower the number the greater the equality. You will find varying calculations for each country, depending on the income sources included and the degree of sensitivity of the analysis (i.e. whether it just divides the population into five broad bands, with 20 per cent of the population in each or, say, 100 bands, with 1 per cent of the population in each). The problem with the Gini coefficient is that it doesn't tell you how inequality is distributed. A given level of inequality might reflect serious absolute poverty along with modest prosperity for the rest, or very low levels of poverty combined with a small minority of very rich individuals, or extreme polarization – serious poverty for a minority, extreme wealth for a minority and relatively equal incomes in between. These situations would have different explanations, and would perhaps evoke different responses.

Quintiles and deciles

An alternative method is to divide the total number of incomes into bands of five (quintiles, each including 20 per cent of the population) or ten (deciles, each including 10 per cent of the population) and to calculate the share of income going to each band and the ratio between different bands. The World Bank uses quintiles, which give a rather crude measure, especially at the top end. It is more illuminating to use deciles, but even this is fairly crude, as we saw in our US example in section 1 – there was a huge variation in income *within* the top decile.

Percentiles: P10, P50, P90

Finally, a method based on the same principle uses percentiles (dividing the population into 100 bands) and compares selected bands. The bands usually selected are P10 (the tenth percentile, or the top of the bottom 10 per cent), P50 (the fiftieth, or the top of the bottom half) and P90 (the ninetieth, immediately below the top 10 per cent). The very poor and very rich are excluded, but we can compare poor (P10), middle (P50) and rich (P90), and the ratios between them.

Paralleling the sudden surge in the incomes of the very rich (see Figure 13.3), the Gini coefficient in the United States has risen steadily over the last forty years, from a situation where it was already the highest in the developed world. The United Kingdom, the original home of the welfare state, and among the more equal of the developed countries in the post-war period, experienced a sharp increase in inequality between 1979 and 1990, the years in which Margaret Thatcher was Prime Minister. As Figure 13.4 shows, it remained in 2000 the most unequal of the developed European countries on all measures. For the UK and the US, then (though not for Canada, whose *overall* level of inequality has not

BOX 13.2 WEALTH AND INEQUALITY IN THE US

The claim that the United States enjoys the world's highest living standard must be evaluated alongside the equally valid claim that the United States enjoys the greatest absolute inequality between the rich and the poor among developed countries. While the rich in America are truly well off by any measure of living standards, many poor Americans at the same time have living standards below those in other nations which are not as rich as the United States.

(Brandolini and Smeeding 2007: 11)

risen in the same way), the data considered here confirm the impression given by the evolution of the incomes of the very rich – a shift towards much greater inequality, rapidly from a low base in the case of the UK, and steadily from an already high base in the case of the US.

Developing and emerging economies

At the same time that the UK and the US have become so much more markedly unequal, the structure of the global economy as a whole has been changing in the same direction. Although the developed countries still dominate, newly emerging economies are taking a steadily growing share of foreign investment and world trade. The so-called BRIC countries (Brazil, Russia, India and China), together accounting for approaching 40 per cent of the global population, have been highlighted in recent years because they have been the favoured new destinations for foreign direct investment (Wilson and Purushothaman 2003). They were only the most prominent examples of a host of emerging economies, concentrated in Asia but also including Mexico and Argentina in Latin America, and South Africa, by far the most industrialized economy in Sub-Saharan Africa.

Among all of these China is easily the most significant. As Figure 13.6 shows, although its impact on global production and trade is as yet limited, its vast reserve of labour and its growth rate of near enough 10 per cent per year (compared to

FIGURE 13.5
Chinese workers labour on the construction of the Shanghai World Financial Centre, 2006.
Photo: AP

	Population (millions) (2004)	1 GDP per capita (PPP) 2000	2 Gini circa 2000	Average growth rate 2001–5	Share of World Exports (%)		Share of Inward World FDI (%)		Share of Outward World FDI (%)	
Inequality and dynamic growth in Russia, Brazil, China and India										
Country					1990	2005	1990	2005	1990	2005
China	1,282,336	4,002	0.43	9.9%	1.8	7.3	1.7	7.9	0.4	1.5
India	1,1116,985	2,644	0.33	6.5%	0.5	1.0	0.1	0.7	–	0.2
Brazil	184	7,194	0.59	2.7%	0.9	1.1	0.5	1.6	0.3	0.3
Russia	144	9,263	0.43	6.1%	1.6	2.3	–	1.6	–	1.7
Total					4.8	11.7	2.3	11.8	0.7	3.7

FIGURE 13.6
Inequality and dynamic growth in Russia, Brazil, China and India. Sources: Columns 1–2: Penn World Tables 6.2; UNCTAD, (2007)

around 2 per cent for the developed countries as a whole) underpin a massive expansion in both exports and inward foreign direct investment (FDI) since 1990; and FDI outwards from China is growing fast, albeit from lower levels. India, almost equally populous, is only beginning to register on the same indicators, but is projected to advance rapidly. Brazil, a focus of much attention in the late twentieth century, has actually fallen back in comparative terms, while Russia is representative of a much larger set of emerging economies in Central Asia, the former Soviet Union and Eastern Europe. Beyond the interest they have attracted in the global economy, these four countries have one thing in common – high or rapidly rising inequality. As Brazil's exceptionally high Gini coefficient shows, it is among the most unequal societies in the world. China and Russia (emerging from decades of socialist rule) and India (with its own post-independence history of broad egalitarianism) share a history of much greater equality. But since the inauguration of pro-capitalist reforms in China in 1978 and in Russia in the 1980s this is changing rapidly, while in India inequality has been rising sharply since neoliberal reforms were launched in the early 1990s – top incomes, for example, show the same trajectory as in the UK and the US (Banerjee and Piketty 2005). In none of these cases is increased integration into the global economy reducing inequality.

RESPONSES
LIBERAL AND DEVELOPMENTAL PERSPECTIVES ON INEQUALITY

The information provided above tells us about emerging patterns of inequality, but it doesn't tell us *why* some people are better off than others. We might imagine that the sharp changes that coincided with the First and Second World Wars and the Depression were unintended consequences of those larger events while the more equal distribution maintained after 1945 was a consequence of conscious policy choice. Policy choices might also explain rising inequality in the UK, the US, China and Russia under the impact of subsequent pro-market reform. If so, we would like to know, for example, why France and Japan share a different pattern, to what extent national cases reflect *regional* variations, and whether the trend towards greater inequality is likely to continue and to spread.

In other words, the information provided so far has identified a *research agenda* (questions we would like to be able to answer), but we haven't found any answers yet. In order to begin to do so, and to address the broader question of *global* patterns of inequality, we need to explore some current approaches to growth and inequality, and the extent to which they are reflected in the policies promoted by governments and international institutions around the world. We begin with liberal globalism, the dominant approach in both academic and policy-making circles, and we contrast it with the global developmentalism that is its principal interlocutor. The following section will question the adequacy of these approaches.

Liberal globalism

Liberal globalists advocate a world of liberal democratic states integrated through the market (Box 13.3), on the grounds that 'growth is good for the poor' (Dollar and Kraay 2002). For Martin Wolf, Associate Editor and Chief Economics Commentator of the London-based *Financial Times*, governments should support markets in their own country, and cooperate to make markets work on a global scale – this is not just the best but the only way to raise living standards around the world.

David Dollar, head of the Macroeconomics and Growth Group in the Research Department of the World Bank, agrees: the answer to global poverty and inequality is more integration, not less (Dollar 2007: 73–4). Liberal globalists tend to take an optimistic view of the impact of growth on poverty reduction, and to argue, for example, that if everyone benefits from growth it doesn't matter if the rich benefit most (Wolf 2004: 139) and that increasing inequality in Russia and China is an inevitable consequence of the abandonment of failed egalitarian policies

Chapter 14 looks in more detail at how and why the liberal approach to poverty reduction has failed.

BOX 13.3 LIBERAL GLOBALISM

A world integrated through the market should be highly beneficial to the vast majority of the world's inhabitants. The market is the most powerful institution for raising living standards ever invented: indeed there are no rivals. But markets need states, just as states need markets. In a proper marriage between the two, one has contemporary liberal democracy, incomparably the best way to manage a society. Its blessing needs to be spread more widely. The problem today is not that there is too much globalization, but that there is far too little. We can do better with the right mix of more liberal markets and more co-operative global governance.

(Martin Wolf 2004: xvii)

(Wolf 2004: 167). Above all, they argue that a degree of inequality is inevitable, as economic growth depends upon private enterprise, and it is therefore essential for states to encourage economic activity across borders and reward entrepreneurs. As the comments above suggest, liberal globalists are not hostile to the state. Rather, they are hostile to state intervention that inhibits the market, but strongly in favour of state support for markets, which they regard as essential at both national and global levels. Finally, liberal globalists are not unconditional defenders of the rich countries, or of the status quo. On the contrary, they condemn the protectionism of the European Union, the United States and Japan, and argue that it is hypo-critical for countries that advocate commitment to liberal principles to refuse to practise them themselves. So for David Dollar: 'After all the rhetoric about globalization is stripped away, many of the practical policy questions come down to whether rich countries are going to make it easy or difficult for poor communities that want to integrate with the world economy' (Dollar 2007: 100). They call, therefore, for *more* liberal reforms, and their extension to *all* countries in the world.

The European Union is explained in **Chapter 9**.

Global developmentalism

Global developmentalists share the commitment of liberal globalists to cooperation between states and the participation of all states in global markets, but they reject the liberal approach on the grounds that it overlooks the privileged position of the rich countries in the global economy as currently constituted, and the tendency for the benefits of growth to be unequally distributed. So Robert Wade

BOX 13.4 GLOBAL DEVELOPMENTALISM

The 'development space' for diversification and upgrading policies in developing countries is being shrunk behind the rhetorical commitment to universal liberalization and privatization. The rules being written into multilateral and bilateral agreements actively prevent developing countries from pursuing the kinds of industrial and technology policies adopted by the newly developed countries of East Asia, and by the older developed countries when they were developing, policies aimed at accelerating the 'internal' articulation of the economy. . . . All this constitutes a shrinkage not only of development space, but also of 'self-determination' space. It ties the hands of developing country governments 'forever' to *the North's interpretation* of a market opening agenda ('you open your markets and remove restrictions on incoming investment, in return for [promises of] improved access to our markets').

(Wade 2003: 622)

argues that the liberalizing measures pushed for by the US, the UK and the European Union in relation to global product and financial markets are shrinking the 'developmental space' open to developing economies.

The enforced liberalization of global markets rules out such things as industrial development strategies that rely for a period on selective protectionism – the very policies that brought about successful development not only in contemporary East Asia, but also in the United States in the past. Linda Weiss similarly argues that 'the rich nations as a group . . . have carved out a multilateral order which best suits their current developmental trajectory' (Weiss 2005: 724), and concludes that global rules support the upgrading of rich country economies while 'kicking away the ladder' (cf. Chang 2002) from under developing countries. Global developmentalists reject the idea that the first requirement of development policy is that it should promote global liberalism; they place greater stress on the continuing relevance of developmental strategy than on the prioritization of further liberal integration. They also tend to be more critical of emerging patterns of inequality. Wade, for example, has maintained that Wolf and others give a misleading account of the potential for liberal reform to address *either* poverty *or* inequality. Dismissing the liberal approach as 'faith-based social science' (Wade 2007: 107), he points to the overall drop in global rates of growth since neoliberal policies were introduced in the 1970s, the extent to which the argument for falling poverty and inequality depends upon the case of China (which has not followed liberal policies) and the widespread evidence (some of it reviewed above) that the benefits of growth have been very poorly distributed – the principal beneficiaries being the top half of the population of the rich countries and China's middle classes (Wade 2007: 110–11).

Liberalism, developmentalism and the international institutions

International institutions over the last two decades, led by the World Bank, have been determined proponents of liberal globalism, unfailingly promoting liberal policies centred on further integration of the global economy. They have argued for greater openness in the global economy, and at national level they have favoured sound macroeconomic policy and a 'market-friendly' orientation on the part of governments. They have made the alleviation or elimination of poverty their major goal, but insisted that it is to be achieved by liberal means. While they have maintained the focus on privatization and reduced state intervention that was prevalent in the early 1990s (and particularly associated with the IMF), they have tended to place greater emphasis on institutional reforms that will underpin a liberal order at national and global levels – the *good governance* agenda. A liberal policy framework, according to these institutions, is still the best hope for the poor.

Chapter 11 explains how international financial institutions such as the World Bank came to be set up.

FIGURE 13.7
The World Bank headquarters in Washington, DC. Photo: AP Images

The World Bank's liberal globalism was best captured in the title of its 2005 World Development Report, *A Better Investment Climate for Everyone* (World Bank 2004), which urged all governments around the world to pursue liberal reforms in order to promote opportunity and entrepreneurship among their citizens. There were two significant features to this approach. The first was that it embraced many aspects of domestic policy, in particular in relation to the reform of tax and welfare regimes and labour markets. In other words, far from concerning themselves with matters of global regulation and integration, the international institutions became increasingly interventionist with regard to domestic policy. The World Bank's Comprehensive Development Framework and the HIPC (Heavily Indebted Poor Countries) and PRSP (Poverty Reduction Strategy Papers) initiatives developed and jointly operated by the IMF and the World Bank reflected this heavy emphasis upon domestic policy in developing countries (Cammack 2002). The second was that over the last two decades international institutions that were once strongly committed to global developmentalism embraced the agenda of global liberalism. The UNDP (United Nations Development Programme), along with UNCTAD (United Nations Conference on Trade and Development) and ECLAC (UN Economic Commission for Latin America and the Caribbean), once the strongest advocates of state intervention in support of national developmentalism, all followed this trend (Cammack 2006).

In all of these cases, the focus has been much more on poverty than on inequality, and where inequality is recognized as an issue (World Bank 2004: 32) the approach advocated is increased access for the poor (whether as workers, consumers or entrepreneurs) to the principal elements of a liberal global economy – work, credit and investment opportunity. In the early years of the twenty-first century there was a consensus, extending beyond the international organizations considered here to the European Union and the OECD (Organization for Economic Cooperation and Development), that the route to prosperity for developing countries lay not only in liberal reform, but in domestic economic and social liberal reform embedding market forces more deeply in society *after* reform.

Chapter 14 raises questions about how we may understand and tackle poverty.

BROADER ISSUES
HISTORICAL MATERIALISM AND THE EXPANSION OF THE GLOBAL WORKING CLASS

Forty years ago there was something approaching a global consensus that governments had a duty to act alongside or against market forces in order to address inequality. In Western Europe, with the UK as a leading example, governments owned and managed key national industries and maintained tax regimes that were intended to bring about a redistribution of national income through high taxes on the rich and substantial investment in a wide range of welfare programmes.

My own experience, as a British citizen born at the beginning of the 1950s, is typical of many. I was born into a working-class family (my father a bus conductor, my mother a nursing auxiliary in a small local 'cottage' hospital) and moved into a newly built council house in the mid-1950s. Through my childhood and into early adulthood I received free medical and dental care, free education and a grant when I went to university that covered all my expenses and left me free of debt on graduation (at the same time, most of my friends, like most working-class children, left school at 15 – only in 1972 was the school-leaving age raised to 16). School-leavers and university graduates were as likely to work for the state in one way or another (in the police, the armed forces, government offices, education or the health service, or in a nationalized industry) as for the private sector. In world politics, the Soviet Union (along with the People's Republic of China) loomed large, not only as a possible enemy, but also as an alternative social and economic system. Between the capitalist and socialist camps, in what was becoming known as the Third World, there was little faith in the market as a solution to the problems of development. On the contrary, there was a consensus that governments (many of them newly established in the wake of decolonization) had a duty to mobilize resources through the state in order to force the pace of change. The dominant model, typified by the case of India under Nehru, was national developmentalism, centred on state ownership, the protection of industry, the active management of exchange rates, interest rates and the money supply, and a broad commitment to egalitarianism. To the extent that there was an alternative, it was not 'reliance on the market', but social revolution – Ernesto 'Che' Guevara's call in 1967 for the creation of 'one, two, three, many Vietnams' captured what turned out to be the high point of revolutionary politics in the Third World.

There is no doubt, then, that the world has changed. The previous sections of this chapter reflect a fundamental shift, the key to which has been a global neoliberal revolution, focused as much on domestic as on international policy. However, the liberal globalist and global developmentalist approaches reviewed on pp. 306–10 capture only a part of this shift, and in particular they touch very

The period when the Soviet Union and its allies were seen as the enemies of 'the West' was known as the Cold War.
See Chapter 19

The term 'Third World' is also from that time.
See Chapter 1

Jawaharlal Nehru was the first Prime Minister of independent India. He was in office from 1947 to 1964.

FIGURE 13.8
Alberto Korda's famous photograph of Che Guevara, 'Guerrillero heroico'. 1960.
© ADAGP, Banque d'images, Paris 2008

lightly on the question of why, in the contemporary world, some people are better off than others. This is because while the first promotes global capitalism and the second promotes national capitalism, neither looks critically at the way in which capitalism itself generates inequality, especially in the forms in which it is currently pursued around the world.

We can best focus on this question by going back 160 years, to the *Manifesto of the Communist Party* written by Karl Marx and Friedrich Engels in 1847–48, and more generally to the analysis of capitalist production offered by historical materialism (Box 13.5).

Karl Marx is introduced in **Chapter 12**.

The starting point for historical materialism is neither the market (as it is for liberal globalism) nor the developmental state (as it is for global developmentalism), but the social relations through which the material production on which social life depends take place; and in this context the relations between the bourgeoisie and the proletariat in the capitalist system, or the capital relation. As capitalism comes to dominate, society is increasingly shaped by the class struggle between the bourgeoisie (owners of the means of production) on the one hand and the proletariat (the majority forced to sell their ability to work in order to live) on the other, and Marx and Engels see this as the driving force behind social change.

The extended analysis of capitalist production that Marx eventually produced was spread across three volumes of *Capital* (1976 [1867]) (with a further three left unwritten) and several thousand further pages of published and unpublished material. Five key concepts extracted from this immense body of work suggest its relevance to understanding contemporary patterns of inequality:

BOX 13.5 HISTORICAL MATERIALISM

The history of all hitherto-existing society is the history of class struggles. . . . The modern bourgeois society that has sprouted from the ruins of feudal society has not done away with class antagonisms. It has established new classes, new conditions of oppression, new forms of struggle in place of the old ones. Our epoch, the epoch of the bourgeoisie, possesses, however, this distinctive feature: it has simplified the class antagonisms. Society as a whole is more and more splitting up into two great hostile camps, into two great classes directly facing each other: Bourgeoisie and Proletariat.

(Marx and Engels 1973 [1848]: 67–8)

1   *Primitive* (or, better, original) *accumulation*: the process by which the bourgeoisie and the proletariat are initially constituted through the twin process of the expropriation of (taking property from) the peasantry and the accumulation of resources in the hands of a minority.

2   The *exploitation of labour*: Marx's claim that the source of profit is the capacity of the capitalists to pay workers for only a part of the surplus their labour creates, and to expropriate the rest for themselves.

3   The *profit motive*: the orientation of the capitalist towards the accumulation of capital, rather than any broader social purpose.

4   The *constant revolution of production*: the pressure on capitalists to compete with each other to reduce the price of production in order to sell their goods in the market, either by obliging workers to accept lower pay or work longer hours, or by innovation and investment that increases the productivity of the worker.

5   Competition on a global scale: the resulting tendency for the production process to spill out beyond national borders and operate on a global scale.

Marx and Engels did not *predict* that capitalism would become global, first, because its development depended on class struggles within and across numerous different societies, the outcome of which could not be known in advance; and, second, because it was inherently subject to periodic crises, with similarly indeterminate outcomes. But they did expect that if it became global it would be through an uneven process of development, the key feature of which would be that the conflict between the bourgeoisie on the one hand and the proletariat on the other would increasingly shape political and social change.

Following this logic, we can see the neoliberal revolution as a victory (perhaps temporary) for capital over labour on a global scale, and we can interpret developments since the 1970s in the light of it. It is not just a question of the opening up of new markets, as liberal globalists argue, but of the drafting in of millions of individuals into a vast new workforce – a global proletariat. This enormously enhances the power of capital by creating new opportunities both for new markets and for new sites of production. What is more, it obliges capitalist enterprises around the world to compete or go under, because of the new intensity of competition on a global scale. Third, governments committed to continued capitalist development have to respond by maintaining as competitive an environment as possible. In other words, they are driven by increasingly intense global competition to create 'a better climate for investment' in their own countries. And a key element of this is the provision of a workforce able to meet the needs of capitalists – in other words, a workforce available at a competitive price, and equipped to respond effectively to the rapidly changing needs of domestic and foreign enterprises.

This perspective immediately illuminates features of contemporary global development noticed by Wade and Dollar, respectively. Wade notes that for the OECD countries (thirty of the most developed economies in the world) as a group there has been a sharp shift of income from labour (the proletariat) to capital (the bourgeoisie): the share of labour remuneration in business revenue fell back from a peak of 72 per cent in 1980 to 64 per cent in the early twenty-first century, while the share going to capital rose from 28 to 36 per cent. A more recent analysis suggests that 'In Western Europe, East Asia, North America and the Middle East and North Africa (MENA) region, labour shares have either remained stagnant or declined during the 1980s and 1990s after rising from 1960 to 1980. In Latin America and Sub-Saharan Africa, negative time trends have persisted through the entire period' (Jayadev 2007: 5). Dollar, otherwise upbeat about the prospects for global growth, notes that 'wage inequality is rising worldwide' (Dollar 2007: 74) – in other words, middle- and higher-wage earners are tending to move away from low-wage earners, with negative consequences for the distribution of income among wage earners as a class. Other sources confirm that this is a powerful contemporary trend (OECD 2007: 12–13).

On this evidence, workers as a whole are losing out to owners of capital, and poor workers are falling back in relation to a minority of favoured top earners. There are three related considerations here. First, the expansion of the global proletariat is the objective both of international organizations and of national governments around the world. The logic of the policies of the World Bank and other international organizations is to increase as much as possible both the size of the global workforce and its utility to or exploitability by capital. This logic is reflected, for example, in the promotion of active labour market policy in developed and developing countries alike, where the emphasis is on ensuring that pension and welfare rights do not limit entry to the labour market, that workers can be 'hired and fired' with ease, and that groups underrepresented in the labour market – lone parents, the disabled and the elderly – are 'encouraged', principally by the removal of benefits, to find work. It is reflected, too, in more 'progressive' aspects of World Bank policy, such as, for example, its genuine commitment to the equal provision of education and work opportunities for girls and boys – progressive in gender terms, but *explained* by the broader goal of building a global proletariat. These policies are promoted with equal enthusiasm by governments from the UK and the US (principal exponents of welfare-to-work or 'active labour market' policies) to India and China. Second, the combination of globally integrated markets and the huge labour reserves in the developing world suggests that this is a fundamental structural feature of the global economy for the foreseeable future: according to the OECD, 22 million new jobs were created in the BRIC economies in the period 2000–5, and there may be as many as 300 million surplus workers in China and India alone (OECD 2007: 26). Compare this with the total workforce of 358 million in all the G7 countries put together (OECD 2007, Table 1.2: 21) and it is clear that the expansion of the global proletariat is neither fortuitous nor temporary, but a likely structural feature of

Chapter 11 argues that in some cases it is useful to think in terms of deproletarianization, that is, a reversion to forced labour or slavery where the workers are not paid anything at all.

Workers in the informal economy often have no protection against exploitation by employers at all.
See Chapter 12

the global economy for the foreseeable future, driven forward deliberately by the policies of governments and international institutions.

CONCLUSION

The OECD expressed concern in 2007 that despite the consensus among economists that globalization is a 'win–win process', public opinion is largely hostile towards it. Its attempt to explain this 'paradox' confirmed the analysis offered in this chapter. First, globalization is taking place on an unprecedented scale, in terms of the number of countries involved, and its extension beyond industry to labour-intensive services. As a result, 'most firms and workers are directly or indirectly competing in today's world economy'. Second, though, 'economic integration is occurring in the context of wider earnings inequality and perceptions of job insecurity' (OECD 2007: 12).

It is no accident, then, that practically every society in the world is becoming more unequal. Inequality within states is growing faster across the whole of the world at present than at any time in the past: a calculation by researchers at the World Institute for Development Economics Research (WIDER) at the UN University for the two decades up to the mid-1990s found 'a surge of within-country inequality' in about two-thirds of the seventy-three developing, developed and transitional countries analysed; only 12 per cent of the countries and 5 per cent of the population surveyed had experienced falling levels of inequality (Cornia *et al.* 2003: 1, 13). The global explosion of inequality over the last thirty years or so and the accumulating evidence of its shameful character and extent have made it a focus of increasing attention in the present century. It is a key feature, and perhaps *the* key feature, of global society today.

In the contemporary world, the reasons why some people are better off than others relate increasingly to policy choices *within* individual countries and across international organizations that favour not only open markets, but also owners of capital. As we have seen, domestic polices are strongly influenced and promoted by international institutions whose principal objective is to increase to the maximum the size of the global workforce and its availability to domestic and foreign capital alike. It follows that the OECD and other international institutions such as the IMF and the World Bank are probably right to suggest that the continuation of the same policies will produce further growth, though it will be interspersed with periodic crashes and crises. But it is a form of growth that also tends to generate inequality, because its commitment to competitiveness on a global scale eventually obliges propertyless workers across the whole of the world to compete with each other. Set against the optimism of governments and international institutions today that the benefits of growth will outweigh the costs of inequality is Marx's suggestion that 'the general tendency of capitalist production is not to raise, but to sink the average standard of wages' (Marx 1951 [1865]: 405). The material presented here suggests that the twenty-first century will see an experiment on a global scale in which these contrasting views will be tested.

FURTHER READING

This chapter has argued that inequality is on a rising trend within practically every country in the world, and that there is nothing either accidental or inevitable about it. On the contrary, it is a consequence of the widespread adoption of neoliberal policies in what has become a genuinely global capitalist economy. Although it was written in 1847–8, the **Communist Manifesto** (Marx and Engels 1973) remains an essential starting point. Callinicos (1996, especially Chapter 6), provides an excellent introduction to Marx's analysis of capitalism. Glyn (2006) explains beautifully, from a similar perspective, how the global political economy has evolved over the last forty years. New sources of contemporary data and debate are appearing all the time. Recent concern about inequality on the part of international institutions is reflected in UNDP (2005, especially Ch. 2) and World Bank (2005), along with their predilection for market-friendly solutions. Birdsall (2005) offers an accessible and humane commentary on the same issues. For the UK, the annual reports by the Institute for Fiscal Studies (e.g. Brewer *et al.* 2007) are very useful, and do a very good job of explaining and analysing different measures of inequality; Dorling *et al.* (2007) is one of a number of excellent Joseph Rowntree Foundation resources. An excellent introduction to the broader debate is the collection of short essays in **Poverty in Focus 11: The Challenge of Inequality** (International Poverty Centre 2007). Some of the same authors appear in Held and Kaya (2007), which offers wider reference to current controversies. My own perspective is developed in Cammack (2003, 2004) and, with colleagues, at www.politicsofglobalcompetitiveness.net. Along with the websites listed below, you should search regularly (on Scopus, Web of Science or Google Scholar, for example) for more recent work by the various contributors identified here.

WEBSITES

Centre for Global Development/Inequality, http://www.cgdiv.org/section/topics/inequality.
    Current research on global inequality.

Inequality.org, http://www.demos.org/inequality/.
    Current research on poverty and inequality in the US.

International Poverty Centre, http://www.undp-povertycentre.org/.
    A joint UNDP/Brazilian government project with a wide range of publications, notably **Poverty in Focus**, and more advanced policy research briefs and working papers.

Joseph Rowntree Foundation, http://www.jrf.org.uk/.
    Current research on poverty and inequality in the UK.

Politics of Global Competitiveness, http://www.politicsofglobalcompetitiveness.net.
Working papers from a Marxist-oriented research group, of which the author is a member, reflecting and extending the arguments presented in this chapter.

UC Atlas of Global Inequality, http://ucatlas.ucsc.edu/home.html.
Excellent interactive resource, with the capacity to generate global, regional and country maps on a range of topics related to global inequality and good links to other related sites.

REFERENCES

Banerjee, Abhijit and Thomas Piketty (2005) 'Top Indian Incomes, 1922–2000', *World Bank Economic Review* 19, 1: 1–20.

Birdsall, Nancy (2005) 'The World Is Not Flat: Inequality and Injustice in Our Global Economy', *WIDER Annual Lecture 9*, UNU-WIDER, Helsinki, Finland, http://www.cgdev.org/doc/commentary/speeches/Birdsall_WIDERpaper.pdf.

Brandolini, Andrea and Timothy M. Smeeding (2007) *Inequality Patterns in Western-Type Democracies: Cross-Country Differences and Time Changes*, Luxembourg Income Study Working Papers Series, No. 458, http://www.lisproject.org/publications/liswps/458.pdf.

Brewer, Mike, Alissa Goodman, Alistair Muriel and Luke Sibieta (2007) *Poverty and Inequality in the UK: 2007*, IFS Briefing Note No. 73, Institute for Fiscal Studies, http://ifs.org.uk/bns/bn73.pdf.

Callinicos, Alex (1996) *The Revolutionary Ideas of Karl Marx*, 2nd corrected edition, London and Sydney: Bookmarks, http://www.istendency.net/pdf/revideas.pdf.

Cammack, Paul (2006) 'UN Imperialism: Unleashing Entrepreneurship in the Developing World', in Colin Mooers (ed.) *The New Imperialists: Ideologies of Empire*, Oxford: Oneworld Publications.

Cammack, Paul (2004) 'What the World Bank Means by Poverty Reduction and Why It Matters', *New Political Economy* 9, 2: 189–211.

Cammack, Paul (2003) 'The Governance of Global Capitalism: A New Materialist Perspective', *Historical Materialism*, 11, 2: 37–59.

Cammack, Paul (2002) 'The Mother of All Governments: The World Bank's Matrix for Global Governance', in Rorden Wilkinson and Steve Hughes (eds) *Global Governance: Critical Perspectives*, London: Routledge.

Chang, Ha-Joon (2002) *Kicking away the Ladder*, London: Anthem Press.

Cornia, Giovanni A., Tony Addison and Sampsa Kiiski (2003) *Income Distribution Changes and Their Impact in the Post-World War II Period*, Discussion Paper No. 2003/28, World Institute for Development Economics Research, Helsinki: United Nations University.

Dollar, David (2007) 'Globalization, Poverty and Inequality since 1980', in David Held and Ayse Kaya (eds) *Global Inequality*, Cambridge: Polity.

Dollar, David and Art Kraay (2002) 'Growth Is Good for the Poor', *Journal of Economic Growth* 7, 3: 195–225.

Dorling, Daniel, Jan Rigby, Ben Wheeler, Dimitris Ballas, Bethan Thomas, Eldin Fahmy, David Gordon and Ruth Lupton (2007) *Poverty, Wealth and Place in Britain, 1968 to 2005*, Bristol: Joseph Rowntree Foundation/Policy Press.

Frank, Robert (2007) *Richistan: A Journey through the American Wealth Boom and the Lives of the New Rich*, New York: Crown Publishers.

Glyn, Andrew (2006) *Capitalism Unleashed: Finance, Globalization, and Welfare*, Oxford: Oxford University Press.

Held, David and Ayse Kaya (eds) (2007) *Global Inequality*, Cambridge: Polity.

International Poverty Centre (2007) *Poverty in Focus 11: The Challenge of Inequality* International Poverty Centre, June, http://www.undp-povertycentre.org/site/PublicationShow.do.

Ip, Greg (2007) 'Income-Inequality Gap Widens', *Wall Street Journal*, 12 October: A2.

Jayadev, Arjun (2007) 'Capital Account Openness and the Labour Share of Income', *Cambridge Journal of Economics* 31, 3: 423–43.

Malone, Nolan, Kaari F. Baluja, Joseph M. Costanzo and Cynthia J. Davis (2003) *The Foreign-Born Population: 2000*, Census 2000 Brief C2KBR-34, Washington, DC: US Census Bureau, US Department of Commerce.

Marx, Karl (1976 [1867]) *Capital*, vol. 1, London: Pelican/New Left Review.

Marx, Karl (1951 [1865]) *Wages, Price and Profit*, in Karl Marx and Friedrich Engels, *Selected Works*, vol. 1, Moscow: Foreign Languages Publishing House.

Marx, Karl and Friedrich Engels (1973 [1848]) 'Manifesto of the Communist Party', in Karl Marx, *The Revolutions of 1848*, edited by David Fernbach, London: Pelican/New Left Review.

OECD (2007) *OECD Employment Outlook 2007*, Paris: OECD.

Piketty, Thomas and Emmanuel Saez (2006) 'The Evolution of Top Incomes: A Historical and International Perspective', *American Economic Review, Papers and Proceedings* 96, 2: 200–5.

Smeeding, Timothy M. (2005) 'Public Policy, Economic Inequality, and Poverty: The United States in Comparative Perspective', *Social Science Quarterly*, Supplement to Volume 86: 955–83.

UNCTAD (2007) *Handbook of Statistics*, United Nations, http://stats.unctad.org/handbook/ReportFolders/ReportFolders.aspx.

UNDP (2005) *Human Development Report 2005: International Cooperation at a Crossroads: Aid, Trade and Security in an Unequal World*, New York: UNDP.

UNESCO (2006) *Education for All Global Monitoring Report 2007*, Paris: UNESCO.

Wade, Robert H. (2007) 'Should We Worry about Income Inequality?', in David Held and Ayse Kaya (eds) *Global Inequality*, Cambridge: Polity.

Wade, Robert H. (2003) 'What Strategies Are Viable for Developing Countries Today? The WTO and the Shrinking of "Development Space"', *Review of International Political Economy* 10, 4: 621–44.

Weinberg, Daniel H. (2004) *Evidence from Census 2000 about Earnings by Detailed Occupation for Men and Women*, Census 2000 Special Reports CENSR-15, Washington, DC: US Census Bureau, US Department of Commerce.

Weiss, Linda (2005) 'Global Governance, National Strategies: How Industrialized States Make Room to Move under the WTO', *Review of International Political Economy* 12, 5: 723–49.

Wilson, Dominic and Roopa Purushothaman (2003) *Dreaming with BRICs: The Path to 2050*, Global Economic Paper No. 99, New York: Goldman Sachs.

Wolf, Martin (2004) *Why Globalization Works*, New Haven, CT and London: Yale University Press.

World Bank (2005) *World Development Report 2006: Equity and Development*, Washington, DC: World Bank.

World Bank (2004) *World Development Report 2005: A Better Investment Climate for Everyone*, Washington, DC: World Bank.

CHAPTER 14

How can we end poverty?

Mustapha Kamal Pasha

- ■ *The question*
  THE GLOBAL POOR AND CAMPAIGNS TO END POVERTY

- ■ *Illustrative example*
  MODERNIZATION AND MICROFINANCE IN SOUTH ASIA

- ■ *Responses*
  THE NEOLIBERAL PROJECT AND THE EXPORT OF AN IDEOLOGY

- ■ *Broader issues*
  ALTERNATIVE VISIONS OF MODERNITY

- ■ **CONCLUSION**

THE QUESTION
THE GLOBAL POOR AND CAMPAIGNS TO END POVERTY

Poverty is a durable face of global politics, one that invades our global public space and imagination with sustained vitality, a face we wish would disappear the moment we see it. We seem to know the poor even though we have not met them. They are an abstraction we embrace, a concrete part in ourselves we deny. Poverty is one of the most visible signs of otherness. It is *the* face of difference, of those who are removed from our space and experience, a connection to others not like us. Poverty consolidates the material divide between us and them, an ideational divide (that is, a divide in terms of how we understand the world). Something tells us that the poor are in a way like us, something we fear the most. Perhaps the anxiety that we could become like them gives us the inspiration to think about helping them, reaching out to them, without becoming like them.

The poor seem to be everywhere, over half of the world's population according to United Nations reports (UNDP 2006), but often in far-flung places removed from our everyday lives. Their existence is a distant presence that does not disrupt the functioning of *our* modern life. Perhaps, their being makes a particular form of life possible for us. We have a name for the place of the poor: the Third World, Bangladesh, Haiti, Africa. The match between the name and the place is not important. It is where poor people live. Faces of malnourished children, squalour, overcrowded slums and waste contrast sharply with our world of affluence, conspicuous consumption, technological advance and the promise of comfort. We are connected to the poor in episodic embrace on the evening telecast. Many feelings and emotions spring to life when we see the face of poverty – pity, sympathy, sorrow, pain, alienation, superiority, disgust.

FIGURE 14.1
A visualization of global income distribution. Photomontage by Dr Kurt Källblad, Malmö, Sweden. Source: 'The Challenge of Inequality', *Poverty in Focus*, International Poverty Centre, June 2007, cover, www.undp.org/povertycentre

Of course, some of 'us' are poor too. At least we live in relative poverty (as defined in Box 14.2 on p. 323) even though we live on far more in real terms than many of the global poor.
See Chapter 13

For more detail on global inequality and how it is measured, see Chapter 13.

It is interesting to think about the ways in which the lifeboat scenario works like the ticking bomb scenario discussed in **Chapter 2**. It tells us what the problem is in such a way that we have no room for manoeuvre.

In the age of digital communication and connectivity (Appadurai 2001), the end of poverty has become *the* truly 'global' public policy issue of our times, eclipsing global warming, human trafficking or illegal drugs. It is a campaign with very few sceptics and critics. A case against helping the poor was widely featured in public consciousness over three decades ago under the rubric of lifeboat ethics. It would be virtually impossible to endorse views of this nature now, although in terms of actual policy, lifeboat ethics is not much different from the logic of neoliberalism.

The poor tend to be differentiated based on particular distinctions and classification: we have 'extreme poverty', 'moderate poverty' and 'relative poverty'. On a global scale, the dividing line typically runs between north and south, between the advanced industrial nations and the developing world, but under conditions of global linkage there may be new lines of material discrimination between prosperity and wretchedness. Nevertheless, the prevailing view suggests that outside the Western Hemisphere, barring a few exceptions in Asia and parts of Latin America, vast populations endure poverty as a regular feature of daily lived reality in their cultural zones.

BOX 14.1 LIFEBOAT ETHICS

According to Garrett Hardin, 'If we divide the world crudely into rich nations and poor nations, two-thirds of them are desperately poor, and only one-third comparatively rich, with the United States the wealthiest of all. Metaphorically each rich nation can be seen as a lifeboat full of comparatively rich people. In the ocean outside each lifeboat swim the poor of the world, who would like to get in, or at least to share some of the wealth. What should the lifeboat passengers do? First, we must recognize the limited capacity of any lifeboat' (Hardin 1974). Hardin's argument is that taking everyone into the lifeboat would swamp the boat and everyone would drown – and thus that we cannot or should not help the poor.

FIGURE 14.2
'Structural adjustment'.
Artist: Kirk Anderson

BOX 14.2 CLASSIFICATION OF POVERTY

Extreme poverty means that households cannot meet basic needs for survival. They are chronically hungry, unable to access health care, lack the amenities of safe drinking water and sanitation, cannot afford education for some or all their children and perhaps lack rudimentary shelter – a roof to keep the rain out of the hut, a chimney to remove the smoke from the cooking stove – and basic articles of clothing, such as shoes. Unlike moderate and relative poverty, extreme poverty occurs only in developing countries. Moderate poverty generally refers to conditions of life in which basic needs are met, but just barely. Relative poverty is generally construed as a household income level below a certain level of average national income. The relatively poor, in high-income countries, lack access to cultural goods, entertainment, recreation, and to quality health care, education, and other prerequisites for upward social mobility (Sachs 2005: 20).

The recognition of poverty as a social problem has been based on different understandings of the factors that cause it. Natural explanations have highlighted geography or population growth as the principal culprits. Some have spoken of cultural factors, including the prevalence of discrimination against women, the lack of an achievement drive or work ethic, even a 'culture of poverty' (Banfield 1958) that keeps poor people trapped in an unchanging stable symbolic world. Others have linked poverty to unequal economic and social structures, the working of a capitalist economy; others to 'entitlement failures' or a case where people lack rights to resources. 'Starvation', Amartya Sen notes, 'is the characteristic of some people not *having* enough food to eat. It is not a characteristic of there *being* not enough food to eat' (Sen 1981: 1). From the perspective of the poorer regions of the global political economy, the colonial experience is *the* major structuring cause of poverty. The working of the current global economic order continues to replicate colonial governmentality.

Chapter 11 shows that neocolonial structures still prevail in global politics.

However, despite decades of international social policy, awareness campaigns and noble intentions, poverty has not disappeared. On the contrary, the greater the effort to end poverty, the more palpable is the failure of imagined solutions.

ILLUSTRATIVE EXAMPLE
MODERNIZATION AND MICROFINANCE IN SOUTH ASIA

In recent years, many grand schemes have been advanced to remove the blot of poverty on human conscience. One of the predominant forms that attempts to end poverty have taken is neoliberal globalization, economic liberalization or market fundamentalism.

FIGURE 14.3
Map of South Asia (India, Pakistan, Bangladesh, Sri Lanka, the Maldives, Bengal, Bhutan and Nepal) and neighbouring regions

To understand how the neoliberal project works, this section looks at the particular context of recent experience in South Asia, a region where nearly half of the world's poor live.

Modernization and the rise of the middle class

In the initial postcolonial decades in South Asia, the idea of modernization (for an excellent critique, see Banuri 1990) captured the imagination of both state and society. Top-down development (development enforced by the state on people and often without their input) was promoted as the panacea to eradicate underdevelopment and cut poverty down to size. For a variety of reasons, including the failure of the state to deliver on its promise for sustainable economic growth within a globalizing world economy and the collapse of the Socialist model of planned economics in the Soviet Union and Eastern Europe, the climate drastically shifted to promote market solutions for what are basically social problems.

The intensification of market relations and a market sensibility in South Asia has produced massive changes in the material and symbolic universe of populations. What is remarkable about the recent shift is the relative ease with which national elites have embraced the neoliberal project. The rise of a new middle class has been heralded as the singular achievement of countries like India in successfully negotiating globalization. A culture of competition is not merely confined to the business elites but has percolated down to the less well off. A great transformation appears to be underway in India, and in neighbouring countries.

A direct effect of growing neoliberal consciousness in India, and to comparable and varied degrees in the adjacent countries, is a rethinking of the discourse on ending poverty. Economic growth, *not* redistribution, is now considered the answer. While economic growth was always regarded as a necessary condition to alleviate poverty, it was accompanied by a wider commitment to development. The latter took the form of welfare, attention to a social wage, food subsidies, but also macro-economic targeting of poor regions for special treatment in the areas of education, infrastructural development and emergency relief. In public consciousness, the legitimacy of the state was interwoven with poverty alleviation.

The present constellation draws many elements from past imaginings and practice. However, the commitment of national elites to globalization has shifted the centre of gravity for poverty alleviation schemes. The poor have new uses in the neoliberal vision. The rise of the new middle classes in India, those with access to global culture and the means to reproduce its translocal variants, is inconceivable without the swelling ranks of the poor. The latter, the poor, provide the labouring capacity that enables the rich to live forms of life more attentive to the compulsions of cultural globalization. Increasingly, the fate of the poor rests on consolidation of middle-class privilege in an already polarized and polarizing social universe, similar to the uses of the poor in Western development experience. The more secure the middle class becomes, the more rigid the structures of poverty.

What we mean by privilege is discussed in **Chapter 4.**

The retreat of the state from development, in public consciousness and policy (Kothari 1993) in favour of non-governmental organizations (NGOs) leaves the question of growing inequality untouched. A second aspect of the deepening of neoliberal consciousness is the emergence of a culture of indifference in South Asia, a region known for its moral economy. The breakdown of the tacit social compact between the rich and the poor against the tide of a lifeboat ethics leaves the fate of the poor to the voluntary sector, a relatively powerless social force without the capacity to challenge the market and the forces of capital behind it.

Finally, the regime of neoliberal globalization extends beyond what is regarded as a self-defeating moral regard for the poor. India is the destination of global pharmaceutical giants testing new drugs on the millions of sickly poor with scant

BOX 14.3 MORAL ECONOMY

The concept of a 'moral economy' is said to have originated with E.P. Thompson. He used it to mean 'a consistent traditional view of social norms and obligations, of the proper economic functions of several parties within the community, which, taken together, can be said to constitute the moral economy of the poor'.

(Source: James Kelly, University College Cork Multitext Project in Irish History, http://multitext.ucc.ie/d/Moral_Economy.

See also E.P. Thompson (1971) 'The Moral Economy of the English Crowd in the 18th Century', *Past & Present* 50: 76–136)

Giorgio Agamben's term 'bare life' refers to the form of life that in sovereign Western forms of politics is produced as distinct from politically qualified life. Treating a person as 'bare life' is to disregard their moral or political standing, and merely ensure their survival.

protections of law or their state. Excluded from the legally barred zones of scientific testing in the economically developed world, these companies have targeted the poorest populations of India (and elsewhere), where protections are in short supply and vulnerability high, in the quest for profits and profitability. The 'bare life' of the poor has entered the global sphere of accumulation in unanticipated ways, not merely providing labouring capacity. Superfluous humanity no more, but a valuable resource for enhancing global capital, the poor are a productive resource. This is a sharp break from the uses of the poor in the moral economy.

Microfinance and emancipation from poverty

An altogether different example from South Asia illustrates the convergence of emancipatory notions of poverty alleviation and the pervasiveness of neoliberal consciousness. The case of microfinance in Bangladesh may not appear as an illustration of neoliberal consciousness. However, upon closer scrutiny, it reveals some curious features of the intrusion of neoliberal ideas into both the social and the individual worlds of the poor who have come to rely on microfinance to undo the effects of poverty. The irony lies in the perception of success and its illusory promise of ending poverty.

A brainchild of Nobel Laureate Muhammad Yunus, the idea of microfinance is a far-reaching departure from standard conceptions of banking. As an ethically charged project to emancipate women from poverty, Grameen Bank has come to play a conspicuous role in alleviating poverty. Although the scale of its achievements is fairly modest given the scope of extreme poverty in Bangladesh, it has

FIGURE 14.4
Muhammad Yunus visits Grameen Bank centres and loan holders, who are mostly women.
Copyright © Grameen Bank Audio Visual Unit, 2006

BOX 14.4 THE GRAMEEN BANK

Grameen Bank methodology is almost the reverse of the conventional banking methodology.
Conventional banking is based on the principle that the more you have, the more you can get. In other
words, if you have little or nothing, you get nothing. As a result, more than half the population of the
world is deprived of the financial services of the conventional banks. Conventional banking is based
on collateral (property used as security against the loan and forfeited if the loan is not repaid).
Grameen Bank is collateral free. Grameen Bank starts with the belief that credit should be accepted as
a human right, and builds a system where one who does not possess anything gets the highest
priority in getting a loan. Grameen methodology is not based on assessing the material possessions
of a person; it is based on the potential of a person. Grameen believes that all human beings,
including the poorest, are endowed with endless potential. Conventional banks look at what has
already been acquired by a person. Grameen looks at the potential that is waiting to be unleashed in a
person. Conventional banks are owned by the rich, generally men. Grameen Bank is owned by poor
women. The overarching objective of the conventional banks is to maximize profits. Grameen Bank's
objective is to bring financial services to the poor, particularly women and the poorest, to help them
fight poverty, stay profitable and financially sound. It is a composite objective, coming out of social
and economic visions (Yunus 2007).

acquired a mythical status as a standard bearer for both market-based solutions to ending poverty and the uplifting of rural women in the poorer quarters of the global economy. Since its inception as a formal bank in 1983 from a small project born in the village of Jobra in 1976, Grameen Bank has lent money to over seven million people, 97 per cent of them women. The Grameen idea reverses the logic of banking to offer the least privileged access to finance.

The Grameen project takes as its point of departure the idea that the rural poor can manage money but also manage it well. Without collateral or legal guarantees, credit is advanced to the poor against the guarantee of a five-member group to which the borrower must belong. Although the group is not responsible for any repayment, there is unspoken moral pressure which ensures that the individual is responsible for the debt. Above all, at present 94 per cent of the equity of the bank is owned by borrowers, with only 6 per cent owned by the government. Against the 'poverty' of received poverty alleviation measures, the Grameen project clearly is a fresh intervention.

The success story of the Grameen Bank has been an example in the development industry and others elsewhere have tried to emulate the model, including sponsors from international intergovernmental agencies like the World Bank. Despite its laudable achievement in helping poor rural women in Bangladesh, a critical assessment presents a sobering qualification to the glow of the Grameen experience. Less apparent in the usual celebrations of microfinance is the deepening of the incapacity to reverse the status of the Third World as such by allowing the poor the mere ability to avoid destitution. Microfinance shifts the focus of attention away from inequality to reducing poverty; it merely deflects deeper questions about the growing wedge between the very rich and those who can barely survive.

Increasing inequality between rich and poor is the subject of **Chapter 13.**

The effects of such finance on the situation of rural women, for example in Bangladesh, have also not received closer examination in accounts of the Grameen story. Microfinance rests on the idea of inculcating habits of competitiveness in local, global or translocal contexts among the poor without necessarily creating the conditions to produce alternative futures. The Grameen example suggests that competitiveness, and therefore neoliberal ideology, plays a significant role in claims about survivability with respect to poverty alleviation schemes. This implicates the non-governmental sector in other parts of the Third World, notably Africa. We now have a socialization process of not mere modernization, but imparting skills to understand the market and embrace efficiency, productivity and cost-reduction. More significantly, the retreat of the state from concerns of development on the promise of empowering civil society and the voluntary sector in virtually all parts of South Asia in effect reproduces lifeboat ethics. Only those who can must survive.

RESPONSES
THE NEOLIBERAL PROJECT AND THE EXPORT OF AN IDEOLOGY

Campaigns to end poverty

In recent years, many ambitious projects to change the fate of the poor have been the staple of highly publicized worldwide campaigns by international development agencies, governments, global rock stars, movie actors and non-governmental relief agencies. At the G8 summit and the World Economic Forum (two annual gatherings of leaders from the rich industrialized countries) in 2005, poverty was recognized as a major concern. This recognition followed the unanimous signing of the United Nations Millennium Declaration by all 191 UN member states in 2002 to achieve eight Millennium Development Goals. Reduction of poverty was the first such goal, with the aim specifically of halving extreme poverty between 1990 and 2015 for the proportion of people whose income is less than a dollar a day and halving between 1990 and 2015 the proportion of people who suffer from hunger. Hardly a day goes by without public discussion of ending poverty. From schemes of debt forgiveness, through fair trade, to development aid, poverty alleviation now has given way to the 'end of poverty' discourse. It is no longer respectable merely to reduce poverty, we have to eliminate it. But from its earliest discovery as a social problem, endless talk and thinking have been devoted to trying to end poverty.

The G8 means the G7 countries – Canada, France, Germany, Italy, Japan, the UK and the US – plus Russia. The G7/G8 holds an annual summit and Russia was first included in 1997.

The neoliberal project has shifted the terrain of poverty alleviation in distinctive ways by decoupling the question of poverty from redistribution. In this revised framework of global governance, the embrace of NGOs and celebrities by state managers and the G8 elites is not coincidental. A voyeuristic culture of celebrity worship has displaced politics, shifting responsibility away from those with actual

FIGURE 14.5
Make Poverty History wristbands.
Photo: Global Call to Action Against Poverty (GCAP)

authority to a nebulous global sphere of liberal good-heartedness and feel-good solidarity with 'the poor'. This sentiment is discernible in recent worldwide campaigns under the Millennium Development Goals umbrella to end poverty. The British Make Poverty History Movement, the Live8 rock concerts to raise public awareness of global poverty and the Johannesburg-based Global Call to Action against Poverty, provide good examples of the shifting meaning and space of politics. Paradoxically, however, publicity also allows an occasional probe into uneasy aspects of the workings of the global economy, including inequality and the gulf between rhetoric and state practice.

The neoliberal solution

The neoliberal project suggests leaving the problem of poverty to the functioning of the market by removing obstacles to its smooth operation. The market, the argument goes, is a social institution designed with human ingenuity to assemble people in a common quest to serve their individual self-interest. Unleashed from the fetters of either tradition or political authority, the market allows people with varied skills, crafts or labours to come together and mutually profit by exchanging what they produce. The idea is not new. What distinguishes its contemporary version from views expressed over two hundred years ago is the conviction that *society comes into being primarily through exchange and is held together by exchange.* Without the market, society does not exist. This is a fairly radical idea with the obvious implication that non-market sociability is either 'primitive' in relation to our modern present or a serious impediment to economic advance. Other socially

Chapter 12 also explains about the idea of the market and where it comes from. Structural Adjustment Programmes and some of these negative implications for the poor are further discussed in Chapter 11.

BOX 14.5 STRUCTURAL ADJUSTMENT PROGRAMMES

A key component of neoliberal globalization is a reliance on Structural Adjustment Programmes, the package of economic measures sponsored by the International Monetary Fund (IMF) and the World Bank to tackle the problem of poverty and underdevelopment in debt-stricken countries. Typically, these measures consist of fiscal discipline and the tightening of monetary policy, combined with an expansion of trade liberalization and privatization of the domestic economy. Within the neoliberal framework, debt relief is linked to Structural Adjustment Programmes: the greater the compliance, the greater the support from the international donor community. In practice, Structural Adjustment Programmes have invariably hurt the more vulnerable sections of society as they reward those who have better capability to profit from opportunities presented by the market. The poor are on a weaker footing to compete, and hence more likely to suffer from welfare retrenchment, which is often the operational effect of Structural Adjustment Programmes.

produced institutions – state, family, community and the cultural trappings in which these institutions come into being and persist – ought to be subordinated to the neutrality of the market. Non-market claims must be treated with circumspection to the degree that they get in the way of the market. The reduction of society to the market or the market principle redirects social life in pursuit of goals produced either within the market or induced by its ever-expanding horizons. From the perspective of this sensibility, the poor are not merely a nuisance or an unintended consequence of the drive to universalize the market, but those who lack the desire, talent or aspiration to compete.

The rupture of the market from other societal norms is a notable feature of the neoliberal project. Once norms intrinsic to the market spread across vast social spaces with ease and without effective resistance, the question of poverty cannot be thought of as having solutions that do not arise within the market.

In a neoliberal universe, the problem of poverty is basically one of a lack of effective market-driven capacity. Once that capacity is created, poverty can become a thing of the past. The enemy for neoliberals is any agency that treats the poor as anything other than potentially rational maximizers. Empowerment lies in providing resources or skills to realize the natural trait to maximize.

The question of treating people as rational subjects arises in the context of strategic thinking in Chapter 17.

A second feature of the neoliberal solution to poverty is in the ability of the poor to effectively negotiate globalization. This suggests building a social world that no longer takes the local and its cultural boundaries as the zone of meaningful sustenance. To discard the local in favour of the global is a confirmation of the evolutionary promise of growth and development.

The neoliberal project is both a belief system and a practice that has come to dominate the management of the global economy. As a belief system, it rests on the notion that development (which is an indispensable condition to eradicate poverty) should occur as an unintended feature of the market rather than planning. The prior assumption that buttresses this notion is that wo/man is primarily a *homo economicus*, a calculating animal seeking to satisfy endless private wants through exchange with other like-minded economic individuals. If governments get out of the way and do not stifle the natural propensity for each individual to participate in the sphere of exchange (or the market) in search of self-interest, all can prosper. The market is the ideal institution to produce wealth, to reward people for their labours, and as a consequence creates social harmony and prosperity. Neoliberals suggest that the primary needs of human beings are material, or their materiality takes precedence over other social, cultural or psychological considerations. If the task of producing wealth is left to the individuals themselves and governments are expected only to guarantee the social conditions for the functioning of the market, there is no reason to expect that poverty cannot be eventually eradicated.

Chapter 2 looks at thinking and practice. A 'belief system' is similar to what was discussed as a 'picture' there.

Critiques of the neoliberal project

Critiques of the neoliberal project have been fairly extensive and far-reaching, questioning both the grounds on which a disembedded economy (Polanyi 1944) can offer social cohesion or meaning as well as its endeavour to universalize a specific form of Western development experience to humanity. On the one hand, these critiques address the limiting vision that informs that project and, on the other, they challenge its export in the non-Western cultural zones.

Exporting Western individualism

In the first instance, the neoliberal project takes the cultural apparatus of (post)-industrial Western capitalism as a model abstracted from history. The experience of one particular zone of humanity (northern Europe and later the United States of America) becomes the universal standard to idealize a success story worthy of global emulation. Absence of significant likeness to the experience of the West serves as the definitive story of poverty in the non-West. The heightened individualism captured in notions of economic rationality, efficiency or performance as normative values superior to those generated in alternative societal or cultural arrangements has become a global currency.

Embedded social practices appear deficient on this canvas of calculability. The atomistic proclivities of neoliberal subjectivity stand in sharp contrast to systems of generalized reciprocity, redistribution and social responsibility. In consuming the neoliberal project in societal and cultural zones less enamoured by its lure, serious obstacles appear on the ground. Without a deepened liberal subjectivity, neoliberalism takes on a coercive character, an imposition by the state to align society to assumed pressures of globalization. The latter dictate rationalization not merely of the economy, but of social relations in their entirety.

On a structural reading of the neoliberal project, the latter development is inevitable. Once human beings are reduced to becoming merely owners of a marketable labouring capacity, their relation to the social world is radically altered: relations with others, division between work and leisure, work and procreation all undergo a great transformation. So long as labouring capacity serves embedded social goals, work and purpose can appear as meaningful activity. The neoliberal project detaches social purpose from labouring capacity, assigning the atomistic individual a fictitious sovereign status. Under these conditions, social meaning takes on the character of individual self-seeking primarily in consumption. To consume means to realize subjectivity.

Despite the realization that the neoliberal project may not serve either deeper social purpose or individual selfhood, globalization has facilitated its reach in uncharted

Problems with the idea of a sovereign subject in control of the world are discussed in **Chapters 6 and 20.**

zones. Virtually everywhere, communities, polities and people live, work and think in words and worlds produced by the expansion of the project, not only the most ardent proponents in the geographically dispersed zones of economic, political and cultural power, but also its alleged detractors. The attraction of neoliberalism lies in its promise to deliver individual happiness in material goods, tangible and within reach. Paradoxically, its hold on the imagination is most pervasive not only in the cultural West, but outside, in the minds of state elites and managers in the non-Western cultural zones, often inspiring mega-projects with unpleasant social and environmental effects, as we saw in section 2 of this chapter. Virtually on a global scale, the zealous commitment to the modernist vision has marginalized real alternatives or radically reshaped them.

Conceptualizing 'the poor'

In large measure, the success or failure of 'end of poverty' schemes depends upon how poverty is conceived and operationalized. Is it possible that the visibility of the poor may in some manner make them invisible? Once we see the poor in particular ways, are we concealing what is the most important feature of poverty?

Common understandings of poverty stress physical needs and their deprivation as the essential ingredient of what it means to be poor. Hence, poverty is said to have a 'vital core' tied to material sustenance. Human beings on this account are intrinsically biological beings. The failure to satisfy those needs qualifies them as

FIGURE 14.6
Price of poverty: Pakistani farmers in Jandala, near Multan, show the scars left after operations to remove their kidneys for cash. Photo: AP

the poor. This idea, however, is not as simple as it seems. The poor are not merely those who lack the means for material sustenance. They are also those whose biological existence is an object of social policy (Dean 1992). In this sense, the poor become 'the poor' only in the process of being classified as such. They have no existence separate from the classification by those who have the authority to classify them. Outside the sphere of classification, poverty is not a problem. It may be a problem of destitution (Nandy 2002). Although poverty has existed for centuries, it is only under modern social conditions that it assumes a particular form of visibility. Modernity engenders particular forms of classifications and distinctions that allow populations to be divided in specific ways that are coterminous with readily perceived 'objective' indices. These indices are highly mobile and can be deployed to advance grand claims. For instance, in the global 'war on terror', poverty increasingly appears as a matter of security, a cause of terror, a source of militancy (Belaala 2004; Willet 2005). Once the poor can be recognized within particular classificatory schemes, they can be linked to danger.

The reduction of life to the satisfaction of physical needs is only one aspect of the problem of conceptualizing the poor. From the perspective of those regarded as 'the poor' there is also the question of the subjective state of the poor that is not easily captured in dominant accounting procedures. As Kirsten Hastrup writes in the context of hunger, 'one of the hardest facts of life is that living is so painful to large numbers of people' (1993: 727). Extending her analysis, sharing the experience of the poor is virtually impossible if suffering takes only the form of visual and numerical representation. Suffering is usually experienced in silence, when speech becomes entirely inadequate. The experience of suffering is severed from the apparatus of meaning-making. Numbers also have the distinctive ability to sanitize the subjective side of human misery.

In public consciousness, poverty does not produce the same heightened anxieties reserved for global terrorism and the latter's potential and real menace to humanity. However, it is also no longer a peripheral global concern buried in stories of modernization and progress and the promises of trickle-down growth. The notion that poverty would eventually disappear with the evolutionary processes of economic development and modernization is not very popular. Yet public consciousness and conscience do not mean that schemes to end poverty are effective. The gulf between the two lies, in part, in particular conceptualizations that detach the poor from their cultural universe or fail to see progress itself as the condition for poverty.

Uncoupling the poor from their cultural universe, and reducing them to data tends to produce the illusion that mere decreases in numbers would connote a process of ending poverty. What gets silenced in this conceptualization of poverty is that the aim of merely securing survival or bare life does serious violence to the poor in the act of salvaging them.

Compare this idea that poverty comes to be problematic by virtue of its classification to the discussion in **Chapter 17** of how particular events or people come to be seen as dangers.

Chapter 13 explains how statistics are used and indeed needed in order to understand and analyse global inequality. But do these statistics allow us to comprehend the suffering involved?

BOX 14.6 GIORGIO AGAMBEN

FIGURE 14.7
Giorgio Agamben

Contemporary Italian philosopher Giorgio Agamben argues that 'sovereign power' – the type of authority most commonly associated with the state – relies on the production of two forms of life as separate (1998). He calls these 'politically qualified life' (the citizen) and 'bare life' (the outlaw, the outsider, or the stateless person, for example). He claims that this separation has now been blurred, and that it no longer holds. Initially, there were certain places, which Agamben describes as 'zones of indistinction', where this blurring could be seen. His first example is the Nazi concentration camp. Here inhabitants no longer had any political or legal status and were subject to the whims of the camp guards. They could be killed without any justification having to be offered: their deaths did not count as murder. More recently, Agamben argues, in our culture of administration, management and capitalist consumerism, we have all potentially become something close to bare life, with no genuine political voice.

BROADER ISSUES
ALTERNATIVE VISIONS OF MODERNITY

Dominant conceptions typically take a statistical threshold to define poverty. Behind that threshold lies a notion of material deficiency or the absence of goods that allow people to survive. What is missing in these understandings is the indivisibility of cultural forms of life and the material universe of people. It is not merely a question of survival, or even culturally ensured form of life, but the ability to be subjects or authors of their own lives rather than subjects or *dramatis personae* in an externally created production. The poor are those that lack not only the material capacity to satisfy culturally informed needs, but the ability to live meaningful lives.

Chapter 13 explains how such statistics work.

Hence, the notion that the poor are simply those who lack money or property misrecognizes the centrality of the idea of poverty. While money or property allows people to pursue goals outside bare survival, unless the idea of self-determination is brought to bear on the analysis, the poor remain trapped in other people's worlds as objects. This is not surprising as the neoliberal idea of finding the solution to poverty in the informal sector (de Soto 2000) and giving entitlement to either a bundle of goods (Sen 1981) or legally recognized token of owning capital (de

See **Chapter 15** for a discussion of the issues that arise when people think that they know what is good for others.

Soto 2000) ultimately takes the poor as the receiving end of policy or ethically inspired aid. The historical link between foreign aid and religiously inspired charity may not be so remote. In both instances, the poor are cast as victims, although in some versions of Christian charity, the poor are singularly blessed with godly favour against the corruptibility of the rich, who cannot enter paradise. Proximity to material goods in the contemporary sense is framed as a solution to make the poor vanish, but the historical evidence has not been very promising in this regard.

The lack of the capacity to produce not simply a particular form of cultural life but the ability to creatively redesign their social and life-worlds, that is, to modify their world, not simply adapt to it (Freire 1996 [1970]) does more violence than is apparent in neoliberal imaginaries. On the other hand, the seduction of statistics that rests on the reducibility of human experience to quantifiable data makes social relations opaque. Hence, the Millennium Development Goal of halving the proportion of the extreme poor appears an achievable and worthy mission. The comforting logic that a statistical decline in the number of the extreme poor justifies international aid as one of the effective ways to end poverty rationalizes the status quo. Without redesigning the architecture of global political economy and infusing a redistributive principle at its centre, aid camouflages the inherent properties of global capitalism, which rests on the stubborn logic of leaving sizeable populations without the capacity to live meaningful lives. In a capitalist universe, the prison-house of poverty offers few escape routes unless people acquire access to the means that allow them to productively enter the world of exchange, not merely the guarantee of subsistence which some poverty alleviation strategies promote.

For Charles Beitz's view of global justice, which revolves around distribution, see **Chapter 2**

The question of poverty cannot be posed with any meaningful determinacy outside modernity. No doubt, the poor have had their uses in pre-modern contexts, as moral brokers in the Manichean world of Sin and Redemption. Helping the poor may open up pathways to Heaven. Traces of this role can be found in pleas for foreign aid, charity and help. Acts of kindness and comfort to the poor have intertwined histories. The moral worth of humanity has rested on the capacity to extend succour and support to the needy, those with the least material possessions. Escape from the enticing world of riches has often been recognized as an essential pathway for spiritual progress and the experience of the sacred. Those who *voluntarily* elected to live in poverty demonstrated their closeness to the deeper wellsprings of life's mysterious purposes. The poor have not been without a productive function after all.

Western conception of modernity

With modernity, the poor tend to lose their cultural meaning, assuming the figure of bare life. Now objects of classification and study, the poor bid farewell to a morally configured world and enter the zone of politics and political economy. In the first instance, the poor are serialized, they become objectified as numbers. They no longer inhabit ethically complex structures of meaning. Within the strict world of modern state practice, the poor are merely objects with potential risks to the polity. Similarly, political economy ruptures the poor from a moral economy, pushing them into the world of labouring. Those outside the modern economy are simply a *social* problem.

The neoliberal project redesigns the problem of the poor. To alleviate poverty is to bring the poor into the world of exchange, and failing that, to supply them as matériel for profit (as the pharmaceutical example suggests). Those who cannot be brought in can be abandoned. However, the attempt to strip the poor from their moral universe is a failed enterprise. The ambivalence towards the poor lies precisely in the difficulty of severing the poor from an ethical world of meaning and judgement. In this context, the conceptualization of the poor as data serves as a surreptitious attempt to represent the poor in ethically neutral terms. The poor continue to enjoy a symbolic quality, and hence they cannot exist outside judgement. Yet, the breach with morality and ethics can allow vast expenditures of liberal guilt without disturbing the status quo. This would entail the unwanted question of whether the world in which the poor live is a world ethically constituted. Poverty alleviation is situated at the faultline of morality and ethics.

In alternative worlds, ethically constituted and culturally embedded, the poor cannot exist as mere data, objects of policy or matériel. They are an intrinsic part of a cultural universe. Embedded economies, that is, economies limited in scope and purpose by ethical considerations, not merely self-serving impulses, recognize the violence entailed in severing people from their cultural contexts.

The rapid spread of the neoliberal project globally has curtailed the possibility to envision alternative worlds. In different cultural zones, with the notable exception of Latin America, a convergence appears to be building to address the problem of poverty, relying on market-based solutions. Those zones that apparently reject modernity reveal a curious mix of delinking the cultural accoutrements of West-centred modernity while embracing its technical rationality. The story of the Islamic Cultural Zones can be read on those lines.

For more on Islam in global politics, see **Chapter 5.**

Islamic conception of modernity

A distinctive feature of any alternative construction of the poor would entail a modified understanding of modernity, one that recognizes the need to harness the pursuit of wealth within a wider framework of cultural and spiritual life. Unlike the hegemonic narrative of Western modernity, which accords accumulation a privileged status in the larger scheme of things, an Islamic conception of

FIGURE 14.8
Islamic banking today in the Gulf States and in Malaysia, where Islamic and 'conventional' banks compete freely. Photo: AP

modernity works with the notion of overlapping sovereignties in which human purpose and intentionality are embedded in concentric spiritual and secular pursuits: in family, community, the state, the *ummah* (community of believers). Humanity might flourish and both vertical and horizontal attachments bear moral and ethical content, not swallowed up by the pursuit of happiness or reasons of state.

An appreciation of a distinctively Islamic conception of modernity (as well as other non-Western modalities of embeddedness) allows a remapping of the place of the economy in society. The pursuit of happiness acquires an expansive, non-economistic character linking other-worldly awareness with material reproduction. The individual makes concessions to societal interests and the well-being of the community, not as residual effects of political economy, but as normative principles for the Good Life. Embeddedness also means making human dignity the foundation of the social order. A key feature of the modern poor is their disconnection from any notion of dignity. Material dispossession means redundancy, unless the poor return to the social order in the shape of matériel to service the economy.

The notion of overlapping sovereignties is not cartographical, but a recognition of multiple commitments to tame the insatiable quest for self-aggrandizement and to prevent state idolatry. An ideal-typical Western conception of sovereignty is a compromise between state idolatry and self-interest, the former allowing the latter. Either the state or the individual serves as the foundation for the social order. An Islamic social order shuns these distinctively secular constructions.

The Western conception of sovereignty and its history is explained in **Chapter 9**.

Difficulties of adopting alternative visions: Islamic Cultural Zones

Alternative visions to Western modernity, however, confront a social universe deeply scared by the unstoppable march of neoliberal globalization, but also the deepening of modernist traits of social organization, thinking and practice. The colonial legacy has ensured that the derivative discourses of state practice would outlive the formal end of colonial rule. Sovereignty follows a modernist script throughout most of the Islamic Cultural Zones. In turn, the process of cultural disembeddeness shows no signs of abatement. Other-worldly concerns have moved to new sites of enunciation, as moral critique of the prevailing social order or as a regressive idiom to avoid objectionable cultural features of neoliberal globalization. In both instances, the institutional form of protest and resistance has taken a modernist turn.

Chapter 11 shows how the colonial legacy still seriously affects people's lives in formerly colonized states.

Within the shrinking spaces of neoliberalism, however, Islamic civil society has become the mainstay of solace and support to the poor throughout most of the Islamic Cultural Zones. The evacuation of the state from its historic commitment to development or welfare is both a cause and an effect of a broadening neoliberal governmentality. Often, the lines between political protest and Islamic variants

---

BOX 14.7 *MURABAHA*

An instance of an Islamic alternative to microfinance is the concept of *murabaha*, originally derived from Islamic jurisprudence, in which it refers simply to a sale (the exchange of a thing of value for another thing of value with mutual agreement). In the contemporary context it has become an integral part of 'interest-free' Islamic banking. In its original formulation, *murabaha* is a transaction which honours transparency: the seller divulges the real cost of the commodity, then adds some additional amount or a percentage as profit. Strict rules of compliance that preserve the transparency of the sale must be observed for a *murabaha* transaction, including the ascertainment of the actual cost of the product. The interesting aspect of *murabaha* lies in the aspiration to disrupt the autonomy of exchange in favour of a desire to recast the notion of profit and embed it in an economy of trust. By contrast, microfinance remains ensconced within a strictly market preserve and the compulsions of opaqueness that characterize the actual workings of a capitalist economy.

For more on how Islamic movements are involved in welfare provision, see Chapter 5.

of social welfare can get blurred, but from the perspective of the poor with nothing to lose, a rediscovery of their faith and sustenance are on a single register. Islamic civil society provides a small semblance of integration in a world falling apart. The promise of an integrated life may be illusory, but it becomes the proxy for thinking in an alternative medium.

The fate of the poor in the Islamic Cultural Zones, as elsewhere, rests on the fate of the hegemonic modern project for organizing social and life-worlds. While resistance to that project may be fragile, disorganized and sporadic, it is not completely devoid of capacities to slow down the processes of cultural dispossession. An Islamic vision to reclaim aspects of humanity acquires greater salience in this context.

Discussions of poverty open up wider queries about the nature of the world order, relations between hegemonic and subaltern forces, normative questions of redistribution and, above all, about the neoliberal trajectory of globalization. The poor have generally avoided the more harmful features of cultural dispossession in the Islamic Cultural Zones. As the neoliberal project has expanded, Islamic civil society has also grown. Can this experience provide an alternative model to alleviate poverty, if not end it?

FIGURE 14.9
Activists of Workers Women's Association chant slogans during a rally to mark International Women's Day, Thursday, 8 March 2007, in Lahore, Pakistan. Thousands of women demonstrated in nationwide rallies on International Women's Day, demanding freedom, equal rights and an end to discriminatory laws in this Muslim nation. Photo: K.M. Chaudary, AP

The inclination to romanticize the poor must be resisted. Equally so, alternatives themselves must be embedded and sustainable, not mere reactions to more powerful tendencies. While the visible salience of Islamic civil society as an alternative site to address poverty can be received with greater openness, the bigger issue of neoliberal globalization cannot be left out of sight. Attempts to end poverty often fall into the trap of detaching understanding of the big picture from encouraging symptoms of change and transformation.

CONCLUSION

Poverty remains a durable feature of international relations. Despite many grand attempts to end poverty, the poor refuse to disappear from the global scene. The basic problem lies in neoliberal prescriptions that rest on economism. Some major shortcomings of neoliberal solutions to ending poverty become apparent in South Asia, including the failings of some innovative schemes like microfinance. The neoliberal project fails to accord the poor any notion of dignity or personhood. Ending poverty may not be possible in the foreseeable future, but an appreciation of cultural embeddedness in other formulations of modernity can restore to the poor some measure of their self-worth. The quest of ending poverty may be better served if the process to transform the poor into 'bare life' can be averted, if not reversed.

FURTHER READING

Davies, Matt and Magnus Ryner (eds) (2006) *Poverty and the Production of World Politics*, Basingstoke: Palgrave.
An exciting recent collection relocating poverty within structures of global political economy.

Davis, Mike (2006) *Planet of Slums*, London: Verso.
A breathtaking account of new forms of poverty produced by runaway urbanization.

Dreze, Jean and Amartya Sen (1989) *Hunger and Public Action*, Oxford: Clarendon Press.
One of the major statements by two leading economists on the need for rethinking public policy to eliminate hunger.

Dreze, Jean and Amartya Sen (1991) *The Political Economy of Hunger*, vols I–III, Oxford: Clarendon Press.
Perhaps the most important studies of hunger and the complexity of under-standing it.

Edkins, Jenny (2000) *Whose Hunger? Concepts of Famine, Practices of Aid*, Minneapolis, MN: University of Minnesota Press.
A highly original book on the limits of received conceptions of eradicating famine.

Escobar, Arturo (1994) *Encountering Development: The Making and Unmaking of the Third World*, Princeton: Princeton University Press.
>One of the most important post-structuralist critiques of modernization and development.

George, Susan (1976) *How the Other Half Dies*, Harmondsworth: Penguin.
>A classic statement on global inequality and its effects.

Goulet, Denis (1971) *The Cruel Choice: A New Concept in the Theory of Development*, New York: Atheneum.
>A key ethical critique of conventional theories of development.

Levine, David P. and S. Abu Turab Rizvi (2005) *Poverty, Work, and Freedom: Political Economy and the Moral Order*, Cambridge: Cambridge University Press.
>One of the most compelling challenges to mainstream wisdom on poverty.

Mahbub ul Haq (1976) *The Poverty Curtain: Choices for the Third World*, New York: Columbia University Press.
>One of the classics in the field of development economics and global inequality.

Schumacher, E.F. (1973) *Small Is Beautiful: A Study of Economics as if People Mattered*, London: Blond and Briggs.
>One of the first books on environmentalism and sustainable development.

South Commission (1990) *The Challenge to the South: The Report of the South Commission*, Oxford: Oxford University Press.
>An important report on Third World development from its perspective.

UNDP (2003) *Human Development Report 2003: Millennium Development Goals: A Compact Among Nations to End Human Poverty*, http://hdr.undp.org/reports/global/2003/.
>A very useful report on recent thinking on eliminating global poverty.

REFERENCES

Agamben, Giorgio (1998) *Homo Sacer: Sovereign Power and Bare Life*, trans. Daniel Heller-Roazen, Stanford, CA: Stanford University Press.

Appadurai, Arjun (2001) *Globalization*, Durham, NC: Duke University Press.

Banfield, Edward C. (1958) *The Moral Basis of a Backward Society*, Glencoe, IL: The Free Press.

Banuri, Tariq (1990) 'Modernization and Its Discontents: A Cultural Perspective on the Theories of Development', in Frederique Apffel Marglin and Stephen A. Marglin (eds) *Dominating Knowledge*, Oxford: Clarendon.

Belaala, Selma (2004) 'Morocco: Slums Breed Jihad', *Le Monde diplomatique (English Language Edition)*, November: 4–5, http://mondediplo.com/2004/11/04/11/04moroccoislamists?var%20recherche=Belaala.

de Soto, Hernando (2000) *The Mystery of Capital: Why Capitalism Triumphs in the West and Fails Everywhere Else*, New York: Basic Books.

Dean, Mitchell (1992) 'A Genealogy of the Government of Poverty', *Economy and Society* 21, 3: 215–51.

Freire, Paulo (1996 [1970]) *Pedagogy of the Oppressed*, trans. by Myra Bergman Ramos, London: Penguin.

Hardin, Garrett (1974) 'Lifeboat Ethics: The Case against Helping the Poor', *Psychology Today* 8: 38, 43; 123–6.

Hastrup, Kirsten (1993) 'Hunger and the Hardness of Facts', *Man*, New Series, 28, 4: 717–39.

Kothari, Rajni (1993) *Poverty: Human Consciousness and the Amnesia of Development*, London: Zed Books.

Nandy, Ashis (2002) 'The Beautiful, Expanding Future of Poverty: Popular Economics as a Psychological Defense', in Mustapha Kamal Pasha and Craig N. Murphy (eds) *International Relations and the New Inequality*, Oxford: Blackwell Publishers.

Polanyi, Karl (1944) *The Great Transformation: The Political and Economic Origins of Our Time*, Boston, MA: Beacon Press.

Sachs, Jeffrey (2005) *The End of Poverty: How We Can Make It Happen in Our Lifetime*, foreword by Bono, London: Penguin Books.

Sen, Amartya (1981) *Poverty and Famines: An Essay on Entitlement and Deprivation*, Oxford: Oxford University Press.

UNDP (2006) *Human Development Report 2006: Beyond Scarcity: Power, Poverty and the Global Water Crisis*, Basingstoke and New York: Palgrave Macmillan for UNDP.

Willet, Susan (2005) 'New Barbarians at the Gate: Losing the Liberal Peace in Africa', *Review of African Political Economy* 106: 569–94.

Yunus, Muhammad (2007) 'Is Grameen Bank Different from Conventional Banks?', June, http://www.grameen-info.org/bank/GBdifferent.htm.

CHAPTER 15

Why do some people think they know what is good for others?

Naeem Inayatullah

- ■ *The question*
  GIVING AND RECEIVING

- ■ *Illustrative example*
  GOD'S PURPOSE: EARLY CHRISTIAN INCURSIONS

- ■ *Responses*
  HISTORY'S PROGRESS: CONTEMPORARY INTERVENTIONS

- ■ *Broader issues*
  DIAGNOSING THE NEED FOR EXCLUSIVE KNOWLEDGE

- ■ **CONCLUSION**

THE QUESTION
GIVING AND RECEIVING

Some people think they know what is good for others because they believe they know something crucial denied to others. For example, a society that believes it has mastered democracy may notice that other societies have authoritarian and dictatorial political institutions that leave their people without a voice. In offering to help create democratic procedures, the 'democratic' society may wish to increase the freedom of others. The George W. Bush and Tony Blair administrations used this motive to justify their occupation of Afghanistan and Iraq. Or, a society with abundant wealth and food supplies might notice the beginning of famine in another part of the world. It might decide to feed the people suffering from famine. Policy makers from wealthy societies might also feel compelled to teach others how to manage their agriculture and reorganize their economy so as to avert future famines. International aid agencies and the World Bank offer such lessons to those who undergo periodic famines. Finally, scientists, social theorists and policy makers in 'democratic' and 'wealthy' societies might believe that the absence of proper political and economic institutions results from a larger and deeper problem with other societies. They may deduce that such societies need a better understanding of the proper relations between humans and humans, between humans and nature, and between humans and the larger cosmos – the universe thought of as an ordered and integrated whole. They may believe that such societies lack the right kind of order and their thinking needs to be reorganized. Europeans have held this posture in their encounters with others for the last 500 years or so. In each case, those with true knowledge believe that they have a responsibility to share their knowledge and thereby improve others' lives.

We can react in two opposite ways to such claims. On one hand, we honour the belief that providing goods for others is an essential part of human responsibility. If we know how to sustain freedom; if we know how to reshape nature so that we can produce great wealth; or if we have learned how to create a social order that produces a vibrant democratic society with abundant wealth, then we must do our utmost to provide such goods for others. Not doing so would be selfish, irresponsible and wasteful. When we accept the role of doing good for others we assume the indispensable value of our knowledge, the inherent sincerity of our motives, and the urgency of the recipient's need. As donors we assume our virtue and delight in our goodness.

Some will of course always dispute that we know how to sustain freedom, reshape nature or produce great wealth in the first place. For example, we may live in a wealthy country but that does not necessarily mean that wealth is abundant for everyone. See Chapter 13

On the other hand, if someone targets us as a recipient of goodness we can become guarded. Perhaps an example will help us understand this wariness. Often parents dutifully try to prepare and guide their young towards future employment. They regard their life experience as a store of knowledge that should help their children replicate their successes and avoid their mistakes. Despite our parents' best intentions, however, we are uneasy and sometimes unwilling recipients of their advice and effort. A part of us questions the relevance of their experience to our current and future plans. Their concern for our career may feel like an intrusion. We may wonder if their worry results from a lack faith in our judgement. When others suggest that they know what is good for us, we imagine that they are actually pointing to our inadequacy. In response, we tend to stress our independence and defend our integrity. We may bristle at the donor's presumption that we are missing a vital perspective. We may even suspect the donor hides self-serving motives in the guise of helping.

Our defensiveness may be hasty and reactive but it may also emerge from deeper issues. How did the donor surmise that the recipient lacks something? Does the donor know the recipient well enough to formulate the recipient's lack? Is the donor's knowledge as vital and necessary to the recipient as the donor believes? Is the donor's duty driven by the desire to reorganize the world according to the donor's self-interested and limited vision? Don't conquerors and imperialists hide their baser motives by clothing them in the good?

On the one side, if we ignore the needs of others we deny our full humanity. On the other side, doing good for others can be intrusive, coercive and detrimental to others' sense of autonomy and freedom. We seem split; stuck in the ethical and political tension between wanting to eradicate ignorance and suspecting that our pursuit of duty endangers others.

Can we find a way to move beyond the split? We can. Notice that we usually jump from one posture to the other without experiencing the tension that lies between them. We skip over the following questions: can we act responsibly towards others without undercutting their autonomy and freedom? Can we offer them democracy, wealth and an alternative social order without colonizing them? From the other side we can ask these questions: how can we receive the 'gifts' and knowledge of donors and nevertheless sustain our political, economic and cultural identity? What can we offer in return? Such questions emerge when we acknowledge the plausibility of both positions – the actual *responsibilities* of the donor and the legitimate *suspicions* of the recipient. When we can feel this tension we can begin to stretch.

Moving past this split requires us to search for the difference between proposing and imposing. Sincere intentions can still be impositions. The more genuinely I believe that I am providing you with a necessary good, the less I am likely to worry about *how* I provide that good and whether you experience it as an imposition. Proposing the good, in contrast, requires that donors re-examine their motivation. Donors may need to motivate their giving not by locating the receiver's deficiency but, paradoxically, by grasping their own lack. When parties seek to overcome their own lack by engaging in cooperative searches for mutual enrichment, then sustainable goods may emerge. Despite this note of hope, we want to bear in mind that even when humans understand how to move beyond this split, they mostly do not do so. The problem of producing the good for others has a long and deep tension that is wrecked with human intransigence. We make a mistake, therefore, if in grasping for a 'solution' to this problem we bypass its complexity.

To illustrate the concerns of this chapter, I might have turned to contemporary events. Interventions by institutions such as the United Nations, NATO, the World Bank, the International Monetary Fund and various inter-state alliances provide familiar examples. Such ready examples, however, are unlikely to help us understand this problem's deep historical roots. My illustrations take us instead

Remember too that when we think about ethics and politics we draw on our pictures of the world, as discussed in **Chapter 2**. You might like to think about the pictures of reason, the subject and political space entailed in this discussion here.

Discussions of colonialism in **Chapter 11** and contemporary interventions in **Chapter 18** are relevant here.

The tricky issue of responsibility towards others is also discussed in **Chapter 20**.

Some of the problems with interventions by international institutions or states acting with their authorization are discussed in **Chapters 11 and 18**.

to the thirteenth and sixteenth centuries. These mostly unfamiliar times present some advantages: they state the issues in clear terms, they show how little the problem has changed over 700 years and they demonstrate the enormous difficulty of our problem. Our challenge remains creating mutually enriching forms of interaction that do not diminish either party. We turn first to Francisco de Vitoria and sixteenth-century Europe.

ILLUSTRATIVE EXAMPLE
GOD'S PURPOSE: EARLY CHRISTIAN INCURSIONS

Spain in the Americas: Francisco de Vitoria's outrage

Catholics and Protestants were waging religious battles against each other in sixteenth-century Europe. Simultaneously, in the early part of that century, Spanish conquistadors were destroying and pillaging the strongest and wealthiest civilizations in the Americas. Francisco de Vitoria, who was among the most influential political theorists and theologians in sixteenth-century Catholic Europe, thought deeply about these two vital issues of the day. On one of these issues his position is clear-cut. He opposed Protestantism. His allegiance was to Catholicism, the Emperor and the Pope. On the subject of Spanish treatment of Indians, he was shocked and embarrassed by the massacre and looting of Indians. In a 1534 letter, he writes that merely thinking about the conquistadors 'freezes the blood' in his veins (Vitoria 1991: 331). Vitoria tried to curtail Spain's invading armies by rejecting their justifications for waging war against the Indians.

Spanish imperialism in South America is also discussed in the context of a general discussion of colonization in **Chapter 11**

BOX 15.1 FRANCISCO DE VITORIA

FIGURE 15.1
Francisco de Vitoria

Francisco de Vitoria (1485–1546) is considered a canonical figure in international law. He was a Dominican theologian and founder of the Salamanca or Spanish school of jurisprudence. He and his students influenced and restructured the theological thinking of Europe.

He was a central figure in the debate of the nature of the Indians in the sixteenth century, especially in his 1539 lectures *De Indis* (*On the American Indians*, published in 1557, after his death). Charles V, Emperor and King of Spain, was among those who consulted Vitoria.

FIGURE 15.2
The Mexica (Aztec) peoples, followers of Moctezuma, face a powerful Spanish force under Hernando Cortés in the 1519–21 campaigns. Source: Fray Diego Durán. *La Historia antigua de la Nueva España*. 1585. Manuscript facsimile, Peter Force Collection, Library of Congress

However, he was not wholehearted in his defence of Indians because he was perplexed and troubled by their deficiencies. These include human sacrifice, cannibalism, a low-level civilization, the absence of Christianity and violations of God's natural order. While Vitoria rebuked the conquistadors he did not believe that the Spaniards should evacuate Indian territories or abandon the natives. His arguments restrained Spanish violence while also providing correctives for Indian deficiencies. Vitoria believed he knew what was good for Indians.

The 'discovery' of the Americas posed a problem for all European thinkers. Were the Indians human? If so, what was their place in the cosmological order (the whole comprising the natural, the social and the spiritual order)? The cosmological problem was also a specific legal concern: was the Spanish conquest and enslavement of Indians legitimate? Pope Alexander VI's 1493 bull *Inter Caetera* permitted Spanish and Portuguese evangelization and territorial acquisition but denied enslavement. In line with this reasoning, Vitoria rejected that the Indians were natural slaves – a popular position inspired by Greek philosopher Aristotle's views of slavery (see Chapter 8). Vitoria accepted Indians as human beings capable of understanding God's laws.

Like most Europeans however, Vitoria, did not *fully* embrace the Indians' humanity. 'Aberrant' and 'unnatural' Indian behaviour indicated that Indians were not sufficiently human (Pagden 1982: 64). Spanish thinkers found themselves in a paradox: if the Indians were irrational and thereby considered natural slaves, it became difficult to account for reports of their technological mastery, their cities and imperial political institutions, and their sophisticated (if satanic) religious practices. Yet if the Indians were deemed rational human beings, then explaining

FIGURE 15.3
'Oh let them go'. Artist: Viv Quillin

their human sacrifices, their relatively primitive agricultural techniques and arts, and especially their acts of cannibalism became complicated. This was no small matter since the legitimacy of Spanish intervention in the Americas rested on the appraisal of Indian culture.

When Vitoria evaluates the reasons for the Spanish conquest of America he considers four oft-cited reasons for depriving the Indians of their rights to self-rule, territorial control and property. The Indians are said to forfeit their rights because they are

- sinners;
- infidels;
- mentally subnormal; or
- intrinsically irrational beings.

(Vitoria 1991: 233)

He easily dismisses the first two reasons (Vitoria 1991: 240–6). Depriving sinners of their natural rights is based on the false belief – attributed to anti-Catholic radicals such as Wycliffe, Hus and various Lutherans – that authority is based on the ruler's purity of faith. Vitoria understood the dangers to the Church if legitimacy of rule is tied to the quality of a ruler's faith: first, because no ruler is without sin; and because someone can always use the claim of greater piety as a means to overthrow the established order. Vitoria refused the belief that sinners lost their rights as a result of their sins. He stood with a long line of thinkers

The link between religion and political authority is explored in **Chapter 6**. **Chapter 5** examines this issue in a contemporary context.

going back hundreds of years who championed the security of the Christian Church against radical reformers.

Nor can the Indians be infidels, Vitoria argued, because infidelity requires prior knowledge of the rejected faith. Indians were ignorant of Christianity. And, if they were originally Christian, as some supposed, then they had degenerated too far from their Christian beliefs to be accountable for their false ideas.

In considering the Indians' deficient mental capacity and their lack of rationality, the third and fourth reasons, Vitoria first weighs the evidence from the Americas and then resists these claims as well, although, as we shall see, he retains something of their rationale, indicating that his opposition is not steadfast. The Indians, he writes, 'have judgment like other men'. They 'have some order in their affairs'. This order is expressed through 'properly organized cities, proper marriages, magistrates and overlords, laws, industries, and commerce, all of which require the use of reason'. They 'likewise have a form of religion' (Vitoria 1991: 250).

On the other side of the ledger, allegations of Indian cannibalism and human sacrifice weigh heavily on Vitoria. He allows the accusation 'that these barbarians are . . . foolish and slow-witted' and further acknowledges their 'sins against the law of nature' (Vitoria 1991: 251, 273). Though he believes that such offences cannot cancel rights, they do indicate intellectual and social chaos in Indian life (Vitoria 1991: 272–5).

Vitoria finds human sacrifice more comprehensible than cannibalism (Vitoria 1991: 212–17). He acknowledges that sacrifice plays a part in Christianity, as in Abraham's willingness to kill his son and, of course, in Christ's own sacrifice on the cross. Despite this sympathy, Vitoria condemns Indian practices. He emphasizes the Indians' confusion about the proper cosmological order, not the similarities between the two systems of religion. He believes that Indians fail to apprehend the most important precepts of God's order. He concludes that they have a distorted vision of reality and that their mental capacity is deficient. Their disorder and deficiency are further expressed in various cultural and technological inadequacies: the Indians possess only a rudimentary knowledge of agriculture, they lack the ability to work iron and other metals, and they are unlettered.

In the end, Vitoria concludes that the Indians are unable to adequately govern their own domains. The following passage summarizes Vitoria's position, though he carefully distances himself from it by insisting that he offers it only for expository reasons:

> these barbarians, though not totally mad, as explained before, are nevertheless so close to being mad, that they are unsuited to setting up or administrating a commonwealth both legitimate and ordered in human and civil terms.

It is interesting to think of the picture of reason used here. How does it differ from the picture of reason employed by the thinkers about global ethics explored in **Chapter 2**?

Hence they have neither appropriate laws nor magistrates fitted to the task. Indeed, they are unsuited even to governing their own households; hence their lack of letters, of arts and crafts (not merely liberal, but even mechanical), of systematic agriculture, of manufacture, and of many other things . . . indispensable for human use.

(Vitoria 1991: 290)

For Vitoria, the Indians are human but inadequately so.

Are there some people we today consider 'human but inadequately so'?

Having diagnosed Indian deficiency, Vitoria moves to the cure. Indians are not permanently foolish or irrational. On the contrary, as human beings they possess reason. The real problem is that they have not activated their dormant reasoning capacity (Vitoria 1991: 250). This failure is due to poor teaching. Vitoria assures us that the fault lies not in their nature, but 'mainly due to their evil and barbarous education', for 'they were so many thousands of years outside the state of salvation' (Vitoria 1991: 250). Notice that Vitoria shifts the status of Indians from slaves to children. Europeans thereby change from being lords and masters to becoming parents and teachers.

Vitoria then provides what today we would call his policy recommendation:

It might therefore be argued that for [the Indians'] own benefit the princes of Spain might take over their administration, and set up urban officers and governors on their behalf, or even give them new masters, so long as this could be proved in their interest . . . and not merely for the profit of the Spaniards.

(Vitoria 1991: 290, 291)

European tutelage will bring enlightenment and order; this is what is good for Indians.

We might sympathize with Vitoria's struggle to reconcile Indian beliefs and practices with his own theological convictions. His Christian beliefs convince him that the Indians are God's children but these beliefs also require him to prescribe Christian instruction. In sum, Vitoria reins in the cruelty of the conquistadors, he refuses to make Indians slaves and he recommends that the civilized world bring in the Indians.

Certainty plays a role in the justifications for torture explored in **Chapter 2.**

If we leave aside the discussion of whether Vitoria is foolish or wise in his beliefs, we can pursue larger questions: why is he so confident in his own faith? Why doesn't an encounter with the Indians raise doubts for him about his own worldview? Before we can turn to these questions, I first want to show that Vitoria's position on the Indians is part of a larger pattern of Christian relations with non-Christian societies, and more generally of relations between self and other.

Relations between self and other are an important part of global politics and are discussed in many chapters in this book. **See particularly Chapters 2 and 4**

BOX 15.2 EXCLUSIVE KNOWLEDGE

Exclusive knowledge is the idea that some group, usually 'our' group, has unique and superior knowledge about how the world works. It contains three specific assumptions:

1   one's own group has special access to knowledge about the order and the workings of natural and social life;
2   there is something superior and final about such knowledge; and
3   others' knowledge claims are inadequate or defective compared to ours.

Later we will discuss how these assumptions work against the great enemy of exclusive knowledge – doubt.

Today, even though contemporary world politics retains much of Vitoria's overall vision, we may regard his views on Indians as ethnocentric. Was Vitoria aware that his worldview was tainted by European and Christian partiality? Unlikely. The deeper source of his certainty derives from what I call exclusive knowledge.

Christian and infidel: Pope Innocent IV

Sinibaldo Fieschi was a leading canon lawyer before he became Pope Innocent IV (1243–54). As pope and lawyer, Innocent synthesized judgements about how Christians should treat non-Christians and he bound these ideas into a legal doctrine. His views illuminated Church thinking for more than 300 years and directly influenced Vitoria's fifteenth-century analysis of Spanish dealings with American Indians (Muldoon 1979: vii–viii, 140–7; Williams 1990: 13, 44). Our examination of Innocent IV's claims to exclusive knowledge remains relevant because we can hear the echoes of his voice in current theory and policy.

Innocent IV raised the following question: 'is it licit to invade the lands that infidels possess, and if it is licit, why is it licit?' (Muldoon 1979: 191–2). ('Licit' means allowed by law.) Innocent was asking if Christians had a right to dispossess non-believers. By contemporary standards, Innocent's question is surprisingly forthright. Nevertheless, despite several hundred years of work by canonists, he was wading into a disputed area. At the time, non-believers included Christian schismatics and heretics, Jews and Muslims living within Christian realms, and Muslims and Mongols beyond the frontiers of Christendom. Though he

FIGURE 15.4
Innocent IV. Source: Library of Congress,
ref. 3644545r

INNOCENTIVS·IIII·PP·IANVENSIS

recognized differences between these groups, he collapsed them into a single category, non-Christian, in order to create a more uniform response to infidels (Muldoon 1979: 3).

Innocent disallows dispossession of infidels simply because they are non-believers. He argues that *dominium* – the basic faculties and rights necessary to human functioning and self-rule, including the right to property and the offices of legitimate authority – rests in the hand of society's rulers regardless of their beliefs. While unpossessed or unruled territories are free for the taking, lands already occupied and ruled are considered the legitimate possessions of their holders. Innocent IV establishes that all peoples, regardless of their faith, have the right to property and self-government.

In which contemporary debates can you find similar considerations and arguments to the ones we are examining here?

We may be surprised that Innocent allows infidels a right to property given that he starts from the premise of exclusive knowledge of Christian truths. His generosity seems all the more astonishing given that, as pope, Innocent considers himself God's vicar. As God's vicar, he can claim universal *dominium* over the planet. Accepting others' right of *dominium* did not mean, however, that Innocent gave up *his* responsibility for *their* souls. He believes that the Church's responsibility for all human souls requires Christians to convert non-believers. However strong or weak the papacy's earthly political power, Innocent retains the pope's ultimate spiritual authority over all peoples, including infidels. He found arguments for dispossessing infidels through this belief.

On the assumption that God's law was evident to all, Innocent argued that infidel rulers forfeited *dominium* when they failed to punish their subjects' violations of natural law. In this circumstance, the pope could mete out justice by authorizing Christian military interventions in infidel societies (Muldoon 1979: 10–11). Innocent leaves unspecified what counts as a violation of natural law, though he mentions sexual perversion and idolatry as particularly serious violations. Such sins, if left unchecked, obligate the pope to summon Christian armies for the purposes of righting the natural order. His armies must withdraw, however, once the mission is concluded.

As long as Christian armies occupy infidel territory why not use them, we may ask, to convert the infidels to Christianity? Christian doctrine disallowed such force because meaningful conversion had to be voluntary. Infidel acquiescence to the sword was no vindication of the true faith. Nevertheless, Innocent recognizes that instructing infidels on proper worship, if not also manners and customs, requires missionary work. Of course, Innocent expects that infidels will resist Christian instruction and block missionary activity. Such resistance, however, amounts to impeding God's way. It justifies the suspension of infidel rights to *dominium* and authorizes Christian invasion. Similarly, the pope may intervene if infidels persecute Christians living under their rule. He may even move to create 'regime change' by replacing noncompliant infidel rulers (Muldoon 1979: 11–12).

Innocent disallows wars of dispossession but retains the claim of exclusive knowledge. On the basis of this knowledge, he then argues that certain kinds of intervention in infidel society are just and necessary. Innocent IV uses the same intellectual apparatus – the same combination of biblical references, Roman law sources and humanist thinking – to establish infidel rights *and* to legitimate dispossession of infidels.

We may ask if Innocent's arguments are tied to Christianity's exclusive knowledge or are they general principles available to all faiths and cultures? Can other faiths marshal these claims and proselytize in Christian society? 'No' replies Innocent. Christians alone have the right to proselytize, to convert others and to intervene militarily for religious purposes. Christian knowledge excludes and exceeds other perspectives on ultimate truth. Innocent tells us why he authorizes Christian missions while blocking all other proselytizers: because 'they are in error and we are on the righteous path' (Muldoon 1979: 14).

In sum, Innocent IV argues *for* the rights of infidels to property and self-government and thereby rejects claims that they can be dispossessed simply because they are not Christians. However, Innocent's defence of infidel *dominium* or, in modern terms, their 'sovereignty', is porous. He offers a justification that legitimates both military intervention and political/spiritual regime change. And,

For a discussion of sovereignty, see **Chapter 6.**

consistent with the claim to exclusive knowledge, intervention is a distinctly one-way Christian prerogative. Like Vitoria, Innocent knows what is good for others. He knows that others lack the knowledge to which he, as a Christian, has full access. Exclusive knowledge and his duty to retrieve the lost souls of non-believers, obligates him to endorse Christian work done for the good of others.

By using the examples of Vitoria and Innocent IV, I am not suggesting that either exclusive knowledge or the belief that one can do good for others is peculiar to Christianity or to Europe. On the contrary, exclusive knowledge seems a common characteristic of many cultures. We can appreciate its pervasiveness by examining an exchange between Christians and Mongols.

BOX 15.3 THE JUST WAR TRADITION

The just war tradition is a way of thinking that is prominent in contemporary politics and academic discussions. It is concerned, at least in part, with doing good for others. Vitoria's work, including his reflections on the legitimacy of the Spanish intervention in the Americas, is seen to have contributed to the development of this tradition and of international law (Bellamy 2006).

The just war tradition is concerned with when it is permissible to fight (this is called *ius ad bellum*) and how it is permissible to fight (*ius in bello*). The precise criteria listed under each heading vary for different just war thinkers. Roughly, the first category requires that a war is fought only

- with the right sorts of aims in mind, such as upholding the law or re-establishing peace (right intention);
- for the right sorts of reasons, such as self-defence against aggression (just cause);
- by the right sorts of political entity, typically now identified as states (right authority);
- for causes that are significant enough (proportionality of ends);
- and when no other means are available (last resort).

The second category requires that the means used in the war remain proportional to the particular objectives (that is, for example, that the least destructive weapon is used to accomplish a particular goal) and that civilians are not targeted (this is called discrimination or non-combatant immunity).

Just war thinkers see this tradition as limiting the ways in which military violence can be used (Coates 1997; Walzer 1992) but they have also justified recent wars. This often takes the form of arguing that we have to do some good for others (such as liberate Afghans from the Taliban or Iraqis from Saddam Hussein) and that we can only do so through war (Elshtain 2003; Walzer 2004).

Christian and Mongol: the encounter with Güyük Khan

In the summer of 1244, Innocent IV moved the papacy from Rome to Lyons to escape the excommunicated emperor Frederick II's attack on Italy. At stake within Western Christendom was the power of the pope versus the emperor. Fear of the powerful Mongols and Muslims multiplied the internal hazards. While both the Muslims and Mongols posed military threats, the Mongols were less known. Innocent IV sent two groups of friars to establish contact and to learn more about the Mongols. He wanted to determine Mongol intentions, ascertain their capabilities and establish an alliance with them against the Muslims. He also hoped to convert the Great Khan and his people to Christianity (Muldoon 1979: 42; Williams 1990: 4). The friars carried two letters from Innocent IV to the Güyük Khan of the Mongols. These letters and the Khan's response provide us with a sense of the encounter.

Innocent explains the central tenets of the Christian view and openly declares his responsibility for the Khan's soul:

> Wherefore we, though unworthy, having become, by the Lord's disposition, the successor of this vicar, do turn our keen attention, before all else is incumbent on us in virtue of our office, to *your* salvation and that of *other* men . . . so that we may be able, with the help of God's grace . . . [to] lead those in error into the way of truth and gain all men for Him.
> (Dawson 1955: 74; emphasis added)

Güyük Khan's response, dated 1246, asks the pertinent question: how does Innocent know he speaks for God?

> Though thou likewise sayest that I should become a trembling . . . Christian, worship God and be an ascetic, how knowest thou whom God absolves, in truth to whom he shows mercy? How dost thou know that such words as thou speakest are with God's sanction?
> (Dawson 1955: 85–6)

How indeed? Güyük poses the question not as a way of opening the debate, but instead to counter-assert his own exclusive intimacy with God: 'From the rising of the sun to its setting, all the lands have been made subject to me. Who could do this contrary to the commands of God?' (Dawson 1955: 86). His exceptionalism is nearly symmetrical to Innocent's:

> The eternal God has slain and annihilated these lands and peoples, because they have neither adhered to Chingis Khan, nor to the Khagan [khan of khans], both of whom have been sent to make known God's command.
> (Dawson 1955: 85)

BOX 15.4 GÜYÜK KHAN

Güyük (*c.* 1206–48) was the son of Ogedei Khan, and grandson of Genghis Khan. He reigned from 1246 to 1248 and was the first khagan, or great khan of the Mongols. Innocent IV hoped to form an alliance with Güyük Khan in order to defeat the Muslims. Güyük Khan's correspondence with Innocent IV reveals how both of them believed the other to be the leader of a relatively inferior people.

FIGURE 15.5
Letter of Güyük Khan to Pope Innocent IV. Vatican Library, http://asv.vatican.va/en/doc/1246.htm

The pope's rightful station, therefore, is not as God's vicar but as Güyük's subordinate:

> Now you should say with a sincere heart: 'I will submit and serve you.' Thou thyself, at the head of all the [Christian] princes, come at once to serve and wait upon us. At that time I shall recognize your submission.
>
> (Dawson 1955: 86)

Does the Khan assume that the pope's submission to him will be good for Innocent and for Christians? Perhaps only in the sense that it would be good for Christians to have their lives spared. Regardless, Güyük Khan believes, much like Innocent and Vitoria, that his knowledge about the world and its workings is absolutely superior. All three assume a form of exclusive knowledge that permits them to suppose they know what is good for others.

RESPONSES
HISTORY'S PROGRESS: CONTEMPORARY INTERVENTIONS

As we shift from the fourteenth to the twenty-first century, can we assume that such claims to exclusive knowledge are relegated to the past? No. It is a mistake to believe that we have moved beyond the powerful pull of exclusive knowledge in contemporary life. Two examples display the strength of that pull. From the left we examine the recently produced Euston Manifesto and from the right the work of British diplomat Robert Cooper. I have selected these examples for two reasons. Both argue with bold fervour and with little regard for upsetting our usual sensibilities. They provide thereby a clarity that helps us to get to the heart of the issue. Second, juxtaposing the similarities of the left and right demonstrates

---

BOX 15.5 KEY POINTS

Keep in mind that as we move from the thirteenth and sixteenth century to the present some things have changed. We can think of this change in two ways.

First, European concern shifts from a social order dominated by religious and theological matters to a secular worldview. Second, history is seen as produced by human action rather than being regarded as the result of God's will.

These shifts nevertheless retain something of the prior vision. History continues to be seen as moving towards an ever more perfect future. Most significant, the certainty that we know God's will shifts to the certainty that the modern period is the apex of progressive human history. Doubts about whether history really contains a progressive purpose or whether it has led humans inevitably towards perfection are hardly taken seriously.

Exclusive knowledge based on Christian beliefs now becomes exclusive knowledge based on European understanding of secular history. In the shift from a Christian to a secular European social order, the hold of exclusive knowledge remains firm across the centuries. Indeed, the attractions of exclusive knowledge may have become all the more powerful in their secular guise.

that the pull of exclusive knowledge reaches not only across centuries but also across ideological divides.

Reform of the British left: the Euston Manifesto

The authors of the Euston Manifesto seek to reform the left. Specifically, they wish to 'draw a line between the forces of the left who remain true to its authentic values' and those who have been 'too flexible' in the face of the forces of cultural relativism (that is, in the face of those who claim that truth or values are not universal but rather differ between cultures). Their supreme belief in modernity is evident in a first principle: 'We reject fear of modernity.' They are for democracy – the liberal pluralist variety. They 'decline to make excuses' for tyranny and they promote universal human rights for all:

> We hold the fundamental human rights codified in the Universal Declaration to be precisely universal, and binding on all states and political movements, indeed on everyone. Violations of these rights are equally to be condemned whoever is responsible for them and *regardless of cultural context*.
> (Euston Manifesto, undated; emphasis added)

Unlike Vitoria and Innocent, the Euston Manifesto does not spell out how such rights are derived. But they are universally binding, regardless of their origins. Presumably the presence of cultural variation means either that some societies have failed to learn the lessons of modern life or that they have simply rejected what is right and good.

Unlike Vitoria and Innocent, the Manifesto writers show little concern for how the powerful can use ideals as masks in order to dispossess the less powerful. This nonchalance comes through forcefully in principle 6, titled 'Opposing anti-Americanism'. They 'reject *without qualification* the anti-Americanism now infecting so much left-liberal (and some conservative) thinking' (Euston Manifesto, undated; emphasis added).

The authors of the Manifesto admit to internal disagreement on one issue – the military intervention in Iraq. They diverge on the intervention's justification, its planning and execution, and the prospects for creating a democracy in Iraq. Nevertheless, they are unified in their view over the

> reactionary, semi-fascist and murderous character of the Baathist regime in Iraq, and *we recognize its overthrow as a liberation of the Iraqi people*. We are also united in the view that, since the day on which this occurred, the proper concern of genuine liberals and members of the Left should have been the battle to put in place in Iraq a democratic political order and to rebuild the

The terms 'left' and 'right' in politics refer to a group's position on a spectrum that ranges from socialist, egalitarian, democratic policies on the left to conservative, republican or libertarian policies on the right.

Just war thinker Michael Walzer was one of the signatories of the Euston Manifesto, but he was not in favour of the war against Iraq, which he argued was unjust.

BOX 15.6 THE EUSTON MANIFESTO

This British-based group dates back to May 2005 after the general election when more than twenty met at a London pub to discuss how to differentiate their own left politics from the anti-war movement and the general state of left politics in the UK. A more formal meeting at a branch of the O'Neill's Irish-themed pub chain on London's Euston Road led to the document's first draft. The Manifesto was first published in the *New Statesman* on 7 April 2006. The first four signers of the manifesto – Norman Geras, Damian Counsell, Alan Johnson and Shalom Lappin – are believed to be the primary theorists of the manifesto.

(The Euston Manifesto, http://eustonmanifesto.org)

country's infrastructure, to create after decades of the most brutal oppression a life for Iraqis which those living in democratic countries take for granted – *rather than picking through the rubble* of the arguments over intervention.

(Euston Manifesto, undated; emphasis added)

In contrast to Vitoria's caution about turning Indian life over to Spanish administrators, these writers express no hesitation in speaking for the Iraqi people and share no misgivings about delineating Iraqi liberation. They are unconcerned about overturning the principle of sovereignty. On the contrary, despite their initial differences, they appear unified in vigorously supporting intervention as a means of promoting modernity in Iraq and elsewhere. In removing significant doubts and arguments against intervention, the Euston Manifesto goes well beyond Vitoria and Innocent IV. The authors of the Euston Manifesto somehow 'know' that modernity and liberal democracy are good for all peoples in all contexts. They 'know', therefore, what is good for the Iraqi people and for all peoples of the Third World.

The authors of the Euston Manifesto might well strongly disagree with the interpretation offered here. We encourage readers to visit their site, http://eustonmanifesto. org, to formulate their own impression.

Benevolent imperialism and the British right: Robert Cooper

If we move from the liberal left to the right, we find in Robert F. Cooper's 'The Post-Modern State' (2002) a parallel claim about doing good for others. Cooper is a British diplomat with experience in Kenya and diplomatic posts in Japan, Germany and Afghanistan. Currently he is Director-General for External and Politico-Military Affairs at the General Secretariat of the Council of the European Union. His arguments revive imperialism and colonialism. Though Cooper is not well published, his ideas have attracted the attention of academics and policy makers on both sides of the Atlantic.

BOX 15.7 IMPERIALISM AND COLONIALISM

There is much debate about the terms colonialism and imperialism. Some use the two terms interchangeably, others want to differentiate between them. Both refer to forms of domination of one group of people, or one state, over others, whether economic, military or cultural, or a combination of all three. Distinctions are sometimes drawn depending on what forms of control are in place. For example, if settlers from one country establish a base in another, that is usually referred to as a colony. Imperialism can be distant control, without settlement but including, for example, the extraction of resources and tribute or taxation. However, this distinction does not avoid overlap: for example, the British Empire, when British subjects lived in and governed vast tracts of the world – or colonized these areas – was referred to as both British imperialism and as a colonial period. The period that followed was a period of decolonization – or a period where those who had been colonized sought a return of self-determination and independence. It is useful to remember that various forms of empire pre-date or exist alongside the modern European state system – the Ottoman Empire, for example, began in 1300 and was at its height in 1683 – and that in the contemporary world some writers refer to US dominance as 'imperialism' or a form of empire. It is interesting to note that 'empires' are sometimes described as 'civilizations', and that the imperial power often sees itself as spreading 'civilization' to 'barbarians'.

FIGURE 15.6
Map of colonial powers, 1914. Source: Peter Mandaville, *Global Political Islam* (Routledge, 2007)

Cooper's use of the term 'postmodern' flouts the usual academic convention wherein 'postmodern' is understood to query if not undermine the assumptions and certainties of modernity. Instead, Cooper treats postmodernity as the last and most advanced of three civilizational stages: premodern, modern, and post-modern. Cooper holds that the postmodern is the final and full realization of modernity. The European Union, Canada, and Japan (and, with some ambiguity, the US) have overcome their 'imperial urge' and reached postmodern statehood (Cooper 2002: 12).

Much like Vitoria's Indian problem, Cooper's concern is that premodern states lack civilization. The less civilized premodern states threaten the emerging postmodern order by following the 'laws of the jungle'. His solution to this problem is that the postmodern state must practice a double standard. Inside their boundaries they can 'keep the law' of civilized society but outside they must operate according to the laws of the jungle:

> Among ourselves, we operate on the basis of laws and open cooperative security. But when dealing with more old-fashioned kinds of states outside the postmodern continent of Europe, we need to revert to the rougher methods of an earlier era – force, pre-emptive attack, deception, whatever is necessary to deal with those who still live in the nineteenth century world of 'every state for itself'.
>
> (Cooper 2002: 16)

As with Vitoria, Innocent IV, Güyük Khan, and the Manifesto writers, knowledge of the absolute truth eclipses concern for the claims of others. Instead, Cooper advocates a return to colonialism and imperialism: 'The most logical way to deal with chaos [caused by the less civilized] . . . is colonization' (Cooper 2002: 17). Civilized states, however, will find returning to an old-fashioned colonialism contrary to their values. For this reason, says Cooper, what the world needs is a benevolent imperialism 'acceptable to the world of human rights and cosmopolitan values' (Cooper 2002: 17).

Faced with a world of infidels, of non-believers in modernity, Cooper follows the tradition of the true believer. He knows that modernity is the highest stage of civilization. He knows that others do not have it and may not like it. He knows that non-believers must be forced to accept modernity for their own good and for the good of all. Nor is Cooper's an isolated argument. The tone and substance of his presentation are widespread in our time. We can find it in the work, for example, of Max Boot (2002), Eliot Cohen (2001), Niall Ferguson (2003), Michael Ignatieff (2003), Robert Kagan (2002), Robert D. Kaplan (2003). The ideology of these mostly academic writers ranges from liberal to conservative, but they all implore the United States to bear responsibility to do good for others by means of creating a benevolent imperialism. We can also perceive the theme of benevolent imperialism in the writing and policy prescriptions of the 'neo-conservatives' involved in the Project for the New American Century (http://www.newamericancentury.org/) and in the highest levels of the current US and UK administrations.

In summary, we can recognize two changes from Innocent's and Vitoria's time to ours. First, there is a shift in the features of the knowledge over which there is certainty. We move from theological convictions about God's purpose to secularized convictions about history's goal. Second, Cooper and the Euston Manifesto writers show *less* concern for the claims of those outside the faith than did Vitoria and Innocent. Nevertheless, each of the thinkers we have examined assumes exclusive knowledge. They believe their exclusive knowledge permits them to know what is good for others.

BROADER ISSUES
DIAGNOSING THE NEED FOR EXCLUSIVE KNOWLEDGE

Recall the tension and the stretch with which we started. On the one side, we feel compelled to shoulder the duty of doing good. On the other side we feel our resistance when we are made good's recipient. I said that we usually jump from one position to the other without considering these two positions simultaneously. What might we learn if we accept the responsibility of doing good for others while also retaining our suspicions? Let us tentatively accept that all humans, cultures and societies have some exclusive knowledge of the world. We may even accept that our desire to share the benefits of such knowledge need not always contain sinister motivations. For these reasons, however, we can imagine that others, whom we picture as recipients of our wisdom, may regard themselves as knowledge givers in their own right. As we envision giving them our gifts, they envision providing us with their gifts. Likewise, as we resist their generosity, they resist ours.

So far, we have assumed that we are either donors or receivers. What we have not done is consider that we are both. Are we not concurrently donors and receivers? Does not a holistic identity require that we acknowledge ourselves as both 'giver' and 'receiver'?

Vitoria, Innocent, Güyük, the Euston Manifesto and Cooper split this whole (Benjamin 1988). They take the whole that is 'giver *and* receiver of knowledge' and split it into two separate entities. They then apportion the role of 'giver' to themselves and 'receiver' to others. Further, by assuming that they have exclusive knowledge, they place the 'giver' on top as the superior being. The tragic result is that as they discharge their responsibility for giving to others, they weave into

What picture of the subject is being suggested here?
See Chapter 2

it their need to feel superior. Superiority turns responsibility towards others into charitable condescension. The tendency to claim exclusive knowledge comes, I think, from a need to claim such superiority.

But why do they and we need this sense of superiority? One answer is that we need this superiority in order to overcome the hidden doubts about the very same exclusive knowledge we espouse. Consider the proposition that no belief can be held without doubt. Doubt is belief's other and its foundation. Doubt is the dock from which the ship of belief sails. Doubt and belief are opposites but they also define each other. Exclusive knowledge – the belief that we have exclusive access to superior knowledge – goes hand in hand with the anxiety that our belief is common and ordinary. The need for superiority emerges from the doubt that perhaps we are inferior or ordinary.

Is such doubt impossible to face? Is that why claims to exclusive knowledge are so pervasive? While we may know people who are able to incorporate the hard kernel of doubt into their beliefs, nevertheless, as we saw in the examples above, holding beliefs and doubts together is difficult. Why? In harbouring doubt, we often begin to contemplate exactly what we want to avoid – our own lack (Fink 1995; Žižek 1993). We avoid that dreaded sense of incompleteness in our knowing and being. In claiming exclusive knowledge our logical rhythm goes something like this: our lack is the source of our doubt; that doubt creates within us a sense of insufficiency; to compensate for that insufficiency we project our superiority both to others and to ourselves; projecting and sustaining superiority requires us to trumpet our exclusive knowledge; this trumpeting cannot be convincing, especially to ourselves, unless others validate our claim; therefore we formulate a mission to convert others to our beliefs. Converting others must not be seen as a way of affirming our superiority but rather as a way of sharing our unique access to the good.

Just as we split knowledge from doubt, we split donor from receiver. A healthy self, however, may require a balanced combination of belief and doubt as well as a sensible mix of giving and receiving knowledge. An insecure self, on the other hand, holds fast to belief and casts doubt adrift. Similarly, an insecure self valorizes the donor while diminishing and cutting loose the receiver.

Remarkably, an insecure self's offerings may still produce something good. Despite the taint of superiority, those who believe that they know what is good for others may nevertheless have something good to give. The Spaniards might have had something worthy for the Indians, Innocent may have offered something of value to non-Christians, and contemporary purveyors of regime change and intervention may identify ways to improve Third World conditions.

If this is true, then why do we find ourselves resisting when others cast us in the role of good receiver? Why don't we simply accept the good they offer? We resist because we sense that the donor needs us to confirm his superiority. Receiving such goods confirms the donor's superiority and affirms our inferiority. Accepting this hierarchy is the real cost of receiving the donor's 'gift' and the crux of the problem (Mauss 2006; Sahlins 2003). From the receiver's perspective, the donor's actions seem far from a faithfully discharged duty. Instead, they seem like an offence against the integrity, self-sufficiency and freedom of the receiver. Receivers resist and rebuke donors as long as the donor's motives are tainted by claims of exclusive knowledge. In response, and compounding the tragedy, donors regard this rejection of their gift as the irrationality of lesser people. Donors seem incapable of perceiving their need for superiority; nor do they search for the deeper reasons for the receiver's rejection. The tragedy plays out in three parts: the receiver's rejection of a potential good, the donor's inability to recognize that donor motivations are tainted and the donor's misunderstanding of the receiver's rejection. Is it any wonder, then, that doing good for others has been so difficult?

Our most difficult and most important step in addressing this difficulty is recognizing the full scope of the tragedy. Can we do more? Let us return to the question raised by this chapter's title: why do some people think they know what is good for others? My answer: we emphasize what is good for others in order to avoid the pain of facing our own lack. If this is so, what happens if we start facing this lack?

If all of us have some unique knowledge of the world, we also suspect that our knowledge is incomplete. We can give and we need to receive; we are both donor and receiver. Recognizing that we are incomplete and that we need others' goods, we can change our posture towards giving. Claiming exclusive knowledge can be replaced by a stance that seeks what we may call knowledge encounters (Bitterli 1993; Geertz 1986; Greenblatt 1976, 1991; Nandy 1983, 1987; Todorov 1984; Verma 1990). The rhythm of this sequence might go like this: our lack is the source of our doubt; that doubt creates within us a sense of insufficiency; to overcome that insufficiency we announce our need to others and to ourselves; we de-emphasize the good we can offer and instead highlight our lack and need; and we search for others who present the same posture, avoiding those projecting missionary values. In sum, we search for opportunities and partners that allow mutual sharing. In this way, we can have access to others' unique knowledge and they to ours.

I am not suggesting that we can easily realign the world so that everyone participates in knowledge encounters. Just one 'exclusive knower' with a powerful mission can disrupt a formative society of 'knowledge encounterers'. Rather, I merely contrast a logical sequence that produces the tragedy of 'exclusive knowing' with a sequence that might produce 'knowledge encounters'.

At a particular moment, others may know what is best for us. However, we may justly reject such knowledge if the donor's delivery is mixed with condescension.

They might indeed know what is best for us but only we can decide to receive that knowledge and integrate it into our actions. Thinking in this way allows us to change the question. We can move from 'why do some people think they know what is best for others?' to 'how can we recognize that we are all a mix of donor and receiver?' And, to 'how do we create social institutions that help us to overcome our incompleteness?'

Are there examples of those who have moved from a posture of 'exclusive knowledge' to that of 'knowledge encounter'? Todorov discusses the case of Las Casas, in his *The Conquest of America* (1984) and Ashis Nandy contrasts the examples of Rudyard Kipling, George Orwell and Mohandas Gandhi to similar effect in *The Intimate Enemy* (1983).

Like Vitoria, Las Casas was outraged that the American Indians were being exterminated. And like Vitoria, he wanted to save the Amerindians from the conquistadors in order to convert them to Christianity. Only later in his life did Las Casas regard the Indians' religiosity as similar to his own belief in Christianity. He defended Indian religious practices by appealing to principles he took to be universal – a desire to worship and serve God. Even 'offensive' Indian religious practices became expressions of principles that underlie all religious practice. In this way, Las Casas moved away from 'exclusive knowledge'. He was unable, however, to use the religious knowledge of the Indians to inform and critique Christian conceptions. Had he done so, he would have moved to a more robust understanding of 'knowledge encounters'. Nandy's examples move us in this direction.

Nandy believes that 'exclusive knowledge' victimizes giver and receiver, both colonizer and colonized. Thus for Nandy, even though Kipling and Orwell support British imperialism they are also its victims. Both were born in India, influenced by their early years there, and sent to boarding school in England, where they were bullied into manhood. Kipling's and Orwell's responses to colonialism, however, differ somewhat. Kipling identifies with the colonizer by denying those parts of him that appreciate India. As an adult writer, he demonstrates precise and intimate knowledge of India but uses that knowledge to legitimate colonization. Orwell also knows India well. He does not identify with the bully and thereby does not celebrate India's victimization. Nor, however, does he identify with the colonized. Orwell remains a divided figure who denies the posture of exclusive knowledge but does not quite know what to do with the partial knowledge offered by his various selves.

Nandy then presents a small but important group – Sister Nivedita, Anne Besant, Mira Behn and C.F. Andrews – who are able to transform their critical knowledge into practical convictions. Andrews finds alternatives within his society's dominant knowledge in order to fight alongside others while also fighting for himself.

Is it significant that three of these four people are women?

According to Nandy, the most creative response to colonialism, however, comes from the colonized. Through his strategy of non-violence Gandhi negotiates two traditions of knowledge: by appealing to the Christian idea of turning the other cheek, he re-presents Western knowledge in terms the West can accept. This method of resisting colonialism minimizes the colonist's strong suit, namely force and domination. Gandhi also reinterprets Indian knowledge so that his appeal to non-violence appears authentically Indian. Andrews and Gandhi encounter and negotiate knowledge that aims to produce cultural transformation in both the British and the Indians. Gandhi reinterprets knowledge so that fighting for India's liberation is simultaneously fighting for Britain's liberation.

CONCLUSION

Those who believe they have exclusive knowledge also tend to believe they know what is good for others. Wishing to share their knowledge and its benefits they devise projects that fulfil their responsibility to others. The problem is that receivers of such missions tend to resist donor plans. Recipients experience such assistance as an intrusion on their self-determination and an imposition on their freedom. As important, they suspect that the donor's claim of exclusive knowledge taints donor efforts. They believe that the donor's ultimate goal is to produce a hierarchy that elevates the donor and diminishes the receiver. Meanwhile, donors perceive receiver resistance as irrational ingratitude. For receivers, in turn, donor condescension confirms that donors are threatening their dignity and equality.

Our challenge is to undo this cycle of mutual incrimination and replace it with a cycle of mutual enrichment. This change becomes possible when we move from a posture of possessing 'exclusive knowledge' to a circumstance where parties who regard themselves as both donors and receivers negotiate partial knowledge.

FURTHER READING

On 'splitting' see Benjamin's *The Bonds of Love* (1988). For more on Vitoria, see Pagden's *The Fall of Natural Man* (1982). Muldoon's *Popes, Lawyers, and Infidels* (1979) provides a context for Innocent IV's ideas. Dawson's *The Mongol Mission* (1955) frames the exchange between Innocent IV and Güyük Khan. Are there examples of those who have moved from a posture of 'exclusive knowledge' to that of 'knowledge negotiating'? Todorov discusses one such case, Las Casas, in his *The Conquest of America* (1984). And Ashis Nandy contrasts the examples of Rudyard Kipling, George Orwell and Mohandas Gandhi to similar effect in *The Intimate Enemy* (1983). On the broader context for how the idea of 'doing good for others' shapes the history and theory of international relations, see Inayatullah and Blaney's *International Relations and the Problem of Difference* (2004).

WEBSITES

The Difference Site, http://www.dif-ferance.org/index2.html.
> Doing good for others requires that we understand how others differ from us. This site is dedicated to understanding how and why difference is crucial to all aspects of life.

Project for a New American Century, http://www.newamericancentury.org/.
> Perhaps the most powerful force on the planet dedicated to doing good for others is this neo-conservative project. This site presents their arguments and the scope of their ambitions.

Charter of the United Nations, http://www.un.org/aboutun/charter/index.html.
> The Charter, like Vitoria and Innocent IV, provides arguments against intervention (chapter I), and arguments for when it is acceptable to intervene in order to do good (chapters VI and VII).

Euston Manifesto, http://eustonmanifesto.org.
> Go to this site if you want clear and concise arguments for intervening in order to promote the good.

Global Policy Forum > Empire > Humanitarian Intervention, http://www.globalpolicy.org/empire/humanint/index.htm.
> This site provides documents, articles and speeches on the debate over humanitarian interventions.

REFERENCES

Bellamy, Alex J. (2006) *Just Wars: From Cicero to Iraq*, Cambridge: Polity.

Benjamin, Jessica (1988) *The Bonds of Love: Psychoanalysis, Feminism, and the Problem of Domination*, New York: Pantheon.

Bitterli, Urs (1993) *Cultures in Conflict: Encounters Between European and Non-European Cultures, 1492–1800*, Stanford, CA: Stanford University Press.

Boot, Max (2002) *Savage Wars of Peace: Small Wars and the Rise of American Power*, New York: Basic Books.

Coates, A.J. (1997) *The Ethics of War*, Manchester: Manchester University Press.

Cohen, Eliot A. (2001) 'World War IV', *Wall Street Journal*, 20 November: A18.

Cooper, Robert F. (2002) 'The Post-Modern State', in Mark Leonard (ed.) *Re-Ordering the World*, London: Foreign Policy Centre.

Dawson, Christopher (1955) *The Mongol Mission: Narratives and Letters of the Franciscan Missionaries in Mongolia and China in the Thirteenth and Fourteenth Centuries*, New York: Sheed and Ward.

Elshtain, Jean Bethke (2003) *Just War against Terror: The Burden of American Power in a Violent World*, New York: Basic Books.

Euston Manifesto (undated) http://eustonmanifesto.org.

Ferguson, Niall (2003) 'America as Empire, Now and in the Future', *In The National Interest* 2, 29: 23 July, http://www.inthenationalinterest.com/Articles/Vol2Issue 29/Issue29Ferguson.html.

Fink, Bruce (1995) *The Lacanian Subject: Between Language and Jouissance*, Princeton, NJ: Princeton University Press.

Geertz, Clifford (1986) 'The Uses of Diversity', *Michigan Quarterly Review* 21, 1: 105–23.

Greenblatt, Stephen J. (1991) *Marvelous Possessions: The Wonder of the New World*, Chicago, IL: University of Chicago Press.

Greenblatt, Stephen J. (1976) 'Learning to Curse: Aspects of Linguistic Colonialism in the Sixteenth Century', in Fredi Chiappelli (ed.) *First Images of America: The Impact of New World on the Old, vol. 2*, Berkeley, CA: University of California Press.

Ignatieff, Michael (2003) 'The Challenge of American Imperial Power', *Naval War College Review* 56, 2: 53–63.

Inayatullah, Naeem and David Blaney (2004) *International Relations and the Problem of Difference*, New York: Routledge.

Kagan, Robert (2002) 'Power and Weakness', *Policy Review*, June/July: 3–28.

Kaplan, Robert (2003) 'Supremacy by Stealth: Ten Rules for Managing the World', *Atlantic Monthly* 292, 1: 66–83.

Mauss, Marcel (2006) *The Gift: The Form and Reason for Exchange in Archaic Societies*, London: Routledge.

Muldoon, James (1979) *Popes, Lawyers, and Infidels: The Church and the Non-Christian World 1250–1550*, Philadelphia, PA: University of Pennsylvania.

Nandy, Ashis (1987) *Traditions, Tyranny and Utopias: Essays in the Politics of Awareness*, Delhi: Oxford University Press.

Nandy, Ashis (1983) *The Intimate Enemy: Loss and Recovery of Self under Colonialism*, Delhi: Oxford University Press.

Pagden, A.R. (1982) *The Fall of Natural Man: The American Indian and the Origins of Comparative Ethnology*, Cambridge: Cambridge University Press.

Sahlins, Marshall (2003) *Stone Age Economics*, London: Routledge.

Todorov, Tzvetan (1984) *The Conquest of America: The Question of the Other*, New York: Harper and Row.

Verma, Nirmal (1990) 'India and Europe: Some Observations on Self and Other', *Kavita Asia* 1, 1: 114–44.

Vitoria, Francisco de (1991) *Political Writings*, ed. A.R. Pagden and Jeremy Lawrance, Cambridge: Cambridge University Press.

Walzer, Michael (2004) *Arguing about War*, New Haven, CT: Yale University Press.

Walzer, Michael (1992) *Just and Unjust Wars: A Moral Argument with Historical Illustrations*, 2nd edn, New York: Basic Books.

Williams, Robert A. (1990) *The American Indian in Western Legal Thought: The Discourses of Conquest*, New York: Oxford.

Žižek, Slavoj (1993) *Tarrying with the Negative: Hegel, Kant, and the Critique of Ideology*, Durham, NC: Duke University Press.

CHAPTER 16

Why does politics turn to violence?

Joanna Bourke

- ■ *The question*
  MASS KILLING AS A CULTURAL PHENOMENON

- ■ *Illustrative example*
  KILLING IN WARTIME

- ■ *Responses*
  BELLIGERENT STATES

- ■ *Broader issues*
  LANGUAGE AND MEMORY

- ■ **CONCLUSION**

THE QUESTION
MASS KILLING AS A CULTURAL PHENOMENON

Mass slaughter at the command of the state was characteristic of the twentieth century. As we approach the second decade of the twenty-first century, it shows no signs of abating. Now is the time to remind ourselves that war is not a metaphor for social crisis (the 'war on drugs') or an excuse for apocalyptic fantasies (the 'war on terror'). War is also much more than the enactment of international 'politics by other means', as the Prussian military theorist Carl von Clausewitz famously put it, through the purposeful destruction of another nation's infrastructure. Rather, war is the deliberate infliction of suffering and death on other people.

BOX 16.1 CARL VON CLAUSEWITZ

Carl von Clausewitz (1780–1831) is still regarded as a major strategic and military theorist, and his ideas continue to be both controversial and influential. His dictum that war is merely an extension of politics by other means, elaborated in his famous book *On War* (1976), has had a significant impact on thinking about war.

For a discussion of his reception over the years since he wrote, see Bassford (1994) and Heuser (2002).

FIGURE 16.1
Carl von Clausewitz. Lithograph by Franz Michaelis after a missing painting by Karl Wilhelm Wach. Source: Bildarchiv Preußischer Kulturbesitz

Steeped (as we are today) in notions of trauma and seduced by catastrophic fantasies, it is easy to forget that the question 'Why does politics turn to violence?' cannot solely be addressed through explorations of statecraft and political failings. Too often, military history reads as though combatants were only on the battlefields to die for their country and its ideologies, rather than to attempt to kill as well. What enabled (and still enables) ordinary men, and sometimes women, to kill others in military conflict? The question becomes even more urgent once we recognise that most of those combatants were not 'socialised warriors', steeped in a military ethos indoctrinated through years of study and service in professional military organisations. Rather, in the major wars of the twentieth century, most combatants were short-term volunteers or conscripts, more comfortable on the shop floor or slumped over their office desks than at the rifle range or on the battlefield. Nevertheless, killing proved remarkably easy.

Warfare in the twenty-first century is discussed in **Chapter 17**, and the question of death in war in **Chapters 1 and 20**.

According to the most conservative estimate, in the last one hundred years, 60 million men, women and children were gratuitously slaughtered in wars legitimately by the state. The perpetrators were not obviously evil; they purported to be rational people engaged in mass killing for particular ends. But their actions cast a pall over that century's history. Two forms of slaughter can be distinguished. The first type involved the large-scale slaughter of service-personnel – an occurrence greatly facilitated by modernity's uncompromising application of aircraft, artillery and explosives. The second type was the slaughter of civilians.

It was only from the 1930s that the slaughter of non-combatants surpassed that of combatants in wartime. Indeed, from 1939, civilians were the victims of choice. While only 5 per cent of deaths in the 1914–18 war were civilian deaths, 66 per cent of deaths in the 1939–45 war were civilians. It is startling to recall that in Britain prior to D-Day (June 1944) more British civilians had been killed in the Second World War than British servicemen. In the 1939–45 war, considerably more civilians than military personnel were killed in Belgium, China, France, Greece, Hungary, the Netherlands, Norway, Poland, the Soviet Union and Yugoslavia. The Holocaust is the pre-eminent instance of the wanton slaughter of non-combatants: aproximately six million Jews were killed, including around two million children. As Hitler admitted in relation to Poland (where one-third of those killed by the Germans were children), destruction was 'our primary task. The aim is not the arrival at a certain line but the annihilation of living forces'. He advised his men to 'Be merciless. Be brutal. It is necessary to proceed with maximum severity. The war is to be a war of annihilation' (Lukas 1990: 89). Although the havoc wrought by Hitler's forces was unprecedented, the Axis powers (a coalition headed by Germany, Italy and Japan that opposed the Allied Powers – France, Britain, the USSR, China and the USA – in the Second World War) were not the only ones who targeted civilians. In the European theatre, one-quarter of American bombs were dropped on the residential or commercial sectors

FIGURE 16.2
Wars, massacres and atrocities of the twentieth century: year by year death toll. Redrawn from graphic and data: Matthew White, 1998

of German cities; according to the United States Strategic Bombing Survey, this was 'almost twice the weight of bombs launched against all manufacturing targets together' (US Strategic Bombing Survey 1945: 71). Most of the victims were women. For every 100 male casualties, there were 181 female casualties in Darmstadt, 160 in Hamburg, 136 in Kassel and 122 in Nuremberg. Around one-fifth of those killed were children under the age of sixteen years and another one-fifth were over the age of sixty (Rumpf 1963: 160–1). In the Asian-Pacific theatre, the American's unilateral atomic bombing of Japan specifically targeted cities. Today, 90 per cent of victims of war are civilians. It has become impossible to understand modern culture without directing one's gaze into the abyss of mass murder. Authorised killing and gratuitous violence are no grotesque accidents – they are a cultural phenomenon, deliberately enacted.

For more on the bombing of German cities, see **Chapter 1**.

Because it targets civilians, terrorism is seen as a particularly objectionable form of violence, but many more civilians are killed in warfare.

What enabled the perpetrators to carry out these gross acts? Evil is not banal. Quite the contrary: violence had infused even the most subtle nuances of the society from which it was born. This is why mass killings could take place with remarkably little psychological trauma for the perpetrators. Afterwards, most perpetrators denied feeling responsible or guilty. This is true even in cases of atrocity and genocide. For instance, many Turks continue to deny that the Armenian genocide of 1915 took place and many Vietnam veterans remain wedded to the defence of 'it was him or me' when justifying the slaughter of

FIGURE 16.3
Hiroshima. Photo: AP/PA Photos

Have a look at the picture of children fleeing a Napalm attack in **Chapter 7**.

unarmed women and children. Prisoners accused of war crimes or crimes against humanity often protest their innocence. This disturbing fact was noted by visitors to refugee camps set up to harbour Hutus after the 1994 genocidal war in Rwanda. In the words of one journalist who described visiting a refugee camp in Goma:

> Perhaps the most disheartening of all is that most of the Hutus – despite their agony – still do not recognise that what happened to the Tutsis was a crime of enormous proportions. There is a state of collective denial by almost everyone you meet in the camps. People do not see their ordeal as self-imposed but as the fault of the Tutsis and the RPF [Rwandan Patriotic Front]: 'We are dying here because of the Tutsis and the cockroaches of the RPF who want to rule over us', said one woman, who was absolutely convinced of the correctness of killing Tutsis.
>
> (Black 1994)

History textbooks have also been influential in denying or, at the very least, understating levels of murderous belligerence. In Japan, for instance, school history textbooks seriously distort Japan's role in the war. In the resulting scandal in the early 1980s, some newspapers drew attention to the way certain phrases had been changed in the revised textbooks. For instance, the phrase 'aggression in North China' had become 'advance into North China'. A similar trend has been observed in Israeli textbooks.

Indeed, the striking thing about mass killing is that it involves almost unimaginable levels of complicity. The Turkish attack on the Armenians was planned at the highest governmental levels, as was the German management of the Holocaust. In Vietnam, official acceptance of the killing of civilians was encapsulated in such terms as 'free fire zones' and 'collateral damage'. In Rwanda, the Hutus were fairly confident of the support of their allies in France, Zaire and Egypt. Hutu perpetrators insisted that they were 'only obeying orders' when they killed. For instance, Robert Kajuga – president of the *interahamwe* militia, the group responsible for a large proportion of the murders – claimed that Hutus acted in self-defence. In his words:

The phrase 'collateral damage' is still used to describe killing that goes beyond what is intended.

> The government authorises us. We go in behind the army. We watch them and learn. . . . We have to defend our country. The government authorises us to defend ourselves by taking up clubs, machetes and whatever guns we could find.
>
> (Hilsum 1994)

Atrocious acts are nourished within political, military and civilian communities; people from all walks of life proved themselves capable of mass killing.

ILLUSTRATIVE EXAMPLE
KILLING IN WARTIME

Most accounts of killing in wartime highlight the aggression of whoever counts as enemies: 'they' killed 'us'. There is a vast literature on the violent behaviour of German and Japanese soldiers during the two world wars in English-language writings, for instance. In contrast, British and American historians have been queasy about dealing with the way what they call 'our men' slaughtered men (uniformed and not), women and children of enemy nations. What enabled British and American servicemen in the years 1914–18 and 1939–45 to kill? It should not surprise us that their languages of mass killing were drawn from the everyday clichés of life. In the diaries and letters of British and American combatants who committed acts of mass killing, there were three excuses that appeared most frequently: retribution, obedience and parallel response.

No prisoners

The first was the language of retribution. In the words of Sergeant John Henry Ewen in Bouganville: 'Our fellows wont [sic] take prisoners. I've seen them kill two or three now in cold-blood. I took a dim view of it the first time, but when you see your mates go, well I'd do it myself now' (Ewen 1944: 60). Or, as a

FIGURE 16.4
Supporting infantry walk forward up the slope into the bombardment during the First World War, the Battle of Ginchy, 9 September 1916. Photo: (Lt) Ernest Brooks. Source: Imperial War Museum

Marine put it: 'Nobody wanted to take prisoners to begin with – nobody who had had a buddy killed, which was almost everybody. And nobody wanted to go somewhere to do it – leave his living buddies to walk the prisoners back behind the lines. Why take the risk? When they first started surrendering, we shot as many as we took.' Allied soldiers had to be bribed with promises of ice-cream and time behind the lines before they could be persuaded to capture more prisoners, as opposed to immediately slaughtering everyone who tried to surrender.

We were only obeying orders

The second was the language of obedience: 'we were only obeying orders'. In the words of psychologist J.F. Brown, writing in 1942, 'the guilt connected with the individual's aggressions in war are projected onto the enemy, and the responsibility for his aggression onto the officers' (Brown 1942: 378). The efficacy of 'obeying orders' as a way of minimising emotional conflict and therefore generating the 'appropriate' response in combatants (that is, murderous aggression) was widely recognised by military instructors who laboriously insisted upon instantaneous obedience to orders so that each man might be able to 'sleep like a child and awaken refreshed – to kill and fear not' (Graham 1919: 3). The unfortunate consequence – that officers would experience more 'collective guilt' about the war than privates – was only rarely commented upon. By 'obeying orders', killing could be reconceptualised as something other than murder.

Thus one of the more notorious examples of the dilemma of 'only obeying orders' took place at a time when combatants *were* under order to obey orders: the July 1943 massacre in Biscari, when American troops of the 45th Infantry Division's 180th Infantry Regiment slaughtered around 70 Italian and German prisoners of war. Captain John C. Compton was one of the men eventually charged with this war crime, but he based his defence on the grounds that Lieutenant General George S. Patton had ordered them to kill prisoners. Evidence was presented, showing, that prior to battle, Patton had addressed the officers in the following way:

> When we land against the enemy, don't forget to hit him and hit him hard. We will bring the fight home to him. When we meet the enemy, we will kill him. We will show him no mercy. He has killed thousands of your comrades, and he must die. If you company officers in leading your men against the enemy find him shouting at you and, when you get within two-hundred yards of him, and he wishes to surrender, oh no! That bastard will die! You will kill him. Stick him between the third and fourth ribs. You will tell your men that. You must have the killer instinct. Tell them to stick him. He can do no good then. Stick them in the liver. We will get the name of killers and killers are immortal.
>
> (Weingartner 1989: 37)

The court accepted Captain Compton's defence and he was acquitted. His co-defendant was less fortunate. Instead of basing his defence on 'obeying orders', he claimed temporary insanity, tiredness and stress. He was sentenced to life imprisonment, and was eventually released after six months imprisonment only on condition that he never spoke about the incident.

What is crucial to understand is that the defence of 'obeying orders' is widely accepted, and not just by serving military personnel in wartime. In particular, this has been demonstrated in two specific contexts: one, a controlled experiment carried out by social psychologist Stanley Milgram about how much pain people would be willing to inflict if ordered to do so by a recognised authority (see Box 16.2 on p. 378) and, two, through questioning people about their beliefs about what they deemed acceptable in the stress of battle. Psychologists Herbert C. Kelman and Lee H. Lawrence were impressed by Milgram's research, but their investigations into aggression were based on a more straightforward method-ology. They simply asked people how they *imagined* they would behave under certain wartime circumstances. To make the question clearer, they presented their subjects with a hypothetical situation in which soldiers in Vietnam were asked to shoot all the inhabitants of a village, including old men, women and children. Sixty-seven per cent of the respondents said that most people would follow orders and shoot, while only 19 per cent said that most people would refuse to shoot. When they were asked 'What would *you* do in this situation?', slightly more than half said that they would shoot and one-third said that they would refuse to shoot. The researchers were particularly struck by this latter response:

> Since it was a hypothetical question, it would have been easy enough for respondents to give themselves the benefit of the doubt and to say that they would refuse to shoot. But the important point . . . is that for many people it is not at all clear that this is the socially desirable response.
>
> (Kelman and Lawrence 1972: 194)

In other words, a majority of respondents felt that the desirable response was to follow orders. These respondents were 'not necessarily admitting to moral weakness; for many of them, in fact, this response represent[ed] what they would view as their moral obligation' (Kelman and Lawrence 1972: 194).

It was either him or me

The third rationale for mass killing (parallel response) was even more prevalent than 'just obeying orders'. If there was one persistent explanation for killing in wartime it was the notion that 'it was either him or me'. War was about 'kill or be killed'. As sociologist Neil J. Smelser pointed out in his study of the determinants of destructive behaviour, 'one of the most profound aspects of evil

US and UK forces have been accused of abusing Iraqi prisoners, in particular at Abu Ghraib prison.
See Chapter 2
Some of them have argued at their courts martial that they were only following orders.

Why we obey is the subject of
Chapter 6.

BOX 16.2 MILGRAM EXPERIMENT

Milgram, a young and ambitious social psychologist at Yale University in the 1960s, was able to show how aggression could be induced in humans. Participants were told that his experiment was to observe the effect of punishment on memory, but actually Milgram wanted to discover what level of electric shock people would be willing to administer to another person when ordered to do so by the experimenter. The male subjects were given the task of teaching another person (who was, unknown to them, an actor) a list of paired associations. They were told to administer an electric shock when an incorrect answer was given. On each error, they were to increase the intensity of electric shock. To Milgram's amazement, some experimenters continued administering the strongest electric shocks, despite being able to hear the intense pain they were apparently causing. Importantly, the men were much more willing to obey the order to hurt the other person when an authority figure (particularly from the prestigious Yale University) was in the room than when he was not present (Milgram 1974). Hiding behind the notion that they were 'only obeying orders', their inhibitions to causing pain petered out.

The teacher is shown how to use the electronic shock apparatus

The teacher helps to strap the learner into the chair and helps place the electrodes

The shock generator showing the switched ranging from 15 to 400 volts

The teacher settles down to begin the experiment; calm and relaxed

FIGURE 16.5
Milgram experiment. From the film *Obedience* © 1968 by Stanley Milgram, © renewed 1993 by Alexandra Milgram and distributed by Penn State, Media Sales

is that he who does the evil is typically convinced that evil is about to be done to him' (Smelser 1971: 17). Repeatedly, men reiterated that their choice was to slay or be slain. As the dedicated killer Sydney Lockwood dryly commented after knocking a German's head off: it 'was not nice but one of us had to die that night' (Lockwood, undated: 10). The sniper Victor Ricketts agreed, admitting:

> It's not too pleasant to have a fellow human in one's sights, with such clarity as to be almost able to see the colour of his eyes, and to have the knowledge that in a matter of seconds, another life has met an untimely end. However, one had to be callous, after all it was, an eye for an eye, a tooth for a tooth.

He then added, 'anyway, it could very well have been in reverse' (Ricketts, undated: 34). Like the other two rationalisations, this one is also entirely unconvincing: long-distance artillery, aerial bombardment, sniping, orders not to take prisoners, and unequal opponents were the norm, not the exception, in modern warfare.

Of course, men and women in wartime were able to glibly recite these rationalisations for wartime killing because of the immense power of the military and the prevalence of martial images within society. Long before any declaration of war, combat art and literature, battle films and war games attracted people to the killing fields. It is not difficult to see the attraction of such representations of war. Everything, and everyone, appeared as nobler and more exotic than everyday environments and encounters. Propaganda depicted the glorious flesh of the imagination: the stoic face of the soldier, the chiselled features of airmen, the muscular bulk of sailors and the fertile curves of mothers, creators of life in the midst of terrible carnage. These representations of gender in war inspired military fervour. Despite the understandable emphasis that many historians have placed on the literature of disillusionment arising out of the ashes of war (see Fussell 1975), the heroic mode has never disappeared. Once our gaze is turned from a narrow canon represented by writers such as Wilfred Owen, Siegfried Sassoon and Edmund Blunden, stock phrases in a glamorous 'high diction' (baptisms of fire, transfigured youth and gallant warriors) emerges as the dominant grammar of war (Bogacz 1986: 643–68). Although such narratives might not directly stimulate enaction, they generate an imaginary arena crowded with murderous potential and provide a linguistic structure or language within which aggressive behaviour might legitimately be fantasised.

Chapter 7 discusses war films and their impact on how we imagine war.

Indeed, emotional and psychological survival in modern warfare depended upon combatants being able to justify their actions to their consciences. The difficulties many combatants experienced in coming to terms with the fact of having killed another human being led some influential officers – including one of the most influential military commentators, S. L. A. Marshall, author of *Men against Fire* (1947) – to argue that 'fear of killing' was actually a more common cause of battle

FIGURE 16.6
US Army trainees practice hand-to-hand combat using pugil sticks during basic combat training at Fort Jackson, South Carolina. Photo: by Air Force Staff Sgt Stacy Pearsall. Courtesy of US Army

Can you imagine killing in war?

fatigue than 'fear of dying' (Marshall 1947: 78). Men grieved for the men they killed as well as for those they fought alongside. After all, they not only *took* souvenirs from their dead victims, they *placed* their own symbols (such as photographs or handkerchiefs) on them (Bourke 1999a).

Eagerness to kill

It could be argued that survival depended upon more than simply 'making sense' of violence or a blunt resilience of imagination – it also relied upon the ability of combatants to forge some degree of pleasure from the world around them. In the field, many ordinary service personnel found that they could enjoy acts of extreme violence against other people. Combatants were often unabashed about their eagerness to kill. Without the threat of *being* killed, killing was even more fun. The Australian William Nagle described killing German paratroopers who were trapped inside their planes on Crete. 'Not one man jumped from any of the planes that I fired at', he observed, admitting that he

> had a feeling of complete exhilaration, full of the hate to kill. I wanted to go on and on. I used up all twenty-four magazines quickly and the rest of the

section were filling the empty ones as fast as I emptied them. I could have kissed the bren [light machine gun] with sheer delight but it was too dammed hot to touch.

(Nagle, undated: 7)

Under what circumstances could men like Nagle feel that killing was exciting, exhilarating even? Clearly the 'outcome' was important. In the aftermath of battle, men were less liable to recall their sense of glee if it was clear that they were on the losing side. Unquestionably, the ultimate failure to protect one's comrades placed a powerful dampener on celebrations and giddy bragging. Even amongst the victors, however, excitement varied according to the branch of service. Airforce personnel were most liable to express pleasure in combat. According to one American survey conducted during the Second World War, three-quarters of combat aircrew expressed a willingness to perform further combat duty, compared with only two-fifths of combat infantrymen. The more 'personal' the fight, the more combat air crew enjoyed their job. Thus, when American aerial combat personnel were asked during the Second World War, 'if you were doing it over again, do you think you would choose to sign up for combat flying', 93 per cent of fighter pilots, 91 per cent of pilots of light bombers, 81 per cent of pilots of medium bombers and 70 per cent of heavy bomber pilots replied, 'Yes' (Stouffer 1949: 333–5). Roderick Chrisholm was a night fighter in the Royal Air Force during the Second World War. On 13 March 1941, he destroyed two enemy aircraft. The experience, he wrote, could 'never be equalled':

> For the rest of that night it was impossible to sleep; there was nothing else I could talk about for days after; there was nothing else I could think about for weeks after . . . it was sweet and very intoxicating.
>
> (Chrisholm 1953: 71)

Equally, the Spitfire pilot Flight-Lieutenant D.M. Crook described the 'moments just before the clash' as 'the most gloriously exciting moments of life'. He was 'absolutely fascinated' by the sight of a plane going down and could not pull his eyes away from the sight. The day after shooting down his first plane, he bragged about it to his wife (readers are told that 'she was delighted') and 'with considerable pride' also informed his family of his success (Crook 1942: 28–31, 75). The fact that the slaughter of fellow human beings could elicit feelings of satisfaction and pleasure was the dirty secret that dared not be uttered if combatants were to settle back into their calm civilian lives, after the war.

This is not to deny widespread disillusionment in war – simply to note that, by the time disillusionment came, it was already too late: the slaughter had already begun. Men who failed to translate their battle experiences into a positive narrative of personal transformation or rite of passage simply went mad. Time and again, we hear the broken voices of combatants who could not 'take it' any

Do you think it matters for these responses that fighter pilots were largely men?

more. These were men whose starkly emotional sentences attested to how 'the sights cannot cannot be explained in writing. Writing is not my line. No fighting either For them that wants to let them fight Because I will never like it no no never', as one stammered from his hospital bed (unnamed soldier in Scholes, undated). There are many such accounts, including more poignant descriptions of fear like the one a private sent to his mother after the Battle of the Somme, simply saying that 'It makes my head jump to think about it' (Hubbard 1916). The Second World War combatant and poet Shawn O'Leary put it best in his poem of 1941 when he wrote:

> And I—
> I mow and gibber like an ape.
> But what can I say, what do?—
> There is no saying and no doing.
>
> (O'Leary 1941: 20)

Or, as another terrorised private who spent time in a military mental hospital put it, 'I admit I am a coward. A bloody, bleeding coward, and I want to be a live Coward [rather] than a dead blasted Hero' (Bourke 1999b: 32).

RESPONSES
BELLIGERENT STATES

For more on explanations of war that revolve around states and their interests, see Chapter 17.

In direct contradiction to the thrust of the chapter thus far, wartime violence is frequently abstracted from the people on the battlefield, centring instead upon the nation-state. Any analysis of wartime violence must acknowledge that war is not declared by citizens or soldiers, but by politicians. War only takes place if a nation's leaders decide either that there will be significant benefits accruing to victory over a (real or imagined) rival or if they see themselves (in reality or potentially) as threatened by an already antagonistic foe.

Of course, this is too simplistic. Experts proffer a vast array of reasons why states become belligerent. Competing explanations can be illustrated by examining the most momentous war of the twentieth century: the Second World War. More has been written about this war than any conflict before or since, yet no one agrees on its origins.

Economics

When examining the European dimension to that war, many historians trace its origins to 1914–18, implying that there was a 'Thirty Years War' of the twentieth century. In particular, imposing the humiliating Treaty of Versailles (which forced Germany to admit war guilt and stripped the country of territory) on the Germans in 1919 and forcing the Germans to mortgage their economy with an outlandish reparations bill, set up a marker for another major conflict. As A.J.P. Taylor famously phrased it in his *Origins of the Second World War*, 'Powers will be Powers' (Taylor 1974: 278–9). In other words, it was inevitable that Germany would seek to regain what it regarded as its rightful place in the world again.

There was an economic imperative for war, as well. In Germany, the Treaty of Versailles had been followed by rampant inflation and then, after a brief breathing space, by a severe economic depression. By 1938, however, under the Nazis, the economic outlook in Germany had changed. The economic recovery fuelled the sense of injustice that had arisen in the aftermath of the First World War. The strength of the German economy had resulted in a balance of payments crisis caused largely by the need to pay for the dramatic increase in imports of food and raw material. Industry and rearmament required ever more resources – and Hitler's regime was increasingly looking outside Germany to meet these needs.

Territorial ambitions

Furthermore, defeat in the First World War had failed to remove Germany's eastward ambitions. Adolf Hitler successfully played upon this national obsession. In this sense, Hitler's policy was fundamentally one of continuity with those of German politicians prior to 1918 and during the Weimar period of 1919–33. When Hitler came to power in 1933, National Socialism seemed to hold out the promise of a revived Germanic nation. Hitler did not invent many of the ideas that led to war. His promotion of the supposed need for *Lebensraum* (or 'living space') can be traced back to the nineteenth century and his racist Social Darwinism was widely accepted by the early twentieth century in Germany. Finally, although Hitler's pathological hatred of the Jews is unquestioned (in his book *Mein Kampf* he called them sub-humans, a cancer that had to be removed), the belief that Jews were responsible for all of Germany's ills – and particularly its fate during the First World War – was widely held by many Germans, on the hard and soft right, and originated in the rise of racial anti-semitism.

Beliefs that the distinctions between different 'races' were biological were widely held at one time. See Chapter 4

An evil leader

This emphasis on the ways Hitler epitomised wider concerns within German society in the 1930s can easily lead to a crude reductionism that employs a very simple equation: no Hitler, no war. It cannot be disputed that Hitler was a domineering political personality in Germany. It is difficult to imagine the Third Reich without him. He possessed a fanatical will and was at the same time an unprincipled opportunist. His desire to gain *Lebensraum* for his 'Aryan race' in Eastern Europe was wholehearted. The borders of 1914 were no longer enough, as he wrote in *Mein Kampf*:

> To demand the borders of 1914 is political nonsense of such a degree and consequence that it appears a crime. . . . The borders of 1914 meant nothing to the German nation. . . . We National Socialists, by contrast, must without wavering keep to our foreign policy aim, which is to secure to the German nation the soil and space to which it is entitled on this earth.
>
> (Remak 1976: 23)

Nor is there disagreement about his willingness to impose his will upon all his subordinates. When any of his subordinates, like his first Foreign Minister, Konstantin von Neurath, seemed reluctant to follow his lead into war, they were replaced.

However, it is far too easy to be carried away by this image of the ultimate in human evil. Indeed, this image of Hitler is largely a construction of Nazi as well as Allied propaganda. It is misleading to place too much emphasis upon Hitler as a cause of the war – whether as a personality in his own right or as someone who managed to epitomise wider and more entrenched national desires and ideologies. Much evidence suggests that Hitler had no coherent plan. Certainly, he was willing to risk millions of his own people in the pursuit of a racially 'pure', rejuvenated Greater Germany. But he was more likely to simply take advantage of things as they happened, rather than working to a pre-planned strategy. Too much of the explanation for the origins of war has been placed on Hitler's lust for domination, and not enough on the expansionist ideology of Nazism.

Competing political ideologies

Chapter 5 has more on ideologies.

However, if focusing on Hitler is a form of reductionism, so too is an excessive emphasis on ideology. Some historians want to claim that the war grew out of a conflict of competing ideologies. Totalitarianism in Germany, Italy and Japan faced up to the liberal democracies of Britain, France and the United States. According to this argument, the Axis countries – and Germany in particular – failed to develop a strong liberal-democratic tradition. In other words, the problem was not Hitler but Germany. Hitler's anti-semitism, virulent nationalism and anti-socialism were simply more extreme than those shared by earlier German leaders and 'ordinary Germans'. This explanation is also unsatisfactory. The problem with blaming 'fascism' is that it fails to differentiate between the very different forms of this political ideology. Italian fascism was very distinct from National Socialism, and neither resembles Japanese totalitarianism.

Strategic concerns

Finally, the origins of the war may also be traced to strategic concerns. War was inevitable if the territorial ambitions of certain nations were to have any hope of being achieved. Germany and Italy believed that they had something to gain from war. Hitler's plan vastly to expand the amount of land available for exploitation by the Aryan race in Eastern Europe has already been mentioned. The Italian dictator Benito Mussolini also pursued a foreign policy that was concerned with the supposed need for *spazio vitale* (again, 'living space') for Italians in North Africa and the Middle East. Mussolini's willingness to act upon this need was clearly signalled in October 1935, when Italian troops from neighbouring Italian Somiland and Eritrea invaded Abyssinia (modern-day Ethiopia). A year later, Italy and Germany militarily supported General Francisco Franco, the fascist dictator in Spain. Franco's victory in 1939 was a major economic as well as political coup for both powers. Spain's iron ore, tin, copper, zinc and mercury were henceforth at their service. Mussolini also had ambitions to establish Italy as one of the Great Powers. Thus, when Mussolini signed the Pact of Steel with Hitler in May 1939 (which committed Italy to support Germany with 'all its military forces on land, sea, and in the air' and Germany to do likewise), he signalled his desire dramatically to extend Italy's 'Roman' empire.

Strategically, the origin of the war was more complex for the Soviet Union. At first, Joseph Stalin pursued a defensive foreign policy. The Soviet–Nazi Non-Aggression Pact of August 1939 decreed that Russia would remain neutral should Germany attack Poland. For Stalin, it was an attempt to protect the Soviet Union from German aggression. Stalin signed the Pact only after his attempts to find agreement with Britain and France were rebuffed. The Pact came as a surprise to the other Great Powers. After all, Hitler regarded the Russians as the 'scum of the earth', while Stalin viewed Hitler as the 'bloody assassin of the workers'. Whatever Stalin's long-term plans involved, it is clear that Hitler always intended the Pact to be a short-term strategy. In the words of the German ambassador to Italy, Ulrich von Hassell, in his diary of 29 August 1939:

> About the Russian pact Hitler said that he was in no wise altering his fundamental anti-bolshevist policies; one had to use Beelzebub to drive away the devil; all means were justified in dealing with the Soviets, even such a pact as this. This was a typical example of his conception of 'Realpolitik'.
>
> (Schweller 1998: 139)

However, in the short term at least, the Pact proffered a great prize to the Soviet Union. The Pact had a secret clause dividing Poland between Germany and the Soviet Union. Stalin clearly understood that the Soviet Union needed to protect itself – and one way Stalin conceived of doing this was by creating a buffer zone. Until Hitler turned on him, Stalin also believed that the USSR had something to gain by belligerence.

FIGURE 16.7
Soviet soldiers raise the red flag over the Reichstag in Berlin on 2 May 1945. Photo:
AP Photo/ITAR-TASS, Yevgeny Khaldei

Are the explanations of
economic reasons,
territorial ambitions, evil
leaders, competing
political ideologies and
strategic concerns still
used to make sense of
contemporary wars?
Which, if any, of these
persuade you most?
Does it depend which
war you are thinking of?

As this brief summary suggests, therefore, historians and political scientists have
given a number of strategic, economic and defensive reasons for why political
leaders committed modern nations to war, including national pride, the need for
economic growth, territorial ambitions, bellicose leaders and warlike ideologies.
The relative weight given to each of these factors depends on the ideological stance
of the analyst as much as any objective reality. The larger question embracing
these, though, is straightforward: how, not why, is violence made possible by social
context?

BROADER ISSUES
LANGUAGE AND MEMORY

Whatever perspective is adopted, wartime killing can never be separated from social
relations more broadly. As we have seen, state authorities initiate processes which
lead to declarations of war. For those doing the fighting, emotions such as fear,

rage and exhilaration, as well as the belief in the need to 'obey orders', were some of the factors that enabled them to be converted into 'effective military personnel' after only perfunctory military training. We have also addressed to some extent the ways language has been used to prepare, facilitate and then rationalise murderous violence in wartime. Some commentators have taken this point further, observing that, in the face of mass killing, language itself was perverted. Words no longer served as bridges, but as bombs. Terror became possible, not through mechanisms of mass organisation but through the *prevention* of affiliations, including linguistic ones. Syntax, grammar and figures of speech were distorted and ritualised. The distinction between 'what is' and 'what ought to be' fractured. With mass killing, language became divorced from experience. A separation of 'act' from 'idea' took place.

Chapters 1 and 7 discuss emotional reactions to accounts of wartime deaths.

Chapter 2 argues that certain ways of using language can help enable torture.

Language of technology

One example might be found by exploring the way technology not only increased the distance between perpetrator and victim, thus bringing into play psychological mechanisms of dehumanisation, but also provided a substitute language with which death could be spoken about. In 1945, sociologist Edward McDonald admitted as much when he witnessed that 'keen discussions' developed between servicemen about the 'rival merits of particular weapons'. These discussions

Chapter 17 explores how technological developments have changed warfare.

> become so involved with physics and ballistics that the participants neglect to realize that the weapon is used to facilitate death. A discussion on the most efficient ways of killing the enemy is not pleasant; however, a technological debate on the range and characteristics of a certain calibre rifle can be challenging and impersonal.
>
> (McDonald 1945: 445–50)

Or, as an American bomb technician admitted in the context of the Vietnam War, 'I don't *feel* like a war criminal. What I was doing is just like screwing fuses into sockets' (Lifton 1974: 347).

Euphemism

Technological languages were only one aspect of the way language was perverted in wartimes. Even more frequently, euphemistic languages were used to deny the experience of meting out death. Thus, for the Turks in 1915, the Armenians were 'suspects' who needed 'resettlement'. The 'deportation' of women, children and the elderly was necessary for 'the restoration of order in the war zone by military measures, rendered necessary by the connivance of the inhabitants with the enemy, treachery and armed support' (Mazian 1990: 78). In other contexts, killing was reconceptualised as 'action', 'severe measures', 'reprisal action', 'rendering harmless', 'evacuating' or 'giving special treatment'. 'Our' boys fought an honourable war 'against fascism' (as opposed to against other humans, many of whom – children, for instance – had an only tenuous attachment to fascism). Even the slaughter of prisoners of war or the wounded – illegal according to military regulation as well as international law – was not 'really' a crime. In the words of one officer commenting on the widespread killing of wounded Japanese, there were 'many grey areas around the Geneva Convention, I suppose' (Fraser 1992: 118). In other words, in the heat of battle, atrocious behaviour easily became an integral part of warfare.

Racist language

In the margin: For more on racism and its impact on global politics, see **Chapters 4 and 8**.

In the modern period, the most trenchant language employed in the task of mass murder was racism. Again, the terrifying application of racist languages occurred long before any killing machines were mobilised. In his classic *War without Mercy* (1986), historian John W. Dower exposed the extent to which linguistic characterisations of the enemy as the ultimate racial 'other' enabled British and American servicemen to act with unsurpassed violence against their Japanese foe. For many British, American and Australian servicemen and women, the Japanese were a brutish population and Allied troops were engaged in exterminating 'slant-eyed gophers' (in Admiral William F. Halsey's words) (Cameron 1994: 1). Equally, in Japan, long-standing derogatory caricatures of the enemy had a similar effect (Dower 1986). Anglo-Americans were described as demons (*oni*), devils (*kichiku*), fiends (*akki and akuma*) and monsters (*kaibutsu*). They also expressed virulent hatred of the Chinese. Shirō Azuma, for instance, was a Japanese soldier who participated in the murders and rapes in Nanjing (China) in 1937. He recalled:

> While the women were fucked, they were considered human, but when we killed them, they were just pigs. We felt no shame about it. No guilt. If we had, we couldn't have done it. When we entered a village, the first thing we'd do was steal food, then we'd take the women and rape them, and finally we'd kill all the men, women, and children to make sure they couldn't slip away and tell the Chinese troops where we were. Otherwise, we wouldn't have been able to sleep at night.
>
> (Schmidt 2000: 87)

In every war, it was important to encourage the fiction that the people being killed were not 'really' human. The Turks had a word for the Armenians: 'dog-food'. Dr Mehmed Resid, Governor of Diyarbekir in 1915 and nicknamed the 'Executioner Governor' in honour of the numerous tortures and murders he oversaw, said:

> Even though I am a physician, I cannot ignore my nationhood. I came into this world a Turk. . . . Armenian traitors had found a niche for themselves in the bosom of the fatherland; they were dangerous microbes. Isn't it the duty of a doctor to destroy these microbes?
>
> (Dadrian 1986: 175)

Nearly eighty years later, in Rwanda, Tutsis were described as 'cockroaches', with the Hutus simply engaged in 'bush-clearing'. Hutus were ordered to 'remove tall weeds' (adults) as well as the 'shoots' (children). Today, in the war in Iraq and Afghanistan, dehumanisation is equally important. As Abu Ghraib prisoner Nori Samir Gunbar Al-Yasseri put it, the American guards

Chapters 4 and 15 examine how others sometimes come to be considered not fully human.

> stripped us naked as a newborn baby. Then they ordered us to hold our penises and stroke it. . . . They started to take photographs as if it was a porn movie. And they treated us like animals not humans. . . . No one showed us mercy. Nothing but cursing and beating. Then they started to write words on our buttocks, which we didn't know what it means. After that they left us for the next two days naked with no clothes, with no mattress, as if we were dogs.
>
> (Danner 2005: 228)

For more on Abu Ghraib, see Chapter 2.

In war, the threshold of the human soars. Large groups of humans are relegated to the level of beasts.

Collective memories

Finally, the link between politics and murderous violence in wartime is generally swept under the carpet after the conflict. War does not begin with the declaration of hostilities, nor does it end with the signing of treaties.

BOX 16.3 WAR AND COLLECTIVE MEMORY

Maurice Halbwachs in *Collective Memory* (1980) and Frances Amelia Yates in *The Art of Memory* (1966) remind historians that it is crucial to examine the ways in which war is 'remembered' by groups, even nations. As historians Jay Winter and Emmanuel Sivan insist, memory is the 'socially-framed property of individuals (or groups of individuals) coming together to share memories of particular events, of time past'. Collective memory is 'the process by which individuals interact socially to articulate their memories' (Winter and Sivan 1999: 6).

Chapter 10 examines counter-memories: in this case stories that challenge dominant narratives of national identity.

The emphasis on the politics of remembrance is crucial: memory itself is a battlefield. After all, national identity and honour depended upon the recitation of selective histories. At times, it required outright denial. This was never more the case than in the context of the Holocaust. As Heinrich Himmler vowed in October 1943, the destruction of the Jews was to be 'an unwritten and never to be written page of glory in our history'. This was one of the reasons why the Nazis built most of the camps in isolated areas and when faced with discovery attempted to hide the evidence, by ploughing over Treblinka and destroying the gas chambers at Auschwitz, for instance.

Blatant denial of violence was a blunt instrument of power, however. More effectively, social and political elites espoused alternative recitals of the past. Accounts of Germans who fought in the International Brigades in Spain between 1936 and 1939, for instance, were employed within East Germany (GDR) to forge a myth of national identity that could be distinguished from that of the West. According to the GDR, their state was portrayed as the heir to the democratic tradition of active resistance as represented by the Brigade. In contrast, West Germany was the heir to Hitler's reactionary Condor Legion. This process of

BOX 16.4 THE BRONZE SOLDIER

The 'Bronze Soldier', a monument depicting 'a Red Army fighter lowering his head in honour of comrades who had fallen during the liberation of Tallinn from Nazi occupation in 1944' (Pettai 2007: 947), has proved a controversial 'site of memory'. 'For years, the memorial had served as a gathering place for mostly Russian Red Army veterans on 9 May (or "Victory Day", as it was known in the Soviet Union). For many Estonians, however, the statue was seen as a hurtful symbol of the Soviet occupation of Estonia and they wanted it removed' (Pettai 2007: 947). After serious protests and counter-protests, 'two special laws were passed [which allowed the government] to remove the monument amid large-scale Russian protests and street violence' (Pettai 2007: 947–8) in April 2007. The statue was moved from its town-centre location to a military cemetery.

FIGURE 16.8
The 'Bronze Soldier', a Soviet soldier inscribed 'To the fallen of the Second World War' in Tallinn, Estonia. Photo: Getty Images

creating a socialist, anti-fascist 'memory' of nationhood was not a benign exercise. After all, it meant sidelining Jewish victims of the Holocaust in the interest of glorifying the active resisters of the Brigadiers and the valour of Soviet soldiers and Communist resisters.

In West Germany too, a collective memory of the Second World War was developed that entailed the creation of a new hierarchy of victims and heroes. Nazi crimes were created 'in the name of' the Germans, as opposed to 'by' Germans. War memorials were built, but sometimes existed alongside Nazi monuments and museums. Nazis who were released after serving their prison terms portrayed themselves as victims of 'victors' justice'. More generally, many Germans promoted an image of themselves as hapless victims. Instead of focusing on German crimes, emphasis was placed on the expulsion of eleven million Germans from Eastern and Central Europe and the many thousands of German POWs (prisoners of war) who died at Soviet hands or who remained in captivity well into the 1950s. Political complicity in such denial was high. Thus, in 1949, the West German Federal Parliament passed legislation that effectively protected from prosecution 800,000 people who had participated in war crimes. Two years later, former civil servants of the Third Reich who had been barred from state service were readmitted. Politically, 'forgetfulness' was pursued. Chillingly, in 1949, nearly 60 per cent of Germans subscribed to the view that National Socialism had been 'a good idea badly carried out', while over 40 per cent still insisted that there was 'more good than evil in Nazism'. It was to be some decades before this national script changed.

Other participating countries were even more reluctant to face their past. In Italy, the fascist past was put to one side and the emphasis placed instead on the role of Italian partisans in resisting the German occupiers from September 1943. Although the myth of resistance was particularly strong on the political left, it was also embraced by the political right (after all, it was King Victor Emmanuel who dismissed Mussolini and declared war on Germany). Dates were equally important in the Soviet Union, where memorials were generally dedicated to the 1941–5 period, denying the Soviet–Nazi Non-Aggression Pact of 1939, the invasion of Finland and the brutal occupation of Poland. War memory in the Soviet Union remains masculine, martial and Russian, leaving little room for women, Jews or other nationalities. Similarly, in Finland, attention was focused on the Winter War of 1939–40 rather than the Continuation War of 1941–4 when the Finns were allies of the Germans. In France, too, it took many decades before the role of French people in persecuting the Jews was recognised. In a typical act of denial, a 1956 documentary called *Night and Fog*, directed by Alain Resnais, was censored by the French to cut a scene showing French police collaborating with the deportations of the Jews. In other words, France reinvented itself: the Vichy regime was cordoned off in a space set unambiguously in the past, while the resistance was elevated into a central place in everyday conceptions of national identity. It was not until 1994 that a monument to the Jewish victims of Vichy

What events in the past
are particularly
important to your
political community? Is
there debate over how to
remember them? Who
gets to decide how
memory is represented
for the community?

was built and 16 July became a 'day of remembrance'. Memory is as much about forgetting as remembering.

Axis powers and the conquered territories were not the only ones keen to manipulate the story of war. War crimes and other atrocities carried out by British and American service-personnel were also written out of the grand narrative of war. In particular, the debate about the legality and morality of the aerial bombing campaign continues to excite furious debate. The mass rapes of French and Japanese women by American, British and Australian soldiers during the Second World War are also rarely discussed. In the words of one American intelligence officer who witnessed the occupation of the German city of Krefeld:

> The behaviour of our troops, I regret to say, was nothing to brag about, particularly after they came upon cases of cognac and barrels of wine. . . . There is a tendency among the naïve or the malicious to think that only Russians loot and rape. After battle, soldiers of every country are pretty much the same, and the warriors of Democracy were no more virtuous than the troops of Communism were reported to be.
>
> (Costello 1985: 144)

As this intelligence officer was aware, euphemistic language (such as 'warriors of Democracy') was just as crucial in the formation of a collective memory as it had been in enabling men to kill in the first place. We have already noted how professional historians play a large part in the creation of collective narratives of the past. The Greek goddess Mnemosyne was not only the goddess of Memory, but the mother of History, as well. As historian Alon Confino dryly observed: 'The often-made contention that the past is constructed not as fact but as myth to serve the interest of a particular community may still sound radical to some, but it cannot (and should not) stupefy most historians' (Confino 1997: 1387). In such a way, historians are complicit in constructing a collective memory of war that elides or leaves out 'our' violence.

In *Les Formes de l'oubli* (1998), French ethnographer Marc Augé reminds us that 'forgetting is an integral part of memory itself'. Memories are 'shaped by forgetting, like the contours of the shore by the sea' (Augé 1998: 21). However, the politics of forgetting can be as morally skewed as those of remembering. In 1998, the former Chilean dictator Pinochet urged that it is 'best to remain silent and to forget. It is the only thing to do' (*Observer*, 29 November 1998). When perpetrators of violence call for the need to 'forget', we are right to be wary. As the Polish poet Zbigniew Herbert expressed it,

> Do not forget truly it is not in your power
> to forgive in the name of those betrayed at dawn.
>
> (Herbert 1977: 79)

CONCLUSION

Should we be pessimistic about a future in which violence is placed outside the realm of possibility? The frustrations resulting from imbalances of power and perceived injustices, the bellicose personalities of politicians and other leading state officials, ideological imperatives and the territorial ambitions will always be with us. Fantasies associated with war remain deeply embedded within our society. A substantial majority of people agree with the statement that 'human nature being what it is, there will always be war and conflict' (Robertson 1980: 55). They are wrong. For long periods of history, wars have been absent. Some societies are more peace-loving than others. One-half of the world's population (that is, women) have been distinctly less keen on battle than the other half.

The anxiety evoked by uncovering the past is not only inevitable, it is also essential in the process of reconciliation. The duty to remember remains strong, particularly if a nation is to move towards a better future. In this way, South Africa's Truth and Reconciliation Commission (for all its faults) has been particularly innovative because its aim was not 'forgetting' but disclosure. Because amnesty for perpetrators of atrocity was predicated upon that person providing a detailed account of their actions, it enabled full public acknowledgement of the harms done to individuals and groups within society. 'Never Forget' is the phrase that has reverberated since the Holocaust. It is at the heart of both individual and collective ways of coming to terms with violent pasts. In the words of Polish writer Czesław Miłosz, 'those who are alive receive a mandate from those who are dead and silent forever: to preserve the truth about the past' (Miłosz 1991: 281). The choice between forgetfulness and remembrance is ours.

Chapter 19 examines how we may move beyond conflict and the role that memory plays in this process.

FURTHER READING

Bartov, Omer (1996) *Murder in Our Midst: The Holocaust, Industrial Killing, and Representation*, Oxford: Oxford University Press.
Bartov reflects on the Holocaust and modernity.

Bourke, Joanna (1999) *An Intimate History of Killing: Face to Face Killing in Twentieth Century History*, London: Granta.
The book gives an overview of the ways in which British, American and Australian soldiers experienced combat.

Braudy, Leo (2003) *From Chivalry to Terrorism: War and the Changing Nature of Masculinity*, New York: Alfred A. Knopf.
Beginning in the Middle Ages and ending with twenty-first-century global terrorism, this book explores the ways in which European and American cultures have established the military ethos. Masculinity is at the heart of his explanations.

Dower, John W. (1986) *War without Mercy: Race and Power in the Pacific War*, New York: Faber and Faber.
This is the best book comparing the experiences of American and Japanese servicemen in combat.

Fussell, Paul (1990) *Wartime: Understanding and Behaviour in the Second World War*, Oxford: Oxford University Press.
This is an analysis of war psychology in the Second World War.

Hughes, Matthew and William J. Philpott (eds) (2006) *Modern Military History*, London: Palgrave Macmillan.
This is the clearest textbook introduction to modern military history.

Keegan, John (2004 [1978]) *The Face of Battle: A Study of Agincourt, Waterloo and the Somme*, London: Pimlico.
This is the classic study of battle psychology and the changing experience of combat over time.

Merridale, Catherine (2000) *Night of Stone: Death and Memory in Russia*, London: Granta Books.
This is an indispensable study of Russian experiences of war.

Overy, Richard (1999) *The Road to War*, London. Penguin Books.
This books provides a clear summary of the main arguments about the political and diplomatic origins of modern war.

REFERENCES

Augé, Marc (1998) *Les Formes de l'oubli*, Paris: Payot and Rivages.

Bassford, Christopher (1994) *Clausewitz in English: The Reception of Clausewitz in Britain and America, 1815–1945*, New York: Oxford University Press, http://www.clausewitz.com/CWZHOME/Bassford/TOC.htm.

Black, Robert (1994) 'A Week in Goma', *Independent on Sunday*, 31 July.

Bogacz, Ted (1986) '"A Tyranny of Words": Language, Poetry, and Antimodernism in the First World War', *Journal of Modern History* 58, 3: 643–68.

Bourke, Joanna (1999a) *An Intimate History of Killing: Face-to-Face Killing in Twentieth Century History*, London: Granta.

Bourke, Joanna (ed.) (1999b) *The Misfit Soldier*, Cork: Cork University Press.

Brown, J.F. (1942) 'The Theory of the Aggressive Urges and War-Time Behavior', *Journal of Social Psychology*, 15: 355–80.

Cameron, Craig M. (1994) *American Samurai: Myth, Imagination and the Conduct of Battle in the First Marine Division, 1941–1951*, Cambridge: Cambridge University Press.

Chrisholm, Roderick (1953) *Cover of Darkness*, London: Chatto and Windus.

Clausewitz, Carl von (1976) *On War*, ed. Michael Howard and Peter Paret, Princeton, NJ: Princeton University Press.

Confino, Alon (1997) 'Collective Memory and Cultural History: Problems of Method', *American Historical Review*, 102, 5: 1386–403.

Costello, John (1985) *Love, Sex and War: Changing Values 1939–45*, London: Collins.

Crook, David M. (1942) *Spitfire Pilot*, London: Faber and Faber.

Dadrian, Vahakn N. (1986) *The Role of Turkish Physicians in the World War I Genocide of Ottoman Armenians*, Oxford: Pergamon Press.

Danner, Mark (2005) *Torture and Truth: America, Abu Ghraib and the War on Terror*, London: Granta Books.

Dower, John W. (1986) *War without Mercy: Race and Power in the Pacific War*, New York: Faber and Faber.

Ewen, John Henry (1944) *Bougainville Campaign*, Australian War Memorial Archives.

Fraser, George MacDonald (1992) *Quartered Safe out Here: A Recollection of the War in Burma*, London: Harvill.

Fussell, Paul (1975) *The Great War and Modern Memory*, London: Oxford University Press.

Graham, Stephen (1919) *A Private in the Guards*, London: Macmillan and Co.

Halbwachs, Maurice (1980) *Collective Memory*, New York: Harper and Row.

Herbert, Zbigniew (1977) *Selected Poems*, Oxford: Oxford University Press.

Heuser, Beatrice (2002) *Reading Clausewitz*, London: Pimlico.

Hilsum, Lindset (1994) 'Hutu Warlord Defends Child Murder', *Observer*, 3 July.

Hubbard, Arthur H. (1916) Letters Written May–November 1916, Imperial War Museum Archives.

Kelman, Herbert C. and Lee H. Lawrence (1972) 'Assignment of Responsibility in the Case of Lt. Calley: Preliminary Report on a National Survey', *Journal of Social Issues* 28, 1: 177–212.

Lifton, Robert Jay (1974) *Home from the War. Vietnam Veterans: Neither Victims nor Executioners*, London: Wildwood House.

Lockwood, Sydney W.D. (undated) **No Man's Land**, Imperial War Memorial Archives.

Lukas, Richard C. (1990) 'The Polish Experience During the Holocaust', in Michael Berenbaum (ed.) *A Mosaic of Victims: Non-Jews Persecuted and Murdered by the Nazis*, New York: New York University Press.

McDonald, Edward C. (1945) 'Social Adjustment to Militarism', *Sociology and Social Research* 29, 6: 449–57.

Marshall, Samuel Lyman Atwood (1947) *Men against Fire: The Problem of Battle Command in Future War*, Washington, DC: William Morrow and Co.

Mazian, Florence (1990) *Why Genocide? The Armenian and Jewish Experiences in Perspective*, Ames, IA: Iowa State University Press.

Milgram, Stanley (1974) *Obedience to Authority: An Experimental View*, London: Tavistock Publications.

Miłosz, Czesław (1991) *Beginning with My Streets*, New York: Farrar, Straus, and Giroux.

Nagle, William (undated) Do You Remember When? Australian War Memorial Archives.

O'Leary, Shawn (1941) 'Shell Shock', in Shawn O'Leary, *Spikenard and Bayonet: Verse of the Front Line*, Melbourne: The Author.

Pettai, Vello (2007) 'Estonia', *European Journal of Political Research* 46, 7–8: 943–8.

Remak, Joachim (1976) *The Origins of the Second World War*, Englewood Cliffs, NJ: Prentice-Hall.

Ricketts, Victor G. (undated) Account of his Service, Imperial War Memorial Archives.

Robertson, Ian (1980) *Sociology*, New York: Worth.

Rumpf, Hans (1963) *The Bombing of Germany*, trans. by Edward Fitzgerald, London: Frederick Muller.

Schmidt, David Andrew (2000) *Ianfu: The Comfort Women of the Japanese Imperial Army of the Pacific War. Broken Silence*, Lewiston, NY: Edwin Mellen Press.

Scholes, Dorothy (undated) Papers of Miss Dorothy Scholes, Wigan Archives Service.

Schweller, Randall L. (1998) *Deadly Imbalances: Tripolarity and Hitler's Strategy of World Conquest*, New York: Columbia University Press.

Smelser, Neil J. (1971) 'Some Determinants of Destructive Behavior', in Nevitt Sanford and Craig Comstock (eds) *Sanctions for Evil*, San Francisco, CA: Jossey-Bass.

Stouffer, Samuel A. (1949) *The American Soldier: Combat and Its Aftermath*, vol. II, Princeton, NJ: Princeton University Press.

Taylor, A.J.P. (1974) *Origins of the Second World War*, London: Penguin.

US Strategic Bombing Survey (1945) *Overall Report (European War)*, Washington, DC: US Government.

Weingartner, James J. (1989) 'Massacre at Biscari: Patton and an American War Crime', *The Historian* 52, 1: 24–39.

Winter, Jay and Emmanuel Sivan (1999) 'Setting the Framework', in Jay Winter and Emmanuel Sivan (eds) *War and Remembrance in the Twentieth Century*, Cambridge: Cambridge University Press.

Yates, Frances Amelia (1966) *The Art of Memory*, London: Routledge and Kegan Paul.

CHAPTER 17

What makes the world dangerous?

Michael Dillon

- ■ *The question*
  LIVING DANGEROUSLY

- ■ *Illustrative example*
  NETWORK-CENTRIC WARFARE

- ■ *Responses*
  THINKING IN TERMS OF STRATEGY AND SECURITY

- ■ *Broader issues*
  UNKNOWN UNKNOWNS

- ■ **CONCLUSION**

THE QUESTION
LIVING DANGEROUSLY

Politics and danger go together like the proverbial horse and cart. We might say that they are intimately correlated. However, we are not all threatened by the same things all of the time. We do not all express the same fears. We do not necessarily interpret danger in the same ways. Things that we feared in Europe at the beginning of the twentieth century are no longer feared now at the beginning of the twenty-first century. Near-elimination of the fear of war between the great powers of Western Europe would be one example. Despite all its failings this is the historical achievement of the European Union. Increasing fear of environmental disaster and global climate change would be another (Dalby 2002). In fact much of politics is an argument about what we do find dangerous, how we should be organised to meet the dangers we think we face and what should be done about them.

In expressing our fears one way rather than another, in prioritising certain dangers over other dangers, we become organised by those fears and dangers. If we become what we eat we also become what we fear. Fear and danger form and express our individual and collective identities. In politics we would say they help constitute our political subjectivity: who we think we are politically, what we find politically acceptable and what binds us together. To meet our fears we will endanger others; those whom we think threaten us; those who do not ally with us against the dangers we say are paramount; and, of course, most tragically of all, those who simply get in the way of the actions we take against what we think poses the most threatening danger to our lives and our ways of life.

Forms of identity and political subjectivity are discussed in **Chapter 4.**

Fear and danger are also like money. They circulate, and they do things. In fact, just like money, fear and danger can only do things when they circulate, when they course through individuals and populations motivating them to one kind of action or another. That is why politicians invest in fear and danger. Their reputations and their political capital become associated with specific fears and dangers. They manipulate and they deal in danger. Danger is therefore one of the single most important currencies of politics. Danger mobilises people, it helps direct their actions, rally support and eliminate opposition.

At the height of the Great Depression of the 1930s, when capitalist economies seemed on the brink of collapse, US President Franklin D. Roosevelt went on national radio to advise the American people that they had 'nothing to fear but

FIGURE 17.1
US President Franklin D. Roosevelt at network radio microphones. Photo: The Franklin D. Roosevelt Presidential Library and Museum

fear itself'. Fear of economic collapse had become a kind of contagion further promoting the economic problems faced by the American economy. Roosevelt had recognised that fear alone was a factor undermining confidence and that this fear had somehow to be addressed. But you cannot, of course, stop fear and danger by simply declaring them bogus. In the event only the massive political, financial and industrial challenge posed by the Second World War finally brought the US economy out of depression.

One of the additional things which this point teaches us is that fear and danger have to be communicated to circulate and do their work. Mass communication is therefore also integral to changing what people fear and how they fear it. This fundamental – I would even say foundational – correlation of politics, danger and communication changes from time to time, from place to place and from one system of communication to another. No political leader today, for example, would think of going on radio to reach a mass audience. And when they use television instead, for example, they speak and communicate in very different ways from the ways once used in political broadcasting by radio. How they communicate is very much determined by the system of communication they use (McLuhan 2001).

For a discussion of the role of the media in circulating images of war and danger, see **Chapter 7**.

I also need to make another basic point. Human beings are mortal. We know that we can be hurt and that ultimately we will die. Therefore everything, in a sense, is potentially dangerous to us. We are vulnerable creatures who suffer pain and death. We are also violent creatures who inflict pain and death. Like dying, danger is simply part of life. It is a reality, brute and inescapable. One way or another, because we live and die we live a life more or less exposed to danger. We live dangerously.

The role of pain and suffering and the pleasure sometimes taken in the infliction of pain are discussed in **Chapter 16**.

In a most basic sense, therefore, what makes the world dangerous for us is the way in which we figure and make it dangerous. Which of all the possible dangers that there are, or could be, are the ones which come to be dangerous to us and which are ignored? Which become politically mobilising and which do not? Asking such basic questions provides a foundation for engaging in a critical approach to enquiring about what makes the world dangerous. It allows us to start posing other challenging questions as well. For example, we do not simply select dangers. They do not sit on supermarket shelves waiting to be chosen. First, dangers have to be formulated. There are traditional ways of formulating dangers. Social, political, economic and religious institutions, for example, are all engaged in authorising and legitimising which dangers are to be considered more important than others. They do it through their truth-telling practices; and all their un-truth-telling practices as well. In many ways, then, we do not choose dangers at all. We inherit them. They come with our forms of life. Once upon a time, for example, smoking tobacco was widespread in our societies. Smoking was a social activity and people learned to smoke because their parents and friends

FIGURE 17.2
'Worried about chemical attacks?' Artist: Glen McDonall

smoked. But we also learned that smoking kills. We inherited a danger, a population of people addicted more or less to nicotine whose health was lethally endangered by the addiction. It has taken time, money, campaigning, political decision, legislation and, finally, knowledge to reduce the danger posed by smoking.

This teaches us another lesson about what makes the world dangerous. We have to know about dangers to make them the dangers that they are. We have to study them, find out about them, measure their intensity and extent, say how dangerous these dangers are and in what ways they are dangerous. In short, there is not only an intimate correlation between danger and politics, and between danger, politics and communication. There is an intimate correlation in our world also between danger, politics, communication and knowledge (Foucault 1988, 2001). What makes the world dangerous for us is therefore not only a question of politics and communication. It is fundamentally also a question of the techno-scientific and social-scientific truth-telling practices of knowledge: of what we know, of how we come to know it (our ways of knowing) and of how our knowledge is validated and distributed so that it becomes 'common knowledge'.

For a discussion of climate change, see Chapter 3.

All sorts of knowledge of weather patterns, of ocean currents, of the Arctic and Antarctic ice shelves and so on is involved, for example, in the analysis of the danger posed by global climate change. But that knowledge is increasingly also made common knowledge through campaigning, which popularises it. Environmental disaster consequent upon the ways in which we act in the world in pursuit of our military and economic interests is therefore now a major new way of problematising danger. Indeed, a whole new form of politics, environmental politics, has arisen out of the ways in which we endanger the world. What that means is that environmentalists call for new forms of rule which respond to the danger they say humankind now poses to the planet. But even environmentalists do not all problematise the danger of environmental disaster in the same ways.

A neat way of summarising the points made so far is to say, in the words of Michel Foucault, that what makes the world dangerous is a matter of problematisation (Foucault 2001). By that Foucault meant the translation, through all the devices to which we have referred (knowledge, communication and political power), of a crude state of affairs into a specific problem or field of problems demanding action and calling for certain solutions; in other words the problematisation of danger concerns how power gives specific form to danger. We could therefore say in answer to the question that what makes the world dangerous critically depends upon how danger comes to be problematised in specific ways by the truth-telling institutions and relations of power which constitute our societies.

For more on Foucault's thinking see **Chapters 6 and 9**. Compare this discussion of problematisation with the discussion of pictures in **Chapter 2**.

Much greater emphasis and recognition has been given in the twenty-first century, however, to how human beings become a danger to themselves (Perrow 1999). Among many other factors the massification, industrialisation and nuclearisation of warfare, together with the recognition of environmental catastrophe, brought that home to many states and societies during the course of the twentieth century. But there is an argument that goes beyond the environmentalist argument that we endanger ourselves because we endanger the environment. An argument is now regularly made instead – or in addition – that it is the very interlinked ways in which our civilisation now functions that circulates, intensifies and precipitates all sorts of new ways in which we endanger ourselves (Barabasi 2003). To the degree that we have become what is called networked societies (Castells 2000), what makes the world dangerous for us is the very close-coupled networks of global–local interchange – illustrated, for example, by the spread of disease and viruses through food chains and transportation networks – which make our societies the societies that they are.

ILLUSTRATIVE EXAMPLE
NETWORK-CENTRIC WARFARE

In the twenty-first century, those calling for peace in the name of the radical interdependence of humankind find themselves making very similar arguments about the networked character of our civilisation to those made by new military

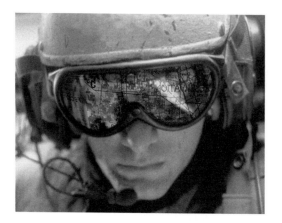

FIGURE 17.3
A reflective view of the Blue Force Tracker (BFT) networking tool. Northrop Grumman Corp

strategic theorists in the United States who have invented a new form of war called network-centric warfare (Cebrowski and Gartska 1998; Alberts *et al.* 1999). What they share is recognition of the networked character of our global civilisation and the ways in which that networking both is central to our economic and social well-being and to questions of peace and security as well as simultaneously also posing dangers to that way of life.

In the vocabulary I introduced in section 1 we can say that while sharing a networked view of global–local relations – and of the central significance of networks – they problematise our network societies differently in terms of the dangers to which our very networked character newly exposes us. In this section I want to outline how network thinking has influenced military strategic thought in particular. In the process I will also say something about contemporary formulations of danger in terms of terror and the threat posed by other civil contingencies such as social breakdown or the disruption of critical national infrastructures like power, finance, information, transportation, water, food and health systems. In both civil and military terms the information revolution, especially, has not only transformed the equipment that we use but also the ways in which we inhabit and think about the world. In terms of the transformations which this has brought to the ways in which danger and threat are now formulated we can do no better than turn our attention first to the so-called Revolution in Military Affairs which characterised the last decade of the twentieth and the first decade of the twenty-first century.

Revolution in Military Affairs

From the 1980s onwards military equipment and military strategic thinking alike began to respond to the information and communication revolution that was revolutionising industrial production and social and cultural life in the Western world (Mathews and Treddenick 2001). The claim was made that the impact of the information and communication revolution on military affairs has brought about what was first called a Military Technical Revolution (MTR) and is now more popularly referred to as a Revolution in Military Affairs (RMA). The RMA refers to two things, equipment and thinking, the second of which is I think even more important than the first.

Equipment

Informationalisation of weapon systems

First the RMA referred to the very many ways in which the information and communication revolution has transformed military equipment. In popular terms we have become familiar with guided missiles, smart bombs that find their own way to the target and the ability to fight 24/7 irrespective of weather and daylight. We now know also that to light up the enemy in electronic terms means you can destroy the enemy with near certainty. Just as weapons were revolutionised through the information revolution so also were military communication systems. These are now global and local. They critically depend upon what the

FIGURE 17.4
US Airmen with the 67th Network Warfare Wing monitor internet activity to maintain security of Air Force computer networks at Lackland Air Force Base, Texas. Photo: Master Sgt Jack Braden, courtesy of US Air Force

US military calls the global information grid, which, with the aid of communication satellites, now covers the world with a fine information net or mesh on which the coordination of large- and small-scale military operations depends (Libicki 2000).

We can summarise the impact of the information and communication revolution on military equipment in terms of what I want to call 'the informationalisation of weapon and communication systems'. The counterpart of the informationalisation of weapons has, however, also been 'the weaponisation of communication and information'.

Weaponisation of communication and information

Just as information has become critical to the performance of weapon systems and their allied command, control and communication systems, so also therefore has information become a new domain of war. Precisely because military and other systems are themselves so dependent upon information, information itself has become weaponised. Here we are not simply referring to the traditional use of information for the purposes of political and military propaganda. We are referring instead to the ways in which information systems themselves are used against other information systems, for example in that new form of war called Cyberwar. Informationalising weapons impacted also on the exercise of military command. To explore this and related changes such as those affecting operational military concepts and doctrines, as well as the training of military personnel, we have to move to the second most important feature of the RMA: changes in how the military think about the world.

Military thinking

In many respects we can say that the changes referred to above are concerned with the impact of information and communication on military equipment. The second and perhaps even more profound impact of the revolution in information and communications on the military has been a change not only in equipment but also in 'cognition'. By that I simply mean that it has changed how the military view the world. They always view the world in terms of danger. That is their profession. The question is how do they now view the world in terms of danger? The answer is that they now comprehensively view it in network terms and increasingly also through ideas, concepts and metaphors which they take from the life sciences such as biology. The impact of that shift in cognition is that they understand the emergence of danger and threats differently and according to different metaphors of how the world is constructed and how dangers arise. Here is how.

What has changed is the military's picture of the world, in the terms used in **Chapter 2.**

Network thinking

Network-centric thinking is consciously modelled on fundamental changes that have taken place in the American and in the global capitalist economy. These draw their inspiration not simply from the revolution in information and communication technology, in fact, but also from the molecular revolution in biology. What the revolution in information and communication technology shares with the revolution in biology that has occurred during the same period is a reduction of material reality to code: information code for ICT (Information and Communications Technology) and genetic code for molecular biology (Dillon 2002, 2004). Here a convergence of thinking based on the overarching idea of code fuels new ways both of doing business and of construing danger in organic and biological ways. Network has become a key term of art for both business and the military since it is also a key term of art in the communication and information as well as in the life sciences.

For example, there is an emphasis on the powers of interconnection, on the speed of interconnection and on the new opportunities thrown up by exploiting interconnectedness. There is similarly also an emphasis on metaphors which construe danger in terms of disease, and of security in terms of immunity and in terms of biological adaptation and change to anticipate and meet new dangers. Danger is in a way also seen in viral terms as something that is able to work on

---

BOX 17.1 NETWORK-CENTRIC WARFARE

FIGURE 17.5
Admiral Arthur
Cebrowski

The single most important architect of this transformation of military cognition was an American admiral, Arthur Cebrowski. It was Cebrowski who virtually invented the term 'network-centric warfare' (NCW) in a leading article published in *The United States Naval Institute Proceedings* in the 1990s. NCW became the official military doctrine of the US in 2002. Almost all the basic ideas are contained in that essay. Cebrowski then went on to head a new Office of Force Transformation (OFT) in the Pentagon, tasked with carrying this revolution in cognition throughout the American military. Championed by the then Secretary of State for Defense Donald Rumsfeld, the RMA suffered a setback with the political and military reverses of the Iraq War. However much these may have arrested the ideological fervour with which the RMA and NCW are being promoted, they have not materially affected the reorganisation of military training deployment, war-fighting and war-thinking that has been inaugurated through NCW by the RMA.

the body because of the ways in which it is also part of the body, whether the body is seen as the biological body or the corporate, social or military body. Security and war in the information age have thus begun to be thought of more in terms of epidemiology, the science of pathology and disease management, or surgical intervention. Threats arise within the system and are not merely posed from outside the system. The system itself is understood as having to develop its own auto-immune responses. Just as the individual biological body is understood in terms of complex networks of information and communication governed by genetic code, so the military body is increasingly understood in terms of complex networks of information and code as well.

Network operations are now claimed, therefore, to deliver to the US military the same powerful advantages that they produced for global capital and American businesses. Military thinking is similarly saturated with the ideas and concepts drawn from the most exciting techno-scientific developments of the age as well; the genetic and the digital revolutions. In network-centric warfare, information, speed, self-synchronisation and flexibility are said to be at a premium just as they are in the global capitalist economy. Nimbler, more efficient and adaptable, closely networked fighting forces are sought against nimbler, more efficient and adaptive, closely networked foes. This new strategy is officially characterised by four themes.

- the shift in focus from the weapons platform – the battle tank, the aircraft carrier, the strategic bomber – to the information network, as the key military unit;
- a shift from individual military actors or units to radical relationality, from viewing actors as independent operators to viewing them as part of continuously adapting military systems operating in constantly changing battlescapes;
- a tendency towards interpreting the operations of complex adaptive military systems in biological terms – like 'natural' organisms, military systems are now said to co-evolve and adapt ecologically through interaction with each other and the battlespace-as-ecosystem that they inhabit;
- the conviction that information is the prime mover in military as in every other aspect of human affairs, the basic constituent of all matter.

This elevation of information does not simply open up new enterprises for the military as it does for business – information warfare and digitised battlespaces for the military, e-commerce and so on for business. Neither does it mean that information is only a force multiplier, as the military say, increasing the firepower and effectiveness of traditional weapon systems. Information has been embraced as the new principle of formation – the 'prime mover', say two of the RAND Corporation's most prolific information and network-centric warfare theorists (Arquilla and Ronfeldt 1997) – for all military systems, initiating a wholesale rethinking of the very basis of military organisation, doctrine, force requirements, procurement policies, training and operational concepts (Dillon and Reid 2001). Military formations no longer simply rally around the flag: increasingly they are obliged to form up, mutate and change through and as information networks.

The strategic debate

Little surprise, then, that, seeking to operationalise and institutionalise the RMA, network-centric warfare became official US military strategic doctrine in May 2000 with the publication of the Pentagon's 'Joint Vision 2020'. Here the RMA was to find its first politically endorsed expression as what is best described as a new military ideology. Joint Vision 2020 commits the US to what the document calls 'Full Spectrum Dominance'. Claiming to look ahead to 2020, the document clearly also was aspiring to a military capable of perfect vision and real-time control to achieve the Information Superiority and the Full Spectrum Dominance that it set as its goal. In every respect Joint Vision 2020 expresses an imperial vision not only of military might but also of fear and danger. Because it fears everything – every virtuality as well as every actuality – the US military now aspires to a form of global control that seeks to govern both space and time. To do that it is planning for forces that are capable of continuous transformation.

For more on the problem of imperialism, see **Chapter 15**.

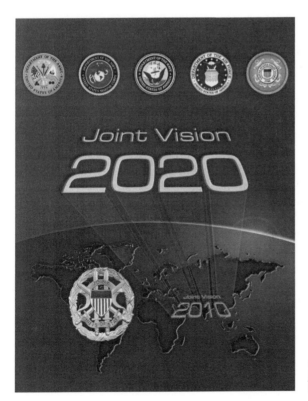

FIGURE 17.6
Joint Vision 2020, from
http://www.dtic.mil/futurejointwarfare/

Network-centric warfare nonetheless remains a controversial and contested strategic doctrine within the US strategic community. The platform specialists (aircraft carriers, main battle tanks as well as fighter and strike aircraft, for example), the individual military service advocates and the old geopolitical warriors, for whom weapon systems, states and territories remain the single most important elements of international politics, all contest its assumptions and loathe its new jargon. Perhaps there are some who also fear the imperial hubris and global overstretch into which it seems to have seduced US decision makers. That is why we are also witnessing a trial of strength between the traditionalists and the network warriors as this internal conflict proceeds, and why we will see an admixture of traditional geo-strategic and network-centric warfare. Indeed the vast expansion of the US defence budget recently announced by President Bush testifies to the continuing power of the warfare traditionalists. But it is the warfare revolutionaries who are leading the way in operations in the war on terror, especially where, despite the term 'homeland security', the distinction between inside and outside is being reformed by network ways of mapping the world in terms of fear, danger and threat (Shapiro 2007).

For more on the war on terror, see **Chapter 19.**

Many protagonists in this strategic debate also try to maintain that the revolution in information and communication technology has not caused much of a so-called Revolution in Military Affairs, or that it has done so only in the US. In one very limited sense these opponents of network-centric warfare and of the information revolution are correct. There has been no exclusive Revolution in Military Affairs. The RMA is the military face of the revolution in global affairs brought about in particular by the coincidence of the fall of the Soviet Union and the revolutionary digitalisation of information and communication technology. Suffice it to say, then, that the RMA is as much an exclusively American way of making war, as capitalism is an exclusively American way of making a living. Everybody now seems to be getting into the business of practising network-centric warfare in one form or another – not least those who orchestrated the destruction of the World Trade Center. For nothing was better designed to send such a powerful, threatening and radically disruptive message around the world's political and military communications networks than the bloody spectacle they engineered on September 11, 2001. The Western European allies of the US are also developing variants on the network theme. The United Kingdom, for example, prides itself on distinguishing the newly emergent British way of war as 'network enabled' (Farrell and Bird 2008; UK Ministry of Defence 2005). This, it says, enables British forces to fight alongside but not as American forces. Some, myself included, think this an example of 'the vanity of insignificant differences'.

The fall of the Soviet Union meant the end of the Cold War, see **Chapter 19.**

For a discussion of capitalism in the global political economy, see **Chapter 12.**

Changing landscape of warfare

Here, then, information is claimed to have become the new fundamental basis of power. With network-centric warfare and information warfare we are in the midst of a radical dissolution of the markers of certainty that gave us all our old – geopolitical and realist – bearings in relation to the problematisation of danger and the military strategic discourse of war.

Traditional forms of conquest, as well as traditional measures of national capability, land or raw materials, for example, recede in significance under the dynamics of network-centric warfare. They do not disappear. But they do become complexly related with these new discourses of threat, danger and war to form an ever more challenging landscape of militarised power relations. Territorial conquest and domination, in particular, does not explain what network-centric warfare is about, albeit traditional geo-strategic factors are still very much also in play, such as those concerning oil, for example as in the 1991 Gulf War at the end of the last century, and the conquest and occupation of Iraq at the beginning of the twenty-first century.

For a discussion of the importance of territory, see **Chapter 9**.

Network forces will not mobilise, march to the front or conduct mass frontal assaults or landings in order to defeat the enemy. Galvanised by information and intelligence garnered through the critical global infrastructures of surveillance and communication systems, it is claimed that network forces will swarm in combined arms and together with hired locals, gather and disperse in different volumes and formations, combinations and directions. So think bees. The many theatres of this network-centric warfare will also be as virtual as geographic, coursing through the capillaries and conduits that comprise network society itself.

FIGURE 17.7
Critical Infrastructures. From 'Information Technology Research for Critical Infrastructure Protection', Shankar Sastry *et al.*, summary of NSF/OSTP workshop, 19–20 September 2002

Conflict will newly configure and exploit these spaces of encounter: re-routing, re-regulating and re-engineering them. The duration of hostilities threatens to be just as indeterminate as the new battlespace. War – the war on terror in particular – thus threatens to become infinite, while danger is seen in every aspect of our networked world (Reid 2007). It has also become big business. Danger has in fact always been big business for the truth-telling institutions of Church, State and Corporations to which we referred earlier. There has, for example, long been what the US President Dwight D. Eisenhower called a 'military industrial complex' in the Western world, but that complex has changed its size and character in the last twenty years. For one thing it has witnessed a massive growth in the privatisation of defence and security and the growth of private military corporations (Shearer 1998).

For more on what James Der Derian calls MIMENET, see **Chapter 7**.

The networking of network-centric warfare now also includes complex networks with every other aspect of our techno-scientific and commercial civilisation nationally and internationally (Der Derian 2001). Most interesting and disturbing of all, however, is the question of who or what is the enemy. For in a world of danger everyone and everything is potentially dangerous and potentially therefore also the enemy; the virtual security business has become as important as the actual security business. Distinguishing friend from enemy becomes a permanent full-time occupation and it is, moreover, conducted within a radical uncertainty of detecting who is friend and who is foe – who looks to be friendly now but who may turn into an enemy at some future date. From the perspective of network-centric warfare, particularly that practised now in the war on terror, it is no longer simply a matter of what makes the world dangerous; it is a matter of everything being in a virtual state of becoming-dangerous (Dillon 2007). We have then to consider briefly how these momentous changes in the military character of our world require changes not only in terms of how the military think about the changing nature of power relations, but also how we are to think about them as well. While alert to transformations in military strategic thinking and practices this does not mean that we must simply take our cue from the military. However important these issues are, there is vastly more at stake ethically and politically in these changes than military success and failure alone.

RESPONSES
THINKING IN TERMS OF STRATEGY AND SECURITY

Defence, security and strategic studies

We seek protection against danger and we seek to secure ourselves against whatever it is that we have come to fear. This was once the preserve of traditional defence, security and strategic studies. They had a monopoly at one time on telling us where danger lay, what things we should be frightened of and also where the solution to dealing with those fears could be found. They were able to do this because for a long time they had a very clear and, at least in the study of international relations, a relatively unopposed view of the world. They claimed to understand reality. Indeed they called themselves Realists (Molloy 2006). What that meant is that they had a very particular understanding of what I want to call the real. I call it the real to draw attention to the fact that, as with danger, there are different ways of problematising reality as well. People fear different things because they inhabit different realities. Our problematisation of the real is intimately tied to our problematisation of danger.

People with different pictures of the world inhabit different realities. **See Chapter 2**

Realist strategic studies and security thinkers and practitioners understood the world this way. They said that the world was inhabited by agents or subjects. The agent or the subject could be an individual or a collective entity. It could be you or me or it could be a state or a nation. It didn't much matter which, because such subjects or entities were thought to all operate in more or less rationally self-interested ways. Since politics was thought to be the sum total of this rationally self-interested calculating by such subjects, then war too was just another instrument in their calculations. That is why traditional strategists and security thinkers continuously appeal to the dictum which the Prussian philosopher of war Carl von Clausewitz made at the beginning of the nineteenth century, that war is merely the extension of politics by other means. Every subject, it was thought, but especially political subjects, was a goal/value-driven subject preoccupied with its own self-interest. They pursued those self-interests in collaboration and cooperation sometimes with other such subjects and often also in violent conflict, if necessary, with other such subjects. In the world of international politics, for example, where this view of the real prevailed throughout most of the twentieth century, it was ritually said that since there was no one sovereign who ruled over all the world, but a world comprised of many sovereign states, then the arbiter of conflict between states would necessarily always have to be war. War was the way in which such rationally calculating subjects operated when they could not settle their differences through bargaining and negotiation or other means of diplomacy and coercion short of war. At the end of the First World War, and then again at the end of the Cold War, liberals challenged this realist account of international relations and war. They did so in the name of a global peace, but that project is now widely discredited as the failing hegemony of states mobilised globally under American military and economic power (Dillon and Reid, 2008).

Strategy was the study of the way such subjects were said to calculate their goal-driven behaviour. It had a lot of affinity with other disciplines like economics which also presumed that the world was populated by such rationally calculating subjects. The strategists' subject of choice was the state rather than, say, the corporation or firm. What these and other disciplines also shared was a way of

For a description of how this works in liberal economics and the thinking of Adam Smith, see **Chapter 12**.

understanding the structure of the real (some people call this ontology) and acquiring knowledge about it (how we do this can be called our epistemology).

First, the real was said to be out there independent of us. Second, it was nonetheless readable by us because it was said to be comprised of accessible universal laws. Third, this meant that it was thought to operate in the same way irrespective of where you were geographically or where you were historically. In other words, these laws were said to operate like mechanical laws of Newtonian physics irrespective of time and place. For example, drop a pencil from a building in Tokyo and it will fall to the ground as assuredly as it will in London. Drop the same pencil tomorrow and it will do the same thing. Pencils always fall to the ground irrespective of where and when you drop them (space shuttle excluded, of course, but that is an example which makes the point I want to make in a moment). The universal law operating here is that formulated by Newton, the law of gravity. Finally, rational subjects, like strategists, were said to be uniquely well equipped with the reasoning mechanisms which could accurately represent the nature of the real. Knowledge for them was thus like a mirror of the real. All they had to do was hold the mirror of knowledge up to the real and reality would be accurately reflected back at them. Follow the dictates of this representational knowledge and things would turn out well for you. This was an article of faith with them. They believed in it and they could not in fact escape from such a significant measure of belief despite their claim to be entirely rational about things because reason itself ultimately depends upon assumptions which cannot be proved by reason alone. This doesn't make reason un-reasonable. It only makes the claim that this kind of reasoning is the only worthwhile kind un-reasonable.

Hence what traditional security and strategic studies taught about the fear, danger and politics which motivated their so-called rational subject reflected this view of the world. Note incidentally how anthropocentric (human-centred) these concerns were. The planet didn't figure. Neither did other species. They only figure now in as much as they add additional issues to the strategic agendas of rationally calculating subjects. The world remains for them a space for rational subjects to use and abuse in pursuit of their interests. Since the essential nature of state behaviour was said to be as fixed as the laws of motion, the issue for such Realists was reduced to polishing up the mirror they held to reality so as to get as clear a reflection as they thought possible. States would be endangered if they forgot or operated in ignorance of the laws reflected back in this representation of the real.

Every account of reality has its heroes as well as its dangers. The hero figure here was very definitely the visionary commander. Until Margaret Thatcher this figure was almost exclusively a male. Statesmanship thus reflected clear vision. Military success followed from applying this clarity of vision with iron will and martial skill irrespective of sentiment. The hero was not only usually male. His or her vision

Environmental thinking sometimes retains this focus on human futures and human needs. **See Chapter 3**

Margaret Thatcher was Prime Minister of Britain from 1979 to 1990.

was almost always expressed in martial terms; a warrior leader equipped with modern rational calculative knowledge.

For these reasons, among others, this view of the real became a very powerful commonsense view. It is one, indeed, which suffuses our entire culture. Traditional security studies taught this modern way of understanding the real. In this way they claimed not only to understand the real way in which the world worked. Through their study of such workings they also claimed to be able to better educate rational subjects in the employment of their reason in pursuit of their interests because they were in general such incompetent rational subjects.

But even as it attained its apogee this account of the real was being undermined from within one of the very establishments which once encouraged and propagated it – the United States Department of Defense and the US Armed Forces. That challenge came in the form not simply of network-centric warfare but through the philosophy which underpinned this form of warfare. That philosophy was the philosophy of transformation enshrined in the Pentagon's Office of Force Transformation (OFT), established in 2001 but broken up in 2006 with the fall of its patron Donald Rumsfeld.

Indeed part of the venom which surrounds the debate about network-centric warfare, and which once surrounded Rumsfeld and the OFT, is precisely the fact that network-centric warriors are relying on a different understanding of the real. This began and remains a fight about the nature of the real as such. On the one side are the old geopolitical warriors schooled in physics, realism and the official history of peoples, states and fear proclaiming universal laws going back to the ancient Greeks and Romans. On the other side are those schooled in cybernetics, information systems, communications theory and molecular biology proclaiming a more biopolitical reality comprised of complex adaptive systems which change

FIGURE 17.8
Donald Rumsfeld as US Defense Secretary, shown on 26 October 2006 during a media briefing at the Pentagon. Photo: Chris Greenberg, AP/PA Photos

their very nature as they behave in co-evolutionary ways with other systems. On the one hand are the old geopoliticians for whom someone or some body – a sovereign of some description – has to be in charge of things. On the other are the newer, let's call them bio-politicians to reflect how much they rely on the idea of evolution and co-evolution between systems and their environments, for whom the world can equally be comprised of complex systems, like capitalism, for example, which are clearly capable of ordering themselves without anyone being in charge, or being sovereign. On the one hand, finally, are the traditionalists who maintain there is nothing new under the sun when it comes to security and war. On the other are the thinkers, like Rumsfeld and Cebrowski, who insisted that transformation was the new name of the strategic game:

> First and foremost, the President and the Secretary elevated transformation to the level of strategy, and that is probably the most important lens through which we should look at transformation.
>
> (Cebrowski 2002)

Moreover, transformation was not only to be continuous, it was to be infinite:

> Transformation should be thought of as a process, not an end state. Hence there is no foreseeable point in the future when the Secretary of Defense will be able to declare that the transformation of the Department has been completed. Instead, the transformation process will continue indefinitely.
>
> (Office of Force Transformation 2004: 4)

And, finally, this was not a representational form of thinking at all; one in which the object was to hold up the mirror of knowledge to provide as clear a reflection of the real as possible. This was an explicitly experimental form of thinking. Its declared objective was not simply to represent or reflect the world as it is. The aim was to experiment in and with the world to create new realities, for example a peaceful, prosperous and democratic Iraq:

> Those responsible for defense transformation must anticipate the future and wherever possible help create it.
>
> (Office of Force Transformation 2004: 4)

This fight over the real persists despite the demotion of OFT. It also tends to run along the line of difference between physics and biology. Unlike traditional physics, time and space do matter for biology. In fact they are foundational to biological understandings of the behaviour of living systems. Change an organism's habitat and it will behave differently. It may prosper through its capacity to adapt to its new geographical location. It may not. It may fail and simply die out. Thus location does matter to the structure and behaviour of living or bio-systems. Moreover, the passage of time profoundly impacts on the

For more on the problems with the idea of someone being sovereign or 'in charge', see **Chapters 6 and 20**.

Of course, since Einstein's work on relativity and the ideas of quantum mechanics, physicists no longer think of time and space in the way they used to. Time does not run at the same rate everywhere, for example, and the world is ultimately unpredictable: general laws no longer apply, and experimental observations change the thing they try to observe.

structure and behaviour of organisms as well. Take hundreds or thousands of years, for example, and evolution teaches that living systems are capable of dramatic change over time. Social systems, including military systems, are having to change much faster than that these days.

Critical security thinking

If, however, the world did operate according to universal laws irrespective of time and place which people had to learn and obey, how come they required so much realist education to understand this? This was odd. It could not all be put down to stupidity, prejudice and ignorance. A seed of doubt was sown. Perhaps the world was not this way at all. Perhaps the real which Realists claimed to understand and explain was not only different from the way they understood it; perhaps it also required different means of understanding to appreciate what the real was like in ways that the Realists had consistently overlooked. In other words, it was not simply the reality which the Realists claimed to understand, it was the means of apprehending that reality – their very understanding of knowledge, or (un)truth-telling, as such – which came under suspicion as well. The reason was clear. It is not possible to experience the real directly. However much 'the real' stands obdurately outside and independent of us, and it does, it is not possible to escape the fact that our experience of the world is necessarily always mediated through the means we have of understanding, interpreting and communicating our different accounts of what the world is like. Even Realists sometimes admitted this. Where they refused to do so, their network-centric warfare counterparts had already sold the pass on them 'ontologically' and 'epistemologically'. By that I mean, as with the point I made above about the shift from representation to experimentation, network-centric thinking understands the nature of reality (ontology) to be different just as it deals with different ways of knowing the world (epistemology). Realism's credentials were not only attacked by critical security studies, for example, they were therefore also undermined from within where they had once been so powerfully accredited. The game of realism began to die where it had once been so alive, at the centre of the US military machine.

If all this was so – and it was – then perhaps the reality which the Realists proclaimed was not as universal and uniform as they said that it was. If there are different ways of accessing the real, and of course there are, as the examples of physics and biology indicate, then perhaps there are different experiences of the real as well. And if there are different experiences of the real, then it follows that there are necessarily also different experiences of danger than those taught us through the (un)truth-telling practices of the Realists.

Here, then, was the Achilles heel of traditional security and strategic studies. It was a fundamental weakness which many critical security studies students began to probe (Booth 2005). There are different schools of critical security studies but they shared at least three basic positions.

First, they challenged the role which the goal-driven subject played in traditional strategic and security studies. There the subject was supposed to come pre-formed unaffected by its terms and conditions of life, just expressing a universal commitment to goal-driven self-interested behaviour. Critical security studies did not deny that humans can be self-interested or goal-driven and so on. They did, however, point out how much this behaviour had to be learned, how much it was conditioned. In other words they argued that the goal-driven subject did not pre-exist the power relations, historical conditioning and learned behaviour that made the subject of security and strategic studies the subject it was said to be. In other words, the 'realist' nation or state seeking security was very much itself a function or outcome of traditional defence and security practices (Campbell 1998).

Second, they observed that there was more than one way of accessing the real. Knowledge is plural not single. It is itself also a form of critical practice in which knowledge changes over time.

Third, they maintained that an intimate relation exists between knowledge and power. Realists too understood that knowledge could be a form of power. But they denied that their own truth-telling knowledge was a form of power, and appealed to the idea instead that their knowledge was a disinterested representation of the real. Critical analysts pointed out that wherever there was knowledge a form of power was also at work. Michel Foucault coined the term power/knowledge to make this point. In other words, they introduced a note of suspicion into the very idea of disinterested knowledge because it was perfectly evident that truth-telling practices – better to use the ambivalent expression (un-)truth-telling practice – are one of the single most important instruments of power. Equally, it was perfectly evident also that that truth-telling practices represent an enormously powerful force in how we live our lives, and even in how we imagine life to be. All knowledge is interested: it is invested with perspective. That does not disqualify it as knowledge. It just teaches us to be more circumspect about knowledge-claims, and always to ask who makes them, who gains, who loses in the advance of certain knowledge-claims and so on. We have, in particular, to get savvy about the power/knowledge games – the truth- and un-truth-telling practices – that teach us how to secure ourselves and what we ought to fear.

For more about Foucault, see **Chapters 6 and 9.**

Robert Cox also argues that theories always imply a perspective. **See Chapter 1**

There are always power and political implications to the pursuit of knowledge. Equally, however, there is always some kind of knowledge at stake in the practices of power and politics as well. Whatever claims are therefore made about the nature of the real, those claims may be made in the language of truth but they will always cash out in the language of politics and power as well. There are different kinds of truths, different kinds of truth-telling practices and different kinds of truth-tellers.

Here I have also used the formula '(un)truth'. One reason at least for this expression will be perfectly clear to you. It is a well-worn cliché to observe that the first casualty of war – and, by extension, discourses of security, fear and danger – is truth. Deception is itself an art of war. It is also integral to discourse of security, fear and danger. The dissimulation – to put it no stronger – practised by the UK and US governments in claiming that Saddam Hussein of Iraq had battlefield-ready weapons of mass destruction will suffice to make the point for us today. Reputedly, a cynical old US newspaper columnist, having learned this lesson the hard way, would advise his young colleagues that when interviewing powerful people they should repeat to themselves: 'Why is this bastard lying to me?' We might well follow that advice especially when listening to political spin-doctors talking the language of security, fear and danger. Recognising that truth is a prize over which powerful forces compete generally teaches us to be circumspect about the truth-claims made by power brokers. Those claims very often also turn out to be self-fulfilling prophecies. Teach people extremes of fear and they will act with extreme hostility towards whatever it is they have been taught to be frightened of. Racist hostility towards Jews and people of colour, for example, as well as homophobia, hostility to strangers and others all teach this lesson.

By using the term '(un)truth' I nonetheless also want to point to a wider issue about truth and knowledge as such. All truth is contoured by un-truth, just as all knowledge is contoured by not knowing. If we knew everything there would be nothing left to learn. If the truth was self-evident to all of us there would be no truths left to bring to our attention. But we are mortals condemned to learn new and often unpalatable truths through the many diverse means of knowing that we have at our disposal, and new ones that we will have to invent if we are to learn new truths about ourselves and our predicament. The modern world once placed an unsustainable burden of hope on the power of representational truth and knowledge to constrain the exercise of power. That we now know the degree to which power relies upon such knowledge, and operates through its truth-telling, does not disqualify the game of knowledge and the passion for the truth as such. It should instead compel us even more strongly to learn how to play these games anew; not least when the stakes are those of survival.

And so we return to danger, because people kill and die for their accounts of the real; the truths and un-truths which they hold dear. The period in which we live is often called the Modern. Modernity itself is an account of the real – or at least a complex of accounts of the real which differed in many ways from the religiously informed Christian accounts of the real which preceded the revolutions of the seventeenth and eighteenth centuries, in and around the Atlantic Basin, which gave birth to the Modern Age. The UK prime minister Tony Blair was also a consistent advocate of modernisation both at home and abroad. But how does modernity in general problematise danger? What makes the world dangerous, especially now, for us moderns?

BROADER ISSUES
UNKNOWN UNKNOWNS

Donald Rumsfeld was appointed US Secretary of State for Defense in January 2001. The White House announced his resignation immediately after the Republican Party losses in the congressional elections of November 2006. Rumsfeld was the great political patron of the RMA, proponent of network-centric warfare and ideologue of the doctrine of transformation. Despite his fall from grace, US military strategic discourse and posture have been changed irreversibly in the last ten years.

Rumsfeld was also widely reviled and parodied for his use of the jargon of network-centric warfare and of force transformation. Apart from justified political opposition to the decisions he was making while defense secretary, such as the

---

BOX 17.2 THE RUMSFELD DOCTRINE

THE UNKNOWN

As we know,
There are known knowns.
There are things we know we know.
We also know
There are known unknowns.
That is to say
We know there are some things
We do not know.
But there are also unknown unknowns,
The ones we don't know
We don't know.

(Donald Rumsfeld, 12 February 2002,
Department of Defense News Briefing)

invasion of Iraq, the way he expressed himself provoked outrage and laughter because his language expressed a different understanding of the real. Incidentally, it was still spoken on behalf of a traditional understanding of the real as well, that of US geopolitical imperial interests. In consequence it contained many contradictions. But contradiction is characteristic of politics, especially security politics. It is often the fuel that drives it. Seeking security, for example, we very often increase the dangers to which we are exposed (consider the case of the balance of terror struck by the nuclear doctrine of Mutual Assured Destruction). Contradictions also afford the gap, however, through which critique enters.

Rumsfeld's reflections, in news briefings especially, spoke of a world of understanding that was relatively novel to defence and security specialists, as well as to the American and to the world's press corps. It was an understanding of the real that has in fact, however, been around for a long time. It, too, goes back to the Greeks, but its teaching had long fallen out of use especially in the study of international relations and strategy. It has been resurrected and refurbished (given modern expression) in the new language of military strategic transformation and change. Rumsfeld's most notorious reflections on it, repeated in Box 17.2 on p. 418, had an almost poetic quality, which is why I record them as a poem.

They nonetheless contain some profound insights, especially about how we moderns problematise danger. I want to end this chapter by drawing out those insights. I especially want to draw attention to three closely related points: first, what Rumsfeld's 'poetry' teaches us about the modern reliance upon knowledge to problematise and deal with danger; second, what his reflections teach us about the intimate modern alliance of power and knowledge (power/knowledge) when problematising danger; third, what Rumsfeld's insistence on the significance of 'unknown unknowns' teaches us about how 'uncertainty' has drifted back into the very epicentre of our problematisation of fear and danger (Cilliers 1998). It is this in particular which calls into question knowledge's capacity to deal with the 'unknown unknowns' which now dominate our global/local landscapes of fear and danger: the unintended consequences, the strategic surprises, the bolts from the blue, the things perhaps to which the very light of our techno-scientific knowledge actually blinds us. In short all that 'shit' which we are unable to see but which Forrest Gump in the 1994 movie says happens and with whose often terrible consequences we are always going to have to deal.

Perfect vision

Recall that the document which authorised network-centric warfare as the military strategic doctrine of the US Armed Forces was, however, entitled Joint Vision 2020. Titles like this should always be taken seriously. Experts spend a lot of time crafting them, and they always give away more than they intend. The 'Joint' in

There is more about the Iraq war in **Chapters 7 and 20**.

Mutual Assured Destruction – or MAD – was the name given to the nuclear posture during the Cold War in which the United States threatened to annihilate the Soviet Union in the event that it should use nuclear weapons against it, even though this would have meant that the Soviet Union would have responded by annihilating the US in turn.

the title obviously refers to the interdependence of land, sea, air and other forces in the US military – joint commands, combined operations and so on. But it was also very clearly meant to invoke connectedness in general – the doctrine of networks as such. Equally, Joint Vision 2020 was not only looking forward twenty years to the year 2020. Again, it was clearly invoking another idea, what opticians refer to as 20/20 vision, by which they mean 'perfect vision'.

Perfect vision is ordinarily associated politically only with hindsight. Only by looking back, it is said, can we see clearly how things really were. But what network-centric warriors are clearly also aspiring to is 20/20 vision in two other respects. The first of these is 20/20 vision in real time so that they can

FIGURE 17.9
Still from Steven Spielberg's science fiction film *Minority Report*. 20th Century Fox/Dreamworks/ The Kobal Collection

comprehend instantly all that is going on in the 'global battlespace'. The second is 20/20 vision as foresight. They do not want to be caught out by what is coming down the pike, because in the end you can only fully escape danger and make everything secure if you can pre-empt the nasty surprises which time itself has in store for us. Think of or watch *Minority Report*, Steven Spielberg's 2002 science fiction film set in the year 2054 AD, where crime is virtually eliminated from Washington, DC thanks to an elite law enforcing squad 'Precrime' (Weber 2006).

Ultimately, perfect vision expresses the desire for perfect security. But perfect security – an end to danger – requires bringing an end to time. Were it possible, 20/20 vision would do just that. The continuous transformation to which network-centric warfare appeals is revealed here in its own terms as the primordial organising dream of political modernity: to bring an end to time here and now in this world through the perfection of our knowledge as the perfect vision of real time, fully transparent and communicable, information and foresight. In net war terms this is called 'shared situation awareness'.

The more we seek to secure, however, the more danger we seem to bring into the world. Spielberg explored these and other themes in his film. There is then a profound paradox at work in this military ideology. It wills the end to the change which the operation of time itself entails. But an end to time would simultaneously also mean the end of us; because we are time's creatures. No time. No us. The will to perfect security expresses the will to bring an end to ourselves. Fortunately life is not so easily secured. The object of security (life) keeps objecting to the ways in which security seeks to secure it. It escapes being secured, and this introduces a point to which I will return in my conclusion. Paradoxical as it may sound, in order to survive we may have to become less obsessed with securing ourselves, recognising that there is more to life, and therefore more to politics, than politics of security which continuously also endangers us.

Recall, as well, the emphasis on continuous adaptability, transformation and change to which the US military now aspires, embracing the idea of co-evolution with the battlespace in order always to prevail over the enemy, whoever and whatever the enemy might be. Transformation is a military strategic vision of permanent revolution, a never-ending event. But what this itself threatens is no profound emancipatory change in the human condition, just permanent revolution of the same, a sameness that escapes time's itself.

And yet Rumsfeld also teaches us a further paradox: that there are unknown unknowns out there which our knowledge cannot reach and which our 20/20 vision will never attain. Note the profound shift that this records in the truth-telling practices of twenty-first-century security. They are founded now in uncertainty. Uncertainty is no mere ignorance which knowledge will eventually overcome. 'Unknown unknowns' have become the basis of its truth-telling practices now. Indeed, everything that we are now taught by Western political, military and police authorities in their war on terror, especially, teaches us that we do not know when the strike will come, we do not know where the strike will come and we cannot estimate how devastating the strike may be. But they are certain of this uncertainty. Uncertainty or radical contingency – not knowing and not being able to know – has paradoxically now at the very height of our techno-scientific civilisation and its dream of 20/20 vision become the very principle of formation around which military strategic and policing powers of the West revolve in their response to the dangers which our globally networked world now presents to us.

Being-in-formation

Excuse the awful pun, but here at the beginning of the twenty-first century the modern vision which Donald Rumsfeld unwittingly poeticised has become one in which every thing is said to be information and everything is said to be continuously in-formation. Things which are continuously undergoing transformation and change are not fixed. They are always on their way to becoming something else. Our military, political and economic leaders, and even some of our teachers, insistently tell us that we have to be skilled at managing our own continuous transformation and change if we are to survive the dangers of the battlespace or the marketplace, and the danger ultimately of becoming outdated. Becoming outdated threatens unemployment, impoverishment, famine, defeat and despoilation. These days becoming outdated spells death. That is the fear we now teach ourselves. And yet that fear breeds another.

FIGURE 17.10
'Well . . . at least we don't have to worry about anarchy any more'. Artist: Ron Cobb, 1968

Becoming-dangerous

If no body, no thing is fixed, if every body is continuously in-formation, then it becomes difficult to secure any body at all since we can never be quite sure what the body is that we set out to secure. While our leaders simultaneous enjoin us to embrace transformation and change, they are simultaneously also terrified by the fact that if we are continuously in formation in the ways that they recommend we may also be continuously becoming-dangerous in ways that simply cannot be anticipated (Dillon and Reid, 2008). No body is able to predict in precisely what ways we are transforming ourselves. Daft as it sounded to the press corps at the briefing in which he made these statements, this was the fear to which Rumsfeld was giving expression. It is the fear of all rulers who rule through the prioritisation of fear and danger. They do not know and cannot know what we are becoming and therefore they do not know and cannot know what dangers we will present to ourselves as well as to others. This recalls us back to that other time in American history and that other President, Franklin Roosevelt. Remember it was Roosevelt who said we had nothing to fear but fear itself. In another time, confronted with other dangers, we might do well to recall those words and reflect on how rule through fear and danger continuously also endangers itself.

CONCLUSION

One of the thoughts which I hope you may have had as you read this chapter is that the more we try to secure ourselves the more we also seem to endanger ourselves. The very instruments and the very preoccupations which tell us what to fear and how to protect ourselves from danger often also threaten us. (The doctrine of Mutual Assured Destruction remains paradigmatic, a primary example of this point.) I am not leaving you therefore with an easy thought. On the contrary I think this thought begins to pose the most difficult and pressing ethical and political questions with which humankind is now faced. There is no easy answer to them and yet we cannot escape them by blaming others for what makes the world dangerous. 'We' make the world dangerous. In trying to escape from danger, we seem also to have made it even more lethally dangerous. How might we, then, govern ourselves differently than through an increasingly terminal preoccupation with governing ourselves through danger? Remember the old adage – when you are in a hole stop digging? What kind of politics might get us out of this hole, or at least reduce the rate at which we are digging ourselves into it? Not one, to be sure, that simply ignored danger. But not one that was blind to everything else but danger, of whatever sort. As a political theorist, a theorist of security in particular and a critic of politics of security especially, this is my problem. But I cannot escape making it your problem as well, since it is a problem that I think we share. Cut your analytical and political teeth on it. A life-affirming intellectual and political challenge such as this is a gift. I could say that it is mine to you. In fact we have been bequeathed it by our history. Enjoy working on it, and good luck.

ACKNOWLEDGEMENT

I want to record my thanks to Manav Guha. Without him I would not have the understanding of network-centric warfare which I have, or be as concerned about it as I am. What I know I have learned through continuous question and answer with him.

FURTHER READING

Reid, Julian (2007) *The Biopolitics of the War on Terror: Life Struggles, Liberal Modernity, and the Defence of Logistical Societies*, Manchester and New York: Manchester University Press.
Application of Foucault and other critical theorists, illustrates how biopolitics makes war on life, explicitly so in the war on terror.

Dillon, Michael and Luis Lobo-Guerrero (2008) 'Biopolitics of Security in the 21st Century: An Introduction', *Review of International Studies* 34, 2.
Provides a general introduction to what happens to security technologies when they take life as their referent object; also touches on the question of what happens to life when it becomes a security object.

Campbell, David (1998) *Writing Security*, Minneapolis, MN: Minnesota University Press.
Pioneering work; deftly counteracted the politics of identity and subjectivity that had dominated international relations and security studies throughout the Cold War period, and beyond.

Dillon, Michael (2008) 'Underwriting Security', *Security Dialogue* 39, 2–3.
Seeks an additional shift in our analytical focus, and empirical field of observation, to the biopolitics of security, which takes 'life' rather than identity as its referent object, and especially to the ways in which the biopoliticisation of security installs 'risk' as one of its single most important devices.

Castells, Manuel (2000) *The Rise of the Network Society*, Oxford: Blackwell.
Explains the rise of globally networked societies and forms a background for understanding the radical interconnectedness of the world today.

Cebrowski, Arthur and John Garstka (1998) 'Network Centric Warfare: Its Origin and Future', *US Naval Institute Proceedings* 124, January: 28–35.
The classic account of network-centric thinking and network-centric warfare. Get your minds around this text and you will understand what is going on, so equipping yourselves to start posing other questions about how our contemporary discourses of danger unite military strategic and other discourses of security.

Foucault, Michel (2001) *Fearless Speech*, New York: Semiotext(e).

Start your adventure thinking about contemporary problematisations of security with the aid of Foucault here; specifically the last lecture, which explains what problematisation means.

WEBSITES

Official website of the Foucault Society, http://www.foucaultsociety.org/.

Rich source of further references by Foucault and on Foucault.

Biopolitics of Security Network, http://www.keele.ac.uk/research/ipj/bos/.

Website devoted to the application of Foucault to questions of security and war.

Office of the now disbanded US Office of Force Transformation, http://www.oft.osd.mil/.

Rich source on the relation of transformation to US military strategic doctrine.

RAND Corporation website on national security, http://www.rand.org/research_areas/national_security/.

Source of military strategic classics on network-centric warfare, information warfare and the war on terror. Paradigmatic of contemporary military strategic discourse and the ways in which it colonises hitherto civil issues.

Home page of the UK Civil Contingencies Secretariat and the strategy of national resilience, http://www.ukresilience.info/cos/aims.aspx.

Use as a resource to track how security as resilience differs from simple military security and is disseminated throughout UK civil society.

Home page of the UK Ministry of Defence, http://www.mod.uk/defenceinternet/home.

Use as a device to track how the UK mimics US military strategic discourse.

US Department of Defense site, http://www.defenselink.mil/.

Use for direct illustration of themes discussed in this chapter.

REFERENCES

Alberts, David S., John J. Garstka, Frederick P. Stein (1999) *Network Centric Warfare: Developing and Leveraging Information Superiority*, 2nd edn, Washington, DC: US Department of Defense, Command and Control Research Program (CCRP).

Arquilla, John and David Ronfeldt (1997) 'Information Power and Grand Strategy: In Athena's Camp', in John Arquilla and David Ronfeldt, *In Athena's Camp: Preparing for Conflict in the Information Age*, Santa Monica, CA: RAND Corporation.

Barabasi, Albert-Laszlo (2003) *Linked: How Everything Is Connected to Everything Else and What It Means*, London: Penguin Books.

Booth, Ken (2005) *Critical Security Studies and World Politics*, Boulder, CO: Lynne Rienner.

Campbell, David (1998) *Writing Security*, Minneapolis, MN: Minnesota University Press.

Castells, Manuel (2000) *The Rise of the Network Society*, Oxford: Blackwell.

Cebrowski, Vice Admiral (Ret.) Arthur K. (2002) Director Office of Force Transformation, Prepared Statement for the US House, Appropriations Committee, 13 March.

Cebrowski, Arthur and John Gartska (1998) 'Network Centric Warfare: Its Origin and Future', *US Naval Institute Proceedings* 124, January: 28–35.

Cilliers, Paul (1998) *Complexity and Postmodernism*, London: Routledge.

Dalby, Simon (2002) *Environmental Security*, Minneapolis, MN: University of Minnesota Press.

Der Derian, James (2001) *Virtuous War: Mapping the Military-Industrial-Media-Entertainment Network*, Boulder, CO: Westview Press.

Dillon, Michael (2007) 'Governing Terror', *International Political Sociology* 1, 1: 7–28.

Dillon, Michael (2004) 'Virtual Security: A New Science of (Dis)order', *Millennium: Journal of International Studies* 32, 3: 531–58.

Dillon, Michael (2002) 'Network Society, Network-Centric Warfare and the State of Emergency', *Theory, Culture and Society* 19, 4: 71–9.

Dillon, Michael and Julian Reid (2001) 'Global Liberal Governance: Biopolitics, Security and War', *Millennium: Journal of International Studies* 30, 1: 1–26.

Dillon, Michael and Julian Reid (2008) *The Liberal Way of War: Killing to make life live*, London: Routledge.

Farrell, Theo and Tim Bird (2008) 'The Transformation of the British Armed Forces', in Terry Terriff, Theo Farrell and Frans Osinga (eds) *The Dynamics of Military Transformation in NATO*, Stanford, CA: Stanford University Press.

Foucault, Michel (2001) *Fearless Speech*, New York: Semiotext(e).

Foucault, Michel (1988) 'Truth and Power', in Colin Gordon (eds) *Power/Knowledge*, Brighton: Harvester Press.

Libicki, Martin (2000) *Who Runs What in the Global Information Grid?*, Santa Monica, CA: RAND.

Mathews, Ron and Jack Treddenick (eds) (2001) *Managing the Revolution in Military Affairs*, London: Palgrave.

McLuhan, Marshall (2001) *Understanding Media*, London: Routledge

Molloy, Sean (2006) *The Hidden History of Realism: A Genealogy of Power*, New York: Palgrave Macmillan.

Office of Force Transformation (2004) *Elements of Defense Transformation*, Washington, DC: US Department of Defense, http://www.oft.osd.mil/library_files/document_383_ElementsOfTransformation_LR.pdf.

Perrow, Charles (1999) *Normal Accidents: Living with High Risk Technologies*, Princeton, NJ: Princeton University Press.

Reid, Julian (2007) *The Biopolitics of the War on Terror: Life Struggles, Liberal Modernity and the Defence of Logistical Societies*, Manchester and New York: Manchester University Press.

Rumsfeld, Donald (2002) Department of Defense News Briefing, 12 February.

Shapiro, Michael J. (2007) 'The New Violent Cartography', *Security Dialogue* 38, 3: 291–313.

Shearer, David (1998) *Private Military Armies*, Adelphi Paper 316, London: IISS.

UK Ministry of Defence (2005) *Network Enabled Capability*, JSP 777, London: Ministry of Defence.

Weber, Cynthia (2006) *Imagining America at War: Morality, Politics and Film*, London: Routledge.

CHAPTER 18

What can we do to stop people harming others?

Anne Orford

- *The question*
  INTERVENING FOR HUMANITY?

- *Illustrative example*
  SAVING TIMOR-LESTE

- *Responses*
  LAW AND THE EXCEPTIONAL

- *Broader issues*
  LEGALITY, LEGITIMACY AND THE POLITICS OF INTERVENTION

- **CONCLUSION**

THE QUESTION
INTERVENING FOR HUMANITY?

During the 1990s, the question 'What can we do to stop people harming others?' animated much public engagement with international politics, at least in the democracies of Western Europe, North America, Australia and New Zealand. In this immediate post-Cold War period, military intervention began to achieve a new respectability, not least because for many it seemed to offer a means for the international community, or at least a liberal alliance of democratic states, to bring human rights and democracy to protect people suffering in situations of genocide, civil war or large-scale human rights violations. Looking back on that period, from an era when security, preventive self-defence and the war on terror dominate the foreign policy agenda of many states, it can be difficult to remember the anguished intensity with which this concern for the situation of suffering others manifested itself. Much changed with the traumas of the violent attacks on the United States of September 11, 2001, and the invasions of Afghanistan and Iraq in response. The use of humanitarian arguments by the US and its allies to justify the resort to force against Afghanistan and Iraq left many convinced that humanitarianism simply functions as an alibi for imperial ambition. Where sentimental emotion dominated public responses to international intervention in the 1990s, cynical reason has resurfaced as the dominant posture of the post-September 11 age.

The idea that force should be used to relieve the suffering of others of course predates the 1990s. Christian Europe was for long centuries inspired to take action by the idea of saving the souls or rescuing the bodies of people elsewhere, and the self-appointed civilising mission of European empire was premised upon the idea that benevolent tutelage in the art of European civilisation was the answer to the suffering of those outside the community of faith. Even in the modern age of the United Nations (UN) Charter, in which states have theoretically renounced recourse to war as an instrument of foreign policy, there are many doctrinal and practical precursors to the concept of humanitarian intervention. Peacekeeping, for example, does not appear in the UN Charter as one of the grounds upon which recourse to force may be authorised. It emerged in the early 1950s, alongside the process of decolonisation, as a means of responding to conflict over territory, threats to the sanctity of former colonial investments and civil war in post-colonial states. The use of force against states in Africa, the Middle East and Latin America was also justified during the Cold War on the basis that intervention was necessary to defend citizens of the home state who were abroad. Such doctrines served to justify armed intervention against Third World states, in the name of defending individuals at risk of harm. Nonetheless, during the Cold War period, the notion that a powerful state or a coalition of allies might intervene to rescue or protect the people of another state could not easily be represented as an apolitical action. The Brezhnev doctrine of intervention to protect the self-determination of socialist countries in the face of capitalist threats and the Reagan doctrine advocating the legitimacy of pro-democratic invasion were met with protest and derision. It was the institutional and ideological conditions of the post-Cold War period which led to the growth of support, amongst policy makers and academics, for the idea that force can legitimately be used as a response to humanitarian challenges.

The institutional conditions which made possible the shift in support for the notion of humanitarian intervention included the post-Cold War revitalisation of the Security Council and the corresponding expansion of its role in maintaining international peace and security. For many years the coercive powers vested by the UN Charter in the Security Council seemed irrelevant. During the Cold War, the Security Council was paralysed by reciprocal use of the veto exercisable by

For more on what is meant by imperialism, see **Chapter 15**.

The thinking that took place around Spanish colonisation is discussed in **Chapter 15**. That chapter also considers the tensions inherent in 'helping others'.

See **Chapter 1** for more on the term 'Third World'.

Leonid Brezhnev was leader of the Soviet Union from 1964 to 1982. Ronald Reagan was President of the United States from 1981 to 1989.

BOX 18.1 THE UN AND USE OF FORCE

The UN Charter was adopted by the fifty founding member states of the new organisation at San Francisco in June 1945. Under Article 24 of the UN Charter, the Security Council is the organ charged with the primary responsibility for maintaining international peace and security. Under Chapters VI and VII of the UN Charter, the Security Council is granted powers to facilitate the pacific settlement of disputes and to decide what measures, including the use of armed force, should be taken to maintain or restore international peace and security. UN member states renounce the use of force as a tool of foreign policy, except in self-defence or where such action is authorised by the Security Council. The jurisdiction of the Security Council under Chapter VII is triggered by the existence of a threat to the peace, a breach of the peace or an act of aggression. Since 1989, the Security Council has proved itself willing to interpret the phrase 'threats to the peace' broadly, to include situations of civil war or humanitarian crises.

FIGURE 18.1
The UN Security Council, United Nations, New York. Photo: Eskinder Debebe

---

the five permanent members (the P5) – China, France, the United Kingdom, the Unites States and what was then the Soviet Union. Under Article 27(3) of the Charter, decisions of the Security Council require the affirmative vote of nine members and the concurring votes of the permanent members. The P5 regularly made use of that veto power during the Cold War to protect against international

The Cold War is also discussed in **Chapter 19.**

interference in their spheres of interest. The ending of the Cold War meant an end to that automatic use of the veto power. The range and nature of resolutions passed by the Security Council in the decade following the end of the Cold War suggested that the Council was willing to treat the failure to guarantee democracy or human rights, or to protect against humanitarian abuses, as a threat to peace and security. The enthusiastic embrace of multilateral intervention (interventions involving more than one intervening country) extended to support for military action undertaken by regional organisations without Security Council authorisation, most notably in the case of the 1999 intervention in Kosovo by NATO (the North Atlantic Treaty Organisation), but also the intervention by the Economic Community of West African States in Sierra Leone.

The ideological climate of the 1990s contributed to the plausibility of the notion that military intervention might be benevolent and disinterested – that powerful states might really come to liberate and not to occupy. A new kind of international law and internationalist spirit seemed to have been made possible in the changed conditions of a world no longer structured around the struggle between communism and capitalism. During the 1990s, many international lawyers suggested that the process of globalisation was contributing to the emergence of an international community by creating the conditions for an increasingly interdependent world, linked by new technologies and the movement of goods, capital and people. In addition, globalisation was thought to promise a degree of integration into a common or harmonised legal system, an increased move towards institutionalisation and a commitment to the shared values of free trade, security, human rights and democracy. While international legal texts still invoke interdependence as a fact and the coming community of shared values as a destination, interdependence post-September 11 is more likely to be figured in terms of a shared vulnerability, and the coming community in terms of the fragility of faith and belief. In this context, the idea that military intervention might be a means of responding to the suffering of others has not disappeared, but it has shifted form, as we shall see below. In order to try to think about the stakes of different approaches to the question 'What can we do to stop people harming others?', I turn to look at an example of humanitarian intervention in action – the case of Timor-Leste.

ILLUSTRATIVE EXAMPLE
SAVING TIMOR-LESTE

Timor was colonised by Portugal in the sixteenth century, and remained under Portuguese occupation until 1942, when it was invaded by Japan. At the end of the Second World War, the Portuguese resumed control over the territory. In 1960, the UN General Assembly placed Timor on its list of non-self-governing territories, with Portugal as the administering power. Following the leftist

The Cold War was seen as a struggle between not only different states but also the ideologies that they subscribed to. **Chapter 19** looks at the role of ideology in conflict and **Chapter 16** discusses competing ideologies as an explanation for war.

For the impact of September 11, 2001 on security policy, see **Chapter 17**; for its impact on immigration policy in the US, see **Chapter 8**; and for changes in perceptions of the place of religion in global politics after September 11, see **Chapter 5**.

Colonialism and its continuing impact today are examined in **Chapter 11**.

FIGURE 18.2
Map of East Timor in the context of Asia and Australia

overthrow of Portugal's authoritarian government in 1974, the new social democratic government in Lisbon reacted favourably to the call by Timorese nationalist movements for independence, but did little to oversee or facilitate the process of Timorese self-determination. The Timorese were left to resolve the difficulties that arose in the preparation for independence, in particular the contest between rival groups advocating independence on the one hand and integration with Indonesia on the other. The most popular among these groups was the pro-independence FRETILIN (Frente Revolucionária do Timor-Leste Independente, or Revolutionary Front for an Independent East Timor), which Indonesian President Suharto was to characterise in conversation with US President Gerald Ford as 'Communist-influenced'.

On 28 November 1975, in the context of repeated cross-border attacks by Indonesian special forces seeking to provoke civil war and thus provide an alibi for intervention, FRETILIN declared Timor's independence. A little over a week later, on 7 December 1975, Indonesia launched a general invasion of Timor, carried out with the knowledge and tacit support of the US, UK and Australian governments. This support was motivated by issues of regional security, concern that an independent Timor might align itself with China and, in the case of

Australia, the desire to secure access to Timor Sea oil and gas. Indonesia was to remain in military occupation of Timor for the next twenty-five years. During that period, an estimated 200,000 Timorese people were killed, and human rights violations were widespread and brutal. Resistance to Indonesian occupation was sustained throughout this period, perhaps most dramatically through the activities of FALANTIL (Forças Armadas de Libertação Nacional de Timor-Leste, or Armed Forces for the National Liberation of East Timor) guerrillas based in the mountains, but also through diplomatic activity by the Timorese diaspora, widespread non-cooperation with Indonesian officials and clandestine resistance activities throughout Timor. The UN condemned Indonesia's aggression and continued to recognise Portugal as the administering authority over the territory. Australia, however, recognised de facto (factual) Indonesian occupation of Timor in 1978, and through the commencement of negotiations over maritime delimitation in the Timor Sea gave de jure (legal) recognition to the occupation. The result was the 1989 conclusion of the Timor Gap Treaty with Indonesia, the terms of which were very favourable to Australia and allowed Australian access to oil and gas fields which would later become the subject of claims by an independent Timor-Leste.

The 1999 intervention and administration

In 1998, Indonesia proposed that Timor be granted limited special autonomy within the Republic of Indonesia. The resulting talks involving Indonesia, Portugal and the UN Secretary-General saw the Secretary-General entrusted with the organisation and conduct of a popular consultation to ascertain whether the Timorese people accepted Indonesia's special autonomy proposal. When the vote rejecting the autonomy proposal in favour of independence resulted in a campaign of violence and destruction waged against the Timorese, the international community responded by sending a multinational force (the International Force for East Timor, or INTERFET) to restore peace and security. International financial institutions also exerted pressure on Indonesia by freezing payments during the post-ballot period. In the following months, the Indonesian armed forces and police withdrew from the territory and militia attacks were controlled. UN Secretary-General Kofi Annan saw these events as significant. For Annan, 'The tragedy of East Timor, coming so soon after that of Kosovo, has focused attention once again on the need for timely intervention by the international community when death and suffering are being inflicted on large numbers of people' (Annan 1999: 49). He welcomed the 'developing international norm in favour of intervention to protect civilians from wholesale slaughter' (Annan 1999: 50). Richard Holbrooke, then US Permanent Representative to the UN, described it as 'the textbook realization of Churchill and Roosevelt's dream when they laid out the principles of the UN' (Traub 2000: 80). Australia's Foreign Minister Alexander Downer also lauded the role played by Australian troops

Chapter 11 explains how international financial institutions came to be set up.

as part of INTERFET in supporting self-determination and relieving suffering in the territory:

> We saw an opportunity to allow East Timorese to decide their own future, and we helped them realise that chance. And when those who lost the ballot sought to overturn it through violence and intimidation, we put Australian lives on the line to end that suffering.
>
> (Downer 1999)

Following the intervention, the UN and the World Bank adopted a major trusteeship role, taking over responsibility for administration in Timor during the period of transition to independence. The idea that the international community has a legitimate role as administrator of post-conflict territories and manager of the reconstruction process gained increasing acceptance at the international level during the 1990s. These developments in international relations flowed from a new faith in the international community as a benign, even civilising, administrator. On 25 October 1999, Security Council Resolution 1272 established the UN Transitional Administration in East Timor (UNTAET) as a peacekeeping operation 'endowed with overall responsibility for the administration of East Timor and . . . empowered to exercise all legislative and executive authority, including the administration of justice'. The UN's view of its role in East Timor was well illustrated by Jean-Christian Cady, the Deputy Transitional Administrator

When we say 'international community' we sometimes mean all the states in the world, sometimes a group of rich and powerful states, sometimes the UN Security Council or – sometimes – the UN General Assembly. We imply that members of the international community share values and obligations. This can ignore or gloss over strong divisions and disagreements, and create legitimacy for a particular view that is not in fact shared by everyone.

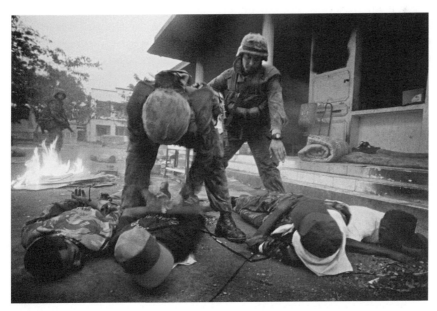

FIGURE 18.3
Australian troops, members of INTERFET, disarm and arrest members of the Aitarak Militia. Dili, East Timor, 21 September 1999. Photo: David Dare Parker

of East Timor. Cady commented that the UN had to 'create a State, with a constitution, administrative, judicial and financial institutions, and a Public Service' and train police, 'not only on police methods and techniques but also on the ethics of a democratic police and respect for human rights, which is of course a new idea in East Timor'. Creating a bureaucracy was portrayed as equally difficult: 'What UNTAET wants to achieve is a Civil Service independent from political affiliations and cronyism, competent and not corrupt. These are ambitious goals anywhere but perhaps more so in this part of the world' (Cady 2000). Hans Strohmeyer, counsel to the Transitional Administrator, understood it as his job to 'invent a Timorese legal system' (Traub 2000: 82). These officials saw Timor as a blank slate in terms of existing knowledge and experience, marked by cronyism, incompetence and corruption. The UN's role was understood in the pedagogical terms that marked colonial discourse – the international community was to bring its tutees in East Timor to political and economic maturity through the creation and transfer of the bureaucratic machinery of the modern nation-state, and the training of the functionaries required to operate that machinery.

The World Bank also played a major role in the administration of East Timor, administering a multilateral trust fund to finance reconstruction and working with Timorese and UNTAET representatives to facilitate economic development. The Bank made clear that certain familiar Bank programmes and priorities were to be implemented in the management of East Timor. It determined as early as 1999 that East Timor was to have a small public sector, with a concomitant contracting out of many areas of service provision to the private sector, and particularly to foreign investors. According to critics, East Timor under UN and World Bank management was overrun by foreign, mainly Australian, companies making large profits out of contracts negotiated with INTERFET or UNTAET (Aditjondro 2000). Non-governmental organisations (NGOs) such as East Timor's La'o Hamutuk argued that the combination of UN paternalism, World Bank development models and unrestrained foreign investment was creating a new form of colonialism, and deepening divisions within the East Timorese community (La'o Hamutuk 2000).

For a discussion of profiteering and the ambiguities of development under structural adjustment regimes put in place by the World Bank in Côte d'Ivoire, see **Chapter 11**.

Independence

In August 2001, during the period of UN administration, democratic elections for a Constituent Assembly were held. FRETILIN won 57 per cent of the vote, and its Secretary-General Mari Alkatiri became Chief Minister. On 20 May 2002, Timor-Leste formally gained its independence and Alkatiri became Prime Minister of the new state. Much of the period following independence was spent in difficult and protracted negotiations with Australia over maritime delimitation in the Timor Sea. Australia was reluctant to lose the access to resources it had secured in negotiations with Indonesia during its occupation of the territory. Two months

FIGURE 18.4
Map of the Timor Sea. Shaded sections of the map represent the areas of overlapping claims, in which Timor-Leste has asked that Australia exercise restraint in exploiting resources in accordance with its obligations under international law. Source: Timor Sea Office, Office of the Prime Minister, Government of Timor-Leste

before Timor-Leste became independent, Australia withdrew from the jurisdiction of the International Court of Justice on maritime issues and the International Tribunal for the Law of the Sea (Downer 2002). The Australian government continued to issue licences for fields in disputed territories where Australian and Timorese claims overlapped (see Figure 18.4). The Australian government also refused to put revenues estimated at $1 million a day from these fields into a trust account pending resolution of the disputed claims to the territory. According to international lawyers from the Australian Attorney-General's department, Australia had no obligation to negotiate claims to these disputed territories, as Australia had exercised 'active jurisdiction' over them while Timor-Leste was occupied (Cleary 2007: 124). After four years of negotiations, the *Treaty on Certain Maritime Arrangements in the Timor Sea* (CMATS) between Australia and Timor-Leste was signed on 12 January 2006.

Eruption of violence and the 2006 intervention

In April 2006, violence between military factions, the police and militias broke out in Timor-Leste. The immediate trigger to this unrest was the dismissal of a group of personnel from within the Timorese defence force, or FALINTIL – Forças Armadas de Defesa de Timor-Leste (F-FDTL). Most of those dismissed were soldiers who were on strike claiming that they had been discriminated against in favour of former members of FALINTIL. Prime Minister Alkatiri characterised the violence in Dili (the capital of Timor-Leste) as an attempted coup and stated that the attacks were directed at 'blocking the democratic institutions' and preventing them from functioning, so that 'the only solution would be for national parliament to be dissolved by the President . . . which would provoke the fall of the Government' (ABC News Online 2006a). On 12 May, the Prime Minister of Australia announced that Australia was deploying two warships to Australia's northern waters 'in case East Timor requested international troops' (ABC News Online 2006b), a move protested by the Timorese government. However, on 24 May, in the context of escalating violence, Timor-Leste sent an official request for military assistance to Australia, Malaysia, New Zealand and Portugal, with the first international forces arriving in response the next day. A new UN peacekeeping force, the United Nations Integrated Mission in Timor-Leste (UNMIT), was created by Security Council Resolution 1704 in August 2006, to operate under Australian command. The renewed unrest and subsequent military intervention had a significant impact on Timorese and Australian politics. Prime Minister Mari Alkatiri resigned on 26 June 2006, as a result of claims aired in Australian media that he had been involved in distributing guns to militias. In February 2007, the Timorese Prosecutor-General announced that he and international advisors had found no evidence in support of these claims, and that the investigation into this matter was closed (Cleary 2007: 255). José Ramos Horta was appointed by President Gusmão as the new Prime Minister on 8 July 2006, and in his first press conference announced that he would ratify the CMATS treaty with Australia. The Australian Defence Department has since announced plans to build a permanent military base in the centre of Dili (Cleary 2007: 258).

While the 1999 UN intervention in Timor was understood within the narrative of humanitarian intervention, the 2006 intervention was quickly characterised in terms of the language of failed states and corrupt governance familiar to the new millennium. The UN treated the outbreak of violence as the expression of

FIGURE 18.5
José Ramos Horta.
Photo: Glenn Campbell

'deep-rooted problems inherent in fragile State institutions and a weak rule of law', and proposed that attention should be paid to 'capacity-building and strengthening of state institutions' (United Nations Independent Special Commission of Inquiry 2006: paras 221–2). In his August 2006 report on the situation in Timor-Leste, the UN Secretary-General focused on the need for 'security sector reform', promotion of the rule of law and increased 'capacity-building' as responses to the civil unrest. The Timorese leadership was condemned by the Australian Prime Minister John Howard: 'There is no point beating around the bush. The country has not been well-governed and I do hope that the sobering experience for those in elected positions of having to call for outside help will induce the appropriate behaviours inside the country' (Cleary 2007: 256). According to such international commentators, the eruption of violence revealed that the Timorese leadership had either failed to understand how a state should function properly or had failed to implement certain technical aspects of governance. Neither the UN nor international experts considered the involvement of outsiders in contributing to the unrest, whether through taking sides in the factional disputes within the military and bureaucracy, or through draining government resources and attention into protracted Timor Sea negotiations.

The 2006 military revolt in Timor-Leste has been interpreted as simply a technical matter – a sign that yet another group of post-colonial tutees require further training in how a state should function and in tenets of the rule of law. For example, the *Economist* describes the situation in May 2006 as resulting from an 'incompetent and faction-ridden government' which 'led to chaos and the dispatch of fresh peacekeepers' (*Economist* 2007). Such analyses strip this situation of any political content and represent Timor-Leste as an inadequate version of a European state, one that 'will need years more babysitting from the UN'.

Chapter 9 examines how the state emerged in Europe.

FIGURE 18.6
'East Timor gas, Bush oil'. Cartoon by Nicholson from *The Australian*, www.nicholson.com.au

It is as if there is only one form of the state, such that we can no longer remember that this uniform model of political order might itself be subject to challenge (see Box 18.2 on p.439). Yet this armed struggle could also be interpreted as a political event – as part of a conflict over the theory of the state which was involved in turning a revolutionary front into the Timor defence force. FALANTIL was initially created in August 1975 as the military arm of FRETILIN. With the creation of the independent state of Timor-Leste, the armed forces were named the F-FDTL (FALINTIL – Força Defensa Timor-Leste). As this name suggests, the military were envisaged as inheriting the political mantle of the revolutionary defenders of an independent Timor-Leste (La'o Hamutuk 2005). The dispute in 2006 resulted from tensions within the military between those soldiers from the western part of the country who claimed they were being discriminated against in favour of soldiers from the eastern part of the country who were active in FALINTIL and the resistance movement. In addition, tension between the military and the police force was fuelled by the ties between the police force and former members of the Indonesian military. Thus the stakes of the unrest in 2006 were in part about a theory of the state which did not treat military power as somehow technical or neutral, and which resisted a vision of the military as somehow above or separate from the people.

RESPONSES
LAW AND THE EXCEPTIONAL

The question – what can we do to stop people harming others? – can be approached as both a political and a legal question. In political terms, we might want to ask – what can we realistically or legitimately do to force or persuade people to stop hurting each other? What is the most effective form of action to achieve this end? What kind of political organisation or world order would best ensure that people are protected from harm? We might also consider this to raise matters of law – what *can* we do, what are we permitted or authorised or obliged to do, to stop people hurting each other? This is a question about the scope and limits of lawful authority in times of emergency or states of exception. In this section, I will introduce a series of ways of thinking about the relation between legality and legitimacy, or norm and exception, which have informed the theory and practice of humanitarian intervention.

For a discussion of why politics turns to violence in the first place, see **Chapter 16**, which discusses war in Europe. See also **Chapter 19** for the argument that moving on after conflict is a difficult and long-term process.

Metaphysical account of law

The first such theory of the relation between legality and legitimacy involves a metaphysical account of law. It is well illustrated by the dominant legal and political response to the NATO intervention in Kosovo in 1999. Commentators

BOX 18.2 THE STATE AND REVOLUTION

FIGURE 18.7
Lenin disguised as
'*Vilén*', wearing a wig
and with his beard
shaved off. Finland,
11 August 1917

In the months prior to the October revolution of 1917, from his exile in Helsinki, Vladimir Lenin finished work on an extraordinary manifesto entitled *The State and Revolution* (Lenin 1951 [1918]). In this book, Lenin broke dramatically with the long tradition of European political thought and practice concerning the relation between church, state and individual (Harding 1996; Žižek 2002). *The State and Revolution*, and the Bolshevik seizure of power which this text anticipates, challenged existing conceptual frameworks for thinking about the proper form of the state and its relation to law.

Lenin argued, following Friedrich Engels, that the state is a form of power which 'arose from society, but places itself above it and alienates itself more and more from it' (Lenin 1951 [1918]: 17). The chief instruments of this state power are a standing army, a police force and a bureaucracy, all separate from the people. The state requires such special bodies of armed men because if the population were armed under conditions of irreconcilable class division and antagonism, armed struggle would result. Lenin argued that in the early twentieth century these aspects of executive power – the military and the bureaucracy – had been strengthened enormously and that repressive measures against the proletariat had intensified. In response, Lenin called for this state machinery to be 'smashed' (Lenin 1951 [1918]: 53). *The State and Revolution* offers a challenge to the conceptualisation of the form of the state as a technical rather than a political question – a conceptualisation underpinning the international project of state-building in Timor-Leste and elsewhere. Lenin's tract serves as a reminder that the relation between the military, the bureaucracy and the people themselves is not a technical question, but one which is at the heart of politics.

such as Bruno Simma and Antonio Cassese argued that the Kosovo intervention was illegal but legitimate (Simma 1999; Cassese 1999). For Simma, Cassese and many others at the time, the question of the legality of the Kosovo intervention was quickly answered – it was illegal as it did not conform to any of the authorised grounds upon which states could have recourse to force under the UN Charter. However, they felt that a commitment to justice required the international community to support the NATO intervention in Kosovo, despite its illegality. Determining whether the intervention was legitimate involved asking whether it was in conformity with universal values which transcended any given legal order.

These interpretations of the legitimacy of the NATO intervention underpinned the position put by then British Prime Minister Tony Blair. Blair portrayed the NATO intervention in Kosovo as a 'just war, based not on territorial ambitions, but on values' (Blair 1999a).

Chapter 15 explains what is meant by a 'just war'.

> This war was not fought for Albanians against Serbs. It was not fought for territory. Still less for NATO aggrandisement. It was fought for a fundamental principle necessary for humanity's progress: that every human being, regardless of race, religion or birth, has the inalienable right to live free from persecution.
>
> (Blair 1999b)

Such accounts are based upon the appeal to a universal law which transcends the rules of any existing legal system. It is reference to this universal law which gives legitimacy to the act of intervention. In such formulations, we see played out what Jennifer Beard has characterised as the metaphysics of modern Western identity (Beard 2006). Such a conception of humanitarian intervention is metaphysical in that it is based on notions of universal values and ideal forms, of which actually existing political communities represent only imperfect copies. Beard has argued compellingly that the impetus for the development of this metaphysics has been the encounters between the Old World and the New, or, in contemporary language, the developed and the developing worlds. The developed world is represented as the embodiment on earth of 'an infinitely distant reality' and a 'potential state of fulfilment', the promise of which will be fulfilled once the peoples of the New World are redeemed (Beard 2006: 3, 4, 11).

Compare the account of the ticking bomb scenario in Chapter 2.

See the discussion of colonial encounters in Chapter 15.

Realist account of law

A second account of the role of law in the global politics of intervention is not concerned with universal norms (as in the metaphysical account) and resists 'any assertion of a place for legitimate authority in the international order' (Carty 2006). This realist approach understands international law purely as an expression of the interests and will of sovereign states. In this familiar vision, global politics is portrayed as anarchic (that is, lacking an over-arching authority), and individual entities such as states are left 'to act instrumentally and calculate power in relative rather than absolute terms' (Huysmans 2006: 154). While norms may be generated by agreement between sovereigns, such norms are not the expression of moral values or of an objectified legal system, but rather of 'an existing historical political order' (Huysmans 2006: 155). Such an account, which finds support from both the left and the right of politics in debates over intervention, dismisses any portrayal of the systematic nature of the international order or any suggestion that international law may bring into being a political community. Instead, the realist approach privileges bilateral relations as at the heart of the existing international order. The international realm in this view is by definition exceptional – the lack of a legal system or a guarantor of law leaves only alienated entities engaged in functional encounters. International lawyers fulfil their tasks when they find ways for these entities to express their national interests or their instrumental objectives in the law they bring into being. In the case of Timor-Leste, this law might include the resolutions of the Security Council authorising intervention in 1999, but the series of treaties that enabled the exploitation of maritime resources in an area subject to conflicting territorial claims would be seen as equally legitimate and valid expressions of national interest and sovereign will.

Decisionist account of law

A third account of the relation between legality and legitimacy is the decisionist account. Key to this account are the claims that the primary role of the state is to protect its citizens, and that the state depends for its survival upon the existence of a sovereign who can guarantee the values and law of the state. In order to begin to analyse the effects of this account of law, I want to turn to the writings of Carl Schmitt. Two aspects of Schmitt's solution are relevant to contemporary debates about humanitarian intervention.

First, Schmitt argued that for the law and governance of a democratic state to be effective, that state must represent a homogenous and unified nation. In order for the state to survive, there must exist a sovereign capable of properly distinguishing between friend and enemy and thus preserving the national homogeneity that was for Schmitt the necessary condition of effective government. The state must be willing to defend the values that bound together the members of a given political community of 'friends'. It was the defence of these particular values, and not some set of universal values that could be determined in advance, that gave legitimacy to the state. In order to protect the state against those who did not share such values, the qualitatively total state must control all aspects of the life of those within it. Thus Schmitt argued, *pace* Hobbes, that the state could not afford to respect individual freedoms such as freedoms of thought or conscience.

Second, Schmitt developed the related argument that an individual could only submit to the law where certain political conditions were in place (Schmitt 2004 [1932]: 20). In particular, there must be only one lawmaker, and that lawmaker must be 'the final guardian of all law, ultimate guarantor of the existing order, conclusive source of all legality, and the last security and protection against injustice' (Schmitt 2004 [1932]: 19). In addition, for a '"formal" concept of law' to be 'conceivable and acceptable', there must be 'congruence between the parliamentary majority and the will of the homogenous people' (Schmitt 2004

Chapter 10 raises questions about the view of a state as populated by a homogenous group of people forming a nation.

Thomas Hobbes is discussed in **Chapter 6**.

BOX 18.3 CARL SCHMITT

FIGURE 18.8
Carl Schmitt

Carl Schmitt (1888–1985) was a German jurist and political theorist whose anti-liberal and anti-parliamentary views provided ideological support for the totalitarian state of Nazi Germany. Schmitt argued that the state has a responsibility to protect its citizens:

> It must be taken into consideration that the totality of this kind of state power always accords with the total responsibility for protecting and securing the safety of citizens and that obedience as well as the renunciation of every right of resistance that can be demanded by this god is only the correlate of the true protection that he guarantees.
>
> (Schmitt 1996: 96)

However, for Schmitt, the state could not – and indeed should not – retain authority if it had no claims to legitimacy other than its capacity to provide protection. Civil society would continually regroup to challenge a state imagined as a kind of soulless, security machine. Schmitt sought to develop a theory of legality and legitimacy which would ground the political authority of the state.

[1932]: 24). Underpinning this conception was the assumption that 'every democracy rests on the presupposition of the indivisibly similar, entire, unified people' (Schmitt 2004 [1932]: 28). If parliament did not represent the will of a unified people, respect for legislation would descend into sterile proceduralism. Schmitt argued that it made no sense to obey statutes passed by a (socialist) parliament simply on the grounds that as a matter of formal process they had been passed by a representative assembly. If the parliament had ceased to represent the will of an 'indivisibly similar, entire, unified people', then the sovereign lawmaker who could act as guarantor of the legal order would have to be found elsewhere.

It is in this context that Schmitt wrote perhaps his most famous sentence: 'Sovereign is he who decides on the exception' (Schmitt 2005 [1934]: 5). For Schmitt, the essence of the legal form 'lies in the concrete decision, one that emanates from a particular authority' (Schmitt 2005 [1934]: 34). And every decision in turn 'contains a constitutive element' (Schmitt 2005 [1934]: 26). The law 'cannot realize itself', this realisation occurs through the decision, and yet the law does not prescribe 'who should decide' (Schmitt 2005 [1934]: 33). This is the constitutive element contained within each decision, and indeed secreted within every legal order. According to this conception of law, whenever 'the legally highest authority does not have the actual capacity to make a decision and impose it according to the established procedures', the legal order comes under pressure (Huysmans 2006: 148). The problem of who can and should guarantee that a decision is made, and thus 'rescue the essence of the legal form', is central to Schmitt's theory of legality and legitimacy (Huysmans 2006: 149). Schmitt argued that in times of emergency, such as are experienced by people caught up in civil war, the preservation of the legal and political order depends upon the existence of a sovereign who can restore the legal form. The essence of the legal form in this conception is the decision. For a legal system to remain legitimate, it must allow for this sovereign decision to be taken if the existing order is under threat. A legal system needs a guarantor of its fundamental values to make such decisions in times of emergency. As we will see in Part 4, this decisionist conception of the relation between law and sovereignty emerges in many contemporary arguments about the legitimacy of humanitarian intervention.

Democratic account of law

The fourth and final account of law which is relevant to understanding the debates about humanitarian intervention we might call democratic. This account of law was developed explicitly in response to Schmitt's constitutional theorising in 1930s Germany. In particular, David Dyzenhaus has argued that the political theory of law developed in the work of Hermann Heller during this period offers a major challenge to Schmittian decisionism (Dyzenhaus 1997). Heller accepted that the question of whether law is valid is a political – rather than a technical or a metaphysical – question. He agreed with Schmitt that the question of the legitimacy of a constitutive law 'cannot, of course, be answered by referring to its coming into existence in accordance with some previously valid positive propositions' (Heller 2002 [1934]: 278). Rather, the determination of the legitimacy and thus the validity of a law requires a justification from principles that are immanent to the law itself. For Dyzenhaus, Heller's account of law requires that the determination of validity involves a consideration of whether any particular law 'is the product of a properly functioning democratic legal order' (Dyzenhaus 1997: 254). Law is understood to constitute and be itself constituted by the (idealised) commitment to understanding relations between individuals (or states) in terms of a political community of equals. In this account of law, all claims to authority or truth, even those made on behalf of law, must remain visible and contestable. Power cannot and should not be made to disappear 'into rational and logical relationships of legality' – rather, there is no outside to politics, including the politics of law (Dyzenhaus 1997: 256–7).

BROADER ISSUES
LEGALITY, LEGITIMACY AND THE POLITICS OF INTERVENTION

How do these different accounts of the relation between legitimacy and legality, or norm and exception, help us to think about what can be done – effectively, responsibly, lawfully – to stop people hurting each other? During the 1990s, a metaphysical account of law often underpinned the answer to this question. From this perspective, the way to stop people harming others is to bring into being a new global community capable of fully representing universal values of justice, peace, human rights and development. Those advocating increased intervention in the name of human rights often sought to elevate certain priorities, decisions or values above political debate. In this new age of wars on terror and in the context of the rise of competing forms of religious militancy, those advocating the use of force are far less likely to make use of universalist claims to be acting in the name of universal values or a common humanity. It is difficult to argue convincingly in such a climate that there exists a stable set of common values animating all states and peoples, or that coalitions of the willing might intervene in the name of defending such values.

For more on how religion and politics mix, see Chapter 5.

In many ways, this is not a bad thing. Metaphysical accounts of humanitarian intervention as illegal but legitimate make it difficult to take responsibility for the practices that are authorised by the claim that one is acting on behalf of universal values to bring into being a global civil society. Where action is understood to be motivated by the need to redeem the lack of law, rights or development in another society, the measure of whether the action is proper will not be its immediate effects upon that society. Rather, the gaze will be upon the coming community which the action is designed to bring into being.

Let me give one example of the way in which this focus upon the future creates problems in the present. The international human rights tradition is committed to constraining executive government, regulating and confining the exercise of emergency or discretionary powers. And yet the approach taken by human rights activists in the debate about humanitarian intervention has been to call for military action to be taken in extreme circumstances to redeem universal values that may transcend particular legal orders. This call for increased intervention by powerful states necessarily relies upon executive governments, militaries and multinational corporations as its agents. While much of the human rights movement has been properly appalled by the abuses carried out by US military and security forces in the war on terror, advocates of humanitarian intervention do not ask whether increased intervention by the US military under its current rules of engagement offers the best strategy for the protection of individuals in Third World states. While much human rights activism has focused on the exploitative practices of multinational corporations in their operations in the

For a discussion of torture and detention, see Chapter 2.

BOX 18.4 HABERMAS AND COSMOPOLITANISM

FIGURE 18.9
Jürgen Habermas

A focus on the coming cosmopolitan community is illustrated well by the work of Jürgen Habermas. Habermas endorsed the Kosovo intervention on the basis that it was understood by continental European states 'as an "anticipation" of an effective law of world citizenship – as a step along the path from classical international law to what Kant 'envisioned as the "status of world citizen" which would afford legal protection to citizens against their own criminal regimes' (Habermas 2004). The measurement of the propriety of this action is then in terms of the extent to which it represents a further step along the path to world citizenship and the coming cosmopolitan order.

Habermas has since published a collection of essays on cosmopolitanism and international law (Habermas 2006 [2004]).

Third World, advocates of humanitarian intervention do not ask whether enabling an increased presence by foreign contractors in the post-conflict period offers the best strategy for ending suffering in the Third World. These concerns are forgotten in the support for increased resort to military action and increased multinational corporate presence implicit in the call for greater international intervention. The metaphysical question 'How can we bring into being a civil society to ensure that universal values are guaranteed to all of humanity?' provides an inadequate grounding for analysing whether humanitarian intervention is in fact a good thing for the people it is designed to serve.

This approach to intervention also makes it difficult to take responsibility for the violence of practices authorised by the international community in the name of ending suffering. The desire to 'do something' to save those at risk of harm in far-off places is often a response to viewing televised images of suffering in the Third World. Images of suffering functioned throughout the 1990s to explain the need for institutional intervention, and in so doing operated also as forms of entertainment and spiritual enrichment for their audiences. The publics of militarily powerful states watched nameless starving, weeping, mourning strangers who appeared as part of a narrative in which the audience was persuaded of the superiority of its nation-state and its capacity to rescue and redeem these others. In contrast, the military actions undertaken by powerful states in the name of humanitarian intervention, such as that undertaken by NATO in response to the Kosovo crisis in 1999, are represented as bloodless. Body counts by intervening forces are often not made available, and the high-tech violence involved in

Media representations of wars impact on how we see the world, see Chapter 7.

The problem of doing something about what is wrong in the world is explored in Chapter 20.

For more on the problem of counting the dead, see Chapter 20.

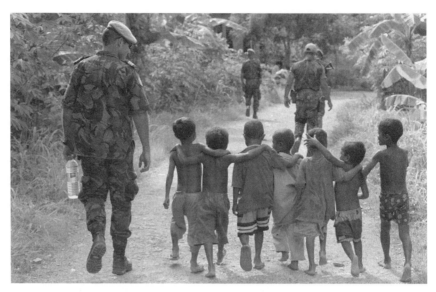

FIGURE 18.10
This photograph appears on many UN and national government websites. The image is of a
United Nations peacekeeping soldier, member of UNTAET's Portuguese contingent,
accompanied by a group of local children as he conducts a security patrol in the Becora district of
Dili, East Timor. UN/DPI Photo# 203225C

bombing is portrayed in televised reports as spectacular rather than brutal. Images
of peacekeepers often portray them as fatherly figures – talking to children,
building schools or fixing roads.

And yet, having pointed to the problems associated with the metaphysical account
of law, the post-sceptical climate of the new millennium has its own dangers. The
first of these is that the tendency to dismiss claims to universalism strengthens a
national-interest based approach to foreign policy and a realist account of law. If
all law is merely a reflection of the interests of powerful states, there is no reason
to hope that anything can or will be done to ensure that the international order
is premised upon a commitment to justice, human rights or equality. In this vision,
law offers no constraint or limit to guide our thinking about what we *can* do in
the world – according to this realist account, we can do whatever we have the
military and economic power to do in situations where this will further our
national interest. To the extent that law ceases to provide an expression of our
national interest, we will withdraw from it, just as Australia withdrew from the
jurisdiction of international tribunals in the context of the Timor Gap negotiations discussed on p. 432. Where such a vision of international law prevails,
humanitarian intervention may serve merely to militarise relations between
powerful and less powerful states. Law may offer some resources for stopping
people harming each other, but only where this end is an expression of the
interests of the entities who make up the existing order.

The post-sceptical environment also fuels the decisionist account of law. Indeed, this approach to law underpins much of the discussion of the emerging notion of the responsibility to protect, which has gradually colonised legal and political debate about intervention since its development by the International Commission on Intervention and State Sovereignty (ICISS) in 2001. ICISS was an international initiative designed to respond to the perceived tension between state sovereignty and humanitarian intervention in the aftermath of the NATO action. Its report proposed a re-characterisation of the humanitarian intervention debate, 'not as an argument about any right at all but rather about a responsibility – one to protect people at grave risk' (Evans 2006: 708). According to ICISS, the state has 'the primary responsibility for the protection of its people' (ICISS 2001). If the state fails in its responsibility, 'a secondary responsibility to protect falls on the international community, acting primarily through the UN' (Evans 2006: 709). ICISS set out three responsibilities incorporated by the responsibility to protect, namely the responsibility to *prevent* conflict or risk to populations, the responsibility to *react*, including in extreme cases with military intervention, and the responsibility to *rebuild*, particularly after military intervention.

Our responsibilities to those beyond our own political community are discussed in **Chapter 2**. **Chapters 15 and 20** also explore responsibility.

The concept of the responsibility to protect was taken up in the Report of the UN High-Level Panel on Threats, Challenges and Change. The Panel argued that what is needed today is a new security consensus:

> The essence of that consensus is simple: we all share responsibility for each other's security. And the test of that consensus will be action.
>
> (United Nations High-Level Panel 2004: 16)

FIGURE 18.11
Kosovars returning from the forced expulsions of 1999. Photo: Gilles Peress

Like ICISS, the Panel developed this notion of a shared responsibility by reference to notions of protection. The Panel endorsed what it referred to as 'the emerging norm that there is a collective international responsibility to protect, exercisable by the Security Council authorizing military intervention as a last resort'. The primacy of protection to the purpose of the state was taken up in the report of the UN Secretary-General to the 2005 World Summit session of the General Assembly. The Secretary-General there stated: 'I believe that we must embrace the responsibility to protect, and, when necessary, we must act on it' (United Nations Secretary-General 2005: para. 135). He continued: 'This responsibility lies, first and foremost, with each individual State, whose primary raison d'être [or reason for being] and duty is to protect its population'. According to the Secretary-General, if 'national authorities' are not able to 'protect their citizens', this responsibility 'shifts to the international community'. The responsibility to protect has since been adopted by the General Assembly, at its World Summit session in September 2005, and been reaffirmed by the Security Council in resolutions dealing with the protection of civilians in armed conflict and the deployment of peacekeepers in Darfur.

A decisionist conception of the need for a sovereign guarantor of law emerges in much of the responsibility to protect literature. This literature assumes that where the existing order threatens to break down, a sovereign must be found who can in fact take the decision that a state of emergency exists. Advocates of humanitarian intervention in these terms focus much of their attention on calling for a decision to be made in times of emergency. So Thomas Weiss, a strong supporter of the notion of humanitarian intervention, comments that 'even if none of the choices are ideal, victims still require decisions about outside help' (Weiss 1999: 2). And the ICISS report states:

> The most compelling task now is to work to ensure that when the call goes out to the community of states for action, that call will be answered.
> (International Commission on Intervention
> and State Sovereignty 2001: 70)

To this degree, the responsibility to protect literature adopts Schmitt's solution to the dilemmas of legitimacy – the need for there to be a guarantor of the values of the legal order. The one who decides on the exception – the Security Council, the United States, the coalition of the willing – is the sovereign guarantor in this sense. This prioritising of the role of the executive as guarantor of the legal order also manifests itself in the post-conflict phase. Intervention is often followed by the creation and legitimisation of strong authoritarian administrations in which executive power is almost unrestrained. Here again we see an echo of 1930s Europe. As Alexander Somek suggests, the effect of authoritarian state theory was to diminish the space for parliamentary participation and expand the space for executive governance in the name of achieving social and economic integration

(Somek 2003). This is precisely the nature and effect of post-conflict governance in the aftermath of international interventions in places such as Timor-Leste, where international administrators suspend democratic participation until political order and economic integration are secured.

At times, the responsibility to protect literature also draws on a more democratic politics of law. This account of the politics of international law treats issues of participation, representation and accountability as essential to establishing the legitimacy of particular forms of authority or of particular decisions. Attention to such questions of political practice has already emerged as a feature of institutional discussion of the responsibility to protect and collective security since 2001. For example, while the High-Level Panel endorsed the responsibility to protect, it spelt out that it is for the Security Council to decide whether or not resort to force is justified. It then stated that not only must such decisions be legal, but there must also be 'the common perception of their legitimacy – their being made on solid evidentiary grounds, and for the right reasons, morally as well as legally' (United Nations High-Level Panel 2004). In its discussion of the question of legitimacy of the global collective security system, the High-Level Panel notes:

> If the Security Council is to win the respect it must have as the primary body in the collective security system, it is critical that the most important and influential decisions, those with large-scale life-and-death impact, be better made, better substantiated and better communicated.
>
> (United Nations High-Level Panel 2004)

The High-Level Panel here seeks to expand the justificatory obligations of the Security Council. It assumes that the Security Council as a political organ representing the otherwise secretive security interests of powerful states is nonetheless part of a political community, to which it must account publicly for the bases of its decisions to authorise (or refuse to authorise) the use of force against Third World states.

As noted above the responsibility to protect concept also directs attention to decisions other than those involved in the resort to force. According to the ICISS report, decisions about protection now involve not simply the decision about whether to use force, but the myriad decisions authorised by the notion that the responsibility to protect involves not just a responsibility to react, but also a responsibility to prevent and to rebuild. Thus the effects of the responsibility to protect will depend on the lawfulness of actions taken in relation to these other aspects of protection. What laws will govern questions of resource ownership, contract allocation and economic restructuring in post-conflict states? How will the powers and responsibilities of the (international) executive and the (local) parliamentary government be determined? Such issues will shape the political orders – both national and international – brought into being through these ongoing acts of intervention.

CONCLUSION

The question 'What can we do to stop people harming others?' registers the demand for justice in an age dominated by internationalist narratives, whether of globalisation and harmonisation, or of high-tech wars on terror and for humanity. In this chapter, I have suggested that there is both a political and a legal aspect to this question.

In political terms, the question of what we can *effectively* do to stop people harming others asks us to reflect upon what measures or actions are demanded of the international community in the name of humanitarian action in the post-Cold War era. This chapter has been critical of the tendency to answer this question by advocating resort to force as the means of protecting people in the Third World. Despite the prohibition against the use of force enshrined in the UN Charter, there has been a persistent trend to militarise the relationship between First and Third Worlds, usually on the basis that an emergency exists justifying, if not requiring, resort to force. The focus on military action as the means to protect those at risk of direct violence at the hands of the state, militias or insurgents detracts attention from the ways in which our world order is built upon other policies and practices which harm people – severe restrictions on asylum, strict controls over immigration, ruthless economic exploitation and an unjust international division of labour. Whether we 'can' change these policies raises questions of our own political capacity to participate in shaping the conditions of our lives and those whose lives we touch.

Examples of restrictions on movement are discussed in **Chapter 8** and economic exploitation in **Chapter 11**.

In legal terms, the question of what we can *properly* do to stop people harming others raises issues of the legal authority to take action and the protocols or procedures for making decisions about matters that affect the lives of others. It also raises questions about who has the authority to speak in the name of law in a particular territory, and how different laws should encounter each other (McVeigh 2007). In this sense, what 'we' can do is not something that can lawfully be determined only by 'us'. Rather than seeing politics as somehow separate from legality, decision-making about protection must be informed by a concept of law which is itself strongly political. Such a concept of law would assume that, in order to be valid, law must be the product of a particular kind of political order and must in turn place obligations upon the members of the community it constitutes. At the least, these obligations would include a commitment to equal participation in the making of law as essential to establishing the legitimacy of particular forms of authority. Bringing decisions about what 'we' can do to help others within a fully political, and thus contestable, account of international law offers some possibility of justice for those the international community claims to protect.

FURTHER READING

Critical readings of humanitarian intervention in the 1990s can be found in Orford (2003), Koskenniemi (2002) and Charlesworth (2002). A useful overview of the emergence of the notion of the responsibility to protect is Evans (2006). A key text on the legacy of the civilising mission for international law is Anghie (2004). Beard (2006) develops a rich account of international law as metaphysics, while Dyzenhaus (1997) provides a detailed analysis of the major constitutionalist theories of law which emerged in Weimar Germany. An analysis of the relationship between these constitutional accounts and the framing of contemporary global politics can be found in Huysmans (2006). Cleary (2007) is a revealing insider's account of the negotiations between Australia and Timor-Leste concerning the Timor Sea oil and gas fields.

WEBSITES

International Centre for Trade and Sustainable Development website, http://www. ictsd.org/.
    News and information relating to trade and development issues and the place to subscribe to the excellent Bridges Weekly Trade News Digest email service.

La'o Hamutuk, www.laohamutuk.org.
    The website of a Timorese NGO, offering incisive analysis of the politics of contemporary international engagement with Timor-Leste.

National Security Archive, http://www.gwu.edu/~nsarchiv/.
    The website of a non-governmental research institute which collects and publishes declassified US government documents, particularly relating to US security and economic policies.

Timor-Leste official government site, http://www.timor-leste.gov.tl/.
    Official website of the Timorese government, providing historical material about Timor-Leste and covering all areas of governmental responsibility.

United Nations Peace and Security website, http://www.un.org/peace/.
    UN website providing access to material relating to peace and security.

REFERENCES

ABC News Online (2006a) 'E Timor Unrest an Attempted Coup: PM', 9 May, http://www.abc.net.au/news/newsitems/200605/s1634598.htm.

ABC News Online (2006b) 'East Timor Rejects Need for Peacekeepers', 12 May, http://www.abc.net.au/news/newsitems/200605/s1637481.htm.

Aditjondro, George (2000) 'From Colony to Global Prize', *Arena Magazine* 47, June: 22–32.

Anghie, Antony (2004) *Imperialism, Sovereignty and the Making of International Law*, Cambridge: Cambridge University Press.

Annan, Kofi (1999) 'Two Concepts of Sovereignty', *Economist*, 18 September: 49–50.

Beard, Jennifer L. (2006) *The Political Economy of Desire: International Law, Development and the Nation State*, London: Cavendish-Routledge.

Blair, Tony (1999a) 'Doctrine of the International Community', speech given to the Economic Club of Chicago, Chicago, 22 April, http://www.fco.gov.uk/news/speechtext.asp?2316.

Blair, Tony (1999b) 'Statement on the Suspension of NATO Air Strikes against Yugoslavia', London, 10 June.

Cady, Jean-Christian (2000) 'Building the New State of East Timor', lecture given at the Centre for International and Public Law, Australian National University, 18 May.

Carty, Antony (2006) 'Visions of the Past of International Society: Law, History or Politics?', *Modern Law Review* 69, 4: 644–60.

Cassese, Antonio (1999) '*Ex iniuria ius oritur:* Are We Moving towards International Legitimation of Forcible Humanitarian Countermeasures in the World Community?', *European Journal of International Law* 10, 1: 23–30.

Charlesworth, Hilary (2002) 'International Law: A Discipline of Crisis', *Modern Law Review* 65, 3: 377–92.

Cleary, Paul (2007) *Shakedown: Australia's Grab for Timor Oil,* New South Wales: Allen & Unwin.

Downer, Alexander (2002) 'Changes to International Dispute Resolution', Media Release, Canberra, 25 March, http://www.foreignminster.gov.au/releases/2002/fa039j_02.html.

Downer, Alexander (1999) Australian Minister for Foreign Affairs, 'East Timor: The Way Ahead', speech given to the Rotary Club of Sydney, 30 November, http://www.foreignminister.gov.au/speeches/1999/991130_rotary_club.html.

Dyzenhaus, David (1997) *Legality and Legitimacy: Carl Schmitt, Hans Kelsen and Hermann Heller in Weimar*, Oxford: Oxford University Press.

Economist (2007) 'Timor-Leste', *Economist Backgrounders*, www.economist.com/research/backgrounders.

Evans, Gareth (2006) 'From Humanitarian Intervention to the Responsibility to Protect', *Wisconsin International Law Journal* 24, 3: 703–22.

Habermas, Jürgen (2006 [2004]) *The Divided West*, trans. Ciaran Cronin, Cambridge: Polity Press.

Habermas, Jürgen (2004) 'America and the World', *Logos: A Journal of Modern Society and Culture* 3.3, http://www.logosjournal.com/issue_3.3.pdf.

Harding, Neil (1996) *Leninism*, Basingstoke: MacMillan.

Heller, Hermann (2002 [1934]) 'The Essence and Structure of the State', in Arthur J. Jacobson and Bernhard Schlink (eds) *Weimar: A Jurisprudence of Crisis*, Berkeley, CA: University of California Press.

Huysmans, Jef (2006) 'International Politics of Exception: Competing Visions of International Political Order between Law and Politics', *Alternatives* 31, 2: 135–65.

International Commission on Intervention and State Sovereignty (2001) *The Responsibility to Protect*, http://www.iciss.ca/report-en.asp.

Koskenniemi, Martti (2002) '"The Lady Doth Protest Too Much": Kosovo and the Turn to Ethics in International Law', *Modern Law Review* 65, 2: 159–75.

La'o Hamutuk (2005) 'An Overview of FALINTIL's Transformation to FDTL and Its Implications', *Bulletin La'o Hamutuk* 6, 1–2: 1–5, http://www.laohamutuk.org/Bulletin/2005/Apr/lhbl6n1e.pdf.

La'o Hamutuk (2000) 'The World Bank in East Timor', *Bulletin La'o Hamutuk* 1, 4: 1, http://www.laohamutuk.org/Bulletin/2000/Dec/lhbul4en.pdf.

Lenin, Vladimir (1951 [1918]) *The State and Revolution*, Moscow: Foreign Languages Publishing House.

McVeigh, Shaun (ed.) (2007) *Jurisprudence of Jurisdiction*, London: Routledge-Cavendish.

Orford, Anne (2006) 'Trade, Human Rights and the Economy of Sacrifice', in Anne Orford (ed.) *International Law and Its Others*, Cambridge: Cambridge University Press.

Orford, Anne (2004) 'The Destiny of International Law', *Leiden Journal of International Law* 17, 3: 441–76.

Orford, Anne (2003) *Reading Humanitarian Intervention: Human Rights and the Use of Force in International Law*, Cambridge: Cambridge University Press.

Schmitt, Carl (2005 [1934]) *Political Theology: Four Chapters on the Concept of Sovereignty*, 2nd edn, trans. George Schwab, Chicago, IL: University of Chicago Press.

Schmitt, Carl (2004 [1932]) *Legality and Legitimacy*, trans. and ed. Jeffrey Seitzer, Durham, NC: Duke University Press.

Schmitt, Carl (2003 [1950]) *The Nomos of the Earth in the International Law of the Jus Publicum Europaeum*, trans. G.L. Ulmen, New York: Telos Press.

Schmitt, Carl (1996) *The Leviathan in the State Theory of Thomas Hobbes: Meaning and Failure of a Political Symbol*, Westport, CT: Greenwood Press.

Simma, Bruno (1999) 'NATO, the UN and the Use of Force: Legal Aspects', *European Journal of International Law* 10, 1: 1–22.

Somek, Alexander (2003) 'Austrian Constitutional Doctrine 1933 to 1938', in Christian Joerges and Navraj Singh Ghaleigh (eds) *Darker Legacies of Law in Europe*, Oxford: Hart Publishing.

Traub, James (2000) 'Inventing East Timor', *Foreign Affairs* 79, 4: 74–89.

United Nations High-Level Panel on Threats, Challenges and Change (2004) *A More Secure World: Our Shared Responsibility*, UN Doc A59/565, http://www.un.org/secureworld/.

United Nations Independent Special Commission of Inquiry for Timor-Leste (2006) Geneva, Report, 2 October, http://www.ohchr.org/Documents/Countries/COI TimorLeste.pdf.

United Nations Secretary-General (2005) *In Larger Freedom: Towards Development, Security and Human Rights for All*, report delivered to the General Assembly, UN Doc A/59/2005, March 21.

Weiss, Thomas (1999) 'Principles, Politics, and Humanitarian Action', *Ethics and International Affairs* 13: 1–22.

Žižek, Slavoj (ed.) (2002) *Revolution at the Gates: Žižek on Lenin – the 1917 Writings*, London: Verso.

CHAPTER 19

Can we move beyond conflict?

Roland Bleiker

- ■ *The question*
  DEALING WITH SEEMINGLY INTRACTABLE CONFLICTS

- ■ *Illustrative example*
  THE CONFLICT IN KOREA

- ■ *Responses*
  CONFRONTATION AND ENGAGEMENT: TWO APPROACHES TO CONFLICT

- ■ *Broader issues*
  DEALING WITH ANTAGONISM

- ■ **CONCLUSION**

THE QUESTION
DEALING WITH SEEMINGLY INTRACTABLE CONFLICTS

This chapter examines one of the oldest and most difficult political problems: how to deal with conflicts that are so deeply entrenched that they seem virtually inevitable. Prospects for peace are particularly slim in societies that have experienced a major trauma, such as genocide or war. From the Middle East to Afghanistan, from Sri Lanka to Somalia, from Iraq to East Timor and from Rwanda to Kashmir, years and often decades of conflict have left societies deeply divided and traumatised. New forms of violence constantly emerge, generating yet more hatred. Commentators speak of so-called intractable conflicts: situations where antagonisms have persisted for so long that they have created a vicious cycle of violence. A particularly influential example of such a position is Robert Kaplan's (2005) analysis of the ethnic conflict that devastated the Balkan region during the first part of the 1990s. Kaplan believes that the political volatility that followed the break-up of Yugoslavia was linked to old ethnic and religious hatreds between Croats, Serbs and Muslims. These deeply seated antagonisms, he stresses, go back hundreds of years to the clash between the Ancient Roman and Byzantine Empires, between a Christian European West and a Muslim Ottoman East.

How can societies that have been torn apart by war and trauma ever become peaceful again? Politicians and scholars are deeply divided about how to answer this question. Numerous commentators strongly oppose the very notion of intractable conflicts. They locate the roots of violence not in ancient hatreds, but in much more recent political manipulations (see Naimark 2002). David Campbell, for instance, provides an interpretation of the conflict in the Balkans that differs fundamentally from Kaplan's. For Campbell (1998: xi) the problem did not lie in ancient ethnic hatreds. The conflict, he believes, was linked to the recent actions of political elites. They opposed multiculturalism and actively generated fear in an attempt to gain and retain power. Ethnicity then became politicised in a way that turned once peaceful neighbours into enemies.

There is another discussion of the break-up of Yugoslavia in **Chapter 4.**

The examples shown here are brief and necessarily incomplete. But they reveal an important point: each conflict is situated in a unique political, social and historical setting. The nature of a conflict can only be understood in the context of its unique environment. No general theory can ever do justice to these complexities. Violence and hatred do not appear without a reason. They emerge as a result of specific grievances and historical struggles. As a result there are no ready-made solutions that can restore order and stability.

Although each conflict is unique, one can still learn from how particular societies have dealt with their political challenges. There are, indeed, numerous cases where seemingly intractable conflicts have eventually given way to more peaceful or at least more stable situations. For instance, many conflicts linked to racial segregation, from the United States to South Africa, have meanwhile been replaced by political orders that promote racial equality, at least at the formal, institutional level. Or look at the situation in Northern Ireland. After several decades of violence and terror the situation today is more stable than it has been for a long time. Another example is the Cold War. After half a century of intense and global confrontations between a communist East and a capitalist West we now live in a world no longer dominated by the competition between two ideologically motivated superpowers.

What, then, can one learn from these positive and negative examples? Why can some conflicts be solved or at least managed while others generate ever more

In **Chapter 16** we consider the opposite question: what brings about the move from politics to violence in the first place. How does armed conflict or organised violence come about?

hatred and violence? Expressed in other words: what is the key to moving beyond conflict? Given the uniqueness of each conflict, this chapter examines the issues at stake not in an abstract manner, but in a concrete political setting: the deeply entrenched conflict on the divided Korean peninsula, where hatred and constant tension continue to dominate politics even half a century after the Korean War. But there is progress too. There are occasional breakthroughs: diplomatic agreements, cross-border visits, gestures of goodwill. And there are setbacks. Again and again. But hope emerges precisely from a more thorough understanding of what actually drives these patterns of progress and regress, conflict and co-operation, hatred and empathy.

Although the chapter illustrates the issues at stake through a case study on Korea, it does not seek to provide an update on the most recent events. Doing so would be impossible, particularly in Korea, where politics is rapidly changing all the time. New events keep happening and the various actors involved regularly reposition themselves. Policy makers in North and South Korea, for instance, often alter their diplomatic attitudes depending on either strategic choices or domestic political struggles. Or look at how the stance of the United States, which plays a key role in Korea, has gone back and forth between an uncompromising confrontational position and a more tolerant attitude, reflecting respective policy debates in Washington. Rather than seeking to capture the latest stage of these ever-changing political struggles the purpose of this chapter is to illuminate the underlying dynamics that have shaped conflict in Korea for decades.

ILLUSTRATIVE EXAMPLE
THE CONFLICT IN KOREA

For the last half a century the Korean peninsula has been divided between a communist North and a capitalist South, each viewing the other as its ideological archrival. Over the years these antagonisms have become so deeply entrenched in societal consciousness that hatred and tension are seen as an inevitable aspect of politics. The reasons for this seemingly intractable conflict are located in particular historical events.

Historical background

Japan occupied Korea in the 1890s and formally annexed the country in 1910. At the end of the Second World War the two dominant victorious countries, the United States and the Soviet Union, dismantled the defeated Japanese colonial empire. In this context they divided the Korean peninsula into two parts along the 38th parallel. The US occupied the southern part and the Soviets the northern one. Separate political regimes were established on each side, reflecting the ideological standpoints of the two superpowers. In the south the Republic of Korea was formed in August 1948. The new country, led by its first president, the Korean expatriate Syngman Rhee, became a close ally of the US. The northern part of the peninsula then became the Democratic People's Republic of Korea. Its first head of state was Kim Il Sung, an anti-Japanese guerrilla fighter. The country adopted a unique nationalist form of communist ideology and became a close ally of both the Soviet Union and China.

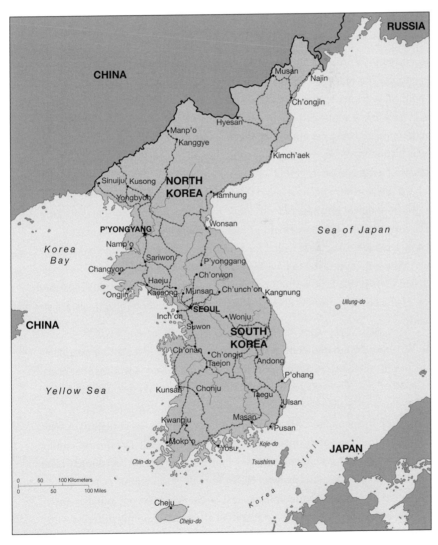

FIGURE 19.1
Map of Korean peninsula

The roots of the ongoing conflict in Korea are located not only in the division of the country but also, and above all, in the three-year war that devastated the peninsula from 1950 to 1953. More than a million people died as a result of the conflict, which saw the North and the South confronting each other. The war also involved several external powers. China intervened on behalf of the North, while the South was supported by a United Nations Command, led by the US. The trauma and hatred that the war generated continues to dominate virtually all aspects of politics today. Feelings of anger and revenge remain deep seated.

BOX 19.1 THE KOREAN WAR, 1950–3

The Korean War lasted from June 1950 until the signing of an Armistice Agreement in July 1953. It killed more than a million people. The most commonly accepted explanation for the war holds that there had been constant political tensions on the peninsula ever since its division at the end of the Second World War. Then, in June 1950, a full-scale war broke out when North Korea launched a surprise attack on the South, trying to bring the entire peninsula under its control. Although the conflict started as a civil war it soon involved, on opposing sides, two of the great powers of the Cold War: first the United States, which intervened, together with other nations, through a United Nations mandate designed to roll back the Northern occupation of the South; and then China, whose involvement saved the North from defeat and secured a military stalemate along the original dividing line at the 38th parallel. The Korean Armistice Agreement of July 1953, which was never signed by South Korea, constitutes only a ceasefire. A clause called for a political conference, on the bases of which the terms of a peace treaty were supposed to have been discussed. This conference, which took place in Geneva in 1954, failed in its prime task. In juridical terms, the two Koreas have thus remained in a state of war ever since. Half a century after the events an estimated ten million individuals are still separated from their families.

The wounds of the Korean War have dominated politics on the peninsula for half a century now. The two opposed Korean states have sponsored black-and-white accounts of the war: accounts that put all blame for the conflict on the other side. The antagonistic historical narratives then became essential elements in the creation of two diametrically opposed notions of nationhood, thus contributing substantially to fuelling conflict on the peninsula. An increasing number of revisionist historians have recently been trying to see beyond the black-and-white images that make up most accounts of conflict on the peninsula. Bruce Cumings (1997), for instance, stresses that intense fighting had already taken place for nine months prior to June 1950. Without denying North Korea's responsibility, Cumings presents the war as a complex set of events with multiple causes. Such revisionist positions on the origins of the war are controversial but also constitute an essential element in coming to terms with such a traumatic event.

On each side, an unusually strong state emerged and was able to promote a particular ideological vision of politics and society: a vision that constructs the other side of the dividing line as an enemy and a source of fear and instability. A passionate anti-capitalist attitude dominates the reclusive North, while a more moderate but still pronounced anti-communist orientation prevails in the South (see Grinker 1998; Hart 1999; Cumings 1997).

These 'ideological visions' are like the pictures that were discussed in **Chapter 2**. They influence people's thinking about the world. The Cold War was often seen as based on competing ideologies. Compare this with the view of contemporary conflicts as a 'clash of civilisations' or as derived from different religious views.
See Chapter 5

Geographical context

The conflict scenario in Korea has been fuelled even more by the unusually important geographical location of the peninsula. Constituting a natural link between the Asian mainland and Japan, Korea has always been an important factor in the security policy of the surrounding powers. In the nineteenth century, two major wars were fought for control over the peninsula, one between Japan and

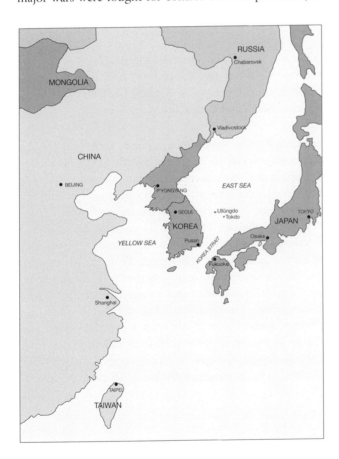

FIGURE 19.2
Map of the geographical location of the Korean peninsula

China (1894–5), the other between Japan and Russia (1904–5). With the development of military technology in the twentieth century, the geographical importance of Korea increased further. The division of the peninsula must to a substantial part be attributed to the strategic and symbolic importance of Korea in the emerging Cold War power struggle between the United States and the Soviet Union. But the competition over the Korean peninsula did not remain a Soviet–American affair. In the early 1960s China became increasingly independent of its communist ally, the Soviet Union. As a result, both of these important powers started to compete for influence over North Korea. Add to this that Japan's post-war reconstruction was so successful the country developed into an important economic force. The political situation in Korea thus became directly linked to the security and economic interests of four great powers, the United States, the Soviet Union, China and Japan.

Developments since the end of the Cold War

Much has changed over the last decade. The Soviet-led global alliance system fell apart in the early 1990s and the Cold War gave way to a new form of international politics. But in Korea strikingly much remains the same. The peninsula is still divided between a communist North and a capitalist South.

The North remains an authoritarian communist regime. It is perhaps the world's most reclusive country. Travel to and from North Korea is severely restricted. The country's population has no access to foreign information sources and the government-controlled media network is tightly censored. Having been devastated by several years of famine and economic mismanagement, North Korea is also one of the world's poorest countries. The South, by contrast, has embarked on a successful path of democratisation and economic development. Here, too, the geographical situation has accentuated differences. With the collapse of the Soviet-led alliance system the communist regime in the North became even more isolated. It lost one of its strongest allies and trading partners, the Soviet Union. Even China, which intervened in the Korean War on behalf of the North and has remained a strong supporter ever since, is now distancing itself increasingly from the regime in Pyongyang, North Korea's capital. Add to this that the US, as the sole remaining superpower, has meanwhile become the single most influential external actor on the peninsula, substantially shaping the security issues at stake.

Neither the collapse of the global Cold War system nor North Korea's increasingly isolated position has eased tension on the peninsula. Quite the contrary, the situation is as volatile as ever. At regular intervals tensions risk escalating into a more direct confrontation.

Economic problems like these are not restricted to communist regimes. Compare the account of strategic adjustment and development in the Ivory Coast in Chapter 11.

BOX 19.2 THE COLD WAR, 1947–89

During the Cold War global politics was largely dominated by the competition between two rival alliance systems. One was led by the United States and advocated democracy and free-market capitalism. The other revolved around the Soviet Union and was driven by communist principles. Although the US and the Soviet Union were allies during the Second World War, an intense ideological rivalry emerged between these two so-called superpowers in the late 1940s.

The Cold War was cold because it did not involve a direct military confrontation between the two superpowers. But for four decades global politics was dominated by an intensive and often dangerous stand-off between them. In most parts of the world politics was driven by the superpowers' attempt to increase and maintain their respective spheres of influence (the areas of the world that they dominated). Numerous regional wars, such as the ones in Korea (1950–3) and Vietnam (1964–75), opposed capitalist and communist alliance partners. Equally problematic was an increasingly intense arms race, which developed because each side was preoccupied with containing and deterring the other. On numerous occasions the arms race threatened to provoke a global conflict. A key event here is the Cuban Missile Crisis of 1962, which nearly led to an open nuclear war between the US and the Soviet Union.

There were moments, as in the 1970s, when the two superpowers adopted a more conciliatory approach. This led to a period of so-called détente. There were also moments when some countries refused to submit to the dictates of either superpower. China, for instance, retained communist policies but started to distance itself increasingly from its communist ally and superpower, the Soviet Union.

The Cold War only ended once the Soviet-led alliance system started to crumble in the late 1980s. By the early 1990s the Soviet Union had disintegrated and most of its allies, particularly in Eastern Europe, abandoned their communist policies and embarked on moves to adopt democratic and free-market-oriented forms of government. As a result, the US emerged as the most powerful global state, a type of sole superpower.

FIGURE 19.3
President John F. Kennedy at the Berlin Wall, Germany, June 1963. Photo: Robert Knudsen, White House. Courtesy of the John F. Kennedy Library, Boston

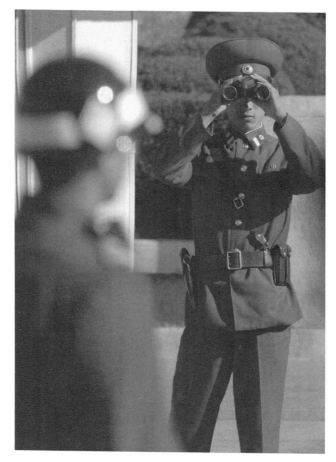

FIGURE 19.4
A North Korean soldier looks through a pair of binoculars as a South Korean solider stands guard in the Demilitarised Zone dividing the two Koreas, in the village of Panmunjom, on the North–South border, 2007. Photo: Jung Yeon-Je/AFP/Getty Images

These 'crises' are perhaps not as serious as those that occurred during the Cold War – the Cuban Missile Crisis, which occurred when the Soviet Union stationed nuclear warheads in Cuba, within easy range of the US, could have led to a nuclear war between the two superpowers.

Of particular importance are the two so-called nuclear crises that haunted the peninsula during the last two decades. The first crisis emerged in the early 1990s. Although Pyongyang had signed the Nuclear Non-Proliferation Treaty in 1985, it retained its ambition to develop a nuclear weapons programme. US intelligence reports drew attention to a plutonium processing plant in Yongbyon. Various negotiation rounds followed. In 1992 North Korea agreed to have its nuclear facility inspected by the International Atomic Energy Agency. But only a few months later disagreements over inspections increased and in March 1993 North Korea declared its intention to withdraw from the Non-Proliferation Treaty. William Perry, then US Secretary of Defense, considered the subsequent crisis the only time during his tenure when he 'believed that the US was in serious danger

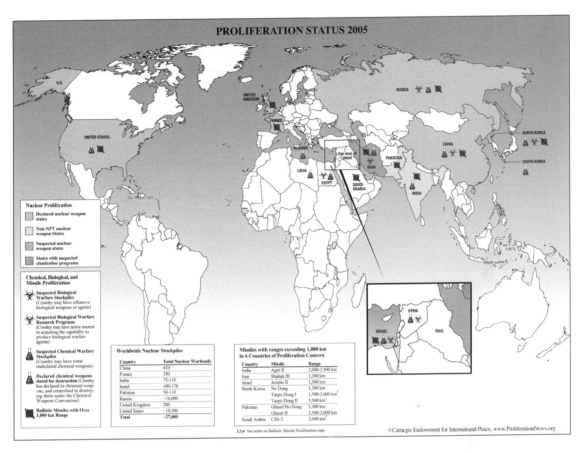

FIGURE 19.5
Nuclear, chemical and biological weapons proliferation status in 2005. © Carnegie Endowment for International Peace, www.ProliferationNews.org

of a major war' (2000: 121). An agreement, signed in October 1994, managed to avert an open conflict. Pyongyang consented to freeze its nuclear programme in return for a number of US, South Korean and Japanese promises, including aid, heating oil and the eventual construction of two light-water nuclear reactors that would provide North Korea with energy sources.

Once the nuclear crisis of 1994 was solved all parties concerned embarked on a more co-operative route. The inauguration of Kim Dae-jung (2000) as South Korea's president in early 1998 signalled the advent of a policy that was more conciliatory, or at least more willing to engage the archenemy across the dividing line. The US administration under President Clinton was strongly supportive of this approach. Of particular significance here is an official policy review, conducted by former Defence Secretary William Perry. This report located the main threat in North Korea's ambition to acquire nuclear weapons or to develop, test and

BOX 19.3 NUCLEAR NON-PROLIFERATION TREATY

The Nuclear Non-Proliferation Treaty, often referred to as the NPT, emerged in the late 1960s and entered into force in 1970. It was designed to stop the spread of nuclear weapons in an effort to reach a more stable and peaceful world. The treaty acknowledges that the five permanent members of the United Nations Security Council are so-called nuclear weapons states, because they tested nuclear devices prior to 1967. These are the United States, the Soviet Union (now in the form of Russia), France, China and the United Kingdom. These five states sought to prevent all other states from acquiring nuclear weapons. In return for agreeing not to develop nuclear weapons, the states that signed up to the NPT were promised assistance from the nuclear weapons states to develop nuclear technology for energy, medical and other peaceful purposes. The nuclear weapon states also promised, under Article VI, to eliminate their nuclear weapons. As this has not happened, the discriminatory nature of the treaty, whereby five states continue to possess nuclear weapons while others are prevented from doing so, has made the NPT controversial. The treaty was extended indefinitely in a landmark Review Conference in 1995.

A total of 189 countries have ratified the Non-Proliferation Treaty. India, Pakistan and Israel have not signed the treaty. The former two are confirmed nuclear powers, while the latter is known to possess nuclear weapons but has not officially confirmed their existence. At numerous points during the last decades smaller states sought to develop nuclear weapons. These include Libya, which has subsequently renounced its programme, and North Korea, which withdrew from the NPT in 2003 and tested its first nuclear device in 2006. Iran's covert uranium enrichment programme has also caused grave concern, although Iran insists that its programme is designed for energy production only.

The International Atomic Energy Agency is the recognised authority that deals with such and other disputes. As a UN agency based in Vienna, its mission is to ensure that non-nuclear weapon states do not develop nuclear weapons and to promote the peaceful use of nuclear technology. More specifically, it foresees that all non-nuclear states that want to develop nuclear technology need to put in place certain safeguards. The respective procedures include opening up nuclear facilities for regular inspections by the International Atomic Energy Agency. These inspections are designed to make sure that the state in question is not diverting its nuclear technology programme to weapons purposes.

FIGURE 19.6
Non-Proliferation Treaty signing ceremony, July 1968, Moscow. US Ambassador Llewellyn E. Thompson, left, signs the treaty in Moscow with Soviet Foreign Minister Andrei A. Gromyko. Among US embassy and Soviet government officials witnessing the ceremony is Soviet Premier Alexei N. Kosygin, standing third from right. Photo: AP Wide World Photos

deploy long-range missiles. At the same time, though, the Perry Report called for a fundamental review of US policy towards Pyongyang, advocating a position that rests not only on military deterrence, but also on a 'new, comprehensive and integrated approach' to negotiations with North Korea (Perry 1999: 8).

The new policy attitudes in Washington and Seoul, capital of South Korea, soon led to several breakthroughs, including the lifting of restrictions on trade with, investment in and travel to North Korea. Pyongyang responded in turn with a variety of gestures, such as a gradual (although still very timid) opening of its borders, agreements on family exchanges with the South and a tuning down of its hostile rhetoric. The process of détente culminated in June 2000 with a historic summit meeting between the two Korean heads of state, Kim Jong-il and Kim Dae-jung. But détente in Korea did not last long.

By early 2002 the fragile security arrangement started to break down. The new US president, George W. Bush, adopted a more confrontational policy, which sharply reversed the conciliatory approach pursued during the Clinton administration. In his first State of the Union address Bush singled out North Korea, together with Iraq and Iran, as one of three nations belonging to an axis of evil. He cited as evidence Pyongyang's export of ballistic missile technology and its lingering ambition to become a nuclear power. Soon afterwards, the Defense Department, in a report to Congress, included North Korea in a group of seven nations that were potential targets of pre-emptive nuclear strikes. Pyongyang reacted in an angry manner, warning that it would abandon the agreed freeze of its nuclear weapons programme, which it subsequently did. The situation then rapidly deteriorated. North Korea officially announced that it would restart its nuclear reactor at Yongbyon. It withdrew from the Nuclear Non-Proliferation Treaty and forced inspectors of the International Atomic Energy Agency to leave the country. The tension culminated in October 2006 when the world community reacted with strong and unanimous protest against Pyongyang's announcement that it had successfully completed a nuclear test. North Korea's demonstrated nuclear ambition substantially increases the risk of a nuclear arms race in the region and an escalation of the security situation, with possible global consequences.

RESPONSES
CONFRONTATION AND ENGAGEMENT: TWO APPROACHES TO CONFLICT

How is it possible to find a way out of the seemingly intractable conflict in Korea? Have decades of antagonisms and hatred created a pattern of conflict that can no longer be overcome? There are, certainly, no easy solutions.

When we say 'international community' we sometimes mean all the states in the world, sometimes a group of rich and powerful states, sometimes the UN Security Council or – sometimes – the UN General Assembly. The term 'international community' is used frequently in **Chapter 18**.

One of the most difficult – and important – tasks is figuring out how to deal with North Korea. Totalitarian and reclusive, ideologically isolated and economically ruined, it is a very unusual country in today's liberal world order. But North Korea keeps surviving, not least because its leaders periodically rely on threats, such as nuclear blackmail, to gain concessions from the international community. The dangers of these policies are evident and much discussed. Miscalculations or a sudden escalation could precipitate a human disaster at any moment.

Equally dangerous, although much less evident, are some of the attitudes with which key regional and global countries, such as the United States, seek to contain the volatile situation. Debates about how to deal with North Korea – and the Korean conflict in general – can be located at two ends of opposing poles. The prevailing approach advocates a confrontational attitude. It relies on economic sanctions and the projection of military threats in an attempt to contain the situation and bring about change within North Korea (Cha 2002; Eberstadt 1997; Rice 2000). The second approach favours engaging North Korea in political, economic and cultural interactions. It assumes that a peaceful solution emerges not from forcing North Korea into submission, but from integrating it into the world community (Harrison 1997; Dujarric 2001; Moon 2001).

Confrontation

First to the most commonly practised stance, which seeks to confront and undermine North Korea through a mixture of military threats and economic sanctions. 'If the North Korean regime is irredeemable', Marcus Noland (2000:

FIGURE 19.7
The British nuclear test code-named Hurricane. Photo: The National Archives, Kew, Richmond, Surrey. Ref: ADM280/966

8) asks, 'should not the rest of the world act to hasten its demise?' Withdrawing support would, undoubtedly, worsen the economic situation in the North and precipitate yet another famine. But is this not the price to pay for bringing about necessary change? Providing Pyongyang with trade possibilities and humanitarian aid would, according to this logic, not only sustain a dictatorial and dangerous regime but also prolong the suffering of the North Korean people. Several non-governmental organisations (NGOs) that provided humanitarian aid, such as Oxfam and Médecins sans Frontières (Doctors without Borders), left North Korea because they were prevented from adequately monitoring and evaluating the impact of their aid, which they feared did not reach the most vulnerable part of the population.

> The question 'Why do some people think they know what is good for others?', which is dealt with in **Chapter 15**, is interesting here.

In the realm of security policy the confrontational approach is exemplified by the foreign policy of the United States under the administration of President George W. Bush. In his first State of the Union address, Bush identified Pyongyang as one of several 'evil' rogue states. With the transition to a post-Cold War order, so-called rogue states replaced the Soviet Union as the main threat. North Korea, together with Iraq and Iran, were seen as the most dangerous of these rogues: totalitarian states that disrespected human rights and aspired to possess weapons of mass destruction. As had already been the case during the Cold War, military means are considered the key methods through which the threat of rogue states is to be opposed. Illustrative here is a US *Nuclear Posture Review* which became public in June 2002. It stipulated that the new US strategic doctrine relied on the possibility of employing pre-emptive nuclear strikes against terrorists and rogue states. North Korea was explicitly cited with regard to two possible scenarios: countering an attack on the South and halting the proliferation of weapons of mass destruction. A few months later Washington made its threats official. The *National Security Strategy* (2002), released in September 2002, outlined in detail how pre-emptive strikes are legitimate and would be employed

> It is important to consider who and what comes to be seen as dangerous and why. **See Chapter 17**

FIGURE 19.8
The heavily mined Demilitarised Zone between North and South Korea seen from a South Korean military observation post. The zone has become a haven for wildlife. Photo: Seokyong Lee for *The New York Times*

BOX 19.4 THE WAR ON TERROR

Terrorism is as old as politics. But recently the phenomenon has gained renewed political significance. The terrorist attacks of September 11, 2001 marked a key turning point in international politics. The death toll alone would not necessarily render the event so central, for many other recent conflicts, from Bosnia to Rwanda, produced far more casualties. September 11 is significant because it fundamentally questioned the prevailing sense of security in the West. The terrorist attack of September 11 represents a type of threat that cannot easily be anticipated, or prevented, through prevailing state-based structures of security. The danger stemmed not from another state, but from a non-state organisation, and one that cannot be precisely defined and located. The conflict was not launched with conventional military equipment, but with simple means. The attack itself took place in surprise, revealing a fundamental weakness in the state's intelligence apparatus. The attack neither involved opposing forces nor was directed at a battlefield or a military target. It struck at the very heart of political, economic and civilian life.

The response by the US and its allies, most notably the UK, was swift and determined. The ensuing so-called 'war on terror' was meant to punish those responsible for the attacks of September 11 and prevent a similar future attack from occurring. An invasion of Afghanistan in 2003 targeted terrorist cells directly. But soon the 'war on terror' was expanded to include so-called rogue states: states that were said to be sympathetic to terrorism or have the ambition to develop nuclear arms and other weapons of mass destruction. The US identified Iraq, Iran and North Korea as rogue states and termed them the axis of evil. The US and its allies then invaded Iraq with the objective of preventing the regime from further developing and using weapons of mass destruction. But no such weapons were ever discovered, nor was there any evidence that could connect the country to the perpetrators of the terrorist attacks of September 11.

Although heralded as a new form of conducting international politics, the 'war on terror' is characterised by a striking similarity with thinking patterns that dominated foreign policy during the Cold War. Once again the world is divided into 'good' and 'evil', and once again military means occupy the key, if not the only, role in protecting the former against the latter.

as a way to 'stop rogue states and their terrorist clients before they are able to threaten or use weapons of mass destruction against the United States'.

The confrontational and militaristic attitude to security does not necessarily exclude negotiations. Diplomacy and dialogue are seen as continuously important, but they occupy only a supporting role. On numerous occasions President Bush publicly declared a willingness to engage Pyongyang in diplomatic

FIGURE 19.9
'Maybe you should reconsider those place cards'. Artist: Dave Carpenter. CartoonStock.
Ref: dcr0435h. www.CartoonStock.com

negotiations. At the same time, though, the projection of threats towards North Korea was carefully maintained, even intensified. Ever since the latest nuclear crisis emerged in Korea, officials in Washington kept stressing that military power is always an option.

Prevailing approaches to security, based on deterrence and the projection of military threats, have failed to deal successfully with the key security challenges in Korea. There are various reasons why the confrontational approach has not worked. Four of them stand out particularly.

First, the use of military power as an instrument of deterrence and pressure has proven to be relatively ineffective with regard to North Korea. The US has, of course, threatened and used military power quite frequently to achieve political goals, most recently in Afghanistan and Iraq. Such actions were aimed either at pressuring a regime to change its behaviour or at actually removing it from power altogether. But strategic experts largely agree that a military solution to the nuclear crisis in Korea is highly problematic. One of the world's biggest cities, Seoul, is only fifty kilometres away from the heavily militarised Demilitarised Zone. Even if pre-emptive strikes were to neutralise North Korea's growing nuclear arsenal, they would not be able to destroy all its conventional weapons.

The latter alone could easily trigger a second Korean war, with disastrous consequences on all sides. Intensifying threats against North Korea would also provide its regime with a welcome source of legitimacy. The result might be a population rallying around its threatened government, no matter how despotic it is.

The second element of the confrontational approach is economic sanctions. Such sanctions were pronounced against North Korea by the UN Security Council in a unanimously accepted resolution on 14 October 2006. Imposed in direct response to Pyongyang's nuclear test, these sanctions were the most far-reaching ones imposed against North Korea since the end of the Korean War in 1953. They included not only any material that could be used to produce nuclear, biological and chemical weapons, but also bans on international travel and a freeze of assets held by people associated with Pyongyang's contentious weapons programmes. The problem with sanctions is that they have historically been of very limited use. Only in rare cases, such as in Libya and Sudan, did they pressure rogue states into adopting a more or less compliant behaviour. Miroslav Nincic (2005) stresses that failure is the norm, as in the cases of Iran, Iraq, Yugoslavia, Afghanistan and North Korea. In fact, Nincic goes as far as believing that comprehensive economic sanctions often had a counter-productive effect, leading to a modification of a regime's ideology and economy that actually ended up strengthening its grip on power.

Third, despite playing lip-service to the idea of negotiations, a confrontational approach forecloses most options other than those based on military means and economic sanctions. 'The opposition between good and evil is not negotiable', Allan Bloom (1987: 142) already noted at the time of Ronald Reagan's presidency. It is a question of principles, and thus 'a cause of war'. Expressed in other words, the rhetoric of evil moves the phenomenon of rogue states into the realm of irrationality. Evil is in essence a term of condemnation for a phenomenon that can neither be fully comprehended nor addressed, except through militaristic forms of power politics. This is why various commentators believe that the rhetoric of evil prevents rather than encourages understanding. They go so far as to argue that it evades accountability, for it leads to policy positions that 'deny negotiations and compromise' (Klusmeyer and Suhrke 2002: 27–9, 35–7; Euben 2002: 4). How is it, indeed, possible to negotiate with evil without being implicated in it?

See **Chapter 2** for a discussion of the importance of language and rhetoric in another case, that of torture.

Fourth, the confrontational approach fails to take into account the interactive nature of conflicts. Very few policy makers, security analysts and journalists ever make the effort to imagine how threats are perceived from the North Korean perspective, and how these perceptions are part of an interactive security dilemma in which the West is implicated too. North Korea does not exist in a vacuum. It cannot be understood outside the insecurities and fear left by four decades of Japanese colonialism, followed by the Korean War and half a century of national division and Cold War tension (Cumings 2004: ix, 151). Particularly significant is the current policy of pre-emptive strikes against rogue states, for it reinforces half a century of American nuclear threats towards North Korea.

Engagement

There are alternatives to confrontation. A second, opposing approach holds that engaging North Korea and integrating it into the world community is the best opportunity to prevent a military escalation and create a more peaceful political environment. Several humanitarian organisations, for instance, stayed behind in North Korea, believing that the possibility of providing humanitarian assistance and development co-operation was essential, even if the conditions were far from ideal. Withdrawing aid, they feared, would only heighten the danger of a confrontation and worsen the situation of the population but not necessarily bring about change for the better. Underlying the logic of this position was the recognition that there are very few cases where famines have brought down an authoritarian regime (Savage and Nautilus Team 2002: 155).

People who advocate engagement with apparently hostile regimes are sometimes accused of being too 'soft'. This can translate into an accusation of not being 'masculine' enough.

South Korea has become the strongest proponent of a policy of engagement with the North. Starting with his inaugural speech in February 1998, South Korea's president, Kim Dae-jung, called for a new approach towards the North. Kim's initiative revolved around moving from a deeply entrenched politics of confrontation towards an attitude that promotes reconciliation and co-operation

FIGURE 19.10
Demilitarized Zone opens for train passage, Paju, South Korea, 17 May 2007.
Photo: Chung Sung-Jun/Getty Images

(Kihl 1998: 23; Moon and Steinberg 1999). Kim's successor, Roh Moo-hyun, supported and continued this approach. The new South Korean president, Lee Myung-bak, signalled a more cautious approach at his inauguration in early 2008. But he largely accepts the need to maintain at least a basic level of engagement with North Korea. During the Clinton administration Washington was highly supportive of South Korea's engagement policy. But with the advent of the Bush administration the US reverted to a much more confrontational attitude that created a major policy rift between the two countries.

The engagement policy is driven by a key emphasis on dialogue. The notion of dialogue goes substantially further than the diplomatic positioning advocated by the confrontational approach. The attempt, rather, consists of engaging the parties to the conflict in genuine negotiations. The most spectacular result of this policy was an unprecedented summit meeting between the two Korean heads of state in June 2000. The most recent success of engagement is an agreement reached in February 2007 between North Korea, South Korea, the US, China, Russia and Japan. The agreement ended, at least temporarily, the tense stand-off that culminated four months earlier with North Korea's first nuclear test. Resembling the agreement reached in 1994, the 2007 deal foresees North Korea abandoning its nuclear weapons programme in exchange for fuel oil, food aid and other economic assistance. The agreement, which was strongly critiqued by conservative policy analysts in Washington, also constitutes an implicit acknowledgement by the Bush administration that confrontation did not work: that engagement offers the most promising approach to solving the security crisis on the Korean peninsula. Half a year after this agreement, in October 2007, there was a second historic summit meeting between the two Korean heads of state, Kim Jong-il and Roh Mo-hyun.

Perhaps even more important than high-level diplomatic negotiations is the fact that the engagement policy generated various forms of low-level cross-border exchanges, from tourist visits, cultural and sports engagements to family reunions. Central here was a substantial increase in cross-border economic activities, which had been all but non-existent until recently. The new 2007 Agreement foresees further cross-border economic activities, such as co-operative shipbuilding complexes, common fishing zones and the opening of a cargo rail service. By international standards these economic activities may be insignificant. But they are spectacular in the context of the hermetically sealed Korean peninsula.

The engagement policy is based on the traditional liberal assumption that increased economic co-operation would eventually engender common interest and understanding. In a context where commercial activities are at stake, the key actors have a strong interest in reducing the likelihood of conflict since it would jeopardise profit and investment (Moon 2001: 188–9). But there is more to cross-border activities than mere interdependence. The ensuing contacts may also help to reduce the deeply entrenched stereotypical perceptions that Koreans have of their compatriots across the dividing line (Chung 1999: 125). This is the case because face-to-face encounters offer perhaps the best opportunity to create true dialogue and to dismantle some of the hostile stereotypes that have fuelled the conflict for decades.

BROADER ISSUES
DEALING WITH ANTAGONISM

Engagement and dialogue offer viable alternatives to confrontation. But they also leave unaddressed larger questions about how to develop the type of tolerance necessary to live with the deep-seated antagonisms that inevitably exist after major traumas. Wars, genocides or terrorist attacks shape people and societies for decades to come. They not only become an essential component of individual and collective identities, but also risk reigniting new forms of tension and violence.

When facing seemingly intractable conflicts, one of the most difficult challenges consists of accepting the existence of deep-seated wounds and grievances without letting them degenerate into violence. The promotion of dialogue is important in this process, but not enough. Just as crucial is a certain level of tolerance: an acceptance that there are – and for the foreseeable future will be – major differences between the conflict parties and their attitudes.

In Korea this challenge largely revolves around coming to terms with the traumatic past, most notably with the legacy of the Korean War. The memory of pain and death is far too present for a single unified understanding of history to emerge. Each side does, in essence, blame the other for causing the war. And each side has rehearsed and institutionalised its particular understanding of the past while making every effort to shield its respective populations from the diametrically opposed position promoted by the other side. Little does it matter that some of the respective historical perspectives, such as North Korea's hero worship of its first leader, Kim Il Sung, are based far more on fiction than on fact. The different understandings of history and society are so deeply entrenched that they cannot easily be overcome, at least not in the near future.

Collective memory after the world wars in Europe is contentious and contested too.
See Chapter 16

Recognising the existence of historical differences is a crucial element in moving beyond conflict. The French philosopher Paul Ricoeur stresses that by 'acknowledging that the history of an event involves a conflict of several interpretations and memories, we in turn open up the future' (1999: 13). Susan Dwyer (1999: 89) takes this idea further and offers a useful way of conceptualising what is at stake in the process of reconciliation. Three steps, she argues, are necessary. The first consists of an effort to find agreement on 'the barest of facts'. The second stage involves an effort to identify a range of different interpretations of the respective events. And the third stage would entail narrowing things down to a limited set of interpretations that the two sides can tolerate. While such a goal of agreeing to disagree seems modest, the path towards it is littered with seemingly insurmountable obstacles. The first hurdle alone is already very difficult, for Dwyer defines agreeing on 'the barest of facts' as finding a clear view on 'who did what to whom and when'. In Korea, these 'bare facts' are, of course, precisely the major point of contention – and the source of trauma and hatred.

Moving beyond conflict requires a compromise between a search for justice and the ability to forgive – a compromise that is all too often neglected by prevailing confrontational approaches. Holding people accountable for past wrongdoings is essential. But so is a willingness to 'forget' some aspects of the traumatic past that continuously fuels conflict. The German philosopher Friedrich Nietzsche stresses that the past suffocates the present unless we forget it. He calls upon people to have the courage to 'break with the past in order to live' (1981: 118). Forgetting, in this sense, does not mean ignoring what happened. Forgetting, after all, is a natural process, an inevitable aspect of remembering; we all do it, whether we want to or not. We cannot possibly remember everything. We cannot give every event the same weight. Our memory of the past is the result of a process through which certain events and interpretations are remembered and prioritised, while others are relegated to secondary importance or forgotten altogether. This is particularly the case with a major event like the Korean War, which is far too complex to be remembered in its totality. The task of historians is to select the few facts, perspectives and interpretations that ought to be remembered. The combination of forgetting and remembering is as inevitable as it is political. Being aware of this inevitability is to explore possibilities for reshaping the past and using this process in the service of creating a better future (Nietzsche 1981: 100). Nietzsche is particularly critical of periods when historical understandings lack critical awareness of this process – situations, say, when illegitimate rulers misappropriate historical events and mythologies to justify their form of dominance (Nietzsche 1981: 106–7, 111). Such is undoubtedly the case in contemporary Korea, where history has been geared far more towards supporting particular regimes than towards actually representing what happened in the past.

> It has been pointed out that we forget much more than we remember: most of what happens is in this sense 'forgotten'.

Politics in Korea also displays signs of what Nietzsche calls 'critical histories': attempts to challenge the notion of a single historical reality and create the political space in which diverging understandings of the past can co-exist in an atmosphere of tolerance. A recent example of a breakthrough in this direction, timid as it may well be, can be found in revisions of school history textbooks in South Korea. The composition and use of school textbooks has always been very tightly controlled by the government. These texts, in turn, were then used to legitimise and spread an ideologically driven perspective on history, society and politics. Several generations of history texts have, for instance, studiously avoided

BOX 19.5 FRIEDRICH NIETZSCHE

FIGURE 19.11
Friedrich Nietzsche

Friedrich Nietzsche is a German philosopher (1844–1900) whose work has shaped a range of contemporary thinkers. Nietzsche's influence has less to do with the particular political views he held, but with the manner in which he approached more fundamental questions of knowledge. In particular, he challenged the deeply entrenched modern search for universal forms of truth, whether they be based in Christian morals or scientific foundations. Nietzsche believed that the search for truth always contained a will to power. Seen from such a vantage-point, a critical investigation into a political issue would need to pay attention to processes of inclusion and exclusion, to how knowledge and power are always intertwined.

even mentioning the role that northern communist guerrillas played in the fight against the Japanese colonial occupiers. Doing so would have been seen as sympathising with the communist North, even if the presented facts are historically accurate. One of six new secondary school history textbooks, released in 2003, for the first time mentions the existence of communist resistance. It does so in a passage dealing with a 1937 clash between Japanese colonial forces and resistance fighters allegedly led by Kim Il Sung, the future leader of North Korea. In addition to these textbook revisions there is an increasing willingness by school administrators, teachers and students to open up a cross-border dialogue about the past. Some government officials have suggested that the North and South could exchange 'narrative memories' by making available, on both sides, a range of commonly agreed upon historical documents and teaching materials, which could then be used in addition to the official textbooks that each side employs. Young teachers in particular appear willing to move beyond existing patterns of hatred. They often supplement the use of the prescribed textbooks with alternative methods, such as historical simulation, television documentaries, cartoons and newspapers (Hoang 2002).

This is a small example that demonstrates how South and North Korea may be able to open up political spaces in which it becomes possible to contemplate the other's memory of the past, even if this memory appears distorted and inherently wrong. But this small example highlights two very important points.

First, an effort to accept deep-seated differences is an important addition to dialogue. But it, too, is not enough. Accepting difference must go beyond acknowledging that people or societies in conflict have diverging understandings of the past. Leaving it at that would only entrench existing antagonisms, and thus legitimise or even intensify the existing conflict. Keith Krause and Michael Williams draw attention to this danger, pointing out that in places like Bosnia and Rwanda an awareness of difference led 'not to celebration but destruction' (1997: xv). The objective, much rather, would be a political attitude that is based on tolerance but that can also generate the type of understanding and respect needed for a commonly acceptable and non-violent relationship between former archenemies.

Second, the greatest push forward towards reconciliation often comes not from politicians, diplomats or generals, but from the realm of the everyday: from normal citizens, grassroots organisations or popular culture. In recent years there have been an increasing number of South Korean films that defy the deeply entrenched tendency to vilify the North. These include *Heuk Su Seon* (*Last Witness*, 2001), *Swiri* (1999) and *Joint Security Area* (or *JSA*, 2000). The domestic and international success of the latter is particularly important, for the film is one of the rare public features that clearly resists perpetuating the entrenched stereotypical image of cold and evil North Koreans. Instead, *JSA* narrates how a small group of soldiers from both sides develop a friendship, secretly and against all odds. In the end conflict becomes inevitable and the respective soldiers must choose country over friendship. But the film is nevertheless a milestone, for it portrays soldiers on both sides as normal Koreans, with a variety of similar emotions, concerns and interests. This contrasts quite sharply with the confrontational approach that prevails among security experts in Korea. It also contrasts with more general outside perceptions of Korea. Consider a relatively recent James Bond film, entitled *Die Another Day*. It portrays North Koreans in the stereotypical role of evil madmen bent on destroying the world. Not surprisingly, there was considerable public protest against the Cold War antics of 007, not only in the North, but also in the South. While her majesty's secret agent, judging the world from neo-imperial London, was clearly out of step with the need for reconciliation on the Korean peninsula, *JSA* has demonstrated that popular films have the potential to open up important spaces for dialogue and common understanding between people from the North and South.

Poets and novelists from both sides of the dividing line have embarked on a similarly innovative grassroots attempt at healing the wounds of national division and war. In 2005 a group of North and South Korean writers issued a joint declaration, aiming to promote reconciliation on the peninsula. Numerous activities followed, such as a visit to the North by ninety-eight South Korean writers – a first in more than sixty years. The delegation was lead by one of the country's most famous poets, Ko Un. Projects that have already emerged from these efforts include plans for a joint magazine, a literary prize and the first unified Korean dictionary.

Novels that resist stereotypes of national identity and that deal with stories of exile and the complicated sense of allegiance and estrangement that many people have in relation to a national community are explored in Chapter 10.

There are many cases where poets have influenced global politics. The war poets in England after the First World War are one example; dissident writers in the Soviet Union are another. Can you think of more? Other forms of cultural output are also important – not only 'high culture' but things like rock music or reggae, for example.

BOX 19.6 KOREAN POET KO UN

FIGURE 19.12
Ko Un

Ko Un is one of South Korea's best-known poets. Born in 1933 he has been shortlisted for the Nobel Prize several times. As a young man, Ko Un directly experienced the atrocities of the Korean War, including the death of several relatives and friends. He then spent ten years as a Buddhist monk, eventually holding several high positions in monastic life. In 1966 he rejoined the secular world to set up a charity on the Korean island of Jejudo. A few years later he moved to Seoul in the context of struggling with alcoholism and making several suicide attempts. During the 1970s and 1980s Ko Un was active in the democracy movement, gaining prominence as an outspoken nationalist poet. As a result he spent two years in prison under the regime of General Chun Doo-Hwan. Released in 1982 as part of a general pardon, Ko Un devoted himself to a life of poetry. Most recently he used his reputation to advance the cause of reconciliation with North Korea. Ko Un's literary output comprises over a hundred volumes of poetry, novels, autobiography, dramas, essays, travel books and translations. He is particularly known for a style that brings everyday language to poetry.

Ko Un has not only played a leading role in bringing together writers from both South and North Korea, but also expressed a vision of moving beyond conflict in his own poetry. Having experienced the trauma of war and national division, Ko Un writes of 'birds that all flew away at the sound of a gun' (2002: 20). He recalls the senseless violence he witnessed as a young man:

> Every morning heaven and earth
> are piled with dead things.
> Our job is to bury them all day long.
>
> (Ko Un 1996)

In an attempt to show a way out of the ensuing cycle of violence, Ko Un believes in a vision for peace, a vision that views security not only in terms of a military-based defence of the state apparatus, but also as a comprehensive endeavour that promotes the rights and well-being of people. In the same vein as his accessibly written poems, Ko Un implies that the key impetus of genuine transformation often stems from the mass of people and not from their leaders. But he also knows that this process is inevitably slow and littered with obstacles. Deeply entrenched hatred and mistrust cannot disappear overnight. But a policy of engagement, combined with a respect for difference, can offer a way forward. Or so suggests one of Ko Un's poems:

> Peace is waves.
> Waves breaking, alive
> and beneath those waves
> swim fish of every kind, alive.

(Ko Un 2002: 7)

CONCLUSION

This chapter has sought to address a political problem that is as old as it is of contemporary relevance: how is it possible to deal with and perhaps even overcome conflicts that are so deeply entrenched that they seem intractable? There are no easy answers to the problems at stake, nor is there a general theory that can offer a comprehensive explanation of conflict and its possible resolution. Each conflict is rooted in particular historical circumstances. Understanding and dealing with these circumstances is essential if conflict is to give way to a more peaceful environment.

The chapter has illustrated the issues at stake by focusing on the seemingly intractable conflict on the divided Korean peninsula, where mutual hatred and constant tensions have dominated politics for over half a century now. One of the most difficult questions today is how to approach a North Korean regime that clearly violates the human rights of its citizens and poses a threat to regional and even global peace. Should one engage in a dialogue with North Korea? Should one try to reach a compromise in order to avoid a dangerous escalation of tension or even a possible war on the peninsula? Or is such an approach merely a policy of appeasement that prolongs the suffering of people and renders the situation in the long run more dangerous? The prevailing approach certainly believes that the latter is the case: it advocates a confrontational stance which relies on military threats and economic sanctions to coerce North Korea into compliant behaviour. Dialogue and negotiations play a role in this policy only to the extent that they reinforce the underlying political and strategic objectives.

The prevailing confrontational approach, which is exemplified by the US policy during the administration of president George W. Bush, has not been able to solve the conflict in Korea. Instead, it has rendered the situation in Korea more volatile than it already was, triggering a new nuclear crisis. The two key instruments of the confrontational approach, namely the threat of a military intervention and the use of economic sanctions, have been ineffective policy instruments. Given North Korea's predictable foreign policy behaviour, no amount of threat will convince Pyongyang to abandon its nuclear programme. To the contrary, American projection of military might, including the explicit threat of pre-emptive nuclear strikes against North Korea, only fuelled Pyongyang's perceived need for a nuclear-based defence.

A policy of engagement, as practised by the South Korean government since the late 1990s, offers a viable alternative to the US-sponsored confrontational approach. The engagement policy advocates genuine negotiations with the North in an attempt to integrate the isolated country into the world community. Essential to this process is the promotion of cultural and economic exchanges across the hermetically sealed dividing line. The ensuing face-to-face encounters between average Koreans have the potential to dismantle at least some of the deeply entrenched antagonistic attitudes that have fuelled conflict in Korea for decades.

Dialogue is crucial in the process of moving beyond conflict. But it is not enough. Just as important is the development of a certain level of tolerance: a willingness to accept that after years of conflict the former enemies will have developed deep-seated differences that cannot easily be removed. Key here is an attempt to come to terms with the influence of traumatic past events: an effort to find a compromise between remembering past atrocities and moving beyond them in the spirit of reconciliation. This can only work if all parties concerned engage questions of tolerance and forgiveness in an attempt to establish a political climate in which former enemies can interact in a respectful, or at least non-violent manner.

Sustained engagement and a genuine acceptance of difference can, of course, not offer ready-made solutions to deeply entrenched conflicts. No conflict is alike. Each has different causes and thus requires different solutions. Not all lessons learned from Korea can automatically be applied to other situations. But at least some aspects of the Korean experience can provide important insights that are of a general nature. This applies as well to the following limits to engagement.

First, there will always be suspicion and mistrust in a political situation that has been dominated by conflict. There is deep and very justified suspicion that North Korea may simply misuse offers of engagement, that it may, for instance, 'cheat' and pursue a nuclear programme in secret, independently of the assurances it gives in public. Dealing with an authoritarian regime also poses a range of difficult moral dilemmas. This is particularly the case when humanitarian aid is involved. But no matter how problematic and porous a policy of dialogue may be, it still offers more opportunity to diffuse conflict than the situation engendered by the confrontational approach, which sees North Korea openly pursuing a nuclear weapons programme that destabilises the entire region.

Second, promoting a policy of engagement and reconciliation inevitably takes time. Entrenched antagonisms cannot be uprooted overnight. But the lessons learned from Korea show that it is crucial to think about the values and implications of different approaches to security and conflict. Based on historical evidence, the engagement policy has the best track record of diffusing tension on the peninsula. The fact that it has only been partially successful cannot be held against it, for the confrontational approach has always played an important and all too often a dominant role. Be it in a realist, neo-conservative or communist version, confrontational attitudes are so deeply entrenched that they have come to fulfil their own promises of doom and gloom.

Third and finally, no amount of engagement and tolerance can absolve decision makers, commentators and individuals from making choices, from separating right from wrong. For instance, engaging North Korea in negotiations and accepting that several decades of conflict have deeply divided the peninsula is not the same as agreeing with or supporting the authoritarian regime in Pyongyang. Even an ethics of difference must, at times, decide about the type of values that are to play a central role in political projects. But the process of articulating and defending these values is likely to be more successful, and less violent, if it is done with the knowledge of and sensitivity towards the complex factors that cause and fuel seemingly intractable conflicts.

FURTHER READING

Bell, Duncan S.A. (ed.) (2006) *Memory, Trauma and World Politics: Reflections on the Relationship between Past and Present*, New York: Palgrave.
   A collection of scholarly investigations that illuminate how traumatic events shape political dynamics and how the ensuing conflicts may be understood and overcome.

Cha, Victor D. (2002) 'Korea's Place in the Axis', *Foreign Affairs* 81, 3: 79–92.
   A concise summary of the confrontational approach to North Korea, as practised by the United States during the presidency of George W. Bush.

Cumings, Bruce (1997) *Korea's Place in the Sun: A Modern History*, New York: W.W. Norton.
   A brief and engagingly presented history of modern Korea, written by one of the most authoritative historians. Cumings' positions are controversial, particularly for challenging the prevailing black-and-white understandings of the Korean War, but they offer very insightful background information about the ongoing conflict in Korea.

Kim, Samuel S. (2006) *The Two Koreas and the Great Powers*, Cambridge: Cambridge University Press.
   A recent analysis by a leading scholar of how the conflict in Korea is intertwined with regional and global political patterns. It focuses, in particular, on questions of identity.

Moon, Chung-in (2001) 'The Kim Dae Jung Government's Peace Policy towards North Korea', *Asian Perspective* 25, 2: 177–98.
   A concise summary of the engagement policy towards North Korea, as practised by South Korea's president Kim Dae-jung.

WEBSITES

The Korea Herald, http://www.koreaherald.co.kr/.
> This is South Korea's most popular English-language newspaper.

KCNA, or the Korean Central News Agency, http://www.kcna.co.jp/index-e.htm.
> This is North Korea's news agency. It publishes a bulletin of news reflecting North Korea's position.

The Korea Web-Weekly, http://www.kimsoft.com/korea.htm.
> A site that aims to be independent and non-partisan, offering a range of useful information and links about Korea, including the political situation.

Ko Un, http://www.koun.co.kr/.
> The website of the Korean poet Ko Un, offering a portrayal of him and his work.

REFERENCES

Bloom, Allan (1987) *The Closing of the American Mind*, New York: Simon and Schuster.

Campbell, David (1998) *National Deconstruction: Violence, Identity, and Justice in Bosnia*, Minneapolis, MN: University of Minnesota Press.

Cha, Victor D. (2002) 'Korea's Place in the Axis', *Foreign Affairs* 81, 3: 79–92.

Chung, Oknim (1999) 'The US–ROK Private Sector Role in Peace and Security on the Korean Peninsula', *Korean Journal of Defense Analysis* 11, 1: 101–26.

Cumings, Bruce (2004) *North Korea: Another Country*, New York: The New Press.

Cumings, Bruce (1997) *Korea's Place in the Sun: A Modern History*, New York: W.W. Norton.

Dujarric, Robert (2001) 'North Korea: Risks and Rewards of Engagement', *Journal of International Affairs* 54, 2: 465–87.

Dwyer, Susan (1999) 'Reconciliation for Realists', *Ethics and International Affairs*, 13: 81–98.

Eberstadt, Nicholas (1997) 'Hastening Korean Unification', *Foreign Affairs* 76, 2: 77–92.

Euben, Roxanne L. (2002) 'Killing (for) Politics: Jihad, Martyrdom, and Political Action', *Political Theory* 30, 1: 4–35.

Grinker, Roy Richard (1998) *Korea and Its Futures: Unification and the Unfinished War*, London: Macmillan.

Harrison, Selig S. (1997) 'Promoting a Soft Landing in Korea', *Foreign Policy* 106: 56–75.

Hart, Dennis (1999) 'Creating the National Other: Opposing Images of Nationalism in South and North Korean Education', *Korean Studies* 23: 68–93.

Hoang, Young-ju (2002) Interviews with administrators and history teachers at Haeundae Girls' High School and Keumjeon High School, South Korea, March and April.

Kaplan, Robert D. (2005) *Balkan Ghosts: A Journey through History*, London: Picador.

Kihl, Young Whan (1998) 'Seoul's Engagement Policy and US–DPRK Relations', *Korean Journal of Defense Analysis* 10, 1: 21–48.

Kim, Dae-jung (2000) 'Presidential Inaugural Address, February 1998', in Yong-ho Ch'oe, Peter H. Lee and Wm Theodore de Bary (eds) *Sources of Korean Tradition: Volume*

II: From the Sixteenth to the Twentieth Centuries, New York: Columbia University Press.

Klusmeyer, Douglas and Astri Suhrke (2002) 'Comprehending "Evil": Challenges for Law and Policy', *Ethics and International Affairs* 16, 1: 27–42.

Ko Un (2002) 'Song of Peace from Jeju Island', in Keun-Min Woo (ed.) *Building Peace and Prosperity in Northeast Asia*, Seoul: Yonsei University Press.

Ko Un (1996) 'Destruction of Life', in *The Sound of my Waves*, translated by Brother Anthony of Taize and Young-Moo Kim, Ithaca, NY: Cornell University East Asia Program.

Krause, Keith and Michael C. Williams (1997) 'Preface', in Keith Krause and Michael C. Williams (eds) *Critical Security Studies*, Minneapolis, MN: University of Minnesota Press.

Moon, Chung-in (2001) 'The Kim Dae Jung Government's Peace Policy towards North Korea', *Asian Perspective* 25, 2: 177–98.

Moon, Chung-in and David I. Steinberg (eds) (1999) *Kim Dae-jung Government and Sunshine Policy*, Seoul: Yonsei University Press.

Naimark, Norman M. (2002) *Fires of Hatred: Ethnic Cleansing in Twentieth-Century Europe*, Cambridge, MA: Harvard University Press.

The National Security Strategy of the United States of America (2002) http://www.whitehouse.gov/nsc/nss.html.

Nietzsche, Friedrich (1981) 'Vom Nutzen und Nachteil der Historie für das Leben' in *Unzeitgemässe Betrachtungen*, Frankfurt: Insel Taschenbuch. Translated by R.J. Hollingdale (1983) as *Untimely Meditations*, Cambridge: Cambridge University Press.

Nincic, Miroslav (2005) *Renegade Regimes: Confronting Deviant Behavior in World Politics*, New York: Columbia University Press.

Noland, Marcus (2000) *Avoiding the Apocalypse: The Future of the Two Koreas*, Washington, DC: Institute for International Economics.

Perry, William J. (2000) 'The United States and the Future of East Asian Security: Korea – Quo Vadis?', in Woo Keun-Min (ed.) *Building Common Peace and Prosperity in Northeast Asia*, Seoul: Yonsei University Press.

Perry, William J. (1999) *Review of United States Policy toward North Korea: Findings and Recommendations*, Washington, DC: US Department of State, http://www.state.gov/www/regions/eap/991012_northkorea_rpt.html (accessed 18/05/06).

Rice, Condoleezza (2000) 'Promoting the National Interest', *Foreign Affairs* 79, 1: 45–62.

Ricoeur, Paul (1999) 'Imagination, Testimony and Trust,' in Richard Kearney and Mark Dooley (eds) *Questioning Ethics: Contemporary Debates in Philosophy*, London: Routledge.

Savage, Timothy and Nautilus Team (2002) 'NGO Engagement with North Korea: Dilemmas and Lessons Learned', *Asian Perspective* 26, 1: 151–67.

CHAPTER **20**

Conclusion

What can we do to change the world?

Maja Zehfuss

- *The question*
  CHANGING WHAT'S WRONG WITH THE WORLD

- *Illustrative example*
  THE IRAQ WAR

- *Responses*
  NO RIGHT WAY FORWARD

- *Broader issues*
  CHANGE AND COMPLICITY

- **CONCLUSION**

THE QUESTION
CHANGING WHAT'S WRONG WITH THE WORLD

Many of the questions we have about global politics are born of a sense of dissatisfaction with the state of the world. We want to know why some people are better off than others because the unequal distribution of wealth seems to us unfair. More than that, many of us will be appalled at widespread poverty and its very serious implications for people's lives. Similarly, we want to know why politics turns to violence because it would be better, we think intuitively, if it did not. We are unsettled by the thought that so many should die, and often at a young age, due to such violence. If we ask whether we can move beyond conflict, we do so because we can think of many cases where this has not happened, often despite people trying very hard. So one question that seems to really vex us and that motivates us to study global politics is how to change what's wrong with the world. Put differently, we would like to know how to respond – and respond effectively – to the sorts of things that we object to: poverty, war, slavery, environmental degradation and so on.

These are extraordinarily important questions. Yet, at the same time, our desire to change the world – to make it a better place – raises all sorts of difficult questions and some of them are often overlooked. After all, how do we decide what is wrong? And why do we think we can – or should – change the world? The question of what we can do to change the world makes some huge assumptions about the world and our role in it. In this conclusion, I want to examine what might be wrong with the idea of changing what's wrong with the world.

Most of us are pretty good at identifying problems with the world. Global politics is certainly replete with states of affairs that we object to: child labour; war; vastly differential access to resources; people having to live in conditions of poverty and violence that many of us find difficult to even imagine; famine; disease; and so on. Thinking about this can be quite frustrating. This is not just because the list of wrongs in the world seems to be very long, but also because it can be difficult to figure out what to do about them. Some of these things seem to be happening in faraway places and it is not clear how, if at all, we could do anything about them. Many of us try, however. We attempt to reduce our 'carbon footprint' in order to make a contribution to fighting climate change. We give money to charities supporting people suffering from poverty in order to help, in a small way, to alleviate the effects of the unequal distribution of resources. At times, we may participate in demonstrations to express our dissatisfaction, for example to protest against war. Often this feels quite unsatisfactory: our contribution appears too small. The world does not change in the way we have envisaged, and we may therefore lose courage. We may begin to think that thinking about the problems of global politics is quite futile: what is the use of identifying wrongs if we cannot rectify them?

This sense of frustration reveals some really interesting underlying assumptions about the world and our role in it. The expectation that we must be able to rectify wrongs, that this is what in a sense justifies our thinking about them, reveals a very particular attitude towards the world. In this vision of the world, we are at its centre and very much in charge. The world is there for us to do with as we please. This seems to go back all the way to the Old Testament: God created man and woman and charged them to 'subdue it: and have dominion over the fish of the sea, and over the fowl of the air, and over every living thing that moveth upon the earth' (Genesis 1: 27–28). Chapter 3 asked what it would mean not to think in human terms: there might be more to this world than just us.

But we approach the world from our point of view. The centrality of the human is firmly lodged at the heart of our thought. This attitude is, if anything, underlined by the way in which God has been displaced from the political universe. As Chapter 6 explained, authority or sovereignty now derives from within our world rather than from a God who is transcendent, somehow beyond our human world. The centrality of the human is therefore reinforced through the Reformation. The Enlightenment, with its ideas of human reason and liberty, further translated this shift into the political sphere. The idea of sovereign 'man' as somehow independent of the world and yet in control of it has proved to be extremely powerful. 'Man' is no longer central just as God's creation, but because 'he' can use reason to decide what to do. 'He' has an impact on the world.

The Enlightenment is discussed in **Chapter 5**.

It is important to ask who we think we are that we want to change the world. Put differently, the idea of changing what's wrong with the world seems to imply that we humans are doing the changing and therefore that we have some kind of control over the world. It implies an idea of sovereign 'man' and with it a rather simplistic idea of power. We can fix things. Chapter 6 discussed the limitations of such a way of conceptualising power and showed that the problem of power in fact raises complex questions about who influences whom and in what way, and indeed about how we would know. It is not just about the ability to make others do what we want them to do or, in terms of our current question, about whether we have the ability to change the world. Power is not something that we 'have' and that we can then use to achieve change. Rather, power is something that happens in all social relations, and that happens precisely because we never have full control. Power relations are productive, not just repressive. This makes the world interesting, but also messy. It's not easy to see how 'we' can simply change the world with others bringing their own views and resources to the world, creating a complicated set of ever-changing power relations.

Chapter 6 discusses Michel Foucault's work on power, which develops these ideas further.

The idea that we need to change what's wrong with the world of course also implies that we are able to identify how the world should be in order for it to be better. This, again, is not easy. We may think that it is obvious that war is a pretty bad idea because of all its negative effects, but there are of course those who believe that some wars are just (see Chapter 15). Often the devil is in the detail. We might spontaneously subscribe to the idea that fighting a war against the Third Reich was right, but does that mean that we approve of civilians being burned to death as their cities were bombed (see Chapter 1)? Chapter 2 talks about the very fundamental questions about who we are and what politics is about that arise and are resolved in some way when we make claims about what it is right to do.

Despite these profound questions and difficulties, many of us do have deeply held convictions about what we should do. There may well be some who endorse war, but that does not mean that you cannot be passionately opposed to it. Because we are not alone in the world, having a clear idea about the right way forward almost always involves having ideas about what others should do and what is good for them. It is altogether likely, for example, that you are opposed to war (if you

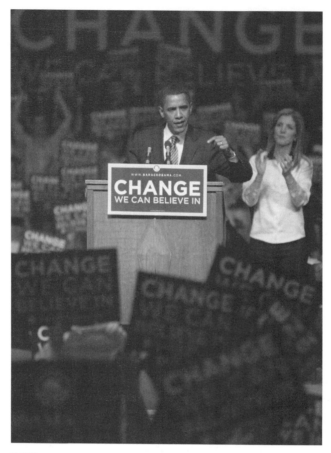

FIGURE 20.1
Barack Obama, US presidential candidate and Illinois senator, on the campaign trail,
applauded by Caroline Kennedy, daughter of late US president John F. Kennedy, 20 April 2008.
Photo: Emmanuel Dunand, AFP/Getty Images

are), not merely because of what it might be doing to you (you wouldn't have
the opportunity to read this book, probably, if you lived in a war zone or were
fighting a war, though you may well know and love people who do), but also –
and perhaps even primarily – because of what it is doing to others: the families
whose lives are disrupted, the women who are raped, the children who go hungry,
miss out on education and might even be killed, the soldiers who have horrifying
experiences and, again, might be killed, to name just a few examples. So you might
think war has to be avoided or overcome because it would be better for these
others if war did not exist. This line of thinking, of course, involves us in the kinds
of problems that were discussed in Chapter 15. Why is it actually that we think
we know what is good for others? You may think that it is obvious that people
would prefer not to live in a war zone (or that developing countries ought not
to be crippled by debt or that we should make real efforts to reduce carbon

emissions, for example), but as we propose our solution we need to be mindful of whether we are not making assumptions about others' needs and our knowledge that are more problematic than we would like to admit.

ILLUSTRATIVE EXAMPLE
THE IRAQ WAR

The 2003 invasion of Iraq was of course seen by its supporters to promote change of a sort we should support. In their view, it was about changing what was wrong with the world. But at the same time many people passionately opposed the war. I want to look at this particular example in a little more detail.

In Chapter 1, we briefly looked into the question of why there are wars and we examined in particular the problem that people get killed, often in gruesome ways. You may recall the story of a survivor of the bombing of Dresden that we recounted: he tells of discovering the bodies of the many people from his street, including his immediate family, who had been killed – asphyxiated – in the air raid shelter during the bombing of Dresden. Having heard this story and perhaps media reports about the impact of contemporary military operations, you may well decide that war is not a very good idea. Many people are opposed to war, and they often express their anger at wars being fought by their countries. Protest against the war in Vietnam was widespread in the 1960s and 1970s, especially amongst students in the United States. In May 1965 a group of students publicly burned their draft cards (the documents that informed them that they were being conscripted into the US armed forces) and it was subsequently made a crime to do so. There were also mass demonstrations against the 1991 Gulf War. 'No blood for oil' was one of the protestors' common slogans. Even though the Federal Republic of Germany, for example, did not deploy its military to the war, many young men there registered as conscientious objectors at the time, to ensure that they could not be compelled to fight. The proposed US-led invasion of Iraq in 2003 met with fierce opposition across the globe. Protests were often co-ordinated such that demonstrations would occur simultaneously across the globe. On 15 February 2003 millions of people in over 600 cities across the world went on marches in order to make their profound opposition to this war heard. Groups have continued to campaign and demonstrate against the war all over the world.

Chapter 7 says more about war and the media.

Many of these campaigns have sought to get us to acknowledge and remember the human cost of war. They have employed different strategies to do so. Sometimes campaigners have been relatives of soldiers killed on duty in Iraq and their actions have drawn attention to the troops' deaths. Military Families Against the War (www.mfaw.org.uk), for example, was founded by Rose Gentle and Reg Keys. Both have sons who were killed in Iraq. The group campaigns to end the

FIGURE 20.2
Anti-war march, London, 15 February 2003. Photo: Jenny Edkins

involvement of UK troops in the war in Iraq, which they consider to be 'based on lies'; they remind us of their loved ones killed – or at risk of being killed or injured – in Iraq. Both the militaries of the UK (Ministry of Defence 2008) and the US (www.defendamerica.mil/fallen.html) have maintained websites to memorialise individual fallen soldiers, often giving a bit of detail about their lives. We learn, for example, that Corporal Paul Joszko, who died in Basra on 28 June 2007, 'always looked scruffy, had a cheeky smile and a cigarette in his hand, but he never failed to deliver the goods' (Ministry of Defence 2007).

In contrast, those killed by these militaries have not been remembered in the same way. Neither the US nor the UK military make any count available of the fatalities that they cause. The failure to provide the public with information about the death toll has been seized upon by critics of the war. Judith Butler (2004), for example, has drawn attention to how Western lives are construed as 'grievable', whilst those of the civilians they kill are not. Through this idea of grievability she wants to pursue larger questions: 'Who counts as human? Whose lives count as lives?' (Butler 2004: 20). She points out that the failure to grieve some lives – those of Iraqi civilians – suggests that other lives are regarded as more valuable.

Various groups have attempted to make up for the militaries' failure to tell us how many people they have killed in Iraq. Iraq Body Count (www.iraqbodycount. org) maintains a database of violent civilian deaths both during the 2003 invasion (the official war which lasted from 20 March until 1 May 2003) and since. Their count covers non-combatants killed by military or paramilitary action and as a consequence of the breakdown of law and order in the aftermath of the invasion. If you go to their website, you will see their current estimate. As I write this, it is 84,328–92,004. In other words, it is not a precise figure. So the first thing we notice, even looking at only this one count, is that it is difficult to come up with a reliable figure. In fact, this is what the US and the UK say: it's really difficult to know how many civilians you've killed in a military operation. Our troops can't be expected to go around counting the dead when they are busy protecting themselves against attack.

Indeed often they may not even know that they have killed someone: if you blow up a building from a distance, how are you to know how many people were in it and whether they were combatants? So, how do groups such as Iraq Body Count figure out how many have been killed? Iraq Body Count relies on media reports (which are cross-checked), figures from hospitals, mortuaries and NGOs and any official figures that are available. Their website does more than count, though: it is an attempt to memorialise the forgotten civilians killed by the war (Zehfuss 2007). This has also been attempted by the 'Eyes Wide Open', exhibition which showed a pair of boots for each of the US military personnel killed in the current war in Iraq and pairs of shoes symbolising civilian deaths.

Even over sixty years after the fact it is not clear how many people were killed by the bombing of German cities during the Second World War.
See Chapter 1

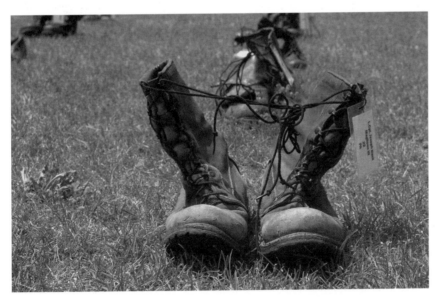

FIGURE 20.3
Boots for 'Eyes Wide Open: the human cost of war' exhibit, 2 July 2004, Philadelphia, PA. The exhibition comprised a pair of boots for each of the US military personnel killed in Iraq and pairs of shoes symbolising the estimated civilian deaths, and was organised by the American Friends Service Committee, see http://www.afsc.org/eyes/. Photo: Terry Foss, AFSC/photographer

War has a very serious effect on people, both on combatants and on civilians. Those opposed to war have often drawn attention to this human cost of war. Yet this does not mean that supporters of war deny the death and destruction caused by war or that they callously disregard it. They may well agree that this is one of the wrongs in the world that we would like to change. In the next section I examine some of the problems that arise in trying to respond to such wrongs.

RESPONSES
NO RIGHT WAY FORWARD

In Chapter 1 we observed that being confronted with the fate of individual people in war – the gruesomeness of their deaths, for example – may produce in you a strong emotional reaction and therefore a desire to do something about it, to respond in some way. But how precisely you will react depends on the circumstances of the particular case. You might disapprove of the UK's role in the Iraq War and approve of its contribution to the Second World War. You might approve of a particular war, but feel profoundly unsettled by a particular incident within it. Your reaction might also depend on an assessment of what your chances are of making a difference. As a rule, there will be a lot of things that you don't actually know. And, worst of all, there is unlikely to be a solution that will be unambiguously good. These things are messy. They don't usually fit in with general rules. Even if you don't think we should kill people, you might struggle with what this means when people are already being killed by others.

There are therefore at least two underlying problems in thinking through the dilemma of war and it is useful to make them explicit. The first concerns the problem that in any given situation we will have responsibilities towards a range of people and we cannot fulfil them all simultaneously. The second is to do with the impossibility of knowing everything before making a decision.

All sorts of claims have been made about the necessity of the war in Iraq by the countries that were part of the invasion. On the one hand it was claimed that Iraq was in illegal possession of weapons of mass destruction and was therefore a threat to the security of Western countries. On the other hand it was argued that the Iraqi leader Saddam Hussein was a cruel dictator and that the Iraqi people had to be liberated from his oppressive rule. US Secretary of State Colin Powell explained in September 2002 that the administration 'would hope that . . . rather than [the war] being seen as an assault, it would be seen as a liberation and it would be seen as the beginning of a new era in that part of the world' ('US Policy Towards Iraq' 2002: 17). His colleague US Secretary of Defense Donald Rumsfeld claimed that the 'goal is to free those people' (United States Department of Defense 2002). And indeed Saddam Hussein was toppled by the

The argument that the overthrow of Saddam Hussein following the military intervention in Iraq constitutes a liberation of the Iraqi people is also made in the Euston Manifesto. **See Chapter 15** invasion, tried for particular crimes against his own population and sentenced to death. However, the country was plunged into a state of war, endangering people and their livelihoods.

I don't want to examine here what the reasons for going to war in Iraq actually were or whether they made any sense. But I would like to draw attention to one aspect of both of the arguments mentioned above. Both propose, in one way or another, to sacrifice some lives in order to achieve, or so it is claimed, the protection of others. Soldiers of the US-led coalition as well as Iraqi soldiers were put into harm's way. So were Iraqi civilians. The first argument suggests that this will protect Western civilians, the second that it will protect Iraqi civilians from a different sort of harm, that inflicted by Saddam Hussein and his supporters. This is, of course, what makes the question of war so difficult: people die. Many of us don't like this idea. But supporters of wars often claim that people will also die if there is no war, in this case Iraqi civilians killed by their own regime and Western civilians at risk from weapons of mass destruction allegedly in Iraq's possession. So there is no obvious way forward that does not involve some wrongs, that is, in this case, people getting killed. To overcome this impasse, some claims to life are privileged over others. If we grant for a moment that the war in Iraq serves to protect Western civilians (which is, of course, an enormously problematic claim, not least because it is difficult to see what evidence would be used to prove this either way), then we have a situation where Western civilians' lives are apparently valued more highly than the lives of those who, for one reason or another, find themselves in the war zone. The war is to protect their lives by sacrificing other lives. As I noted earlier, this privileging of some lives over others can be seen in the way in which some deaths are grieved whilst others appear not to be grievable in the same way, as Butler (2004) puts it.

This apparent need to sacrifice some lives to protect others makes for a tricky moral dilemma. People often try to resolve these sorts of dilemmas by arguing for a general rule that will settle the matter. One could argue, for example, that we have duties towards members of our own community that we do not have towards others (see Chapter 2). So if a choice has to be made between protecting US civilians and Iraqi civilians (and, remember, this is what is *claimed* by some, but that does not necessarily make it true), the US government is right to opt for the former. I do not think that this sort of argument works.

The dilemma we seem to confront when contemplating the possibility of war seems based on something that Jacques Derrida calls an aporia: there is no way forward, the path is blocked (2006: 63). There is no course of action that would resolve or escape the dilemma. In such a situation, anything you might do involves you in committing some wrong. Put differently, if you take responsibility towards one person or group of people – say Iraqi civilians who will be liberated from an oppressive regime – this involves you in not taking responsibility

Another way of deciding whether the human cost of war is justified involves applying the criteria of just war thinking, explained in **Chapter 15.**

The idea of taking responsibility for others also raises a host of further tricky questions. See Chapter 15

towards others – the combatants and Iraqi civilians killed in the process. More generally speaking, if you expend your resources on this conflict, you might not be able to intervene in another, say in Darfur, and thereby you fail in your responsibility towards those others affected by the other conflict. This is a problem we constantly face: to whose call do we respond? And whom do we end up ignoring? It is not possible to act responsibly towards everyone at the same time. We simply do not have the capacity. In Derrida's words, 'I cannot respond to the call, the request, the obligation, or even the love of another without sacrificing the other other, the other others' (Derrida 1995: 68). Whilst we give our support to one person, for example, another may be in need of our attention, too, but we are already occupied. So there is a paradox at the heart of responsibility: 'As soon as I enter into a relation with the other, with the gaze, look, request, love, command, or call of the other, I know that I can respond only by sacrificing ethics, that is, by sacrificing whatever obliges me also to respond, in the same way, in the same instant, to all the others' (Derrida 1995: 68). Acting responsibly therefore does not mean doing good rather than evil. It means negotiating a difficult situation in which no purely good way forward is possible.

This is why you have to make a decision: there are many demands on you, and you cannot respond to them all simultaneously. Some of them may contradict each other. Moreover, you often have to respond under less than ideal circumstances because the matter is urgent (Derrida 2002: 296). Urgency means not least that you will be unable to gather all the knowledge that you might want before making your decision. Whilst you are gathering more information about the precise circumstances of a conflict, for example, people could already be dying. At some point, you need to make your choice, even if you do not know

BOX 20.1 JACQUES DERRIDA

FIGURE 20.4
Jacques Derrida. Photo: Joel Robine, AFP/Getty Images

Jacques Derrida (1930–2004) is one of the most important contemporary philosophers. His work is a radical critique of the inescapable tensions within Western thought (Derrida 1998). His strategy of 'deconstruction' involves showing how arguments rely on assumptions that at the same time undermine them. This has profound political implications. Derrida (1992) shows that accepted institutions such as the state monopoly of power are logically unfounded and that it is impossible to arrive at justice through applying rules. Rather, justice or responsibility become necessary when knowledge does not provide an answer. It requires a leap, what he calls the madness of decision.

everything that could be useful in helping you make your decision. Derrida also points out that it is anyway a mistake to think that there is some piece of knowledge that will somehow settle the matter and tell us the right way forward. For him knowledge is one thing, but an ethico-political decision is quite another. We should certainly try to know as much as possible, but knowledge is not enough. An ethico-political decision involves a leap of faith (Derrida 2003: 118). Although we may be under pressure to make a decision, at times it actually feels like the decision has already been made. So the idea of a decision is tricky and Derrida has quite a bit to say about it. What is important here is that the decision that we may make in response to others' demands is not under our control. I have already mentioned that it involves a leap of faith. Derrida also talks of a decision being 'the Other's decision in me, or through me' (2006: 103). That is, even when we make a decision, we are not somehow separate from the world that we respond to. I will say more about our inextricable involvement in the world and what that means in the next section.

A decision involves committing to one way, despite not knowing the right way forward. It is not possible to keep all the options open. The invasion of Iraq on 20 March 2003 closed down the possibility of non-intervention. Waiting and not intervening often looks like it keeps more options open, and in some ways it does. But if you wait you cannot go back. You may choose what looks like the same option later, but by then the situation will already have changed. Whatever you do, you will have made a choice. Nevertheless, making a choice, under these circumstances, is not for the faint-hearted. You know that it is impossible to act responsibly towards everyone. On top of that, whatever you may know about the situation is actually not enough to lead to the right decision. So you cannot get this entirely right. You need some courage to make a decision despite knowing this, though you cannot actually avoid a decision altogether either. After all, you are involved. You need some courage to admit that your position – where you stand – is not determined by secure knowledge. Whilst you might be prepared to passionately stand up for your views, you know that you don't know whether you are right. You could be wrong. No: you are wrong, at least in part, because there is no option that makes everything all right. More generally, there is no way forward that you could take that would rectify all that is wrong with the world and change it for the better.

This is similar to the situation in **Chapter 15** where the 'stretch' inherent in thinking about 'exclusive knowledge' is explored.

BROADER ISSUES
CHANGE AND COMPLICITY

I want now to turn to different and broader issues the idea of change entails. When we ask how to change what's wrong with the world we make a number of assumptions about the world and our role in it, and I want to use this section to draw some of them out more explicitly. We seem not only to think that we can identify what is wrong with the world, but we also seem to expect that we should be able to rectify what is wrong. So there is an assumption here about what we know, but also about what we are in control of, the sort of power that we might have in relation to the world. These are assumptions about how the world works and about our role within that world. In some way, the question seems to suggest that we are separate from this world – able to step back and diagnose the problem. But at the same time we seem to expect to be able to act upon the world – able to act on the diagnosis and solve the problem. These are assumptions about knowledge and power, about thought and action. They are also assumptions about identity: who is the 'we' that we assume has the ability to change the world?

In Chapter 1 we talked about Robert Cox's ideas about different sorts of theories, which he calls problem-solving theory and critical theory. Problem-solving theory assumes that the world is as it is, with particular power and social relationships that frame the possibility for action; it is 'a guide to solve the problems posed within the terms of the particular perspective which was the point of departure' (Cox 1981: 128). Critical theory, in contrast, calls the prevailing institutions and power relationships into question; it is 'directed towards an appraisal of the very framework for action' (Cox 1981: 128). Problem-solving theory seems to be just the thing we need when we want to fix what's wrong with the world. This sort of theory should be able to tell us how the global economy works and what we therefore need to do if we want to reduce inequality, for example. Or it should tell us what causes wars and what we need therefore to do to avoid them. This is what many scholars studying global politics have in fact tried to do, but they don't seem to have succeeded. Cox thinks that this way of thinking is based on a false premise. It involves looking at particular problems in isolation and fails to appreciate the larger picture. It assumes that the social order is fixed and that we must solve problems within this fixed order.

Cox argues that the social and political order changes, at least in the longer term (1981: 129). Chapter 6 examined some very fundamental changes in the political order that were related to changes in the way people conceived of their own being in the world. How we think and how we act within the world are deeply connected. After the Enlightenment, the legitimacy of the political order could no longer be derived from God and therefore had to come from somewhere within our world. This makes a very big difference and historically we therefore saw a shift towards democracy. Problem-solving theory seems to be unable to cope with such change. Cox argues that such theory is conservative. By acting as a guide to action within the prevailing order it implicitly accepts this order and therefore reinforces the status quo. Measures such as debt relief or development aid may alleviate global inequality in a small way. They may appear to rectify what's wrong with the world, but they achieve only very limited change. Such 'solutions' seem to assume that the system of global capitalism is malfunctioning in a particular way and that this can be fixed. They make the global economy run more smoothly. But what if the global economy as we know it is the cause of global inequality in the first place? Then this is not a very good solution. If we want to reduce global inequality and if global capitalism produces such inequality not when it is malfunctioning but when it is working perfectly, then we need to do something other than propose measures that take the system of global capitalism as given. Similarly, the idea that there are some bad states that are violent towards their own citizens and others – sometimes called 'rogue states' – and that this is in some way against the values of the international community which must therefore intervene to bring such states back into the fold, makes out that the system is just fine. Saddam Hussein's Iraq was a problem that needed to be fixed. But what if the existence of such regimes is an inevitable outcome of the system of state sovereignty? Then we would need to change something far more fundamental to get away from politics turning to violence. This is where critical theory is important.

The idea of an 'international community' that shares values is often used to support claims in favour of intervention, but this is quite problematic. For more on this, see **Chapter 18**.

Critical theory is concerned with possible alternative orders. As Cox puts it, 'critical theory can be a guide to strategic action for bringing about an alternative order, whereas problem-solving theory is a guide to tactical actions which, intended or unintended, sustain the existing order' (1981: 130). So critical theory is interested in how we might actually get out of the system that is causing the problems that we then need to fix. Cox works this through in one particular way and you might wish to follow up these arguments by reading his article. What is important here is that how we think about the world and how we act within it are not two separate issues. They are inextricably linked. Sometimes we cannot see an alternative, but that does not mean that there can never be one. What is conceivable has changed over time and therefore there is no reason to assume that the world as we know it now will or must remain as it is. One of our problems is that we are caught up in the world as it is. We cannot step back from the world and identify its problems objectively: what appears to us to be a problem is already related to who we are and where we are situated in the world. We are in a sense part of the problem that we are trying to respond to.

Nevertheless we do, of course, respond. Acting is not an optional extra, a choice we make after identifying a problem and figuring out a solution. Often we do not quite know what to do. As I noted earlier, we might not have all the information that we might wish to have before acting. And we might be quite unable to identify a right way forward. But we are involved, whether we like it or not. In fact, this is what makes us so frustrated at times. You might be against the war in Iraq and yet, if you pay tax in one of the countries that are part of the US-led coalition, you are in some way contributing to the war effort. Or you might feel passionately that the conditions under which people have to work in some parts of the developing world are appalling, but it is altogether likely that you have bought products made by them. The issue is not that you have control over war or exploitation. But you are involved.

Chapter 6 discusses different ways of thinking about power; this is also relevant to the issues of involvement and control raised here.

Thinking through what it means to respond from this position of being *involved* but not *in control* helps us to understand more about what Cox means when he talks of critical theory. We observed in Chapter 1 that there seem to be two ways in which one might think of responding to a question: by thinking it through or by taking some form of action in response to it. We noted then that different chapters seemed to emphasise one or other way of conceptualising response but that these two are by no means quite as different or separate as might appear to be the case. Thinking about something in a different way can already be an intervention, part of changing the world. Chapter 4 showed, for example, how the ways in which feminists rethought the world had significant political implications. That is not to say that you can just think differently about something and expect that the world will suddenly be different: after all, it took a committed feminist movement – the efforts of many women and indeed men – in order to bring about changes. Change is difficult precisely because we are already involved. We are always already part of a social context and our critique, our attempt at change, is part of it too. We, as people, or subjects, who think and speak, confront language as a system that already exists (Edkins 1999). When we speak we draw on this system: the system is what allows us to communicate. Therefore language also limits what may be said. If we try to say something that is not envisaged in the system, something for which there is literally no language, this is very difficult and we risk becoming unintelligible. Over time, of course, language and its rules may and do change. This happens, for example, when language users persist in doing something new – say, in using a new word, such as 'blog'. The new word or rule becomes part of the system and can then be used by others. But you can't just change the language on your own, by thinking about the language differently. Language can change if others are involved. Your new use of language only works if it is understood by others. In fact, all social action is like this. We, as social beings, are always already part of a context that both enables action and circumscribes what we may do. It is possible to move things, to change work patterns such that they allow for people having family commitments at the same time, for example, but it takes effort. Such change is often actively resisted and sometimes people are stuck in their ways and cannot see how what they are doing is creating difficult conditions for others.

This way in which language or discourse always already exists is also discussed in Chapter 4.

So changing what is wrong with the world is difficult, but that is not because change is impossible. Significant change involves changing the prevailing order. Problem-solving as defined by Cox may appear to be easier and indeed more effective because it seems that you can know what can be done within the prevailing order. When we start talking about really changing the world, then things can be quite uncertain. What exactly would be put in the place of global capitalism? Would any alternative not have its own problems? Even if it was possible to have a different system, would it end global inequality? You can see how someone proposing a shift to the whole system could be in a difficult position. Such a shift would only be possible if others agreed to it, and how do you persuade someone to contribute to an outcome that you can't be quite certain is better in any respect than what we already have?

No doubt being able to convince people that you are certain about something is a powerful political move. There are those, for example, who have undermined environmental policy for years with the argument that there isn't really enough scientific evidence that climate change is happening. But the debate about climate change, discussed in Chapter 3, is very interesting in this context, because of course many people argue that we need to do something even if we might not be entirely sure. Certainty about the precise mechanisms underpinning climate change really is neither here nor there for them, as the consequences of not doing anything might just be devastating.

Certainty can even be dangerous. When people are very certain about something we do not agree with, we often see them as fanatics. More pragmatically, if you are completely convinced that you are right, then you might see no need to talk to and listen to others. But this can seriously damage your chances of implementing your policy. In politics you typically need to get people to co-operate with you and, whilst you may persuade some with the strength of your convictions (your certainty that you are right), those who disagree with you will be likely to feel disrespected and have little desire to co-operate.

Chapter 17 explores the issue of certainty and uncertainty in the context of thinking about security.

Sometimes people have come together, fought for change to the prevailing order and accomplished something. We have mentioned the feminist movement already. The Black Power movement would be another such example (see Chapter 4). Successfully promoting change often involves many people doing things in some way together. If great numbers of people were to decide to avoid behaviours and products that are damaging to the environment, this will have some impact, not least because companies want to sell us their products and services and so they'll play to our preferences. Sometimes the actions of ordinary people dramatically alter the expected course of events. This effect is often called 'people power'.

Chapter 6 examined one such example, the fall of the Berlin Wall in 1989. This was something that was considered quite unthinkable at the time. So it's really unlikely that this is what all the people who went to checkpoints between East and West Berlin on the evening of 9 November 1989 had in mind. They took considerable risks to go into the border area, and yet from the stories that Chapter 6 examines it seems that people just wanted to find out whether it really was possible to travel to the other part of the city as the press release earlier that day had seemed to suggest. They were not planning on changing the world, or at any rate not all of them were. A number of them had left their children asleep in their beds (Hertle and Elsner, undated: 145): they clearly intended to be back to the routine of their lives later in the night. Some just wanted to see for a couple of hours what 'the West' was really like. Some only turned up because there were so many people already and they went to figure out what the fuss was about. They challenged the authorities at no small risk to themselves, but they did not expect to set off German unification or the end of the Cold War. Yet if so many people had not turned up at the checkpoints on that one night in November 1989, it is possible that the authorities in the GDR might have been able to persist with their plan to issue visas to a limited number of people who would have had to apply for them in an orderly fashion with the correct government authority (Hertle and Elsner, undated). Things could have turned out differently.

On 9 November 1989 no one had the outcome under their control, neither the authorities nor the people. But as it turned out life happened and significant change ensued. This is important because we have still been talking here of change and response as though we are at the centre of the universe and somehow in control of it. This view of the world is rather limited – we have seen that social action and power are much more complex – and it also makes it easy for us to slide into a conceptualisation of the world where 'we' are responsible for 'them'. We have to be really careful so that this does not end up as just another way of suggesting that we know what is good for them. The problem that we face is that we are so used to thinking of us as separate from the world that surrounds us that we find it really difficult to absorb the insight that it really makes no sense to imagine ourselves as separate from the social world. We are always already within it, subject to demands from others, but also to what they offer. It is difficult to see ourselves as always already tied into the social world because we have no fully developed language for it. In contrast, we do have a language for being in charge. The subject that we outlined at the beginning of the chapter is at the heart of English and other Western languages: it acts. But who is this subject? Who is this 'we' that is to change the world? I have observed that the question seems to assume a 'we' that can know what is wrong and know how to put it right, a 'we' that is separate from the world and able to act upon it. But when we thought this through we found something quite different. We found that our knowledge of the wrongs is imperfect, as is our ability to identify a right way forward. We found that we are not in control but that we are always already implicated in the social and political order that produces the wrongs that we want to rectify. We found that we cannot respond to the wrongs in the world in a way that would allow us to know that we have done the right thing.

So there is actually something wrong with the idea of changing what's wrong with the world. It is a question that envisages us at the centre of the universe, able to make things all right. It imagines us as potential heroes, and if we lived up to this idea of ourselves we would be able to feel really good. But of course we realise that this is not how things are, and so at times we get frustrated at our apparent inability to change what's wrong with the world. Yet what we may experience as an inability is in many ways no bad thing. Being heroes who change what's wrong with the world would mean imposing our views on others, disregarding them. So when we find that we cannot be such heroes, that instead we are involved in creating the problems in the first place – that we are complicit – this is no reason to despair. It is, not least, a reminder that we are not alone. This is often difficult, but just occasionally something happens that is totally unexpected and at the same time quite wonderful – such as the peaceful opening of the Berlin Wall – to remind us that it is our being with others that makes life worthwhile in the first place'.

CONCLUSION

We are, all of us, already involved in global politics. We often treat the question of how to respond as a really big issue that causes us considerable anxiety. Yet whenever we look closely at issues – in particular those that involve the sort of wrongs that we might want to fix – we find that people are already there, responding, every day. People drop water in the US–Mexico border region to save those trying to cross without authorisation from dying of dehydration. They set up alternative banking schemes to provide opportunities to those who traditionally find it difficult to get credit (see Chapter 14). They try to move beyond conflict (see Chapter 19).

FIGURE 20.5
'The world would be a better place'. Artist: Betsy Streeter. CartoonStock. Ref: bstn29h.
www.CartoonStock.com

Many of us have a passionate interest in global politics precisely because we think there are things wrong with the world. Even though it is often difficult to know what to do, it is good that we care. What we have tried to show is that in responding to global politics we have to tackle many large and fascinating questions. Many of them remain unresolved. Over some we may disagree in the strongest possible terms. The problem is, of course, that the world is full of other people and they do not always agree with us. So one really difficult question that we often face in global politics is how we know the right way forward when things are contested. Often other people think quite differently from us. But at the same time this is what makes global politics endlessly fascinating. Other people are, after all, also the best bit about our world. Learning about different ways of thinking about and tackling a problem can be quite an experience. Being able to do that requires remembering that others' views are important, even if we may disagree with them or if they appear to be strange. Our 'solutions' will not work if we cannot get others to join in and co-operate. Learning from and about global politics requires therefore a certain generosity or hospitality, if you will. Sometimes we find that hard because we cannot see what assumptions we are making in our own views, whilst it is apparent to us that others do make assumptions, at times ones we might wish to contest. The answers to larger questions flow from the answers we give to the question of 'life, the universe and everything'. In the end, this is what makes politics, and in particular global politics, so important: it is an arena in which hugely important questions are raised, on which people disagree.

REFERENCES

Butler, Judith (2004) *Precarious Life: The Powers of Mourning and Violence*, London: Verso.

Cox, Robert W. (1981) 'Social Forces, States and World Orders', *Millennium: Journal of International Studies* 10, 2: 126–55.

Derrida, Jacques (2006) *Deconstruction Engaged: The Sydney Seminars*, ed. Paul Patton and Terry Smith, Sydney: Power Publications.

Derrida, Jacques (2003) 'Autoimmunity: Real and Symbolic Suicides', in Giovanna Borradori, *Philosophy in a Time of Terror: Dialogues with Jürgen Habermas and Jacques Derrida*, Chicago, IL: The University of Chicago Press.

Derrida, Jacques (2002) *Negotiations: Interventions and Interviews 1971–2001*, ed. and trans. Elizabeth Rottenberg, Stanford, CA: Stanford University Press.

Derrida, Jacques (1998) *Of Grammatology*, trans. Gayatri Chakravorty Spivak, corrected edn, Baltimore, MD: Johns Hopkins University Press.

Derrida, Jacques (1995) *The Gift of Death*, trans. David Wills, Chicago, IL: University of Chicago Press.

Derrida, Jacques (1992) 'Force of Law: The "Mystical Foundation of Authority"', in David Gray Carlson, Drucilla Cornell and Michel Rosenfeld (eds) *Deconstruction and the Possibility of Justice*, Routledge: London.

Edkins, Jenny (1999) *Poststructualism and International Relations: Bringing the Political Back In*, Boulder, CO: Lynne Rienner.

Hertle, Hans-Hermann and Kathrin Elsner (undated) *Mein 9. November: Der Tag an dem die Mauer fiel*, Berlin: Nicolai.

Ministry of Defence (2008) 'Operations in Iraq: British Fatalities', http://www.mod.uk/DefenceInternet/FactSheets/OperationsFactsheets/OperationsInIraqBritishFatalities.htm.

Ministry of Defence (2007) 'Corporal Paul Joszko and Privates Scott Kennedy and James Kerr Killed in Basra Roadside Bomb Attack on 28 June 2007', http://www.mod.uk/DefenceInternet/DefenceNews/MilitaryOperations/CorporalPaulJoszkoAndPrivatesScottKennedyAndJamesKerrKilledInBasraRoadsideBombAttackOn28June2007.htm.

United States Department of Defense (2002) *News Transcript: Secretary Rumsfeld Interview with Fox Affiliate – WAGA Channel 5, Atlanta, Ga.*, 27 September, http://www.defenselink.mil/transcripts/transcript.aspx?transcriptid_3672.

'US Policy Towards Iraq: Administration Views' (2002) *Hearing before the Committee on International Relations, House of Representatives*, 107th Congress, 2nd session, 19 September, Serial No. 107–117.

Zehfuss, Maja (2007) 'Subjectivity and Vulnerability: On the War with Iraq', *International Politics* 44, 1: 58–71.

Index

eBooks – at www.eBookstore.tandf.co.uk

A library at your fingertips!

eBooks are electronic versions of printed books. You can store them on your PC/laptop or browse them online.

They have advantages for anyone needing rapid access to a wide variety of published, copyright information.

eBooks can help your research by enabling you to bookmark chapters, annotate text and use instant searches to find specific words or phrases. Several eBook files would fit on even a small laptop or PDA.

NEW: Save money by eSubscribing: cheap, online access to any eBook for as long as you need it.

Annual subscription packages

We now offer special low-cost bulk subscriptions to packages of eBooks in certain subject areas. These are available to libraries or to individuals.

For more information please contact webmaster.ebooks@tandf.co.uk

We're continually developing the eBook concept, so keep up to date by visiting the website.

www.eBookstore.tandf.co.uk

RELATED TITLES
FROM ROUTLEDGE

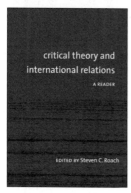

Critical Theory and International Relations: A Reader
Steven C. Roach

This innovative new Reader provides students, scholars, and practitioners with a comprehensive overview of essential works of critical theory and critical international relations (IR) theory, including the writings of Kant, Hegel, Marx, Nietzsche, Freud, Weber, Horkheimer, Adorno, Marcuse, Habermas, Linklater, and Honneth, among others.

Steven Roach frames each chapter showing the major tensions of four periods of the extension of critical theory into critical IR theory. This rich narrative, telling the story of how critical theory entered into international relations theory, seeks to deepen the reader's historical and sociological understanding of the emancipatory project of critical IR theory. Postmodernist and feminist texts are included to give context to the question of whether the discipline is in crisis or is working toward a cohesive and reflexive framework.

2006: 246x174: 424p
Hb: 978-0-415-95418 -1 **£75.00** • Pb: 978-0-415-95419-8 **£21.99**

International Relations Theory for the Twenty-First Century: An Introduction
Martin Griffiths

International Relations Theory for the Twenty-First Century is the first comprehensive textbook to provide an overview of all the most important theories within international relations. Written by an international team of experts in the field, the book covers both traditional approaches, such as realism and liberal internationalism, as well as new developments such as constructivism, poststructuralism and postcolonialism.

The book's comprehensive coverage of IR theory makes it the ideal textbook for teachers and students who want an up-to-date survey of the rich variety of theoretical work and for readers with no prior exposure to the subject.

2007: 246x174: 200pp
Hb: 978-0-415-38075-1 **£70.00** • Pb: 978-0-415-38076-8 **£19.99** • ebook: 978-0-203-93903-1

International Relations Theory : A Critical Introduction
Cynthia Weber

This introduces students to the main theories in international relations. It explains and analyzes each theory, allowing students to understand and critically engage with the myths and assumptions behind them. Each theory is illustrated using the example of a popular film.

Key features of this textbook include:

- discussion of all the main theories: realism and neo-realism, idealism and neo-idealism, liberalism, constructivism, postmodernism, gender and globalization

- two new chapters on the 'clash of civilizations' and Hardt and Negri's Empire

- innovative use of narratives from films that students will be familiar with: Lord of the Flies, Independence Day, Wag the Dog, Fatal Attraction, The Truman Show, East is East and Memento

- an accessible and exciting writing style which is well-illustrated with film stills, boxed key concepts and guides to further reading.

This breakthrough textbook has been designed to unravel the complexities of international relations theory in a way that gives students a clearer idea of how the theories work, and of the myths associated with them.

2004: 246x174: 208pp
Hb: 978-0-415-34207-0 **£90.00** • Pb: 978-0-415-34208-7 **£19.99** • ebook: 978-0-203-48146 -2

Available at all good bookshops

For ordering and further information please visit: **www.routledge.com/politics**

Routledge
Taylor & Francis Group

RELATED TITLE FROM ROUTLEDGE

CRITICAL THEORISTS AND INTERNATIONAL RELATIONS

Edited by **Jenny Edkins**, University of Aberystwyth
and **Nick Vaughan-Williams**, University of Exeter

Covering a broad range of approaches within critical theory including Marxism and post-Marxism, the Frankfurt School, hermeneutics, phenomenology, postcolonialism, feminism, queer theory, poststructuralism, pragmatism, scientific realism, deconstruction and psychoanalysis, this book provides students with a comprehensive and accessible introduction to 32 key critical theorists whose work has been influential in the field of international relations.

February 2009: 234x156: 368pp
Hb: 978-0-415-47465-8 **£75.00**   Pb: 978-0-415-47466-5 **£21.99**

Contents: Introduction *Jenny Edkins* and *Nick Vaughan-Williams* 1. Theodor Adorno *Columba Peoples* 2. Giorgio Agamben *Nick Vaughan-Williams* 3. Hannah Arendt *Patricia Owens* 4. Alain Badiou *Claudia Aradau* 5. Jean Baudrillard *François Debrix* 6. Simone de Beauvoir *Kimberly Hutchings* 7. Walter Benjamin *Angharad Closs Stephens* 8. Roy Bhaskar *Milja Kurki* 9. Pierre Bourdieu *Peter Jackson* 10. Judith Butler *Cristina Masters* 11. Gilles Deleuze *Robin Durie* 12. Jacques Derrida *Maja Zehfuss* 13. Franz Fanon *Himadeep Muppidi* 14. Michel Foucault *Andrew Neal* 15. Sigmund Freud *Vanessa Pupavac* 16. Antonio Gramsci *Mark Rupert* 17. Jürgen Habermas *Neta Crawford* 18. G.W.F. Hegel *Ritu Vij* 19. Martin Heidegger *Louiza Odysseos* 20. Immanuel Kant *Kimberly Hutchings* 21. Julia Kristeva *Vivienne Jabri* 22. Emmanuel Levinas *Elizabeth Dauphinee* 23. Karl Marx *Milja Kurki* 24. Jean-Luc Nancy *Martin Coward* 25. Friedrich Nietzsche *Robin Durie* 26. Jacques Rancière *Rens van Munster* 27. Richard Rorty *James Brassett* 28. Edward Said *Latha Varadarajan* 29. Carl Schmitt *Louiza Odysseos* and *Fabio Petito* 30. Gayatri Chakravorty Spivak *Catarina Kinnvall* 31. Paul Virilio *James Der Derian* 32. Slavoj Zizek *Diane Rubenstein*

'Edkins and Vaughan-Williams have produced a very helpful collection of introductions to the thinking of a wide variety of writers who have been influential in the critical analysis of international relations. This comprehensive set of accessible introductions helps the reader understand the core contributions of writers who have been seminal in the development of a critical account of international relations.'
– *Professor Steve Smith, Vice-Chancellor, University of Exeter*

'Global politics has provided an important context of critical theory. Yet its growing complexity has also called attention to the ongoing task of articulating and reflecting upon the roles of identity, power, order, and resistance in International Relations. *Critical Theorists and International Relations* is a splendid and much-needed volume that addresses and fills, in a truly original manner, this important niche. Providing comprehensive and authoritative analyses of the key critical theorists, this edited volume will continue to remind us of the ever-present need to wrestle harder with the contextual and overlapping meanings of critical theory in International Relations.'
– *Steven C. Roach, Editor of* Critical Theory and International Relations: A Reader

Available at all good bookshops
For ordering and further information please visit:

www.routledge.com/politics

Routledge
Taylor & Francis Group